BILL MONROE

MUSIC IN AMERICAN LIFE

A list of books in the series appears at the end of this book.

BILL MONROE

The Life and Music of the Blue Grass Man

TOM EWING

**UNIVERSITY OF
ILLINOIS PRESS**
Urbana, Chicago, and Springfield

Publication of this book is supported by the Otto Kinkeldey
Endowment of the American Musicological Society, funded
in part by the National Endowment for the Humanities
and the Andrew W. Mellon Foundation, and by a grant
from the L. J. and Mary C. Skaggs Folklore Fund.

Library of Congress Control Number: 2018947543

ISBN 9780252041891 (hardcover) | ISBN 9780252050589 (e-book)

CONTENTS

Preface   vii

Acknowledgments   xi

Prologue   xv

Chapter One. 1892–1919   1

Chapter Two. 1920–1929   22

Chapter Three. 1930–1939   46

Chapter Four. 1940–1949   109

Chapter Five. 1950–1959   158

Chapter Six. 1960–1969   227

Chapter Seven. 1970–1979   314

Chapter Eight. 1980–1989   379

Chapter Nine. 1990–1996   434

Epilogue   469

Appendix: Blue Grass Boys   471

Notes   479

Selected Bibliography   577

Index   579

PREFACE

This book is not necessarily a biography. It is, more accurately, a chronicle, documenting many of the most important events involving, or relating to, Bill Monroe, the Father of Bluegrass Music, in the hope that the commentary accompanying them will provide readers with insights into the life and music of this extraordinary individual.

At the end of the 1930s, after establishing a reputation as a phenomenal mandolin player and tenor singer with the Monroe Brothers, Bill joined the cast of WSM's *Grand Ole Opry*, then heard throughout the eastern United States and Canada with much less interference than today. With his crackerjack band, the Blue Grass Boys, doing their best to enhance his playing and singing, in his words, "it turned out to be" a new country music genre.

Other performers from Kentucky had appeared on the *Opry*, but Bill was the first to clearly identify his connection with "the Blue Grass State," emphasized by the name of his band. As a result, he would soon be considered the show's Kentucky representative, the man from the Blue Grass State: the Blue Grass Man. Eventually, in the 1950s, it appears that the use of "Blue Grass" as a substitute for his name may have influenced the naming of the new genre: "bluegrass."

In 1945, Bill hired banjo player Earl Scruggs, who added an exciting dimension to the music with his driving three-finger-style picking. Later, this would inspire the ongoing debate regarding the beginnings of bluegrass, with many believing it began when Scruggs joined the band. Meanwhile, there are many others who agree with Bill's firm conviction that bluegrass began in 1939, prior to his *Opry* debut. (I should state here that I appreciate the dramatic difference Scruggs made. But it's clear that all the other elements that make bluegrass a distinctive genre were already in place when Scruggs was hired.)

In 1961, when I first became aware of Bill Monroe, he was a virtual unknown in the urban, middle-class world I'd grown up in. He'd been a star of the *Grand Ole Opry* for more than twenty years, yet the majority of Americans were completely unaware of him. Mainstream record stores didn't carry his recordings, and I bought my first Bill Monroe album in a country music record store. This was soon to change, thanks to the popularity of folk music at the time, which identified the folk-derived elements in bluegrass, making Bill a kind of folk musician. Reading about him in a folk music magazine in 1963, I was fascinated with the story of his early life and career.

About twenty years later, at age forty, I joined the Blue Grass Boys. Early on, I told Bill I thought I was more of a guitar player than a singer; thereafter he insisted that I sing at every opportunity. In the latter half of my ten-year tenure, he became very changeable. From day to day, I never knew what to expect of him. Some days, I was a friend; other days, I was a stranger. Yet, through it all, when he did acknowledge me, I felt a level of respect that was completely disarming. Many times I knew he was suffering physically, yet he was determined to carry on, making whatever problem I was having seem insignificant. (In this book, as a part of his story, I will refer to myself in the third person.)

I was one of 149 Blue Grass Boys, by my reckoning: thirty-nine guitar players, thirty-seven banjo pickers, thirty-three fiddlers, twenty-three bassists, fifteen musicians who played more than one instrument, an accordionist, and a spoon-playing jug blower. Bill was also helped by innumerable musicians who filled in over the years, making it possible for him to play a few shows or record a session when he needed a temporary replacement in the band. Naturally, the fill-ins consider themselves to have been Blue Grass Boys; it was an honor to be associated with Bill on any basis. But, in order to limit this book to fewer than a thousand pages, I've had to be selective, limiting band membership to those who worked with Bill for an extended period. Their full names, birthplaces, birthdates, and, in some cases, death dates can be found in the Appendix of this book. A few years after Bill died, in 2000, a biography was published that I didn't feel was adequate, and I started work on this book. I was able to raise enough money via donations to visit every place Bill had lived after leaving home, to see what I could find of him there. In 2006, I moved to the area where he was born and raised, Ohio County, Kentucky, and scoured local newspapers on microfilm at the library in Hartford for mentions of the Monroe family beginning in the 1800s, learning a great deal about the area in the process. This proved to be one of the best moves I ever made, for, not only were the papers full of useful information, I met several Ohio Countians who were happy to help me in my quest for knowledge just for the sake of helping.

For this book, I interviewed sixty-eight former Blue Grass Boys, almost all of the former band members still living during the time of my research. They lived all over the United States (and one in New Zealand), so I conducted most of the interviews by phone, due to the expense involved with travel. Only a few members did not respond to my request for an interview.

The results follow, beginning with a Prologue concerned with people and events prior to the twentieth century (the century Bill lived in, from 1911 to 1996). If you aren't interested in Bill's ancestors, the early lives of his parents, the story of one of his most popular songs, "Molly and Tenbrooks," or the history of the village he called his hometown, you (as they say in Ohio County) might ought to skip it.

ACKNOWLEDGMENTS

Early on, I applied for financial help from the National Endowment for the Humanities and was turned down, twice. So, I contacted friends, and friends of friends, asking for donations. The following people contributed substantially: Robert Hunter, Richard Keldsen of Saga Musical Instruments, and Rick Shubb of Shubb Capos. Other contributors were Tom Adler, Hank Arbaugh, Todd Autry, John Averill, Fred Bartenstein, Tom Bekeny, Norman and Nancy Blake, Mike Blankenship, Mack Blevins, Fletcher Bright, Tom and Ruby Brooks, Leonard and Ruth Brotherton, Gary Bushorn, Greg Cahill, Jeffrey Cohen, Ray Edlund, Bill Emerson, Stuart Evans, Mike Fletcher, Robert and Lillian Fraker, Pete Goble, Bob Hammond, John Hedgecoth, Roger and Carol Johnson, Annie Johnston, Joe Karson, Terry C. Keller, Charlie King, Bill Knowlton, Les Leverett, Lizzie Lewis, Mike Long and Gloria Belle Flickinger, Virginia Long, Bill Lowe, Tim Lynch, Robbie Macdonald, Mike Manetas, George Martin, Dr. Robert Mavian, John C. Maynard, Jesse and Joy McReynolds, Barry Melton, Buddy Merriam, Bill and Wilma Millsaps, Tom Mindte, Pat Mullen, Bob and Pat Myers, Ed and Brijet Neff, David "Hagar" Nelson, Alan O'Bryant, Jim Opie, Annette Panek, Fred and Mary Lou Pement, Joel and Michelle Putnam, John R. Qualls, Evan Reilly, John Rossbach, Sandy Rothman, Mark Royal, Dennis Satterlee, Dr. Dan Scullin, Pete Seeger, Michael Sheats, Mayne Smith, Bob Stone, Johnnie and Peggy Stringer, Ron Stuckey, John Thierman, Larry and Barbara Wallace, Butch Waller, Charlie Walls, Beth Weil, and Jon Weisberger.

I am also very grateful for a 2007 grant from the Rex Foundation.

Special thanks to: history advisor and son Sam Ewing, legal advisors Robert Cogswell and David Crow, medical advisor Dr. Daniel Scullin, and musical advisor Glen Duncan; Bill Monroe fans Leonard and Ruth Brotherton and Bill Hawkins; computer expert Cody Bilbro; genealogists Helen McKeown and Larry Warren; musicians and music business experts Willard Lake Brickey, Gloria Belle Flickinger. Randy Franks, Vic Gabany, Melvin Goins, Russ Hooper, Tim Lynch, Raymond McLain, James McReynolds, Jeff Miller, Alan Munde, James Alan Shelton, Steve Waller, and George Winn; Ohio Countians Gladys Burgess, Rebecca Sue Carter, Sandra Crumes, Linda Decker, Darrell Dukes, Anna Laura Duncan, Loretta (Shultz) Finn, Gracie Frizzell, Frances Harvey, Bob and Geraldean Jones, Campbell Mercer, Marcia Murphy, Rita Stewart, and, from nearby counties, Nila Morgan (Butler County) and Byron Oost (Daviess County); photographers Les Leverett and J. Chris McGlone; proofreaders Carl Ferre and Sandy Rothman; researchers Hank Arbaugh, Bill Archer, John Arms, Greg Ernest, Hank Edenborn, Victor Evdokimoff, Barb, Bob, Jane, and Steve Good, Doug Hutchens, Tom Isenhour, Robert Montgomery, Jerry Steinberg, Richard Thompson, and Marshall Wyatt; scholars and writers Tom Adler, Fred Bartenstein, Bob Carlin, Wayne Daniel, Michael Gray, Tom Hanchett, Murphy Henry, Michael J. Kramer, Jerry Long, Judith McCulloh, Penny Parsons, Bob Pinson, Jeff Place, Jerry Prescott, Ronnie Pugh, Gary Reid, Jim Rooney, Neil V. Rosenberg, John Rumble, Dave Samuelson, Dennis Satterlee, Walt Saunders, Harry D. Tinsley, Ivan Tribe, Bobby O. Wallace, and John Wright; the staff of the Ohio County Public Library (particularly Jill Barrett, Lori Tichenor, and Melanie Warga), and University of Illinois Press director Laurie Matheson.

Many thanks to those I interviewed who were willing to share their stories with readers and to those who provided the photographs that enliven the writing.

Above all, this book would not have been possible without the help and encouragement of Merlene Austin, Margaret "Peggy" Ewing, and Sandy Rothman. I will never be able to thank them enough.

Tom Ewing, Hartford, Kentucky, 2017

For my father, Kenneth S. Ewing (1920–2005),
a serious contemporary jazz fan who encouraged
a love of all music

PROLOGUE

Bill Monroe never knew his grandparents. John Jesse and Lydia Charlotte Monroe and Joseph M. and Munerba Jane Vandiver all died long before he was born. So a tangible connection with his family's past was lacking, and Bill later admitted he could recall little of what he heard as a child about his ancestors, leaving him able to name only the foreign lands they came from. "I don't know too much about my mother's side of our family," he said, "and I don't know near as much about the Monroes as I should know." Then he joked, "I was the last one [born] in the family and I think they know the least of anybody in the family."[1]

Now, thanks to recent genealogical research, we can know a lot about the early Monroes and Vandivers. Brief histories, beginning with their arrivals in the New World in the 1600s, can be pieced together. Through them, we can see the striving to succeed by the Monroes and the inability to stay in one place by the Vandivers, characteristics that were passed on to Bill by the two people who gave him life and that directly influenced the tremendous success of his music, bluegrass.

Bill's Monroe ancestors came to America from Scotland in the mid-1600s. They lived in the colony of Maryland briefly, but eventually settled in the Virginia colony, in Westmoreland County, bordered on the east by the Potomac River. Several generations later, the first to venture forth from the then-state of Virginia was Bill's great-great-grandfather, John Monroe. Born on November 10, 1749, farmer John volunteered to fight in the Revolutionary War in 1775, rising from the rank of private to second lieutenant with various militia units during the six years of war. In 1778, in the midst of the struggle, he married Winifred Berryman, and during their twenty years together, they had ten children (four died before age three). When Winifred died in 1798, John and the children moved away to neighboring King George County but returned to Westmoreland County in 1801. Then, in 1805, after the death of eldest daughter Rebecca at age twenty-three, it appears John began to consider another move, this time to faraway Kentucky.[2]

In 1807, at a time when Kentucky's western border was part of the western boundary of the United States, fifty-seven-year-old John and his children (William, twenty-seven; Elizabeth, twenty-three; Mary Ann, twenty; Eleanor, sixteen; and Andrew, twelve) undertook the long and perilous journey. Traveling a distance of five hundred miles, they probably entered Kentucky by passing through Cumberland Gap, and headed to the northeastern part of the state known later as the Blue Grass region, to Scott County (east of Frankfort, the state capital), where John would farm for the next nine years. Then, in 1816, the Monroes moved to Woodford County (west of Lexington).[3]

During the next eight years (1816–24), James Monroe was president of the United States. Like John Monroe, he was born in the Virginia colony's Westmoreland County (on April 28, 1758, about eight years after John). His grandfather, Andrew, and John's grandfather, William, were brothers, making James and John "distant cousins" (and Bill Monroe, descended from John, was, likewise, a distant cousin of the president's). James and John were probably also distant socially. According to James Monroe biographer Harry Ammon, the future president left Westmoreland County, never to return, when he was sixteen. So, although it's possible that James and John may have met when James was very young, it's unlikely that there would have been any contact between them after that. Still, John must have been very proud of cousin James.[4]

Around 1827, John's youngest son, Andrew (Bill's great-grandfather), then thirty-two, left his Woodford County home and traveled west across Kentucky about a hundred and twenty miles to Ohio County, so named because its northern border had originally (1798) extended all the way to the Ohio River. There, in the region later called the Western Coalfield, he met teenaged Ailsey Q. Harris, and they were married with her father's permission on October 30, 1828.[5]

Andrew and Ailsey returned to Woodford County to live with John, and the first of their nine children was named for him: John Jesse Monroe (Bill's grandfather), born on July 19, 1829. Two years later, in 1831, possibly due to Ailsey extolling the beauty of the western lands (or cheap land prices), John sold his farm, and the entire Monroe clan relocated to Ailsey's native Ohio County. Exactly where they settled isn't known for certain, but twenty-four years later, when John Jesse Monroe married Lydia Charlotte Stevens of Hartford (the county seat) in 1855, they settled down near the village of Elm Lick (later renamed Horton) on a low hill called Pigeon Ridge, and it's likely that their farm adjoined the original Monroe homestead.[6]

John Jesse and Lydia's first child, Arabella, was born on December 20, 1855, then James Buchanan (Bill's father) was born on October 28, 1857. Born thereafter were Andrew Smith (1859), John Henry (1861), Ida Anne (1864), William (1867), Burch (1871), and Susan Mary (1874).[7]

James Buchanan Monroe was born during a time of tumult over the issue of slavery, midway between the publication in 1853 of *Uncle Tom's Cabin* (with its story set in Kentucky) and the beginning of the Civil War in 1861. Monroes had been slave owners since the early 1700s, and James's parents were no exception. They owned seven slaves (a mother and her six children) and were among the minority of Kentucky farmers who could afford them. Proud of their status and firm in their belief in slavery, they named their first son in honor of James Buchanan, a proslavery Democrat from Pennsylvania, elected president in 1856, with John C. Breckinridge, a Kentuckian, his vice president.[8]

James and at least one of the slave children were friends. In an interview years later, Bill recalled a regular visitor to his father's farm when he was a child: "There was an old negro there, George Monroe. We owned him when he was a slave to us, you know? And he'd come spend a Sunday with us once a year when he got real old." According to historians Lowell Harrison and James Klotter in *A New History of Kentucky*, a relationship like this was more likely in Kentucky, where the number of slaves per farm was small and "masters were more likely to work alongside their slaves than were the plantation owners in the Lower South." James and the slave children on the Monroe farm would have worked and played together throughout the Civil War, as the Emancipation Proclamation of January 1, 1863, didn't apply to slaves living in Kentucky or other states allied with the Union.[9]

In October 1863, James turned six and should have started school, but his education may have been delayed, due to a shortage of teachers in Kentucky, gone to fight or find a safer place to teach. But he would complete the eighth grade, considered the highest level attainable for the average child in rural Kentucky for many years to come.[10]

The end of the war brought an end to James's childhood. After slavery was abolished in December 1865, John Jesse would have needed help with the farm, and his eldest son would start working in the fields at age eight. From then on, James's life alternated between school and farm work, and he was given the nickname "Buck," possibly for his tenacity on the job (or because his presidential namesake was nicknamed "Old Buck"). Before long, he was joined in the work by brothers Andrew and "Jack" (John Henry). By tradition in Kentucky, sons were bound to the family farm until they turned twenty-one, and Buck reached that age in 1878.[11]

Three months before Buck's birthday, on the Fourth of July, 1878, a much-promoted "challenge race" was held at the Louisville Jockey Club (later, Churchill Downs) between two of America's fastest thoroughbreds: Mollie McCarthy, a brown mare from California, and Ten Broeck, a bay horse (brown with black mane, tail, and legs) from Kentucky. Named for Richard Ten Broeck, the first American to race horses in England, Ten Broeck ran unsuccessfully in the first Kentucky Derby in 1875. But by 1877, as he matured, mentions of speed records he was breaking began to appear in Kentucky newspapers, including Ohio County's four-page *Hartford Herald*: "At Louisville, Ten Broeck ran a mile against time in 1:39 $^3/_4$, beating the fastest time ever accomplished by three seconds." Meanwhile, it was said that Mollie had won every race she'd entered, and a competitive rivalry began to develop between California, the first of the new states in the west, and Old Kentucky. A race was scheduled, and a purse of $10,000, one of the largest ever wagered, would go to the winner of two of the three four-mile heats they were to run. A national news event, even the *New York Times* sent a reporter to cover it. And as race time approached, in spite of the sweltering July weather, a crowd of thirty thousand spectators jammed the stands.[12]

"Ten Broeck was the first to make an appearance," wrote a *Louisville Courier-Journal* reporter, in an account that also ran in the *Hartford Herald*:

> The King was most royally received, and Billy Walker, his rider, was for the nonce [for the moment] the most important personage on the ground. . . . When the horse was stripped he showed in most beautiful form, his satin coat gleaming in the sunlight, and the brilliant rosettes of yellow and red knotted in his mane

gave him the appearance of having just sprung from a milliner's bandbox. Shortly afterward Mollie McCarthy came in sight and a shout arose hardly less long and loud than that which had saluted her opponent. When stripped she showed just as "pretty as a picture." . . . She was simply attired, and she arched her beautiful neck in proud consciousness that she, of all others, had been selected to cut the wings of the Kentucky conqueror.[13]

For the first two miles of the first heat, it appeared that Mollie would do just that, as she was usually in the lead, with Ten Broeck straining to keep up. "The impression . . . seemed to settle like a cloud upon the Kentuckians that the Queen ['of the Pacific Slope'] was destined to win the heat, as she was going with all ease and at a very pretty stride." Three-eighths of a mile farther, however, the elements conspired against her. The heat and humidity, and the muddy condition of the track, appear to have caused her muscles to cramp, bringing her to a full stop, while Ten Broeck ran on to an easy victory. He had "distanced" her, crossing the finish line several lengths ahead and, according to the rules, the need for two more heats was eliminated.

> There was, of course, a grand rush for the track at once. Mr. Harper [Ten Broeck's owner, F. B. Harper] was taken off his feet and carried by the crowd of yelling, hat-tossing men. The grandstand was in a state of Vesuvian eruption. People screamed until their throats refused to perform their functions. The poverty of glory in the race was not considered.[14]

Nonetheless, the event captured the popular imagination. A rumor spread that Mollie had died (she would, in fact, live and race for several more years), and a multistanzaed folksong arose from the black population of Louisville, later to become one of the most popular songs in Bill Monroe's repertoire, "Molly and Tenbrooks." In 1915, some of its stanzas were collected for the first time by a folklorist from a singer in Kentucky who "learned it from a Negro source," and this was probably Bill's source as well. When asked about it in 1963, he said, "When I was a little boy down in Kentucky, I remember the folks that would be singin' that. Somebody would sing a little of it . . . and so I learned it there."[15]

According to plan and tradition, Buck should have left home in 1878 to make his own way in the world, but he probably didn't. With the nation suffering through one of the worst depressions of the nineteenth century (1873–79), he stayed at home. But as the depression eased, it appears he was making an effort to get started: in the 1880 census, the notation "farmer" next to his name indicates he was working for another landowner in the area.

(Brother Andrew, nearly twenty-one, was designated "laborer," indicating he too was working elsewhere.) For the Monroe family it was a good arrangement: with their "boys" coming home in the evenings, the family circle would remain unbroken. But this happy circumstance didn't last long. On June 10, 1881, their mother, Lydia Monroe, died at age forty-eight of "consumption" (tuberculosis), a common killer in those days.[16]

In 1883, on the other side of the world, northwest of Australia on a small island between the larger islands of Sumatra and Java, a volcano called Krakatoa erupted on August 27, resulting in one of the largest explosions on Earth in recorded history. Volcanic dust was blown into the upper atmosphere, affecting the color of sunrises and sunsets throughout the world for years afterward. The dust also caused "vivid and highly unusual colorations" of the moon, making it appear to be blue (and sometimes green) for nearly two years. This and other rare occurrences of the moon "turning" blue influenced the expression "once in a blue moon" (and it was this kind of moon that Buck's son would years later refer to when he wrote "Blue Moon of Kentucky," not the second full moon in a month, also called a "blue moon.")[17]

That fall, it appears that Buck and Andrew began to consider an alternative to farming. The closing of the Wilson & Jones General Store in Horton in October 1883 may have inspired it—they would open their own general store. Both were in their twenties, confident in their ability to run such a business and know what the average farming family wanted to buy. And, most important, they were overdue to try their wings and be on their own.[18]

As planning for the store progressed, Buck became "J. B." and Andrew, "A. S.," using their initials like other big businessmen of the time. Jack ("J. H."), twenty-two, loaned his older brothers $334, becoming a "junior member of the firm."[19]

The J. B. & A. S. Monroe General Store opened in September 1884, offering a wide variety of goods for sale. Among its grocery items were necessities like sugar, flour, and coffee (beans sold green, to be roasted and ground at home), but there were also niceties like raisins, canned oysters, salmon, and peaches. A full line of clothing was available and, to name just a few other things: baskets, buttons, cologne, dishes, hair oil, Jew's harps, nails, pencils, pocket combs, shoe polish, tobacco in many forms, thimbles, and even violin strings ("the new steel wire kind"). Much of the stock was purchased on credit, a few items from local suppliers (like corn meal from a mill in the town of Rosine, about three-and-a-half miles east of Horton), but most of it from companies in faraway Louisville and Cincinnati. Initially, J. B. and A. S. worked in the store, but early in 1885, they hired J. H. to clerk. Then in April, one Mollie Walla of Horton was brought in to manage "the millinery department."[20]

Before the end of 1885, however, the Monroe brothers' general store business had failed, due primarily, it appears, to the weather. In Ohio County, 1884 began with extreme cold and heavy snows, followed by heavy rain and flooding in February and March, followed by alternating drought and heavy rain thereafter, ruining crops by the time the store opened. In 1885, blizzards and cold temperatures lasted until April, seventeen-year locusts emerged in May, and a drought in July and August withered every growing thing. Farmers had little or no money to spend, and if they bought on credit, their accounts went unpaid. By early 1885, to make ends meet, J. B. and Andrew were working for others as timbermen, while Jack and Miss Walla ran the store. Then, in June, Jack was stricken with "bilious malarial fever."[21]

In October 1885, lawyers for more than a dozen creditors filed claims at the Hartford courthouse, demanding payment for goods totaling nearly $3,500 (more than $65,000 in today's currency). Even brother Jack, after he recovered, sued for the amount he loaned his brothers plus his pay as a clerk, which he claimed he was never paid ("$15 a month for six months and 16 days"). Legal proceedings dragged on for months. On J. B.'s twenty-ninth birthday, October 28, 1886, the Statue of Liberty was unveiled in New York Harbor with grand ceremony. But J. B. wouldn't have been in the mood for a celebration of any kind. Eventually, by 1887, all of the store's debts were paid, but J. B. and Andrew had lost nearly everything.[22]

Being the eldest brother, J. B. probably shouldered the weight of the failure himself. After turning his back on farming, he may have resolved to become the most successful farmer ever. But many years would pass before he could begin to achieve that goal.

Bill's Vandiver ancestors came from the Netherlands (often referred to as "Holland," one of its provinces). They arrived in the late 1600s and, apparently afflicted with wanderlust, slowly moved south during the next one hundred years, living in Virginia, North Carolina, and South Carolina, before returning to North Carolina.

As with Bill's Monroe ancestors, it was his Vandiver great-great-grandfather who led the way to Kentucky. Farmer George Vandiver, born in Virginia around 1774, his wife Nancy, and their five sons (William, ten; George H., eight; Charles, five; Henry, four; and Hiram, two) moved from North Carolina to Tennessee in 1810, where they lived four years (and three daughters were born there: Mahala, Lucinda, and Malinda). Probably unable to stay put, the growing family moved to western Kentucky in 1815—about fifteen years before the Monroes—settling in Muhlenberg County (southwest of Ohio County), in a northern section that later became part of McLean County. They bought land on Cypress Creek, between the towns of Sacramento and Island, and a fourth daughter, Grace, was born there in 1816. Her father, George, Bill's great-great-grandfather, died later that year.

Eight years later, in 1824, namesake son George H. Vandiver (Bill's great-grandfather), married Elizabeth Miller (née Mishler, in Virginia in 1807), and they had two children, Joseph M. in 1825 and Nancy C. in 1827. When George H. died around 1830, Elizabeth carried on alone. Never remarrying, she ran their Muhlenberg County farm and raised the children herself. By 1833, she had purchased one hundred additional acres for her farm, a rare accomplishment for a woman in those days.

Elizabeth's son, Joseph M. Vandiver (Bill's grandfather) married Martha Beales in 1843 when he was seventeen. After the birth of first child Louisa in 1845, Vandiver wanderlust reemerged. The couple moved from Muhlenberg County to Butler County (south of Ohio County), where their second child, Nancy Catherine, was born in 1846. But they were back in Muhlenberg County when their third child, John Henry, was born in 1847. Shortly thereafter, Martha died, and Joseph arranged for the children to be raised by relatives.

Joseph wed again in 1852, marrying Munerba Jane Pharris (Bill's grandmother). Born in Knox County, Tennessee, sometime in the 1820s, her mother was from Knox County, Kentucky, and her father from Tennessee. Munerba and Joseph had four children during the next eight years—Martha Jane (1853), George Robert (1856), Stanley Singleton (1857), and William J. (1859)—and they bought land near Sacramento, in that northern part of Muhlenberg County that had become southern McLean County in 1854.[23]

Around 1860, the family moved again, this time to Ohio County, settling in an area west of Hartford. For a brief time (1863–64) during the Civil War, Joseph served with the 87th Kentucky Regiment of Enrolled Militia, a Union home guard. His apparent sympathies with the North would have put him at odds with the slave-owning Monroes, but it's doubtful they knew each other, since they lived in different parts of the county. While Joseph and Munerba lived in Ohio County, two more children were born to them: Joseph Levi (1862) and Mahala (1864).[24]

In early 1865, with the war ending, the Vandivers moved to Muhlenberg County. Born there were Joseph and Munerba's last two children: James Pendleton in 1867 and Malissa Ann (Bill's mother) in March 1870. In July 1870, when the census was taken, the Vandivers were included among those living near the town of South Carrollton. Listed last in the family was little "Not Named"—Malissa—yet to be given a name, and in the column labeled "If born within year, state month," the abbreviation "Mar." for March.[25]

In 1870, when Bill's mother was born, the tracks of a new railroad were being laid down in western Kentucky. The Elizabethtown and Paducah Railroad (E&P) would soon cross Ohio County to connect Elizabethtown (forty miles south of Louisville) with the Ohio River town of Paducah. The path the E&P would take was likely influenced by the coal known to be buried in southern Ohio County. Passing through villages that happened to lie along the way, the E&P's tracks would head straight for the county's most extensive deposits of the flammable mineral.[26]

At the time, most of the coal used in Kentucky was imported from Pittsburgh, Pennsylvania. But an increase in demand encouraged the opening of several mines within Kentucky, particularly in the western part of the state. Once the E&P provided a way of moving the coal efficiently to large population centers (like Louisville), it appeared that Ohio County could become a center of coal production for the entire state (which is exactly what happened). Meanwhile, undoubtedly intrigued by this development was an Ohio County lawyer and politician with the improbable name of Henry D. McHenry.[27]

The son of a successful lawyer and politician, Henry Davis McHenry was born in Hartford, Kentucky, on February 7, 1826. He graduated from law school in 1845 and began his practice that year at age nineteen. He was elected to a two-year term in the State House of Representatives in 1851, and married Martha Jane "Jennie" Taylor of Hardinsburg (Breckinridge County, northeast of Ohio County) in 1856. The new Mrs. McHenry was a poetess who used the pen name "Rosine" when her first poem was published in the *Louisville Daily Journal*, a forerunner of the *Courier-Journal*, in 1858.

HOME AGAIN
By Rosine

I'm back again in my dear old home,
'Mong the scenes of my sunny youth to roam.
The sky is bright and the morn is fair,
And the fresh cool breeze toys with my hair.
My heart is glad and my spirit free,
Nothing is wanting, dear one, but thee.
One bright young bird on yon old peach limb
Is twittering so sweetly his morning hymn,
All fearless of winds and a stormy sky,
For he knows his sheltering nest is nigh.
Like that bird, I'll sing, for my heart is wild
And bounds as lightly as when, a child,
I played in the love and warmth of home,
Ere thy winning smile taught my heart to roam
From its cottage walls, its birds and flowers,
From the hearts that cherished my childhood hours.
But, as Time relentless steals on apace,
He touches but lightly this sacred place,
Still laugh bright waters, there stand the old trees,
The flowers are here that then perfumed the breeze,
Just waiting for Spring to come o'er the plain,
To burst into sweetness and beauty again.
The friends, that then loved me, all welcome me yet,
And cold be this heart, when their love I forget.
Ah! no; e'en though cloudlets should dim the world's truth,
Still fondly I'd cling to the friends of my youth.
The past it was joyous, the present is bright,
The future, hope clothes it with beauty and light,
And if thorns shall e'er lurk in this pathway of ours,
Still, dear one, we'll take all the thorns for the flowers.
Loving virtue and truth, trusting Heaven and thee,
Can this beautiful world have a sorrow for me!

New poetry was an almost daily feature of the *Journal*, and its poets usually used one name ("Olla," "Lulie") to identify themselves. One of Jennie McHenry's most prolific and popular predecessors was "Rosa" (Rosa Vertner Jeffrey), whom the *Journal*'s editor once called "the Queen of Southern Poetry." Perhaps in deference to her, Mrs. McHenry chose a diminutive form of Rosa—"Rosine"—as her pen name.[28]

A few years later, during the Civil War, Henry D. McHenry reentered state politics, serving in the Kentucky Senate during 1861–65, then returned to the House in 1865 for another two-year term. Thereafter, he tried national politics but lost in a close race for the U.S. Senate in 1867, the year a book of his wife's poems, *Forget Me Not*, was first published. He ran again in 1870 and was elected to the U.S. House of Representatives. While there, probably based on his knowledge of Kentucky railroads (including the E&P), he was appointed to the Pacific Railroad Committee, a governmental body involved with the country's first transcontinental rail line.[29]

After the E&P had crossed Ohio County and the connection was made with Paducah in September 1872, it appears that Representative McHenry began to act on the potential that the railroad offered to him personally. His first move involved one of the smallest Ohio County villages on the E&P's route, a former stagecoach stop called Pigeon Roost, named for the flocks of pigeons that once roosted in cedar trees on the banks of nearby Pigeon Creek, flocks so numerous, it was said, they broke the branches.[30]

Taking advantage of his standing in the county and claims to land in the area, McHenry virtually took over Pigeon Roost. By June 1873, it was formally renamed "Rosine" in honor of his wife. He had the area surveyed and, in September, a "Plat of the Town of Rosine" was filed at the courthouse in Hartford: a diagram of the rectangular town-to-be, with twenty-five equally sized blocks separated by sixty-foot-wide streets. For McHenry, it was an opportunity to profit from the sale or leasing of its property as a shipping center, with streets wide enough to accommodate wagon traffic, where area farmers would bring their produce to the railroad, drink in its taverns, and stay overnight in its hotels. (McHenry also established the McHenry Coal Mine, about eight miles to the southwest of Rosine. In 1874, the town nearest the mine and the railroad's tracks, Render, was renamed "McHenry").[31]

While Pigeon Roost was being transformed into Rosine, the Vandivers moved from Muhlenberg County to Butler County—the last move they would make as a family—returning to the county where Joseph and his first family lived twenty-six years earlier. This time, they settled in an area just south of the Ohio County line, near Indian Camp Creek and the town of Banock, in a farming community called the Burdens. They would live there until the late 1880s, the longest time they ever lived in one place.[32]

During that time, in February 1886, Arnold Shultz, later one of Bill Monroe's most important musical influences, was born in the town of Cromwell, across the Ohio County line from Banock. The third of David and Elizabeth Shultz's eight children, his father, a former slave, was forty-two and his mother, born free, was barely sixteen. By 1900, fourteen-year-old Shultz had attended school (according to the census, he could read and write) and he was working with his father in the coal mines. It was then that half-brother Ed Shultz, a riverboat roustabout, gave him his first guitar.[33]

One month after Arnold Shultz was born, Malissa Vandiver turned sixteen. Unable to read or write, according to censuses, she probably hadn't attended school. Instead, after farm work, she devoted her free time to learning songs and playing the fiddle, button accordion, and harmonica. By the time of her birthday in 1886, all of her siblings had married and left home, except for nineteen-year-old brother James Pendleton, called "Pen." He concentrated on playing the fiddle but also learned the rudiments of several other instruments. Their preoccupation with music was likely seen as natural by their parents, for, as Bill later pointed out, "Seemed like the Vandivers were gifted in music, just in their family. They could all play, they could all sing some, and they could fiddle the old-time breakdown numbers. And they played just to listen to [it] and they liked it themselves." In other words, music was a personal pursuit for them. They played for their own enjoyment first, then for the enjoyment of others. They weren't musicians who played solely to entertain an audience.[34]

Bill wasn't sure how his parents met: "They was at a dance or a church, and my father met my mother there." Only about ten miles separated the Burdens in Butler County from Horton in Ohio County. Perhaps Pen traveled to Ohio County to play for a dance and brought his sister with him, and J. B. happened to be there. Malissa, possibly six feet tall or taller, with long red hair, fair complexion, and blue eyes, would have quickly caught his eye. Blue-eyed J. B., about 5"10" and sporting the moustache many men wore at the time, was twelve years her senior. He had a very serious, almost stern demeanor, so he would have surprised everyone with his lively buck-and-wing–style dancing. Charmed, Malissa may have showed off with the tricky buckdancing step she knew called the "Kentucky backstep." On the other hand, it's possible that the Monroe and Vandiver families both journeyed to a distant church, drawn to a revival, one of many held during that time, and they met there.[35]

J. B. and Malissa's courtship followed. In the 1970s, Bill told a newspaper columnist an intriguing story in which Pen "squired [Malissa] to the banks of the Green River, to a spot where [J. B.] would swim across and court her."

The only problem with this charming bit of Monroe family lore is that the Horton and Burdens areas aren't separated by the Green River. It may have actually been a branch of the Green River, such as Indian Camp Creek, swollen by spring rains. But it's likely that J. B. would have been more than willing to swim a river if it had been in the way.[36]

In 1888, Joseph and Munerba Vandiver separated (but never divorced), and Joseph moved to Ohio County. Their son William also moved to Ohio County after the death of his first wife that year. Pen turned twenty-one in 1888, and he and Malissa may have followed their father and brother to Ohio County by about 1890, leaving their mother behind. (She died in 1897 or 1898.)[37]

Also during the late 1880s, Jack, J. B. and Andrew's former "junior partner," was working full time as a timberman and saving his earnings. In 1889, he began buying land, making a series of purchases—sometimes large, sometimes small—that totaled more than eight hundred acres by 1902. Some of the properties he acquired were located in or near Rosine.[38]

On January 24, 1890, J. B.'s father, sixty-year-old widower John Jesse Monroe, married forty-five-year-old divorcée Mary (Watson) Renfrow. Mary and first husband John Renfrow, who divorced in 1880, were former neighbors of John Jesse and Lydia Monroe.[39]

On December 17, 1890, a small, hastily printed insert in the *Herald* notified readers of the death "this morning" of Hartford resident Henry D. McHenry, age sixty-four. A younger brother, John Hardin McHenry Jr., had served with the Union army during the Civil War, surviving several major battles, including Shiloh, and attaining the rank of colonel. His brother Henry was also called "Colonel," as an obituary published a few days later explained, "because of the invariable courtesy of his bearing and the gentleness of his disposition." His widow, Jennie "Rosine" McHenry, would move to Louisville in 1897, returning to Ohio County for occasional visits.[40]

BILL MONROE

CHAPTER ONE
1892–1919

J. B. and Malissa Are Wed

On Wednesday, August 3, 1892, in that week's edition of the *Hartford Herald*, the following announcement appeared on page 3:

> J. B. Monroe and Miss Malissa Vandiver were united in the holy bonds of matrimony at the bride's home near Horton yesterday.

Seeming terse by modern standards, most wedding announcements in the *Herald* were about this length at the time. J. B. and Malissa's names would never again appear together in print during their lives, and they would not announce the births of their children in the newspaper, as others often did. (They were issued a marriage license on August 2. But according to their marriage certificate, signed after the ceremony, they were actually married on August 3.)[1]

On their wedding day, Malissa was twenty-two and J. B., thirty-four. The day may have been part of a "downtime" for farmers in western Kentucky— the wheat and oat harvests were usually completed by then and the tobacco harvest wouldn't begin until later—and the couple probably planned it that way. The ceremony was actually held at a cousin's house (not "the bride's home"), but was still in keeping with the long-standing Southern tradition of weddings being held at home. If only the immediate family was invited, there must have been quite a crowd, considering the nine brothers, four sisters, four aunts, and four uncles that J. B. and Malissa had. And after the ceremony, there was surely music and dancing, with Pen fiddling.[2]

It was 1892, the one hundredth anniversary of Kentucky's statehood. Benjamin Harrison's single term as president of the United States was coming to an end. Before leaving office, he issued a proclamation endorsing the daily recitation of the newly composed "Pledge of Allegiance" in all public schools. Down in Nashville, Tennessee, at 116 Fifth Avenue North, construction of the Union Gospel Tabernacle (later called the Ryman Auditorium) had recently been completed.[3]

J. B. and Malissa settled down on Pigeon Ridge, on a small portion of land given by J. B.'s father. There, on that plateau about 150 feet above the countryside surrounding it, J. B. set about building a log cabin, probably with the help of his younger brothers.[4]

The newlyweds wasted little time starting a family. Four of their eight children were born before 1900: Harry Carlisle Monroe, born September 8, 1893, may have been named for the recently departed Republican president, "Harry" being short for "Harrison"; Speed Vorhees Monroe, born November 30, 1895, his first name possibly from noted Kentucky Republican James Speed, attorney general for Presidents Lincoln and Johnson (or an old synonym for "success"); John Justine Monroe, born May 16, 1897, named in honor of J. B.'s father, John Jesse, who died on December 30, 1899; and Maude Bell Monroe, born November 17, 1898, her first name inspired by another Maude Monroe, distant kin from Indiana whose family lived in Beaver Dam, about four-and-a-half miles west of Horton.[5]

J. B.: Farming and Logging

During this time (1893–98), Mother Nature again challenged the survival of farmers in western Kentucky, including J. B. Monroe. In 1893, heavy rains and flooding washed crops away, and in 1894, a late frost killed crops planted too soon and a three-month drought followed. By 1895, with a wife and child to feed (and Speed on the way), J. B. teamed up again with Andrew and Jack, this time to start a logging business. In November, the *Herald* took note in a report from Beaver Dam's train depot: "The Monroe Brothers are having a great quantity of very fine timber delivered and loaded here" (for shipment via the east-west rail line, then owned by the Illinois Central Railroad).[6]

Another late frost came in 1896, and a cutworm infestation decimated the corn crop. Heavy rains and flooding returned in early 1897, followed by another drought so severe that travel by boat was suspended on the Ohio River between Louisville and Evansville, Indiana (about forty miles northwest of Ohio County), due to low water levels. In 1898, the weather improved, but the fall brought swarms of voracious grasshoppers, and harvested tobacco was badly damaged by heat and humidity. Meanwhile, the war with Spain began in April 1898, two months after the sinking of the USS Maine in Havana harbor, increasing the demand for raw materials, including timber. Until the destruction of the Spanish fleet in July 1898, the brothers would have been busy supplying the demand.[7]

When the Monroe brothers began logging, about half of the forest that covered Ohio County when the first settlers arrived was still standing. In an 1898 report to the *Herald*, a newsman visited one of the county's logging camps:

> We found an oak tree, which they had fallen, which measured five feet three inches in diameter at the butt, from which forty-five feet had been taken off, the top end of which was four feet and five inches. This, we thought, was a large tree; it was a beautiful log, no limbs or knots and as straight as an arrow; but a little farther on we found one of the same variety with an actual measurement of seven feet nine inches in diameter, which, when standing, extended into the heavens 135 feet.[8]

The effort involved in dealing with these behemoths without power tools nearly defies modern comprehension. A long crosscut saw, with a man at each end, was used to cut the trees down. Logs were wrestled up ramps into wagons pulled by cattle or oxen, the stronger ones close to the wheels called "wheelers" or "wheel cattle." Hauled to a portable sawmill powered by a steam engine, the logs were cut into lumber.[9] The Monroes took the sawn lumber to town in wagons pulled by teams of horses; those closest to the wheels were called "wheel horses." Like wheel cattle, they were "responsible for the brunt of the actual work in breaking the inertia of a heavily-loaded wagon, as well as for maneuvering the turns," according to an album's liner notes for "Wheel Hoss," which Bill recorded in 1954. (Bill always preferred to call the tune "Wheel Horse.")[10]

Malissa and Her Music

While J. B. was "working in the timber," Malissa had her hands full by 1899, with three boys (Harry, five; Speed, three; John, two) and newborn Maude. Her life revolved around (a biographer once wrote) "raising chickens and turkeys for market, doing the chores about the house and farm, caring for the children, and gardening, canning, and cooking for her family." To cope, it appears she relied on an old friend, her music, beginning a daily ritual of playing and singing whenever she had time, leaving her instruments out and ready to play. If, indeed, she found help this way, she was lucky. There would be more to cope with soon.[11]

J. B. and Malissa's fifth child, Birch Monroe, was born on Thursday, May 16 (the same as brother John) in 1901. He was named for J. B.'s youngest brother, Burch (the spelling here differentiates the two; in Kentucky, it could be spelled either way). Like him, Birch wasn't given a middle name, probably honoring the precedent.

The sixth child, Charles Pendleton Monroe, was born on the Fourth of July in 1903. Given J. B. and Malissa's penchant for naming their children after well-known public figures and a lack of national politicians named Charles, his first name might have been inspired by Charles M. Schwab, the first president of US Steel and one of the wealthiest men in America at the time. The source of "Pendleton" was, of course, Malissa's brother, James Pendleton Vandiver.[12]

These early years of the twentieth century saw a wide array of other developments within the family circle: J. B. began participating in local politics in 1900, serving as an election officer at the Rosine polling place for Democratic primaries and regular elections, a duty he continued to perform for nearly twenty years. That spring, J. B.'s brother William, thirty-three and married with a young son, was involved in the new "national pastime," playing shortstop with the Beaver Dam baseball team. On July 21, 1900, J. B.'s brother-in-law Pen Vandiver, thirty-four, married fifteen-year-old Anna Belle Johnson. Then, in 1902, J. B.'s twenty-seven-year-old baby sister, Susan, a teacher in Ohio County, left for "a summer's course of study" in Chautauqua, New York, and thereafter moved to Riverside County, California. In February 1903, brother Jack, forty-one, married Eleanor Mary "Eldamary" (Crowder) Pierce, a thirty-year-old widow with three children. That same year, Pen and Anna Belle's first child, Cecil E. Vandiver, was born. (And on December 17, 1903, the Wright brothers made their first successful aircraft flights in Kitty Hawk, North Carolina. In their leisure time, Wilbur Wright enjoyed playing harmonica and Orville Wright, the mandolin.)[13]

J. B. Buying Land

Also in 1903, shortly after Charlie's birth, J. B. began buying land, using the hard-earned money he'd made in logging to establish a large-scale farming enterprise. His initial purchases were on Pigeon Ridge, a total of about 502 acres bought from newlywed brother Jack for around $1,845 (the equivalent of nearly $40,000 today). A few years later, in 1907 and 1911, he acquired about 104 more acres from a neighbor. According to one of the deeds, forty-two of the acres were located on what was variously named as "Gernsden," "Geruslen," or "Gerslen" Ridge (later called "Jerusalem" Ridge), just south of and contiguous with Pigeon Ridge, yet rising slightly higher above it. One small purchase in 1910, of an acre for $150, included a house. And after the purchase of about 182 additional acres (in partnership with Jack) on Christmas Eve 1912, J. B. had amassed nearly 790 acres, the measure of his land for the next several years. By this time, all of his brothers owned smaller farms near to or adjoining his, with "the entire neighborhood belonging in effect to the Monroes," as Robert Cantwell aptly described the area in *Bluegrass Breakdown*.[14]

Between 1904 and 1912, an entrepreneurial J. B. also bought several lots in the town of Rosine, some that were owned by Jennie McHenry, properties he rented or leased. But within a few years he would sell them to Jack and others.[15]

In the midst of these busy but happy times, there were also troubles and sorrows, especially for Malissa and the Vandivers. Around 1902, Malissa's brother William, who came to Ohio County in 1888 and remarried in 1890, died of pneumonia at age forty-three. In April 1905, Malissa's father, eighty-year-old Joseph, was killed after being struck by a train shifting in position in the railroad yard at White Run, about five miles east of Rosine (and was buried in an unmarked grave in Rosine Cemetery). And in December 1906, Malissa's oldest sister, Martha Jane (Vandiver) Cook, died of typhoid fever at age fifty-three. The following year, it appears that Pen and young wife "Annie" separated, for as J. B. noted in one of the ledgers he kept of all his transactions on the farm, "Moved in my House—Feb. 19, 1907—Pen Vandiver." By this time, J. B. was hiring workers for his expanding acreage, and Pen worked alongside them, making a dollar a day, the going pay rate at the time. But Pen and Annie were soon reunited. A daughter, Lena B., was born in 1907 or 1908, and in 1910, they and seven-year-old Cecil moved to a small, seventy-acre farm near White Run.[16]

Life in Ohio County

Life in rural Ohio County continued as it had during Civil War times. Electricity for street lights came to Hartford in 1905, but it wouldn't be widely available in the surrounding farm country until after World War II. Dirt roads, maintained by those living near them, were the norm (paved roads wouldn't arrive until the mid-1930s). Given the roads' unpredictable quality, especially after it rained, mechanized vehicles of any kind (the first Model T rolled off the assembly line in 1908) were seldom seen. Country folks walked, rode horses or mules, or traveled in wagons pulled by horses or mules well into the 1940s. And indoor plumbing was a luxury limited to larger towns. According to Harrison and Klotter, "As late as 1940 . . . ninety-six percent [of rural dwellings in Kentucky] had no running water."[17]

Meanwhile, the town that J. B. and Malissa lived closest to, Rosine, had already begun to shrink in size; from a population of more than two thousand in the 1880s, it would have only 166 by 1910. Unpredictable weather probably caused many to leave, and economic opportunities in the industrial North beckoned. Also, as one of the few places in dry Ohio County where liquor could be bought, Rosine had developed a reputation for the violence fueled by drink. But it wasn't the only town losing residents—Kentucky in general experienced a dramatic decline in population growth after 1900. Record numbers of immigrants were coming to America, but most were going elsewhere. Kentucky was becoming "more and more self-contained," according to Harrison and Klotter, and the area around Rosine more and more isolated.[18]

On Friday, July 17, 1908, J. B. and Malissa's seventh child, Bertha Lee Monroe, was born. Malissa may have borrowed the baby's first name from her eight-year-old niece, Bertha Vandiver, the youngest child of her brother Stanley and wife Martha, who lived in Butler County. "Lee" may have come from Butler County too, where there were many Lees.[19]

Interviewed recently, Rosine native Frances Harvey said that around 1909–10, her grandmother, Caroline Goff, an old friend of Malissa's, would come up from Butler County with husband Robert to visit on Sunday afternoons, and Malissa and she would race their husbands' horses at a homemade race track south of Rosine. As told to Harvey by her mother, Mae Goff Harvey (Caroline Goff's daughter, then about eleven years old), they threw themselves into it: "They was as close as sisters otherwise, but when they got on those horses, there was no holds barred. She said each one was tryin' their durnedest to beat the other one." In 1910, the Goff family moved to Ohio County, and Robert Goff began working with J. B. in the timber.[20]

Around this time, the singular event of Malissa's fiddling for a dance may have occurred. When the fiddler hired to play for a dance at the nearby Wright house failed to show up, Mr. Wright rode over to the Monroe place to ask J. B. if he could "borrow" Malissa, bringing a horse with him for her to ride. As Charlie told it:

Dad said, "Malissa, put on your coat, [take] what you need, get on the horse and ride over with Mr. Wright, play the fiddle for them to dance a little bit." Mom got right on the horse, rode off, and the man followed right behind her on his horse. They rode over, she got right off and walked right on in where the crowd was, took her fiddle out, and you never heard such fiddling in all your life. Just sawed it to death. Stood up—wouldn't sit down—just stood up (and she was a tall-like woman) . . . and fiddled those old fiddle tunes . . . and just put the music right in your feet![21]

By 1910, the days and nights of Malissa breastfeeding her seventh baby, which limited her ability to get pregnant again, had ended. Both she and J. B. were from families with eight children, so having eight themselves would have been almost preordained.[22]

Financially, it was a good time for another child. The economic hard times of 1907–08 were over. The peak year of the timber boom (1870–1920) had come in 1909, with more than a billion board feet of lumber produced in Kentucky. That year there was also a record harvest in the United States. With increases in rail and factory construction, the nation had begun to experience a "general wave of prosperity," according to an authoritative source. By 1910, J. B. was easily able to buy an additional acre of ground with a house (which he may have rented previously, as Bertha was reportedly born there in 1908).[23]

During the spring and summer of 1911, the entire northeastern quadrant of the United States, including Kentucky, was suffering from extreme high temperatures and lack of rain. The drought finally ended in late August and the crops were saved, but the intense heat continued. On September 12, on a sweltering Tuesday afternoon, Caroline Goff, her daughter Mae, and son Gordon left their cabin east of Rosine and walked up to the recently purchased Monroe house on Pigeon Ridge. Goff knew that Malissa's time was near, and she wanted to see how her friend was doing. As Mae Goff Harvey later told daughter Frances Harvey, "She was settin' on her porch, playing music, barefooted—her feet were swollen—and she had on an old loose dress. Malissa said, 'Caroline, the only relief I can get in this heat from this baby is playin' my music.'"[24]

Bill's First Days on Earth

The next day, Wednesday, September 13, 1911, Malissa gave birth to a baby boy. Thanks to Kentucky's Vital Statistics Law of 1910, which, for the first time, required a birth certificate for every child, we know he was born at home at 10:30 in the morning. Helping to bring him into this world was a midwife ("That's the way we was all brought," Bill said later of his siblings and himself). In a few days, he would be examined by Dr. Adam L. Schanzenbacher, Rosine's doctor at the time, who filled out the birth certificate, listing the mother's maiden name as "Lizzie Vandiveer."

On September 13, 1911, J. B. was fifty-three and Malissa, forty-one. While many women nowadays might be reluctant to have a baby at that age, it was not unusual in that place and time: a survey of women Malissa's age or older, who lived in Ohio County in 1910, revealed that nearly 20 percent had given birth between the ages of forty-one and fifty, and the majority were forty-one to forty-three years old.[25]

On the morning the baby was born, most of J. B. and Malissa's other children would have been conveniently out of the way, at Horton School. This one-room schoolhouse, also on Pigeon Ridge, was about a mile and a half to the southwest of the Monroe house. Harry had turned eighteen five days earlier but was still attending; Speed was fifteen-going-on-sixteen; John was fourteen; Maude was twelve-going-on-thirteen; Birch was ten, and Charlie was eight. Three-year-old Bertha was probably taken to the home of one of the other Monroes nearby.[26]

J. B. and Malissa named their eighth child William Smith Monroe. His first name may have been chosen to honor J. B.'s baseball-playing brother William, but may also have been given in remembrance of Malissa's late brother William. William Howard Taft was president, so the name satisfied any urge to name the baby after a prominent politician. "Smith" probably came from J. B.'s brother Andrew Smith Monroe, his general store partner of 1884–85. But, as William Smith Monroe himself would have put it later, both names "went way on back" in the history of the Monroe family: the father, grandfather, and great-grandfather of John Monroe, who came to Kentucky in 1807, were all named William, and the maiden name of John's mother, Jemima, was Smith.[27]

An otherwise healthy baby, Bill was born with serious vision problems. Increasingly obvious during the first weeks of his life was an eye disorder called strabismus or "cross-eyes," and in his case, it was his left eye that turned inward (esotropia). Today, medical science has effective ways of dealing with strabismus, but back in 1911, J. B. and Malissa were probably told by Dr. Schanzenbacher that Bill would eventually outgrow it. Not apparent, however, was the fact that he was also severely farsighted (objects far away were clearer than those up close). This manifested itself later, when he was unable to focus on objects in low-light conditions: "[W]hen I was real young, I looked like I was gonna go blind. Of a night, I couldn't see anything, hardly." But this particular symptom seems to have corrected itself ("And it just seemed like my sight got to comin' back better"), causing his farsightedness to be overlooked for several years. Visually handicapped, Bill learned to rely on his sense of hearing to compensate for his inadequate sense of sight, and a heightened sensitivity to sound developed as a result.[28]

Primary Musical Influences

The first musical sounds Bill heard came from Malissa. He once described a scene he would have observed nearly every day during his early years:

> My mother, she used to walk through the house singing, you know? And she could play the fiddle. But she had to cook for, you know, eight children and for her husband, my father, and so, that taken a lot of her time. She'd go by the bed where she left her fiddle and pick it up and play a number, you know, an old-time fiddle number, and it was just wonderful.[29]

Malissa filled the house with her music, playing on her fiddle, accordion, or harmonica such lively dance tunes as "Old Joe Clark" or "Heel and Toe Polka," singing unaccompanied, with "a high, clear voice," funny songs like "How Old Are You?" or ballads like "The Butcher Boy."

> In London city, where I did dwell,
> A butcher boy I loved so well.
> He courted me my life away
> And with me then, he would not stay.
>
> There is a tavern in this town
> Where he goes in and he sets down.
> He takes another girl on his knee
> And tells her things that he won't tell me.
>
> I have to grieve. I'll tell you why:
> Because she has more gold than I.
> Her gold will melt, her silver fly.
> In time of need, she's poor as I.
>
> Must I go bound and he go free?
> Must I love a boy that don't love me?
> Alas, alas, t'will have to be,
> 'Till oranges grows on apple trees.

And when her father first came home,
"Where is my daughter? Where has she gone?"
He went upstairs to give her hope.
He found her hanging to a rope.

He took his knife. He cut her down
And in her bosom, these words he found,

"Go dig my grave both wide and deep.
Put a marble stone at my head and feet.
Upon my grave, a snow white dove,
To show the world I died for love."[30]

Although her praises as a musical influence have been generally unsung, it's clear that Malissa was the first and, arguably, most important one in Bill's life. She fostered in him a love of the traditional music she loved, a love that would guide his musical thinking for the rest of his life. In the late 1970s, when he first spoke of the "ancient tones" in bluegrass, he was recalling the timeless songs and tunes he'd marveled at in early childhood, sung and played by his mother. Also, by the example Malissa set, playing to satisfy herself first and then others, Bill too would come to view music as a very personal pursuit, causing him to look deep within himself early on to find his own voice. Years later, his mother's influence was evident in one of his first widely circulated public statements: "If you're singing a song to satisfy your heart and feeling, you won't sing it the same way every time."[31]

As she'd done for all of her other children, Malissa introduced Bill to the fiddle, providing him with a standard to appreciate the abilities of others who played the instrument. Unique to her sensitive youngest son, this would instill a life-long preoccupation with the fiddle, both as the basis of his own playing and as an integral part of the music he would father. And, as Malissa was more inclined toward religious worship than J. B., it was she who took her children to the churches in Rosine. There they made their first acquaintance with harmony singing. As Bill recalled: "[B]ack in the early days, with the Methodist and the Baptist churches, everybody come there to hear the singing and the preaching. They had a Methodist church there at Rosine and a Baptist church." Malissa and her flock were able to go to both services, due to differing start times. Her inability to read the lyrics in hymnals may have hindered her from singing in the choirs, but several of her sons eventually participated in them, with John earning a reputation early on as a fine bass singer.[32]

Malissa probably sang her favorite hymns by heart when the family gathered together to sing. Bill said, "I can remember them singing around home ever since I was big enough to remember anything." And, sometimes, "Our neighbors would come in and we'd get together and sing one or two nights of the week. We didn't have any music [instruments] back then. We'd just sing."[33]

Second only to Malissa in importance as one of Bill's musical influences was her brother Pen. When Bill was born, Harry, Speed, John, and Birch were all fiddling some around home, initially inspired by their mother. But Birch later named Pen as his teacher, and he probably helped teach the others as well. He was also a role model for the boys, a man who could play the fiddle and do it well. Tall, gangly, and easygoing (Birch said he "never did get in a hurry about anything"), Pen was much in demand for dances held nearly every weekend at someone's house, so well known that, according to Bill, "Everybody in the country just called him 'Uncle Pen.'" "If they was going to have a square dance up there around Rosine, why, Uncle Pen was the man they called for, if they could get him." In those days, a fiddle alone was enough for a dance, particularly if the fiddler played with a steady beat. "He had the most perfect time of any fiddler," said Bill, who also praised his uncle's ability to enhance the rhythm, by the way he moved his bow up and down on the strings—the "shuffle."

> Uncle Pen had the greatest shuffle you ever seen. He didn't note so good [his left-hand technique wasn't the best], like a lot of fellers [who used] all four fingers, but he had a shuffle that was out of this world, man. And it was good to listen to, and he got the tone. He tuned his fiddle up, what they called the "bass and counter up" [A/E/A/E, rather than standard G/D/A/E], a lot of times, and he played right on the note. It wasn't neither sharp nor flat, and it was good.[34]

Pen visited the Monroe family many times over the years, staying with them whenever he played for dances in the Horton-Rosine area. By September 1911, at age forty-four, he'd been fiddling for more than thirty years. But it's likely he seldom had a more appreciative audience than his sister's children, who, thanks to her, could recognize that his music was something very special. As an extra added attraction, he'd always bring along some hard stick candy for the youngsters. By 1913 or so, little "William" was among them. "When I first can remember him," he said, "he'd bring his fiddle and he'd stay a night or so, and after supper, why, we'd get him to fiddle. We didn't have no guitar or anything, we'd just all gang up around him and listen to him fiddle—maybe for an hour, hour and a half. My father would call bedtime then."[35]

J. B. and Malissa

At the time, J. B. Monroe was a busy man. He'd acquired the equivalent of more than one square mile of land, and his job was to make it as productive and profitable as possible. He cultivated huge fields, plowing with teams of mules, planting the staples of Kentucky agriculture, corn and tobacco. Huge fields required hired hands to maintain, and J. B. undoubtedly worked with them while supervising. He was also mining coal on his property, helped by his older sons, selling it in the fall to local customers and supplying the Rosine Methodist Church with free fuel for its heating stove. The mine eventually extended several hundred feet into the side of a hollow, with tracks for a coal car to carry the "black gold" out. And J. B. was still cutting timber, although on his own land only. The trees weren't as large, but the effort involved in creating telephone poles and railroad crossties to sell, hewn with a portable sawmill, was only slightly less strenuous. When his sons were old enough, all were his helpers here: "Us boys," Charlie said, "we cut timber and we drug logs and we worked a sawmill." Otherwise, J. B. had to cultivate a large garden, to help feed his family. He had livestock, fox hounds, and game chickens to tend to, and fences to mend. And he took time to account for every penny in his ledger books. (Americans were required to pay annual income taxes for the first time in 1914. Married couples who earned more than $4,000 in 1913 paid 1 percent of their taxable income.)[36]

Charlie spoke of his parents in these days in an interview published in 1973. Always jovial in public, he began by telling an old joke as if his father had actually said it about his offspring ("Malissa, I wouldn't take a thousand dollars for all of the children, but I wouldn't give a dime for another one!"). Included was the story of a childhood escapade involving Birch and himself (Bill was still too young), loading up the coal car with playmates and pushing it as fast as it would go until it jumped the track ("Little kids scattered all over everywheres!"). Ultimately, Charlie had to confess to his father, and the way J. B. calmly resolved the matter (simply putting the car back on the track and warning Charlie not to do it again) reveals that even though sometimes stern ("He could look at you harder than any man you ever seen in your life"), J. B. could also be very patient.

Charlie also told of his mother's efforts to encourage his music-making: In early 1914, at the age of "about eleven," Charlie bought his first guitar in Rosine for $3—on credit—

> An old guitar, had one string on it. . . . I told mama along in the week, I said, "Mama, I've got to have five more strings." She said, "Well, if you got to have five more strings, we'd better pick up a few chickens"—frying chickens—"and take 'em to town." So we took them little old frying chickens to town. Carried 'em—walked and carried 'em—and she bought me five strings. And I brought 'em home and strung that old guitar up, and I don't guess I slept over two hours the whole night long, beating around [on] that old guitar. Out of tune! Couldn't sing, couldn't chord, nothing![37]

Pen probably showed Charlie his first chords, and he definitely helped him thereafter with his rhythm: "I'd just love to follow him," Charlie said, "because he had the best time of any man to follow. . . . I was just learning the guitar then . . . just from what I could pick up, here and yonder."[38]

Shortly before Bill's third birthday, on September 8, 1914, oldest brother Harry turned twenty-one, and a tradition was established within the family: when J. B.'s sons reached that age, he would offer them the choice of $100 or a horse. It's not known which Harry chose, but a few months later, on December 28, he married eighteen-year-old Nola "Nolie" Goff (Robert and Caroline Goff's niece), so either would have been welcome. (In the interim, on November 14, 1914, eighty-two-year-old Jennie Taylor McHenry died in Hartford. The *Herald* reported that several poems from *Forget Me Not* were read aloud at her funeral, but no mention was made of her connection with Rosine. J. B., a *Herald* subscriber, would have known of her passing.)[39]

Bill and His Dad

With Harry gone, J. B.'s workload increased, and his youngest son saw even less of his father than before. Like most little boys, Bill idolized his father and stayed close whenever he was around. Many years later, Bill's son James wrote a biographical profile of his father and carefully paraphrased Bill's words on the subject:

> As a youngster, Bill followed his father around wherever he went and watched every move he made very closely. He wanted to learn to do all the things his father did and he thought by watching him closely, when he grew up he could do the

work around the farm as well as his father. He listened intently to everything his father told him and obeyed him without question. Bill never got a whipping from his father and thought his father was the greatest man in the world.

In those days, however, mothers were usually the disciplinarians, so if a whipping was called for, it would have been Malissa who administered it. As Bill once recalled: "When I was real small, you know, I was too small to go with [my father]. He worked hard and he had men that worked for him and I wanted to go, and when I couldn't go, maybe I would say something about it. I remember my mother would really get me."[40]

Bill was often separated from his brothers, too. By 1914–15, all of them, including eleven-year-old Charlie, were among the "men" who worked with their father, and Bill was still a child. As such, he stayed close to home, helping his mother by digging potatoes in the garden, gathering eggs, carrying in wood, fetching water from a nearby spring, or whatever else he could do for her. But he and his father and brothers were together in the evenings, and sometimes J. B. would take him along when he went fox hunting on Jerusalem Ridge, half a mile or so south of the Monroe farm, where his fox hounds were turned loose to chase the fox. Bill later described one of these outings, revealing his youthful insecurity: "I was real small, and I would set down by a fence post, and I would get real sleepy. And he'd be standing up and listening to the hounds run, and I just *knew* I was gonna go to sleep, and I was afraid he'd go off and leave me there." (Nevertheless, in later years, Bill still had positive feelings for Jerusalem Ridge, saying, "I have loved that area since I was a kid.")[41]

Occasionally, the whole family would visit kinfolks, or kinfolks would visit them, as Bill recalled:

> I can remember Uncle Pen coming around to visit us on Sunday, bringing his family along and driving up with a team of mules. Either that or they would have a buggy—more so it was a wagon. I can remember them coming and spending a Sunday, or coming Saturday night and staying Saturday night and awhile Sunday and then going back home. And we got to visit them once in awhile like that, and I thought it was great to get to go to one of my aunts on the Vandiver's side and stay a weekend.

(At the time, only one of Bill's Vandiver aunts, Mahala, was living. "Aunt Halley" [Hay-lee] lived near Rattlesnake Knob, not far from the town of Dogwalk—now gone—about six miles southeast of Rosine.)[42]

Arnold Shultz was twenty-five years old when Bill was born. At the time, he was playing guitar around Ohio County with the Shultz Family Band, with three of his cousins, brothers Luther (string bass) and Hardin Shultz (banjo) and their sister Ella (fiddle). Around 1914 or 1915, he drifted away from them to roustabout on riverboats traveling the Green, Ohio, and Mississippi Rivers. During this time, according to folklorist William Lightfoot, he established a regular routine: "When he returned from these trips, Arnold would visit his relatives [in Ohio County], . . . hang around a few days, then disappear without a word."[43]

Singing Conventions

In 1915, Bill was taken to his first singing convention. An important social and religious event, the convention brought together choirs from several Methodist and Baptist churches to meet at one church, with each choir singing a few selections, often new compositions. New hymns were learned at a "singing school," a series of lessons and rehearsals held at each church, led by a singing schoolteacher, a specialist hired by the church who taught proper singing technique and music reading, and was familiar with the newest songs. To learn the harmony parts of new songs quickly, choir members had to read music—in this case, the shape-note system of music notation. Commonly used in hymnals of the time, the system transformed the seven notes of the standard musical scale (then, doe-rae-me-faw-sole-law-*see*-doe) into a different geometric shape, theoretically making sight reading easier.[44]

Singing conventions were first held in Ohio County in 1910 at churches in northern areas of the county, too far away for the Monroes to travel to them. So, when the first convention was held near Rosine, on Sunday, August 29, 1915, at Bethel Methodist Church near Horton, it's very likely that Malissa and the children attended, with Bill watching in awe as his big brothers sang with the Rosine Methodist Church choir.[45]

"Another Baby Comin' Around"

A few days after the Convention, Harry and Nolie arrived for an extended stay with J. B. and Malissa. Nolie's first child was due, and J. B. and Malissa's home was the perfect haven for the young, inexperienced couple. On the evening of September 8, Harry's twenty-second birthday, Nolie went into labor. Birch, fourteen; Charlie, twelve; Bertha, seven; and Bill, almost four, were herded out of the house to spend the night in the farm's large (30' × 12') corn crib. "The next mornin'," Bill recalled, "our father came and told us that there was a new baby at the house." Then they were ushered in to meet Charlotte, their first niece, born on Nolie's nineteenth birthday.[46]

Malissa's pampering of her first grandchild was briefly upsetting to sensitive young Bill. "That was the first time that I'd ever heard of anything like that," he said sixty years later, " 'cause I was the youngest in the family—about another baby comin' around." Revealing that he had been pampered, he noted that "back in them days, a kid was babied and petted more than they are today." Then he continued, somewhat overdramatically: "And so, when she [Charlotte] came in the picture, that kindly shoved me out. My mother would hold her and I'd have to stand down beside of her and wish that I was in her lap. So, from that time on, I was just shoved out like that. It made it a sad life, you know, a lonesome life." Seeming to realize he'd gone a bit too far, he quickly summed up, "Any kid's jealous of another one." It was simply little Bill's realization that he was no longer the only baby in his mother's life.[47]

It was probably about this time that Bill was taken to his first "musical," a gathering where folks would listen, rather than dance, to music. Recalling that night, Bill referred to it as "the first music I heard," meaning the first string band music he heard:

> The first music I heard was Uncle Pen and Uncle Burch [Monroe] and Clarence Wilson, and they played numbers like "Soldier's Joy." . . . Clarence Wilson, he played five-string banjo. . . . It's not the clawhammer style, that rapping style. It's a little different than that—with a thumb and a finger . . . and my Uncle Burch, he'd set down and play the bass [probably a cello] and play it with a bow.[48]

Bill also remembered another musical, possibly as much for the journey getting there as for the music:

> There's a long ridge back home called Jerusalem Ridge, and I remember we had to cross that and go on down about a mile to where we come to this real old house called the Leisure [Lie-shur] place, and this man, Cleve Baize that played the fiddle, he lived there. We'd walk back there with a coal oil lantern, and we got there that night and there was a good many in the room listening to them play and they sat in the middle of the room, and I thought that was awful pretty music. . . . Numbers like "Turkey in the Straw" and that kind of stuff. They'd play "Cacklin' Hen" and he could really play that. It was something to go, knowing you was going to hear some music that night.[49]

By 1916, Charlie's guitar playing had improved, and Bertha was trying to play guitar too, probably using his instrument. Birch's fiddling was getting better, especially after he was given his own fiddle by his cello-playing Uncle Burch. Oldest sister Maude "didn't ever fool with [music] any," according to Birch, so she and youngest brother Bill would have been their audience. But Bill wasn't going to be a bystander for long: "If somebody laid an instrument down, I had my hands on it, you know?"[50]

World War and a New House

Speed turned twenty-one on November 30, 1916, but continued to live at home, uncertain of his future. By then the World War had been going on for more than two years and the *Herald* was full of news from various battle-fronts. Finally, on April 6, 1917, the United States declared war on Germany. Registration for the draft was required for men aged twenty-one to thirty, and Harry and Speed dutifully complied. Harry, a married man, was exempt, but Speed, knowing he would be drafted anyway, enlisted on October 5. The next morning, he and forty other recruits boarded a train in Hartford, bound for Louisville and training at Camp Zachary Taylor.[51]

It appears that between the time of the declaration of war and Speed's departure, a new Monroe house was built. Nineteen seventeen was the year of J. B. and Malissa's twenty-fifth anniversary, a fitting time for such a special gift.[52]

A simple yet distinctive one-story dwelling, the house was built in the "cruciform" design of southern vernacular architecture. Seen from above, its two rectangular sections formed the letter T, with the "arm" or top of the T (16' wide × 32' long) on the eastern side and the "stem" of the T (16' wide × 38' long) on the western side. Within were five rooms, two in the arm of about the same size, and three in the stem, arranged east-to-west from smallest to largest.

Uniquely, this relatively small wooden structure was given seventeen windows (each extending almost the 9' 8" distance from floor to ceiling) and ten exterior doors, all providing ventilation in summer and direct entrance into and exit out of each room. Slabs of sandstone served as steps up to five of the doors. The others opened onto nearly six-foot-wide front and back porches, extending the full length of the stem. The entire house was perched on more than a dozen sandstone "pillar rocks" (ranging in size from 9" to 35"), leveling the structure on uneven ground and discouraging snakes from entering.

In the arm, Maude and Bertha shared the room in the northern half and J. B. and Malissa's room was in the southern half (both approximately 15'6" × 13'6"). For heat in the winter, these rooms had back-to-back fireplaces made of sandstone blocks, venting into a single chimney. In the stem, the first and smallest room (15'6" × 7'11") may have been designed to be the main entryway into the house. But, since there was still a "baby" in the family (Bill, five-going-on-six), Malissa may have decided it should be a room just for him, to "protect" him from older brothers. (Even though given his own space, Bill complained about it years later, saying, "He had to sleep by hisself in a room.") It had no windows but did have doors to the porches with panes of glass in their upper sections, like others in the stem. Next in line was the kitchen-dining room (15'6" × 13'8"), with a large wood-burning cookstove, and just beyond it was the largest room (15'6" × 15'8"), for the rest of the boys, with a small free-standing woodstove.[53]

In 2001, before restoration of the Monroe homeplace's house began, there was some speculation that it was constructed on the site of an older house and was built around the back-to-back fireplaces. The Kentucky Archaeological Survey examined the site and found no conclusive evidence of a previous structure. Thirty years prior to the Survey's examination, however, the house was described in a local newspaper article as being "surrounded by a square of twelve maple trees and three walnuts on the east end." Many of these trees were gone by the 2001 examination, but they were much older than the 1917 house, and this seems to confirm that the area within the square was once occupied by *something* and that the new house was built on the site of this older structure.[54]

Bill Goes Off to School

In the 1910s in rural Ohio County, where everyone farmed for a living, the school year ran from July to February, allowing children to be available to help during spring planting. And, even though enrollment records do not exist, it appears that Bill's first day of school may have been in July 1917, while the house was being built. A class photo taken at Horton School that year, published many years later in a local newspaper, includes an unidentified little boy, wearing a tie, with an inwardly turned left eye.[55]

It wasn't long after the house was completed that sixteen-year-old Birch earned the dubious distinction of being the first in the family to be stricken with a serious illness, "double pneumonia," inflammation in both lungs.

In those days, without antibiotics, it was often deadly. "They give Birch up to die," Bill said later, adding that Speed was sent home from the army in anticipation of his passing. But he recovered, possibly due to the cleanliness of his new home.[56]

The First Insults

Bill was probably in the front yard of his new house when the first insults about his eyes reached his ears. The house was located on one of the main roads on the ridge, and some of the travelers on the road made fun of his appearance. "People used to come to this house," he said, "and since I was cross-eyed, strangers would laugh at me. . . . After awhile, when I saw strangers coming down the road, I would go and hide in the barn." The house also served as a hiding place: raised off the ground on "pillar rocks," it could be crawled under. "I'd get under the floor, if I could, just anything to get away from 'em, so I could see them and they couldn't see me." And it was about this time in 1917 that Bill said he began using his sensitive ears to concentrate on more pleasant sounds, particularly those of his Uncle Pen: "I would say from around six years old, something like that, on up through to ten and twelve years old, I listened to him close."[57]

Six months later, in February 1918, Private Speed Monroe, Company K, 336th Infantry Regiment, was on his way to France. He'd completed his basic training and, after his visit home, he was sent to Camp Merritt in New Jersey before boarding the ship in Hoboken that carried him across the Atlantic Ocean. The passage was dangerous: on February 5, 1918, eleven days before Speed left, 166 American soldiers aboard the British troopship *Tuscania* died when it was sunk by a German submarine.[58]

On May 18, 1918, John Monroe turned twenty-one and registered for the draft. At that point, most of the American forces in Europe would not be involved in the fighting until the end of June. That month an influenza epidemic began spreading through the ranks and, according to one historian, "More American soldiers were to die of influenza in France than by bullets of the enemy." When the pandemic arrived in the United States in the fall, hundreds of thousands died. Eventually, draft calls were cancelled, possibly saving John from dying during the last days of the war.[59]

In 1918, school started on July 8, and students registered at Horton School included Birch, Charlie, Bertha, and "William S. Monroe." During the school year, they and the other children were expected to help at home whenever help was needed, so absence was prevalent and accepted in farm country. As a result, many students were unable to complete the work of one grade level during a school year, and it would be another term or longer before they could pass on to the next level. It took determination to complete eighth grade, the highest level before high school.[60]

Shultz Comes Home to Stay

Arnold Shultz is said to have returned from his travels in 1918, to remain in western Kentucky for the rest of his all-too-brief life. By day, he worked in the McHenry coal mines; by night, he made the rounds of the taverns, singing and playing for tips tossed in his big black hat. He also busked on street corners in several towns with a black mandolin player named Walter Taylor. Shultz had become a versatile instrumentalist, able to play guitar using several different techniques or play a hoedown on the fiddle when white folks called for it, and word of his abilities began to spread.[61]

World War I officially ended on "the eleventh hour of the eleventh day of the eleventh month" in 1918. But it took a long time to bring two million American soldiers back to the United States by ship. On May 12, 1919, Speed was discharged at Camp Taylor in Louisville, then put on the train back to Hartford. After arriving at the depot, he and a few of his soldier buddies from the Horton-Rosine area decided to walk home, a distance of some seven or eight miles. Bill, out of school, said he heard them approaching, singing an old hymn, "We'll Understand It Better By and By." Speed's daughter Rosetta, not yet born at the time, liked to tell a story she'd been told about her father whistling as he drew close to the homeplace and Malissa running to meet him.[62]

Malissa Finds an Instrument for Bill

By mid-1919, when Bill was around eight years old, he had made some progress playing Charlie's guitar and Birch's fiddle with his Uncle Pen's help. But the guitar was too big for him and likewise a full-sized fiddle, and Malissa knew young William was struggling to play instruments that weren't really his. (Of his fiddling, Bill would later say, "Never was good enough for me to hardly listen to, much less somebody else.") As the youngest of eight herself, Malissa knew he needed something of his own, something that would be easier to play, something small to fit his stature.[63]

Malissa's choice was the mandolin, a child-sized combination of the two instruments her son was trying to play, "a fiddle with frets that could be plucked or picked like a guitar," as Robert Cantwell described it. She knew that one of the farm workers, twenty-four-year-old Hubert Stringfield, played one, so she took Bill to hear him play it. Bill later said he was "the first man I ever heard play the mandolin" and that "he could tremble one [tremolo, moving the pick back and forth rapidly on the strings] and play different numbers and I thought it was real nice." Malissa paid $3 for it and presented Bill with it, an American-made (probably), Italian-styled instrument with a bowl-shaped body resembling the back of a potato beetle—a "tater bug." But Bill chose blame on his brothers for it.

> I *had* to take the mandolin. I was put on that. Birch was older and he'd taken the fiddle. Charlie was older than I was, so he got the guitar. I woulda liked to have played a guitar or a fiddle either, but . . . so they thought they played a fiddle and guitar, so I'd better get another instrument. Wound up with mandolin.[64]

That summer of 1919, Maude contracted tuberculosis, still a common killer more than thirty-five years after J. B.'s mother had died from it. Everything that could be done in those pre-antibiotic days was done, including sending her to the expensive Hazelwood Sanatorium in Louisville, a facility that treated TB with rest, healthful food, and sunshine. It appears she was well enough to return home by November 17, 1919, her twenty-first birthday.[65]

CHAPTER TWO
1920–1929

Birch and Charlie Take Charge of Bill

By 1920, eight-year-old Bill had learned to play chords on his mandolin, taught by his Uncle Pen, who stressed the importance of rhythm: "One thing that he learnt me how to do was keep time," Bill said. He was soon "playing rhythm" (strumming rhythmically, emphasizing the off beat) with Birch, eighteen, and Charlie, sixteen. It must have been exciting for him—so exciting that he flogged the tater bug for all it was worth, eagerly trying to equal their volume level. Probably due to Birch and Charlie's complaints, Malissa approved of the removal of one string from each of the mandolin's four pairs, because, as Bill put it, "They didn't want me to play too loud."[1]

Although this "solution" might offend modern sensibilities, in those days parents seldom considered the rights and inner feelings of their children. For Malissa, regardless of Bill's hurt, it was the easiest way to solve the problem, and it was probably effective—he learned a lesson and the strings were soon put back on. However, since the idea for it probably came from Birch and Charlie, the solution also served to "put him in his place" and ensure their authority over him.

During the next fourteen years, whenever Bill played music with Birch and Charlie, he would primarily play rhythm on the mandolin. This was appropriate in the early 1920s, when the mandolin's primary role in string band music was to provide rhythmic support. But later, as it emerged as a soloing instrument, Bill's efforts were inhibited by Birch and Charlie, who told him what they wanted. "They wanted me to play rhythm," he said. By then, not only were they maintaining dominance, they were also dependent on him playing rhythm to keep their music on track. Hinting at this, Birch later admitted, "I got to have good seconds [rhythm players] if I do anything. . . . It takes somebody on the ball for me to be any account. 'Cause if you fool along, I fool along. I couldn't pull you to save my life."[2]

In 1920, almost everyone in the family sang occasionally when they played together, but Bill's voice had yet to be heard. After his playing had been put down, he was unsure about his singing, so he only sang when no one else was around: "I used to get out in the field, maybe [a] quarter of a mile from where any of 'em was at, so they couldn't hear me. I was seeing if I could sing numbers like 'Old Joe Clark' and that kind of stuff, like some of the older ones in the family could do." It would awaken early his personal musical values: "I would be singin' just to get to hear the tune and [see] how it would make me feel."[3]

After he turned nine in September, he was given a little more responsibility in his daily chores:

> Bill's job was to water the four work horses [Percherons] at noon at a creek about a quarter of a mile from his house. He and three friends, the sons of a family who worked for Bill's parents, would race bareback every time they went to the creek. Bill recalls one time in particular when racing each other, his horse jumped sideways across a bad place in the road; Bill lost his balance and was thrown into some brush and logs. The boys rushed to help him and got him home. This was his last horse race, as he walked with a limp to favor his leg. To keep his folks from getting after him about racing the horses, he wouldn't say what was causing him to limp. His parents thought he had been playing around big stacks of lumber which had been left to "season," and had fallen. After awhile his father called the doctor who just took hold of Bill's leg and jerked it out straight.

In his later years, Bill seemed to recover quickly from broken bones and various surgeries, and was able to perform long before others could have. Clearly his stoicism started early.[4]

It was probably with these boys, not his brothers, that Bill first played baseball, the sport he later named his favorite. His brothers didn't include him in their play because they were much older and naturally wanted to play with boys their own age. As it was, Bill's vision problems would have made playing ball difficult for him, even after he was fitted for eyeglasses about this time. But he did play ball and, based on the testimony of someone who actually played with him a time or two in the late 1920s, being cross-eyed didn't slow him down. "If it did, I didn't notice it," said boyhood friend Elvis Hines. However, Bill would never be good enough to be a member of an official team, so his pride caused him to deny he ever played the game, as in 1971, when he was quoted saying, "I couldn't see well enough to play ball." Eventually though, in 1986, he finally set the record straight when asked about his childhood ball playing. "I could play all right," he said.[5]

Near the end of 1920, on Tuesday, November 2, the first commercial radio station in the United States, KDKA in Pittsburgh, Pennsylvania, began regular weekly broadcasts. This "free" entertainment would soon challenge the burgeoning "talking machine" business, causing it to look for new ways to sell its "records," including offering "old time music" to listeners. That same Tuesday, American women voted in a national election for the first time, helping Republican presidential candidate Warren G. Harding win a landslide victory over Democrat James M. Cox. Cox had visited western Kentucky in October, speaking in Beaver Dam and Horse Branch (five miles east of Rosine), traveling in a train that carried him right past the northern edge of the J. B. Monroe farm. (Most of the trains that used these tracks at the bottom of Pigeon Ridge carried coal eastward, making "the lonesome sigh of a train going by" a familiar sound to everyone in the area, including Bill.)[6]

The Death of Malissa Monroe

The year 1921 was not a good one. Heavy snow blanketed Ohio County in February, and cold weather wiped out the fruit crop in April. Prices paid to farmers for their produce during the war dropped to an all-time low. Ohio County's coal production lagged behind the mines in eastern Kentucky, and many miners were out of work. In June, the house Uncle Burch lived in, the one he and his brothers and sisters had grown up in, burned to the ground. The only bright spot came in September with a visit from Aunt Susan, who was living in Columbia, South Carolina, at the time. Then, in October, a few weeks after Bill's tenth birthday, his mother fell ill.[7]

On October 19, Dr. Newton J. Rains of Rosine was summoned to the farm. The pain in Malissa's back was already intense. His diagnosis was "antero myelitis," now called osteomyelitis, an infection of the bone, which, in this case, had invaded her spinal column. Usually caused by staphylococcus bacteria in the bloodstream, it could've begun with a cut on the finger from a germy paring knife. Today, osteomyelitis is easily treated with antibiotics, but without them, there was little Dr. Rains could do (recalling the scenario of a song Bill recorded in 1962, "There Was Nothing We Could Do"). He would have given her painkillers, but they were less and less effective. J. B.'s sixty-fourth birthday came and went on October 28. Three days later, on October 31, fifty-one-year-old Malissa died. She was buried in Rosine Cemetery the next day.[8]

Bill later wrote in his song "Memories of Mother and Dad" that "our home was silent and so sad." Not only was the house devoid of the usual talking and laughter, but Malissa's daily music making had ended forever. Without it, the house was unnaturally quiet.[9]

The stillness was especially noticeable to Bill, quiet himself. As the youngest in his family, this was natural, according to birth-order specialist Frank Sulloway: "As [the number of siblings] increases, firstborns become more outgoing and laterborns become more reserved." After the insults of strangers passing the house and insecurities promoted by his brothers, it's likely that Bill was already quiet. The trauma of losing his mother at age ten would have worsened his condition. As Sulloway points out: "Childhood dispositions to shyness are sometimes reinforced by the early loss of a parent," especially the mother. In Bill's case, he would be shy for the rest of his life.[10]

J. B. appears to have been temporarily incapacitated, even unable to arrange for an obituary in the *Herald*, something a Monroe husband hadn't failed to do for a wife in forty years. Pen came to live with J. B. and the children for a while. In spite of his own sorrow, someone had to take charge of them.[11]

Bill Plowing at Age Ten

When spring came in 1922, life went on, mainly because farming had to continue. J. B. enlisted Bill to help break ground for the first time, providing him with a team of mules described as "gentle" and "easy to handle."

> If you was raised on a farm [Bill said later], you would know of hard times, and you didn't get things as a kid that you do now. On Saturday I would get a nickel to buy some candy with and that's all I got all week. And one pair of shoes a year and two pairs of overalls. Have shoes to wear in the wintertime and go barefooted in the summertime [normal for youngsters in the country]. If you plowed for your father, it felt good to your feet to follow that plow and stay in that furrow with the fresh ground turning over there. You didn't mind.

Like his father's, ten-year-old Bill's childhood had ended early, but, as he said, he didn't mind—he had finally become one of the men who worked for his dad.[12]

For Pen, the spring of 1922 brought the beginning of the end of his marriage to Annie. They were legally separated on March 28. Pen and nineteen-year-old son Cecil moved away from the White Run farm, leaving it to Annie and fifteen-year-old daughter Lena. On June 1, Pen bought a ninety-acre farm near the town of Horse Branch. His and Annie's divorce would be final on October 30, 1922.[13]

Also that spring, on May 16, Birch turned twenty-one. Like Speed, then twenty-six, and John, whose twenty-fifth birthday also came on May 16, Birch continued to live and work at home. Maude, twenty-three, and Bertha, thirteen, took over the cooking chores for the family and for the farm workers, and were evidently backward around all the men. Earl Austin, a neighbor who helped J. B. cut hay, told daughter Mildred that Maude and Bertha would fix a meal for the hands, put it on the table, and " . . . Zoom!—Disappear! You wouldn't never see 'em no more." (Austin also recalled Bill being assigned to pick blackberries whenever his sisters made blackberry cobbler.)[14]

Bill, eleven by September 1922, worked tirelessly, like a man was supposed to do, and was eventually invited to join the others when they went hunting for game. "They didn't have to go far because there was plenty of good hunting right on their farm," Bill's son James noted later, referring to squirrels, rabbits, raccoons, and possums. (Deer and wild turkeys, plentiful there now, had been hunted to near extinction in Kentucky, and deer hunting was outlawed in the state at the time.)[15]

During 1922, Arnold Shultz was playing in his Cromwell hometown in a band led by a fellow coal miner, drummer Forrest "Boots" Faught. "I had a four-piece outfit then and Arnold made five," Faught said. "He was the only colored man in the band. He was the first man I ever heard to play the lead on a guitar." They played regularly in an old one-room schoolhouse made into a tavern, where illegal booze was readily available.[16]

Prohibition had been in effect since 1919, but enforcement varied in Ohio County, with some of the most diligent lawmen found around Hartford. One of their most determined efforts was made on Saturday, November 11, 1922, when, according to the *Herald*, five "Federal Prohibition Enforcement Officers" chased a car containing "three McHenry negroes" for six miles on the road from Owensboro (thirty miles north) to Hartford, with the chase ending at the bridge just north of Hartford's downtown. In the car, officers found "Did" Crumpton (the driver), "Bud" Walker, and Arnold Shultz, along with a "one quart bottle and some smaller bottles of white liquor." The *Hartford Republican* (the *Herald*'s new competitor) reported that the men were taken to Owensboro and "delivered to the Federal Authorities." Records of the case couldn't be found, so the final outcome isn't known. But the three probably avoided prosecution due to a then-recent Court of Appeals decision noted in the *Herald* "that automobiles could only be searched by authority of a search warrant." The experience may have been life-changing for Shultz. During the next few years, he could be found in or near the quiet villages of Horton and Rosine, much to the benefit of Bill Monroe.[17]

Learning to Drive

When spring came in 1923, Bill said he was almost continuously busy: "You worked from Monday mornin' 'til Saturday afternoon, then you had Saturday evenin' off." J. B. would drive a wagon into Rosine on Saturday afternoons to buy coffee, sugar, lamp oil, and other supplies for the coming week, and Bill, typically staying close to his father, usually went with him. While J. B. shopped, Bill waited in the wagon and practiced his driving, a skill his father was already teaching him.

> Even though the team was tied to a post in the front of the store, Bill decided he would get some driving in while his father was inside. He pulled them up two or three steps and then backed them up, pulled them ahead and backed them up. . . . Sometimes he would continue this for an hour or more, depending on how long it took his father to get the shopping done.

Driving a wagon was usually limited to adults, twenty-one years old or older. Eleven-year-old Bill, man enough to work for his father, probably wasn't happy that he couldn't drive the wagon, but he was going to be ready when the time came.[18]

It was also during this time that Bill's involvement with music began to move away from home. With full bands becoming more and more popular, Birch, Charlie, and Bill started playing for dances around Rosine, and the brothers also played with their fifty-six-year-old Uncle Pen. "We played quite a bit together," Bill said, "but we still would all get in and play with Uncle Pen, you know, if we could, because he was old. . . . We wouldn't never take no playing away from him [play a dance without him], if he could play." But sometimes it was just Bill playing mandolin or a borrowed guitar to "second" (accompany) his uncle.[19]

Aside from fiddling, as Pen grew older, he turned to other ways of making a living, as Bill later described:

> He was a farmer, and then later on in life he done a lot of trading. Like, if he stayed the weekend with us, he'd start out on Monday morning and he'd go from one friend's house [to another], or on through to whoever he could run into. If he started out with a mule or a horse a-ridin', if he had a pocketknife or something, he would keep trading, and maybe he'd come back at the end of that week with the same horse and a cow, . . . so he must've been a good trader. I guess he enjoyed doing it and made a little something out of it.[20]

Bill's Appendicitis

That summer of 1923, not long after his mother's death, young Bill became aware of his own mortality. On August 27, shortly before his twelfth birthday, he suffered an attack of appendicitis, possibly caused by swallowing a seed from an apple eaten in the fields. He couldn't be stoic this time; the pain was excruciating. It was clear to J. B. that his son needed to be seen by a doctor as soon as possible, but a bumpy ride to town in a wagon would have been torture—he would have to be transported some other way. Luckily, the farm workers were there and J. B. was able to recruit six volunteers: Archa "Archie" Autry, Denver Basham, and William A. "Willie" Johnson, plus three others, possibly Speed, John, and Birch. Bill was laid on a metal-framed cot and, with four carrying and two running alongside to relieve them, they set off for Rosine, a mile and a half away.[21]

After they got there, accounts differ as to what happened next. Apparently, however, Dr. Rains wasn't available and a train to Horse Branch, the nearest town with a doctor, wasn't due soon. So, the six men heroically carried him on to Horse Branch themselves. They knew the distance was five miles by road and four by rail, so they took the shorter route, walking on or beside the railroad tracks. When they finally got to Horse Branch, Dr. R. A. Byers recognized Bill's affliction and had him put aboard "the Peggy," a passenger train that made three round trips a day from Horse Branch to Owensboro. Once there, he was taken to Owensboro City Hospital for emergency surgery—just in time. As Bill recalled in 1987, "The doctors said if we'd gotten there forty-five minutes later, I wouldn't have made it."[22]

Bill Hears Arnold Shultz

It wasn't long after surviving this ordeal that Bill turned twelve and, possibly that fall, heard Arnold Shultz playing music for the first time. Bill recalled that "him and two other colored men come there to Rosine to play for the dance" and "they had a guitar, banjo, and fiddle. Arnold played the guitar." Black men playing for white folks was not uncommon in Ohio County, especially if they played string band music *and* if one of them was thirty-six-year-old Arnold Shultz. "Arnold was always welcome in the best of white homes," according to "Boots" Faught, the Cromwell bandleader. Bill was awestruck.

> If he played a guitar behind a fiddle and he used a straight pick [a flat pick], nobody today plays anything like it. And it's a shame somebody can't play a guitar the way he played with a straight pick. . . . He could just run from one chord to another the prettiest you've ever heard. I tried to keep in mind a little of it—runs that I use in a lot of my music. I don't say that I make them the same way that he could make them, 'cause he was powerful with it.[23]

As 1923 turned into 1924, a new national trend was growing in popularity: nostalgia. Historian Harvey Green believes its appeal was as strong as the allure of rapidly advancing technology: "Equally powerful for the middle class and the wealthy was a yearning for the past that they thought simpler, and therefore more comforting. Images of idyllic rural small towns of harmony and unity coexisted with the new world of the future." Record companies, anxious to sell records, had catered to the trend since 1922, offering sounds of a simpler past. First came fiddlers (including A. C. "Eck" Robertson, Fiddlin' John Carson, and Gid Tanner), then singers (among them, Vernon Dalhart, Henry Whitter, and Riley Puckett). Competitor radio, harking back to days when dances were held in barns, began broadcasting "Barn Dance" shows, most significantly from WLS in Chicago, Illinois, beginning in April 1924. A small (500-watt) station owned by Sears, Roebuck and Company (the "World's Largest Store"), WLS's early *Barn Dance* performers were unknowns who had yet to record, including a square dance band led by fiddler Tommy Dandurand of Iowa, with calls by Tom Owens of Missouri. The show's first announcer was Indiana native George D. Hay, already called "the Solemn Old Judge" for the comedic columns he'd written for a Memphis, Tennessee, newspaper, portraying a white judge and black defendants.[24]

That spring of 1924, Bill's next encounter with Arnold Shultz may have come when Shultz was busking on a street corner in Horton or Rosine. Just one of the crowd gathered around him, Bill listened in wonderment as Shultz sang the blues and fingerpicked his guitar. "He played the old slow blues," Bill said later, "where he could pull the strings and make it really sound blue." It was a revelation.

> That's where the blues come into my life—hearing old Arnold Shultz play 'em. He was the best blues player around in our part of the country there in Kentucky, and that's where most of the people that plays a guitar today [1966]—that's all come from Arnold Shultz. It come on down from Mose Rager, from him into Merle Travis, and from him into Chet Atkins. That's where all that style of playing come from.

Shultz never recorded, so there's no way to know how good he was, but more than forty years after first hearing him, Bill was still in awe of his abilities: "There's no colored man today could play blues with him. Nobody in the world could play blues with that man."[25]

Singing with the Choir

That summer, Bill may have sung with the choir at the Rosine Methodist Church for the first time. Brother John probably pushed the painfully shy twelve-year-old into it, but he didn't have to push too hard. Bill already knew which harmony part he liked the best: "I thought I would love to sing bass, 'cause I had some brothers that could really sing bass—John Monroe and Birch Monroe. That was the first singin' I ever done [in public], was bass." A singing convention was scheduled at Rosine on August 31, and the singing school for it began in June. There, Bill first encountered the basics of music notation, but his vision problems made reading the shape notes frustratingly difficult. However, he discovered he could remember his part after hearing it sung once or twice, leading to a resolution: "I just decided that I would learn my music by ear and always do it that way." (Bill would sing with the choir for about six months, until the end of 1924.)[26]

Meanwhile, Charlie turned twenty-one on July 4, 1924, and decided to take the horse his father offered for his birthday. Combined with another he'd bought from John, he had a team to work with.

> So when I become twenty-one, I put them horses up and told my dad, I said, "Dad, I'm going to sell my horses and I'm going to public work [work in a town or city]." He said, "Well, son, I hope you know what you're doing." That's all he said. I loafed just about two weeks, and I met this girl in the little town of Rosine.

Pretty soon I changed my mind, that I wasn't going to leave! So I went back to my dad and I said, "Dad, I've just about decided to stay on." He always called me "Charger." He said, "Charger, that's the nicest thing you've ever said, when you said you'd changed your mind." He said, "We need you so bad."

I worked right along with them big horses [Percherons], drug logs, hauled coal, or anything that needed to be done, and I done that for a suit of overalls—an overall jacket and overalls—and what I could eat all year long. And I worked! I drug as many logs as any dollar-and-a-half man he had. Dollar and a half was top price, at them times.

And, sir, went on, played on the ball team at Rosine. I played I believe it was thirty-two games and got twenty-eight home runs! Pretty good for a country boy!

Bill must have been envious of Charlie's ability to play baseball. It's no wonder he claimed to have not played, compared to his brother's impressive performance.[27]

Even though Bill couldn't play ball as well as Charlie, he had something else he had begun to take pride in—his musical ability. He had sung with the church choir, and could remember complicated harmony parts by ear. And he had successfully accompanied his Uncle Pen, a musician he greatly admired, and he had discovered a newfound ability to play tunes on his mandolin he'd heard Pen play. But instead of trying to play like him, it appears Bill recognized it was his uncle's individuality and high musical standards, not just the notes he played, that made him great. In the words of Ralph Rinzler, who wrote the first meaningful biographical profile of Bill, he "resolved, at the age of thirteen, to play the mandolin in a way that nobody else had ever played it and to play his music cleaner and better than anyone."[28]

Charlie and Birch's First Trip North

In early 1925, Charlie's mind changed back. He and his girlfriend "had a spat—that took care of everything," he said. He sold his horses, and he and Birch left for Detroit, Michigan. They found jobs at the Briggs Manufacturing Company, maker of car and pickup truck bodies for Ford, and after work, they played at friends' parties. "We'd set and play for them to dance," Charlie said. "Never was a spat, never was an argument, no drinking. Everybody there to have a good time." The brothers boarded with family friends Enos and Hazel Wallace, and at the Wallace home they had access to a Victrola for the first time and started buying records. "We bought everything we seen," Charlie said, including, it appears, the first Columbia release by Charlie Poole and the North Carolina Ramblers, "Don't Let Your Deal Go Down Blues" / "May I Sleep in Your Barn Tonight, Mister?" Charlie learned "May I Sleep," a tale of the woes of infidelity, and later said it was "the first song I ever sung in my life" (probably the first song he ever sang solo in public).[29]

With Charlie and Birch gone to Detroit, Bill was put to work "yarding timber" for the first time, dragging logs with a mule to a spot where they were trimmed into crossties. After the ties were loaded into a wagon, he would ride into Rosine with J. B. to help unload them in the tie yard at the Rosine depot.[30]

Bill Plays with Shultz

By the spring of 1925, Arnold Shultz was living in Hartford and playing throughout the area, and that may have been when Bill first heard him play the fiddle: "He played just a little blues in his fiddlin'," Bill recalled. "If he played 'Sally Goodin,' there'd be just touches in there where he'd touch that was a little blues way he'd do it. And if we played it in A, why, he'd play it in G. He didn't play like a white man plays." It may have been then that Shultz first heard Bill play guitar, and after hearing his solid rhythm, he asked the youngster if he would be willing to play a dance with him.

> Me and him played for a dance there one night and he played the fiddle and we started at sundown and the next morning at daylight we was still playing music—all night long. And, of course, that automatically made you be dancing on Sunday, but that is really the truth—I could say that I have played for a dance all night long. I played guitar with him. I could just second fair—probably any guitar man in the country could've beaten me, but anyhow, I played guitar for him.

Bill said once that Shultz only knew five or six fiddle tunes, so they probably played each one several times that night. On Sunday morning, Bill was paid $5, possibly the largest sum he'd ever been paid to play music. Asked if other white folks said anything to him about playing with a black man, Bill said, "They mighta thought that they wouldn't have done it, but he was a real musician and I thought it was an honor to get to play with him. And he woulda played with me if I coulda played a fiddle, of course, you know? He was a real man, a real colored man." Old-style notions of racial supremacy were common where Bill lived, and even he was not completely free of them, but thanks to his father's friendship with former slave George Monroe, he had an open-mindedness that other whites didn't have, particularly when it came to musicians like Shultz.[31]

It may have been after this "all-nighter" that Bill's father began to rein in his youngest son. Bill's son James wrote in his profile of Bill that he "remembers that his father and he would stay home Saturday nights because his father thought he was too young to go to town." But it would ultimately be beneficial for both father and son, bringing them closer than they'd ever been before.

> So I stayed home with my father. That's what leads back to where me and him would listen to the foxhounds, you know, and it'd be on a Saturday night. But he was up in his late sixties, goin' on seventy years old [sixty-seven in the summer of 1925], and that's probably all he wanted to do. My mother had gone. And he would never marry again—didn't want to. So to hear a good pack of foxhounds was what he loved. I stayed close to him and there wasn't nothin' to be scared about. 'Cause he was the most wonderful father in the world and a straight, honest man, truthful. I don't guess you could be any closer than me and him was. I had the feeling in me that he was a wonderful man and I was proud to be his son.[32]

Out under the stars, they sat and listened to the barking of J. B.'s foxhounds (as many as thirty-two at one point, each with a distinctive "voice" that J. B. could discern in its bark), temporarily driving a marauding chicken-killer away. Johnnie Ragland of Rosine, then twenty-three, worked for J. B. during this time and was sometimes invited to stay for the fox hunts. Years later, he told his daughter Thelma that J. B. heard the chorus of dogs in the distance one night and asked him, "Ain't that the prettiest music you ever heard, Johnnie?"[33]

Uncle Pen

Bill's weekend ramblings may have been limited, but it seems he was still permitted to play with his Uncle Pen: "When some of the other boys had left home and gone out to Detroit and places, Uncle Pen and me would go play for a dance, or where they would want some playing. We'd ride horseback to get there."[34]

That fall in 1925, after Bill turned fourteen, Pen's son Cecil died of pneumonia at age twenty-one or twenty-two. No death certificate was filed, and he was buried in Rosine Cemetery in an unmarked grave, indications that Pen was having financial troubles (he'd presumably sold the ninety-acre farm, and he and Cecil had been living on a three-acre plot near Rosine, which Pen bought earlier that year). J. B. and his children attended the burial ceremony, and Bill, ever after, remembered seeing his Uncle Pen cry and hearing a hymn sung that day, "Take Courage Un' Tomorrow."

> If your soul was veiled in darkness
> And your heart was filled with care,
> T'would be better than the Master,
> For the cross he had to bear.
> Then take courage un' tomorrow.
> All the clouds will pass away.
> Live and trust, and faith believe in.
> Then there'll come a happy day.[35]

Thereafter, Pen moved in with his old friend Clarence Wilson (who played banjo with Pen and Burch when Bill heard his first string band music). Wilson owned a three-hundred-acre farm about a mile west of J. B. Monroe's place, and during the next two years, Pen lived with Wilson, wife Minnie, teenaged daughter Flossie, and young son Tommie. This arrangement was clearly good for both men. As Flossie Wilson recalled, "He and Dad [about ten years Pen's junior] never did have a cross word. They were jolly. Every day [they] would get up like two boys going to play."[36]

In October 1925, radio station WSM went on the air in Nashville, Tennessee, broadcasting with 1,000 watts from the home office building of its owner, the National Life and Accident Insurance Company (its motto: *We Shield Millions*). By November, the company had hired George D. Hay away from WLS to be its station manager, and he promoted a radio barn dance featuring Uncle Jimmy Thompson, a grandfatherly fiddler cut from a mold similar to Uncle Pen. The *WSM Barn Dance* would soon become a regular part of the station's Saturday night programming. (But the Monroes had no radio.)[37]

Charlie and Birch, laid off at Briggs in Detroit, returned home just before Christmas. The two were hooked on records, and it appears they brought their interest home with them. Soon a newfangled phonograph occupied the Monroe house: "We had that kind of record player where you had to wind it up," Bill recalled, "and they started buyin' records." New releases in the early months of 1926 included "Watermelon Hanging on the Vine," by Gid Tanner and His Skillet Lickers, and "Put My Little Shoes Away," sung by Riley Puckett, one of the Skillet Lickers (both on Columbia).[38]

Another facet of the fascination with old-time music was the popularity of the "Old Fiddlers Contest." The new year in Ohio County began with one, held on Saturday night, January 2, 1926, at the courthouse in Hartford and reported on by the *Herald*. More than 350 spectators came in the dead of winter to hear fourteen fiddlers from all over the county. Among the tunes played were "Going Across the Sea," "Turkey in the Straw," "Jennie Lind," "Devil's Dream," and "Sallie Goodin," and on hand to accompany the contestants were "Mr. John Phipps, of Hartford, and Arnold Shultz, colored, also of this city."[39]

That spring, forty-year-old Shultz moved to Horton, where he worked at the "Gold Nugget" coal mine and lived in a two-room shanty in Coal Bank Hollow, a wooded area just west of town. One day, he reportedly showed up at the nearby Clarence Wilson farm, wanting to buy one of the cured hams Wilson was well-known for. Thereafter, Wilson, Uncle Pen, and Shultz played some dances together. It is said that Bill played with them sometimes (although not at dances). If so, the combination of instruments, with Shultz on guitar, Pen on fiddle, Wilson on banjo, and Bill on mandolin, was similar to that used later to play "bluegrass" music.[40]

Birch, Charlie, and Bill: 1926

Playing together again that spring and summer of 1926 were Birch, twenty-five, Charlie, twenty-three, and fourteen-year-old Bill. Noble Stewart, whose family lived in Rosine, recalled the three were in the town "all the time, playin' music" at their Uncle Jack's big, two-story house on the south side of the railroad tracks. Noble, then about six years old, watched as Birch taught Charlie and Bill a new tune: "Birch would have his feet on both of their feet and he would mash on 'em when it came time to change chords." (This adds a new dimension to a comment Bill made in a 1974 interview: "I know when I started I didn't hear the changes like they should've been made, and had to learn all of that stuff.")[41]

During this time, Birch was courting a young lady from Rosine named Leora Baize (not related to Cleve Baize). Running low on funds, Birch asked his Uncle Pen, the successful trader, for a loan. Pen had appointed Clarence Wilson to be his "banker," so daughter Flossie Wilson knew the details: "Birch wanted [Pen] to buy him a suit of clothes, and we got so tickled. He was goin' with a Baize girl. . . . Birch wanted him to buy him a suit, and Pen said, 'Why, I ain't even got a suit myself!'"[42]

Still needing money, Birch and Charlie left home again in August 1926, their departure noted in the new weekly newspaper, the *Ohio County News*: "Messrs. Birch and Charlie Monroe left Saturday [August 14] for Whiting, Ind., to seek employment." Located just across the line from Chicago, Illinois, the community of Whiting is sandwiched between the Indiana towns of Hammond to the west and East Chicago to the east. Together with the city of Gary, east of East Chicago, they combined to form "the Calumet," an area then crammed with oil refineries, steel mills, and manufacturing plants. Many Ohio Countians had already moved to Whiting, some even buying homes there, and they had reported back home that work was "plentiful."[43]

That fall in 1926, the sad saga of Pen's personal life continued with the death of ex-wife Annie of an unknown cause. After she and Pen divorced in 1922, Annie married one Monroe Hayes in December 1925, but by July 1926, records indicate she was married to another man (James Higgs). Within a year of her death, daughter Lena died, also of an unknown cause, at age twenty. Both mother and daughter were buried in unmarked graves in Old Bethel Cemetery, near Horton.[44]

A few months after Birch and Charlie left, they came home again, but just for Christmas. According to the *News* of December 31, "Messrs. Birch and Charlie Monroe, who have been employed at Whiting, Ind., are spending the holidays with their father, Mr. Buck Monroe, and family." When 1927 began, they were gone again, back to the Calumet for their longest stay yet away from home.[45]

Birch and Charlie on Radio

During this time, Birch and Charlie's involvement with music was noticeably increasing. Charlie later wrote in his first songbook about making his radio debut, just east of East Chicago: "My first program was on a station at Gary, Indiana, in 1927. At that time there were not many radios. My father rode a horse about 2 miles to hear that first broadcast. My brother Birch worked with me then." To hear what was likely a one-time appearance on someone else's show, J. B. would have ridden a horse to C. E. Crowder's General Merchandise Store in Horton, the location of the only radio in the area at the time.[46]

For Bill, 1927 seems to have been the loneliest year of his youth, and not just because Charlie and Birch were gone. The health of his sixty-nine-year-old father had begun to decline. J. B. needed to start each day by drinking "a dram of bourbon," probably at least a shot glass of the Kentucky whiskey (available by prescription during Prohibition, to dull aches and pains), which he sometimes shared fraternally with his youngest son. There is also evidence that some form of dementia was overtaking J. B.. Bill's care was left in the hands of brothers and sisters: "I guess they'd see that I had clean clothes, you know, for the weekend [and] to go to school. But they had their own life to live and I guess that they thought that that might have come first." Previously pampered, he felt abandoned: "Just had to kindly grow up like a little dog outside, makin' his own way, you know; tryin' to make out the best way he could."[47]

Pen's Accident

Adding to Bill's loneliness was the lack of music following Uncle Pen's accident: in early 1927, Pen had moved away from the Wilson farm to a cabin about two miles west of Rosine, just across from the Illinois Central's tracks. The mule he was riding was startled by a train and threw him (or, according to another source, fell on him). Pen's leg was broken and the scroll (head-stock) of his fiddle was broken off. Treated by Dr. Pal T. Willis of Beaver Dam, one of the best physicians in the area, his leg "never would set up no more," Flossie Wilson said. "[The doctor] had to break it twice. It would just fall over, and he'd have to walk on crutches." During his long convalescence, Pen again stayed with the Wilsons.[48]

In the evenings, Bill would drift down to Crowder's store, where the radio, now equipped with speakers, was tuned on Saturday nights to the *WSM Barn Dance* (before it became the "Grand Ole Opry" in late 1927). The store owner's grandson, Kenneth Stevens, recalled seeing him with his mandolin: "I remember Bill sitting on the steps that went up to the second level in the store. Everybody urged him to sing, but he didn't want to sing very much, by himself. He'd sing some, but he'd [just] play most of the time." At that point, Bill preferred to think of himself as a harmony singer. "I loved tenor," he said later.[49]

Newly popular in country music at the time were recordings of the duet, a precise combination of two voices singing every word of a song as closely together as possible. Pioneered by blind singers Lester McFarland and Robert Gardner (Mac and Bob) in 1926 and by Tom Darby and Jimmie Tarlton (Darby and Tarlton) in 1927, duet singing would later be dominated by sisters and brothers (including Charlie and Bill Monroe) whose vocal inflections matched naturally. But for the next several years, Mac and Bob and Darby and Tarlton would be its chief practitioners. (Meanwhile, during the first days of August 1927, the Carter Family [August 1] and Jimmie Rodgers [August 4] were recorded for the first time.)[50]

Arnold Shultz was working in Rosine around this time, loading crossties at the depot for the Bond Brothers Lumber Company and teaching guitar between loads. The work was backbreaking, and opportunities to play music may have begun to thin out, so he'd decided it was time to move on. Possibly while helping deliver a load of ties, Bill was able to speak to him before he left:

> I believe it was the next day about ten o'clock, there was a passing train come down through and stopped at Rosine, and I believe he caught that train and went back home, and that was about the last time I ever saw him. I believe if there's ever an old gentleman that passed away and is resting in peace, it was Arnold Shultz—I really believe that.

Shultz moved to Morgantown, the seat of Butler County, and again played with an all-black string band. He died at age forty-five on April 14, 1931. According to folklorist William Lightfoot, his death was "officially of heart disease, unofficially in regional lore of either 'bad' whiskey or poison administered by white musicians jealous of his musicianship." A cousin claimed that someone in his band poisoned him.[51]

Despite his passing, Arnold Shultz would live on in Bill's understanding of and appreciation for the blues. Indicative of the depth of Shultz's influence on him, Bill once said that, instead of mandolin, he would have preferred to play guitar "the way Arnold Shultz played it with a straight pick. If I'd fooled with the guitar, I would have been a blues singer and I never would have fooled with a mandolin, and me and Charlie would never have worked together. It might have been a different setup all the way around. I'd probably have been a blues singer playing the guitar."[52]

Bill turned sixteen in 1927 and, desperate for companionship, he was willing to play with boys less than half his age. Noble Stewart, who had watched the Monroe brothers play music at their Uncle Jack's a year earlier, remembered playing a version of hide-and-seek with Bill that fall. His father worked for J. B. in the timber, and after work, Stewart, age seven, and his six-year-old playmate, Harry Carlisle Monroe Jr. (brother Harry's son) were allowed to ride the work horses. Stewart and "H. C." pretended to be "lawmen" and Bill was "an outlaw."

> They had those big old Perchin [Percheron] horses [Stewart said]. We just barely could straddle across 'em. Bill had a little ol' bay mare. He'd get started [a head

start]. We'd get on them ol' horses on that ol' ridge and [go] through them woods. 'Course you could see the leaves turned up where he went. We'd hunt him down and tell him he was under arrest.

Sometimes the boys couldn't find him: "We'd lose him a time or two. We'd stomp back out and he'd come in after a while." Recalling those days, Stewart added wistfully, "Bill—he was a lot of fun."[53]

As Christmas time drew near, Birch and Charlie came home again. Bill walked down to the Rosine depot to meet them and, as he confided later to one of his Blue Grass Boys, "They got off that train and they were just talking to each other and never even looked at me—just walked right up the road. Wouldn't even pay no attention to me at all." Chances are it was a practical joke they'd decided to play on their "backward" brother, who usually had little to say. Bill, however, would never forget what he perceived as a slight.[54]

The Death of J. B. Monroe

At the time of Birch and Charlie's arrival, pneumonia was widespread in the area, and sixty-year-old Uncle Pen was sick with it. With everyone fearing the worst, he'd been taken to the home of Harry and Nolie Monroe, to be with next of kin. By the end of December, however, he was reported to be "slightly improved," and, although his health would continue to be poor, he managed to survive.[55]

J. B. Monroe would not be so fortunate. Shortly after the beginning of 1928, the seventy-year-old came down with the dreaded "pneumonie fever" ("Dad took sick," Bill later wrote in his "Memories of Mother and Dad"). On Tuesday, January 10, J. B. was seen by Dr. Willis, but, again, without antibiotics, little could be done. Three nights later, Noble Stewart's father, Arthur T. Stewart (whom J. B. called "T"), was sitting up with his bedfast employer and friend, watching over him. In the wee hours of January 14, according to Noble Stewart, "[Dad] said he got up to put some wood on the fireplace. Buck said, 'T, come here a minute.' He said he came over there. Buck said, 'All my life I haven't believed in God, but now I know that something's gonna happen, and I believe in Him.' And then he died."[56]

The following day, James Buchanan "Buck" Monroe, called "a well-known farmer" in his *News* obituary, was buried in Rosine Cemetery next to Malissa. A gray granite tombstone to match hers, simple but beautiful, was later placed on his grave. Inscribed beneath their birth and death dates were epitaphs seen on several tombstones of that era in Ohio County: on Malissa's, "Gone, but not forgotten," and on J. B.'s, "We will meet again." Reminiscent of Malissa's "The Butcher Boy," with the heroine asking for "a marble stone at my head and feet," footstones with the initials "M.A.M." and "J.B.M." marked the lower ends of their graves.[57]

Only after the death of his mother, when Bill became "a man," had he really begun to get close to his father:

> [L]ater on, I got to seeing what kind of a man he really was, the kind of man I really wanted to follow. He was a truthful man, and honest, and would do you a favor. And I'm this much like him, if I do you a favor, I might ask you for one. That was the kind of man he was and I have tried to grow up under what kind of man I thought he was like. I know I have an awful soft heart and I've often wondered about him—I imagine he did too.

Bill was fifty-seven when he spoke these words, still trying to measure up to the image he had of his father. Sadly, he never knew him well enough to be sure if he was soft hearted.[58]

In February 1928, with Jack as administrator of his late brother's estate, an appraisal was made of everything on the farm that could be sold to pay off J. B.'s debts and burial expenses. With Clarence Wilson as one of three appraisers, a list was made that included farming implements, wagons, livestock, lumber, and even stacks of hay. It ended with items "set apart" for the youngest children: for Bill, a gray mare named "Pat" (of less value than the bay mare), a cot, a trunk, a "chist" (chest), and a fox horn; for Bertha, three dining room tables, three "bedstids" (bedsteads), four quilts, a sewing machine, and "all of the dishes." An auction followed in March, with most of the inventory purchased by J. B.'s brothers Jack and Burch and older sons Harry and John. Spending the most otherwise was Reverend Ward Taylor of the Rosine Methodist Church, who had preached at J. B.'s graveside service. Charlie bid $11.50 and won one of the stacks of hay, which he may have given to Bill to feed Pat.[59]

During this time, Pen, now hobbling on crutches, once again came to the Monroe house to take care of the survivors. However, bachelors Speed, thirty-two, and John, thirty, were living elsewhere, possibly in the nearby cabin where they were born. "There wasn't nobody left but just me and my two sisters," Bill said later, not mentioning Birch and Charlie, who were there, but really only visiting. "Then later on, why, Maude [twenty-nine] and Bertha [nineteen] moved [in] with some of my other uncles and I stayed on with Uncle Pen."[60]

Bill Lives with Uncle Jack, Then Uncle Pen

Pen and Bill left the Monroe house in the spring of 1928. As Bill later wrote:

> Soon my childhood days were over.
> I had to leave my old home,
> For Dad and Mother was called to Heaven.
> I was left in this world all alone.

Separated from brothers and sisters forced to look out for themselves, he did, indeed, feel like he was "all alone." Thankfully, he wasn't alone for long: invited by his Uncle Jack to stay with him and his family, he would actually live *in* Rosine for a while in Jack's big house, just south of the railroad tracks and Front Street. While there, Bill tried to farm, on land that belonged to Jack. "[H]e went out on his own," son James wrote, "and farmed five acres of corn and two and one-half acres of cane." Meanwhile, Pen moved into another cabin on the Rosine–Renfrow Road (now "Uncle Pen Lane"), southeast of Rosine on a hill above the town. A small cabin (with one large front room with a small kitchen behind), it was built with huge, thick logs.[61]

During June 1928, three months after Bill moved in with Uncle Jack, nearly eleven inches of rain fell on Ohio County, drowning many crops. Adding to the misery, there was an outbreak of measles in the area, and soon two of Jack's children (Lafe, seventeen, and Smith, fifteen) were sick with the disease. After Bill was advised to relocate until his cousins were well again, he walked up to Pen's cabin. "Uncle Pen, he was by hisself and he was lonely and would like for me to stay there, so that's where I stayed," Bill said.[62]

After he moved in, Bill went back to school in July as he had every year since 1917. It was a long way from Uncle Pen's cabin to Horton (about three miles), but Bill had Pat to ride to and from school now. When he wasn't riding, Bill kept Pat in his Uncle Jack's barn, behind the house on the south side of the railroad tracks in Rosine.[63]

On July 24, 1928, the day after school started, Bill's brother John left "to seek employment" in Gary, Indiana. He'd endured the measles, and the rain had washed out his crops, so he was bound for the steel mills of the Calumet.[64]

The Incident in Rosine

By the end of September, Birch and Charlie were still in Ohio County. Somehow or other, they acquired a car, a Model T, according to those who recalled the incident, and may have decided to go for a joyride in stodgy old Rosine, where a motorized vehicle was extremely rare. After they'd driven around one of the blocks a few times at top speed, a crowd began to gather near Willis Peach's barbershop on the south side of Front Street. Someone yelled, probably in fun, that Charlie was having "a running fit," comparing him to a dog afflicted with worms, and he heard it. Stopping the car, he got out and stormed back to the barbershop. Determined to find out who said it, six-foot-two Charlie grabbed diminutive barber Willis Peach, threw him to the floor and climbed on top of him. Peach, defending himself, reached in his pants pocket for his knife and slashed the left side of Charlie's throat with it. (He later told a friend, "I'm sure glad that that knife was dull. Otherwise, I would have cut his face off.") As Charlie was pulled off Peach, blood gushed from the wound, and Birch fainted.[65]

The gash in Charlie's throat was quickly and inexpertly sewn up. He would carry an obvious scar for the rest of his life, causing him to turn the right side of his face toward the camera whenever he was photographed. Within a couple of weeks, he and Birch returned to Detroit.[66]

Not long afterward, in November 1928, farmers in Ohio County were harvesting their corn. Bill's crop, like many others, was decimated by rain, but his two-and-a-half acres of cane had thrived. Son James noted, "When the cane was milled into syrup, Bill received fifty-five gallons. He kept some of it and sold the rest for $1.00 per gallon." The sorghum "syrup" he kept was shared with his Uncle Pen. "He done the cooking for the two of us," Bill wrote years later for an album's liner notes. "We had fat back, sorghum molasses, and hoe cakes for breakfast, followed up with black-eyed peas with fat back, and cornbread and sorghum for dinner and supper." Bill helped out by fetching wood and water for his crippled uncle. "We just made out," he told writer Peter Guralnick. "That was hard days, man. Hard days."[67]

After the harvest, Bill began working for his Uncle Andrew, who had carried on with the logging after J. B.'s death. Bill again yarded timber and transported the finished products to the Rosine depot. In a rare public reflection on the past, onstage at a bluegrass festival in 1983, Bill spoke of himself in those days in the third-person:

He worked and he hauled crossties and he hauled telephone poles. You might not believe this, but he learned all this under his father, too. How to chain 'em down—"boom" 'em down [securing the load in the wagon]—and he drove four horses from sixteen until he was eighteen. He hauled thirty crossties on a wagon, and he would haul five twenty-five-foot telephone poles on a load, or if they was forty-five, he would haul three. I'll put my hand up to the good Lord that that's the truth. But he went up and down some powerful big hills, and he knew how to brake and rough-lock [immobilizing one of the back wheels with a heavy chain wrapped between its spokes], do it so the wagon would go down the hill real easy, [and] when he'd get down there, he'd have to unlock and he would have to pull [up] a powerful hill over there on the other side. Going into Rosine, Kentucky, that was a powerful hill there where [the road crossed] the railroad crossing, right there in town. And people would walk up on that road . . . to see him pull that hill there with these four horses. . . . [A]nd I was really proud of him for doing that. . . .

It definitely was a sight to see, this youngster who could drive a wagon so expertly, with an uncanny ability to control his horses, getting them to do his bidding with such ease. For Bill, it was a performance, and he liked the feeling of people watching his every move, admiration shining in their eyes.[68]

Bill's Last School Days

On February 1, 1929, when the school year ended, Bill's school days were over forever. He had completed the work of the fifth grade level and, if he started in 1917, it had taken twelve years to do it. Judging by grades he received in later years (in conduct, spelling, reading, writing, arithmetic, and language-grammar), he was an outstanding student. Given absences due to farm work and his impaired vision, it must have been a struggle for him, but he did very well.[69]

"Late in the Evenin', about Sundown"

Bill continued working for Uncle Andrew and, when spring came, he also worked for Uncle Jack, plowing and planting his crops. For this, he was paid $1.50 a day "plus his dinner" (lunch). After work, as day turned into evening, he would put the work horses up in Jack's barn and, in the quiet, he could hear Pen, way off in the distance.

I could hear him playing many evenings after I'd get through work. I would put my teams up downtown [in] a barn there, and I could hear him playing out on the back porch [of the cabin] with that [fiddle]. There wasn't no radios—there wasn't no other music in that town going but that. You know, I've heard him set out there and play them old-timers a lot of years, and that fiddle would come down across the town . . . and I guess it was three quarters of a mile up there.

Pen, like Malissa, was playing for his own enjoyment first. And, in the process, he was also revealing to Bill one of the primary "secrets" of playing music: in order to be really good at it, one had to play a lot.[70]

With interest in old-time music growing, Uncle Pen's fiddling was more in demand in 1929 than ever before. He and Bill played somewhere every weekend, both Friday and Saturday nights, and they would ride double on Pen's mule to get there.

> He could still get on that mule with his crutches and I'd get on up behind him and we'd go play for square dances. Used to be they'd have them in Rosine, Kentucky, every Saturday night. . . . They generally would start about eight o'clock and go on up till midnight. Sometimes [when the dances were elsewhere] we'd have to go a mile and a half, two miles, three miles. . . . Of course, that was right back through dirt roads, you know. That was the kind of roads we was on.

The dances in Rosine were often held behind Will Dever's General Store on the north side of Front Street, and when the weather was dry, they'd have "a dance in sawdust," with the ground covered up to keep the dust down.[71]

Pen and Bill also played at parties: "We did a lot of house parties, and some of them had square dances there at [in] the house. The people would all dance and they would donate fifteen cents a set." This amounted to anywhere from $2.50 to $5, "never over five dollars a night," according to Bill. (Today, this would be the equivalent of approximately $90 to $180.) But, Bill said, whatever they made, Pen always gave him half. It was an indication not only of Pen's fairness but that he now considered his nephew to be an equal.[72]

Learning Uncle Pen's Tunes

Bill's status as an equal appears to have encouraged him to study a body of music now readily available: his uncle's repertoire of fiddle tunes. He learned to play as many as he could on his mandolin, so intensely that they became a part of him. Forty years later, he admitted to having lost only a small percentage: "One thing that did stay in my mind—and I can remember most of them, you know?—is the fiddle numbers that Uncle Pen played. Now that really stuck to me. I can play ninety-five percent of every tune that he played, and can still remember them. I must've listened to him awful close when he was playing."[73]

Bill had learned several tunes during the ten years he'd been playing mandolin, but, in his eyes, this was a new beginning: "Learning his numbers gave me something to start on." Gradually, he began to see that his way of playing them was leading to something unique: "When I got up, I'd say around eighteen years old, then I knew that I was on to a style of my own ... nobody else played that style of mandolin ... and I wasn't going to follow nobody then, after I seen that I really had another style ... I was going to master it if I could, and that's what happened."[74]

On August 1, 1929, Birch and Charlie came home, bringing John with them. He had worked in Gary, Indiana, for about a year, then joined them in the Motor City. This time the *News* reported the three planned to "spend their vacation with relatives."[75]

During this time, the *News* mentioned many young men leaving the area to find work in the industrialized North. But for the time being, Bill seems to have been happy where he was, primarily because the wise old gentleman he bached with knew exactly how to handle him: "Uncle Pen treated me right—he treated me good. . . . He would tell me things that he thought I should do, and if he never told me anything, I knew I was doing pretty well right."[76]

Around the time of the beginning of the Great Depression ("Black Tuesday," October 29, 1929), with dances and parties tapering off in the fall, sixty-two-year-old Pen was showing eighteen-year-old Bill how to supplement their income and their diet: "[W]e'd set snares and traps for foxes [to sell the hides] and rabbits [to eat]. And I would set them in the evening, and the next morning, he would go around on the trail where I had them set, and he would bring in what I had caught. And I've seen him bring in as high as eight rabbits of a morning. Now that's something."[77]

Bill's big brothers' "vacation" turned into a four-month stay and, during it, Birch and Charlie undoubtedly got together with Bill. Impressed with his new skill on the mandolin, they wouldn't have praised him too much, preferring he stick with what was best for them: playing rhythm. Missing his rhythmic support, they may have suggested he come along when they got ready to leave. But Bill wasn't ready. "You wondered what life would have been like in a town or a city," he said later, "but I was afraid to tackle it."[78]

On November 26, 1929, John, Birch, and Charlie returned to Detroit.[79]

CHAPTER THREE
1930–1939

Bill Leaves Home

Bill, eighteen, was still in Kentucky when spring came in 1930, but not for long. Uncles Andrew and Jack might have encouraged him to "go to public work" like John, Birch, Charlie, and Speed. Speed, thirty-four, had recently come home after working in Owensboro and married thirty-one-year-old divorcée Geanie (Clark) Whitehead. "I reckon my people figured I would never make anything there," Bill said, "and that they should try to get me out of there to where I could make a decent living."[1]

Possibly delaying his decision to go was a brief romance. All he ever said about it was, "I never had a date 'til I was eighteen. I never kissed a girl 'til I was eighteen years old. I didn't know what I was doin'." It may have inspired many "what ifs" in the years to come.

> I could have stayed in Kentucky and been a farmer. I'd have been satisfied with that. I could've probably planned a married life and raised a family. But my people went and talked me into leaving Kentucky and going up to where there was money. I was afraid to leave Kentucky because I'd never been around no place like that. I didn't know whether I could find my way around or not.[2]

Shortly after they returned to Detroit, Birch and Charlie were laid off again, so they and brother John headed back to the Calumet. A letter home may have convinced Bill to join them in Whiting, where they could all live together cheaply.[3]

On the morning of Wednesday, April 30, 1930, after the crops had been planted, Bill said goodbye to Uncle Pen, whom he had lived with for nearly two years. Bill never spoke of this parting, but it couldn't have been easy: "He done a lot of good things for me. A man that old, and crippled, that would cook for you and see that you had a bed and a place to stay and something for breakfast and dinner and supper, and you know it come hard for him. . . . Maybe, if I hadn't heard of him, I'd have never learned anything about music at all." Bill carried his suitcase and tater bug (stowed in a pillowcase, it's said) down to the Rosine depot and was met there by Speed. "It never hurt him so bad as anything in his life to put his little brother on a train goin' north," said Frances Harvey, who had heard about that morning. With tears in his eyes, Speed gave Bill a twenty-dollar bill and sent him on his way.[4]

"I didn't have music on my mind. I went up there to work," Bill said. But finding a job wasn't easy; by the end of June, he was still unemployed. Charlie was working at the Sinclair Oil Refinery in East Chicago, southeast of Whiting, and in July he used his influence as a standout player on the company baseball team to get Bill hired: "[The] manager of the team was my boss at the plant—Max Tucker. . . . I said, 'Max, I've got a brother here, eighteen years old. Now, he's not well. Now, if we can't get him through that gate out there, I'm going to have to leave Sinclair's ball team and company.'" Charlie played on Tucker's sympathies, using Bill's cross-eyed appearance to claim he wasn't completely normal. But it worked, and he was given a job.[5]

At that time, Jimmie Rodgers was in Hollywood, California, recording for Victor Records. He had been dubbed "America's Blue Yodeler" for the series of "blue yodels" he'd recorded, combining his black-sounding blues singing with a seemingly effortless yodel (which, for some early listeners, confirmed he was white). On July 11, 1930, he recorded a new one, "Blue Yodel No. 8," subtitled "Mule Skinner Blues," and when it was released, Bill's avid record buying brothers would've bought it immediately. Bill would've been easily drawn to it, with its frank mention of using a whip "on a mule's behind" and of working for "a dollar and a half a day," something he himself had done recently.[6]

Bill was assigned to "the barrel house" at Sinclair, cleaning and stacking empty oil barrels. In later years he described his job, which, like logging in the 1890s, seems to define hard work.

> Many's a day I've stacked a thousand barrels—two thousand barrels. We could unload a freight car in forty-five minutes. There would be two inside the car and two or three of us outside and they would spin those barrels down on you and

you would have to catch them—just like playing ball. And then we would clean
barrels with gasoline. Some of them weighed one hundred and fifty pounds.[7]

I learned how to handle those barrels just like a man throwing a ball, throwing
a curve. I got to where I could handle a drum—you'd be surprised at what I could
do with it and how far I could throw it and make it set up. I believe I could clean
thirty-six drums in fifteen minutes and have them all setting in the dryer.[8]

With Charlie and Bill both working, sisters Maude and Bertha were encouraged to come to Whiting and, after they arrived from Rosine on August
5, they moved in with their four brothers. Then Charlie's temper flared and
he was fired at Sinclair after a fistfight with a co-worker. Bill, earning $65
every two weeks, was suddenly the sole breadwinner for six Monroes. He
recalled:

Well, there was a time when my brothers couldn't find work. And my two sisters
were there, and they wasn't workin' either. But I worked every day. The people out
at the Sinclair refineries, some of them was from Kentucky, and they knew that
I needed the money to take care of everything—pay our rent and buy groceries.
And they let me work thirty days in the month, 'cause they knew I needed the
work. And I took care of everything. I would work there, and I'd go out on the
streetcar to go to work, and my brothers would go out and pick up my check.
They'd take it back and get it cashed, and pay all the bills. And I'd hang in there
and work.

It was a situation that appears to have happened more than once during the
next few years. "I never could put any money aside," Bill said later. "I've often
wondered if I was doing the right thing. I guess I was. It wouldn't be right
not to support your people."[9]

After work, Bill was surrounded by new worlds of entertainment: movie
theaters with "talking pictures" (which he had not yet seen), nightclubs,
vaudeville shows, dance halls. Even old familiar radio seemed new, with
numerous local stations coming in loud and clear, unlike the static-filled
signals he'd heard at Crowder's store. Most powerful was WLS in nearby
Chicago, then a 5,000-watt station owned by the *Prairie Farmer* newspaper.
In 1930, the stars of its Saturday night *Barn Dance* included cowboy singer
Arkie, called the Arkansas Woodchopper (Luther Ossenbrink of Missouri,
who wore riding britches as part of his stage costume); Kentucky folksinger
Bradley Kincaid (whose repertoire included "The Butcher Boy"); and the
original Cumberland Ridge Runners (Karl Davis, mandolin; Doctor How-
ard "Doc" Hopkins, banjo; leader John Lair, jug; Gene Ruppe, fiddle; and

Hartford Connecticut "Harty" Taylor, guitar), all from Kentucky. Bill must have heard they were all earning a better living than he was by just singing and playing on the radio.[10]

Before long, Charlie found a job at Sinclair's competitor, Standard Oil in Hammond, due south of Whiting; Maude and Bertha were hired at the Queen Anne Candy Company (famous for their chocolate-covered cherries), also in Hammond; and Birch went to work at Sinclair. With some time off, Bill made a bold move: no longer worried about "finding his way around," he took his tater bug, journeyed to a small radio station in Hammond he'd been listening to, 100-watt WWAE, and guested on one of its many live shows. "I was the first Monroe to go on radio," he told John Hartford in 1990 (forgetting, at age seventy-eight, about Charlie and Birch's radio debut in 1927), "and the next day, the Monroe Brothers was together—we's all on it." Thereafter, the three visited WWAE occasionally, but their main musical activity remained playing for parties. As Bill later put it, "We'd play wherever we'd get to play, anybody that wanted us, they didn't have to pay us nothing, we just wanted the experience. We thought it was great for somebody to want us to play."[11]

After most of the Monroes were employed, they began looking for a new place to live, closer to their jobs. That fall they moved into an apartment building in East Chicago at 4714 Magoun [Ma-goon] Avenue, near the busy intersection of Chicago Avenue and Forsythe Avenue (now Indianapolis Boulevard). It was a short streetcar ride for Bill and Birch to Sinclair, and Charlie had only another half mile farther north to go to get to Standard Oil in Hammond. The Queen Anne factory in Hammond was less than a mile to the west of the apartment building for Maude and Bertha. Brother John, meanwhile, couldn't find work and returned to Rosine in November 1930.[12]

By 1931, Bill had a reputation as a solid and dependable worker. As was his style throughout life, he thrived on hard work, but he then had the happy-go-lucky attitude of youth. "I weighed about 165 pounds and was young then," he said in 1977. "I got kind of a kick out of doing it." Co-worker Roy Hatton and Bill would pick up and deliver oil barrels and building materials around the refinery, with Hatton driving a tractor and Bill riding in a wagon behind it. Hatton remembered nineteen-year-old Bill singing and yodeling at the top of his voice as they traveled around the huge Sinclair facility.[13]

While Bill worked, the *WLS Barn Dance* grew in popularity, especially after WLS boosted its power to 50,000 watts in early 1931 (a year before WSM in Nashville). Joining the *Barn Dance* cast that year were duet pioneers Mac and Bob (Kentuckian Lester McFarland, tenor singer and mandolinist, and Tennessean Robert Gardner, lead singer and guitarist). Bill would learn a great deal from McFarland, especially about using a mandolin to accompany singing. Also new were twenty-four-year-old Gene Autry, then an interpreter of Jimmie Rodgers's songs; tenor-voiced Hugh Cross, who replaced Doc Hopkins with the Cumberland Ridge Runners and sang a song called "Footprints in the Snow"; and comic Max Terhune, "the Hoosier Mimic," who could "make all kinds of funny noises" and "keep a crowd happy for hours at a stretch."[14]

As the Depression deepened, two new duet-singing duos emerged in 1931—the Delmore Brothers (of Alabama) and Karl and Harty (Karl Davis and Harty Taylor of the Cumberland Ridge Runners)—and both recorded near the end of the year. But sales were limited, and both would have to wait until 1934 before they had another record released.[15]

In early 1932, the news from home was mixed. Uncle Andrew, J. B.'s general store partner, died on February 1 of cancer and double pneumonia at age seventy-two. Then, on March 27, thirty-four-year-old brother John, once again farming, married thirty-two-year-old divorcée Clara Wilson (not related to Clarence Wilson). But there is no indication that the Monroes of East Chicago returned home during this time.[16]

That March, the *WLS Barn Dance* moved from a small studio to the 1,200-seat Eighth Street Theater, to accommodate the crowds thronging to see it. Caught up in the rising "hillbilly fever," little WWAE began to increase its country music programs. Live shows titled *Old Time Music* or *Old Time Tunes* were broadcast three to five times a week, and a weekly *Old Time Midnight Frolic* was added on Wednesday nights. Birch, Charlie, and Bill undoubtedly guested on these shows, and, before long, were approached about doing a show of their own.[17]

The Death of Uncle Pen

Meanwhile, down in Rosine, sixty-three-year-old Uncle Pen was dying. In May, an ongoing bronchitis had worsened (he may have been a smoker) and he was again stricken with pneumonia. Speed and Geanie moved in with him and tried to nurse him back to health. Years later, Geanie told Rosine historian Wendell Allen about Pen's last days; Allen paraphrased her recollections in a letter to Ralph Rinzler:

> Mrs. Monroe [Geanie] recalled that Uncle Pen seemed improved on the day before his death—he had eaten well. Speed went to the store and post office in

Rosine. Uncle Pen managed to get out of bed and go to an outdoor toilet, where he fell. She said she partly dragged and carried him back to the house, while sending her oldest daughter, Ruth [Whitehead, from her previous marriage], down to Rosine to get her husband [Speed]. A doctor was sent for and Dr. Pal T. Willis came. Uncle Pen was considerable weaker and his breathing labored. Dr. Willis told them that he couldn't last much longer. Dr. Willis left with Speed in the doctor's car, to bring back some medicine. Speed walked all the nine miles back from Beaver Dam to Rosine with the medicine for Uncle Pen. Uncle Pen died the next day [June 22, 1932].[18]

Pen was "washed, shaved, and dressed" by a neighbor, and a local undertaker arranged for his burial in Rosine Cemetery, in an unmarked grave near son Cecil's unmarked grave, in the cemetery where Pen's father had been buried in an unmarked grave twenty-five years earlier. No death certificate was filed. Pen's nieces and nephews in Whiting didn't have a telephone, so they probably learned of his passing and burial by mail. "That's the worst part of all of my life, that I didn't get to go to his funeral," Bill said years later. But, like Arnold Shultz, James Pendleton Vandiver would live on within Bill: "He was a wonderful uncle and I could always remember how he sounded—what kind of timin' he had to his music."[19]

Their Own Radio Show

On July 17, 1932, the Monroe Brothers' first radio show was broadcast on WWAE, on a Sunday night from 9:00 to 9:30. Probably a program of religious music, it appears the trio was already specializing in the kind of songs Charlie and Bill would later be famous for. With Birch singing bass, Charlie lead, and Bill tenor, they reprised many of the hymns they'd learned in church back home. Accompaniment was sparse, with Birch probably not fiddling, so the emphasis was on the remarkable way their voices combined. The following week, the secular side of their music was heard on the *Saturday Night Frolic*. By August, they were broadcasting twice a week on WWAE, once on various weekday evenings and always on Sunday night. In the *Hammond Times* radio logs of Wednesday, August 24, they were listed for the first time with a nickname they would use for the next several years, "Kentucky Songbirds."[20]

For all of this early radio work, they were paid either nothing or, at best, a nominal fee. As Bill later explained, "At that time you couldn't hardly get a job playing music [on radio] that paid any money. WLS in Chicago was about the only place up there that really paid any good money, and you got very little on smaller stations without you didn't have a sponsor, you know; they would take you in and give you so much a week." However, their shows allowed them to plug the square dances they were playing throughout the Calumet, where the money was: "If you went out and played for a square dance, you might [each] make three, or four, or five dollars a night [depending on attendance]. We'd get maybe twenty-five dollars for the three of us, or the four of us if somebody was playing bass or something" (an intriguing indication they welcomed other instruments, including upright bass, a newcomer to country music in 1932).[21]

Dancing for WLS

In those days, if Birch, Charlie, and Bill weren't playing for a square dance, they were usually dancing at one with their girlfriends. And, at a hoedown in Hammond in September 1932, while square dancing with friends Larry Moore and his wife, they were spotted by WLS's Tom Owens. Owens, now the leader of the "Exhibition Square Dancers," a popular feature of the *WLS Barn Dance*, was looking for a new set of dancers for one of WLS's road shows, scaled-down versions of the *Barn Dance* that toured the Midwest, playing at theaters and high schools. According to Charlie, "Tom came around after the dance and said, 'How would you boys like to dance on the stage, for a living?' Well, that sounded pretty good. So we told him . . . we would like it very much." Then Owens, who'd heard the Monroes sing and play earlier that night, also offered the tantalizing possibility of appearing on the *Barn Dance*: "'Another thing, you boys might break into WLS.' But he said, 'I'll tell you before you go, they got an awful lot of talent.'" That doesn't appear to have deterred them.[22]

Birch, Charlie, Bill, their girlfriends, and the Moores were soon on tour, initially away from the Calumet for two weeks at a stretch. Bill had evidently earned plenty of vacation days at Sinclair after two years of work, so taking time off wasn't a problem ("I'd take off two weeks and then I'd go back"). Later, the touring schedule would be heavier and, as Bill recalled, "then I'd get a relief of absence [a leave of absence] and stay off from work maybe a month." Birch and Charlie's work situations aren't known, but if they had to quit their jobs to go, WLS paid their dancers well ($22.50 a week each), so money would not have been as seriously lacking as before. During this busy time, from October 1932 through February 1933, the brothers were heard on WWAE only twice: Sunday, October 16, 1932, and Wednesday, January 18, 1933.[23]

The new square dancers usually danced to the music of Rube Tronson and his Texas Cowboys, led by old-time fiddler Tronson of Wisconsin, with clarinet, accordion, tenor banjo, drums, guitar, and a second, more polished fiddler. But Tronson fiddled for the dancers: "He played 'Waggoner' and 'Billy in the Lowground' and them tunes," Birch said, "and he played them so you could dance." Like their radio counterparts, the male dancers wore overalls and white shirts with red bandanas tied around their necks, while their partners were dressed in beltless frocks with hemlines cut below the knees.[24]

Bill later remembered many of the main acts on the early tours: Arkie the Arkansas Woodchopper, the Cumberland Ridge Runners (with Karl and Harty), harmonica player Lonnie Glosson of Arkansas, the barbershop harmony-singing Maple City Four of Indiana, and the Three Little Maids, the gentle-voiced Overstake sisters of Illinois.

> We played [put on the show] a lot of times seven days a week. We [the square dancers] had a Packard we would travel in. We played mostly through Indiana and Illinois and maybe a few days in Wisconsin and Michigan. It give us some experience and give us a chance to travel. That's something I never had done before then, you know, was to travel any, you might say.

Traveling like this (sleeping in the car, washing up in gas station restrooms, eating on the run in roadside cafés and truck stops) doesn't appeal to most people. Twenty-one-year-old Bill took to it like a proverbial duck to water. Wanderlust, after all, was in his blood, and the hardships didn't bother him.[25]

With a little extra money from the tours, Bill was able to buy a better-quality mandolin to replace his tater bug. (He once said of his days in the Calumet, "All I got out of it was I spent forty dollars for a mandolin and I got a couple of suits of clothes.") While on tour, he asked Karl Davis if he could try his Gibson A-4, the same model Lester McFarland played. According to Davis, "Bill said, 'Could I see your mandolin?' and he took this mandolin and I've never heard anybody play as fast in my life, and I went across the stage and got Red Foley and Linda Parker [both had joined the Cumberland Ridge Runners during 1932] and Harty [Taylor] and I said, 'Come over here and listen to this man play this mandolin.'" Bill was apparently playing tunes he learned from his Uncle Pen. Shortly thereafter, Bill bought an A-4 with the same teardrop-shaped body, black-painted top, and oval sound hole as Davis and McFarland's, but one with a distinctively different "snakehead" headstock. (Its design is credited to Gibson acoustical engineer Lloyd Loar, one of the designers of the Gibson F-5 mandolin that Bill would play later.)[26]

Probably influencing Bill's choice was Charles "Chick" Hurt of Metcalfe County, Kentucky, who owned and played a snakehead A-4 (but who usually picked a mandola or tenor banjo) and whose musicianship and style had a definite impact on Bill. In late 1932, Hurt joined the *Barn Dance* cast as a member of the Kentucky Ramblers, which soon became the Prairie Ramblers, honoring WLS's new *Prairie Farmer* owner. The Ramblers also included Rosine, Kentucky, native Shelby "Tex" Atchison, possibly inspiring hopes of *Barn Dance* stardom for other Rosine natives. Raised in McHenry, left-handed fiddler Atchison had known Arnold Shultz too, and later credited him with teaching him the long bow style of fiddling.[27]

Economic conditions in America, meanwhile, continued to decline, and, while the Monroe brothers and sisters seem to have glided through it, the Depression was at its worst during this time. Even elite RCA Victor reduced its prices to stay in business: in January 1933, using the name "Bluebird" for a low-priced "budget" label, the company issued a series of previously released recordings, selling them for twenty-five (later thirty-five) cents each, instead of the usual seventy-five cents. (A few months later, they were also issued on the Montgomery Ward label, to sell cheaply in the retail giant's stores and mail-order catalogs.)[28]

After Bill's skill with a mandolin was revealed to Karl Davis, WLS agent Joe Frank arranged an audition for Charlie and Bill as a potential duo on the *Barn Dance* (with a band like the Monroe Brothers trio not needed after the Prairie Ramblers were hired). The audition was held at the Palace Theater in Chicago, and the brothers were the opening act of the show—a burlesque show. They were told that when they finished their set, they were to dance off the stage behind a string of twenty-six scantily-clad strippers while playing "She'll Be Coming 'Round the Mountain When She Comes." As Charlie recalled:

> We sung out fifteen minutes worth of singing . . . started the show, and danced off behind the girls on the way out. But Rube Tronson [and] the Arkansas Wood-chopper, all of them came down, to see how we got along. And that Joe Franks set back there and laughed like a daggone fool at us hillbillies—he called us "hillbillies"—following these burlesque girls off'n that stage. We were so afraid someone might bump into us or something might happen, we was just guarding everything! Scared smack dab to death.

They had confirmed they were "hillbillies," not at all the showbiz-savvy professionals who performed on the *WLS Barn Dance*. At this point, they'd had little or no experience "putting on a show," and talent alone was not going to be enough to make them members of the cast. Franks may have advised them to get some experience singing and playing for listening audiences.[29]

With the road show schedule thinning out, they did just that. During March and April 1933, as Franklin D. Roosevelt began his first term as president and the Delmore Brothers debuted on the *Grand Ole Opry*, the Monroe Brothers started performing for revivals and "Southern Nights" at churches in Hammond and East Chicago. They were also heard on WWAE again, on occasional Monday and Thursday evenings at 6:45 in March and April. When touring stopped during May, June, and July, they were on almost every Monday and Thursday evening at 6:45.[30]

On Friday, May 26, 1933, Jimmie Rodgers died at the age of thirty-five. He'd gone to New York City to record and finished on Wednesday the 24th. His lungs hemorrhaged violently the next night, and in the morning he finally succumbed to the tuberculosis he'd suffered with since 1924. (Just a few weeks earlier, RCA Victor reissued its first Rodgers recordings on Bluebird. "Rock All Our Babies to Sleep" / "Moonlight and Skies" wasn't the first Bluebird release, but it was given the new label's first release number, B-5000.)[31]

By this time, Bluebird was such a success that RCA Victor began issuing new recordings on the label. Among the first country music performers to record for Bluebird, in July 1933, was the *WLS Barn Dance*'s newest act, the Girls of the Golden West. Sisters "Dolly" and "Millie" Good (Dorothy and Mildred Goad of southern Illinois) were an instant hit on the *Barn Dance* with their exceptionally close duet singing. Their repertoire was mainly cowboy-western, but they also sang old Tin Pan Alley tearjerkers like "When the Bees Are in the Hive" (recorded later by Bill).[32]

Playing on WWAE and WJKS (WIND)

During this time (May–July 1933), while the Monroe Brothers were playing regularly on WWAE, they were also playing on WJKS, a much more powerful radio station (1,250 watts daytime, 1,000 watts nighttime) in the Calumet's largest city, Gary. When the brothers first played there isn't known, since listings of morning shows weren't published in Gary's newspapers, but it's certain they were heard on WJKS at 5:00 A.M., Monday through Saturday, in the summer of 1933.[33]

WJKS was founded in 1927 by Chicago lawyer Thomas Johnson and wife Frances Kennedy, its call letters deriving from their surnames plus "S" for their son, but in 1928, it adopted the slogan "Where Joy Kills Sorrow," based on the letters. The station was about nine miles east of the Monroes' place, a long way to travel compared to WWAE (only two miles west), so, luckily, Ray Pierce, a friend from Rosine living in Hammond, was willing to drive them there. Six days a week, their day began with a road trip in the pre-dawn darkness to sign the station on, and for this they were paid their first substantial radio wages, $11 a week each. (WJKS was sold just prior to the brothers' arrival and its call letters changed to WIND about a month later. They continued to play on WIND, but for how long isn't known.)[34]

Touring resumed in August 1933 with a special performance of the *WLS Barn Dance* (including its road show dancers) at the Chicago World's Fair. Held outdoors on Wednesday the 16th, during "Farmer's Week," the free show attracted a crowd of about 30,000, most of them standing. Arrangements were made for five more performances in August and September, including one on Wednesday, September 13, Bill's twenty-second birthday.[35]

Shortly after the World's Fair shows, one of the *Barn Dance*'s sponsors, Dr. Miles Laboratories, paid for a segment of the Saturday night show to be syndicated to eighteen NBC-affiliated stations, to sell its new product, Alka-Seltzer. The broadcast, on September 30, 1933, "was not truly national, because the stations were all from Omaha eastward," according to WLS historian James F. Evans, but, from then on, Chicago's *WLS Barn Dance* would be known as the *National Barn Dance*. Chicago was now a center of "national" country music activity, so it was natural for the Delmore Brothers of WSM and the Prairie Ramblers of WLS to record their first Bluebird sessions there on December 6. The *Barn Dance* road show, meanwhile, played closer to the Calumet, and the Monroe Brothers could play regularly on WWAE. Beginning on Sunday, October 1, they were heard every Sunday from 7:00 to 7:30 P.M., including shows on Christmas Eve and New Year's Eve.[36]

During this time, Bill may have had an operation to align his inwardly turned left eye, due to an awareness that his and his brothers' futures lay in show business. Their first audition for WLS was unsuccessful, but there was no reason to believe they wouldn't make it the next time. Linda Parker of the Cumberland Ridge Runners (born Genevieve Meunich in Covington, Kentucky) had gotten her start at WWAE, and now she was a star of the *National Barn Dance*. The Monroe Brothers were making every effort to be a success, and a major hindrance was Bill's cross-eyed appearance. An operation was needed to change this, and it might have happened when the brothers weren't busy.[37]

After the operation, Bill's eyes appeared "normal," but his ability to see hadn't improved. If strabismus is corrected early, the eyes and the brain are able to begin working together, and normal, three-dimensional vision results. But if treatment is delayed, the natural ability of the eyes to coordinate with the brain deteriorates, and the dominant eye continues to do most of the seeing. Using one or the other eye to see with (mainly his right one), Bill's perception of depth had always been poor, and it would continue to be so. He saw the world in only two dimensions before the operation, and he saw it that way afterward.[38]

The "new, improved" Monroe Brothers continued gaining experience during January, February, and March of 1934, at revivals and other church-related functions. Sometimes they didn't even have to leave home. On January 3, 1934, they played for a meeting of thirty-two Methodist ladies at their Magoun Avenue apartment building, and their performance in Mrs. Della Boszar's apartment that evening was mentioned in the *Hammond Times*:

> The Monroe brothers, popular radio entertainers over stations WWAE and WIND, of Hammond and Gary, respectively, were the guest artists. Their program of vocal selections included "This Home Is Not My Own" ["This World Is Not My Home"], "If I Could Hear My Mother Pray Again," "Lonesome Valley," "Twenty-One Years," and "You Will Miss Me Again" ["You're Gonna Miss Me When I'm Gone"].[39]

The brothers continued playing almost every Sunday evening on WWAE until April 1934, when their WLS road show unit began making extended visits to several Midwestern locations. On the road almost constantly, they would no longer be heard on WWAE. Bill had to quit his job at Sinclair to go, but it was worth it. Fifty years later, he still remembered some of the places they visited.

> We danced for 'em one time for about three months. We were in Peoria, Aurora, Springfield, Decatur, and on up into Wisconsin, and down into South Bend and Indianapolis. We played a lot of theaters. They had us working with the Maple City Four, Red Foley, Arkie the Arkansas Woodchopper, Rube Tronson and the Texas Cowboys, and the Hoosier Hotshots.

Foley, of the Cumberland Ridge Runners, was often being featured as a soloist. The newly arrived Hoosier Hotshots, using a washboard and virtuosic slide whistle, played a wide variety of pop and jazz numbers, including a tune they called "Milenberg Joys" (recorded later by Bill as "Milenburg Joy").[40]

Texas Crystals

When the tour ended in June, Charlie and Bill were able to get their jobs back at Standard and Sinclair. Then Charlie got a call from an agent of a WIND sponsor, Texas Crystals, a purgative made by the Dollar Crystal Company of Omaha, Nebraska. He'd heard the Monroe Brothers trio, but particularly liked Charlie's singing, and asked if he would be willing to go to Shenandoah, Iowa, to sing on a radio station there, sponsored by Texas Crystals. Never a soloist, Charlie said he would go if one of his brothers could accompany him. So, an audition was arranged.[41]

With duet singing so popular at the time, Bill was clearly the one to audition with Charlie. Birch was undoubtedly disappointed, but he'd recently landed a good-paying job with Cities Service Company, a natural gas supplier. Maude and Bertha needed someone to supplement their income if they could continue living in the city. It looked like it was going to be him.[42]

Charlie and Bill's audition was an unscheduled, after-midnight show broadcast on WIND, sponsored by Texas Crystals. Listening in Omaha was the company's president James S. Thompson, via a telephone held to the speaker of a radio in Gary, overcoming WIND's limited broadcasting range. After the show, "Old Man Thompson" (as Charlie called him) phoned the station to offer Charlie $25 a week each for him and his brother, plus two weeks off with pay before starting work in Shenandoah. Charlie agreed with Thompson's offer and decided it was time for a visit to Rosine.[43]

The brothers spent the last week of June and the first week of July 1934, including Charlie's thirty-first birthday, in and around the old hometown, their first visit in more than four years. They might have been surprised to find brother Speed and his family (wife Geanie; stepdaughter Ruth Whitehead, thirteen; daughter Rosetta, four; and son Scottie, two) living in the house at the Monroe homeplace. The brothers posed for photographs at the nearby farm of Uncle William's son, cousin Hallie Monroe, including a memorable one with Charlie and Bill standing in a wheelbarrow. A week after they left town, they were mentioned in the new *Ohio County Messenger*: "Charlie, Birch, and William Monroe of East Chicago, Ind., who have been spending their vacation with relatives and friends here, returned home Saturday [July 7]." But no mention was made about the impending trip to Iowa.[44]

After they returned to East Chicago, Charlie and Bill should have left straightaway for Iowa, but they didn't. WLS probably wanted them to stay until replacements were found. In August, they, along with Birch, once again danced with the *Barn Dance* show at the World's Fair when it reopened. Finally, after shows there on Thursday, Friday, and Saturday of August 16, 17, and 18, 1934, Charlie and Bill headed west to the Tall Corn State. The Monroe Brothers as we know them today were on their way.[45]

Charlie and Bill Go to Iowa

At the time, with nearly 25 percent of the country's workforce unemployed, twenty-two-year-old Bill was apprehensive: "It was taking a big chance, leaving a good job and going into music." And he was unsure of his ability to "play lead" (play the melody of a song): "I didn't know how to play a lead. I couldn't play lead. I didn't know anything about it." But this was "Charlie's show" and he had picked Bill to go with him—so, in spite of his apprehensions, Bill felt obligated to do the best he could.[46]

Following Old Man Thompson's directions, they took the "Big Four" train from East Chicago into Chicago and transferred to the "Burlington Route" for the trip to Omaha, Nebraska, over four hundred miles west. After reporting to company headquarters in the Redick Towers building at Fifteenth and Harney Streets in downtown Omaha, they might have been loaned a car by the company. Crossing the nearby Missouri River into the state of Iowa, they drove southeast about thirty-five miles to Shenandoah. There on Sycamore Street, near the center of downtown, was radio station KFNF.[47]

Created by Henry Field to sell his line of seeds, KFNF went on the air in 1924, and by 1925, Field owned "the largest mail order seed company in the world." But when Charlie and Bill arrived in August 1934, the company was nearly broke and the station was dependent on outside advertisers like Texas Crystals. Field had lost control of his company, but he was a frequent on-air host of KFNF's shows. Based on a description of him by an associate, he may have made a lasting impression on Bill: "He was a man who never failed to speak his mind, regardless of where he was or who happened to be present. He never seemed to care whether the other fellow liked him and his ideas or not. Anything he thought was right was right, and everyone should see it that way."[48]

Field preferred that KFNF's call letters stand for *K*nown *F*or *N*eighborly *F*olks, and he wanted the music played on the station to be "old fashioned," and his preferences were honored. Other than Charlie and Bill, those providing the music were local amateurs, including seed company employees, so Bill would not have been under any pressure as he began to develop his lead playing.[49]

KFNF's studio was located in a distinctive Spanish Mission–styled building, where the Monroe Brothers broadcast two Texas Crystals–sponsored shows every day, Monday through Friday, 7:00 to 7:15 A.M. and noon to 12:15, on the 2,000-watt station. One of the studio's walls was a seventeen-by-seven-foot pane of plate glass, usually covered with a curtain. But on Saturday nights, when the *KFNF Barn Dance* was broadcast, the curtain was opened and the audience in the adjoining auditorium looked through the glass into the studio-become-a-stage to see the show's performers.[50]

Bill Meets Carolyn Brown

It was at the *Barn Dance* that Bill met his future wife, twenty-one-year-old Carolyn Brown, who was born Carolyn Minnie Phipps in Marshalltown, Iowa, on May 15, 1913; her father was part Native American, possibly Sioux. When her mother died in 1923 or 1924, she was adopted by George Brown, an Episcopal priest, and wife Carrie. Carolyn graduated from high school in Marshalltown and attended a business college, then headed to Minnesota to work in the Minneapolis–St. Paul area. She soon returned to Iowa, however, and when she and Bill met in 1934, she was living with a cousin in Red Oak, about eighteen miles north of Shenandoah.[51]

Charlie and Bill played on KFNF for about three months. The Dollar Crystal Company employed several performers on several radio stations, rotating them at intervals, and in November 1934 the Monroe Brothers were moved up to Omaha. On Monday, November 12, they were again broadcasting two fifteen-minute shows a day, Monday through Saturday, at 8:00 A.M. and 3:00 P.M., on 500-watt WAAW (*Where Agriculture Accumulates Wealth*). Omaha's first licensed station, WAAW was owned by the Omaha Grain Exchange, with studios in the Exchange's impressive eight-story building on the corner of Nineteenth and Harney Streets, close to Dollar Crystal Company headquarters and a short walk from Charlie and Bill's rooming house at 2017 Douglas Street.[52]

The Old Hired Hand

Now that Dollar Crystal Company executives heard the Monroe Brothers' broadcasts regularly, it appears they were not completely satisfied with

Charlie's ability to sell Texas Crystals. As a result, the brothers were teamed with an experienced salesman, Byron Parker, a native of Hastings (near Red Oak), Iowa. "He was the announcer," Charlie said, "and a good one! That man could sell water. Put it in a bottle, he could sell it. And get cash for it." (Little did Charlie think when interviewed in 1972 that bottles of water would eventually be sold by the millions daily.) Only a week older than Bill (born September 6, 1911), Parker dubbed himself "the Old Hired Hand." He had gotten his start on KFNF a few years earlier, singing with an act called the Gospel Twins. Learning of his singing talent, the Monroes enlisted him to sing bass on some of their gospel songs.[53]

The Move to the Southeast

Charlie and Bill had played on WAAW for about eight months when they found out they were being moved again, to Columbia, South Carolina, nearly a thousand miles to the southeast. The news couldn't have been very welcome. Their weekly radio pay had increased to $45 each, and they were playing good-paying showdates in the area, booked by Parker. They had been able to afford new instruments: Charlie, a new model Gibson "Jumbo" guitar, and Bill, a Gibson F-7 mandolin with a fancy "scroll" headstock and f-holes in its top, like a fiddle. Nevertheless, they dutifully went to see Dollar Crystal president Thompson before leaving, to thank him and to say good-bye. Thompson, a busybody, knew about Bill and Carolyn and, suspecting that Bill was planning to take her along, he advised Bill to leave her behind. Around the first of August 1935, Byron Parker, his wife Deanne, Charlie, Bill, *and* Carolyn left Omaha together, bound for Rosine, Kentucky.[54]

With another two weeks off with pay, on Sunday, August 4, Charlie and Bill were singing in the old hometown. As noted in the *Ohio County Messenger*: "The people of this place were entertained Sunday evening after preaching service at the M. E. [Methodist Episcopal] Church, with a musical rendered by [the] Monroe brothers and their announcer Mr. Byron Parker. The program consisted of a number of sacred hymns." The following week, they and a bunch of others visited a famous tourist attraction in western Kentucky, also noted by the *Messenger*: "Mr. and Mrs. Byron Parker; Charlie and Billie Monroe, of Omaha, Neb.; Misses Carolyn Brown of Iowa; Zonia Jones of Hartford; Leora Baize; Mr. Smith Monroe; Mr. and Mrs. John Monroe; [and] Mr. and Mrs. Lafe Monroe of Rosine motored to Mammoth Cave last week. Everyone reported a very enjoyable trip." (During this time, RCA Victor was in Atlanta, Georgia, recording the first session by J. E. Mainer's

Mountaineers, and among the songs released from it was the band's biggest hit, "Maple on the Hill," a duet sung by J. E.'s banjo-picking younger brother Wade Mainer and guitarist Zeke Morris.)[55]

During the third week of August 1935, Charlie, Bill, Carolyn, and the Parkers arrived in Columbia, the capital of South Carolina, rested and ready for work. Shortly thereafter, the Monroe Brothers and the Old Hired Hand began broadcasting their Texas Crystals–sponsored programs from WIS (its motto: *Wonderful Iodine State*), a 100-watts-daytime, 500-watts-nighttime station at 1809 Main Street, near the state capitol building. Unfortunately, local newspapers didn't list radio programs, so further details of their debut in the Southeast are not known. However, these details seem superfluous now in view of the brevity of their stay in Columbia.[56]

In September, less than a month after their arrival, the Dollar Crystal Company suddenly dropped its sponsorship of all of its performers and "left us hanging," Charlie said. Bill said, "I guess they just figured they had advertised enough in those particular parts of the country." In the Carolinas at least, it's more likely that Texas Crystals was unable to compete with Crazy Water Crystals.[57]

Crazy Water Crystals

The best-known of several crystalline purgatives on the market, Crazy Water Crystals was made by the Crazy Water Crystals Company of Mineral Wells, Texas. The product's name derived from the name of a well dug there in 1881 by one Uncle Billy Wiggins. According to local legend, a woman suffering from a mental disorder began drinking from Uncle Billy's well and, in time, became sane. The therapeutic fount acquired the nickname "Crazy Woman Well," which was shortened to "Crazy Well," and Uncle Billy's well water became "Crazy Water."

Later found to contain lithium, a mineral used to treat manic depression, the water at this and other wells in the east Texas town was also promoted as a cure for other diseases, due to its "eliminating properties" that cleansed the digestive system of "toxins and poisons." The Crazy Well was eventually sold, and in 1930 its new owners began selling Crazy Water Crystals, "the snowy white residue left after evaporation of the waters," which could be reconstituted in tap water anywhere. It was so popular that several copycat brands, including Texas Crystals, were available by 1933. That year, a Crazy sales manager, James Wesley "J. W." Fincher, arrived in Charlotte, North

Carolina, the state's largest city, to organize an aggressive advertising campaign utilizing radio and country music. By 1935, he had created a network of fourteen stations in the Carolinas and Georgia carrying Crazy-sponsored shows with the best hillbilly duos and bands in the Southeast. So it was to Fincher in Charlotte that Charlie and Bill (and Parker) went when they were dumped by the Dollar Crystal Company.[58]

Fincher and his musical advisor, Fisher Hendley, leader of a band called the Aristocratic Pigs, agreed to audition them at Crazy headquarters at 239 North Tryon Street in downtown Charlotte. Pleasantly surprised by what they heard, Fincher hired them to play on the network's flagship station, WBT, a 50,000-watt giant at 237 South Tryon Street, on Crazy's fifteen-minute shows Monday through Saturday at 7:15 A.M. and 12:15 P.M. And on Saturday nights from 8:00 to 9:00, they would play on the *Crazy Barn Dance* with J. E. Mainer's Mountaineers, the Dixon Brothers, Dick Hartman's Tennessee Ramblers, the Three Tobacco Tags (featuring twin mandolins), and lesser-known local acts like the Jenkins String Band, with banjoist DeWitt "Snuffy" Jenkins, and Homer "Pappy" Sherrill's East Hickory String Band, with banjoist Lute Isenhower. Both banjo pickers used a "three-finger style," which the Monroes had probably not heard before. (Earl Scruggs, born in nearby Cleveland County, North Carolina, in 1924, grew up hearing three-finger style banjo playing, but he once dated the beginnings of his own three-finger picking to this time in 1935, when banjo music from Charlotte filled the airwaves on Saturday nights.)[59]

Gaining the sponsorship of Crazy Water Crystals was a tremendous step up for the Monroe Brothers. They were now on one of the most powerful radio stations in the country, capable of transmitting their music to the entire southeastern United States. Fincher wasn't paying them much, but the exposure made up for it when requests for personal appearances rolled in, *and* Fincher covered travel expenses, allowing Charlie and Bill to keep all of their showdate pay.[60]

The Monroe entourage quickly moved to Charlotte, to a downtown rooming house on Fifth Street, near where it crosses North Tryon Street, close to Crazy headquarters and not far from WBT. Then, in October, Fincher asked the brothers to take over a show in Greenville, South Carolina—a hundred miles to the southwest—Monday through Sunday afternoons from 12:30 to 12:45 on 1,000-watt WFBC (founded by the *F*irst *B*aptist *C*hurch), while maintaining the 7:15 A.M. show on WBT in Charlotte. It was a long way to travel every day, but Fincher was paying expenses, so they agreed to do it.[61]

After their broadcasts in Greenville, on the way back to Charlotte, the Monroes and Parker played showdates on the "kerosene circuit," usually rural schoolhouses without electricity. According to music historian Pat Ahrens,

> Back in the days of the kerosene circuit, when lamps lit the stage, the roads were muddy, unpaved, and seldom well marked. Other than announcing on [the performers'] radio shows, there was little "advance publicity." Word of mouth or a sign tacked in the window of the local grocery or hardware store served as sufficient notice. Southern towns were spread apart and usually the largest public building for a country music performance was the local schoolhouse.

Homer "Pappy" Sherrill remembered playing music on the circuit:

> Back in those days you just rode and rode and played and played. It didn't matter how small the buildings were, you played 'em anyway, and just put on the full show. And you got up there and picked your heart out—with no p.a. system, sweat running off your elbows. . . . Man, that was rough days then. We played many a place that had no electricity. They'd have an old gas [kerosene] lantern, setting on each side of the stage; that's all the light you had.

After the show, they would head back to their Fifth Street rooming house and start all over again the next morning.[62]

During the next couple of weeks, while they traveled between Greenville and Charlotte, Crazy Water Crystals and WBT were negotiating certain "financial questions." By the end of October, Crazy decided to end its relationship with WBT, and Charlie and Bill played their last show on the station on Saturday, November 9, barely two months after starting there. But they would continue playing on WFBC: on Monday, November 11, they were listed in the *Greenville News* at 12:30, not as the Monroe Brothers but as "Kentucky Colonels" (appropriated from the Honorable Order of Kentucky Colonels, a benevolent society that had only recently begun to formally organize).[63]

Then near-disaster struck. On Tuesday morning, November 12, the car carrying "the Kentucky Colonels" from Charlotte (where they still lived) to Greenville collided with another car near Gaffney, South Carolina. The circumstances of the accident couldn't be determined, but it appears that Parker was driving and wife Deanne was in the front seat, judging by the injuries they received—she, a fractured skull and broken ankle, and he, "a badly injured shoulder and head injuries." Charlie and Bill, in the backseat, were unhurt, but they remained off the air until the Old Hired Hand could rejoin them on November 27, 1935.[64]

During the interim, the Monroe entourage moved to Greenville. Aunt Susan had lived there earlier in the 1930s, at 427 Buncombe Street on the west side, so she probably advised them to locate in the same neighborhood, and they moved into a rooming house there at 312 Butler Avenue. The day after they returned to the air, Uncle Jack died at age seventy-four of "pneumonia, with complications of heart and nervous troubles," according to the *Ohio County Messenger*. For his nephews, going home for the funeral was out of the question.[65]

Bessie Lee Mauldin

The Kentucky Colonels were soon back on the road, to North Carolina and a high school in the town of Norwood, just east of Charlotte. The school had held a contest to sell tickets to the show, and whoever sold the most would win the prize of a visit backstage with the famous Monroe Brothers. The winner was a freshman, Bessie Lee Mauldin.

> Bill, that night, asked my mother, could he take me home and she said, "Look, she's only a child." And he kept begging and begging. She said, "Bill, she's only fourteen. I don't allow her to date." He kept insisting. She said—because he and Charlie did a lot of religious songs—she said, "Well, O.K., as long as you bring her straight home and her oldest sister can ride with you."
>
> From then on, he wrote . . . he would not leave me alone. I heard from him constantly.

Mauldin, born December 28, 1920, was actually closer to fifteen at the time. She would become the first "other woman" in Bill's life, the first of many. Now that he had discovered his fascination with women, and they would discover their fascination with him, there would be no limit.[66]

In December, the Kentucky Colonels were cut back to six days a week on WFBC, losing Sunday but gaining a little time off. They had trouble deciding on their listing in the *Greenville News*, changing from Kentucky Colonels to the old "Kentucky Songbirds" nickname, then back to Kentucky Colonels, finally settling on Kentucky Songbirds, to emphasize Charlie and Bill's singing, by mid-January 1936. But their fans weren't confused. By January 25, with overflow crowds at the WFBC studio (in the Imperial Hotel, 201 West Washington Street), it was arranged for the Songbirds to broadcast on Saturdays from the nearby Butler Guards Armory Hall (16$^{1}/_{2}$ South Laurens Street), and their time was increased to thirty minutes (12:15–12:45).[67]

Bluebird Records

It's likely that this show, including the whooping and hollering of its audience, was heard up in Charlotte by RCA Victor producer Eli Oberstein, preparing for Bluebird sessions there in February. He sent a telegram to Charlie and Bill, insisting they record for him, but they demurred, apparently feigning disinterest in recording. Oberstein came to Greenville the next day, offering them more than the standard royalty (a half-cent per record was standard; Bill said they received a cent and a half), and they agreed to sign a contract.[68]

By this time, Carolyn was pregnant. Elsewhere, much has been made of her being unmarried and "in the family way," but in South Carolina at that time, Carolyn and Bill's common-law marriage was just as legally honored and binding as any formal marriage. Carolyn *was* married, even without a license or wedding ceremony. She and Bill would attend to these formalities when there was time, but there just didn't seem to be any then.[69]

Beginning February 2, 1936, the Kentucky Songbirds were once again heard on Sundays on WFBC, from 2:30 to 3:00. Then on Monday, February 17, after their 12:30 show, Charlie and Bill drove to Charlotte for their first recording session. Held in a makeshift studio, it was recorded on portable equipment in the storeroom of RCA Victor's local distributor, the Southern Radio Corporation, at 208 South Tryon Street, familiar territory for the former Charlotte residents. Sessions had begun there on February 12, and several acts had already recorded, including the new duo of Wade Mainer and Zeke Morris. On February 17, the last day for recording, the Delmore Brothers had completed their session, waxing sixteen songs (including "The Nashville Blues"), and were providing backup for fellow *Opry* star "Fiddlin'" Arthur Smith. He had recorded six pieces (including "There's More Pretty Girls than One") when Charlie and Bill arrived around 3:30. Smith and the Delmores were asked to stop so the Monroes could record and have time to get to a showdate that night. Right off the road, they recorded ten songs (nine were duets) in about two hours, nearly all on the first take.[70]

None of the songs recorded by the Monroe Brothers at this or later sessions was original ("Neither one of us had never ever written a song," Charlie said. "Didn't know how to start one"), and only nine of the sixty songs they would eventually record had not been released previously by others. (Two of the nine, "My Long Journey Home" and "What Would You Give in Exchange," were recorded at the first session, both learned by the brothers while at home.) This lack of originality was unusual at a time when most recording companies wanted newly composed works, for the profits that could be made publishing them. But it was the remarkable way the Monroes sang and played, not necessarily their songs, that minimized the importance of this lack. They could sing high or low, they could play fast or slow, or even in a free tempo ("Drifting Too Far from the Shore"), all with the same ease and unity, the result of hours of practice and performance combined with the natural cohesion of brothers. Most remarkable instrumentally, of course, was Bill's mandolin playing, causing the kind of excitement among listeners then that Earl Scruggs's banjo picking would later. After only two years of playing lead, Bill was a phenomenon.[71]

Wade Mainer and Zeke Morris

Other musicians were already listening closely to Charlie and Bill, evidenced by the attempt to "steal" their signature song, "What Would You Give In Exchange," by Wade Mainer and Zeke Morris. They had undoubtedly heard the brothers sing it on WFBC and recorded it three days before the Monroes' February 17 session. When Charlie and Bill found out about it, they complained to Oberstein, and the release of the Mainer-Morris recording was delayed until 1937 on Montgomery Ward and 1939 on Bluebird.[72]

About a week after the Monroe Brothers' first session, Crazy Water Crystals sent them to Atlanta, Georgia, to promote Crazy's new shows on the city's 500-watt WGST. They were heard there from February 25 through March 3 for fifteen minutes at 7:00 A.M. and noon. Filling in for them at WFBC were the Blue Ridge Hillbillies, teenaged brothers Bill (mandolin) and Earl (guitar) Bolick, later known as the Blue Sky Boys, with fiddler Homer "Pappy" Sherrill.[73]

While the Monroes were gone, WFBC increased its daytime power to 5,000 watts, and when they returned, their Monday-through-Saturday show was moved to noon and their Sunday show dropped, giving them the day off again for awhile. On Monday, March 16, 1936, after the noontime show, thirty-two-year-old Charlie married twenty-five-year-old "Betty" Miller. Born Elizabeth Branch on August 5, 1910, in North Wilkesboro, North Carolina, she was the eldest of four children of Presbyterian minister and biblical scholar James Bennett Branch of North Carolina and Kentucky native Nora (Pryce) Branch. Betty was married in the early 1930s to one S. M. Miller, a "chain store operator" in Georgia, and had probably lived in relative luxury, but they divorced in 1934. Six-foot-two Charlie once described his five-foot-ten wife as a "tall-like woman," just like he'd described his mother. Remembered as a smiling, happy person, she seems to have been the perfect match for her outgoing husband.[74]

In the works during this time was the Monroe Brothers' first songbook, *Favorite Hymns and Mountain Songs*, a keepsake for their fans and a source of extra income for the brothers. Handbook-sized, it began with a brief biography, informing the world for the first time that they were from Rosine, Kentucky. The lyrics to seventeen songs followed, eight hymns and eight "mountain songs," separated by one that bridged both categories, "What Is Home without Love?" It and two others they'd recorded recently were included, but most were likely audience favorites, songs they never recorded, like "Working and Singing," "Smoky Mountain Bill," and "Down in Arkansaw."[75]

By now, other companies besides Crazy were interested in the Monroe Brothers' music and the Old Hired Hand's salesmanship. Shortly after they returned to Greenville, the Gillespie Service Station (a Sinclair affiliate at 34 South Laurens Street, near the armory) began sponsoring the brothers on a daily 7:30–7:45 A.M. show. By May 16, they were playing two fifteen-minute shows a day for Gillespie, at 7:30 and 11:00 A.M., while continuing to broadcast for Crazy at noon. (Banjoist Don Reno, born in Spartanburg, South Carolina, in 1927, but living near Asheville, North Carolina, in the 1930s, recalled first hearing the Monroe Brothers during this time.)[76]

In April 1936, Bluebird released the Monroe Brothers' first record: "What Would You Give in Exchange?" / "This World Is Not My Home." "It really sold good," Bill said. "It was a powerful hit in the Carolinas." Likely influencing its success were the many deeply religious textile mill workers in the two states. (Charlie and Bill's second release, "What Is Home Without Love?" / "Drifting Too Far from the Shore," came in June or July, and the third, "My Long Journey Home" / "Nine Pound Hammer," in August. Beginning with the fourth, "God Holds the Future in His Hands" / "You've Got to Walk That Lonesome Valley," in October, Bluebird would release at least one Monroe Brothers record nearly every month until July 1938.)[77]

The brothers had little time to savor the success of their first record; they had to get ready for the next recording session, on Sunday, June 21, their day off. Once again in Charlotte in the storeroom "studio," they again recorded ten songs. Only one, "Just a Song of Old Kentucky," hadn't been released before, its composer unknown to Charlie and Bill. Also once again, Wade

Mainer and Zeke Morris recorded before them, on June 15. This time they re-corded *two* songs that Charlie and Bill planned to record, "Lonesome Valley" and "Watermelon on the Vine." Six days later, when the Monroes kicked off their session with "Watermelon," this seems to have inspired a certain extra intensity in both Charlie and Bill. In fact, they literally flew through it with an incredible display of up-tempo playing, leaving little doubt about whose song it really was. (All the recordings from this session are between 1.2 and 1.5 semitones [half-steps] below standard pitch, probably due to improperly adjusted portable recording equipment.)[78]

Two weeks after the second session, on July 4 (Charlie's thirty-third birth-day), Crazy dropped its sponsorship of the Kentucky Songbirds on WFBC. On July 18, the Carlisle Brothers, Cliff and Bill, took over the noon Crazy show. The Songbirds would broadcast for Gillespie during the rest of July, but then on August 2, a headline appeared in the *Greenville News*: "Ken-tucky Songbirds, Hired Hand to Take Air Vacation." They were taking a few weeks off, "in the hills of Kentucky," returning on September 7 (Ohio County newspapers made no mention of them being in Rosine, however). When they returned, it appears a compromise was reached: they had one show for Gillespie, Monday through Saturday at 7:30 A.M., and one show for Crazy beginning September 23, Monday through Saturday at noon. In the *Greenville News*, they were briefly listed as "Kentucky Songbirds" for Gillespie and "Monroe Brothers" for Crazy.[79]

The Birth of Melissa Kathleen Monroe

Shortly before the Monroe Brothers returned to the noontime Crazy show, on Thursday, September 17, 1936, Bill and Carolyn's first child, Melissa Kath-leen Monroe, was born. Her first name was Bill's mother's and, according to brother James, her middle name was simply one that Carolyn liked (pos-sibly from a song included in Charlie and Bill's first songbook, "My Lovin' Kathleen," a Carlisle Brothers original).[80]

The brothers' third recording session was on Monday, October 12, regard-less of the complications a baby had brought into Bill's life. Bill sounded tired, as if he'd been up all night with Melissa. His tenor singing was notice-ably subdued, his voice even cracking at one point (on "We Read of a Place That's Called Heaven"). Wade Mainer and Zeke Morris again recorded before Charlie and Bill and, again, they recorded a song the brothers planned to record, "There's Just One Way to the Pearly Gates." As a result, the Monroe

Brothers' recording was retitled "The Old Crossroad," a phrase used many times in the song (and not a similarly titled song recorded later by Bill). Among others they recorded was a little-known novelty song they helped make one of the best-known country songs in the world: "Roll in My Sweet Baby's Arms."[81]

Six days later, on Sunday, October 18, twenty-five-year-old Bill and twenty-three-year-old Carolyn were married in Spartanburg, South Carolina, about thirty miles northeast of Greenville. Gillespie had added a Sunday-afternoon Songbirds program from 3:15 to 3:30 beginning October 11, so Bill and Carolyn's wedding day, like Charlie and Betty's, included a radio broadcast.[82]

Life seemed to level off in November 1936, one year after the move to Greenville. But in December the Monroes and the Parkers learned that Crazy Water Crystals was moving them to Raleigh, North Carolina, nearly three hundred miles to the northeast. On Christmas morning, the Songbirds played their Friday morning show for Gillespie, their last show on WFBC.[83]

The Monroe entourage was given a week off for the holidays and two weeks more to resettle in Raleigh, North Carolina's capital. After living in close proximity since 1930, in January 1937 the Monroe brothers found separate places to live, a harbinger of things to come. Charlie and Betty (and presumably the Parkers as well) moved into a downtown rooming house at 614 South Salisbury Street, near their new radio home, WPTF, at 330 Fayetteville Street. Bill and Carolyn, with four-month-old Melissa, rented a house at 1208 Filmore Street, about two miles north of WPTF, in the suburbs of Raleigh.[84]

At the time, 5,000-watt WPTF (its motto: *We Protect The Family*) featured a rich variety of country music every day except Sunday. Regulars included the Three Tobacco Tags (Monday through Saturday, noon to 12:15) and Wade Mainer and Zeke Morris, now calling themselves the "Singing Rangers" (Saturday mornings, 7:45 to 8:00). New to the station like the Monroes *and* from WFBC was a former member of Fisher Hendley's Aristocratic Pigs, guitarist-singer Boyd Carpenter, broadcasting as the "Hillbilly Kid" (Monday, Wednesday, and Friday evenings, 7:00 to 7:15).[85]

Beginning Monday, February 8, Charlie and Bill and the Old Hired Hand were on the air Monday, Wednesday, and Friday mornings from 10:15 to 10:30, listed as "Monroe Brothers" in the Raleigh *News and Observer*. Exactly one week later, on Monday, February 15, Charlie and Bill were on their way back to Charlotte to record their fourth session.[86]

This time, the session was held at the Hotel Charlotte, on the corner of West Trade and South Poplar Streets, not far from the Southern Radio

Corporation offices. RCA Victor's mobile studio was now in three rooms on the top floor of the ten-story hotel, probably due to extraneous noises heard in the background of previous recordings, including a few by the Monroe Brothers ("Don't Forget Me," in particular). In surroundings more conducive to quality recording, Charlie and Bill began with two previously unreleased sacred songs they had undoubtedly learned in Rosine, "I Am Ready to Go" and "What Would the Profit Be?" The Mainer-Morris team recorded the next day (February 16) and, for the first time, there was no "borrowing" of material by them.[87]

Thereafter, Charlie and Bill began playing an entirely new kerosene circuit, again booked by Parker. To please their North Carolina audiences, known to favor the combination of banjo and fiddle, the brothers acquired the instruments and tried to play them on their shows. According to Charlie, "Bill took up fiddling, and see-sawed around, and he could make the sourest notes of anybody you ever heard in your life. I got ahold of a banjo and got to where I could play it in the old time clawhammer style." However, their efforts were too often laughed at, and they decided to stick with guitar and mandolin.[88]

In March 1937, Bluebird released "Where Is My Sailor Boy?" by the Monroe Brothers, and on the flip side, "The Carter Family and Jimmie Rodgers in Texas," a dialog skit recorded in 1931. Being combined with such illustrious company may be seen as a sign that Charlie and Bill had "arrived." On April 5, they were given the prestigious first show of the day on WPTF, Monday through Saturday from 7:00 to 7:15 A.M. But it was then that Byron Parker quit, possibly feeling left out of the Monroe Brothers' increasing fame. He may also have foreseen that the end was near for their sponsor, the Crazy Water Crystals Company. It was constantly fighting and losing legal battles with the Federal Trade Commission, and sales had steadily declined. Sales manager Fincher had cut back on groups being sponsored, and the branch office in Atlanta would soon close. Presumably thanks to the Monroe Brothers' popularity, Crazy continued to sponsor them, for the time being.[89]

The Old Hired Hand returned to WIS in Columbia, South Carolina, to work as an announcer and form his own band with Homer "Pappy" Sherrill and DeWitt "Snuffy" Jenkins. Charlie and Bill hired Boyd Carpenter, the Hillbilly Kid, to replace Parker as their pitchman.[90]

That summer the brothers began preparing early for their fifth recording session, scheduled for Tuesday, August 3, at the Hotel Charlotte. RCA Victor had apparently commissioned an anonymous songwriter to create three sequels to their "What Would You Give in Exchange" hit, and it took extra time to learn and rehearse them. Other than the sequels (which went nowhere commercially), all the songs they recorded had been released before. "All the Good Times Are Past and Gone" was one of two songs recorded by the little-known Fred and Gertrude Gossett in 1930, but thanks to the Monroe Brothers, it would become a standard in the bluegrass repertoire. On "He Will Set Your Fields on Fire," Bill attempted to duplicate the resonant bass voice of the now-departed Byron Parker. On the next song, "Sinner, You Better Get Ready," Bill sang lead and Charlie sang tenor. Sung in the key of E♭, Bill tuned up a half-step in order to play his mandolin in D position. (As in the second session of June 21, 1936, all of the recordings from this session are between 1.2 and 1.5 semitones below standard pitch, probably due again to improperly adjusted portable recording equipment.)[91]

During late-1937–early 1938, there were two significant developments on the national country music scene, of which Charlie and Bill were undoubtedly aware. John Lair, former leader of the Cumberland Ridge Runners, left the *National Barn Dance* in September 1937 to organize his *Renfro Valley Barn Dance* (eventually locating in Kentucky). Also leaving WLS were the Girls of the Golden West and rising star Red Foley, briefly joining Lair for his first show in Cincinnati, Ohio, on October 9. Later that same month, Roy Acuff of near Knoxville, Tennessee, auditioned for the *Grand Ole Opry* in Nashville, making a guest appearance arranged for by agent Joe Frank, who had arranged for the Monroe Brothers' burlesque audition for WLS in 1933. Acuff's audition was less than a rousing success, but he appeared on the *Opry* again on February 5, 1938, and joined the cast two weeks later, quickly becoming a country-music sensation.[92]

As these events were unfolding, the Monroe Brothers were in faraway Raleigh, about as far away from these centers of country music as they could be. Gibson Musical Instruments had profiled the brothers for their catalog in the fall of 1937, an indication of their new national stature, but they were misidentified as artists from Norfolk, Virginia, suggesting the relative lack of importance of the outpost where they were actually located. By January 5, 1938, they had risen at daybreak to play their 7 A.M. show on WPTF for nine months in a row, longer than any other early morning show they'd had previously.[93]

Sharing WPTF's airwaves with the Monroe Brothers during this time was a band called the Swing Billies. It was led by James Clay Poole, son of Charlie Poole of North Carolina Ramblers' fame, who went by the name "Charlie

Poole Jr.," and sang with a smooth, crooning voice. With fiddle, guitars, and tenor banjo, the Swing Billies played an up-tempo swing rendition of the elder Poole's "White House Blues" (which they had recorded for Bluebird in August 1937 as "From Buffalo to Washington"). Charlie Monroe would soon be singing the song as a solo.[94]

The Monroe Brothers recorded their sixth (and final) session for Bluebird on Friday, January 28, 1938, on the last of six days of recording activity at the Hotel Charlotte. Several bands recorded—a clear indication of the increasing popularity of bands (and the declining popularity of duos). Among them were Mainer's Mountaineers and Wade Mainer's new group, the Sons of the Mountaineers (with Clyde Moody on guitar). On the 28th, the brothers recorded their usual ten, but only one that was previously unreleased, an obscure camp meeting song titled "On My Way Back Home" (sung "On My Road Back Home"). On "A Beautiful Life," Bill again tried to sing bass like the Old Hired Hand.[95]

Next on the agenda was getting ready for the "New Show of 1938," as it was advertised, for which Charlie and Bill went all out. They put together a new songbook, *The Monroe Brothers: Their Life, Their Songs*, with a new cover photograph of themselves and a more detailed biography. As usual, the songbook contained favorites from their shows, including three Delmore Brothers songs, but this time there were more that Charlie and Bill had recorded (nine). Also, for their road shows, they hired a comedy act, Gladys and Rusty Scott, a husband-and-wife team who did a blackface routine in the style of "Amos 'n' Andy," two of America's favorite radio comedians in the 1930s.[96]

There were soon major changes in the brothers' radio schedule. For two weeks starting April 11, they were moved to noon on Mondays, Wednesdays, and Fridays and to 7:00 A.M. on Tuesdays and Thursdays. Then, on April 25, their weekday shows were shifted to 1:00 P.M. and Saturdays were added at 7:00 A.M. These changes may indicate a withdrawal of Crazy sponsorship, with WPTF sponsoring them whenever they could fit them in. President Roosevelt's Pure Food and Drug Administration had discredited Crazy's curative claims, forcing it to be sold as a laxative only, and "sales had dropped off to a mere trickle," according to the biographer of Crazy's president. The company remained in business, sponsoring portions of the *Grand Ole Opry* (it was, in fact, the show's first outside advertiser), but it could no longer afford to back groups. Bluebird held sessions in Charlotte in early June, but Charlie and Bill may have been too busy dealing with the upheaval to participate. Without a sponsor, the brothers knew they would probably have to go elsewhere. They bought house trailers to have inexpensive places to live during the uncertain days ahead, and by Saturday, June 25, when they played their last show on WPTF, they were already living in them.[97]

The Breakup

After June 25, the only question was when would they leave Raleigh, or, more exactly, who was in charge. As far as thirty-four-year-old Charlie was concerned, it was still "his show." He'd always made the decisions, and he wanted to leave right away. Twenty-six-year-old Bill, feeling his importance to the duo, thought he deserved a say in the matter. He wanted to stay until they played the dates already booked in the area ("about thirty days or more," Bill said later). They'd had arguments before: "Lot of times, we didn't get along," said Bill, "and I don't think brothers ever get along smooth all the time . . . and I had my feelin', you know, he wanted somebody else or a group of his own" (the latter a real possibility with the rising popularity of bands). As Charlie recalled:

> We'd had several little disagreements. . . . I went down that morning [to see him]. I said, "Bill, now, we're not doing any good like this. We are arguing. We're not seeing the business alike. Now, I'm going to go back out to my trailer. I've already got it jacked up. If you're not out there in ten minutes, I'm going to let her down on my car, and I'm going to pull out of here." Oh, it made him hot! He got hot as a firecracker! He told me, "You wouldn't leave me! . . . You'd starve to death, you know you would!" I said, . . ."[N]either one of us is going to starve to death. But we're better together. . . . If you've got one grain, you'll admit that." But . . . he didn't come, so I just backed [up to] my trailer . . . and pulled out.

That was probably it (although we'll never know for sure)—just an ultimatum presented by Charlie, and Bill's refusal to budge. The trailer park must have been very quiet after Charlie left, and Bill would have suddenly realized he was on his own. Thankfully, he had Carolyn to help him now.[98]

By standing up to Charlie, Bill was on his way out of the shyness that had plagued him since childhood. Birth-order specialist Frank Sulloway writes that "overcoming shyness generally represents a personal 'revolution'" that begins "among later-borns [like Bill] who have successfully rebelled against domination by older siblings." And those most successful at conquering shyness, according to Sulloway, are those who accept a challenge wholeheartedly. Bill would go forth, accepting the challenge of whatever (or whoever) came his way and always trying to make the best of it. Although never an extrovert, he would become a much more complete human being, capable of leading others and expressing himself in increasingly creative ways.[99]

Charlie, meanwhile, was seemingly prepared for Bill's response. He picked up the Scotts, rounded up mandolinist-tenor singer Bill Calhoun (who also played guitar) and left-handed mandolinist Emmett "Lefty" McDaniel (misidentified later by Charlie as Lefty "Frizzell"), and they all headed west to Knoxville, Tennessee. Charlie was soon featured on the *Mid-Day Merry-Go-Round* variety show on WNOX (5,000 watts daytime, 1,000 watts nighttime) and "in three days, I was booked solid," he said. It appears he planned to follow in the footsteps of Roy Acuff—play with success on a small Tennessee radio station (in this case, the very station Acuff had played on), and an invitation to play on the *Grand Ole Opry* was likely to follow.[100]

Bill Goes to Memphis

Bill left Raleigh with Carolyn and Melissa and returned to Charlotte, where he met secretly with Bessie Lee Mauldin, then seventeen, at the Clayton Hotel. Afterward, "I didn't hear from him for about a year," Mauldin said. Then Bill and family went home to Rosine and visited brother John, who may have given Bill some much-needed encouragement. What occurred next is open to further speculation, since no one ever asked Bill about it. But based on what actually happened: Bill, as keen as Charlie to get on the *Opry*, knew his brother had gone to Knoxville in eastern Tennessee, so he decided he would go to a city in western Tennessee—Memphis.[101]

Arriving in Memphis during the first week in July 1938, Bill went to the city's best-known radio station, WMC. Unfortunately, there were no openings there, but he learned of a spot on a station in Little Rock, Arkansas, 140 miles farther west. It wasn't in Tennessee as Bill had hoped, but it *was* west of Nashville, and he would make the best of it. He made arrangements to be at Little Rock's KARK the following week.[102]

Bill then asked about local musicians and was given the phone number of Mississippi fiddler Bob "Handy" Jamieson, a regular at the station. Bill called twenty-two-year-old Jamieson, who was living on his parents' farm near Ripley, Mississippi, about fifty miles south of Memphis, and they agreed to meet where Bill had parked his 1938 Hudson Terraplane and trailer, at a park on the south side of Memphis. The first tune they played together was

"Eighth of January," and after a few more, Bill asked Jamieson to help him form a band, saying he wanted a guitar picker and a bass player who were "clean-cut." Jamieson named his suggestions: a young bassist from Memphis, Charles "Chuck" Haire, and a guitarist and singer from western Tennessee, Willie "Bill" Wesbrooks (later to play with Bill in the 1940s as "Cousin Wilbur"). Bill wrote down the names of those in his potential band, beginning with his own name first, followed by "Bob Jamieson." ("He didn't even ask me about it," said Jamieson, "he just put my name down!") The group met the next day at a shelter in the park, and Bill informed them of his plan to go to Arkansas and to call the band "the Kentucky Blue Grass Boys." They were all for it, according to Jamieson, and left Memphis the following day, with Jamieson's new bride, nineteen-year-old Florence, going with them.[103]

Playing in Arkansas

The first stop in Little Rock was a western store where Bill bought the band matching "cowboy" outfits. "Man, we had them boots and everything," Jamieson recalled. "We wore black hats and he had him a white hat." Then it was on to downtown Little Rock, to audition at KARK (1,000 watts daytime, 500 watts nighttime), with studios on the eleventh floor of the National Standard Building (now the Union Life Building), 212 Center Street. On Friday, July 15, the "Kentucky Blue Grass Boys" (as listed in the evening *Arkansas Democrat*) debuted with a fifteen-minute, once-a-week show at 1:45 P.M. Also on KARK that day was former WLS star Lonnie Glosson and his Sugar Creek Gang at 8:00 A.M. and the western swing of the Light Crust Doughboys at 12:30 P.M.[104]

Three of the Kentucky Blue Grass Boys found rooms in downtown Little Rock. Bill, the fourth Kentucky Blue Grass Boy for the time being, settled into a trailer park with Carolyn and Melissa just across the Arkansas River in North Little Rock. After four broadcasts (through August 12) they were off the air for six weeks, promised an eventual Monday-through-Saturday morning show by KARK. But word had already spread that Bill Monroe was in Arkansas. "We had all the work we could have," Jamieson said, and although he didn't remember them playing outside of "the Natural State," he recalled many long trips within it.[105]

Bill's first band was succeeding, but Bill had yet to take a dominant role as bandleader. "He wouldn't do anything to hurt your feelings," Jamieson said. "If somebody made a mistake, he'd say, 'Somebody is messin' up.' He never called your name." He continued to just play mandolin and sing tenor, and didn't sing solos or play guitar on stage. Haire and Wesbrooks both sang lead vocals or solos, with Haire switching to guitar and Wesbrooks to bass whenever Haire sang. Wesbrooks emceed and told jokes, but he hadn't developed his comedic "Cousin Wilbur" persona yet. Jamieson could fiddle whatever he wanted, but he did learn to "read" Bill: "I'd always look at him, and if he'd draw a tight lip, I could tell . . . he didn't like it. I could look at him and tell, almost, what he was thinkin'."[106]

In September 1938 word came from East Chicago that sister Bertha, thirty, had married Bernard Charles Kurth, a twenty-two-year-old railroad fireman from Wisconsin. Bertha, born July 17, 1908, gave her birthdate as July 17, 1911, on the marriage license application, trying to reduce the disparity in their ages.[107]

The band returned to KARK on September 26, broadcasting Monday through Saturday mornings at varying times for about eight weeks. Jamieson was elected to cross the Arkansas River to wake Bill up, and after the rest of the band arrived at the trailer park, they crossed back over the river together to the station. During this time, they were listed in the *Arkansas Democrat* as "Bill Monroe and Kentuckians." Most significant, Bill's name was now out front, where it would remain for the rest of his career. Otherwise, the band's name appears to have changed, but when asked about this, Jamieson insisted it was always "the Kentucky Blue Grass Boys." It appears that when "Bill Monroe" was added, the entire band name was too long for the *Democrat*'s narrow, one-column KARK listings, and it was shortened by editors to make it fit. Meanwhile, on September 29 in Rock Hill, South Carolina, Charlie recorded ten songs (including a cover of Roy Acuff's hit, "The Great Speckled Bird") at his first session for Bluebird, with Bill Calhoun on second guitar and Wade Mainer's singing partner, Zeke Morris, on mandolin. When the records were released, the band was called "Charlie Monroe's Boys" or "The Monroe Boys."[108]

By November, Bill would have heard of Charlie's recordings and reckoned it was time to make his move. He turned in his notice to KARK, and the band played its last show there on November 16. "Bill just decided he wanted to go on to Nashville," to audition for the *Opry*, Jamieson said. "He done had his mind made up." First, however, band members went home for Thanksgiving, with Bill, Carolyn, and Melissa going with the Jamiesons to Florence's parents' farm, just outside Ripley. Back home again after four months, the young Jamiesons talked it all over, and shortly thereafter Bob Jamieson told Bill that he and his wife "had other fish to fry" and he couldn't continue to be a professional musician. Bill told him he understood. But the next morning, the Jamiesons woke up to find the Monroes gone.[109]

Bill wasn't willing to proceed to Nashville without his fiddler. Not knowing another as good, he would have to look elsewhere, and the sooner he got started, the better. He was bitterly disappointed, but he couldn't tell Jamieson this, and thus his sudden departure. In later years, it appears Bill preferred to think of this episode as separate from the rest of his career, and instead of a connection with later bands, he would always refer to his first as "the Kentuckians," the abbreviated name in the *Arkansas Democrat*.

Bill knew he needed to go where there were lots of musicians, and he needed to move quickly to get to the *Opry* before Charlie. He knew Birmingham, Alabama, had several country music radio stations and was only about a hundred and fifty miles to the southeast of Ripley, so that's where he pointed his Terraplane. He spent the next several weeks looking, but according to the only credible account of his time there, "He couldn't find what he wanted." Atlanta, Georgia, the South's most prominent country music center of the time, was only another hundred and fifty miles to the east. Surely his luck would change there.[110]

Atlanta, Georgia

Arriving in Georgia's capital near the beginning of 1939, Bill parked his trailer just south of downtown in a Sinclair service station lot at Central Avenue and Fair Street (now Memorial Drive). There he could plug into the station's electrical supply and the family could use the restrooms to clean up. Bill's status as a former Sinclair employee may have reduced the fee that stations ordinarily charged travelers with trailers.[111]

After deciding that what Bill needed most was someone to sing with, a classified ad was placed in the *Atlanta Journal*, the evening newspaper, to run Thursday, Friday, and Saturday, January 5–7. In the "Employment" section under "Help Wanted—Male," it read: "HILLBILLY singer to pick guitar; collection old-time songs required. Sinclair Serv. Sta., cor. Central Ave. & Fair St." The term "hillbilly" was commonly used in those days, but Bill once told an interviewer, "I have never liked the name, the word 'hillbilly,'" which suggests that Carolyn may have written the ad.[112]

That weekend, several applicants showed up, including nineteen-year-old Cleo Davis, born near Antioch, Georgia, just west of Atlanta. He'd taught himself to play guitar but had played mainly around home. Leaving his guitar behind, he came to Atlanta to find regular work and was living with cousin

Henry Gallimore when family friend Ed Daniel noticed the ad. Daniel and Gallimore insisted that Davis respond to it, and in spite of his reluctance, Gallimore bought him a substitute guitar and went with him to make sure he didn't back out. Arriving at the trailer, they waited briefly while others auditioned. As Davis recalled,

> We were then invited in, and I trailed in last. Introductions were passed around, but I never did get his name. He said, "Well, who plays the guitar?" I eventually pulled it out from behind me, where I had it hid, and said, "I do, sir." He asked, "Well, what can you play?" "Oh, maybe a verse or two of 'This World Is Not My Home' or 'What Would You Give in Exchange for Your Soul?'," not knowing at that moment who I was talking to.

After a verse and chorus of "What Would You Give?," Davis realized who it was and froze, unable to sing. According to Bill (as told to son James), when Davis heard him sing, "he commented that he sounded like Bill Monroe, to which Bill answered, 'I *am* Bill Monroe.' This unnerved him and he couldn't finish his audition." But as Davis told it, he recovered enough to start singing "This World," but froze again in mid-song. He said Bill told him with a laugh, "You'll get over that," and they tried the song again.

> His wife . . . was sitting at the end of the trailer, listening. He said, "Carolyn, what do you think?" She said I sounded more like Charlie than any man she ever heard not to be Charlie Monroe. I seen a grin come over Bill's face and he said, "Let's try that number again." I think we did it still a little better that time and he turned around and told Carolyn that "I think I found what I've been looking for."[113]

The next day, Bill bought Davis a better guitar, then matching suits and Stetson hats for the two of them. Thereafter, they rehearsed daily, and Bill taught Davis other Monroe Brothers songs and even some of Charlie's guitar licks. As they practiced, Charlie returned to Rock Hill to record his second session for Bluebird on February 5, 1939, with just Zeke Morris singing tenor and playing mandolin. But these attempts to duplicate the Monroe Brothers sound were clearly not successful sellers: Charlie would not record again until 1946.[114]

In mid-February Bill and Davis auditioned for the *Cross Roads Follies*, a popular midday country variety show on Atlanta's 50,000-watt WSB that featured several Kentucky bands. But at the audition, Davis panicked.

> We walked up to the microphone and we used a verse and chorus of "What Would You Give in Exchange for Your Soul?," which we was extremely good at, and I lost my voice completely. I was scared so bad—it was the first microphone

I'd ever seen. Bill said it was mike fright. I don't know what it was. To me, I was about to have a heart attack.

WSB station manager Lambdin Kay appears to have taken pity on them, however.

[A]fter we auditioned, the manager told us they only used groups, not duets. He told Bill to go out and pick up a few other guys and that he'd make a place for him on the Cross Roads Follies. Bill chose a few choice words and told the manager that that wasn't what he had in mind, and we walked out.

It was the first documented flash of the famous Bill Monroe temper. But it appears Bill wanted to begin again with a Monroe Brothers–style duo, and Davis agreed: "The Monroe Brothers name and sound was very popular throughout the lower Appalachians, and I think Bill was tryin' to . . . regain notoriety over the airwaves as he was buildin' his own group."[115]

Bill and Davis then tried auditioning at Atlanta's WGST (where the Monroe Brothers had guested in 1936), but the Blue Sky Boys were playing there and another duo wasn't needed. "Bill was rather disgusted," Davis recalled, "so we went back home."[116]

Bill had run out of options in Atlanta, so he decided to try WFBC in Greenville, South Carolina, where he and Charlie had been so successful during 1935–36. The new Monroe entourage traveled 140 miles northeast to Greenville but didn't even get to audition—the Delmore Brothers had just started at WFBC, sponsored by the Gillespie Tire Company, the service station's sideline, and, again, another duo wasn't needed. The Delmores had left the *Opry* in September 1938, singing "What Would You Give in Exchange for Your Soul?" as their last song. They'd gone to Raleigh to play on WPTF, then played theaters and schools in Winston-Salem and Asheville, North Carolina, before coming to WFBC. Bill might have consulted with them about where to go next, and, if so, it appears they advised him to try Asheville.[117]

Asheville, North Carolina

Bill left Carolyn and Melissa in the trailer in Greenville, and he and Davis headed north about fifty miles to western North Carolina. There, in late February 1939, Bill finally found a place to "regain notoriety over the airwaves"— Asheville's 1,000-watt WWNC (the same wattage as KARK). The only radio station in town, it was owned by the Asheville Citizen-Times Company, publisher of the city's newspapers, the morning *Citizen* and the evening *Times*. Bill and Davis were offered a fifteen-minute, Monday-through-Friday show called *Mountain Music Time*. There was just one catch: it already featured one "Sunset Slim," who was only a few weeks into a two-month contract. Bill and Davis would have to wait until April for the program to be theirs. Bill was determined to make the best of the opportunity. He had waited several weeks for a show in Little Rock; he could do the same here. He agreed to take the show when it opened up.[118]

Bill and Davis returned to Greenville to pick up wife, daughter, and trailer, and on the trip back to Asheville, Davis asked Bill what he intended to call their duo, not yet knowing of his plans to form a band. Bill answered, "Bill Monroe and the Blue Grass Boys." When asked why that name, Bill said it mainly identified him: "I'm from Kentucky, you know, where the bluegrass grows, and it's just got a good ring to it. I like that." Once in Asheville, Bill parked his trailer at a service station, and Davis settled nearby: "I got a room across the street for a dollar and a half a week, plus a meal ticket to the Asheville Lunch Room [110 Patton Avenue], and, boy, we were set!"[119]

For the next several weeks, during record cold weather, Bill and Davis continued to rehearse and even played a few shows. WWNC, meanwhile, moved around the corner, from the Flat Iron Building at 20 Battery Park Street to the brand new Citizen-Times Building at 14 O. Henry Avenue. On Monday, April 3, 1939, Bill and Davis went on the air at 1:30 P.M., just as the weather began to improve. "We walked up to the radio station each day and played our fifteen-minute program," Davis said. "I believe the announcer referred to us as 'Bill Monroe and Cleo Davis,' although quite often our mail was addressed to the Monroe Brothers." In the mail were a growing number of invitations to play, and Carolyn started handling the bookings. But after only five days, the unsponsored *Mountain Music Time* was bumped off the air by a new soap opera, *Your Family and Mine*, sponsored by Sealtest ice cream. When *Mountain Music Time* returned on April 18 at 1:45, it was bumped off again for two days of public service programs, then on for about a week, then moved to 12:45 for a week beginning May 1.[120]

During these three disjointed weeks, Bill used the air time to invite musicians to audition for his Blue Grass Boys. One of the first to try out was fiddler Art Wooten of Sparta, North Carolina. Nearly six years older than Bill, Wooten was a carpenter by trade but had fiddled since childhood and was well known at the then-new Galax (Virginia) Old Fiddlers' Convention, just across the state line. Making the band a foursome was Tommy Millard [MILL-urd] of Chattanooga, Tennessee. A contemporary of Bill's, he got his start doing blackface comedy with medicine shows. Hired to do comedy and emcee, he also played spoons or bone clappers on instrumentals. The newcomers began appearing on showdates with Bill and Davis, the entire band dressing in the style of the Monroe Brothers: Stetson hats, riding britches, tall boots, white shirts, and ties. But Wooten and Millard did not play on WWNC's *Mountain Music Time*.[121]

The Return to Greenville, South Carolina

With the on-again, off-again situation at WWNC, Bill had kept in touch with WFBC and the Gillespie Tire Company in Greenville, South Carolina, so when the Delmore Brothers left to play elsewhere, he and the band were ready. On Monday, May 8, 1939, three days after Bill and Davis played their last show on WWNC, Bill and all of the Blue Grass Boys played their first radio show together on WFBC (then 1,000 watts daytime, 5,000 watts nighttime) at 7:30 A.M. Their fifteen-minute show would be heard at this time for about four weeks, sponsored by the station on Mondays, Wednesdays, and Fridays and by Gillespie on Tuesdays, Thursdays, and Saturdays.[122]

Bill had, as usual, parked his trailer at a service station, and although it's not certain that it was a Sinclair station, it is certain that the owner was a fan. He offered the use of his grease house behind the station as a place to rehearse, if Bill and the boys would just clean it up some. And soon, their daily practice sessions were drawing crowds. Davis recalled,

> We had so many good times, so many laughs in there. Bill started working on "Footprints in the Snow," a song I'd heard my mother singing when I was a little boy. Bill started singing it, and I didn't think he was singing it the way it was supposed to go. He changed it around to suit himself, and it worked. People really loved it. Also in the grease house, Bill started working on "Mule Skinner Blues." I thought he had written it. I'd never heard Jimmie Rodgers do it until later.

Bill had never sung solos like these before.

> I didn't sing a solo until I was twenty-seven years old. I'd always sung tenor. But with training to be a tenor singer, to get up and hit high notes, when I started singing solo, there wasn't any trouble for me to hit any note, you see? I'd trained my voice and cultivated everything and my throat was in fine shape—I never smoked nor drank—and I could hit any note, didn't make any difference.

He could also "hit any note" because he'd developed the ability to sing in falsetto without it being obvious: "When I learnt I could do that, then I went to workin' on it and trainin' for it and smoothin' it to where I could go from one voice into the other and not show it, you know?" Bill was convinced that a singer singing a solo ought to play guitar, so he and Davis switched instruments whenever he sang "Footprints," "Mule Skinner," or "I'm Thinking Tonight of My Blue Eyes." "We used it ["Blue Eyes"] in a comedy skit," Davis said. "Tommy Millard came out in blackface [as Snowball] while Bill was singing that song. Millard would be crying as Bill was singing 'Blue Eyes,' so sad and lonesome. Millard would lean on Bill's shoulder, almost going into convulsions." (It was a routine handed down from the Monroe Brothers and a song Charlie sang as a solo.)[123]

As Bill was new to singing solos, so Wooten was to playing songs. "He'd never played him a song until he went to fiddlin' for me," Bill said. Wooten had mastered the technical aspects of playing fiddle tunes, but not playing the melody of a song, providing sympathetic backup for singers, or playing with feeling appropriate to the song. This further encouraged Bill's role as teacher, begun with Davis. Now, unlike his laissez-faire approach with the Kentuckians, Bill began to impose his ideas and standards on the musicians who worked for him. During rehearsals, he used his mandolin to show Wooten exactly what he wanted him to do.

Wooten's mastery of things technical included the mechanical "one-man-band" he built, which Davis described:

> It was like half an organ, with Art sitting with his knees under the thing. He . . . had a five-string banjo and a guitar built into it. He picked it with one foot and chorded it with the other, while at the same time playing the fiddle. He also had a harmonica rack around his neck, and played the fiddle and the harmonica at the same time. We used that act on stage with the Blue Grass Boys many times.[124]

Bill was now intent on making music based on his ideas, preferences, and high standards—music that showcased his talents: "I went to building around myself to form the music I wanted." He wasn't consciously trying to create a new kind of music—that's just what resulted from his efforts: "In forming the other instruments around the mandolin and my singing, it turned out to be bluegrass music." Whatever they called it (and they wouldn't call it "bluegrass" for another ten years or so), in his view, it would always be "his music": "I was just gonna carve out a music of my own."[125]

After a month, in June 1939, Gillespie dropped its sponsorship, but WFBC continued to carry Bill and the Blue Grass Boys at 2:15 P.M., Monday through

Friday, and at 9:00 on Saturday mornings. On July 24 the group found a new sponsor: Green Spot Orangeade, a precursor of orange soda pop, bottled at local dairies and delivered by milkmen. Green Spot maintained the weekday shows at 2:15, while WFBC covered Saturday shows at 2:00 P.M. Meanwhile, in July, the *Grand Ole Opry* moved from the Dixie Tabernacle to the War Memorial Auditorium, and admission (twenty-five cents) was charged for the first time. By the end of July, Carolyn was pregnant again. Suddenly, the financial security that an *Opry* membership could provide made it an even more attractive goal.[126]

"Snowball" Millard left the band in July, his wife expecting their first baby. He was replaced not by a comedian but by a talented upright bass player, Walter Franklin "Amos" Garren, a North Carolina native then living in Greenville. His ability to sing gave the band four musicians who were also singers, encouraging the development of a special feature of the band's performances: gospel songs by "the Blue Grass Quartet." As Davis recalled, "I sang bass. . . . My good friend Amos Garren did the lead, Bill sang tenor, and Fiddlin' Art Wooten did the baritone." Religious singing at their shows was especially timely. On September 1, 1939, Germany invaded Poland, the beginning of World War II in Europe. President Roosevelt, upon hearing of the invasion from William Bullitt, his ambassador to Russia, said, "Well, Bill, it has come at last. God help us all."[127]

Charlie had also formed a new band in 1939, the Kentucky Pardners. By July 1939, they were playing on 10,000-watt WWVA in Wheeling, West Virginia, and Charlie was writing to WSM, asking for an *Opry* audition. Bill was reportedly writing to WSM for an audition too, and it appears both were told there were no openings. But Charlie persisted. In August, long-time *Opry* regulars the Binkley Brothers' Dixie Clodhoppers left the show, "leaving vacant a key slot for a string band," according to *Opry* historian Charles Wolfe. Soon after, Charlie secured an audition, scheduled for early November.[128]

Green Spot Orangeade continued to sponsor Bill and the Blue Grass Boys throughout August 1939, and the band was working steadily around Greenville, South Carolina. As Davis recalled:

> I can't say I believe that Bill was a rich man, and, certainly we were not makin' very much money. We wouldn't sometimes take in more than twenty-five to thirty dollars at those little shows back then, which we'd play somewhere, generally, every night. From eighteen to . . . twenty-three dollars was . . . average pay for a

week [for a worker] back then—might've been tops for general types of work. So, if a man [like Bill] was able to take in two hundred [or so] dollars a week [and] pay three of us boys fifteen dollars [each] a week out of it, he was still, generally, ahead of the game.[129]

The *Grand Ole Opry*

After Green Spot ended its sponsorship on September 22, the band left WFBC, but they continued playing in the Greenville area through the first three weeks of October. In Wheeling, Charlie told his Kentucky Pardners they were going to Nashville in a few weeks to try out for the *Grand Ole Opry*. It appears that, somehow, Bill found out about it and immediately contacted Cleo Davis:

> One day, Bill called me up [at] the [rooming] house and asked me what I thought about going to the *Grand Ole Opry*. I foolishly said, "Do you think we're good enough?" He laughed and said, "We're as good as the best over there and, right now, we're better than most of the rest." I thought that if Bill Monroe thought we were good enough, we were good enough. I said, "Man, I'm for it!" . . . He told me to go back and tell the other boys to get their toothbrushes ready; we're going to Nashville.[130]

Driving overnight, the band arrived in Nashville on Monday morning, October 23. They headed straight for the National Life building, at Seventh Avenue North and Union Street, and the fifth-floor headquarters of WSM. As Bill recalled in 1974:

> I come in on Monday and I believe that they told me that Wednesday was their day to listen, but they would be back—Judge Hay [George D. Hay, "the Solemn Old Judge"] and Harry Stone [WSM station manager] and David Stone [younger brother and WSM announcer] was all going out to get coffee—as I got off the elevator on the fifth floor they was going out. And they come back and I played the "Mule Skinner Blues" for them, and "Bile Them Cabbage Down," "John Henry," and another one, and they said I had the music that National Life [the National Life and Accident Insurance Co., owners of WSM] needed—that the *Grand Ole Opry* needed. Said I had more perfect music for the station than any music they'd ever heard. One thing they told me that made me feel good: They said, "If you ever leave the station, you'll have to fire yourself."

Bill told this story many times over the years without much variation, but on one occasion he added, "So they told me I could go to work that Saturday, or

I could go on lookin' for another job, some other radio station, Louisville or some place—maybe I could make more money. And I told 'em, no, I wanted to stay at the *Grand Ole Opry*. And they said, 'Well, you're here, and if you ever leave, you'll have to fire yourself.'"

Cleo Davis's recollection differed primarily regarding what they played (but also revealed that Hay and the Stone brothers listened in another room while Bill and the band performed using a microphone).

> They put us in one of the studios and we really put on the dog. We started out with "Foggy Mountain Top," then Bill and I did a duet tune with a duet yodel, fast as white lightning. We came back with the "Mule Skinner Blues," and "Fire on the Mountain," and I think that really sewed it up. [They] came walking in and asked Bill if he could take over the first spot on the *Grand Ole Opry* on Saturday night. Bill said, "Yes, sir."

Both Bill and Davis agree, however, on "Mule Skinner Blues," and it was undoubtedly this song that really "sewed it up" with Hay. An adaption of the distinctive blue yodel by the beloved Jimmie Rodgers, with a swinging tempo set by Bill, it begins with a black man (the mule skinner) talking to a white man (the captain), reminiscent of the humorous newspaper columns Hay used to write, so popular they were published in book form (*Howdy Judge*) in 1926. Bill couldn't have picked another song as "in tune" with the Solemn Old Judge as this one.[131]

The band raced back to Greenville to pick up wives, children, and trailer, and quickly returned to Nashville (where Bill parked the trailer at Jefferson Street and First Avenue North, on the banks of the Cumberland River). Bill was not going to be late for his first show as a member of the *Grand Ole Opry*. That first show was not, however, "the first spot" that Saturday night, October 28, but the fourth "portion" (as the *Opry*'s segments were called), from 8:45 to 9:00 P.M. central time. The *Opry* began at eight o'clock with the Golden West Cowboys, a new western swing band, followed by "the grand old man" of the *Opry*, Uncle Dave Macon, at 8:15, and at 8:30 by the comedy singing team of Monk and Sam, new *Opry* members from Zanesville, Ohio. Then, introduced by Judge Hay at 8:45, Bill Monroe and the Blue Grass Boys. As Davis recalled, "I believe we opened up with 'Foggy Mountain Top,' with that wild duet yodel that we had [à la the Carter Family's recording], and came right back with 'Mule Skinner Blues,' [then] some fast [fiddle] tune like 'Fire on the Mountain' or 'Katy Hill,' [and then] 'Roll in My Sweet Baby's Arms.'"[132]

The *Opry* audience, both in the 2,200-seat War Memorial and at home, had never experienced anything quite like this before on the *Opry*. They'd heard a wide variety of string bands and several fine duos, but never one group that combined instrumental performance and duet singing this way. They'd heard bands playing "fast," but never with the same precision and drive as this one, urged on by twenty-eight-year-old Bill's unrelenting rhythm mandolin. "[T]here was absolutely nobody living that ever played with the speed, the tempo, and the perfection that the Blue Grass Boys had," said Davis. Then there was "Mule Skinner Blues," sung with a high-pitched voice that cut through the air like a siren. "I know that when we started there that 'Mule Skinner' was the first number to ever get an encore there," Bill once said. If so, he and the Blue Grass Boys had empowered the *Opry* audience to demand more with its applause, a practice that would continue from then on.[133]

In Wheeling, Charlie was listening to the *Opry* that night with band member Curly Seckler. Seckler remembered Charlie's reaction when they heard the band introduced: "[Judge Hay] said, 'It's Bill Monroe and his Blue Grass Boys!' Charlie said, 'Good Lord! He beat me there by just a couple of weeks.'" (Charlie soon moved to another 50,000-watt station, WHAS, in Louisville, Kentucky.)[134]

Following Bill and the band, there was more western swing with Jack Shook and the Missouri Mountaineers (9:00), crooner Ford Rush with son Junior on guitar (9:15), Roy Acuff and the Smoky Mountain Boys (9:30), Uncle Dave again (9:45), the Golden West Cowboys again (10:00), the old-timey Possum Hunters string band (10:15), and the Andrews Brothers, replacements for the Delmores (10:30). By 10:45, even the *Opry*'s cast members were ready to hear more from Bill Monroe and the Blue Grass Boys. As Davis recalled: "When we hit the stage, such performers as Roy Acuff, Uncle Dave Macon, and Sam and Kirk McGee, who were standing in the wings watching the Blue Grass Boys when they pulled the curtain on us, could not believe when we took off so fast and furious. Those people couldn't even think as fast as we played, I believe."[135]

What Bill and the band did on their second show isn't known, but they might have finished with a gospel quartet, the traditional way of closing a show. Bill said the first quartet he sang on the *Opry* was "Farther Along," then still a new song, with Bill singing high lead above three harmonizing voices, and it may have been their closer that night.

Bill's "Blue Grass Quartet" wasn't the first quartet on the *Opry*, but it was the first with four singers who were also members of a string band. Old-timer

Uncle Dave Macon, sometime leader of his own string band, took note. Bill said later, "When I come to the *Grand Ole Opry*, I had a quartet. I hadn't been there two or three weeks till Uncle Dave had him a quartet." (The Blue Grass Quartet would be advertised as a separate unit at Bill's shows and credited as such on Columbia and early Decca records.)[136]

Bill Monroe and his Blue Grass Boys would now be heard every Saturday night throughout most of eastern North America, thanks to WSM's 50,000 watts. On November 25, 1939, the band guested for the first time on the R. J. Reynolds Tobacco Company–sponsored half-hour portion of the *Opry*, carried to an even wider audience by the NBC network. By 1943, the *Prince Albert [Smoking Tobacco] Show* was heard from coast to coast. The cost of this "free publicity," making *Opry* members household names, was loyalty—no matter where they were, they were supposed to return to Nashville every weekend to appear on the *Grand Ole Opry*.[137]

The band was trapped in Nashville by heavy snows during its first month in Tennessee's capital. Carolyn was finally able to book a show nearby, at Florence School in Murfreesboro, on November 25 (the day after Thanksgiving that year). To advertise it, Bill placed the first of countless orders for show posters with the now-famous Hatch Show Print Company. The company's record of purchases and payments would provide an excellent source of information about Bill's showdates during the next thirty years, with the date and location to be imprinted on the posters carefully noted. From these "receipts," we know that after Florence School and the band's appearance on the *Opry* on November 25, they returned to their normal schedule, playing Monday through Friday for three weeks in a row at schools in western North Carolina (all near Greensboro) and just across the border in southwestern Virginia. The band's last showdate of 1939 was at Axton High School in Axton, Virginia, on Friday, December 15. That night, the movie version of *Gone with the Wind* premiered in Atlanta, with opening ceremonies, including the arrival of Clark Gable, broadcast live by WSM. The next night, Bill Monroe and his Blue Grass Boys were featured on WSM's *Grand Ole Opry*.[138]

Horton School, the one-room schoolhouse Bill and his siblings
attended, about a mile and a half from the Monroe Homeplace.
The damage to the front door was done after the school was no
longer used. (Photo courtesy of Logan Leach)

Horton High School · 1912

This photograph and the Horse Branch High School picture are the third in a series of old photographs being furnished to THE TIMES by Wendell Allen, through the courtesy of Smith Monroe, both of Rosine. THE TIMES also wishes to thank Mrs. Jess Stevens of Beaver Dam for identifying those persons pictured in the Horton School photo, and Mrs. Raymond Renfrow of Horse Branch for identifying the 1928 photo of Horse Branch students.

This Horton School photo of about 1912 captures many of Ohio County's leading citizens in their early school years. In the first row from left to right are: Bertha Monroe, Myrl Crowder, Josephine Thompson, Alma Crowder, Lucy Smith, Stoy Crowder, Not Identified, Carlos Crowder, and Marion O'Connell Crowder. Standing in the second row are: Nacie Crowder - Teacher, Grace Crowder, Ruth Wright, Maud Monroe, Not Identified, Ira Smith, Birch Monroe. Those in the third row also from left to right are: Martin Thompson, Hallie Monroe, Jess Smith, John Monroe, and Speed Monroe.

The picture was taken by Leonard "Doc" Wallace of Mt. Pleasant. Wallace became a photographer while serving in the U. S. Army. He retired from the Army in 1916, but did not give up his talent as a photographer. Wallace died December 3rd, 1949.

Horton School, Class of 1917: In the front row, Bill is third from right and Bertha is
first from left. Of the six in the second row, Birch is first from right and Maude is third
from left. In the third row, Speed is first from right and John is second from right. The
newspaper caption "Horton High School – 1912" is incorrect. (Photo courtesy of Merlene
Austin)

Charlie and Birch Monroe, ca. 1925. (Photo courtesy of David Mahan)

Bill and puppies, ca. 1925. (Photo courtesy of James Monroe)

Uncle Pen Vandiver and Flossie Wilson, ca. 1927. (Photo courtesy of Merlene Austin)

Carolyn (Phipps) Brown, age eighteen, in 1931, three years before she met Bill. (Photo courtesy of James Monroe)

Bill and Charlie, Rosine, ca. 1934. (Photo courtesy of Merlene Austin)

Robert "Handy" Jamieson, fiddler with the Kentucky Blue Grass Boys. (Photo courtesy of Robert E. Jamieson and the Tippah County Historical Museum, Ripley, Miss.)

Bill, age twenty-seven, in Arkansas, 1938. (Photo courtesy of Robert Jamieson)

This classified ad, from the January 5, 1939, edition of the *Atlanta Journal*, attracted the first member of the Blue Grass Boys, Cleo Davis. (Author's collection)

Music and Dramatics

PRIVATE instruction by teacher of piano; also trombone. JA..3821.

EMPLOYMENT

IN answering help wanted ads with box numbers do not send original or valuable papers. Copies will do just as well.

Help Wanted—Male

HILLBILLY singer to pick guitar; collection old-time songs required. Sinclair Serv. Sta., cor. Central Ave. & Fair St.

BARBER WANTED. HARRY JONES, COLUMBUS, GA.

Employment Agency—Male

COMMUNITY EMPLOYMENT SERVICE. WA. 3142.

Salesmen

NATIONALLY known punchboard manufacturer has opening for reliable, experienced salesman, with car; must be resident of the state of Georgia; repre-

Bill and Earl Scruggs, ca. 1946. (Photo courtesy of Merlene Austin)

Lester Flatt, on the road, ca. 1946. (Photo courtesy of Merlene Austin)

Robert "Chubby" Wise, ca. 1946. (Photo courtesy of Merlene Austin)

Howard Watts, early 1940s, prior to joining the Blue Grass Boys. (Photo courtesy of Merlene Austin)

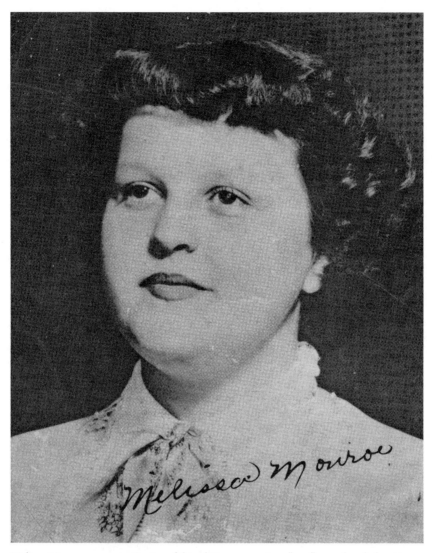

Melissa Monroe, ca. 1950. Copies of this photo, measuring 5" × 4", were handed out to promote her Columbia releases. (Photo courtesy of Merlene Austin)

The Mayfield Brothers: (*left to right*) Herb, Smokey, and Edd, ca. 1954. (Photo courtesy of Fred Mayfield)

Bill Monroe, 1954. (Author's collection)

Ralph Rinzler, 1963. (Photo by Kelly Hand, courtesy of Barry Olivier and the Charles Deering McCormick Library of Special Collections, Northwestern University Libraries)

Virginia Stauffer and Bill, 1966. (Photo courtesy of Marlene and the late Dan Stauffer)

103

Bill Monroe and his Blue Grass Boys at the Brown County Jamboree, Oct. 13, 1963: (*left to right*) Bessie Mauldin, Bill, Bill "Brad" Keith, Joe Stuart (hidden), and Del McCoury. (Photo by Jim Peva)

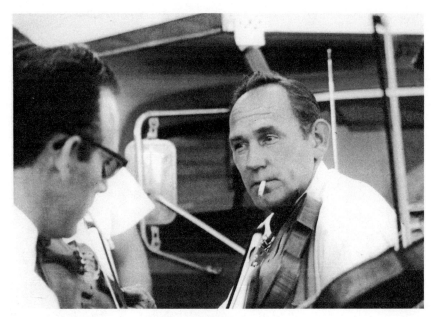

Kenny Baker, September 1967. (Photo by Dennis Satterlee)

Bill and his son, James, at the Bean Blossom festival, June 1969. (Photo by Marty and Frank Godbey)

Bill and Doc Watson, August 1970. (Photo by Carl Fleischhauer)

Bill and Lester Flatt, reunited at the Bean Blossom festival, singing "Little Cabin Home on the Hill," June 1971. (Photo by Ron Petronko)

The house at the Monroe Homeplace, 1972. (Photo by Carl Fleischhauer)

"Gettin' down" while playing "Southern Flavor" with (*left to right*) Billy Rose, Bill, Tom Ewing, and Sonny Osborne videotaping, Bean Blossom, June 1989. (Photo by Michelle Putnam)

Melissa Monroe welcoming her father home from Japan at Nashville International Airport, September 1989. Denise Painter used this photo to bring Melissa out of her withdrawal. (Photo by Denise Painter Easter)

Bill Monroe, June 27, 1993. (Photo by Gene Lowinger)

At one of Bill's last sessions with his Blue Grass Boys, Imagine Studios, Nashville, November 14, 1993, with (*left to right*) Vic Gabany, Robert Bowlin, Clarence "Tater" Tate, Dana Cupp, Bill, recording engineer Kurt Storey, and Tom Ewing. (Photo by Ronnie McCoury, courtesy of Vic Gabany)

CHAPTER FOUR
1940–1949

The Cost of Stardom

At the beginning of 1940, due primarily to the relocation to Nashville, show-dates for Bill and the Blue Grass Boys were limited, but the band survived thanks to the WSM Artist Service Bureau, the *Opry*'s booking agency. The three shows the Bureau booked at schools near Columbia, Tennessee, must have been very welcome, for there was a lack of any other work in January and early February. The downside: the agency collected 15 percent of the gate receipts for its efforts. *Opry* members also paid WSM 15 percent commission for showdates they booked themselves, for the privilege of advertising their *Grand Ole Opry* affiliation.[1]

In March the band was again playing five nights a week in western North Carolina and southern Virginia, not ranging too far from Nashville, where they were expected to be every Saturday night. Then in April the band traveled farther east and north, testing the limits of their range. They were in eastern North Carolina on the 8th and made a long jump back to western Virginia on the 9th. On the 10th, with a day off, they might have visited WDBJ in Roanoke to promote the next night's show in Bedford, twenty miles east. If so, it might have been the day Bill first met Lester Flatt. Twenty-five-year-old Flatt was living in Covington, Virginia, about thirty-five miles north of Roanoke, and playing on WDBJ with a band called the Harmonizers. He had been a Monroe fan for several years: "My first radio experience with this type of music was from the Monroe Brothers. . . . They were singing good country and gospel songs and it was the kind of music that we had been raised to." Flatt invited the band to his home for supper, but never mentioned his musical activities to Bill: "I didn't tell him that I even tried to sing."[2]

Also in April 1940, on the 12th, Roy Acuff recorded "Mule Skinner Blues" in Bill's style for Columbia Records, six months before Bill had a chance to record it. It's not known if Bill was angry or if he confronted the then-most-popular singer on the *Opry* about it. But, in the end, when it was released, there was little reason for a confrontation. Straining to sing the song at the top of his vocal range, Acuff only succeeded in highlighting the disparity between his singing and Bill's.[3]

The Demands of the Road

Bill's Blue Grass Boys were now making $25 a week, up ten dollars from their Greenville days, plus $5 each for playing the *Opry*, adequate amounts for that time. But the trips were longer, and the ride back to Nashville for the *Opry* was often made at death-defying speeds. DeFord Bailey, "the harmonica wizard" of the *Opry*, toured with Bill during this time. He'd traveled with several bands and once said they all drove fast. "None of them walked along," he said, "but Bill Monroe was the fastest, though. . . . He would often drive at ninety or ninety-five miles an hour down country roads at night. I looked down on ninety-five many a time with Bill Monroe and him still mashing down on the gas—and it raining. Once he ran off the shoulder of the road, and I got him to slow down a little for the rest of the trip." Being one of the Blue Grass Boys was more demanding, especially for those with no previous road experience. Leaving in June or July of 1940 was Wooten, replaced by Tommy Magness. Born in the same northwestern corner of Georgia as Cleo Davis, Magness had traveled widely and waxed the original recording of "Orange Blossom Special" in 1938. "He had that fine old-time touch," Bill said, "rich and pure, but he was able to put a touch of blues to it. He was the first man I heard play 'Orange Blossom Special,' and he could put a lot more in it than they do today."[4]

The next to go was Garren, replaced by Willie Wesbrooks, one of Bill's Kentucky Blue Grass Boys of 1938. He had been playing bass and doing rube comedy as "Cousin Wilbur" when he arrived in Nashville looking for work. Bill and the band were on their first tour to West Virginia in early August 1940. "So I waited for Bill to come in," Wesbrooks said. "Then Bill told me,

'I'll let you go with me this next week and see how it works out.' So I went along with him the following week, and then the next week, and Bill never did hire me. He would just drive up and I'd get in the car. And I stayed with him for four years [1940–43] like that."[5]

Shortly thereafter, Bill got a call at the *Opry* from Clyde Moody. Bill, keenly aware of musicians he heard on his car radio, had liked Moody's singing and guitar playing since 1938, when he was with Wade Mainer. Moody was looking for a job, and evidently Bill couldn't resist. By then, RCA Victor had probably contacted him about recording for Bluebird and may have been worried that Cleo Davis would freeze in the recording studio, as he had in other new situations. To hire "a sure thing" like Moody, however, he had to let Davis go. Bill offered him a two-weeks' notice or two weeks' pay and, after the *Opry* on August 31, Davis took the money and left. Moody met up with the band for a show in Bluefield, West Virginia, on Friday, September 6. (During the following week, Bill and the band were seen for the first time by brothers Carter Stanley, fifteen, and Ralph Stanley, thirteen, at Ervinton High School in Nora, Virginia. "It was the first stage show we ever saw," Ralph Stanley said later, "and it really got me and Carter excited.")[6]

The First Bluegrass Session

Less than thirty days after Moody joined, on Monday, October 7, 1940, Bill and the band were in Atlanta to record their first session. Considering the short time they'd been together, the tightness of the group is remarkable. Of the eight numbers they cut for Bluebird, the most original were Bill's vocal solos, "Mule Skinner Blues" and "Dog House Blues"; his instrumental solo, "Tennessee Blues"; and Moody's solo vocal, "Six White Horses." Bill played Moody's D-18 Martin guitar on the first two, providing a driving rhythm that exemplified the style later called "bluegrass." This rhythm influenced many early white country blues players (soon to be known as "rock and rollers"), a fact not lost on Bill: "Bluegrass time—now, if you check it back, you'll see that a lot of rock and roll plays the same kind of time that we play. Of course, we play it in a country style and I know we was before rock and roll." Bill's "Tennessee Blues" was a deceptively simple-sounding "composition"—Bill's first—but it was light-years away from any other country mandolin playing of the day. Moody's "Six White Horses," a blues not previously recorded by a white performer, was the first of only three solo vocals ever commercially recorded by one of the Blue Grass Boys. (The session's other songs, recorded previously by others, are not discussed here.)[7]

Immediately after their session, the Blue Grass Boys provided backup for a session by the legendary fiddler Arthur Smith. He had recently had problems with *Opry* management due to his drinking and "was kind of down on his luck," according to Wesbrooks. Four years earlier, Smith (and the Delmores) stepped aside for the Monroe Brothers to record, and Bill was undoubtedly glad to return the favor. He took Smith to Atlanta with him and let him use the Blue Grass Boys to record, including eight numbers with Moody and Wesbrooks playing backup and Magness and Smith fiddling together on "K. C. Stomp." (On October 9, Magness, with Bill's permission, recorded with Roy Hall and the Blue Ridge Entertainers, cutting one of their most popular songs, "Don't Let Your Sweet Love Die." On October 11, twenty-year-old Mississippi native Pete Pyle recorded his first session, playing guitar and singing eight solo vocals accompanied by the mandolin playing of songwriter Edward Crowe. Pyle would soon be joining the *Grand Ole Opry.*)[8]

After the sessions, Bill and the band returned to the Monday-through-Friday grind—a series of small-town movie theaters, playing brief shows before, in between, and after the featured films. Sleep usually happened in the car. Occasionally, if the next town wasn't too far away, a Blue Grass Boy could sleep in a bed, but he had to pay for it. As Wesbrooks remembered it,

> We rode in a Hudson that Bill had—a Country Club Eight that cost sixteen hundred dollars, the highest-priced Hudson that you could buy. There'd be four or five people in the car. We'd always take my bass fiddle and put it on top of the car in a waterproof case. . . . Sometimes we'd go play as many as seven states a week. . . . Union scale at that time was only twenty-five dollars a week, and you paid your own hotel bills. . . . We had to pay for our eats and our clean shirt every day, and buy the riding pants, boots, and hat that Bill always wore. So when we slept in a hotel, it'd be a dollar and a half or two dollars a person—and there would be two people sleeping in one bed.[9]

In November 1940 President Roosevelt was elected to an unprecedented third term in office and, in December, there was an early Christmas present: the first release by Bill Monroe and the Blue Grass Boys on Bluebird, "Mule Skinner Blues" backed with "Six White Horses." (Years later, concerning the former on the relatively new coin-operated record-playing machine, Bill said, "'Mule Skinner Blues' was so hot back in the early 1940s that it would lock a machine three times in the run of a week because that is all people would play on the jukebox.")[10]

The Birth of James William Monroe

The band played at schools at the beginning of 1941, only occasionally playing a theater for several months. In February, as the birth of Bill and Carolyn's second child drew near, four-year-old Melissa was taken to Rosine to stay with Uncle John and Aunt Clara, then living in the house at the Monroe homeplace (Speed and family had moved to Cleveland, Ohio, to find work). On Saturday, March 15, James William Monroe was born in Nashville, named for his grandfather, James Buchanan Monroe, and for his father. Luckily, his father was in town that day to play the *Opry*. But the next day he was gone, to play a theater in eastern Kentucky.[11]

That spring, the *Grand Ole Opry* sponsored its first tent show. With a tent 80 feet by 220 feet, seating sixteen hundred, the show traveled the country until fall, playing one-night stands that brought the *Opry* to those who couldn't afford the trip to Nashville. It was the brainchild of Lee Davis "Honey" Wilds of the blackface comedy team of Jam-Up and Honey, *Opry* stars since 1932.

> It took twenty-five roughnecks to move it, and we moved it every cotton-picking day, feeding the roughnecks three hot meals a day in the process. With salaries, lot rent, advertising, and licenses, our daily operating expenses fluctuated between $550 and $600 a day. In other words, we had to make $600 a day before Jam-Up and I would make a nickel. Everybody said we were crazy.

But there were "monstrous" crowds, according to Wilds, drawn by Roy Acuff and his Smoky Mountain Boys, Uncle Dave Macon, and the ever-popular Jam-Up and Honey.[12]

Buoyed by the fame of recording with Bill Monroe, Clyde Moody left the Blue Grass Boys after a few months. The sudden lack of a lead singer was dealt with as personnel problems often were, by Bill relying on whoever was close at hand—in this case, the new featured singer on the *Opry*, Pete Pyle. (Moody, meanwhile, re-formed his Happy-Go-Lucky Boys with new tenor singer and guitarist Lester Flatt.)[13]

Magness left the Blue Grass Boys in the summer of 1941 to play with Roy Hall. When Hall and the Blue Ridge Entertainers recorded again, the band included seventeen-year-old Jim Eanes singing a new Johnny Bond song, "I Wonder Where You Are Tonight." After a year off the road, Art Wooten returned to fiddle with the Blue Grass Boys.[14]

Up to this point, recordings by the Monroe Brothers and Bill and the Blue Grass Boys had been marketed primarily as country music. In July 1941 RCA Victor released *Smoky Mountain Ballads*, a collection of five 78s in a binder resembling a family album. Produced by seventy-three-year-old folklorist John Lomax, pioneering popularizer of American folksongs, with its selections chosen by John's twenty-six-year-old son Alan Lomax, it included recordings by Uncle Dave Macon, Arthur Smith, the Carter Family, and the Monroe Brothers (singing "Darling Corey"). According to music historian Richard Spottswood, this "album" introduced these performers "to many northern listeners for the first time, implicitly transforming their status from hillbillies to folk singers."[15]

Bessie Mauldin in Nashville

In early September 1941 Bill, nearing thirty, decided to bring Bessie Lee Mauldin, nearing twenty-one, to Nashville. "He came to North Carolina and got me," she said. He installed her in the Tulane Hotel, on the northeast corner of Eighth Avenue North and Church Street, not far from the National Life building. She said that between 1938 and 1940, she had given birth to a baby, a girl, and it appears Mauldin showed the child to Bill early on. (He later said he "knew her from the time she was a baby.") But Mauldin did not claim that Bill was the father at this time. He, meanwhile, was certain that "she was not my child or anything," due to the time that he and Mauldin had been apart. Mauldin told Bill she was going to give the baby to friends or relatives in Georgia, so she could be free to move to Nashville with him.[16]

Meeting Bill during this time was Bill "Hawk" Hawkins, in later years a friend and frequent guest backstage at the *Opry*. Bill and the band came to Hawkins's hometown, Lafayette, Tennessee, on September 12, 1941, and Bill rode a white horse around the town square, a tactic he frequently used to "ballyhoo" his shows in those days. Sixteen-year-old Hawkins went to the square carrying his mandolin and Bill noticed him. "He came up and looked at my mandolin and we were talking about playing, and I said, 'I'd sure like to learn to play like you.' And I never forgot what he told me. He says, 'No, you don't want to play like me. You want to play like you.'"[17]

Bill and the band's second recording session was, as before, held in October in Atlanta. This time, they were in the middle of a hectic touring schedule. On September 29, 1941, they played in Elizabethton, Tennessee, and raced two hundred miles south to Atlanta so Pyle could record his second session for Bluebird on September 30. Then they drove back to eastern Tennessee to play that night in the town of Roan Mountain and, afterward, drove back to Atlanta with, thankfully, October 1 off. But on Thursday, October 2, they had to record early in the morning in order to be in Russellville, Alabama, two hundred miles to the west, that night.[18]

Needless to say, the session was rushed—the band didn't even take time to tune their instruments to standard pitch, so all of the recordings were nearly half a step above standard tuning. Making an already tense situation worse, RCA Victor executives informed Bill that Pyle was an exclusive solo artist for Bluebird and they would not allow his voice on a Bill Monroe recording. As a result, two songs Pyle and Bill had rehearsed as duets, Jimmie Davis's "Sweethearts or Strangers" and Wiley Walker and Gene Sullivan's "Live and Let Live," were not recorded.[19]

The most original performances survived, including "Shake My Mother's Hand for Me" and "Were You There?" (on which Pyle was permitted to sing baritone or bass). Both had been recorded by Wade Mainer and the Sons of the Mountaineers, the first just three days earlier in Atlanta and the second in 1939, and it's likely they had been "borrowed" from Bill via radio broadcasts. Made new was Bill's solo vocal on "Blue Yodel No. 7," a follow-up to "Mule Skinner Blues" ("Blue Yodel No. 8"). After Bill sings that Texas women "done got the best of me," Wesbrooks says, "North Carolina women killin' me," possibly a sly reference to North Carolina's Bessie Mauldin. It was hoped that Bill's new instrumental, "Honky Tonk Swing," would be another jukebox jammer. On it and "No. 7," Wesbrooks plays intentionally humorous bass breaks. "The Coupon Song," sung solo by Wesbrooks, was the second of only three solo vocals recorded by one of the Blue Grass Boys. (Other songs, recorded previously by others, are not discussed here.)[20]

First House in Nashville

Before the end of 1941, Bill, Carolyn, five-year-old Melissa, and baby James moved into a house at 618 McFerrin Avenue on Nashville's near-northeast side. On Saturday night, December 6, the band played the *Opry*, and Bill was probably at home on Sunday, December 7, when Japan attacked Pearl Harbor. On Thursday, December 11, the day Germany and Italy declared war on the United States, Bill played in his native Ohio County, Kentucky, for the first time since joining the *Opry*, appearing at the high school in Horse Branch. No mention of the show was made in the local papers.[21]

Pete Pyle was drafted in early 1942 and Clyde Moody returned to the Blue Grass Boys. After his Happy-Go-Lucky Boys disbanded in 1941, Moody reportedly served in the army briefly. (Pyle would serve briefly too, returning to the *Opry* in 1943 to replace Ernest Tubb as lead singer with Pee Wee King and the Golden West Cowboys.)[22]

In the spring of 1942, Bill and the Blue Grass Boys were the stars of Jam-Up and Honey's *Grand Ole Opry* tent show, a clear indication of the growing popularity of Bill and his music. Providing music for Jam-Up and Honey's act were fiddler Howard "Howdy" Forrester and his wife, guitarist-singer Wilene [Will-een] Forrester. She also sang with Dixie Belle Buchanan in a duo called "The Kentucky Sweethearts," and he also fiddled for guitarist-singer-songwriter Tommy Thompson, dubbed "the Singing Range Rider" on the *Opry*. While on the tour, Bill asked Thompson to write lyrics to a melody he'd written, resulting in "Kentucky Waltz."[23]

During the tent show season (April through November), the tour took a break every two weeks or so, and Bill booked open-air variety shows on Saturday or Sunday afternoons with guest stars like Uncle Dave Macon and DeFord Bailey. Bailey was fired by the *Opry* in May 1941 but remained a major draw. He would continue to tour with Bill in the 1940s and, in later years, spoke highly of him: "He was a good fellow to work with and a good musician. He'd treat you right." In those days of segregated restaurants, Bailey often had to eat in the car: "It didn't matter what I wanted to eat, he'd get it for me. He'd see I'd eat." If the group stayed at a hotel, it was usually for whites only, so Bill had to find him a place to stay in the black community. As Bill recalled,

> We'd walk the streets together, two, three o'clock in the morning, nobody out, in the roughest parts of town, we'd be down there getting him a place to stay. We wore riding pants and hats back in them days, and I suppose they thought we was the law and nobody would ever bother us. Then he would get in the room and lock the door and stay there until I went to get him the next day.[24]

The Recording Ban and Columbia Records

In the summer of 1942 all of the major record labels in the United States stopped recording. American Federation of Musicians President James Petrillo, determined to make record companies pay royalties to all musicians' union members, ordered a nationwide strike that began at midnight on July 31, 1942, to end only when the companies agreed to pay. Thinking the "recording ban" wouldn't last long, Bill ended his association with RCA Victor and signed with Columbia Records on October 26, 1942. The difficulties involving Pete Pyle at 1941's session had convinced him that it was time for a change, but, due to the continuing ban, he would not record again until 1945.[25]

In the meantime, Wooten joined the navy in the summer of 1942 and was replaced by the fiddler closest at hand, Howdy Forrester. A devotee of Texas-style fiddling, which emphasized variations on the melody, Forrester's familiarity with the fingerboard allowed him to play in any key. This, in turn, allowed Bill to sing in keys that better suited his voice, including B-flat and B major ("B natural," as he called it). Less capable fiddlers complained, according to Bill: "Fiddle men had a fit and they wouldn't hardly tackle it and they'd swear that they wanted to play straight stuff and they figured that that's where I should sing." But, thanks to Forrester, Bill and the Blue Grass Boys began to achieve a higher level of musicianship, leaving behind the days of 1939–40, when Cleo Davis couldn't recall using a capo (the device that attaches to an instrument's neck to alter the pitch of the strings), or the sessions of 1940–41, when most of the recordings were in the keys of G, C, D, or A.[26]

Charlie finally auditioned for the *Grand Ole Opry* in the summer of 1942 but was turned down. Approaching age forty, he may have begun to consider retirement thereafter. At the end of the year, he bought 109 acres of land that once belonged to his father, midway between Horton and Rosine, and started making plans to build a house there. (This was the first of several land purchases Charlie would make in the area, eventually amassing over a thousand acres by 1963.)[27]

The 1942 tent show season with Jam-Up and Honey was successful, and Bill was making more money than he'd ever seen in his life. "Right in '42–'43 was my greatest years in bluegrass," he said later. "In the early days . . . they [audiences] were hungry for it, and there was a demand for it, and we had big crowds back there in wartime." By mid-1942, he began to think in terms of mounting his own tent show, as Roy Acuff had done that year. This may have been when Bill, knowing he would need as much variety and comedy as possible, offered a job to five-string banjo player DeWitt "Snuffy" Jenkins. Bill had not forgotten his three-finger picking, and Jenkins was widely known in the Southeast as a comedian. Still working in a band led by Byron Parker, thirty-one-year-old Jenkins was reportedly averse to Bill's demanding travel schedule and declined the offer.[28]

The honor of being Bill's first banjo player would go, instead, to twenty-six-year-old David Akeman from eastern Kentucky, who'd written to Bill asking for a job (actually someone must have written for him; he couldn't read or write). Tall and skinny, as a comedian he was known as "String Beans" (later "Stringbean"). He'd worked successfully in brother Charlie's Kentucky Pardners during 1940–41 and played five-string banjo in the various styles of his idol Uncle Dave Macon. He wasn't a three-finger picker, but Bill overlooked this because of Akeman's comedic abilities: "I needed a comedian, you see, is the reason Stringbean got the job with me." Bill wanted him to team up with Wesbrooks, to have an act like Jam-Up and Honey: "Two working together, they was really powerful onstage, you know? They could really get the laughs." Akeman was playing with the band full-time by the end of 1942, the first musician from Kentucky to join the Blue Grass Boys.[29]

The search for ways to entertain audiences may have inspired a now-legendary stunt in which Bill, like a circus "strong man," carried his Blue Grass Boys. "I would put one on top of my shoulders," he said, "and one around my back. Then I'd hold one with my right arm, and one with my left." Bill was, without a doubt, "stout" (his word for "strong"), but the combined weight of Akeman, Forrester, Moody, and Wesbrooks—which he estimated at nine hundred sixty pounds—must have strained his back, and the stunt didn't last. But word of Bill's strength would live on.[30]

Howdy Forrester, meanwhile, received his draft notice on August 8, 1942, and signed up for the navy. But he couldn't be inducted until after he turned twenty-one (on March 31, 1943), so he continued playing with Bill during the rest of 1942. (Bill himself was exempt from the draft; his poor vision and status as a father disqualified him.)[31]

Shortly after 1943 began, on February 1, Bill's namesake uncle, baseball-playing William Monroe, died of heart disease at the age of seventy-five. Years later, Bill remembered "Uncle Willie" giving him twenty cents on his birthday when he was young: "Two dimes looked like he'd carried for a year, just as shiny as they could be. Nobody give you money in them days because they didn't have it to give."[32]

By February 1943, it appears Forrester was the "primary" fiddler, playing only on the *Opry*, while others fiddled on a temporary or trial basis on the road: Magness returned briefly, then a young fiddler and singer from North Carolina, Carl Story, worked with the band off and on, while Clarence "Mac" McGarr and Floyd Ethridge, featured *Opry* soloists, filled in. But none were capable of replacing Forrester. As Bill later said, "He's the first man to play with me that played double-stop [two strings played together, creating a harmony], and [he] knows that neck all the way, and he knows how to get that tone out, [to] give the fiddle a chance." Finally, in March 1943, Bill announced Forrester's departure on the *Opry*, calling for a replacement.[33]

Listening down in Gainesville, Florida, was twenty-seven-year-old semiprofessional fiddler Robert Russell "Chubby" Wise. After hearing Bill's announcement, he recalled saying to himself, "Bill's going to need a fiddle player."

> The next Monday, after hearing that Saturday night, I took a train to Nashville. I just sat around there till the weekend. On Saturday night, I just threw my fiddle under my arm, went backstage [at the *Opry*]—I told the man at the door, "My name's Wise. I'm from Florida. I've come to see Bill Monroe. I want to have a job. Now, he's got to have a fiddle player and I'm a fiddler." [S]o he said, "Alright, he's in the dressing room." And I walked in and shook his hand, said, "Are you Bill Monroe?" He said, "Yup." I said, "My name's Russell Wise (I didn't use my [nick] name) and I'm a fiddle player and I hear you're a-huntin' a fiddler." He said, "Do any of my stuff?" I says, "Yeah." He said, "Play me a hoedown." I'll never forget, the first thing I played for him was "Katy Hill." Then he said, "How about playing something that I sing? How about 'Footprints in the Snow'?" So he sang and I backed him up on "Footprints in the Snow." He looked around and said, "You got your clothes with you?" And I said, "By God, no. They're over at the hotel." And he said, "Well, go get 'em."[34]

They headed out that night, Wise hired on a trial basis. Others, including Story, McGarr, and Ethridge, fiddled at some shows instead of him. They all knew that whenever Forrester returned from the service, the job would revert back to him. But Bill could see that Wise's swing-influenced style was right for the times (western swing was all the rage) so, as with Davis and Wooten, Bill became his teacher.

> Bill Monroe taught me how to play bluegrass. He taught me the long blue notes. Many a day, in motels and hotels—him with that mandolin and I'd have my fiddle—he taught me to play bluegrass music. He'd say, "Now do it this way," and I'd try. And he'd say, "No, that's not what I want." And he'd show me on the mandolin—"Now this is what I want." And finally when I'd get it, he'd say, "Yep, that's what I want."

Ethridge praised Wise's abilities to Bill, and Bill arranged for him to teach Wise the old-time fiddle tunes he knew. Wise was an eager and appreciative student.[35]

Bill's First Tent Show—1943

It wasn't long before Bill's own *Grand Ole Opry*–endorsed tent show began in May 1943 in Georgia, traveling through Tennessee, North Carolina, Virginia, South Carolina, and then back to Georgia in mid-November. There were usually short distances between shows. "Back in days like that," Bill said, "say, you played here today, you might play five or ten miles down the road the next day." The tent and its crew were leased from noted tent showman Billy Wehle [Whale-ee] of Louisville, Kentucky. Uncle Dave Macon and Sam and Kirk McGee were Bill's special guest stars, and he hired several other musicians for the show, including Howdy Forrester's twenty-year-old wife Wilene "Billie" Forrester. Dubbed "Sally Ann" by Bill, she was featured as a solo singer, occasionally backed by Bill and the Blue Grass Boys. She sold tickets to the shows and took care of the gate receipts as well. Bill also hired harmonica player Elliott "Curley" Bradshaw, thirty-one, from central Kentucky. Bradshaw was featured playing solos in the styles of DeFord Bailey or Lonnie Glosson, but, otherwise, he played a second rhythm guitar whenever he joined in with the Blue Grass Boys. By the end of the season, both Bradshaw and Forrester were regular members of the band, with Bradshaw billed as "King of the Harmonica" and Forrester—born in New Mexico and raised in Oklahoma—"The Kentucky Song Bird."[36]

By then, "Sally Ann" Forrester was also playing accordion with the Blue Grass Boys. A piano player since childhood, she transitioned to keyboard accordion easily, and she may have suggested to Bill that she play it with the band. In 1975 Ralph Rinzler wrote that "Bill has said that the inclusion of the accordion [in his band] . . . was directly traceable to his memory of his mother's playing"—so, her suggestion was easy for him to accept. The same could be said for harmonica, which his mother also played, and the banjo, which Clarence Wilson played. At any rate, all three instruments were being used in many mainstream country music bands of the time. (One of Forrester's instrumental specialties was "Heel and Toe Polka," a tune Malissa used to play on her little button accordion, and Akeman usually picked banjo "two-finger" style, using his thumb and forefinger like Clarence Wilson.)[37]

Shortly after the 1943 tent show season began, the State of Tennessee invited the *Grand Ole Opry* to leave the War Memorial Auditorium. Too many Saturday-night visitors had used their knives to carve "their initials in the War Memorial's fine leather seats," so the *Opry* moved to the largest showplace in town, the Ryman Auditorium, near Fifth Avenue North and Broadway. It seated 3,574—over a thousand more than the War Memorial's 2,200 capacity. The transition happened so smoothly that many forgot when the first *Opry* performance was broadcast from the Ryman. It was June 5, 1943. (During 1943–44, Mauldin was living at the Victory Hotel, on Seventh Avenue North, a short walk from the Ryman.)[38]

The best known star of Bill's tent show was Uncle Dave Macon, then approaching age seventy-three. Bill later remembered him fondly as an amusing challenge for a then-young showman.

> Uncle Dave was . . . one of the finest entertainers you ever seen. If he could really sell to the audience—if they liked him—he could really turn on. But if they didn't like him, he wouldn't stay on the stage over five minutes. And he'd turn it over to me, and I'd really have to go to work! And if we went to a place that, say, we had a big crowd, why, "Boy, the old man can still draw 'em in"—that's what he would say. But if we went to a place and had about twenty-five or thirty people, [he] said, "Mr. Bill, you're not drawing so good tonight."[39]

In September, while the tour was in South Carolina, the troupe stayed in Spartanburg at the Franklin Hotel, just across the street from radio station WSPA. Sixteen-year-old Don Reno was playing on it at the time, picking three-finger-style banjo with the Carolina Hillbillies, with sixteen-year-old John Palmer on bass. Reno and a slightly older teenaged acquaintance from North Carolina, Earl Scruggs (age nineteen), had independently managed to improve on the style they'd heard "Snuffy" Jenkins and others play, and the sound was still new (and relatively unrefined).[40]

Moody, Wesbrooks, and Wise crossed the street to do a guest spot on WSPA to advertise the tent show, and as Reno later recalled,

> When Clyde (Moody) heard me play banjo, he immediately had to take me over to the hotel to let the other fellows hear me. They kept me playing just about all day over there, [but] they had to save me till Bill got in, so he could hear me. And when he did, right away he said, "Boy, you want a job?" I told him I would love to have one, but I had to wait and see if I was going in the army or not, and if I didn't have to go, I'd come to work with him. But I went in the army.

Bill (then thirty-two, twice Reno's age) played three hours with the group at the hotel that day, telling Moody at one point, "This is the sound right here that I want." (Reno would survive World War II and return to play with Bill later.)[41]

Charlie, meanwhile, built a house on the land he'd bought in Ohio County, but he didn't retire, and during 1943 and 1944, Lester Flatt was playing mandolin and singing tenor with him. The job with the Kentucky Pardners required Flatt to sing and play like Bill and, even though he never went far on the mandolin, he was very good at singing Bill's style of tenor. Able to study Charlie's guitar playing at close range, he would later use one of Charlie's licks, his "G-run" (which fans called "the Lester Flatt G-run"). One of the songs Flatt sang solo was one he'd written, "Will You Be Loving Another Man?" This may have inspired Charlie to write songs too, and one of the first was "Who's Calling You Sweetheart?" Brother Birch worked with the Pardners during this time, lured away from the East Chicago job he'd kept since Charlie and Bill left Indiana in 1934.[42]

In early 1944 Wesbrooks called it quits. "I left [Bill] on good terms," he wrote in his autobiography. "Of course, he didn't want me to leave. And I can understand why, because I did the type of comedy that he wanted. One of his brothers, John, said, 'Bill, Wilbur's the only comedian there are in the country as far as we're concerned.'" Clearly, Bill needed a good comedian, and Wise said he knew one: Howard Watts. A fellow Floridian who worked there with Wise in a band called the Jubilee Hillbillies, thirty-year-old Watts had been honing his comedy skills with various bands since the mid-1930s. Since 1941, he was "Arizona Slim" in *Opry* star Paul Howard's Arkansas Cotton Pickers, a western swing band. Also with Howard in the Cotton Pickers was James "Tex" Willis, another of the Jubilee Hillbillies, alternating bass and guitar with Watts. Bill had undoubtedly heard them playing at the *Opry* and knew how musically talented Watts was.[43]

Watts's comedy routines were very successful on Bill's shows, and prior to the beginning of the 1944 tent-show season, he and Bill collaborated on a new stage name for him, originally with mock dignity, "C. Cedric Rainwater." It was eventually shortened by fans to just "Cedric Rainwater," and that's what Watts would be called from then on, his real name virtually forgotten.[44]

Regrettably, no recordings of Watts's routines have survived, but "A Letter to a Nephew" was included in one of his souvenir booklets, and an excerpt provides a hint of the richness of his humor.

As I have time, because I ain't so busy, I thought I would write you a few lines— eight or ten pages—and let you know the up-to-date news, about six months old. We are all as well as can be expected for the condition we're in. We ain't sick, we just don't feel good. I am feeling fine. Aunt Martha is dead. I hope this letter finds you the same. I suppose you will want to hear about us moving from West

Virginia to Caliwood, Hollyfornia. We never started moving until we left, never turned off until we came to a cross-road, and stayed on the road that went there. It didn't take us any longer than from the time we started until the time we arrived. The trip was the best part of all. If you ever come out here, don't miss that.

They didn't expect to see us until we arrived and most of the people we were acquainted with, we knew, and the people we didn't know seemed like strangers. We still live at the same place we moved to last, which is beside our nearest neighbors, across the road from the other side. John says he thinks we will stay here until we move or go someplace else. We are very busy farming. We have three cows, but are going to sell one because we can't milk him. Eggs are a good price. That's the reason they are so high. I sure hope we get a lot of them. We just bought twenty-five roosters and one old hen. Some of the ground is so poor, you can't raise an umbrella on it, but we have a fine crop of potatoes—some the size of a hickory nut, some the size of a pea, and then a whole lot of little ones. We also have a fine crop of corn. I think we will make about five gallons to the acre. Some worms got in our corn last year, but we just fished them out and drank it anyway.[45]

Baseball–1944

Aside from a new comedian and the new solid sound of the band (thanks to Watts's bass playing), Bill's 1944 tent show also featured the latest nationwide preoccupation—baseball. The war had robbed major league teams of star players, and interest in the game had shifted to the local level. "Back before television," Bill recalled later, "baseball was really popular all over the country. Every town had a ball club." Cashing in on this, Bill and the Blue Grass Boys would challenge each town's team to a game before the show and attract the entire community. Neil Rosenberg has written that pop music's big bands may have devised the ploy, but Bill's use of it "seems to have been unique in the country music of the time."[46]

Although all of the band members took part, Moody and Akeman were especially talented athletes. Both had played semi-pro ball and both pitched for the Blue Grass Boys (Watts was their catcher), but, according to Bill, Akeman could play any position well *and* he was a good hitter: "He was a hard man to strike out, boy. He went one year, and I think maybe they only struck him out a couple of times."[47]

The Blue Grass Special

For the 1944 season, which took the troupe through Tennessee, Kentucky, Virginia, North Carolina, Georgia, and northern Florida, Bill purchased his own tent. A three-thousand-seat giant, it nearly doubled his seating capacity. He also bought a 1941 Chevrolet airport limousine, the first Blue Grass Special. Then called a "bus," it could transport up to ten people, including the band and guest stars. According to Bill,

> After you got a lot permit for the show, there was nothing anybody could do to give you any trouble. It was like owning your house, until you left the next day. At one time, I had five trucks I traveled with, besides a long, stretched-out bus we had. One truck hauled folding seats, another hauled the tent, another hauled the light plant [generator], another was a kitchen on wheels, and the fifth truck hauled the long tent poles. All the trucks would try to arrive at a certain place outside of a town at a certain time. Then we would drive through the town in a procession to promote the show.
>
> The people would be watching for you. They knew you were coming because you'd been advertised for two or three weeks, and they'd be standing on the street corners and sidewalks, you know, watching the show come in. Around half-past ten or eleven [A.M.], we'd go out to where the tent would be put up. First you'd stretch the tent out, then drive the stakes down to where you could put the ropes up, just like the old carnival days.[48]

Birch left Charlie (who was considering retirement again) and went to work for Bill, running the tent show's refreshment stand. His nephew, Bill's three-year-old son James, recalled visiting the shows with his dad and seven-year-old sister Melissa.

> When we was kids, we would go with him to tent shows. He had my sister put on a box, with Clyde Moody a-backin' her up [when she sang], and she would be, like, a little part of the act. There was a blackfaced act that he had on the show [Akeman and Watts]. . . . I'd just be out there a-runnin' around, you know how kids are. I'd be gettin' popcorn from my Uncle Birch. He'd be out there sellin' at concessions. I'd take the Cokes and run around and play with my dog and stuff.

James also recalled "the bus" and the longing to be with his always-on-the-go dad. He admired his father, just like Bill admired his dad when he was a boy.

> My father used to have an old car, a stretched out Chevrolet bus with a big . . . rack on top of it where they could carry the instruments [covered with waterproof canvas]. I wanted to go on the road with him so much, because he'd only come in [to Nashville] for a day. I'd hide up on top of that thing and I'd go to sleep up there, and he'd want to see me before he left. He'd see my sister, and his boys would

always find me up there a-sleepin' on top of that [bus], hoping that they wouldn't find me so I could go with 'em. He'd only come to do the *Opry* on Saturday, and I'd be cryin' every time he left. I couldn't stand it. So I'd hide.[49]

On Tuesday, June 6, 1944—D-Day—Allied forces landed at Normandy, hastening the end of World War II in Europe. That same morning, Texas native Jesse Granderson "Grant" Turner reported to work for his first day as a WSM announcer (later to be called "the Voice of the *Grand Ole Opry*"). In November, after the tent show season ended, he was assigned to the station's early morning shift (5:00 to 7:00 A.M.), a cavalcade of fifteen-minute shows by the most popular *Opry* stars, and his first show featured Bill Monroe.[50]

President Roosevelt was elected to a fourth term on November 7, 1944. A month earlier, he had pleaded with musicians' union president Petrillo to end the recording ban, and four days after the election, the strike was settled. Rather than pay royalties to musicians individually, record companies agreed to contribute to a trust fund to aid out-of-work union members and finance free performances.[51]

The end of the recording ban brought a flurry of session schedulings; one for Bill was set by Columbia Records for February 1945. Recording contracts for new artists were plentiful, and Moody seized the opportunity, leaving the band to sign with Columbia. Bill suddenly needed a new lead singer, and by the end of November 1944, he had taken Watts's recommendation and hired his and Wise's former bandmate, Georgia native Tex Willis, who played "slap-," "chop-," or "sock-style" rhythm guitar.[52]

Bill Finds His First F-5

It's probably not a coincidence that Bill and the band played in Florida more often during 1945 than ever before (due to Watts and Wise), including the first documented trip to the southern part of the Sunshine State in January. And, while they were in Miami, on January 10 or 11, it appears that Bill found his new primary instrument, a Gibson F-5 mandolin (serial number 73987), signed by one of its designers, Lloyd Loar, after it was completed on July 9, 1923. As Bill told mandolinist David Grisman in 1977, "I was in Miami, Florida, and I was just shopping around, you know, looking in store windows, things like that. I passed by this barbershop and this mandolin was laying in the window there and had this little card up there with the price on it: $150. I went in and listened just a little, played it a number or so, and bought it." In pristine condition, the top-of-the-line instrument was also a bargain: In 1923, the list price of an F-5 was $250.[53]

During this time, Lester Flatt came to Nashville and stayed with former Happy-Go-Lucky Boys bandmate Clyde Moody until he could audition for Bill (who was in town for the *Opry* on January 13 and 20, 1945). Finding that Willis had already been hired, Flatt returned to Burlington, North Carolina, with a promise that he would be contacted when there was a change.[54]

In February, Bill, his new F-5 mandolin, and the band traveled to Chicago to record on Tuesday, February 13, in Studio 12 of radio station WBBM, a Columbia Broadcasting System affiliate, on the second floor of the stately Wrigley Building. Columbia producer Art Satherley asked Bill for solo vocals, and he delivered, recording four of the most enduring ones in his career repertoire: "Rocky Road Blues" (which Akeman had given him), "Kentucky Waltz" (co-written by Bill and Tommy Thompson), "Goodbye Old Pal" (which Bill purchased from Cliff Carlisle for $5; previously, Charlie had sung it as a solo), and "Footprints in the Snow" (learned from Hugh Cross of WLS). Only two of the remaining five numbers recorded that day would be released in the 1940s: the duet "True Life Blues," written by Pete Pyle, who gave it to Bill, not thinking much of it, and a blues instrumental, "Blue Grass Special" (named for the Chevrolet bus) and played in the same key as "Tennessee Blues" (A), but with a more typical ("12-bar") blues chord progression.[55]

Of the nine items recorded on February 13, only three derive directly from Bill: "Blue Grass Special," the co-authored "Kentucky Waltz," and one of the songs not released in the 1940s, Bill's "Come Back to Me in My Dreams." Although "typical" in chord structure, "Blue Grass Special" is completely atypical with regard to Bill's playing. His picking here, in the words of country music historian Doug Green, "solidified his position as one of country music's great instrumentalists." Bill once said he wrote the melody of "Kentucky Waltz" in 1935, when he and Charlie arrived in the Southeast. Initially featured by Clyde Moody, who sang it in the key of D, the song was recorded by Bill in the same key, even though it was pitched low for him, causing him to sing in a quieter, more relaxed-sounding style for the first time. "Come Back to Me in My Dreams," possibly the first song Bill wrote by himself, was shelved indefinitely, and the rejection was disappointing (but he would not give up on it, recording a new rendition in 1957).[56]

A few weeks after the session, in early March 1945, Howard Watts's father died in Florida. Watts asked Bill for a leave of absence, and so did Willis and Wise, who had both known Joseph Jarrett Watts. Bill, knowing there were capable fill-ins waiting in the wings, agreed to let them go, loaning them his Hudson Terraplane for the trip. While in Florida, Watts offered to arrange for bookings wherever he could for Bill and other *Opry* acts. Taking their wives with them, Watts, Wise, and Willis left Nashville planning to rejoin the band when the tent show season began at the end of April.[57]

Immediately thereafter, Lester Flatt received a telegram from Bill, and within an hour or so he was on a bus bound for Nashville. To fill in for Watts, Bill hired another Floridian, Andy Boyett, a blackface comedian nicknamed "Bijou" (also the name of a blacks-only theater in Nashville). And Bill called twenty-three-year-old fiddler Jim Shumate, whom he'd heard on radio in Hickory, North Carolina. Shumate recalled, "The telephone rang and a voice said, 'This is Bill Monroe.' That shook me up, you know? He said, 'Now, you play the fiddle, don't you? You've got Howdy Forrester, Tommy Magness, and three or four others all mixed up together. If you play that type of fiddle, that's what I want.'" Within a few days, Shumate too was on a bus to Nashville.[58]

Bill's First Farm

Bill had just purchased his first farm, forty-four acres on the outskirts of Nashville (near the northwest corner of Dickerson Road and Old Hickory Boulevard). After considering it since early 1943, he was finally able to purchase the property with the profits from the previous year's tent show. "Tell 'em I'm a farmer with a mandolin and a high tenor voice," he would tell the writer of a souvenir picture book published in the spring of 1945. The truth was, however, that even though he was finally a farm owner, when the new tent show season began, he would have little time for farming.[59]

President Roosevelt died on Thursday, April 12, 1945, while at his Warm Springs, Georgia, retreat south of Atlanta, with his mistress of twenty-seven years, Lucy Mercer, at his bedside. A three-day period of national mourning was declared and, honoring it, the *Grand Ole Opry* was cancelled for the first time, on April 14. Germany surrendered about three weeks later.[60]

When Watts returned at the end of April, Boyett was let go. Willis and Wise chose not to return, Wise joining Curley Williams and the Georgia Peach Pickers, a western swing band, touring California with them. This allowed Flatt to be hired full-time and Shumate to become the primary replacement for Howdy Forrester. Bradshaw left during this time; his open-string guitar playing (heard on recordings of "Kentucky Waltz," "True Life Blues," "Goodbye Old Pal," and others) was in the hands of Flatt now. That summer of 1945, while the United States continued to battle Japan, the band included Akeman on banjo; Flatt, guitar; Forrester, accordion; Shumate, fiddle; and Watts, bass.[61]

Watts wouldn't stay long, however. By the end of July 1945, his wife Alice was about to give birth to the couple's first child, and he took another leave of absence to be with her. Bill enlisted brother Birch to play bass temporarily. Howard Watts Jr. was born on August 2, but complications would keep Watts Sr. home for eight months, taking care of wife and baby. On August 6, the United States dropped an atomic bomb on Hiroshima, then another on Nagasaki three days later. Japan surrendered on August 15, and suddenly World War II was over.[62]

During the war years, three-finger-style banjo player Earl Scruggs had been working in a textile mill in North Carolina, maintaining a draft deferment to support his widowed mother and younger sister. With the end of the war, restrictions on where he could work were lifted, and he returned to playing music full time, joining the band of guitarist-singer "Lost John" Miller, previously with Pee Wee King's Golden West Cowboys (1938–40). Miller and his Allied Kentuckians had a daily show on WNOX in Knoxville, sponsored by the Allied Drug Company, and played locally five nights a week. A few weeks after twenty-one-year-old Scruggs joined, they started traveling to Nashville to do a Saturday morning show on WSM.[63]

Bessie Mauldin Marries Nelson Gann

Bessie Lee Mauldin had been in Nashville about four years at this point, and it appears that she and Bill had grown apart. During one of his extended absences, she had gotten acquainted with Nelson Gann, a Tennessee Highway Patrol officer. On September 4, 1945, they were married in Franklin, Kentucky, just north of Nashville on the Kentucky-Tennessee border, where quick and cheap wedding ceremonies were performed.[64]

"Blue Moon of Kentucky"

Bill never spoke publicly about his relationship with Mauldin, but her departure appears to have caused him to write one of his best-known songs, "Blue Moon of Kentucky." The use of blue moon imagery wasn't new: Richard Rodgers and Lorenz Hart's pop "Blue Moon" had been around since 1934, and Walker and Sullivan's "When My Blue Moon Turns to Gold Again" was a country hit in 1943. But uniquely, in Bill's song, he actually speaks to the blue moon, telling it to change its seldom-seen ways and "keep on shinin'" on his lost love. Bill once told an interviewer he wrote the song while driving back from one of the band's trips to Florida. Indeed, there was a full moon at the end of March 1945, as the band returned from playing a few shows there, and Bill may have already known of Mauldin's involvement with Gann by then. Bill's earliest-known performance of "Blue Moon of Kentucky" was on the *Opry* broadcast of August 25, 1945, ten days before the Mauldin-Gann nuptials.[65]

In mid-September 1945, Shumate went home to North Carolina for a few weeks for the birth of his second child, and Bill used whomever he could get from the *Opry* to fiddle. At that point, Akeman decided to enlist in the army, figuring it was safe now that the war was over. Bill hired Jim Andrews, one of the Andrews Brothers duo from the *Opry*, to do comedy, and he played tenor banjo with the band. But he left within a couple of weeks when Akeman came back, likely dismissed for his inability to read. When Shumate returned in mid-October, he rode a bus to the Mississippi town nearest the tent show, then took a taxi to the tent site.

> The tent was settin' out in the field. I started walkin' across the field toward the tent, about four o'clock in the evenin'. Bill saw me comin'. He come runnin' just like a child, just a-flyin'. Grabbed me up, held me up over his head, and went round and round, me and that fiddle. He set me back down. He said, "I have never been as glad to see somebody in all my life! I've had half the fiddlers in Nashville with me all week, can't none of 'em fiddle a lick."[66]

The first biographical writing about Bill to appear in book form was published about this time by its author, *Opry* founder George D. Hay, in his *A Story of the Grand Ole Opry*. A brief but surprisingly accurate portrayal of Bill's past, Hay's sketch also mentioned the newly purchased forty-four-acre farm. At the other extreme was his description of Bill's singing: "There is that authentic wail in his high-pitched voice that one hears in the evening in the country when Mother Nature sighs and retires for the night."[67]

When the tent season ended in early November 1945, Akeman decided to leave again, to team up with new *Opry* member Lew Childre, a guest on Bill's tent show. "Bill told me that Stringbean was quittin'," Shumate said, "and asked me if I knew anybody in North Carolina that could play the banjo. I said, 'Yeah, I know a fella, but he don't play Stringbean-style.' He said, 'Who is he?' I said, 'Earl Scruggs, lives in Shelby'" (he had met Scruggs in North

Carolina and thought he still lived there). Bill asked him to get in touch with Scruggs, and Shumate eventually learned he was playing at WSM in Nashville on Saturday mornings with Lost John Miller. He found him at the National Life building studios and encouraged him to quit Miller and audition with Bill, but Scruggs later said he was reluctant at first.

> I wasn't the type to jump from one pasture to another, and I didn't know Bill's nature as to whether he would even go for my style of picking at all. Lost John was treating me good and I told Jim [Shumate], "No, I can't take a chance." Shortly thereafter, Lost John decided to get off the road, for financial reasons. When that happened, I met Jim down at the coffee shop in [the Tulane Hotel] in Nashville and told him I was free to make a change.

Shumate called Bill, and within an hour or so on Saturday, December 1, 1945, the three were in Shumate's room at the hotel.[68]

Shumate recalled that Scruggs was a little nervous in the presence of Bill Monroe. "I'd always worshipped the Monroe Brothers," Scruggs said later. After they got their instruments out, Scruggs picked the familiar "Sally Goodin," then the less familiar "Dear Old Dixie." "He picked the hound out of that banjo," Shumate recalled. Bill, showing little reaction, asked Scruggs to come to the *Opry* that night, to see what his picking sounded like with the entire band. But secretly, he was very impressed, as Shumate revealed: "I said, 'What do you think of him, Bill?' He said, 'Gosh, he's good. I think I'll hire him, if he'll work.'" Bill wasn't sure Scruggs would be willing to work for what he was paying: $50 a week, $60 a week during the tent-show season.[69]

Lester Flatt thought they were doing fine without a banjo: "[Akeman] had been gone a few weeks, and I was enjoying not having a banjo around when Bill told me onstage there was a banjo player backstage wanting to try out for the group. I told Bill, as far as I was concerned, this fellow Scruggs could leave his banjo in its case. It was later a surprise to everyone, and certainly to me, to hear a banjo played the way Scruggs did it." That evening at the *Opry*, they played nonstop in the dressing room (only). Flatt recalled Bill asking for his opinion: "Bill said, 'What do you think?' and I said if you can hire him, get him, whatever it costs." After awhile, Scruggs began to notice it was getting late:

> His closing show was at 10 [Scruggs recalled]. The last bus out of Nashville was at 10, or 10:05, or something like that. Bill still hadn't said anything about whether he wanted me to go to work with him or not. So I just picked up my banjo and

said, "That's it. I've got to catch this bus." He looked at me and said, "We'll leave at 10 [A.M.] Monday," just like that. I said, "I can't." At the time, I had a touch of the flu and, for another thing, my clothes were in Knoxville. So I told him, "I've got to go to Carolina for a few days," and he said, "Well, be back next Saturday," and that's how I began working for him.

That audition night was Shumate's last with the Blue Grass Boys; Howdy Forrester had returned from the navy to reclaim his job. The next Saturday night, December 8, Shumate was home in North Carolina and tuned in the *Opry* to hear Scruggs's first night as a Blue Grass Boy: "When Earl hit the stage, he really tore that place up."[70]

After Howdy Forrester returned, Bill agreed to hire his older brother, Joe Forrester, a survivor of the D-Day invasion, as bass player and comedian. Birch continued to work with the band, singing bass on gospel songs and fiddling old-time hoedowns, billed as "the South's Champion Square Dance Fiddler." And rehired was Jim Andrews, mainly as a second comedian. After December 8, Bill and the Blue Grass Boys played close to home for the next two weeks, then took two weeks off for the holidays (except for the *Opry*s of December 22 and 29).[71]

Bill's First Hit: "Kentucky Waltz"

At the beginning of 1946, the first record from the 1945 Columbia session, "Kentucky Waltz" / "Rocky Road Blues," was released. It had been more than three years since Bill's last record ("Honky Tonk Swing" / "Back Up and Push"), and during those years, the country music record business had become big business, fostered by a new national prosperity. The music-business journal *Billboard* began providing a "Most-Played Juke Box Folk Records" chart ("Folk" meaning any white artist with country or hillbilly tendencies), informing jukebox distributors of customer preferences nationwide, allowing them to profit, too. By April 1946, after six weeks on the chart, "Kentucky Waltz" peaked (reached its highest level) at number 3 of five entries. Limited though the chart may have been, it was populated by only the biggest stars in country music, and Bill's inclusion is a clear indication that he had risen to a new level of prominence.[72]

During this time (January–April 1946), Bill and the band played mainly in the Southeast's schools, city auditoriums, and courthouses, with one exception: the Carolina Theatre in Shelby, North Carolina, Scruggs's hometown,

on January 16, ten days after his twenty-second birthday. Meanwhile, Joe
Forrester recalled one courthouse in particular:

> We were playing in this courthouse one night. It was upstairs, and we were
> singing the gospel songs. And some guy in the back was mouthing off about
> something—he wouldn't be quiet. Bill asked him two or three times to be quiet,
> and we sang another verse or two, and that guy just kept on. Bill said, "Carry
> on, Lester." And we started out on another gospel song and Bill went back there
> and he must have thrown that guy down the steps. We heard something going
> on. But Bill was very serious about singing gospel songs. . . . [H]e thought you
> should be very solemn about that. . . . He was a religious man, but you wouldn't
> know it for sure, just how religious he was. He really believed.[73]

By March 1946, Joe, Howdy, and Sally Ann Forrester had turned in their
notices and were gone. Bill, Flatt, and Scruggs played the *Opry* on March 23
and were joined there by Howard Watts, finally returning to the band to play
bass. Recorded live that night, Bill is heard singing the opening line of "Little
Maggie"—"Over yonder stands little Maggie"—with Watts (in character as
Cedric Rainwater) wondering out loud, "Where?"[74]

The following week, again on the *Opry* and recorded live, Judge Hay is
heard introducing them, saying, "The number will be by Bill and brother
Earl with that fancy banjo." Indeed, it was "fancy"—both to listen to (when
Scruggs picked it) and to look at—a Gibson RB-11 with its headstock and
fingerboard covered with shiny imitation mother-of-pearl ("pearloid"),
painted-on "inlays" of black and red, and its wooden parts coated with a
blue-tinted finish. It was one of Gibson's cheaper instruments, described in
the company's 1935 catalog as "the flashiest five-string banjo made."[75]

Chubby Wise, back from California in April, undoubtedly knew the time
was right to reclaim his job. Bill would have welcomed the return of his star
pupil; he knew the band was scheduled to record in September and needed
to start preparing for it. Once Bill, Flatt, Scruggs, Watts, and Wise were finally
together, Bill took charge, refining the instrumental interplay and insisting
they all listen to each other, not just themselves, a crucial directive. "He
would spend a lot of time just tightening up the band," said Scruggs. "Some
rehearsals we wouldn't sing a song. We would just concentrate on the sound
of the band."[76]

It's likely that five of the twelve songs they would record in September
were already in the works then, including Bill's "Blue Moon of Kentucky,"
"How Will I Explain about You?" (a song Bill bought for $10 from Arthur

Q. Smith, the eccentric Knoxville songwriter who sold several great songs for a pittance), and another Jimmie Rodgers adaptation, "Blue Yodel No. 4" (actually, three stanzas from "No. 3" plus one devised by Bill, apparently equaling "4," to his way of thinking). There was also Flatt's "Will You Be Loving Another Man?" and another song he was probably already working on, "Why Did You Wander?" Composer credits would list Bill's name as well as his on these two, as usual, according to Flatt: "It was almost mandatory to give the bandleader a half interest in your songs." In return, Flatt could make money on them before they were released. According to Bill, "[Flatt] thought it was the most wonderful thing in the world that I could get advance money for him from BMI." (Broadcast Music Incorporated, the music licensing organization, collects a fee from broadcasters for each use of a composition registered with it.)[77]

Only Bill's name appeared as the writer of the other songs they would record, but it's likely that at least a few were written with the help of the entire band, in a "co-op" songwriting process Bill began to use at this time. Ralph Rinzler once witnessed the process in the 1960s, while on the road with the band.

> Sometimes . . . Bill would come up with a melody which he'd either sing or pick out on the mandolin. Sometimes he might have a refrain [chorus] to go with it or would ask the group in the car to help him set words to the refrain. He would then teach the vocal lead to his singer and they would rehearse the song without any verses, as a means of honing it and establishing it in memory.

In 1946 the primary members of the cooperative were Flatt and Scruggs. According to Scruggs, "We'd ride a lot of nights after a show, going to another gig, and sit back there [in the back seats of the bus] and pick. [Bill] was writing some new songs, Lester was writing some new songs, and I was helping." Later, a song might be copyrighted in Bill's name only, but no one complained publicly while he was living. Scruggs spoke out in 2006 when asked if he'd written any songs before 1948: "I'd written some stuff, but most of the time Bill Monroe got the credit for my ideas."[78]

A "fun" product of this co-op process was likely "Heavy Traffic Ahead," an in-joke the entire group might have contributed to. It was initially inspired by a road sign's warning, near Flatt's hometown of Sparta, Tennessee, on the road they often took eastward from Nashville, State Route 70. According to Scruggs, "[T]here weren't over three cars a day that went through there, I don't guess." (He also said the line about the Blue Grass Boys being "never late" was a laugh, since they were often one to three hours late wherever they played.) Another possible co-op product is "Toy Heart," a novelty song using double meanings, which Bill probably wouldn't have written on his own (or it may have been another song Bill bought from Arthur Q. Smith). Other possibles are the gospel songs recorded in 1946, "Mansions for Me," "Shining Path," and "Wicked Path of Sin." Flatt, Scruggs, and Watts would all write gospel songs later in their careers, and all could have helped Bill write these. At the time, it would have been much easier for the band to devote its energies to songwriting. During the 1946 tent-show season, when Bill was lacking good baseball players like Moody and Akeman, he decided to stop featuring the ball games.[79]

Speed Monroe and Family

The tent show rolled through Tennessee, North Carolina, Georgia, and Kentucky in April, May, and June 1946, and Bill had left his farm unattended. Brother Speed, recently returned from Ohio, was renting a house in Rosine and needing a job, so when Bill asked him to move to Nashville to take charge of his farm, Speed readily accepted, bringing with him wife Geanie, daughters Rosetta, now sixteen, and Earrol Dean, ten, and son Scottie, thirteen. An added bonus was the companionship the children would provide their cousins Melissa, nearing ten, and James, five.[80]

It appears the popularity of the new sound of Bill and the Blue Grass Boys was spreading, judging by a tour they played about a month later. The tent show came to a halt while the band played a long series of one-nighters, culminating in Bill's first extended visit to the Northeast. The tour began on the 4th of July in Blytheville, Arkansas, and Scruggs recalled that day clearly:

> We were playing out in a field . . . on a truck bed . . . in a pasture, and people bought their tickets and were standing around listening to the show. We were picking, and came up one of those famous afternoon thunderstorms real quick, and we just kept picking. . . . By the time we quit playing, we headed for [a nearby] barn and that [RB-11] banjo was soaking wet. [It] had a lot of plastic on it and it started breaking loose and I was forced to get another banjo. I couldn't afford it, but I found another banjo—a [1934] Gibson Mastertone.

For the next two weeks, the band played in a different location in the South each day, returning to Nashville on Saturdays, as usual. Then, after the *Opry* of July 20, they flew via American Airlines to Washington, D.C. (probably the first flight for all of them, except for Flatt, who hated planes and may have driven), to begin their visit to the Northeast with a five-day stand (July 21–25) at nearby Sunset Park, the new open-air country music showplace near West Grove, Pennsylvania, with special guest Tommy Thompson, co-writer of "Kentucky Waltz." For the next eleven days, they played in Pennsylvania, Ohio, Delaware, and Maryland at other country music parks, traveling as far north as Allentown, Pennsylvania.[81]

"The Classic Band" Records

The tent show was restarted in West Virginia and traveled through Tennessee, Alabama, and Mississippi during August and early September 1946. From Mississippi, Bill and the band headed north to play the *Opry* on September 14, then continued northward to Chicago to record for Columbia (Birch went with them, to sing bass on one song and play bass on another). As in the previous year, they were again on the second floor of the Wrigley Building with producer Satherley, though this time there would be three short sessions instead of one long one, two on Monday evening the 16th and one on Tuesday afternoon the 17th, easing some of the pressure. Scruggs was apprehensive:

> I didn't know how anybody would take to my style of playing when I came to Nashville, and I had the same feeling when I went to record. [But] that Art Satherley had a way to make you feel good. We went in and went through a tune, and he was in the control room. He came out and said, "Bill, where did you find this young man?" He said, "You've got the best band I've ever heard you have. Hang on to what you got." And that made me feel like I had something that was pleasing to him, so I could relax a little in the studio.[82]

All twelve recordings were made with one microphone. "We was used to workin' one mike for personal appearances," Scruggs recalled. Still, before the first take of a song was cut, they had to rehearse the moves they would make, to maintain the right volume level for each voice and instrument. Acceptable first takes were rare, combining the right moves, familiarity with the song, and luck. Only two songs were recorded acceptably on the first take, the duet "Mansions for Me" and "Mother's Only Sleeping" (they would also make up the first release from the sessions). The band attempted a second take of "Toy Heart" unsuccessfully, so the first was deemed acceptable (it would not be released until 1949, however). "Shining Path" (with Birch playing bass and Wise, guitar) was dropped after one take, possibly due to Scruggs's slightly off-pitch bass singing. Most of the rest ("Heavy Traffic Ahead," "Why Did You Wander?," "Blue Moon of Kentucky," "Blue Yodel No. 4," "Will You Be Loving Another Man?," and "Wicked Path of Sin") were recorded in two takes. Only two songs required more: "How Will I Explain About You?" (three) and "Summertime Is Past and Gone" (five).[83]

Not counting "Blue Yodel No. 4," only one song had been recorded and released before: "Mother's Only Sleeping." Mainer's Mountaineers were the first to record it, released in July 1946 (King), probably learned from Charlie Monroe's radio broadcasts. Charlie's Kentucky Pardners once included the song's original writers, Lance and Maynard Spencer, often featured singing their "Mother's Just Sleeping." After the Spencers left, Lester Flatt learned the song from Charlie, who had rewritten and retitled it "Mother's Only Sleeping." Flatt wrote his own verses, and it was this version he eventually gave to Bill. On September 30, two weeks after Bill waxed it, Charlie recorded his own version, titled "Mother's Not Dead, She's Only Sleeping," at his first session in more than seven years, now on RCA Victor, competing with his brother.[84]

Bill and the band returned to the tent show in Mississippi following the September sessions, traveling through Louisiana and Texas until mid-November 1946. Joining the tent crew during this time was twenty-year-old Bill Myrick, born in Mississippi and raised in Monroe, Louisiana. One day there was time to kill before showtime. As Myrick remembered,

> I was just kinda standing around, and we had everything set up and ready to go. The band was [elsewhere] and the instruments was laying there. So, I reached and got the guitar and serenaded myself about fifteen minutes. Then I figure I'd better put ol' Lester's guitar up. He's liable to "scob my knob," 'cause I don't know him. I raised the sidewall on the tent to put the guitar [behind it] and there was five pair of feet! And it was Bill, Lester and Earl, Chubby, and Cedric. And, of course, Lester was just standin' there grinnin'. All Bill said was, "You didn't tell me you could sing, boy." I said, "Well, nobody asked me." That was all that was said, and Lester just kinda winked at me and went on.
>
> Later that night, I was watching the show from the side and talking to Tommy Thompson, and when Bill looked over there, he saw me. He come to the edge of the stage and said, "You'd better get ready. I'm gonna put you on." So I told Tommy, "Man, I can't go up there." He said, "You'd better take my guitar, 'cause you're fixin' to go up there."

Myrick sang Roy Acuff's "Great Speckled Bird" and went over big, he said. (Acuff had left the *Opry* in April, after his demand for higher pay was refused.

National Barn Dance star Red Foley was hired to replace him as host of the *Opry*'s nationally broadcast *Prince Albert Show*. Acuff would return in April 1947.) During the next four years, Myrick would work off and on with Bill, doing everything except actually joining the Blue Grass Boys.[85]

Bessie Mauldin Returns

On this leg of the tour, Myrick witnessed the return of Bessie Lee Mauldin, who, it appears, was estranged from her husband after only a year of marriage. She caused a scene at one of the shows, sticking her head out of the curtain while the show was going on, to draw attention to herself after another woman flirted with Bill. Myrick overheard Flatt tell Bill, "Monroe, if she belonged to me, I'd have popped her right in the mouth." (Nelson Gann and Mauldin divorced in 1946–1947).[86]

In October 1946, Columbia released the second record from the 1945 session, "Footprints in the Snow" / "True Life Blues," more than nine months after the first release. (Around the first of November, Carter and Ralph Stanley formed the Stanley Brothers and Clinch Mountain Boys, with twenty-two-year-old West Virginia mandolinist and tenor singer Darrell Lambert, five-foot-two or -three and nicknamed "Pee Wee." One of the first serious Bill Monroe mandolin imitators, Lambert influenced the brothers to play in Bill's style.)[87]

Meanwhile, the tour was in Louisiana when the troupe stopped to eat in a café and Wise heard a Cajun song called "Sidewalk Waltz" on the jukebox.

> I was listening to a fiddle player . . . Harry [Choates], he's dead now . . . I thought it was the most beautiful thing I ever heard. And I played it three or four times [on the jukebox] . . . I couldn't get it out of my head. And when I got to Houston in the hotel [on November 2], I took my fiddle out, I was sitting right on the side of the bed there and just drove around that tune and came up with the [melody of] "Shenandoah Waltz" in about fifteen or twenty minutes.

(Wise would later play the tune for Clyde Moody, who wrote lyrics for it, and they would record it for King in 1947.) It was on the long return trip from Texas, Bill later recalled, that he wrote "The Old Cross Road" all by himself: "I wrote it in the car while everyone was asleep." Once back in Nashville, Watts took another leave of absence, to take care of his wife and one-year-old son. He would occasionally play the *Opry* with the band, but for the next several months, Birch filled in for him again.[88]

Bill's Second Hit: "Footprints in the Snow"

On December 7, "Footprints in the Snow" arrived in *Billboard*'s "Most-Played Juke Box Folk Records" chart, Bill's second charting record of 1946. It peaked after four weeks, in a three-way tie for number 5 among seven entries. (As Christmas time drew near, Pee Wee King and his Golden West Cowboys' lead singer, Henry "Redd" Stewart, happened to hear Bill's first hit, "Kentucky Waltz," on the radio. King told him he should write a waltz for his home state, Tennessee, and, lacking paper, Stewart scribbled lyrics on a matchbox cover. They were set to King's "No-Name Waltz," a tune he'd used as a closing theme since 1939, and the "Tennessee Waltz" was born.)[89]

Nineteen forty-seven followed, the only year Bill's Blue Grass Boys included Flatt, Scruggs, and Wise for its entire twelve months. It began with the band playing movie theaters in the Deep South. Scruggs recalled they would sometimes get there just before the first show, after cleaning up in the "bus" on the way: "We'd shave, sometimes, goin' down the road with a Coke bottle of water." Then, in February, they were in West Virginia and Ohio, where they headlined an *Opry* package show tour, playing at several large auditoriums.[90]

At Memorial Hall in Dayton, Ohio, on February 9, 1947, more than four thousand came to two shows featuring Bill and the Blue Grass Boys, Jam-Up and Honey, Grandpa Jones, and the York Brothers. In the audience with his family at one show was fifteen-year-old Bobby Osborne. He had been following Ernest Tubb, trying to sing like him until his voice changed, pitching his voice higher rather than lower. Then he started getting interested in Bill.

> I didn't even know what Bill played. I never had any idea he played the mandolin. I didn't even know what it was. But I was under the impression Monroe played the fiddle until I saw him in person in 1947. . . . About '47, I really got to listening to Bill and . . . I got to singing Bill's songs and playing the guitar and I had me a thumb pick and a finger pick—I seen Flatt play with one of them so I got me a thumbpick.

(In a couple of years, Osborne would be playing with banjo picker Larry Richardson, causing eleven-year-old brother Sonny Osborne to take an interest in the banjo.)[91]

An abbreviated tent show season followed, beginning in late February 1947 in Miami and lasting through the end of April. It appears that Bill and Jam-Up and Honey teamed up for this brief tour through Florida, Georgia, and

Alabama. During it, in March, the first record featuring Bill's current band was released, "Mansions for Me" / "Mother's Only Sleeping." The label may have released these first because they were reminiscent of Monroe Brothers recordings.[92]

The First Bill Monroe Songbook

Work started that spring on the first Bill Monroe songbook, financed by publisher Peer International. Two "shoots" for the book's photographs took place on Bill's farm and in downtown Nashville. On the farm, Bill posed with a thoroughbred Tennessee Walking Horse named King Wilkie (so-named by its original owner), shook hands with a collie dog (a Scotish breed), and, with Birch, proudly displayed two of their game chickens (like father, like sons). Downtown, the band was photographed in a studio in the National Life building and in a nearby parking lot with an extremely clean and shiny Blue Grass Special. Wearing their Stetson hats but otherwise dressed casually, they looked like they were ready to travel, and they probably were.[93]

Not long afterward, possibly while the tent show was in Georgia, Bill hired James "Chick" Stripling to do comedy and share bass playing duties with Birch. Stripling was a star of Atlanta's popular *WSB Barn Dance* (which replaced the Cross Roads Follies in 1940), and was only on temporary leave from it. Also, while on the road during that spring or summer of 1947, the Martin D-28 guitar Bill had bought in 1939 disappeared. According to Scruggs, "Bill had a D-28 and Lester played it for a good while. It got stolen off the top of the car. . . . There was no space in the trunk [for instruments]. It's a wonder they hadn't all got stolen." (The guitar was a "herringbone," nicknamed for the herringbone-patterned trim around the front edges of its body, inlayed on all Martin D-28s built between 1933 and 1946. Bill would replacc it with another herringbone, sometime in 1948–49.)[94]

In April 1947, while the band was on the tour, three WSM engineers moved their sideline recording business from the radio station to the Tulane Hotel. There, they opened the Castle Recording Studio, Nashville's first, located in the hotel's old dining room on the mezzanine level, between the first and second floors. That month, a young singer-songwriter from Alabama, Hank Williams, began recording there for MGM, and within a few months Ernest Tubb would become a regular, recording for Decca. (It would be more than two years before Bill recorded there, however.) In May, Tubb opened his Ernest Tubb Record Shop at 720 Commerce Street, not far from the Tulane Hotel, the first large-scale all-country record store in the United States. Its mail-order service could provide almost any country music record, and Tubb's radio advertisement for it, the *Midnite Jamboree,* would soon be broadcast from there after the *Opry.* And, at the *Opry,* Jim Denny, director of the Artist Service Bureau, took over the duties of George D. Hay, becoming the "house manager." Born the same year as Bill, Denny was first employed at National Life, WSM's owner, as a mailroom clerk.[95]

Bill and the band, meanwhile, were taking their music farther north than ever before, traveling to Michigan in May to play shows in Kalamazoo (where they toured the Gibson Instruments factory), Grand Rapids, and Detroit. Then, between *Oprys* on June 7 and 14, they went east to West Virginia for six consecutive days, followed by a week off.[96]

Possibly during one of his days off, Bill happened to hear a brother duo, Mel and Stan Hankinson, auditioning at WSM. Born in eastern Kentucky but raised in western Pennsylvania, they called themselves "The Kentucky Twins," even though Mel was three years younger than Stan. Nonetheless, Bill liked their Delmore Brothers–influenced style and one of their original songs, "Tennessee Gambler," and he became their benefactor. Using his influence, they were given a morning show on WSM and began appearing regularly on the *Grand Ole Opry* (featured there until 1949).[97]

Also in June 1947, the first batch of Bill's first songbooks arrived. *Bill Monroe's WSM Grand Ole Opry Song Folio No. 1* was an impressive 9" by 12" booklet featuring the photographs taken in the spring and the words *and* music to twenty-one songs. Among the fifteen Bill Monroe songs, four had yet to be recorded: "Ten-Brooks and Molly" [*sic*], "I'm Goin' Back to Old Kentucky," "Sweetheart, You Done Me Wrong," and "Little Cabin Home on the Hill." (The last two bear the credit "Words and Music by Lester Flatt and Bill Monroe," but in later listings Bill would be credited as the sole composer.) Six other songs, not from Bill's repertoire, were included, solely because they were published by Peer International, the songbook's publisher.[98]

In July, as Bill and the band again played movie theaters throughout the South, Columbia released "Will You Be Loving Another Man?" / "Blue Yodel No. 4," the first record to feature Scruggs's three-finger-style banjo picking. It went nowhere in *Billboard*'s jukebox chart, possibly due to the war-related scenario of "Loving Another Man," too out of date by then.[99]

That summer of 1947, Bill and the band knew more recording sessions were coming at the end of October. Columbia, heeding rumors of another musicians' union strike, had asked for sixteen rather than twelve new selections, to have enough releases to survive a long ban. Everyone in the band was working hard to develop new material, including "Blue Grass Breakdown." According to Scruggs,

> Going up and down the highway, a lot of times traveling day and night, I'd sit back there in about the third seat, pick tunes and work out tunes. You get bored riding, but anyway—I came up with that "Blue Grass Breakdown." . . . [A]t that time Lester was writing some songs, and he'd give Bill credit to record them, you know. . . . And I came up, really, with what was called "Blue Grass Breakdown," and Bill, he just took it all.[100]

Then, in September, they made another trip up north to play at Sunset Park and several other country music parks in Pennsylvania. Twenty-one-year-old singer-guitarist and future bluegrass bandleader William "Mac" Martin was at one on September 11, two days before Bill's thirty-sixth birthday.

> Golden Oaks Park was about sixty miles from my hometown, Pittsburgh. . . . It was a beautiful fall evening, as I remember it, [but] because of the lack of publicity, there were fewer than a hundred people [there when I arrived]. . . . Earl Scruggs was warming up, picking the banjo on the steps at the back of the stage [and] a crowd stood around [him]. . . . Lester Flatt was sleeping, stretched out across the backseat [of their car].
>
>   I saw Bill Monroe just before the show . . . and I asked him to play "John Henry." [As soon as] the band came on stage, Bill announced that he had a request for "John Henry, the Steel-Driving Man," and Chubby Wise did the kick off. . . . Playing bass that evening and doing comedy was Chick Stripling. Chubby was called upon to act as Chick's straight man.
>
>   When I left home in 1943, Bill had a powerful duet with Clyde Moody . . . I thought it could not get any better. But that Thursday night, I found out differently, [after] Lester and Bill did "Why Did You Wander?" and "How Will I Explain About You?" [the latter not yet released].

Martin also recalled Bill singing "Blue Moon of Kentucky." The Columbia recording would be released about two weeks later, backed with "Goodbye Old Pal." Neither registered on *Billboard*'s chart, but "Blue Moon of Kentucky" would become one of Bill's most popular songs and add significantly to his stature as *the* country music representative of the Blue Grass State.[101]

At the end of September 1947, Howard Watts returned to the band and Stripling went back to Atlanta. Watts had some catching up to do, probably familiar with only a few of the numbers they planned to record. But one, "Remember the Cross," he knew well—he and wife Alice had written it (she the lyrics, he the melody) in late 1945. Bill told Watts, "I'll record it for half," according to Watts's son Jarrett, so Bill and Watts share the copyright. A live recording from January 1947, with Watts singing bass, reveals the rest of the band knew it too.[102]

With the sessions coming up in a few weeks, the band could have taken some time off for rest and rehearsals, but the schedule of showdates continued unabated. The only concession: the dates were mostly close to home, in West Virginia and Kentucky. On the 25th, after the *Opry*, the band headed for Chicago.[103]

"The Classic Band" Records Again

Again they returned to the Wrigley Building to work with producer Art Satherley. This time, on Monday, October 27, and Tuesday, October 28, two sessions were held each day with longer breaks in between. The band was again well prepared, completing most of the sixteen numbers in two or three takes, including "My Rose of Old Kentucky" in two and "Blue Grass Breakdown" in three. Only two required more: "Sweetheart, You Done Me Wrong" (five) and "The Old Cross Road" (six). They finished four songs on the first take: "I Hear a Sweet Voice Calling," "When You Are Lonely" (credited to "Monroe-Flatt"), "I'm Going Back to Old Kentucky" (which Bill had been singing since 1943), and "Little Community Church." (Two additional takes were made on the last two, trying to improve on the originals.)

This innovative band still honored tradition by using mandolin and guitar (the latter played by Wise) to back five gospel quartets: "That Home Above," "Remember the Cross," "Little Community Church," "Shine, Hallelujah, Shine," and "I'm Travelin' On and On." Watts sang bass this time. Birch had left to marry and settle down in the house on the Monroe homeplace with a woman he met in 1945, now known only as "Jimmie." (The marriage ended in 1949, and Birch would return to Nashville to work for Bill as a booking agent.)[104]

The only song recorded previously was "Molly and Tenbrooks," a variant of it, recorded in 1929 by the Carver Boys, a trio from south central Kentucky, released with the title "Tim Brook" (Paramount), but sung "Ten Brooks." As with Bill's rendition, banjo was the featured instrument and, intriguingly, the chord changes were the same as those played by Flatt (I-IV-V-I-V-I). But "Tim Brooks" lyrics are different, and it has a chorus: the phrase "Ten Brooks skippin' and a-gone away, Ten Brooks skippin' and a-flyin'" is repeated twice.[105]

Regarding songs most directly traceable, or original, to Bill, one likely candidate is "It's Mighty Dark to Travel." Bill once told of hearing a black man use the phrase, then Bill said, "I had my song right there," an indication it was, indeed, his. "Along About Daybreak," supposedly based on a quarrel he had with Carolyn, was his first autobiographical song (a "true song" in his words), and, as such, is also very likely his. Already mentioned was "The Old Cross Road," which Bill said he wrote "while everyone was asleep." Most uncertain are four of the quartets: "That Home Above," "Little Community Church," "Shine, Hallelujah, Shine," and "I'm Traveling On and On," all credited solely to Bill. Based on the complexity of their lyrics, it appears he may have had a "ghost" co-writer, possibly Carolyn, raised by an Episcopal priest.[106]

After the sessions, the Hatch Show Print record of the band's appearances is unusually vague for nearly three weeks (posters were ordered, but for no specific location). This may have been the time Jake Lambert writes of in his biography of Flatt when Benny Martin, a nineteen-year-old fiddler from Flatt's hometown, filled in for Wise during a quick, barnstorming trip to Oklahoma:

> Chubby was getting some dental work done, so Benny joined the Blue Grass Boys on a [tour]. . . . When Chubby returned to the group, Benny stayed on, playing the guitar and, sometimes, even the mandolin. . . . Benny and Monroe played twin mandolins in concerts and on the *Opry*. . . . At other times, Monroe played the guitar, leaving the mandolin work to Benny.

Wise may have had "dental work done," but his real reason for staying in Nashville was to record with Hank Williams. On November 6 and 7, 1947, at the Castle studio, he fiddled on eight songs, including "Honky Tonkin'," "My Sweet Love Ain't Around," and "A Mansion on the Hill" (MGM). Around this time, Columbia released "How Will I Explain About You?" / "Blue Grass Special," another Bill Monroe record that went nowhere in the charts.[107]

Bill and the band "reappear" in the Hatch receipts on November 20, with a two-day stand at a movie theater in Little Rock, Arkansas. After Thanksgiving, they ended the year in north Georgia, playing a courthouse and a series of high schools from December 15 to 19. At the courthouse in Clayton, bassist Joel Price, from the nearby town of Gumlog, auditioned. Except for the *Opry*s of December 20 and 27, the band had the rest of 1947 off.[108]

There had to have been some dissatisfaction among the Blue Grass Boys concerning their recordings, if nothing else, at this point. Of all the material they'd recorded, only six songs had been released in nearly two years, and none had made the Most Played chart. The royalties of one that Flatt wrote ("Will You Be Loving Another Man?") had to be split with Bill. And even though it was natural for Bill's songs (ones he claimed to have written) to be released first, it must have displeased Flatt that more songs with his name on them hadn't been released yet.[109]

During the 1947 holidays Lester and Gladys Flatt, Earl Scruggs and wife-to-be Louise Certain, and Howard Watts got together at Flatt's house trailer in a north Nashville trailer park, and grievances must have been aired. Chief among them was the work schedule, which they knew was not going to ease in 1948. Flatt, speaking later for himself and Scruggs, said, "We both just got tired of being on the road. Sometimes we would go three days without taking our shoes off. Earl and I had done most of the driving for Monroe's group and we were just tired of traveling." Scruggs said, "I enjoyed working with Bill, but he had no management about him. He said he'd pick you up about eight o'clock; well, it may be twelve before he'd come." And, concerning the pay, Scruggs said, "I just got enough of it [playing in Bill's band] from the standpoint that I learned I could make more money working for myself."[110]

Another Recording Ban

The anticipated recording ban began on January 1, 1948, and lasted throughout the year. Musicians' union president Petrillo wanted a share of the profits from the use of records by radio stations and jukebox operators, and, to get it, the possibility that he would stop live radio performances by union musicians was very real for awhile.[111]

Near the end of January, Columbia released "Shine, Hallelujah, Shine" / "I'm Traveling On and On." The latter would have been an appropriate theme song for the Blue Grass Boys during this time.[112] The new year for Bill and the band began with two weeks in Kentucky, a week in Alabama, and a week in West Virginia. By the time they reached West Virginia on January 25, Wise was gone, leaving to play with "Shenandoah Waltz" co-writer Clyde Moody on WARL in Arlington, Virginia. Benny Martin now joined full time.[113]

Mauldin Remarries Gann

Bessie Lee Mauldin also left, to marry Nelson Gann a second time with another quickie ceremony in Franklin, Kentucky, on February 7. Scruggs may have turned in his two-weeks' notice on the same day. It appears he played his last on February 21 at the *Opry*. Then Flatt turned in his notice. (A banjo picker named Tommy Goad was seen with Bill in Virginia during the week of February 22. Lloyd McCraw from Shelby, North Carolina, is said to have played banjo with Bill on the *Opry* of February 28, but he apparently didn't stay either.)[114]

Don Reno, meanwhile, had returned from overseas and was back at WSPA in Spartanburg, South Carolina, playing with the Carolina Hillbillies and listening to Bill on the radio. Hearing him on the *Opry* without a banjo on March 6, Reno said he "came to the conclusion that Earl [Scruggs] wasn't there anymore." He drove to Nashville, finding Bill had left town to play in Virginia and North Carolina. So, he "doubled back," arriving in Taylorsville, North Carolina, where Bill and the band (without a banjo) were playing to a packed house at the Bijou Theatre (this one for whites only) on Tuesday, March 9. "I got to Taylorsville just as they were starting their show," Reno said. "I went backstage, took my banjo out of the case, and walked onstage and started playing. Bill said, 'Boy, I've been trying to find you,' and I said, 'Well, I finally made it.'"[115]

Reno, unlike Scruggs, had never used a capo. He later said he didn't know of one when he was learning to play and noted that his mentor, Snuffy Jenkins, never used one either. On stage that night, Bill asked him where his capo was.

> I said, "Capo, for a banjo?" I'd never heard of one. I asked him if he used one on his mandolin. Well, he played everything in sharps and flats that night to test me out. I think we played [only] one number in an open chord [one that didn't require a capo]. When I was working with him, he did ask me if I would use a capo on some stuff, and after all, I was working for him and he was paying me; whatever he wanted, I'd do.[116]

In the band that night, Joel Price was playing bass and doing comedy as "Cousin Horsefly," filling in for Watts. Playing electric "lap" steel (without pedals) was Virginia native Jackie Phelps, filling the instrumental gaps left by the lack of a banjo. He had been hired only the week before at a show in Portsmouth, near his home, and although he had auditioned as lead singer, he would continue to play steel for awhile, since Flatt was still with the band. After Reno had played a few days, he recalled that Bill brought up the subject of pay: "[He] said, 'I don't know how much you're used to making.' I said that money wasn't the thing. I didn't care what he was paying. He was paying ninety dollars a week and fifteen dollars extra on Sundays."[117]

It appears that Flatt and Watts formally departed the Blue Grass Boys about the same time, in mid-March 1948 ("Before my notice was up," Flatt said, "Cedric Rainwater turned in his notice."). Then Joel Price was hired.

According to Flatt, "[Watts] proposed that Scruggs and I start our own group. He told me, 'Why don't you and Earl form a band and let me work with you?'" This may have been all the encouragement they needed.[118]

What most people consider to have been Bill's finest group of Blue Grass Boys was now gone. Bill wasn't angry with them. He had seen many band members come and go, and they had stayed longer than most. He *was* disappointed, after his efforts to encourage and promote their talents. He was certainly saddened with the loss of the great way they fit together musically. And, to his way of thinking, his Blue Grass Boys belonged to him, so he didn't like for them to leave him. He later singled out only Flatt for comment on this subject, saying in 1971, "Now, I didn't care to see Lester go. I'd have liked for him to stay." He even tried to change Flatt's mind, revealed by his widow, Gladys Flatt, in 2002: "Bill came to me and asked for my help. He asked if I would beg Lester to not quit."[119]

Bill had, in fact, been able to keep all of the elements of the band except Flatt's singing. Phelps knew Bill's songs, but his singing was just not the same. In early April 1948 Columbia released "My Rose of Old Kentucky" / "Sweetheart, You Done Me Wrong," and the latter made what was lacking even clearer. Hoping to restore it, Bill sent a telegram to a young singer with a similar crooning style, Jim Eanes of southern Virginia, inviting him to join the Blue Grass Boys. (It arrived while Eanes was working with Flatt, Scruggs, and Watts at WDVA in Danville, Virginia, as they tried to get their own band, the Foggy Mountain Boys, off the ground. Bill had been aware of Eanes since 1941's "I Wonder Where You Are Tonight.") Eanes dropped everything and headed for Nashville.[120]

Unfortunately, Eanes's vocal range made it too difficult for him to sing all of Bill's material. He told an interviewer later that he "had to stand on his tiptoes and strain to hit the notes" during his first *Opry* appearance in late April. Within a month, he would be gone, replaced in May and June by nineteen-year-old Florida native Doyle Wright. When Wright left, for reasons unknown, Phelps switched from steel to flattop guitar, and Reno became the band's banjo-picking lead singer.[121]

Bill's Last Tent Show

In May 1948, what would be Bill's last tent show season got underway in Kentucky and Tennessee, with the Kentucky Twins guesting. The tour was successful, but it was hard to find help. "We couldn't keep a [tent] crew together," Reno said, "and me and Joel Price and Bill put the tent up and took it down more than anybody else did. Bill loved to work. Nobody could work him down." In June, "Sweetheart, You Done Me Wrong" appeared in *Billboard*'s "Most Played" chart. It was there for only a week at number 11, but Bill was finally "back in the charts." But the July release of "I Hear a Sweet Voice Calling" / "Little Cabin Home on the Hill" went nowhere.[122]

By the summer of 1948, Flatt and Scruggs were based in Bristol, Tennessee-Virginia, broadcasting on WCYB. Their band now included former Blue Grass Boys fiddler Jim Shumate; bassist Watts; and a twenty-three-year-old singer-guitarist from northern Virginia who usually sang tenor, Mac Wiseman. That summer, Bill and the Blue Grass Boys were in the Bristol area, and Flatt and Scruggs invited them to play on their radio show. As Scruggs recalled, "Don [Reno] decided that he wanted to trade banjos with me. I had a good Mastertone at the time, but I just heard something in his banjo that I liked." So, they traded, Reno adding a new Martin D-28 "to boot," to make up for the rough condition of his banjo, bought from "Snuffy" Jenkins in 1941. But what happened when the two bands played on the same show isn't known. It's clear that there were no ill feelings at this point, but they were not yet competitors.[123]

In August, September, and October 1948, the tent show traveled throughout the Ozark region of southern Missouri and northern Arkansas. Bill later remembered one of the "good people" who lived in the area: "A lot of times, I'd be short [of] men, you know, and I would be in helping put the tent up, and there would be some feller dressed up real nice come along [and] he would help me set chairs, or whatever I was doin'. And he would ask me, sayin', 'I wonder when Bill Monroe's gonna get here?' I said, 'Don't you never worry about him—he'll be here.'"[124]

Reno, the lead singer, remembered a time when he could only recall the chorus of a song Bill sang with Flatt on the *Opry*, so he made them up on the spot.

> All I had heard was the chorus of "When You Are Lonely" and the song stuck in my mind. So I was singing duets with [Bill]. . . . We were in a tent show in Missouri. I said let's sing "When You're Lonely." O.K. We sung the thing for about three weeks and I sung different verses every night. [I]t took Bill about three weeks before he asked me if I was singing the same verses to it. I told him I didn't know. He said, "I thought I heard some different verses."[125]

The Shenandoah Valley Trio

During this time (July through October 1948), Bill revived baseball at his shows and, again, everyone in the band played. Bill filled out his team with good players who were also musicians and they became an added attraction, the Shenandoah Valley Trio, singing popular country songs of the day in three-part harmony. Originally, the Trio consisted of Phelps on steel, singer-guitarist G. W. Wilkerson Jr., son of the leader of the *Opry*'s Fruit Jar Drinkers, and Mack Carger of Arkansas, former bassist with the *Opry*'s York Brothers. Mel and Stan, the Kentucky Twins, also played on the team. According to Reno, "Phelps and Carger and Wilkerson, and Mel and Stan, were all excellent ball players. Myself and Joel Price and Benny Martin weren't nearly that good, but we played fairly decently. I think we'd scare the other teams a lot of the time, so that we'd beat them psychologically."[126]

Occasionally, the band and team would leave the circuit, traveling in a 1946 Packard limousine, teaming up with Stringbean for special appearances. Such was the case one sweltering Sunday, July 11, 1948, when they came to Rosine, Kentucky, to play the Rosine Red Legs at the ballpark just west of town. Darrel Dukes, then seventeen, was among the three-hundred-or-so spectators. He recalled that Bill and the band played music before the game, then "String" pitched for an inning or two, keeping everyone in stitches: "He'd do a little jig, then he'd wind up and throw that ball hard." Red Legs first baseman James Paul Burden, then sixteen, was sure that a former pro pitcher relieved String. Left fielder Leslie "Bud" Raley laughed as he recalled "manager" Bill (who didn't play): "He beat our socks off." But only pitcher Joe Wright remembered the exact score: 15 to 2. "We were outclassed," he said, "but we had a good time." (A washtub filled with ice and bottles of beer is said to have been available in the nearby woods.)[127]

In September 1948, Rich-R'-Tone Records released "Wicked Path of Sin" by Wilma Lee and Stoney Cooper and "Molly and Tenbrooks" by the Stanley Brothers, both before Bill's recordings were released. Nowadays, this is seen in a "positive" light: the Stanleys' record in particular, as Neil Rosenberg has written, "marks the transition from the sound of Monroe's band to the musical genre known as bluegrass." But, at the time, Bill's experiences with song appropriation caused him to view it as more of the same, and he communicated his displeasure to both parties directly. Of this, Ralph Stanley would later say only that "way back then, Bill didn't want . . . us doing his songs . . . [and] he just let you know he didn't want you to do 'em." The recordings weren't nationally distributed or noticed by *Billboard*, but it appears that just in case, Columbia arranged for the early release of Bill's "Wicked Path of Sin" (backed with "Summertime Is Past and Gone") during the first week of October.[128]

In the meantime, *Billboard* had added a new chart category, "Best-Selling Retail Folk Records," and Bill could take some satisfaction in the appearance of his "Wicked Path of Sin" in the chart on November 6 (for one week at number 13). Then "Little Community Church" appeared there on November 27, two days after its release, remaining in the chart for five nonconsecutive weeks, peaking at number 11.[129]

The recording ban of 1948 ended on December 14 with the establishment of a welfare fund for union musicians unable to work. Another positive result: RCA Victor, short of material, rereleased four of the 1940–41 recordings ("Mule Skinner Blues" / "Blue Yodel No. 7" and "Katy Hill" / "Back Up and Push"), keeping these early bluegrass classics in circulation.[130]

The *Grand Ole Opry* was broadcast on Christmas night that year, and Bill arranged for twelve-year-old daughter Melissa to make her national singing debut on the show that evening. And on the 27th, Columbia released the song Reno had trouble remembering, the Monroe-Flatt collaboration "When You Are Lonely," backed with Bill's "It's Mighty Dark to Travel."[131]

The first record by Flatt and Scruggs and the Foggy Mountain Boys, "God Loves His Children" / "I'm Going to Make Heaven My Home," was released on January 15, 1949, by Mercury Records. Intriguingly, not a note of banjo, mandolin, or fiddle was heard on either, and the performance style was more akin to the Brown's Ferry Four, with Scruggs's guitar picking featured on both. Mac Wiseman, who sang tenor on both, had left the band by the time of the release, taking a job as a featured singer on WSB in Atlanta.[132]

It was during this time, Reno recalled, that Bill and the band took their first trips in an actual bus. Bill had bought a used city bus in Florida the previous summer, to haul the tent show crew from town to town, and it lacked a heater.

> We were in Nebraska during that winter [of 1949] and the temperature was well below zero. Joel Price . . . had a habit of taking so much Bromo Seltzer that we took to calling him "Bromo." He and I were lying on mattresses in the back of the bus, trying to keep warm. Joel wanted a dose of Bromo, so he reached over for a jar of water that he always carried and poured the powder into it. Well, he took a swig and jumped up screaming. The water had frozen over, and Joel got a mouthful of powder. He looked like he was foaming at the mouth. Later that

night we got a kerosene heater and I burned my coattails on it, trying to keep warm. What a bus! Everybody tried to think up ways to blow up the engine so we wouldn't have to ride in it anymore.[133]

By February 1949, Bill learned that Columbia Records had signed the Stanley Brothers, and he was not happy. Producer Art Satherley tried to convince him that the label was doing him a favor, that it could "control them" and limit their popularity, but Bill didn't buy it. And, as it turned out, he was right. His admonition to the Stanleys not to do his material had encouraged Carter Stanley to write songs, and his efforts would ensure the brothers' success. On the first day of March at the Castle Studio, the Stanleys recorded some of Carter Stanley's most compelling compositions, including "A Vision of Mother," "The White Dove," and "The Angels Are Singing (in Heaven Tonight)."[134]

Bill's "Toy Heart" and "Blue Grass Breakdown" were released on March 14, while he and the band were in Georgia. Phelps had quit ("I had worked myself and traveled myself just about down," he said later) and Stan Hankinson was filling in on guitar. Bill had kept tabs on Mac Wiseman's whereabouts, so he stopped by WSB studios in Atlanta to guest on Wiseman's fifteen-minute show. As Wiseman recalled, "We were working with WSB when Bill Monroe came through up there and he made the remark on the air, 'Well, if you ever get tired of working here, come see me about a job in Nashville,' which was very flattering. The *WSB Barn Dance* dwindled out in the spring of '49, so I called Bill and he said, 'Sure, come up.'" Wiseman played his first show with Bill on April 15 at the National Guard Armory in Huntsville, Alabama.

> You're constantly asked about your most embarrassing moment—well, the night that I first met Bill to go to work with him, I didn't know any of his dern songs! Not one could I think of! I was most embarrassed 'cause he had really caught me off guard—it looked like I had hired in with a man who was very popular, and I hadn't bothered to learn his songs.

The next day, "Toy Heart" appeared in *Billboard's* "Best-Selling Retail" chart at number 12, remaining there for two weeks.[135]

By then in 1949, it was clear that Bill Monroe's style of music was spreading, particularly after the release of the second Flatt and Scruggs Mercury record on April 1 ("My Cabin in Caroline" / "We'll Meet Again, Sweetheart") and the first Stanley Brothers Columbia record on April 4 ("The White Dove" / "Gathering Flowers for the Master's Bouquet"). The Flatt and Scruggs sides included banjo and fiddle, and the music was, of course, reminiscent of Bill's new style, played by those who helped him establish it. But Flatt and Scruggs had tried to be different, avoiding the use of the mandolin and featuring jazzier fiddling. Much more imitative were the two by the Stanley Brothers, with Lambert playing mandolin as much like Bill as possible. ("White Dove," concerning the death of "mother and daddy," seemed autobiographical but wasn't—the Stanleys' parents were very much alive at the time.)[136]

Bill Myrick rejoined the Monroe organization that spring of 1949, hired to drive a Greyhound-style bus ("a late forties Flxible" [sic]) Bill had bought. Myrick recalled that Carger of the Shenandoah Valley Trio had become the Blue Grass Boys' bass player, replacing Price, who'd left to work with new *Opry* star George Morgan (returning when Morgan wasn't touring). Myrick was featured as a solo singer and also sang bass with the Blue Grass Quartet. About this time, Bill spoke to *Billboard*, mentioning plans "to line up fifteen [baseball] players . . . to play all comers on afternoon dates, with his show set for the evening." He would put together a team of talented high school and college players known as "the Blue Grass Boys Team" or "Bill Monroe's Ball Club," and for the next several months, Bill and the band (Martin, fiddle; Reno, banjo; Wiseman, guitar) played showdates with them at ballparks, stadiums, and athletic fields. (On May 2, Columbia released "Remember the Cross" / "The Old Cross Road.")

Opry comedians Lonzo and Oscar (Lloyd George, later known as "Ken Marvin," and Rollin Sullivan, respectively) appeared with Bill during April and May, and the duo sometimes took the team with them to appearances while Bill and the band played elsewhere (including what may have been Bill's first appearance at a drive-in theater, on May 15, 1949, in Salisbury, North Carolina). Stringbean replaced Lonzo and Oscar at the end of May, performing and coaching the team until the end of August. Bill would join in the games "every now and then," according to Myrick. "He could pitch! Man, I got out there and was tryin' to catch for him—he'd knock you over backwards with that ball."[137]

Mauldin Returns Again

Also returning that spring of 1949 was Bessie Lee Mauldin, her second union with Nelson Gann having lasted a little over a year (but they would not divorce until 1951). Many stories about the storminess of her and Bill's relationship begin to appear at this point. Women were attracted to him and threw themselves at him and, soon, the slightest flirtation could cause an extremely jealous Mauldin to "go crazy." Wiseman remembered a time in a restaurant when a woman spoke to Bill, after which Mauldin took the car they were traveling in and drove it wildly around and around the block. Bill tried to stop her by stepping in front of it, but she nearly ran him down. Finally, Wiseman was able to get her to stop long enough to grab the key from the ignition. Another time, when they were traveling in the Flxible bus, Myrick recalled Bill locked Mauldin out of it after she had a jealous fit. In a rage, she smashed the windshield with bricks. It appears that to calm her down at some point, Bill began writing "My Little Georgia Rose," a song about the little girl she claimed was her daughter, then ten or eleven and living in Georgia, whom Bill had said he'd seen (although Wiseman did not recall seeing her during his time in the band).[138]

Meanwhile, Benny Martin left in early June 1949 to work briefly with Roy Acuff, and *Opry* fiddler Floyd Ethridge filled in again. Bill would sometimes be gone, "chasing Bessie," according to Wiseman, trying to make up with her again, and Wiseman would take the band, Stringbean, and the team out himself.

> Excuses were made to the promoter [Wiseman said]—Bill just couldn't make it or something. With the ball team, we didn't have to put on a full-length show. Seems to me like forty-five minutes to an hour at home plate [where the band usually played], then get on with the ball game. Where you was playing their local team, they was revved up about that, and really didn't give a damn if we put on much of a show or not.[139]

Hank Williams made his first appearance on the *Grand Ole Opry* on June 11, 1949. Guesting on the Warren Paint–sponsored portion (9:30–10:00), he followed Lew Childre, host Ernest Tubb, and Bill. Williams sang "Lovesick Blues," number 1 on both of *Billboard*'s "Folk" charts the previous week, and got six encores. *Opry* management knew of his reputation as an alcoholic, but his reception ensured he would become a member of the cast (bolstered, reportedly, by publisher Fred Rose's offer to name WSM executives Jack Stapp and Harry Stone as composers of "Chattanoogie Shoe Shine Boy," if they accepted him).[140]

Columbia released its second Stanley Brothers record, "Let Me Be Your Friend" / "Little Glass of Wine," on June 18. The melody of "Let Me Be Your

Friend" was the same as Bill's recently released "It's Mighty Dark to Travel." It's likely that this encouraged Bill to begin negotiating with other recording companies. Decca Records of New York, one of the first major labels to record in Nashville on a regular basis, was a leading contender.[141]

Bill's new fiddler, Tennessee native Gene Christian, played his first show in Middletown, Ohio, on Sunday, June 19. He had been playing with country singer "Big Jeff" Bess on WSM's local competitor, WLAC, and in bars Bess owned (wife Tootsie Bess would later open her Orchid Lounge in downtown Nashville). Christian said he'd auditioned for Bill "a dozen times" before he got the job.[142]

On July 3, while "String" and the Shenandoah Valley Trio went to Tennessee with the ball team, Bill and the band headed back to the country music parks of Pennsylvania for a week, and Mauldin went along. At some point, she and Bill had a spat: Christian recalled, "I was in the back seat with 'em . . . , and I was sittin' on the right-hand side and Bill was on the left side and Bessie was in the middle. And he hit at her and she ducked and he slapped me with that damn ham of meat of a hand, and I seen stars for twenty minutes."[143]

Reno left in mid-July 1949, saying later he wanted to form a group with his nephew Verlon (who would die in a swimming accident in 1950) and to recover from a lingering case of malaria caught in the service. On July 18, Columbia released "Heavy Traffic Ahead" / "Along About Daybreak."[144]

On July 22, Bill and the band, minus one, arrived in Mt. Airy, North Carolina. "He . . . didn't have a banjo player," said Rudy Lyle, then nineteen and picking banjo in a band led by Dobro player Uncle Joe Johnson, "so I tuned up and went out there with him. . . . After the show I told Bill that I'd sure like to work for him, and he said that he would like for me to, but didn't want to take me away from Uncle Joe. . . . I respect Bill for that."[145]

About two weeks later, on August 6, "When You Are Lonely" appeared at number 12 in *Billboard*'s "Most-Played Juke Box Folk Records" chart, nearly eight months after its release, an early indication that Bill's recordings did well in the long run, rather than skyrocketing to the top. However, it would be his last *Billboard* chart appearance until 1958.[146]

Bill waited until mid-August to call Lyle (whom he usually called "Lyles," probably due to a family named Liles who lived near Rosine): "He . . . asked me if I wanted to come to work. I said yes, I was ready." When Lyle arrived in Nashville, Christian had been replaced by Chubby Wise, back from eighteen months with Clyde Moody's Radio Ranchmen, and Carger had been replaced on bass by Jack Thompson, formerly guitarist and straight man for Stringbean.[147]

Within a few weeks, baseball as a feature of Bill's shows ended for the year. Bill and the Blue Grass Boys, with the Shenandoah Valley Trio (Myrick, Thompson, and Wilkerson), were once again playing at schools, theaters, and drive-ins in Ohio, West Virginia, Kentucky, and Tennessee. Melissa, twelve, also traveled and performed with her dad during this time. On September 12, the day before Bill's thirty-eighth birthday, Columbia released the last of his recordings with Flatt, Scruggs, Watts, and Wise: "I'm Going Back to Old Kentucky" / "Molly and Tenbrooks." By then, the current band knew they would be recording soon, but they may not have known it would be the last for Columbia. Bill had informed the label of his intention to leave and, according to country music historian John Rumble, " . . . [Art] Satherley exercised his option to extend [Bill's] contract and refused to release him from it until he cut more sides."[148]

Bill and Hank Williams

In early October 1949 Bill and new *Opry* star Hank Williams were the featured performers for several days at the Michigan State Fair in Detroit. During this time, according to Rinzler, "Hank happened to hear a new tune that Bill had just put together and he set . . . words to it. They sang ["I'm Blue, I'm Lonesome"] backstage for their own amusement though they never performed it together."[149]

On October 15, a week before the Columbia session, twenty-two-year-old Jimmy Martin took a bus to Nashville. He'd been playing with "Tex" Climer and the Blue Band Coffee Boys on tiny WCRK in Morristown, Tennessee, near his home in Sneedville, and had been fired from his job as a house painter (for singing on the job, he later said), so he decided to go to the *Opry*. "Really, when I went to visit the *Grand Ole Opry*, I went to see Bill Monroe, period."[150]

There are conflicting stories about what happened next, with Martin's published accounts changing with every retelling. According to Myrick, the Shenandoah Valley Trio needed a replacement.

> We had G. W. Wilkerson singing tenor. Then, all of a sudden, he quit. We was standing backstage at the *Opry* and Bill said, "Hey, you'd better find you a tenor for your Trio." I said, "What do you mean, '*my* Trio'? When did it become mine?" He said, "Just now." I said, "Well, thanks a lot." So I walked out [of the Ryman] to get a cup of coffee, and this kid had a guitar slung around his neck, singin'

for two or three gals in the alley out there, and I heard him hit some pretty high notes. When I came back, he was still there, so I walked up and said, "What are you doin'? Are you lookin' for a job or what?" He said, "Oh, I might be. Workin' for who?" I said, "Bill Monroe." He said, "Oh, I can sing any of his stuff."

Thinking he was auditioning for the Blue Grass Boys, Martin was taken inside to sing and play with Bill backstage. He was familiar with Bill's recently released duet "The Old Cross Road," but, as he admitted in his first published interview, it was the only song of Bill's he knew: "When I tried out singing with Bill Monroe, the first night I seen him on the *Grand Ole Opry*, I didn't tell Bill I didn't know his songs. He just liked what I done and hired me on the spot." Bill offered to pay him $20 a week and expenses for a two-week tryout with the Shenandoah Trio.[151]

Bill, band, and Trio had played six days in a row in Arkansas prior to this, and following the *Opry* and two days off, they returned there, playing a high school on October 18, and movie theaters from the 19th to the 21st. At every show, Martin said, Bill brought him out to sing with him, presumably impressed with his ability to duplicate the singing and playing of Lester Flatt on "The Old Cross Road."[152]

They arrived back in Nashville on the morning of Saturday, October 22, with Bill and the band (Lyle, banjo; Thompson, bass; Wise, fiddle; Wiseman, guitar) scheduled to record their first session at Castle Studio, and the last for Columbia, that afternoon. Only four items were recorded, but the band had not rehearsed thoroughly, so numerous takes were required for three. First of the three was "Can't You Hear Me Callin'?," written by Bill about Mauldin, which the band had previously sung with a trio chorus in a lower key. Then, recorded in only two takes, was "Travelin' This Lonesome Road," which Bill had also written about Mauldin, with a melody that derives from "Sweet Betsy from Pike." "Blue Grass Stomp" was next, Bill's fourth blues instrumental, but the first in the key of D. It features the only banjo break of the session, uniquely Lyle in style. Finally, Bill sang "The Girl in the Blue Velvet Band," originally an "epic" poem with as many as thirty-eight stanzas, the story of a "hophead" (the girl) and her willing victim. In Bill's recording, they meet "on the corner of Cherry and Pine," but in the poem it's "Kearney and Pine," two streets that actually intersect in San Francisco.[153]

After the session, Wiseman remembered Bill saying, "We sounded better than I thought we would"—a dubious compliment. That night, they played the *Opry*, and the next Saturday night, October 29, marked Bill's tenth anniversary on the show.[154]

Bill Visits the Monroe Homeplace

From November 7 to November 10, Bill and the band played several dates in western Kentucky, all near Rosine, and this time Bill decided to visit the old homeplace. John and Clara had shared the house with Birch and "Jimmie" until their brief marriage ended in early 1949. Then John and Clara, whom Bill expected to find there, moved to northern Indiana.

A gravel road went up the ridge only so far; then Bill had to get out of his car and walk up the old wagon road.

> I went up there one time when I'd come back to Kentucky. I'd been out workin' different places, you know, and come back, and I thought I'd go up to the old homeplace and some of my brothers would be livin' there. Well, when I went up there, there wasn't a soul livin' there. The lights was all out. There wasn't nobody livin' there.
>
> When I left the old homeplace up there that night and walked way on back down the road to where the car was at, I had to cry. Oh, everybody was gone from there, you know?

Afterward, Bill began writing "I'm On My Way [Back] to the Old Home." Wiseman helped complete it by providing the last verse ("High in the hills . . ."), again without credit. "I don't remember him ever saying thank you, which is all right," Wiseman said. "It was his idea and his song."[155]

On November 11, Bill was in Montgomery, Alabama, headlining an *Opry* package show at the City Auditorium with local-boy-made-good Hank Williams and Little Jimmy Dickens, a new *Opry* member at that point. For the finale, the three teamed up to sing Williams's still-new "I Saw the Light."[156]

Decca Records

A mention of Bill in the November 12 issue of *Billboard* noted his imminent departure from Columbia Records:

> Bill Monroe, for years a standby of the Columbia rustic roster, has reportedly been dissatisfied with his treatment by that waxery for months and is now dickering with several firms. It is known that Paul Cohen, of Decca, and others have made concerted pitches to the WSM, Nashville, star. Monroe's original gripe with Columbia was their inking of the Stanley Brothers, a combo which he felt sounded too much like his own.

Bill had provided the *Billboard* reporter with these details because he was about to reach an agreement with producer Cohen, a deal they would seal with a handshake in the WSM men's room (where musicians rehearsed before they played) at the National Life building, an agreement that would last for more than forty years.[157]

During the rest of November and into December, Bill and the band were again playing at movie theaters. A highlight was a week in Illinois, Indiana, and Ohio with Stringbean and former *National Barn Dance* star Max Terhune. Terhune had already had a long career in Hollywood B-westerns, featured as a comic sidekick, and the tour was probably in support of one of several films he made in 1949.[158]

Exactly one month after the *Billboard* blurb, on December 12, Columbia released "The Girl in the Blue Velvet Band" / "Blue Grass Stomp." Two others recorded in October, "Can't You Hear Me Callin'?" and "Travelin' This Lonesome Road," arguably more significant, would not be released until March 13, 1950.[159]

By mid-December 1949, Bill had informed Wiseman he was letting him go. Bill wanted to regain the sound he had with Flatt, and Martin appeared to be the one who could help him do it. Wiseman had been hoping to land a recording contract for himself while in Nashville, "but it hadn't materialized," he said, so he was probably ready to move on anyway. He left town at Christmastime to return to Bristol and WCYB.[160]

CHAPTER FIVE
1950–1959

Bill's New Band

Wise left shortly after 1950 began. His replacement was twenty-one-year-old Vassar Clements, a fellow Floridian whom Wise began giving pointers in the mid-1940s. "I helped him start," Wise said later. "I showed him some of the first things he ever knew about bluegrass when I was with Monroe and he was a shaver kind of boy." Joel Price had already returned, first as comedian, then as comedian and bass player when Thompson left to return to Stringbean.[1]

Bill and his new band (Clements, fiddle; Lyle, banjo; Martin, guitar; Price, bass) played at movie theaters for three weeks in January, then took the last week off for rehearsals before the first Decca sessions, scheduled for Friday, February 3, at Castle Studio. There were five new songs and a new instrumental, plus a revision of "Mule Skinner Blues" to be practiced. Bill had written his own revision in 1946 and sang it once on the *Opry*. It began with a clever first stanza:

> Daddy was a mule skinner.
> I think I'll be the same.
> I'll quit poppin' my initials—
> I'm goin' to write my name.

Producer Cohen may not have been satisfied with the other stanzas, so he commissioned singer-songwriter George Vaughn Horton to write a new set of lyrics (later credited to "George Vaughn"). Horton was a good choice: he and Rodgers had been friends; Rodgers had even sung at his wedding in 1932.[2]

The new instrumental was the first thing recorded that afternoon, Bill's mandolin-driven "Blue Grass Ramble," using his first different-than-standard tuning (from lowest to highest: AA, EE, AA, C#E; an open A chord). He said later, "Uncle Pen tuned his fiddle different, you know, in a lot of those old tunes . . . and so I just started [to] . . . see what I could do in the way of tuning the mandolin like he did and also in harmonies." "New Mule Skinner Blues" followed, with Bill adding something else new: a mandolin break. Next was Bill's first "true" song recorded for Decca, "My Little Georgia Rose," which Martin later claimed he helped write. Price "walked" his bass throughout, reminiscent of Watts. And the three-hour session ended with Martin's voice being recorded for the first time on Bill's "Memories of You." Bill made a small change in tuning for it, raising one of his mandolin's G strings to A and lowering the other to F#, making a large difference in the sound of this moody love song.[3]

After a two-hour break, they returned to the studio for another three-hour session, beginning with another true song, "I'm On My Way to the Old Home." It was Bill's first time to sing lead on the verses and tenor on the choruses, a common practice for him in the years ahead. Then he sang solo on "Alabama Waltz," written by Hank Williams, who had asked him to record it, followed by the Williams-Monroe collaboration "I'm Blue, I'm Lonesome." Thereafter, six of these seven recordings were released during 1950. Held back for more than two years was "I'm On My Way to the Old Home," not released until March 1952. This may have been due to Columbia's release of "The Old Home" by the Stanley Brothers shortly after Bill's sessions and Decca's reluctance to release a recording with a similar theme.[4]

Mauldin's Claim

During the rest of February and March 1950 the band returned to the movie-theater grind in Ohio, Indiana, Kentucky, Tennessee, Alabama, and Georgia. Mauldin went along sometimes, and Myrick called it quits in mid-February after she threw "a temper fit" over him carrying her bags into a hotel without her permission. Before he left, Bill invited him to his house for supper. Afterward, they went for a walk around the farm, and Bill revealed to him that, after he recorded "My Little Georgia Rose," Mauldin had informed him that he, Bill, was the girl's father. According to Myrick, Bill didn't know whether to believe her or not—"All he knew is what she told him"—but he was very worried it would cost him his *Opry* membership if word of it ever got out. (Jimmy Martin, once certain that Bill was the father, later said, "I thought that Bill was her daddy and I can't really say that he was, 'cause I didn't ask him, but I took providin' [for granted] that he was.)[5]

Released almost simultaneously in March 1950 were Bill's Columbia record of "Can't You Hear Me Callin'" / "Travelin' This Lonesome Road," his Decca record of "New Mule Skinner Blues" / "My Little Georgia Rose," and Flatt and Scruggs's Mercury record of "Foggy Mountain Breakdown" / "No Mother or Dad."[6]

That spring, Howard Watts left Flatt and Scruggs, then based in Lexington, Kentucky, and returned to Nashville. When he asked Bill for his job back, Martin recalled Bill wouldn't hire him. But it probably had more to do with Bill's reluctance to fire Price than with whatever anger there may have been toward Watts. The turndown would prove to be for the best, however, for within a few months, Watts would replace Hillous Butram in Hank Williams's Drifting Cowboys and make a legendary contribution to another band.[7]

Bill was ready to record again soon, and a session was scheduled for Saturday, April 8, 1950, just prior to the *Opry*. Lacking from the first sessions were sacred songs, and Bill solved that with one he'd written, "I'll Meet You in Church Sunday Morning," and one co-written with Price, "Boat of Love." Noteworthy on the first, Martin sang falsetto tenor on the chorus, a technique he probably learned from Bill, and on the second, brother Birch sang bass, recording with Bill right after a session with Charlie for RCA Victor on March 25. Then Bill recorded a novelty song Decca had acquired and asked him to do, "The Old Fiddler," and he dutifully learned it. With a melody similar to "Wreck of the Old 97," it was about "a spry old" fiddler named Uncle Ben. Decca quickly released it, backed with "Alabama Waltz," a month later.[8]

Bill and the band played movie theaters in Ohio, Indiana, Kentucky, North and South Carolina, and Virginia during the rest of April and May, then "baseball season" started again in June. Two weeks into it, on June 17, Bill's Uncle Burch died of heart disease at age seventy-nine. The last surviving brother of J. B. Monroe, he had played in the first string band Bill heard. About a week later, on June 25, North Korea invaded South Korea and the Korean War began.[9]

One of the players on the ball team that summer was pitcher Russell Petty, just graduated from high school. Scouts from major league teams advised that he would make more money in "the bigs" if he worked a season for Bill, so he signed up to play for $65 a week. He was one of the youngest players: "Most of the boys were a lot older than I was. Some of 'em had been in pro ball. . . . Others were college boys." There were now two buses, one for the team and one for the band, and the team's was definitely older: "In 1950, I believe that bus was 100 years old! It had one double-wide bed across the back end," Petty remembered, "and it was always a fight to see who could get the bed, while the rest of us would sleep sitting up in the seats." Melissa, then thirteen, went along that summer: "Sometimes she'd ride with us on the team bus," Petty said. The daily routine varied:

> They'd put on the show and we'd play the local team, or we'd play the team and then they would put on the show sometimes.
>
> Sometimes the crowds weren't real big; we played for crowds as small as two or three hundred in some of the little towns. Sometimes the crowd might be a thousand or so, if they had a nice stadium. Best I can remember, a lot of times Bill and the boys didn't even use a sound system, so they had to be loud!
>
> . . . A lot of times, if we were going to ride all night, we'd stop and Bill would rent a couple of rooms in a hotel or motel and we'd go in and take a shower and change clothes and get back on the bus and ride all night to the next game. It was a lot of fun, it was!

Petty noticed a few musicians having fun in other ways: "And sometimes they were in pretty bad shape before the show! I didn't drink, but some of them were pretty bad about drinking. But you'd never know it when it came time to play." Bill, however, probably knew and wasn't happy about it, due to his dislike of alcohol.[10]

Clements left the Blue Grass Boys that summer, replaced by Mississippian Merle "Red" Taylor, a young fiddler who was already an *Opry* veteran, having worked with "Cousin Wilbur" Wesbrooks, Paul Howard, and Little Jimmy Dickens. Noticing Bill was without a fiddler, Taylor joined in one night while the band rehearsed in an *Opry* dressing room, and Bill asked if he would be interested in playing with him. "Well, what fiddler in his right mind wouldn't be interested in playing with Bill Monroe? I definitely was!" Taylor said later.[11]

Writing "Uncle Pen"

Bill began writing one of his best-known true songs shortly after Taylor joined. The band had arrived early in Danville, Virginia, on August 4 to play the City Auditorium that night. It was then, Taylor said, that Bill asked for his help.

> I remember when we were staying in a hotel up near Danville, Virginia. Bill brought his mandolin up to my room one morning and said, "I've got a song here I'm trying to write about an uncle of mine. His name was Pendleton Vandiver." And he strummed a little bit of what he had. He said he wanted a melody with an old timey sound that would match his uncle's fiddling, 'cause Uncle Pen had been an old-time fiddle player.
>
> Well, I liked the idea and I stayed shut up in that hotel room all day long 'til I thought I had what Bill was looking for. Then I called his room and played it for him and he said, "That's exactly what I wanted!"[12]

Melissa Records for Columbia

Two days later, Melissa Monroe recorded for Columbia Records, a month shy of her fourteenth birthday. Columbia's paperwork reveals she was to record "4 sides [songs] per year," so it appears to have been an experiment, to see how well she would do, years before the first recordings of youngsters like Molly Bee (Capitol, 1952) and Brenda Lee (Decca, 1956). Decca may have passed on it, but was willing to let another label try, so on that Saturday afternoon, August 6, Melissa recorded four new country songs: "You Rule My Heart," "Guilty Tears," "Stop, Look, and Listen," and "Oh, How I Miss You" with Red Taylor, fiddle; Jimmy Martin, rhythm guitar; Jimmy Selph (possibly), steel guitar; Hank Garland, electric lead guitar; and Joel Price, bass.

With the current Shenandoah Valley Trio (Taylor, Martin, and Price) already in the studio, it was convenient for them to record a session for Columbia next (and use Selph and Garland again), with studio musician Ernie Newton playing bass while Price concentrated on his singing. But the primary purpose of the session was to record four songs that may have been written by Birch Monroe: "While I'm Reading Your Letter," "Let Me Rest (at the End of My Journey)," "Little Sunshine Girl," and "Cabin of Love." The Trio's rendition of the latter included a verse Bill did not use when he recorded it about a year later:

> Too late, too late to reconsider,
> Too late to start life anew.
> I'm left alone in my cabin,
> Alone in this world without you.

It was the only session a Shenandoah Valley Trio would ever record.[13]

Bill continued working on "Uncle Pen" while traveling in Pennsylvania in mid-August. Lyle remembered him writing the song "in the back seat of the car up on the Pennsylvania Turnpike," on the way to Lancaster, Pennsylvania, and Rainbow Park. Managing the country music park then were Bud Reed, his wife Ola Belle, and her brother Alex Campbell. They would open their own park, New River Ranch, in Rising Sun, Maryland, in 1951.[14]

By the end of August 1950, the first hit recording from the "folk music revival" in America, "Goodnight, Irene" by the Weavers on Decca, was number 1 on *all* of *Billboard*'s charts. Pete Seeger's five-string banjo—an exciting new sound for urban listeners—could be heard about halfway through it. Meanwhile, the titles of *Billboard*'s country music charts changed to "Most Played Jukebox Folk (Country & Western) Records" and "Best Selling Retail Folk (Country & Western) Records," the first indication of the dissatisfaction with calling country music "folk."[15]

In early September, Bill and the band were playing at the State Theatre in Bluefield, West Virginia, where they "split the bill" with the Lonesome Pine Fiddlers (leader Ezra Cline, bass; Ray Morgan, fiddle; Larry Richardson, banjo; and Bobby Osborne, guitar), regulars on radio in Bluefield. Osborne recalled: "Bill Monroe came to the theater on our show that day to advertise the show that night and do a song, and I met Jimmy Martin there." Later that day: "I got to know Jimmy when he broke a string on the show and I got him one. Jimmy and I got together and sang some that day."[16]

By late September, Bill and the band were in Alabama (26, Decatur; 27, Hartselle; 28, Russellville; 29, Ardmore). Eighteen-year-old local fiddler Gordon Terry went to all of the shows and eventually worked up the courage to audition for Bill. Later, he recalled what happened after the Ardmore show:

> Soon as they got loaded up, we went down to this little restaurant. And the Blue Grass Boys . . . was sitting at a table by themselves, and me, Bill, and Bessie was sitting over here. [N]othing was said about no music, hiring nobody, or nothing. Bill ate and got through. He just got up and walked out [to] the front of the little bitty old restaurant, and Bessie started kicking me under the table. . . . I looked at her and she knew I didn't know what was happening. She said, "Go out front! Bill wants to talk to you." I wondered how did she know that. He hadn't said nothing. So, I went outside and he told me, "The next time I need a fiddle player,

I'll call you. I'll want you to sing bass in the quartet, sing in the Shenandoah Valley Trio, emcee some, and introduce me when I come out." I knew then I had to confess. I said, "Bill, I've just got to tell you, I've never sang bass in a quartet, never sang in a trio. Now, I have sung a little, just by myself. . . ." He said, "Well, I think you can do it."

Bill returned to Nashville and Terry went back to his job at a chicken-packing plant where he would wait for Bill's call.[17]

At the time of Bill's next session, Sunday, October 15, his herringbone D-28 guitar had been sent back to the Martin factory in Nazareth, Pennsylvania, for new frets. Jimmy Martin, who had been using it, later said Bill insisted on going ahead with the session, so, according to Martin, he had to make do with a guitar that was "laying around" the Castle Studio, country singer George Morgan's Gibson. "I was hittin' it as hard as I could," Martin said, "but it [the sound] wouldn't come out"—most evident on the first song, "Uncle Pen." Next was "When the Golden Leaves Begin to Fall," a love song Bill said was written when Mac Wiseman was with him, suggesting Wiseman helped to write it, too. Both songs had trio choruses, but "Golden Leaves" featured a "high baritone" harmony (with the baritone part an octave higher than usual, higher than the tenor), an arrangement used by the Stanley Brothers in recent releases, suggesting their influence on Bill. Also recorded were two songs by the Blue Grass Quartet, "Lord, Protect My Soul" and "River of Death," sung with the tradition-based accompaniment of just guitar and mandolin, last used on Bill's recordings in 1947.[18]

The Second Bill Monroe Songbook

This particular Blue Grass Quartet was pictured and its members identified by name in Bill's second songbook, *Bill Monroe's Blue Grass Country Songs*, published in 1950 by song publishers Hill and Range Songs Inc., in partnership with Bill's new publishing company, Bill Monroe Music Inc. The songbook's title is the first in-print reference connecting Bill, the *Opry*'s primary representative of the Blue Grass State, with his "Blue Grass" songs, and may have influenced the naming of bluegrass music. The collection included eight of Bill's songs and a piano arrangement for "Blue Grass Breakdown," all of them recorded with the Flatt, Scruggs, Watts, and Wise band in 1947. There were also five Hill and Range songs Bill had not recorded, including the Hankinson Twins' "Tennessee Gambler" with Bill listed as co-writer (to reward him for helping the Hankinsons). On the cover, Bill was pictured

playing a 1930s Strand-model mandolin made by Epiphone, a Gibson competitor before the two companies merged.[19]

Bill's plans for baseball in 1951 were revealed in the songbook's introduction by an uncredited writer: "He had so many calls for his club to play at
various parks last season [1950] that he [has] decided to organize a second
club." (Confusing matters somewhat, the writer then wrote of "the first club"
being "coached by Bill's sidekick, Stringbean," referring not to one of these
two teams, but to the 1949 team, which was, indeed, coached by Akeman.)[20]

After Myrick left Bill, he moved to the panhandle region of west Texas,
invited there by an army buddy he'd met during World War II, Edd Mayfield.
They formed a band, Bill Myrick and the Mayfield Brothers, with Myrick
and Edd Mayfield, guitars; Herb Mayfield, mandolin; and Arlie "Smokey"
Mayfield, fiddle, and played in the Lubbock area with growing success. In
the late fall of 1950, Myrick booked Bill and the Blue Grass Boys for two
weeks in west Texas, with himself and the Mayfields as the opening act, and
it was then that Bill first heard the high-ranging voice and distinctive guitar
playing of Edd Mayfield.[21]

Bill and the band went on from there to play in nearby Louisiana, Mississippi, and Alabama. In mid-December, about the time "Uncle Pen" was
released, Taylor let Bill know he was leaving. Bill had told Gordon Terry he
would call when he needed a fiddler and, true to his word, he called Terry,
now nineteen, at the chicken-packing plant in Alabama on Thursday, December 28.

> He said, "Be [here] Saturday in time to play the *Opry*." I thought we would re-
> hearse and I went up the next day. [H]e was up at the Andrew Jackson Hotel [at
> 6th Avenue and Deaderick Street in downtown Nashville, where Bill was staying
> when in town, now evidently separated from Carolyn]. I'd never been in a hotel
> in my life. I went up to the desk and I asked what room Bill was in. They told me
> and I walked around through the lobby. I didn't see any stairs. . . . Finally, I went
> back over there and said, "How do I get up there?" . . . They said, "The elevator is
> over there." . . . I got on there and told the girl, "Let me off at 928." . . . I found his
> room. It must have been, maybe, ten o'clock in the morning. I knocked . . . and
> Bill came to the door [and he] might have been barefooted. . . . I said, "Well, I'm
> here." He said, "Well, the boys are on Christmas vacation and won't be back until
> noon [tomorrow]." Finally, he said to come on in. He said, "Go on down and get
> you a room." [I] went down, got me a room, then came right back to his room.[22]

The band had two more weeks off after that, so 1951 began on January 15
with a week of high schools and city auditoriums in Georgia. That month,

sheet music for Bill's recently released "Uncle Pen" was published. On its cover was an actual photograph of Pen, taken in 1927 by Clarence Wilson's daughter, Flossie, while he was recuperating from his accident. Bill was able to provide it, probably given to him by Flossie Wilson Hines, who married and continued to live in the Rosine-Horton area.[23]

The fifth Decca session was held on Saturday, January 20, and even though Red Taylor had left the band, he would fiddle on it. First up was the duet "Letter from My Darling" (with a melody similar to "The Old Cross Road"), a true song Bill had seemingly been working on for some time, since he and its subject (Mauldin) had been back together since 1949. Next was another duet, "On the Old Kentucky Shore," a true song Bill wrote about Birch's Rosine girlfriend, Leora Baize, who died of tuberculosis in 1939 at age twenty-seven. It appears Bill borrowed the phrase "on the old Kentucky shore" from the minstrel favorite, "Darling Nellie Gray." Bill's instrumental masterpiece "Raw Hide" was next, named for the movie *Rawhide*, featuring old friend Max Terhune in a small and uncredited role (as Mr. Slade, early in the film). It appears to have been Bill's answer to the challenge of Flatt and Scruggs's dynamic instrumental "Foggy Mountain Breakdown." And last was "Poison Love," Bill's first "cover" (or copy) of a current performer's recording, in this case, a hit by country singers Johnnie and Jack (RCA Victor).[24]

A week after the session, Martin was unavailable for some reason. Singer-guitarist Vern Young, a newcomer to Nashville whom Lyle had befriended, was backstage at the *Opry* on January 27, and Bill asked him to fill in that coming week. "I happened to be at the right spot at the right time," Young said later. "I only knew one of Monroe's songs, 'Toy Heart,' but . . . we left that morning at about one o'clock for Evansville, Indiana, along with the Carter Sisters and Stringbean [to play the Coliseum]." The band also played at movie theaters in Missouri for three days thereafter. Born and raised in New York, near Rochester, Young was the first "Yankee" to work with Bill, although only as a fill-in. Martin returned the following Saturday, and the band headed to Georgia to play movie theaters in the South through March 1951.[25]

By then, Decca knew Eddy Arnold had recorded Bill's "Kentucky Waltz" for RCA Victor, during the current "state waltz craze," and it was scheduled for release in early April. Anything Arnold touched was sure to turn to gold, so Decca wanted Bill's cover available then *and* in Arnold's mainstream style. A session was arranged for Saturday, March 17, with some of Nashville's best country music session players, including drummer Ferris Coursey, fiddler Tommy Jackson, electric guitarist Grady Martin, bassist Ernie Newton, and producer Paul Cohen's assistant, Owen Bradley, playing organ and piano. Bill, Lyle, and Martin were flown in from Florida for it.

"Kentucky Waltz" was recorded first, with an instrumental break that included twin fiddles (played by Jackson with Grady Martin switching briefly to fiddle). It was the first time harmonizing fiddles were used on a Bill Monroe recording, probably instigated by the musicians themselves. Bill also sang two other solos, country standards "The Prisoner's Song" and "Swing Low, Sweet Chariot," and a new gospel song, "Angels, Rock Me to Sleep," with Lyle, Martin, and an uncredited bass singer.[26]

Two weeks later, on March 29, Bill was back in the Castle Studio again, this time with all of the Blue Grass Boys. Taking Terry's place was *Opry* veteran James "Hal" Smith, previously fiddler for Pee Wee King and Ernest Tubb. They recorded three Jimmie Rodgers songs, to be included with five others in a planned tribute album (four 78 disks in a binder): "Brakeman's Blues," "Travelin' Blues," and "When the Cactus Is in Bloom" (on which, unlike Rodgers, Bill sings, "When the cactus *are* in bloom").[27]

Everett Lilly joined Flatt and Scruggs at this time (March 1951), singing tenor and playing mandolin in a band that included Chubby Wise. Lilly began to notice people using the word "bluegrass" more often.

> . . . I do recall people saying this to us, they would ask Lester and Earl to do a Bill Monroe tune. Lester and Earl didn't want to hear that name—or I don't believe they did—and I believe the public could feel that. The public began to say, "Boys, would you please do us one of them old Blue Grass tunes like you used to do?" They knowed me and Lester could sing them duets like him and Bill. They'd say, "Would you please do an old bluegrass tune?" . . . [T]he public named bluegrass music . . . through the fear to speak Bill's name to [Flatt and Scruggs].

Contrary to generally accepted explanations, that the name of the music derives from the name of Bill's band, or was inspired by the title of Bill's songbook, Lilly's observation seems to offer an equally likely possibility: that "bluegrass" was originally a substitute for the name of the well-known representative of the Blue Grass State: The Blue Grass Man, Bill Monroe.[28]

Bill's 1951 baseball season appears to have run from April to August. Games were no longer advertised with posters, probably to reduce expenses, so there is no record of where the band appeared with the team. But in the 1960s, Bill discussed his baseball years, and some of his comments refer to the 1951 season in particular:

I had two ballclubs—one that traveled and one that worked out of [played in] Nashville. . . . The road club was called "The Blue Grass All-Stars" and the one out of Nashville was called "The Blue Grass Ballclub" [which probably played teams visiting Nashville to see the *Opry*]. . . . I paid each man ten dollars a day and five or ten dollars if they hit a home run. . . . The club I had on the road I don't think was beat but only a couple or three times all season. They was really a wonderful club.

We played about six games a week. Saturdays I would have to go into Nashville to play the *Opry*. But if the Shenandoah Valley Trio was out and there was enough show [bookings], then they would go right ahead and play seven days a week. . . . You made a lot of money. 'Course it cost a lot of money. I carried thirteen or fourteen players at ten dollars a man, besides the musicians. But you could play any little town.[29]

The "Kentucky Waltz" Suit

In mid-April 1951, as Eddy Arnold's "Kentucky Waltz" was climbing the *Billboard* charts, co-writer Tommy Thompson filed a civil suit demanding half of the song's royalties. According to Nashville's *Tennessean*, "Thompson claims he wrote the lyrics . . . on the agreement that they would split the income from it." Bill's reply, via his lawyer, soon appeared in the paper: "Monroe, in his answer, admits he asked Thompson to write the lyrics, but claims they are not his 'exclusive compositions' [he didn't write all of the lyrics]. He denies he agreed to copyright in both names [which Thompson may have assumed he would do] and declared that Thompson has repeatedly asked for a settlement. Monroe claims he bought the lyrics for a valuable consideration, and that the statute of limitations prevents Thompson's recovery." That, and a cash settlement, appear to have ended the matter. (On June 2, Arnold's "Kentucky Waltz" was number 1 in *Billboard*'s "Most Played" and "Best-Selling" charts for one week.)[30]

In the midst of dealing with Thompson's lawsuit, Bill was back in the Castle Studio on Monday, April 23, recording five more Jimmie Rodgers songs and a new song by former Blue Grass Boys member Pete Pyle. The success of Bill's "Kentucky Waltz" session, at which he recorded a musically mainstream version of the song, might have caused producer Cohen to insist on similar accompaniment this time. Most of the same musicians returned (except Bradley), and only Blue Grass Boys Lyle and Smith were included. Recorded during the two sessions were "Sailor's Plea," "My Carolina Sunshine Girl,"

"Ben Dewberry's Final Run," "Peach Picking Time in Georgia," and "Those Gambler's Blues," plus, in the wee hours of April 24, Bill's original waxing of Pyle's "Highway of Sorrow." Regrettably, only two of these recordings were released in the 1950s ("Highway of Sorrow" in 1951 and "Sailor's Plea" in 1952), and the projected Rodgers album was scrapped, reportedly due to Decca's or Bill's dissatisfaction with this removal of Bill from his regular sound.[31]

Jimmy Martin left the band in May 1951. He never discussed his reasons for leaving this first time. (Mauldin later told Rinzler that Bill fired him, due to twenty-three-year-old Martin's flirtations with fourteen-year-old Melissa.) He did say, "When I got away from Bill, I decided I wanted to be like Lester [Flatt] and Earl [Scruggs] and I wanted to get a banjo player. I wanted to go as Jimmy Martin and whoever the banjo player was." It was to have been Larry Richardson, whom he'd met in Bluefield about nine months earlier, but Richardson had other plans. Instead, Martin teamed up with Bobby Osborne (who began playing mandolin after Martin told him, "If you're gonna sing tenor, you're gonna have to play the mandolin"), and they initially worked with the Lonesome Pine Fiddlers (with newcomer Charlie Cline on banjo). Martin and Osborne soon formed their own band and recorded four songs for King Records.[32]

Pete Pyle returned to the Blue Grass Boys, replacing Martin, but found he was unable to do what he once did with Bill: "I come back and tried to play with him, but I had lost it." He was followed by Vic Daniels of Independence (near Galax), Virginia. Then Carter Stanley called to offer his services as a lead singer. Bookings were scarce for the Stanley Brothers, the Korean War had robbed them of band members, and brother Ralph was having second thoughts about music as a career (he'd planned to study veterinary medicine), so they had disbanded. When Carter Stanley replaced Daniels, it ended the animosity between Bill and the Stanleys and fostered an enduring friendship.[33]

It appears that Hal Smith left after Martin departed, and Gordon Terry returned. Then Joel Price left to work with Little Jimmy Dickens, but Bill had trouble finding a replacement. Bessie Mauldin was already a regular on the road, and Bill needed to fulfill contracts that stipulated five musicians. So, he bought her a blonde Epiphone bass in a North Carolina music store and convinced her to act like she could play it before she knew how.[34]

In mid-June, Bill and the band appeared with Pee Wee King and his Golden West Cowboys at the Hippodrome Theater in Baltimore, Maryland.

Backstage, emcee and local deejay Ray Davis told Bill and Carter Stanley about a clever new recording he'd been featuring on his radio show. He used a portable record player to play a copy of "Sugar Coated Love" by western swingster "Tex" Williams (Capitol).[35]

Bill recorded his tenth session for Decca on Sunday, July 1, with Lyle, Stanley, Terry, and studio bassist Ernie Newton reappearing (Mauldin was still learning). Newton had developed a new rhythm-enhancing technique, using a small drum-like attachment on his bass that he slapped on the off-beat with a drummer's brush held in his right hand, and he used it with Bill for the first time here. Bill was again recording covers, but this time, something different—topical protest songs—"Rotation Blues" (to the tune of "Rocky Road Blues"), about conditions for soldiers in Korea, and "Lonesome Truck Driver's Blues," dealing with problems of long-haul drivers. Both required the ability to yodel, so Bill may have been the only one in Decca's stable of singers who could handle them.[36]

Bill and the band played drive-in theaters in northwestern Arkansas on July 3 and 5, then drove all night, about five hundred miles, to be in Nashville to record a session that began at 8:30 A.M. on July 6. It appears bassist Newton didn't work that early, so Bill asked Howard Watts, confirming there were no hard feelings. In spite of the early-morning circumstances, the band recorded four memorable performances, beginning with a duet rendition of "Sugar Coated Love." Bill and Stanley's version did not include the third verse of the original:

> And now that we are done and through, I hope you're satisfied.
> You took the best out of my life, you cheated and you lied.
> I hope the next man that you catch and put upon your string
> Can tell it's sugar-coated love and not the genuine thing.

The second duet of the session, "Cabin of Love," was much more effective than the recent recording by the Shenandoah Valley Trio. Two gospel quartets followed, both credited to Bill: "You're Drifting Away," resurrected from the live performance repertoire of the Flatt-Scruggs-Watts-Wise band, and the new "Get Down on Your Knees and Pray." The latter was the first of Bill's recordings to undergo surgery by recording technicians: its ending phrase, "You'd better get down on your knees and pray," was recorded separately, then cut and spliced onto the end of an otherwise perfect third take. Both quartets were recorded with just guitar and mandolin, the last time this tradition-based accompaniment would be used on one of Bill's recordings.[37]

Rudy Lyle, age twenty-one, was drafted on August 3 and sent to Korea. Without a readily available replacement, Bill arranged for *Renfro Valley Barn Dance* star Manuel "Old Joe" Clark, an old-time banjo-playing comedian, to play shows with him. (Maintaining his solo-act identity, Clark would not become a member of the band but would continue to work for Bill off and on during the Korean War years, also playing bass on occasion.) Carter Stanley, meanwhile, convinced brother Ralph Stanley to pick banjo with Bill, which he agreed to do as a fill-in. "I just never did like to work for anybody," he said later. After the Stanley Brothers played with Bill about a week, Carter Stanley was stricken with laryngitis, and it's said that Bill switched to guitar and sang lead while Pee Wee Lambert of the Clinch Mountain Boys played mandolin and sang tenor. It's also said that Bill was so determined to change Ralph Stanley's mind, he offered to change the name of his band to "Bill Monroe and the Stanley Brothers." If the latter is true, it was to no avail. After Ralph Stanley picked with Bill, he and Lambert were critically injured in a car wreck while returning home from a show.[38]

Melissa's Second and Last Session

Meanwhile, Melissa Monroe recorded her second session for Columbia on August 5, shortly before her fifteenth birthday. She again sang four songs ("Peppermint Sticks and Lemon Drops," "I'm Waiting Just for You," "Oceans of Tears," and "There's No Room in My Heart for the Blues"), most of them closer to pop than country. The backing musicians are not known, although the fiddling sounds like Chubby Wise, who was working with Flatt and Scruggs at the time. Melissa would not record in a studio again.[39]

Near the end of August 1951, new *Opry* star Hank Snow was involved in a one-car accident in downtown Nashville, reportedly the result of drinking and reckless driving. Married man Snow and "a female companion" were thrown from the car, with Snow suffering a fractured skull, and his companion a broken back (she would recover). Bill filled in for Snow at a show in South Boston, Virginia, on September 6, backed by Snow's Rainbow Ranch Boys (Hillous Butram, guitar; Buford Gentry, steel; "Sleepy" McDaniel, bass; Tommy Vaden, fiddle).[40]

After Bill's baseball season ended in early September, he hired a new banjo player, twenty-two-year-old Joe Drumright, then with the band of deejay Carl Tipton at WLAC in Nashville. Drumright couldn't make it to his first show with Bill, so local musician Johnny Vipperman filled in on Monday, September 10, at a theater in Mt. Airy, North Carolina. On Thursday September 13—Bill's fortieth birthday—Bill "called in sick," so Vipperman filled in for him and played Bill's mandolin at a theater in Roxboro, North Carolina. It was Carter Stanley's last day (the Stanley Brothers would soon restart their band), but Vipperman said he didn't try out for the lead singing spot because he was about to be drafted and Stanley had already recommended a replacement, Kentuckian South Salyer. Also, on the recommendation of Old Joe Clark, Bill hired Oscar "Shorty" Shehan to play bass while Mauldin continued to learn. Shehan had played music with Clark in the early 1940s.[41]

Bill's First Reunion Show with Charlie

On Sunday, September 16, 1951, Bill played a show with brother Charlie for the first time in nearly thirteen years, at the YMCA Auditorium in Corbin, Kentucky. It was the first of a series of shows that week featuring the brothers with their bands and as a duo. "Crowds traveled hundreds of miles to see the Monroe Brothers together again," according to a contemporary report, and many hoped the reunion would be permanent. But it was not to be.[42]

South Salyer soon realized that life on the road wasn't for him, and Bill called Edd Mayfield, who'd offered his services shortly after they met in Texas in 1950. Mayfield arrived in Nashville in late September, and Bill made him audition like everyone else, calling Drumright to come to the Andrew Jackson Hotel to help.

> So I walked in and there stood that old boy with that big Texas hat, that big Martin [guitar], and a thumbpick [which was all he used to play guitar]. I thought, "What kind of turkey is this?"—until I played about two tunes with him. He was just great. You couldn't get him out of time and he played some of the best backing notes you ever heard in your life. Edd was way ahead of his time. There wasn't anyone even close to him back then.

Unfortunately, Drumright's army reserve commitment caused him to miss many shows with Bill during this time. James Garfield "Gar" Bowers of Winston-Salem, North Carolina, filled in and eventually replaced him in November. Bowers hadn't anticipated being hired because he didn't sing. (In the future, Drumright would return several times to fill in, "whenever [Bill] ran out of banjo pickers," he said.)[43]

"Christmas Time's A-Comin'"

On October 14, Bill and the band returned to Baltimore for a package show at the Coliseum with Cowboy Copas, Hawkshaw Hawkins, Flatt and Scruggs, and Wilma Lee and Stoney Cooper and the Clinch Mountain Clan. After the show, two of the Clan, fiddler Benjamin Franklin "Tex" Logan and resonator guitarist Burkett "Buck" Graves, approached Bill. "I told Bill I'd written a Christmas song for him," said Logan, "and hoped he would listen to it. He would; so Buck and I started in, and right away, Bill joined in on the chorus. When we finished, he said three big rapid-fire words, 'I'll record it.'" Bill asked Logan to come to Nashville the following weekend, to show "Christmas Time's A-Comin'" to the band, and at that rehearsal, he was invited to fiddle on the recording session the next weekend (Sunday, October 28). Planning to meet at the Castle Studio, Logan went on to Texas to visit family and Bill and the band headed for Indiana.[44]

The Brown County Jamboree

On Sunday, October 21, 1951, Bill played for the first time at a country music showplace called "the Brown County Jamboree" in the village of Bean Blossom, Indiana, about thirty-five miles south of Indianapolis. Bass player Shehan had lived in the area and may have been responsible for booking Bill there. Operated by Francis Rund and family since 1941, the Jamboree was first held in a circus tent. Then, during 1942–43, Rund used the lumber from an old barn to build the venue's "Jamboree Barn." It was reportedly packed for Bill's appearance and, perhaps, when the show was over that night, someone (possibly tobacco-chewing soundman Denzel "Spurts" Ragsdale, later known as "Silver Spur") told Bill the Brown County Jamboree was for sale.[45]

By Thursday, October 25, Bill was back in Nashville. Knowing Tex Logan was in Big Spring, Texas, but not knowing exactly where, he sent a telegram: "Will Record Sunday. Have Song OK. Let Me Hear From You At Once." Logan called the next day, telling Bill he'd had car trouble and couldn't make it to the session. Later he recalled, "[Bill] said they would go ahead and try ["Christmas Time's A-Comin'"] and play it back to me over the phone, and then, if I didn't like it, to come in the next weekend." Logan had originally played it with his fiddle in a unique tuning (lowest to highest: B/F#/B/E), but with the help of Shehan, whose main instrument was fiddle, Terry simplified the tuning to B/E/B/E, making it easier to play, and that's the way it was recorded on Sunday the 28th. Paul Cohen's assistant Owen Bradley added a "Christmasy" touch, playing vibes. As promised, Bill called Logan: "It sounded so good that I said, 'Let 'er go, Bill.'" Also recorded that evening was a new duet Bill had written, "The First Whippoorwill," in which the now-forty-year-old wrote, "I know I'm over the hill." Mayfield's voice never faltered despite a cold he'd caught in Indiana.[46]

At the time, television was quickly becoming the most popular entertainment medium in America. In 1949 there were fewer than a million TV sets in the United States, most of them in major cities, but by the end of 1952, there would be 19 million. On October 29, 1951, the day after Bill's session, millions of viewers watched the third episode of a new show called *I Love Lucy*, starring Lucille Ball (born on August 6, 1911, about six weeks before Bill).[47]

Bill and the Blue Grass Boys returned to Indiana to finish out October in high school auditoriums. Thereafter, they mainly played movie theaters in Missouri, Tennessee, and North Carolina, then took a week off at Thanksgiving time. During that week, on November 28, Mauldin's second divorce from Nelson Gann became final, with the court's decree stating that "the defendant [Gann] has abandoned the complainant, turned her out of doors, and refused to provide for her."[48]

By Thanksgiving, negotiations may have begun for Bill's purchase of the Brown County Jamboree, including its Jamboree Barn, three "tourist cabins" Rund had built and the fifty-one acres they sat on. Bill later said the sale was finalized "soon after Christmas"—before the end of 1951. According to Bean Blossom historian Tom Adler, the price was "purportedly between thirty-two and thirty-eight thousand dollars" (paid in monthly installments during the ensuing eight years). Brother Birch, who had been handling Bill's bookings, agreed to manage the venue, and the land contract for the property was put in his name, since he would be in charge of it (even though it belonged to Bill). Ernest Tubb had his Record Shop, Roy Acuff had his Dunbar Cave, a resort-showplace near Clarksville, Tennessee, and now Bill Monroe had his Brown County Jamboree.[49]

By the end of 1951, Shehan had left the band and Old Joe Clark was filling in on bass. Bowers left in late January or early February 1952, replaced by former Lonesome Pine Fiddler Larry Richardson of Virginia. Terry, about to be drafted, also left in January-February. Bill was in need of a fiddler, and Richardson recommended another Lonesome Pine Fiddler, banjo-playing fiddler Charlie Cline. Stopping in Bluefield on the way to a show in nearby Beckley, Bill called Cline and invited him to play with the band that night.

By the end of the evening, the twenty-year-old West Virginia native was hired.[50]

James Monroe turned eleven on March 15, 1952, and, during Bill's visits home to his forty-four-acre farm north of Nashville, he began to involve his son in farm work, as J. B. Monroe had done when Bill was about eleven. "He was a hard man to work for," James told an interviewer in 1972. "He expected the most out of you. He learned me to hitch a team [of horses] when I was eleven and he only showed me once." A biographical sketch of James, published about that time, revealed the extent of the farming on the property and Bill's views on how it should be done.

> [James] took care of the work that had to be done on the farm, like feeding about thirty horses [and] some game chickens, and cutting and raking hay. This was done with a mowing machine pulled by two horses, the old-time way. His father didn't believe in having a tractor, so it was this way that James learned to farm. About twenty foxhounds had to be fed, and corn had to be shocked [the stalks bundled together into a shock]. Jim received a salary of fifteen dollars a week for his work.[51]

At the end of March, Decca finally released "I'm On My Way to the Old Home," recorded two years earlier, backed with "The First Whippoorwill," which had already been released in November 1951, on the flip side of "Christmas Time's A-Comin.'" It was the first of several oversights by Decca-MCA.[52]

Birch Moves to Bean Blossom

In the spring of 1952, Birch moved to the Brown County Jamboree park in Bean Blossom, Indiana, and settled into one of the tourist cabins on the property to begin his job as manager. Tom Adler, in his *Bean Blossom*, describes Birch's duties:

> He booked local bands, advertised the shows, and put up showcard posters to promote the Jamboree. He oversaw minor maintenance of the property—lawn mowing, mostly, and periodic cleaning of the barn's interior—and he directed the workers in his concession stand and ticket booth. He emceed most Jamboree shows, often making a guest appearance with the featured artist of the week. If opportunity presented, he might also perform his own modest set of old-time fiddle tunes.

Birch, "always wearing his trademark white shirt and tie," also initiated, hosted, and fiddled for a "Big Round and Square Dance" every Saturday night during the Jamboree's May-to-November schedule. On Sundays he played bass with the house band—the Brown County Fox Hunters—"warming up" the audience before the featured artist performed. The Fox Hunters during the 1952 season included Pete Pyle (guitar)—whom Bill picked to lead the band—Shorty Shehan (fiddle), and Shorty's wife Juanita. (One of the songs the band worked up was a new gospel song by Pyle, "Happy on My Way.")[53]

That spring in Dayton, Ohio, twenty-two-year-old singer-guitarist Harley "Red" Allen met seventeen-year-old mandolinist Frank Wakefield, and Allen took him to Dayton's Memorial Hall to see Bill. Backstage, Bill invited Wakefield to play his mandolin, and Wakefield showed him what he knew of Jesse McReynolds's new style of mandolin picking, inspired by the rolling notes of Scruggs's banjo. McReynolds and brother James of western Virginia were then playing on radio in Middletown, Ohio, near Dayton, as "Jesse and James," and McReynolds's picking had not yet been widely heard. Wakefield would go on to emulate Bill's mandolin style so faithfully that by 1961, Bill would tell him, "You can play like me as good, or near as good, as I can. Now you've got to go out and find your own style."[54]

By the spring of 1952, Flatt and Scruggs had been recording for Columbia for more than a year, but Mercury was still releasing their 1950 recordings. On the first of May, Mercury released their "Pike County Breakdown." Scruggs later wrote, "I know I learned it from him [Bill]. . . . When I recorded it, I gave him credit as the author. Anyway, it did start out as a mandolin tune." Ill feelings of Bill with Flatt and Scruggs may have begun with this unauthorized use of one of his tunes, in spite of the fact that he was credited.[55]

On Sunday, May 4, Bill and the Blue Grass Boys (Cline, fiddle; Mayfield, guitar; Old Joe Clark, bass; Richardson, banjo) were the first featured act at the Brown County Jamboree under its new ownership. Thereafter, Bill's *Opry* cohorts were often featured on Sundays, beginning with Lew Childre and Stringbean on May 11, and the Carter Sisters with Chet Atkins on May 18.[56]

Bill Sends His F-5 to Gibson

Bill's main mandolin was in need of some serious repair work at that point. Lacking qualified instrument repairmen in Nashville in those days, he shipped it to the Gibson Instrument Company in Kalamazoo, Michigan, as he had done several times before. "Once a year," he said later, "I'd send it back and get a new fingerboard put on it. I don't know how many fingerboards have been put on that mandolin. Choking your mandolin to beat rhythm, it eats a fingerboard up." By then, however, his F-5 was in need of more extensive help: "This time that I sent it back [in May 1952], the neck had been broke off [the neck joint had loosened]; it needed a new fingerboard; it needed refinishing [cosmetic touching up to hide scratches]; it needed [tuning] keys—it needed everything, mind you." He would be without it for several months.[57]

By the end of June 1952, Mayfield and Richardson were gone, possibly due to the demanding road schedule when baseball season began in June. When these shows were combined with the *Opry* on Saturday and the Brown County Jamboree on Sunday (where Cline said they went if there were no other bookings), Bill and the band were on the go all the time. Seeking some relief, Mayfield and Richardson left, and during this time Bill hired an inexperienced lead singer-guitarist, Bill "Billy" Price from Monroe, North Carolina, and Cline doubled on fiddle and banjo. Jimmy Martin, meanwhile, was performing in Middletown, Ohio, sometimes playing on radio with fourteen-year-old Sonny Osborne picking banjo (while older brother Bobby Osborne was with the marines in Korea). According to Martin, "[Bill] called up and they wanted him to cut an album [five disks in a binder] and he didn't have nobody to help him record and asked me would I come back down and record an album with him. I said, 'Why, sure.'"[58]

Sonny Osborne's recollection of events was somewhat different: "[Martin and I] went to Bean Blossom . . . they had the old park back there [in] the back [an open-air stage in the wooded area of the property, as in later years]. . . . Bill come up there that Sunday [July 6, 1952] with his Blue Grass Boy, which was Charlie Cline at the time, and so Jimmy worked that day with him and asked if we could have . . . the job and he said yeah." But Sonny Osborne did not play that day, so it appears Bill's mind was not entirely made up about him yet.[59]

Martin and Osborne drove to Nashville to play the *Opry* with Bill on July 12, probably arriving just in time to tune up and hit the stage. As Osborne recalled:

> I still hadn't said a word to Bill. Nobody had introduced me to him. He was God to me—I was gonna go to work for God and I didn't know him yet. [T]he hardest thing you could probably ever do, for a young banjo player, would be to do "Raw Hide." . . . I got down there, fourteen years old, standing on the stage of the *Grand Ole Opry* and literally knees shaking . . . Bill came out there and he still hadn't spoken a word to me yet—not one word. . . . I was fourteen years old and scared to death and he said, "Here's a song I wrote called 'Raw Hide,'" and he went into it and I thought, "Oh, my God. I'll never get through this."[60]

Osborne survived this "baptism of fire," but he was not yet hired, and he would not see Bill again until Friday, July 18, when he recorded with him at the Castle Studio. At the first session, new renditions of "In the Pines" and "Footprints in the Snow" were recorded, as well as the first of a proposed album's two religious songs, "Walking in Jerusalem," previously recorded only by black quartets in the 1920s. It was sung with just guitar accompaniment, the only time this was done on one of Bill's recordings. Cline sang baritone, and singing bass was Boudleaux Bryant (later the co-writer of "Rocky Top"). Playing bass was studio musician Ernie Newton, who, from this point on, played on all of Bill's sessions through 1954.[61]

There was a three-hour break before the next session, during which negotiations regarding Osborne's membership in the band took place in the coffee shop of the Tulane Hotel. As big and as tall as Bill, Sonny Osborne was legally still a child (and would always be the youngest person ever to work with Bill). Martin recalled using his lead singing services as leverage.

> So I told him, "I'll work this summer, Bill, if you'll let Sonny work with you." . . . He said, "No, he's too young, Jimmy. I can't hire him." I said, "Well, I guess I'll have to go back up [to Middletown], 'cause I wanted Sonny to be around me so I could help him on his baritone singing and help him on timing . . . on the banjo." . . . Bill said, "The only way I'll let him go to work with us is you be responsible." I said, "Why, sure, Bill. I'll be responsible. We'll just stay together." [So] me and Sonny roomed together.[62]

Returning to the studio, Bill and the band recorded five more songs, including three of Bill's most intriguing duet compositions. "Memories of Mother and Dad," a true song, was possibly written during Martin's first tenure (1950–51). Martin later told of Bill taking him to the Rosine Cemetery early on, to remove weeds around his parents' headstones, and of being surprised to see the words from the song on them. (Recorded in the key of F sharp, legend has it that Bill was angry with Cline and he chose a difficult key for a fiddler to play in, just to punish him.) Next was "The Little Girl and the Dreadful Snake," written in the fall of 1950, after Bill learned that his eighteen-month-old step-great-niece, Jill Raley (daughter of Speed Monroe's stepdaughter, Ruth Whitehead Raley) had been bitten by a non-poisonous chicken snake. Carter Stanley recalled learning the song after joining the band in early 1951. "My Dying Bed" may have been a look into the future by Bill. Decca seemingly didn't know what to do with this disturbing confessional; it would remain unissued until 1966. A similar fate would befall

Bill's solo vocal on Pete Pyle's "Don't Put Off 'til Tomorrow." The proposed album's second sacred song, this impassioned plea for religious conversion wouldn't be released until 1969. However, Bill's solo vocal on the commercial "Country Waltz" (written by one Claude V. Breland) would be released before any other song recorded at this session (in July 1953).[63]

A two-song session, about a week later (July 26, 1952), was required to complete the ten-item album project. First was a cover of "A Mighty Pretty Waltz," a pop love song released in June by Decca's sultry-voiced Jeri Southern. It was the second of Bill's recordings to have a new ending recorded for it, to be spliced onto the original later. Next was Bill's version of "Pike County Breakdown," released three months earlier by Flatt and Scruggs and, according to Sonny Osborne, "on every jukebox in the world." Osborne wondered if he was supposed to duplicate Scruggs's picking: "I asked Bill if he wanted me to play it like 'the other record.' Very bluntly he told me, 'What other record? Play it the way the tune goes.'" (A few weeks after the session, Osborne recalled, "We were at a place between Nashville and Knoxville eating and I spotted Lester and Earl's record on the jukebox and played it. I told [Bill], 'This is the other record of "Pike County Breakdown."' He didn't say anything, [just] looked at me, and, although I didn't know it at the time, being a fourteen-year-old kid had its advantages.") Decca would release these recordings almost immediately (on August 18), confident of the popularity of the love song and wanting to cash in on the success of "the other record." But, possibly due to recordings it considered unreleasable (like "My Dying Bed"), the company again cancelled plans for an album by Bill.[64]

Shortly before Martin and Osborne came to Nashville, Hank Williams and wife Audrey were divorced on July 10. Williams recorded "You Win Again" on July 11, introduced "Jambalaya" on the *Opry* July 12 (the same night Sonny Osborne was confronted with "Raw Hide"), and then started drinking again. On August 11, after Williams failed to show up for the *Opry* and an *Opry*-sponsored showdate, *Opry* house manager and artist service director Jim Denny fired him.[65]

Bill's Mandolin Returned

Bill's main mandolin was returned about this time, after four months at the Gibson factory. Years later he said, "They sent it back to me with just the neck put back on and that was about all." Then elsewhere he said, "All they'd done was the fingerboard, and I got so aggravated that I just took the Gibson name right off it. Cut it out with a pocket knife" (referring to the inlaid mother-of-pearl "Gibson" on the headstock). Reportedly, Gibson hadn't touched up the scratches and they were unable to replace the old-style tuning keys, but, as was their usual practice, they sprayed the mandolin with a thin coat of lacquer, to make it look "like new." Osborne said it was probably in Grundy, Virginia (at the Lynwood Theater on August 19, 1952), and the Blue Grass Boys had just returned from eating between shows: "We hear this scrapin' sound . . . and we go back there and Bill is workin' on his mandolin, on the finish of his mandolin with a little penknife. . . . And I'm thinkin', 'What's he doin'? He couldn't be doin' this for the sound.' He said, 'It won't be so pretty now. Maybe nobody will want to pick it up.'"[66]

Shortly thereafter, in September 1952, Osborne returned to school in Dayton, Ohio. Bill had probably been listening to Knoxville's WROL on the road, hearing Carl and Pearl Butler's banjo player, eighteen-year-old Jim Smoak from South Carolina. Arriving in Knoxville on September 22, Martin called the station and arranged to meet Smoak on a street corner near the station. "Bill sat in the backseat of the car [a 1952 Chrysler Imperial] with the door open and his feet on the ground and I stood on the sidewalk with my banjo," Smoak said, "and he and I picked a few tunes." He wanted to know if I could leave right now and I said, yeah, I could." They were headed to eastern North Carolina.[67]

Mauldin was singing solos with the band by then, dubbed "the Carolina Songbird" by Bill, and she liked to sing "Tennessee Ernie Ford's stuff," according to Charlie Cline. She'd also started bringing along her little Pekingese dog, "Chappie." Smoak said Mauldin's presence depended on how her and Bill's relationship was going: "Bill and Bessie had their ups and downs." He definitely remembered her being on his first trip: "Bill and Bessie got in such an argument in the car—I'd never heard anything like that in my life. I was shocked—I didn't know what to say or do. They were using foul language at each other. Bill wanted to put her out on the side of the road there in the mountains. We stopped the car and they cooled down." In Nashville, Mauldin had a room at the Hermitage Hotel, a block or so from Bill at the Andrew Jackson. While this provided the appearance of propriety, it's clear that it also provided separate corners to go to when a time-out was needed.[68]

October 1952 was busy, with a steady stream of theaters and high schools to play in Indiana, Kentucky, and Alabama. Then, in November, Dwight David Eisenhower was elected president, Bill's first season as owner of the

Brown County Jamboree ended, and the first "Deejay Convention" was held in Nashville, attended by a hundred disc jockeys, all of whom stayed at the Andrew Jackson Hotel. In December, Bill's road schedule slowed to a crawl, with a show in Akron, Ohio, on the 7th, promoted by local deejay Cliff Rodgers, and a week of schools and theaters in Tennessee and Mississippi from the 15th to the 19th.[69]

Sometime during the last hours of New Year's Eve 1952 and the first hours of New Year's Day 1953, twenty-nine-year-old Hank Williams died in the backseat of his Cadillac, a victim of booze and the drugs he took for back pain. He was being driven to Canton, Ohio, just south of Akron, to play the Memorial Auditorium with Homer and Jethro, Hawkshaw Hawkins, Autry Inman, and Red Taylor, then featured as a singer-songwriter as well as fiddler. Cliff Rodgers, the deejay who had promoted Bill's show in Akron, announced Williams's death to cast and crew. Then, somehow, the show went on.[70]

The funeral was held on Sunday, January 4, 1953, at the City Auditorium in Montgomery, Alabama. Roger M. Williams, in his *Sing a Sad Song*, observed that "save for the awesome turnout for the martyred Dr. Martin Luther King, Jr., fifteen years later, it was the most spectacular funeral the South has ever seen." Midway through the service, the *Opry*'s Roy Acuff, Red Foley, Jimmy Dickens, Carl Smith, Lew Childre, and Bill, joined by Webb Pierce from the Louisiana Hayride, sang two choruses of "I Saw the Light," with a verse between them sung by Acuff.[71]

During a two-week lull in bookings that followed, Cline left the Blue Grass Boys to rejoin the Lonesome Pine Fiddlers in Detroit. Bill and the band, with Gordon Terry filling in on fiddle, played the *Opry* on January 10 and a few early-morning shows for WSM at the National Life building. Then Bill left town to go fox hunting in White House, Tennessee, about twenty miles north of Nashville, promising to be back for a morning show at WSM on Friday the 16th.[72]

The Accident–1953

As promised, in the predawn hours of a cold January 16, Bill was headed south on one of the main roads into Nashville, 31W, with Mauldin by his side and a hunting dog in the Chrysler's trunk. He saw a car coming toward him, crossing into his lane. "I was makin' this [bend in] the road," he said. "Well, this drunk come in on the same curve I was on, and he just kept comin' right over in the middle of the road 'til he come right up on me." Bill stubbornly refused to avoid him—"I didn't give a inch," he said later—and they collided head-on. Mauldin said she went through the windshield, but, other than broken bones in her right foot, her injuries were minor. Bill suffered nineteen fractures: three in his skull, five in his back, and others in his left arm and legs. His left eye was also dislodged slightly from its socket, but, as he later told son James, he managed to push it back into place himself. Luckily, someone Bill and Mauldin knew happened to drive by. "Bill picked me up and put me in [their] car," Mauldin said, and they were taken into Nashville, Bill to General Hospital, then Mauldin to Baptist Hospital. As stoic as ever (and still in shock), Bill insisted on walking into the hospital, which would have been painful but not unbearable, since the fractures in his legs were likely in the fibulas, the smaller of the two bones between the knee and ankle. (Bill chose General Hospital, on Hermitage Avenue just southeast of downtown, because his sisters were both working there. Maude had moved to Nashville in the late 1940s, becoming a practical nurse, and Bertha joined her there after she and Bernard Kurth divorced.)[73]

The Blue Grass Boys were at WSM when they got the word. "Grant Turner popped around the corner and told us that Bill was in the hospital," said Smoak. They left immediately to see him, not doing the show, and found him in a cast covering his entire body except for his head, feet, and right arm. During the next few weeks, WSM permitted Martin and Smoak to play Bill's *Opry* spots, but they weren't paid much. Smoak was offered a job with the Jimmy Dickens band, and when he told Bill about it, Bill encouraged him to take it. Martin returned to Knoxville, to work on grocery store magnate Caswell "Cas" Walker's *Farm and Home Hour* radio show on WROL, where he had been prior to Middletown, Ohio.[74]

Mauldin got out of the hospital after about a month and began taking small rubber balls to Bill, so he could exercise his hands. "The doctors said he would never be able to work again," she told Rinzler, but she and Bill were determined to prove them wrong. He was still in traction when WSM sponsored a benefit show at the Louisville, Kentucky, Armory on Sunday, February 22, featuring many *Opry* stars, including Roy Acuff, Red Foley, Pee Wee King, Hank Snow, and Ernest Tubb. Seventeen thousand attended two shows, and more than $8,600 was raised for Bill (some of which was used to buy a 1953 baby-blue Cadillac limousine for the band).[75]

Another source of income was *Bill Monroe's WSM Grand Ole Opry Song Folio No. 2*, published at this time. Not a new songbook, it was a recycled *No.*

1 with nine fewer songs. Its cover was the same as *No. 1*, except the number "2" had been printed over the number "1" in its title.[76]

The second season at the Brown County Jamboree was being planned by then. For the Brown County Fox Hunters, Birch hired Edd Mayfield and Larry Richardson. Mayfield arrived from Texas with pregnant wife Jody and young son Fred, and they moved into one of the tourist cabins in February. Jody Mayfield recalled the birth of their second son: "Carl was born in March and the snow was deep. Edd carried me [from the car to the cabin] in knee-deep snow." Mayfield and Richardson would play in the house band throughout the spring and summer of 1953.[77]

At the end of March, Bill's body cast was finally removed, but he still had to wear a metal brace to support his back. "I wore that back brace a long, long time," he said later. He was still in the hospital recuperating in early April when Columbia Records released "Thinking About You" and "Why Did You Wander?" by Flatt and Scruggs. The latter, originally recorded in 1946 when they were with Bill, may have caused further annoyance, due again to its unauthorized use, but this may have lessened somewhat when the royalty checks arrived.[78]

On the weekend of April 17, 1953, near Philadelphia, the eighth annual folk festival at Swarthmore College featured Pete Seeger, performing as a soloist while still one of the Weavers. In the audience was Ralph Rinzler, an eighteen-year-old freshman from Passaic, New Jersey (near New York City), later to play a key role in Bill's career. The son of a doctor, Rinzler had grown up listening to southern folk music recorded "in the field" by John and Alan Lomax and issued by the Library of Congress on records his Uncle Sam gave to him on birthdays and Christmases. Hearing Seeger sing and play the banjo renewed his love for the music.[79]

Bill was released from the hospital in mid-April. When the band reunited, Martin had recruited fiddler L. E. White of Knoxville, and Cline (back in Nashville) was put on banjo. North Carolinian Leslie "Les" Sandy filled in on bass at a show in South Carolina in May. Already working with another band, he would join the Blue Grass Boys when they played in North Carolina in June.[80]

Bill with Cline, Martin, and White were featured at the Brown County Jamboree on Sunday, May 24, then headed south to Mississippi, picking up brother Charlie in Kentucky on the way. In Meridian, birthplace of Jimmie

Rodgers, avid fans Hank Snow and Ernest Tubb had arranged for a tribute to him on May 26, 1953, the twentieth anniversary of his death. A monument to Rodgers was dedicated and a locomotive welded in place nearby "to serve as a permanent memorial for deceased Meridian railroaders" (including Rodgers). Bill and Charlie and the Blue Grass Boys were a small part of a huge four-hour concert at the Junior College Stadium with, among many others, Roy Acuff, the original Carter Family, Jimmie Davis, and Jimmie Skinner.[81]

At the end of May, having quit school to play music, Sonny Osborne asked for his job back. Cline, just filling in, he said, until Bill found someone, returned to the Lonesome Pine Fiddlers. Osborne, now fifteen, not only replaced Cline on banjo, he also took over his job as primary driver, even though he lacked a driver's license. "[Bill] still had the back brace from his hips to the top of his shoulders," he recalled, "and late at night, if I hit a rough place in the road, I could hear him moan in the backseat, but he never complained. He was tough, very tough." (Bill would continue to wear back supports of various kinds throughout his life, particularly when he had to stand for long periods.)[82]

On June 1, Flatt and Scruggs debuted on the *Martha White Biscuit Time* radio show, broadcast live from Nashville on WSM, Monday through Friday from 5:45 to 6:00 A.M., Central Time. Their hot and peppy brand of Bill's music had already made them his main competition, and now they were right in his backyard. They would continue to do the show live for over a year, maintaining a full schedule of showdates otherwise.

Also that June, Mississippi native Elvis Presley graduated from L. C. Humes High School in Memphis, Tennessee. He recorded two songs as a gift for his mother at the Memphis Recording Service (for four dollars), and the tape was heard by owner Sam Phillips. But it would be nearly a year before Presley would record for Phillips's Sun Records.[83]

After bassist Les Sandy joined the band in June 1953, he began doing comedy as "Uncle Puny" (inspired by his previous band's leader, Charles "Slim" Mims, who was "Uncle Ugly"). Bill, often his straight man, carried a newspaper onstage in one routine, announcing he was now in the newspaper business. Not to be outdone, Uncle Puny claimed he was in the newspaper business, too. Bill demanded proof.

> And I reach in my pockets everywhere and pull out a little bitty piece of paper. I say, "This is a copy of my newspaper." Bill says, "Uncle Puny, you can't print half

as much in that as I can in this big newspaper." Then I tell him, "You go ahead—I've got everything in here that you've got in that newspaper." So, he's reading and says, "All right, Uncle Puny, see if you've got this in your newspaper." He reads, 'Chicago, Illinois—In order to have a cleaner city, the city of Chicago is gettin' rid of all its telephone poles, parking meters, and fire hydrants.' And Bill says, "Have you got that in your newspaper?" I look in there real good and say, "Yeah, here it says, 'Chicago, Illinois—Ten thousand dogs commit suicide.'"[84]

Bill Meets Carlton Haney

That summer of 1953, Bill first encountered Lawrence Carlton "Carlton" Haney. The Reidsville, North Carolina, native, then twenty-four, was working in a battery factory in nearby Danville, Virginia. He had been befriended by former Blue Grass Boy Clyde Moody, and Haney started booking shows for him. At the time, sixteen-year-old Melissa Monroe happened to be living with Moody and his wife in Danville, sent there, reportedly, to again shield her from the amorous advances of Jimmy Martin. (She reportedly told Haney it was to separate her from Mauldin, whom she had attacked while visiting Bill in the hospital.) Haney soon fell in love with Melissa and began developing an interest in her father's music. During a visit to see his daughter, Bill met Haney and asked him to book some shows for him.[85]

The Korean War came to an end in late July 1953. At that point, Sonny Osborne knew his brother was on his way home and, since they planned to team up, he also knew his days as one of the Blue Grass Boys were numbered. He remembered one of his last nights with Bill, at the high school in Sandy Ridge, North Carolina, near Raleigh, on August 5:

> [Bill] opened his case, and where he had put a set of strings (which came in a cardboard box in those days)—under the peghead—and closed the case down on [it], the neck was broken out of his mandolin at the heel. I just looked at him and he grinned. . . . Well, not to be defeated on this night, he took a piece of wood and put it under the fingerboard extension [to hold the neck in place], which still left the strings really high, and he played on. Not very well, but he played.

Obviously, the work Gibson had done on the neck the year before didn't hold; Bill would soon send his main instrument back to the factory again. On August 8, Osborne learned his brother had been released from the marines: "I didn't give [Bill] notice of nothing. I just left. I told him, 'I'm gonna go home tonight,' and that's it. I went home" (knowing his replacement, Rudy Lyle, would soon be returning from Korea too).[86]

When Bill's mandolin arrived in Kalamazoo, Gibson employees would have immediately noticed his "modifications," especially the gouged-out "Gibson" on the headstock, so it was probably shortly thereafter that company executives arrived in Nashville to talk to him.

> They come to the Grand Ole Opry and they'd heard about what I'd done, you know, taken the name off . . . and I told 'em, "Well, you didn't do me right." They said, "Well, we've got other good mandolins." I said, "Yeah, but not as good as this." They said, "We can make one as good." I said, "No, you can't!" So we had a good many people at the *Opry* and they all told 'em, "No, you can't make one like this. You don't have one like this."

Gibson's boast, that they could duplicate his mandolin, was ridiculous, and anyone who knew mandolins knew it. Bill was convinced he had been wronged, and, since Gibson was apparently unwilling to apologize, that's where the matter would stand for more than twenty-five years.[87]

Rudy Lyle did return soon to claim his job. "When I came back from the army [in 1953]," Lyle said, "Flatt and Scruggs were doing the morning Martha White show at WSM. They were in one studio and [Bill and the band] were in the other [also doing a radio show]. Me and Earl was good buddies. He would come by ever so often. I remember one Sunday they were working [Acuff's] Dunbar Cave in Clarksville and Carter Stanley and me went up there with Earl."[88]

On September 13, Bill's forty-second birthday, the Stanley Brothers were the headliners at the Brown County Jamboree, and it's likely that Bill and the Blue Grass Boys were there also. The brothers had recently signed with Mercury Records, and, to celebrate, Bill gave them a new gospel song he and Mauldin had co-written, "A Voice from On High." (The Stanleys recorded it on November 25, 1953, about two months before Bill.)[89]

The 1953 season at the Brown County Jamboree showcased some of the biggest stars in country music, including Roy Acuff, Johnnie and Jack with Kitty Wells, and the Jordanaires. Also scheduled was a Monroe Brothers reunion on November 8, with Bill, Charlie, and Birch performing together, joined by seventeen-year-old Melissa on a few quartets. Years later, Birch recalled those days: "We had big crowds, 'cause we had *Opry* acts coming in all the time. And . . . we could get 'em cheaper then, of course, [and] you could make a little money on 'em. They'd charge all the way from hundred and fifty to three, four hundred. . . . [A]t the time, the price [at the door] was only a dollar. . . ." (However, possibly due to the expense of running the Jamboree, there doesn't appear to have been a "baseball season" during 1953.)[90]

That fall, L. E. White left the band to work with the Osborne Brothers, and Cline returned again, this time to fiddle. On Saturday, November 28, Bill and the band were in the Castle Studio to record a pop-country "Wishing Waltz" and two solid bluegrass entries. The first was the duet "I Hope You Have Learned." Then Bill demonstrated he had recovered from his second near-death experience with "Get Up John"—a relentlessly driving and dynamic adaption of his Uncle Pen's "Sleepy John." Bill had devised yet another tuning for it, with the mandolin's G strings tuned to F# and A and its E strings to A and D. Bill's main mandolin may have been returned to him prior to this session, and the reunion inspired the tune.[91]

Bill and the band headed west after the *Opry* that night to play auditoriums in Kansas, Nebraska, Iowa, and Missouri for the next three weeks. The Brown County Jamboree's season had ended, but Bill and the band played there one more time, on December 13, before heading to West Virginia for a week of schools and theaters. Afterward, Les Sandy left the band and Mauldin played bass.[92]

By the beginning of 1954, Decca had released everything Bill had recorded since 1950 that it considered releasable. So, the first two weeks of the new year were devoted to replenishing the musical larder. Five of the twelve songs recorded, however, would not be released for two or more years, probably due to the "rock and roll revolution" that began that summer. Decca's country music division would soon be struggling to stay in business, and the time between Bill's releases would be several months instead of one or two.[93]

Researchers aren't sure where all of Bill's 1954 sessions took place. Most may have been held, experimentally, at the "Bradley Studio," built in an alley near Nashville's Vanderbilt University by Paul Cohen's assistant Owen Bradley and his guitarist brother Harold Bradley. Bill was experimenting, too: first to be recorded on Thursday, January 7, was "On and On," a trio (sung in three-part harmony throughout), something new for Bill and for bluegrass, played at a moderately fast tempo. Next was another trio, this one a waltz: "I Believed in You, Darling." It was followed by two driving uptempo vocal solos, "New John Henry Blues" and "White House Blues." Bill had been singing "John Henry" for years. He later told Ralph Rinzler the first recording he heard of it was "an old record that belonged to Charlie," but none of several old recordings have all of the stanzas in Bill's version (including the Shelton Brothers' 1935 Decca recording of "New John Henry Blues," the only one with this title). Bill also told Rinzler that "lots of people knew it down home," suggesting he actually learned it in Kentucky. He often sang three stanzas in live performance that weren't included in his recording:

> John Henry hammered on the right-hand side
> And the steam drill hammered on the left.
> "Before I'd let that stranger beat me down,
> I'd hammer my fool self to death." (x2)
>
> The man that invented that big steam drill,
> He thought he had something fine.
> John Henry sunkered fourteen feet,
> The steam drill only sunkered nine. (x2)
>
> When the women in Chicago heard that John Henry's dead,
> Went out all dressed in red.
> When the people asked them where they was a-goin',
> "We're goin' where John Henry fell dead." (x2)

It's known that Bill had heard "White House Blues" since the 1920s, but, as mentioned earlier, it was probably the Swing Billies in the 1930s that caused Charlie to sing the song. Now Bill was making it his own.[94]

The next day, Friday, January 8, 1954, Bill and the band recorded four more. Bill later said he wrote the duet "Sitting Alone in the Moonlight" (sung: "Settin' alone in the moonlight") when the band had gone out to eat, leaving him alone with a toothache, and he wrote it to distract himself. "Plant Some Flowers by My Grave" is credited to country singer Jimmie Davis, who wrote it between terms as governor of Louisiana (1944–48 and 1960–64). According to Cline, Davis was in the studio to hear Bill record his song. "Changing Partners" and "Y'All Come" were covers, the former a hit for Patti Page on Mercury and the latter a hit for its composer, Arlie Duff, on the new Starday label. (Around 1958, Bill would begin using "Y'All Come" as the closing theme song on his shows.)[95]

The next session, on Thursday, January 14, 1954, was devoted to gospel music, three quartets and a trio—four of the most distinctive religious songs in Bill's repertoire: "Happy on My Way" (written by Pete Pyle, which the Brown County Fox Hunters sang in 1952), "I'm Working on a Building" (from the Carter Family, a song Bill had sung since the 1940s), "A Voice from On High" (a trio, written by Bill and Mauldin, previously recorded by the Stanley Brothers), and "He Will Set Your Fields on Fire" (an old standard, said to have been the song Bill and Charlie won a singing contest with in their younger days and the first song from the Monroe Brothers repertoire that Bill recorded). Singing bass on the quartets was Milton Estes, former spokesman for Martha White Mills. A dynamic salesman, he's credited with coining the company's slogan, "Goodness gracious, it's good."[96]

Bill's Second Farm

In the works during these sessions, Bill had decided to buy land near Nashville where he could raise foxhounds and do his fox hunting close to home, and the sale was completed on January 21, 1954. The five adjoining tracts were in Sumner County, about ten miles northeast of his Davidson County farm, totaling 288 acres. After paying $1,000 down, Bill would pay $14,500 in monthly installments of $250 (reputedly with help from Mauldin, at least initially). Only about three miles from the village of Goodlettsville (via Long Hollow Pike), it was far removed from city life, surrounded by hills on three sides, at the dead end of Allen Road. Near the entrance was an old log cabin, said to have been built in the 1860s, and nearby, a small concrete-block dairy barn of more recent vintage.[97]

Lyle left after the January sessions, about six months after he'd returned from the war. "Things weren't the same," he said later, and although he continued to play music, he would never pick banjo on a recording again. Bill contacted Jim Smoak, home after leaving Dickens, and he rejoined the band. Still lacking a regular bass player, on a trip through Knoxville, Martin recommended "Little Robert" Van Winkle (real name: Ralph Guenther), then on radio there, to fill in (he'd played bass with Martin and Osborne when they recorded for King in 1951). Thirty-nine inches tall, his upper torso was normal, but his legs were those of a dwarf. He'd written a song called "Close By" and was featured singing it during the week or two he worked with Bill. Cline left again near the end of January, to rejoin the Lonesome Pine Fiddlers, and Bill used Red Taylor or Gordon Terry on the road, plus in-demand sideman Dale Potter on the *Opry*.[98]

By February 1954, it was clear Martin was getting ready to leave too. "Jimmy was planning on making a move," said Smoak. "We all knew it. I don't know how much Bill knew about it." Martin said later he told Bill that Columbia, Decca, and RCA Victor had offered him recording contracts, but Bill wouldn't allow him to record for them while he was in his band. Bill knew this wouldn't please him, but he couldn't allow one of his band members to be in competition with him. Martin responded by turning in his two-weeks' notice and blaming Bill: "Bill asked me, 'What have I done? Why are you leaving?' I said, 'Bill, if you don't know, I'm not gonna tell you.'" It might have taken a while for his replacement, Edd Mayfield, to arrive. According to Martin, "I wound up working a six-week notice instead of two weeks." When it was finally time for him to leave, he said Bill told him, "If you get out there and need your job back, all you need to do is just call me." But he would never return.[99]

Mayfield arrived in March 1954, and for the next few months Bill and the band played mainly in theaters and drive-ins in Arkansas. In April, fiddler Jack Youngblood joined the Blue Grass Boys. An Alabama native, he had been working with country star William "Lefty" Frizzell and, thanks to Frizzell's connection with Columbia, Youngblood had recorded his own release for the label ("Bile Dem Cabbage Down" / "Wednesday Night Waltz"). Comedian James Alvie "Lazy Jim" Day went along to open shows and fill in on bass, on loan from country star Lloyd "Cowboy" Copas. (Copas and Bill enjoyed playing fiddle tunes together backstage at the *Opry*, according to Copas biographer John Simon.) And Day was a fellow western Kentuckian, born less than a month after Bill, on October 10, 1911, in Grayson County, just east of Ohio County.[100]

That April, the featured performers at the ninth annual Swarthmore Folk Festival were Mike and Peggy Seeger, Pete Seeger's half-brother and half-sister, singing and playing old-time southern folk music. Mike Seeger had recently gotten interested in bluegrass after seeing Flatt and Scruggs ("Incredible! It was like a religious experience," he once said), so when the Seegers and sophomore Rinzler met at a jam session, Mike Seeger suggested that next year's festival might feature the Stanley Brothers, then unknown to Rinzler. As it turned out, the Stanleys would never play there, but Rinzler's interest in bluegrass was kindled.[101]

During a two-day stand at a theater in Hot Springs, Arkansas, in early May 1954, Bill showed his new band (Mayfield, guitar; Smoak, banjo; Youngblood, fiddle) a tune he didn't have a name for yet, and they worked out an arrangement for it. Smoak suggested they call it "Old Cheyenne"; Mayfield simplified it to "Cheyenne," the name of an American Indian tribe as well as a town in Oklahoma and the capital of Wyoming. Smoak said it was the result of Mauldin being absent on this trip: "When she wasn't along, Bill was kinda like one of the boys, you know? We had a lot more fun. You could even play a few tunes together [offstage] sometimes. That's how we worked up 'Cheyenne'—We worked it up because he wasn't fooling around with her." Later, Youngblood recalled it was an instant hit with audiences. He would soon be moving on, however. Shortly after recording another session for Columbia on May 22, with Mayfield and Smoak backing him on "Hitch Hiker's Blues" and "Twinkle, Twinkle Little Star," he took a playing job in Louisiana that didn't require much traveling.[102]

Bill returned to using former fiddlers Taylor, Terry, and Cline (back again!) on a catch-as-catch-can basis, and, soon, two of them convinced him to use all three, as a fiddling trio. According to Taylor, "Me and Gordon talked Bill into 'the three-fiddle thing' with us and Charlie Cline. Bill was a little reluctant to give it a try at first, but after the three of us played some things like 'Blue Moon of Kentucky' and 'Put My Little Shoes Away,' he decided that he liked the sound and we [including Paul Cohen and Owen Bradley] decided to cut some of it." A three-song session, Bill's twentieth for Decca, was scheduled for Saturday, June 26. Smoak remembered the session being held at the Castle Studio, making it Bill's last session there. (Castle Studio closed in 1955 and the Tulane Hotel was torn down in 1956).[103]

Recording technology had progressed to the point of using several microphones to capture the various sounds of the band, and Smoak recalled that they used four at the June 26 session: one for Bill's voice and mandolin, one for the banjo, one for the guitar and bass (with Ernie Newton playing bass on a platform, bringing it up closer to the mike), and one for the fiddlers three (Terry playing lead; Taylor, tenor; and Cline, baritone). The engineer, using a "plot" of who-did-what-and-when, adjusted the levels of the four channels, mixing the songs as they were being recorded.[104]

First up was "Close By," the song written by "Little Robert" Van Winkle that he'd featured with Bill about six months earlier. Then came a second recording of "My Little Georgia Rose." Bill may have been reluctant to dredge this up, but they recorded it because the fiddlers had worked it out. (Decca executives later decided that another rendition was not needed, and it would be shelved for twelve years.) Third was "Put My Little Shoes Away," a turn-of-the-century tearjerker and one of the first songs recorded in Nashville, by Paul Warmack and his Gully Jumpers, in 1928. Bill recorded it because he knew his country audience loved this kind of song, not because he had a "fascination . . . with dying or neglected children," as Wolfe later suggested.[105]

Elvis Presley and "Blue Moon of Kentucky"

About a week later, on July 5, 1954, Elvis Presley recorded his first session in Memphis, Tennessee (where Bill found his Kentucky Blue Grass Boys). Sun Records producer Sam Phillips, hoping for a hit record by combining rhythm and blues with country and western, teamed the black-sounding youngster with two members of a country band called the Starlite Wranglers, electric guitarist Scotty Moore and upright bassist Bill Black. "Fooling around" in the studio, they recorded black bluesman Arthur "Big Boy" Crudup's "That's All Right," then they needed a "B side." According to Moore, "We started going through different songs, then Bill [Black] this time came up with it. Same deal—we're taking a break when Bill [Black] started clowning around and doing Bill Monroe's 'Blue Moon [of Kentucky]' uptempo, doing a high falsetto voice, where Monroe had done it slow. Well, Elvis knew that song and just joined in and it kinda fell into place." (Black may have heard rockabilly singer-songwriter Carl Perkins doing the song this way in some west Tennessee honky-tonk. Perkins, a longtime Monroe fan, said he'd played an uptempo rendition of "Blue Moon" in "the tonks" since 1947. Presley didn't know it that well—he sang the wrong lyrics.) Presley's first Sun record was released about two weeks later (July 19, 1954).[106]

The Death of Harry Monroe

Bill and the Blue Grass Boys were on the road almost continuously during July and most of August. The long series of showdates ended on August 20, and on that day, Bill's oldest brother Harry died of a heart attack at age sixty. Harry and wife Nolie (whose first child, Charlotte, displaced Bill as the baby) had divorced in 1929. Harry moved to Whiting, Indiana, where he managed a hotel restaurant. His funeral was held in Rosine at the new Methodist church, built on the site of the old church where Malissa Monroe had taken her children. All of Harry's younger brothers and sisters were there, including Speed, who had recently left Bill's farm and moved back home with his family. Harry's grandson, David Mahan, thirteen at the time, recalled that Bill was the most "torn up" of them all.[107]

Smoak had turned in his notice two weeks before the tour ended and left to work with Youngblood in Louisiana. The following weekend, the Stanley Brothers came to Nashville and visited Bill at the *Opry* before their recording session for Mercury the next day (August 29). As Carter Stanley recalled,

[Bill] said, "After the *Opry*, we'll go eat and . . . then I want to [go] up to WSM studios [in the National Life building]. There's something up there I want to hear." He had the record with him—"Blue Moon of Kentucky" by Elvis Presley. And we had to go up there where there was a machine, you know? So, he said, "I want you to hear something," and he had never said anything like that to me before. So, we went up [there] and that's what we heard. . . . I laughed a little bit and looked around and everybody else was laughing except Bill. He said, "You better do that number tomorrow if you want to sell some records."

Bill came to the Stanleys' session, bringing Charlie Cline with him to play fingerpicking lead guitar on "Blue Moon." Then Cline played on the session's four other songs, playing on two of them some of the earliest bluegrass-style flat-picking lead on a major label. It was the first time the Stanleys featured lead guitar on their recordings, later a hallmark of their style.[108]

Bill had not found a replacement for Smoak, but told the Stanleys on the 29th that he was going to record "Blue Moon" himself in a week, so it seems he was prepared to do it with or without a banjo. And, sure enough, at the one-song session on Saturday, September 4, 1954, he recorded without one. The lack actually focused attention on the other instruments—three fiddles (played by the fiddlers who used "Blue Moon" to convince him to use them), guitar (with Mayfield's marvelous runs), and mandolin (with some "hot" picking by Bill)—and on the new arrangement, dramatically shifting from the original waltz time into Presley's swinging 4/4. (It also was the first song recorded by what would later be called "the classic bluegrass band" to be rerecorded by Bill in a studio and released by Decca-MCA.) [109]

That night after the *Opry*, Bill and the band left for Missouri, playing there through September 10, with Terry on fiddle, Cline again on banjo, and Les Sandy back to do comedy and play bass. On the 19th, they were at the Brown County Jamboree, and one of their shows can still be heard today, thanks to local radio and TV dealer Marvin Hedrick using the latest technology—a portable tape recorder. On (probably) the first recording of a bluegrass band's stage show made by a fan, the music is often interrupted by short comedic outbursts: "Hey, Bill," Uncle Puny calls out after "Bile Them Cabbage Down."

> "Yes, sir," Bill answers in mock seriousness.
>
> "You know, I went down yonder awhile ago at the rooster-rant, I mean, rest-a-rant."
>
> "Restaurant," Bill corrects impatiently.
>
> "Yeah, I went down there and I eat some chicken awhile ago. I eat so much chicken, I'm in *fowl* shape."

Later, Bill introduces "Blue Moon of Kentucky," explaining that it's "a new arrangement" and that "[It] looks like it's gonna make a good comeback." As usual, he was being straightforward with his audience; his song having a new life was just as important to him as selling a lot of records. By the end of the month, Presley's "Blue Moon" would be number 1 in *Billboard*'s "Country and Western Territorial Best Sellers" list (for Memphis), while "That's All Right" was number 4.[110]

Sandy would not last long this time. A talented singer, he had auditioned for Decca but wasn't offered a contract, and he went home. Bill needed a bass player (and he and Mauldin were quarreling), so, with shows in North Carolina coming up, he called Tar Heel booking agent Carlton Haney. Haney contacted Tar Heel fiddler Bobby Hicks and asked if he would play bass with Bill. Hicks, who had fiddled on sessions in Nashville with former Blue Grass Boy Jim Eanes for Decca, readily agreed. Bill featured him fiddling a tune on every show, and when the tour ended, he asked him to come to Nashville with him. "I had just turned twenty-one," Hicks said later, "and I was so happy to come to the *Grand Ole Opry* . . . because that was *the* thing back then."[111]

The popularity of Elvis Presley's "Blue Moon of Kentucky" helped producer Sam Phillips arrange a guest spot on the *Opry* for Presley and his "Blue Moon Boys" (as Moore and Black were now called) on October 2, 1954, their first major appearance anywhere. Presley sang his rocking "Blue Moon," but audience reaction was "tepid," according to biographer Bobbie Ann Mason. William "Buddy" Killen, a frequent fill-in musician at the *Opry* (and later music-publishing executive) who was there, wrote: "He received an enthusiastic round of applause, but there was no earthshaking response. He didn't bring down the house and there was no encore." Afterward, Presley approached Bill and apologized for changing his song. "The record company told him that he needed a style of his own," said Bill, recalling what Presley said, " . . . so that's what he was searching for when he recorded 'Blue Moon of Kentucky'. . . . I told him if it would help him get [his own style], then I was one hundred percent for [it]." Bill, who had changed "Mule Skinner Blues" while finding his own style, may have seen himself in nineteen-year-old Presley, so his encouraging words were probably not influenced solely by the promise of large royalty checks. Years later, he told *Record World* columnist Red O'Donnell, "He need not have apologized. It was a boost for the song and me and bluegrass music."[112]

Bill's fifteenth year on the *Opry* was acknowledged with a rare feature article in the November 15 issue of *Pickin' and Singin' News*, a fan newspaper published in Nashville, recently acquired by George D. Hay. Hay himself wrote the article, borrowing two paragraphs from his sketch of Bill in *A Story of the Grand Ole Opry*, prefaced by a couple of new ones:

> Bill Monroe, The Blue Grass Boy from dear old Kentucky, one of the most beloved stars of the WSM Grand Ole Opry, celebrated his fifteenth anniversary as a member of the world's foremost country music show on Saturday, October 30th. It's about as easy to get news out of Bill Monroe as it is to walk across the Cumberland River without a boat, but it finally leaked out.
>
> ... His quiet manner and genuinely honest approach to life make him stand out as a man of high character and he is quick to go to the aid of a friend or anyone who needs help.

Feature articles about Bill were rare because he never permitted his managers to promote (or control) him. "No man will ever manage me," he once told Charlie before the breakup in 1938. But perhaps by 1954 he was willing to be managed by a woman: a half-page ad in that edition of the *News* welcomed deejays to the third annual convention, announced Bill's latest Decca releases, and proclaimed, "EXCLUSIVE MANAGEMENT: BESSIE MAULDIN." And so it may have been for a while—long enough for her to arrange for the article and the ad. During this time, she moved into the Andrew Jackson, evidently to be near her "client." In the future, even though she was replaced by other managers, it appears Mauldin continued to see herself as a manager of Bill.

Published for the first time in the ad was a new photograph of Bill, taken at Nashville's Fabry Studio, the now-iconic shot of him wearing a new white western hat and holding the neck of his mandolin with both hands, with the gouged-out space for "Gibson" clearly visible. Mauldin, as his manager, may have also arranged for this photo. In it, Bill appears to have aged about ten years in the four since the photos in *Blue Grass Country Songs* of 1950.[113]

Edd Mayfield's second departure from the band came at this time. He returned to Texas to raise stock for rodeos and to ride the rodeo circuit as a contestant. Replacing him was Jackie Phelps, who had played guitar while Don Reno was picking banjo and singing lead in 1948–49. Bill and the band (with Cline on banjo and Hicks fiddling) worked steadily through November and December 1954. After the *Opry* on Christmas night, they were off for the rest of the year (or so they thought). Hicks went home to Greensboro, North Carolina, where Carlton Haney and banjo picker Hubert Davis (who had recorded the Eanes sessions with Hicks) visited one evening. As Davis recalled,

> Me and [Bobby Hicks] and Carlton was sittin' around [that] night at Bobby's when
> the phone rang. Carlton [answered it and then] says, "Bobby, it's Bill. We're going
> to have to get back to Nashville. You're goin' to have a session to cut a record, and
> he said if we knew a banjo player to bring him." And I hear Carlton say [to Bill],
> "Well, I've got the best right here with me." [Bill] says, "Well, who is it?" and he
> says, "Hubert Davis," and [Bill] says, "Bring him on."

Bill had known Davis since the 1940s and even offered him the banjo spot when Lyle left, but Davis didn't accept the offer. "I was just young and didn't have nothin' like that on my mind," he said.[114]

Bill and his hastily assembled band recorded on New Year's Eve afternoon, from 1:45 to 4:45. During those three hours they cut three of Bill's most popular instrumentals: "Wheel Hoss," "Cheyenne," and "Roanoke." "Wheel Hoss" is played at a moderate tempo (not the frenetic pace favored by some today) and, alternating between dominant and seventh chords in its first part, it casts a nearly hypnotic spell. Bill, who preferred to call the tune "Wheel Horse," is plainly heard hollering, "Watch that wheel horse, boys!" (thereafter whooping and laughing delightedly). "Cheyenne," written earlier in 1954, begins and ends with an eerie Native American–sounding chant by Bill, adding to its western flavor. Jackie Phelps's guitar break was the first in Bill's music since 1945, fingerpicked like Cline at the Stanley session. "Roanoke" was the newest of the three, written in August or October when the band played in or near the Virginia town and during further dental distress: Bill later said, "When I wrote 'Roanoke' I had the toothache the worst anybody had ever in this world. Everybody had gone out of the theater there in Roanoke but me, and I felt so bad and I started playing and that's what I come up with." It was Bill's idea for twin fiddlers Cline and Hicks to solo on the first part and to take turns doing it, beginning with Hicks. The only vocal was "You'll Find Her Name Written There," written by country fiddler Harold Hensley, a member of Paul Howard's Arkansas Cotton Pickers when it included Howard Watts and Tex Willis. Hensley wrote the song for his mother when her death seemed imminent (she recovered from leukemia-like symptoms). It had been recorded in 1949 by Mauldin's favorite, Tennessee Ernie Ford (Capitol), and in May 1951 by brother Charlie (RCA Victor), but Bill made the song more effective by changing its original waltz time to $^4/_4$ (reminiscent of Elvis Presley and "Blue Moon of Kentucky").[115]

The session was an indication of the "boost" that Presley's record had given Bill, part of a brief surge of recognition, causing Decca to ask for new recordings. Also, on January 15, 1955, the *Opry* gave Bill top billing on the Prince Albert portion of the show, broadcast nationwide on NBC.[116]

Back in the recording studio on Friday, January 28, Bill could have chosen something bluesy or swinging to show his connection with rock and roll, but instead, he chose gospel songs. First was "Wait a Little Longer, Please Jesus," a hit on Capitol Records by California bandleader Chester Smith and the song's composer, his singer-guitarist, Hazel Houser of Modesto. In Bill's cover, three fiddles (Cline, Hicks, and possibly Taylor) are heard in the background only. "Let the Light Shine Down on Me" was sung as a quartet with just guitar, mandolin, and bass (the latter played by Buddy Killen, at the *Opry* when Elvis was there), written by Dottie Swan of Radio Dot and Smokey.[117]

During this time, Flatt and Scruggs moved to Nashville to do a live TV show for Martha White Mills on Saturday evenings (initially on WSM-TV only, it eventually required them to travel to five other cities to broadcast live on other nights), and the company began campaigning to get them on the *Grand Ole Opry*. Bill was convinced that imitators of his style, who were not cast members, were not worthy to perform on the *Opry*, and WSM executives were inclined to agree with him. However, when Martha White owner Cohen Williams threatened to withdraw his advertising on WSM, Flatt and Scruggs began appearing on portions of the *Opry* sponsored by his company in January 1955. From this point on, Bill considered Flatt and Scruggs his rivals.[118]

In February, America was gripped by the "Davy Crockett" craze, a mania that began in December 1954 when "The King of the Wild Frontier" miniseries debuted on the new "Disneyland" TV show. On February 7, 1955, Decca released Bill's single of "Cheyenne" / "Roanoke." One of the first to hear it in Knoxville was a twenty-eight-year-old eastern Kentucky coal miner turned professional fiddler, Kenny Baker: "I played swing fiddle until I heard 'Roanoke' and 'Wheel Hoss' [released later in 1955]. The first time I ever heard 'Roanoke,' I thought it was the prettiest piece of music I'd ever heard. I'll bet you I put three dollars worth of damn nickels in that jukebox in Knoxville."[119]

The Country Show

In late February, filming continued on *The Country Show: With Stars of the Grand Ole Opry*, a syndicated half-hour TV series produced by Albert Gannaway for Flamingo Films of Hollywood. Begun in November 1954, *The*

Country Show provided the first national television exposure for many of Nashville's finest performers, including Bill and the Blue Grass Boys. Filmed in color (anticipating that color television would be available someday) with sensitive microphones suspended overhead, the show captured live performances with remarkable clarity. In the first-ever footage of Bill in action, he has a commanding presence, but he is also singular, serious, and seemingly oblivious to those around him. Standing straight (thanks to his back brace), he seems twice the size of those in his band (regulars Cline, Hicks, and Phelps, supplemented by Newton, Taylor, and Terry). Unfortunately, producer Gannaway packed his shows with as many performers as possible and preferred rapid-fire pacing, causing many performances (including all of Bill's) to be abbreviated. (Sponsored by Pillsbury Flour, *The Country Show* would be halted in 1956 after ninety-two episodes, due to complaints of "favoritism" by Martha White Mills.)[120]

Bill's North Carolina agent, Carlton Haney, came to Nashville about this time (late February 1955) to become Bill's "manager"—more like an agent with a modicum of authority who ran errands. His arrival appears to mark the end of Mauldin's "exclusive management" and the beginning of her playing bass on the road full time, bringing along *two* Pekingese dogs, male "Chappie" and female "Kewpie."[121]

Also arriving in Nashville then were two eastern Kentucky natives, guitarist-singer Carlos Brock and banjo picker Noah Crase, leaving their homes in Ohio to join the Blue Grass Boys. Brock had auditioned for Bill at the *Opry* in the summer of 1954, and the audition ended in a jam session that included Crase (who had come along for moral support) on banjo. In February 1955 Mauldin called Brock, telling him Bill said to come to Nashville and "bring that banjo player with you." When they arrived, Brock got the guitar spot, Phelps temporarily shifted to banjo (which he played in the old two-finger style), and Cline moved from banjo to fiddle. (It was in this configuration a couple of days later that Bill and band were filmed cutting loose on "Roanoke" in episode 26 of *The Country Show*.) Carlton Haney, meanwhile, had brought an unnamed banjo picker with him to audition for the banjo job, and both Crase and he played on shows for about a week until Bill sent the North Carolinian home and hired Crase. Phelps left shortly thereafter to work with Hawkshaw Hawkins.[122]

Crase recalled his first night on the *Grand Ole Opry* with the band, in March 1955, with special pride:

It was pretty rare for Bill to feature you the first night at the *Opry*. We were backstage, getting ready to go on with "Wait a Little Longer, Please Jesus." Earl Scruggs was onstage picking and Bill turned around to me and said, "Want to play an instrumental, boy?"

I said, "Yeah, sure."

"What do you want to play?"

"Lonesome Road Blues."

"O.K."

I remember, Bill turned around [to me, while Hicks and Cline were fiddling] and said, "Give me another break, boy."

It was a sure indication that it was going well. (Crase would leave the band in May, however, due to responsibilities at home, and Cline returned to banjo.)[123]

Brock had purchased a new Martin D-28 guitar in anticipation of working with Bill, but he soon learned that "new" wasn't always "best."

I thought my new Martin sounded just fine. I was on the road two weeks and Charlie Cline told me that when we got back to Nashville, we'd go up to Bill's room and get the guitar Bill has in there. Charlie told me it sounded better than mine. I thought, what does Charlie know anyway? Bill kept a room at the Clarkston Hotel, where he kept records, various instruments, clothing, etc. So when we got back to Nashville, Charlie walked me up to the room and pulled out a battered old guitar case. It had an old 1936 herringbone D-28 in it. Because it was beat-up looking, I kind of frowned on it. Then I played it. I could not believe the difference! It astonished me! I shipped my new guitar back home and didn't play it again. I came to find out that most of the [previous] Blue Grass Boys had played that guitar.

Actually, this was the herringbone Bill purchased to replace the one stolen when Flatt was with him. It had a distinctive, extra-large pickguard and, based on a 1949 photo of the band, it appears Wiseman was the first member of the Blue Grass Boys to play it.[124]

The Stanley Brothers were back in Nashville to record for Mercury on April 5, 1955. They recorded two more of Bill's songs, the new (and now little-known) "I Hear My Savior Calling" and a song written during Reno's tenure, "You'd Better Get Right," dimly remembered by Carter Stanley from his days with the Blue Grass Boys in 1951: "All I knew of that song was the chorus . . . [so] I just kindly took a word here and there, from what I'd heard [Bill] do, and added a few words to 'em and done our version. Of course, I give him credit for [being] the writer of the song because I think that was right. It was his idea, his tune, and everything."[125]

Seeger Takes Rinzler to See Bill

About three weeks later, on Sunday, April 24, the Stanleys were at New River Ranch in Rising Sun, Maryland, and Mike Seeger took Ralph Rinzler to see them there in person for the first time. Two Sundays after that, on May 8, Seeger again took Rinzler to the Ranch, this time to see Bill Monroe in person for the first time (at a joint appearance with brother Charlie). "It was clear," Rinzler wrote later, "that [Bill] was a unique synthesizer, a cultural figure of signal importance in our time. Having grown up listening to Library of Congress field recordings, [both Mike and I] were aware of the degree to which Bill integrated elements of varied secular and sacred music traditions and styles. We shared observations and speculated about the figure who we knew was the originator and shaper of 'bluegrass music.'"[126]

Meanwhile, the *Opry* had decided to revive its tent show. The "Grand Ole Opry Tent Show No. 1," headlined by Bill and the band (Brock, Cline, Hicks, and Mauldin), also featured Cowboy Copas and Radio Dot and Smokey, with Billy Wehle of the 1940s tent shows returning to manage it. Opening in Kokomo, Indiana, in mid-May 1955, it was scheduled to play in Ohio, Pennsylvania, and New York in June, Canada in July. Bill would be on the road most of this time, so he assigned Carlton Haney to help Birch handle the Brown County Jamboree while he was gone, and Haney moved to Bean Blossom, taking Virginia-born, North Carolina–raised fiddler Roger Smith with him. Smith played with the house band, then a country music outfit led by local singer-guitarist "Tex" Watson, with pedal steel, electric lead guitar, and electric bass (and Smith occasionally picked banjo, adding a touch of bluegrass). Haney and Smith lived in one of the tourist cabins, using the nearby pond for bathing and cooking. "That was our water," Smith said, "and if you wanted to use the restroom, you went around behind the cabin."[127]

Tent Show No. 1 came to an early end, due to what *Billboard* called "a hassle" between WSM and owners of the tent, and its last show was in Maine on June 26. Bill and the band stayed on in the Northeast, playing quickly arranged showdates. Brock left in early July, thinking he was about to be drafted, so Cline switched to guitar and Hicks alternated between fiddle and banjo. Shortly thereafter, Bill slipped and fell as he was getting out of a hotel bathtub in Brattleboro, Vermont, breaking his collarbone. His left arm was placed in a sling to limit movement, and he was unable to play for about eight weeks. Unstoppable, of course, he went on making appearances with the band, returning to New River Ranch on July 31 to again appear with brother

Charlie (with Cline picking mandolin for Bill and Charlie's performances). Then it was on to Canada for Bill's first visit there.[128]

After Canada, Bill and the band continued to pick up work in the northeastern United States, and on Wednesday, August 17, they were playing in Harrisburg, Pennsylvania. At the show that evening was Tennessee-born, North Carolina–raised Joe Stuart, with a night off from the band he was working with in the area. Multi-instrumentalist Stuart had played in Knoxville in the late 1940s (leading his own band, the Midnight Ramblers), and he'd worked briefly with Flatt and Scruggs (playing bass) in 1953. He played mandolin with Bill that night in 1955, auditioned on banjo the next, and joined the Blue Grass Boys for the first of several stints over the next twenty years. (He would eventually play every instrument except mandolin on Bill's recordings and become one of his closest friends.)[129]

Things in Bean Blossom, meanwhile, were not going well. Birch's pennypinching ways of managing the Jamboree clashed with Haney's promotional schemes (including buying time on local radio for daily shows by the house band). According to Haney, Birch was upset enough by the end of August to threaten him with an axe (after Bill told Birch to let Haney "take over," according to Adler in *Bean Blossom*). "In September," wrote Haney's friend Fred Bartenstein, "[Haney] was sent home to Reidsville, North Carolina, in a car with bald tires [which he couldn't afford to replace], with little to show for his efforts." He and Bill continued to be friends, but Haney managed other acts thereafter, most notably the new band of Don Reno, Arthur "Red" Smiley, and the Tennessee Cutups.[130]

At Swarthmore College in Pennsylvania, twenty-one-year-old Ralph Rinzler was about to begin his senior year. His listing in 1955's student directory reflected his growing interest in bluegrass, particularly the Stanley Brothers: he had changed his name from Ralph Charles Rinzler to "Ralph Carter Rinzler."[131]

Bill's next session was on Friday, September 16, 1955, three days after his forty-fourth birthday, at the new Bradley Film and Recording Studio, 804 Sixteenth Avenue South, closer to downtown Nashville (where he would record for the next fourteen years). It was the first session for new banjo picker Stuart and for new bass player Mauldin, who acquitted herself nicely after playing, off and on, for only four years. First recorded was Bill's "Used To Be," at a tempo that might have appealed to rock and roll dancers, with

Vassar Clements, Bobby Hicks, and Gordon Terry fiddling. Cline played both rhythm and lead guitar, effortlessly switching to fingerpicking for his break. Two of the three fiddlers took a turn playing lead on the next two items (with Hicks playing harmony): Gordon Terry on "Tall Timber" and Vassar Clements on "Brown County Breakdown." "Tall Timber," a variation of "Katy Hill," was, by far, the wildest-sounding recording Bill ever made. "Brown County Breakdown," written backstage at the Jamboree, was more complex, with another fingerpicked break by Cline. It may have been the tune Bill once showed to recently departed Crase, who complained it was hard to play. "Anything hard to play's good, boy," Bill had told him. Lamentably, none of these recordings would be released for at least nine years, as rock and roll caused Decca to cut back to its most profitable releases. (Reno and Smiley's King recording of "Used To Be" was released in 1962, two years before the release of Bill's recording.)[132]

Bill and the band had played in the Northeast that summer, and in the fall, after the session, they played in the upper Midwest, mainly theaters in North Dakota and South Dakota and neighboring Minnesota for almost all of October and the first half of November. While in the Minneapolis–St. Paul area, they played on the *Sunset Valley Barn Dance*, broadcast on radio *and* TV, an *Opry*-style show founded by David Stone after he left WSM. There Bill met singer-songwriter Chuck Carson, a *Barn Dance* regular he would later collaborate with on some memorable songs. Things hadn't changed much between Bill and Mauldin, according to Hicks: "Every time we were in the car traveling . . . they'd get into the damnedest cuss fight you ever heard in the backseat of that car. She was just damned jealous of him, [always] talking about other women. . . . It was just a constant argument about him and someone else." Somehow, a new instrumental tune was written during this time—"Big Mon" (Hicks and Cline's nickname for Bill, pronounced "Big Mun")—but it would be forgotten for a few years.[133]

By November, Elvis Presley had found a new manager, Colonel Tom Parker, who bought Presley's Sun recording contract and offered it to the highest bidder. Decca's offer of $5,000 and Dot's $7,500 were easily outclassed by RCA Victor's bid of $35,000. Presley's record sales surged.[134]

Bill's First West Coast Trip—1955

In December, as the boost to Bill from Presley was spreading nationwide, plans for Bill's first trip to the West Coast were finalized. Expensive air travel was out of the question, so Bill and the band (with Vassar Clements added to twin fiddle with Hicks) traversed the two thousand miles in the 1953 baby-blue Cadillac limo. An added attraction at each show was a reunion with brother Charlie, and he and wife Betty followed the Caddy in a station wagon driven by Brown County Jamboree soundman "Silver Spur" Ragsdale (who equipped the wagon with a loudspeaker to ballyhoo their shows). Cline had decided he'd had enough traveling on dry land and joined the navy, leaving Bill without a guitarist–lead singer. Hicks, on a recent trip home, had heard Arnold Terry (not related to Gordon) of Virginia, singing on radio, so on December 17 Terry auditioned for Bill at the *Opry*. The next morning, they headed west.[135]

On the way, they played at the municipal auditorium in Phoenix, Arizona, on December 23. New lead singer Terry sang Jimmy Newman's hit "Cry, Cry Darlin'" as his solo (previously featured by the Shenandoah Valley Trio). On Christmas Eve they arrived in Los Angeles and appeared on the area's top country music TV show, *Town Hall Party*, with regulars Merle Travis and Johnny Bond. The Monroe Brothers reunited for two numbers, and Mauldin sang tenor with the band on the new "Wait a Little Longer, Please Jesus." They played on the show again on Christmas Day and, afterward, Clements went out drinking and ended up in jail. His whereabouts would not be known for more than a week.[136]

The Monroe entourage had to go on, to join a package show with Lefty Frizzell and Freddie Hart. They raced north to Salinas and Modesto (near San Francisco) for December 28 and 29, then back south to San Diego (south of Los Angeles) for December 30. Due in Oakland (east of San Francisco) on December 31, Bill and Mauldin took a plane, while the rest of the troupe (including Charlie and Betty) drove. After the show, Mauldin and Bill decided to go to Fisherman's Wharf to eat seafood on New Year's Eve, and Terry volunteered to drive them. On the way back to Oakland, the Cadillac broke down at a toll booth on the Bay Bridge, where Terry said they spent the night waiting for a tow truck and "like to froze to death." On January 1, 1956, the package show appeared in Medford, Oregon, then Bill and band played a show in Washington before returning to California to bail out Clements in Los Angeles. Then it was on to Amarillo, Texas, for a show on January 5.[137]

Relations between Bill and Charlie were already strained by then ("The more they were together, the more they wore on each other," Terry said), much of it due to Mauldin, who was bossy and meddlesome, according to Terry. When they reached New Mexico on January 6, Bill relieved the tension by putting Charlie and Betty on a plane to Nashville, evening the score for his and Mauldin's flight to Oakland. Bill and the band played in Arizona on January 7 and 8, New Mexico on the 10th, then shows in Texas on the 11th, 12th, and 13th, and the *Big D Jamboree* radio show in Dallas on the 14th before heading home.[138]

The band was given a few days off when they got back to Nashville, and it appears Bill visited Knoxville, guesting on the noontime *Mid-Day Merry-Go-Round* radio show on WNOX. One of the show's regulars was country singer-songwriter Don Gibson, whose band included fiddler Kenny Baker, and Bill seemed to take an interest in him: "I'd do an instrumental tune every day on the show," Baker said, "and I noticed Bill would be settin' right out in the audience when I would be doin' my number." Eventually, Baker said Bill spoke to him, saying, "'If you ever get dissatisfied with where you're workin', just call me.' Then he looked at me and said, 'Don't call me—just come on.'" Bill and the Blue Grass Boys played the *Mid-Day Merry-Go-Round* later in 1956, and he would repeat the offer.[139]

The year 1956 was the beginning of hard times for many country music performers, due to the success of rock and roll in general and Elvis Presley in particular. It was the "Year of Elvis," according to Presley biographer Mason, with hit record after hit record, his first movie ("Love Me Tender"), and several national TV appearances. Bill's schedule continued to be full, but it appears his showdates were not as well attended, and profits declined where pay was based on attendance. To make up for losses, Bill played more of the profitable Saturday night shows than before, thanks to the *Opry* finally reducing its fifty-two-Saturday-nights requirement to twenty-six. Like many country artists, Bill would not record in 1956, as Decca Records favored its pop artists (Bing Crosby, Bill Haley, and "9 Year Old Sensation" [sic] Brenda Lee) to survive the Presley–RCA Victor onslaught. Decca's involvement with country music was limited to its bigger sellers (Red Foley, Red Sovine, Ernest Tubb, and Bob Wills), plus a few lesser-knowns and unknowns, hoping another Elvis would come out of nowhere and tickle the public's fancy. One of the lesser-knowns was former Blue Grass Boy Jimmy Martin, who recorded two sessions for the label in 1956. His first single, "Hit Parade of Love" / "You'll Be a Lost Ball," would be released at the end of the year. Decca was then the label of Bill Monroe and Jimmy Martin.

One of the unknowns was Charles "Buddy" Holly of Lubbock, Texas, who recorded two sessions for Decca before his twentieth birthday and one after it in 1956. But his first recordings (including an early "That'll Be the Day") were not successful. According to a biography by Goldrosen and Beecher,

"His records received little promotion of any sort in any market." In his teens, Holly was interested in bluegrass and learned to play mandolin and banjo, and he might have seen Bill and the band in Lubbock in 1950, when they appeared there with Myrick and the Mayfields. But little is said about the influence of Bill Monroe in his biography.[140]

Arnold Terry left the band on March 2, and his replacement showed up at the *Opry* on March 3. Lucky Saylor (his real name), another southwestern Virginian, came there to sell an F-5 mandolin, slipped backstage, and encountered Joe Stuart, whom he'd played music with years earlier in Knoxville. "Joe Stuart and I were good friends, so Joe said [to Bill], 'Bill, here's a guitar player right here.'" The band headed south, where Saylor soon heard about Bill and Mauldin's relationship: "There, in a motel in Florida, I woke up one morning and I set up in bed, and Joe was settin' up, and I said, 'What is that?' Bam! Wham! Bam! Sounded like big rocks hittin' the wall. He said, 'That's Bill and Bessie fightin'.' They'd fight like cats and dogs, but they loved one another."

Saylor recalled one of Bill's favorite "games" on the road: "Bill would tell me that Joe was gonna whip me. He'd go to Joe and tell him that I was gonna whip him. I figured it out and said [to Bill], 'You're just pullin' that damn stuff to get the two of us to fight.' If there *was* a fight, he'd stop it. He'd get a kick out of that." Saylor stayed a couple of months, leaving when his car was repossessed. "Monroe wasn't doing that great then," he said. "He just wasn't making the money to pay the guys, really." Shortly thereafter, Bill bought a new 1956 Cadillac. Money was tight, but comfortable and reliable transportation had to be provided, and an image of success maintained.[141]

On April 30, Decca released Bill's only single of 1956, "On and On" / "I Believed in You, Darling," both recorded more than two years earlier. At the same time, the label released its first Bill Monroe EPs, one secular and one sacred (gospel), with four songs on each disc from 1950–54 that played at 45 rpm.[142]

Saylor was replaced by North Carolinian Yates Green, whom Bill had heard on radio in a band that included banjo picker Hubert Davis. Beginning April 30, Bill and the Blue Grass Boys played two solid weeks of mainly theaters in North Carolina and Virginia, and then headed to Maryland, to play New River Ranch on May 13. Bill, wanting something special for it, arranged for Rudy Lyle (then playing electric lead guitar with country bands around D.C.) to pick banjo, while Hicks and Stuart played twin fiddles. Taping the show that day was Jeremy Foster, a high school friend of Mike Seeger's, and with him girlfriend Alice Gerrard (soon to be Mrs. Foster), both students at Antioch College in Yellow Springs, Ohio.[143]

By May 23, Bill and the band (Green, Hicks, Stuart, and Mauldin) were in Texas with a package show that included the Maddox Brothers and Rose. Then they headed west, returning to California and Oregon for about two weeks. "Silver Spur" Ragsdale went along to ballyhoo again, and back for a second stint with Bill was Chick Stripling, to do comedy. Green said Stripling kept the band laughing, teasing Bill by reading his name on posters as "Bill Roemonk." But Stripling wasn't fond of Chappie and Kewpie, often saying they ate better than the Blue Grass Boys and that if they lived with him, "there'd be nothin' fannin' around but a ball of fur."[144]

Mauldin was not one of Green's favorites: "The way I found her, she liked to spend Bill's money. She was pretty haughty at times. She wanted to boss Bill. There's places he wouldn't take that." Green recalled that Bill bought a watch on the road for son James, for his eighth-grade graduation in June 1956 (then fifteen, James would attend Goodlettsville High School that fall). "Bessie had a fit over that and she fussed on him [Bill] and he had to put her in her place."[145]

ABC-TV's Live Opry Show

After the band returned to Nashville and played the *Opry* on June 16, 1956, Green left to get married. Coming up the next Saturday (June 23) was one in a series of live ABC-TV shows featuring the *Opry* on national TV for the first time. Caught without a lead singer, Bill assigned Stuart to play guitar, then called Noah Crase in Ohio to pick banjo. According to Crase, producers made them rehearse the one song they were to do, "Uncle Pen," for a week (with Buddy Killen filling in on bass). During the band's recent trip out west, country singer Porter Wagoner's RCA Victor recording of the song peaked at number 14 (of 15) in *Billboard*'s "Most Played by Jockeys" chart, and that appears to have caused Bill and the band to play it on the live, one-hour show titled, simply, "Grand Ole Opry."[146]

The next day (June 24), Bill and the band played in St. Louis, Missouri. Crase had gone home, so Bill called Roger Smith in Indiana (where he'd stayed when Carlton Haney left, playing in a bar and teaching guitar), and he alternated guitar and banjo with Stuart. In the audience, seeing Bill for the first time, were Robert "Red" Cravens and the Bray brothers (Francis, Harley, and Nate) from Champaign, Illinois, later to emerge as one of the best young Northern bluegrass bands. They had been intensely studying Bill's recordings and, as Harley Bray recalled, "Every time those guys would pick a solo, we'd just come out of our seats."[147]

Following a Carlton Haney–arranged tour with Reno and Smiley in the Carolinas, Bill and the band returned to the Brown County Jamboree on July 1. They shared that day's shows with Charlie Monroe and his Kentucky Pardners, so apparently there were no hard feelings over the West Coast trip. (Charlie would retire from music in 1957 and begin mining coal on the Monroe family property in Ohio County, Kentucky.)[148]

Besides "On and On" and "I Believed in You, Darling," the only other recording by Bill to see the light of day in 1956 was "New John Henry Blues," released only in Great Britain in July on Decca's subsidiary, Brunswick (with "Put My Little Shoes Away," already released in the United States). Hugely successful in Britain at the time was "skiffle" music, with a recording of "John Henry" by Scotland's Lonnie Donegan (on British Decca) on the charts, and the craze would soon spread to the States. Decca, meanwhile, said they withheld the American release of "New John Henry Blues" due to racially sensitive language (Bill singing "John Henry was a little colored boy").[149]

The Stanley Brothers recorded a new song, "Who Will Call You Sweetheart?," credited to Bill Monroe and Carter Stanley, at a July 16, 1956, session. Ralph Stanley recalled that Bill had sung the chorus for his brother at some point, and Carter Stanley asked Bill if he could write verses for it. It would not be released until 1958, on the Stanleys' first Mercury album.[150]

Bill was again using Jackie Phelps to play guitar during a lull at the beginning of August 1956. Bobby Hicks recalled going fox hunting with Bill several times on the Goodlettsville property.

> He'd go out there a-ways and turn the dogs loose and just sit down and listen to 'em run. That's what he liked to do—just to hear 'em run. He didn't care if they caught anything or not. We'd sit there and listen to them dogs run. He really got a big kick out of that, and I got to where I really enjoyed listening to 'em, too, 'cause every once in awhile he would say something about what was happening: "Ol' What's-His-Name, he's gettin' ready to tree there. Listen at him!"

Hicks was about to be drafted. Before he left, eighteen-year-old Charlie Smith (no kin to Roger) auditioned on fiddle for Bill on September 8. A Nashville native studying electrical engineering at Vanderbilt University, Smith had recently discovered bluegrass while playing violin and viola with the Nashville Symphony Orchestra. He noted in his diary, "Monroe said I was good but needed a little more practice, and he didn't need a fiddler right now" (he would begin filling in at the *Opry* in 1957). After Hicks left on September 15, another eighteen-year-old, Tommy Williams, filled in between shows with *Opry* star Ferlin Huskey. Soon, Clarence "Tater" Tate of Virginia was hired to replace Hicks. Just returned from army duty in the Panama Canal Zone, Tate, twenty-five, had played professionally since 1948 in Knoxville (where Cas Walker nicknamed him "Tater"), and Bill offered him the fiddling spot in 1954, just before he was drafted.[151]

On September 23, 1956, Bill and the band returned to New River Ranch, sharing the day with Reno and Smiley. Bill again brought something special with him to the Ranch—Edd Mayfield (instead of Phelps). While visiting Nashville, it appears Mayfield agreed to play the date as a favor to his former boss (and Jeremy Foster again taped the proceedings). Later that evening, after the shows were over, Mike Seeger asked Joe Stuart to pick a few tunes for his tape recorder. These were the first Seeger recorded for a collection of banjo music that Folkways Records of New York City had commissioned him to produce, soon to be released on a relatively new medium for popular music, the "album" (as in the binders of the past) which was "long-playing" (thus the alternate name: "LP").[152]

Flatt and Scruggs Join the Opry—1956

On September 24, 1956, WSM president Jack DeWitt fired *Grand Ole Opry* house manager and Artist Service Bureau chief Jim Denny. He was replaced by Walter David "D." Kilpatrick, the first person after George D. Hay to be considered "a real manager" of the *Opry*, according to country music historian John Rumble. Previously associated with Mercury Records, Kilpatrick made former Mercury artists Flatt and Scruggs full members of the *Opry* before the end of 1956. Denny, meanwhile, established his own booking agency, and Bill, like many *Opry* stars, would forsake WSM's Artist Service Bureau to sign with the Jim Denny Artist Bureau (in Bill's case, it may have been in exchange for Denny's help in keeping Flatt and Scruggs off the *Opry*).[153]

Rockabilly Bill Monroe fan Carl Perkins made his first guest appearance on the *Opry* that fall, "rendered breathless" to see Bill "strolling casually around the backstage area," according to biographer David McGee. While on the road, Perkins had met Chuck Berry and, Perkins told McGee, Berry was a serious fan of both Jimmie Rodgers and Bill.[154]

After Mayfield went home to Texas, Stuart called another old friend in Knoxville, Enos Johnson, offering the guitar spot for "$90 a week, plus hotel bills." Johnson had played mandolin with Tex Climer and the Blue Band Coffee Boys in 1949, when the group included Jimmy Martin, and played guitar with the Osborne Brothers when they were in Knoxville in 1953. He would work with Bill for a couple of months. On October 13, Tate left the band, replaced by fiddler Ralph "Joe" Meadows, previously with the Stanley Brothers.[155]

The "Million Dollar Quartet"

Jerry Lee Lewis's first record for Sun ("Crazy Arms" / "End of the Road") had just been released when he played piano on Carl Perkins's Sun session of December 4. Visiting the studio were Johnny Cash, a Sun veteran who had recently joined the *Grand Ole Opry*, and Sun's most famous son, Elvis Presley. A photographer from the local newspaper was called, catching the four of them gathered around a piano. (The next day a story appeared, calling them the "Million Dollar Quartet.") After the pictures were taken, Cash left, and Lewis, Perkins, and Presley carried on, enjoying themselves while the tape rolled. They sang snatches of many old favorites, including four learned from Bill's band of 1946–48: "Little Cabin Home on the Hill," "Summertime Is Past and Gone," "I Hear a Sweet Voice Calling," and "Sweetheart, You Done Me Wrong," all released in 1948, when Lewis and Presley were thirteen and Perkins was sixteen.[156]

In early December 1956, twenty-one-year-old Carl Vanover replaced lead singer Enos Johnson. Born in Virginia and raised in Kentucky, Vanover and his family moved to Michigan in the 1940s, and he was playing around Detroit when he was heard by Jimmy Martin. Vanover recalled auditioning backstage at the *Opry* and Bill quickly hiring him: "He said, 'Son, tonight you're gonna sing on the *Grand Ole Opry*.' My legs started shakin', I was so scared." He sang, but because he was not in the local musicians' union, someone else played guitar.[157]

With the new year, Decca Records appears to have realized its neglect of Bill, releasing two songs on January 7, 1957, that had gathered dust on its shelves since 1954: "You'll Find Her Name Written There" and "Sitting Alone in the Moonlight."[158]

The Folkways album Mike Seeger began recording in September 1956 was also released in January 1957. *American Banjo Tunes and Songs in Scruggs Style* featured fifteen banjo pickers, including former and current Blue Grass Boys Larry Richardson and Joe Stuart. Later called "the first bluegrass album," it actually dealt with only one aspect of the music—banjo picking—and was the first scholarly attempt to explain what many neophytes believed was the music's defining characteristic. Seeger's friend and recent Swarthmore graduate Ralph Rinzler wrote the album's notes, revealing a very limited knowledge of Bill and his music.

> During the fifteen year period from 1930 to 1945 the five-string banjo was used rarely in commercial country music. In 1945, however, a well known mandolin picker and lead singer in Kentucky, Bill Monroe organized a different type of band from those already in existence. His new-found banjo picker, Earl Scruggs had developed a style of three-finger picking which enabled the banjo to play the lead or melody. . . . The term "bluegrass" refers to that section of Kentucky where Bill Monroe originally lived and where the music was most popular at the outset. [Punctuation as in original. The last sentence is completely incorrect.]

After graduate school in Vermont, Rinzler studied French language and literature at the Sorbonne in Paris. During 1957–58 he served as an accompanist (on banjo and mandolin) for English folksingers A. L. Lloyd and Ewan MacColl, and he became friends with expatriate folklorist Alan Lomax.[159]

Bill, meanwhile, was having trouble keeping a band together. Newlywed Vanover's wife didn't like living alone in a Nashville hotel while her husband was on the road, so Vanover left the band in early January 1957. Filling in again briefly, as he'd done prior to both Johnson and Vanover joining, was lead singer-guitarist Bob Metzel, a young York, Pennsylvania, native. Then, leaving in late January–early February was fiddler Joe Meadows. Mauldin tried writing to Mayfield, asking him to come back: "Bill needs someone that can keep his band strong, especially a good guitar man." But it didn't work.[160]

In early 1957, when interest in bluegrass banjo picking was high, Bill hired a banjo picker worthy of that interest: West Virginia native Don Stover. Bill had been aware of him as far back as 1952, when Stover was working with the Lilly Brothers and "Christmas Time's A-Comin'" composer Tex Logan in Boston. When Stover joined the Blue Grass Boys, Stuart was again moved to guitar. Returning to fiddle with Bill at this time was Gordon Terry (who had been pursuing a solo career).[161]

By 1957, fifty-five-year-old Birch Monroe had lived in a tourist cabin on the grounds of the Brown County Jamboree for about four years. ("The winter gets awful cold in them cabins," he once said. "[They] was just about like being outside.") He'd become friends with guitar player Kyle Wells and wife Cordie, who lived near Martinsville, Indiana, about fifteen miles north of

Bean Blossom, and when Birch didn't visit as usual, they grew worried. "Me and Kyle hadn't seen him for several days," Cordie Wells told Tom Adler, "and Kyle said, 'Something's wrong. Monroe ain't been over here.' [We] went over there and he was real sick . . . 'bout pneumonia, and so Kyle said, 'You can't stay over here by yourself. We'll just take you home with us.'" Birch would live with them for about a year, then move into Martinsville in 1958. Kyle Wells helped him get a job as a janitor at Martinsville's Twigg Industries, manufacturer of jet engine components, where Birch would work for thirteen years. He began relying on others to help with the Jamboree, even having a few manage it for him.[162]

Yet another *Grand Ole Opry* tent show was organized in the spring of 1957, to run, off and on, through October at county fairs as far east as New Jersey and as far west as North Dakota. Naturally, tent-show trouper Bill Monroe was chosen to headline, joined by new *Opry* member Jimmy Newman (later, Jimmy C. Newman), a rock and roll band (Pat Kelly and the Shamrocks), and a young duo who had knocked around Knoxville and Nashville since 1953, the Everly Brothers (whose parents were western Kentucky natives). When the show opened on April 2, 1957, eighteen-year-old Phil Everly and twenty-year-old Don Everly's first record, "Bye Bye Love" / "I Wonder If I Care As Much," on the Cadence label, was about to be released. As Phil Everly remembered it,

> It was fifty cents to get in and another quarter to sit in the segregated part, otherwise you'd have to sit with the blacks. . . . The first five rows would fill up with all the rough kids in town, because they threatened to cut the tent down unless you let them in free. Don and I played the country section, and then they charged everybody another quarter to see the rock and roll show, which was all of us again doing rock and roll songs.

"Bye Bye Love" began climbing the country charts in mid-May 1957. By May 27, the brothers were made members of the *Opry* and soon quit the tent show.[163]

Comedy, still a tent show necessity, was handled by Jack Paget, a Canadian who played steel with Jimmy Newman and doubled as "Uncle Hiram." He also filled in on bass for Mauldin whenever she had "standin' troubles," as Bill described it (painful varicose veins).[164]

Meanwhile, after ignoring Bill for nearly a year and a half, Decca asked him to record covers of two recent country releases, Jimmy Newman's "A Fallen Star" (on Dot) and Jim Reeves's "Four Walls" (RCA Victor). Neither had entered the charts yet, but both were considered likely hits. Rather than jeopardize his relationship with Decca, Bill agreed to do it, and his twenty-fifth session for the label followed on Saturday morning, April 20. By this time, Bill had heard Newman sing "A Fallen Star" several times at the tent show. Studio fiddler Tommy Jackson twinned with Gordon Terry on it, but Terry played an appropriately bluesy solo fiddle on "Four Walls." Bill was fortunate to have Joe Stuart on guitar, capable of the distinctive playing on the latter.[165]

Bill's First Album

Bill's handling of these songs appears to have opened Decca's eyes to a singer who had been silenced long enough. Arrangements were made for him to record an album, something several fellow *Opry* members had already accomplished at this point: Hank Snow and Ernest Tubb had two; Roy Acuff, the Louvin Brothers, Webb Pierce, Kitty Wells, and Del Wood each had one. Work on Bill's first, to feature his solo singing, was due to begin in mid-May.[166]

At the beginning of May, former Blue Grass Boy Les Sandy called Bill at the *Opry*. "I told him I wanted to go back to work with him and he told me to come on up there." As it turned out, there wasn't much work then, but there were a few showdates after Bill's upcoming sessions, so Sandy stuck around.[167]

On the afternoon of Tuesday, May 14, almost the same group that had recorded on April 20 returned. Three fiddles were again called for, so another studio fiddler, Dale Potter, joined Jackson and Terry. Potter reportedly took charge, telling the others what to play and assigning Terry to play all of the bluesy fills. First on the agenda was "A Good Woman's Love," written by pop-country songwriter Cy Coben (né Cyrus Cohen of New Jersey). Hank Locklin had the original release (RCA Victor) in 1956, but Bill's rendition would make the song a standard. Next was another Jimmy Newman song, "Cry, Cry Darlin," this one Newman himself had written. Arnold Terry's use of it as a solo in 1955–56 probably caught Bill's ear. And last was the original bluegrass recording of the folk blues "Sittin' on Top of the World" ("Sittin'" sung as "Settin'"), which Bill might have learned from the Light Crust Doughboys at KARK in Little Rock in 1938 (and which Decca confused in its credits with the pop song "I'm Sittin' on Top of the World").[168]

It may not have been known until the last minute that Tommy Jackson couldn't make it to the next session on Wednesday afternoon, May 15. Again fortunately for Bill, Joe Stuart could play fiddle, so the three-fiddle sound could be maintained, and Les Sandy was available to play guitar, his skill with the instrument Bill knew well. "Many times I'd see Bill playing [backstage] and I'd pick up the guitar and play along with him," Sandy said.[169]

Six songs needed to be recorded that day. Everyone involved ignored a musicians' union regulation, limiting sessions to three hours, in order to do it. They played an hour or so longer and were paid for two sessions, one falsely dated May 5 on official forms. They cut the six songs quickly, as a comment by Stover suggests: "When I went down there to [record] with Monroe, there wasn't no rehearsing going on—just 'Here's what we're doing next.'" Three of the six ("Goodbye Old Pal," "Molly and Tenbrooks," and "Come Back to Me in My Dreams") were remakes and needed little rehearsal ("Molly and Tenbrooks" the second "classic bluegrass band" song rerecorded by Bill). The other half needed rehearsing, beginning with "Out in the Cold World," which Bill probably learned from a 1930 McFarland and Gardner recording. He once said he learned the next song, the traditional east Tennessee murder ballad "Roane County Prison," from Tommy Magness in 1940. Finally there was Bill's "In Despair," with a trio chorus. Intriguingly, Bill used the same mandolin tuning as 1953's "Get Up John" (lowest to highest: F#A, DD, AA, AD) to play his break.[170]

Sandy left shortly after the session. Stover lasted about another month, unhappy with the way Bill used his band members: "Sometimes he'd call over to the hotel room and say, 'Let's go,' and we'd figure we were going out to do a show. In the end, we'd be over on his farm, plowing with a mule or loading hay bales." After Stover left, Stuart again picked banjo and Bill relied on several talented but less experienced guitarists–lead singers, including Ernie Graves of Morristown, Tennessee, and Bill "Chum" Duncan of Charleston, West Virginia (whom Bill nicknamed to distinguish between the two of them).[171]

Into this less-than-ideal situation in the summer of 1957 came fiddler Kenny Baker. Luckily for Bill, Baker was more concerned with learning to play bluegrass than with the quality of the band: "I decided before I ever went there, I just knew I could play that kind of music without even thinking about it. I found out that I didn't know near what I thought I did." Eventually, he spoke to Bill about it: "I was trying to make myself believe that I couldn't play what he wanted. . . . I explained to Bill that I couldn't put the stuff in there. . . . He said, 'Now, don't listen to what somebody else is playing. You play what you feel and what you hear. That's why I want you.'" Soon, Bill was telling him about some fiddle tunes he'd learned in Kentucky: "After I got to playing his stuff a little bit, he told me about these old numbers of his Uncle Pen's. He said he was saving them back for the right fiddler, the man he thought could play them and do them right."[172]

Stover's complaint about working on Bill's farm reveals the increased activities on the Goodlettsville property. Earlier in 1957, son James, then sixteen, had provided a place for those hay bales to be loaded: he and a friend disassembled a barn on the Dickerson Road farm and transported the pieces to Goodlettsville, where workmen put it back together. Financial hard times also caused Bill and the band to use the property as living quarters: lead singer Duncan said he swept out a stall in the dairy barn and asked Bill for a mattress. "He went to town and came back with four new mattresses tied on top of his car." Duncan recalled that Baker and his family lived on the property too, "in a little house on up the holler" that had been recently built (about seventy-five yards from the old cabin). Bill and Mauldin had planned to live in it, but to provide for the Bakers, they moved into the cabin instead. Then, in July, Bill's 1956 Cadillac was repossessed (he would later be sued for nearly $2,000 when it didn't sell for the amount he owed on it). He and the band began using Mauldin's 1956 Buick.[173]

On October 4, 1957, the Soviet Union launched the first man-made satellite, "Sputnik," into orbit around the Earth. Three days later, Columbia Records released the first bluegrass album, *Foggy Mountain Jamboree*, by Flatt and Scruggs. It was, however, not really new: eleven of its twelve selections were recorded between 1951 and 1955, and only one, "Shuckin' the Corn," was recorded in 1957. Meanwhile, Bill's first album languished. The reason for the delay isn't known. Bill may have wanted 1954's "Plant Some Flowers" and 1955's "Used to Be" to be released on it, while Decca continued to insist on all new material.[174]

Carlton Haney, briefly Bill's manager in 1955, was now manager of one of bluegrass music's most successful bands, Reno and Smiley and the Tennessee Cut-Ups. One reason for their success was the *Old Dominion Barn Dance*, an *Opry*-style show broadcast on 50,000-watt WRVA from the Lyric Theater in Richmond, Virginia, heard throughout the Eastern Seaboard. When the show folded in early 1957, Haney organized its replacement, the *New Dominion Barn Dance*, which debuted in the same location on Saturday night, October 19, 1957.[175]

Subsequently, Haney brought Reno and Smiley to Nashville in November 1957 for a guest appearance on the *Opry*, during the annual DJ Convention.

Haney said later he had been ambivalent about bluegrass, but his experience that night changed his mind:

> [W]hile we was backstage, Don [Reno] had the banjo and . . . Chubby Wise was in that dressing room [then working with Hank Snow] . . . and Jimmy Martin was there, and I asked Jimmy Martin and Bill to sing a couple of duets like they used to, and Don was gonna play banjo and Red [Smiley] was there, too, with the guitar, and they decided to do "Live and Let Live" [one of the songs Bill and Pete Pyle planned to record in 1941, but no one present had recorded yet]. Jimmy started it twice and Bill stopped both times, and then Bill said, "Let me start it," and when he started it, it was in [an] entirely different time than I'd ever heard music in, and that must have been the first time that I really got interested in bluegrass.[176]

By then, it appears Decca had persuaded Bill to record three new songs to complete his first album. The label had learned that Dot was about to release the second bluegrass album, Mac Wiseman's 'Tis Sweet to Be Remembered, a collection of his recordings from 1951–54, and it responded by issuing Bill's "Molly and Tenbrooks" / "Sittin' on Top of the World," a single promoting the release of his first album. It also appears that one of Bill's new songs was chosen at the last minute, as recalled by singer-songwriter Doug Kershaw, who with brother Rusty had recently joined the *Opry*.

> December 14, 1957, I wrote "Sally-Jo." That night, backstage at the *Opry*, in one of the small dressing rooms at the Ryman Auditorium, I was sitting on the floor with my guitar, with my back to the door, singing this brand-new song. When I finished singing, I hear this most recognizable voice say, "Boy, meet me [tomorrow] at Decca Records studio. I want to record that song," and he walked away. I stuck my head out the door to make sure it was Bill Monroe, and it was. Bill kept walking, then turned his head and said, "And bring that hot guitar lick with you."[177]

The next afternoon, they met at the studio. Bill was lacking a guitarist–lead singer ("Chum" Duncan had left in October), so he used Kershaw and his "lick" on "Sally-Jo" and the other songs recorded at the session, "Brand New Shoes" and "A Lonesome Road (to Travel)." Country singer George Jones had shown "Shoes" to Bill, and Bill's friend Joe Stuart had written "A Lonesome Road." Kershaw played his guitar in an open D tuning on "Sally-Jo" (lowest to highest: D, G, D, G, B, D), capoed at the seventh fret, but he used standard tuning on the others. Jimmy Elrod, a recent addition to the Clinch Mountain Clan of new *Opry* members Wilma Lee and Stoney Cooper, was brought in to pick banjo, allowing Stuart to twin with Baker. By suppertime on December 15, Bill's first album was completed (but it would not be released until June 1958).[178]

Stuart left the band shortly thereafter. His replacement on banjo was an eighteen-year-old picker whom Don Reno had recommended, Earl Snead of Danville, Virginia. "It was exciting to me," he said later, "being right off the farm in Virginia and getting to play with Bill Monroe and be on the *Grand Ole Opry*. That was my greatest ambition, my greatest dream as a young man, and I fulfilled it." But plans would soon be hatched to record an album without banjo.[179]

Recording a Gospel Album

Owen Bradley had just become Bill's producer at Decca—Paul Cohen had moved on to new subsidiary Coral—and it appears Bradley (also vice president of Decca's Nashville division) decided the label would enter the bluegrass LP market in 1958 with a splash—releasing back-to-back Bill Monroe albums, one secular and one sacred, like the EPs in 1957. All Bill needed to do was record a gospel album as soon as possible.

Bill again contacted Edd Mayfield, offering him "the little house up the holler" if he would come back, a rent-free place where he and his family could live in Nashville. Mayfield was then one of only a few lead singer-guitarists capable of successfully recording an album of gospel songs with Bill, particularly one using the accompaniment of just mandolin and guitar. "He was a wonderful guitar man and a wonderful singer, I thought," Bill said later. "I thought he was as good as I ever had." Charlie Smith, who had filled in on fiddle several times at the *Opry*, served as lead singer-guitarist until Mayfield arrived in mid-February 1958.[180]

The album was recorded in four three-song sessions on February 25 and March 19, 20, and 21. Gordon Terry, who had sung bass on "You're Drifting Away" and "Get Down on Your Knees and Pray" in 1951, sang bass on the first session, but bass singer Culley Holt, one of the original Jordanaires, sang on the others. Baker sang baritone, helped by Holt: "When I'd go to singin', if I needed to go up to get my part, he'd point up. If it was down, he'd point down. He kept me in line—I watched him all the time." Producer Bradley played organ on four songs (prominently on only two, "Life's Railway to Heaven" and "Precious Memories"), a sound influenced by one of the best-selling country albums of the 1950s, Tennessee Ernie Ford's *Hymns* (Capitol), released in 1956.[181]

Helping speed the recording process was the fact that those involved were at least familiar with the twelve songs, all of which others had previously recorded—"Life's Railway to Heaven" as early as 1918 on cylinder. Bill once said he learned "Wayfaring Stranger" from Charlie Cline (Tennessee Ernie Ford included a variant, "Wayfaring Pilgrim," on his *Spirituals*, a companion album of *Hymns*). Newest were Hank Williams's songs "I Saw the Light" and "House of Gold," both included on a Williams gospel album, *I Saw the Light* (MGM), released posthumously in 1956.[182]

In February 1958, as Bill was preparing to record, King appears to have appropriated Decca's plan, releasing back-to-back Reno and Smiley albums, *Sacred Songs* and *Instrumentals*. Then Mercury released three bluegrass albums at once, *Gospel Quartet Favorites* by Carl Story and the Rambling Mountaineers, *Country Pickin' and Singin'* by the Stanley Brothers, and *Country Music* by Flatt and Scruggs. At that point, Flatt and Scruggs and Reno and Smiley had two albums; the Stanleys, Carl Story, and Mac Wiseman each had one. Bill still had none.[183]

In New York City that spring, the Greenbriar Boys, one of the first "city bluegrass bands," was formed. Lead singer-guitarist John Herald (né Serabian), then nineteen, had traveled to Nashville in 1957 to see Bill on the *Opry*. With nineteen-year-old Eric Weissberg on mandolin and twenty-one-year-old Bob Yellin on banjo, the threesome played regularly at what Yellin called "the gathering of folkies" in New York's Washington Square Park on Sunday afternoons.[184]

After the gospel album was recorded, Bill returned to the studio on Tuesday, April 8, 1958, and, possibly taking a cue from Reno and Smiley's *Instrumentals* album, recorded two instrumentals, "Panhandle Country" and "Scotland." Snead had just left the band, so Joe Drumright filled in on banjo. Hicks was in town on leave from the army, so he played harmony fiddle to Baker's lead. "Panhandle Country" came from Dave Akeman in the 1940s, and Bill had played it for his own amusement since then, but now that someone in the band was actually from the Texas panhandle (Mayfield), Bill decided to record it. Mayfield nearly "stole the show" with his walking-bass-styled guitar break, played using just a thumbpick. "Scotland" was a new composition by Bill, and working it out in the studio reportedly took a long time.[185]

The next day, Bill and the band began playing a series of drive-ins and movie theaters in Kentucky, Alabama, and Tennessee that extended through

May. On Sunday, April 20, they took a side trip to Bean Blossom for the Brown County Jamboree. The following afternoon there was a fire in the Jamboree Barn, possibly caused by the overheated chimney of one of the barn's wood stoves, according to Jamboree historian Adler. Luckily discovered soon after it started, it was quickly extinguished by firefighters. Most of the damage was smoke and water related, but a section of the roof caved in. "I think they repaired it quickly," Adler said, "though some charring was evident to observers inside the barn from then on." The Jamboree reopened on May 18, featuring Porter Wagoner and Bill.[186]

Picking banjo with Bill at that show was another young picker from Virginia, nineteen-year-old Eddie Adcock (hired in late April–early May). He had already played with several bands, including Mac Wiseman and the Country Boys on the *Old Dominion Barn Dance* in 1954, but times had changed.

> I was with Bill . . . at a time when he wasn't drawing flies. That's not to say anything bad about him, because all of bluegrass music was rough then. We worked some places that didn't even have floors. Sometimes I went two or three days without food. I helped Bill on his farm also. We would work six to eight hours during a day and then we would go do a show that night.

Adcock said that Baker left the band just as he arrived in Nashville ("He was coming down the stairs of the Clarkston as I was going up"), and Red Taylor returned. Mauldin didn't play bass during this time, due to a spat she and Bill were having (and he couldn't remember the name of her substitute). Adcock would leave the band near the end of June.[187]

On June 23, 1958, six months after recordings for it were completed, Decca finally released Bill's first album, *Knee Deep in Blue Grass*, its title an apparent play on the title of a 1957 Marty Robbins hit, "Knee Deep in the Blues" (Columbia). According to its liner notes, "After becoming a mandolin expert, Bill formed the Blue Grass Boys and the group soon was singing, playing and performing for several miles around Rosine, Kentucky, his home town."[188]

The Death of Edd Mayfield

Barely two weeks after Bill's long-awaited first album was available, on July 7, 1958, thirty-two-year-old Edd Mayfield died of leukemia while on the road. The week before, Bill and the band (just Mayfield and Red Taylor) were scheduled to play a series of shows in southern West Virginia and western

Virginia with singer-guitarist Melvin Goins and his brother, banjoist Ray Goins, formerly of the Lonesome Pine Fiddlers, then playing on their own in Bluefield, West Virginia.

> We left Nashville one time from the farm [Bill said]. I could tell [Mayfield] was looking bad. He didn't look good. We got up the road and I could tell there was something coming in on him. We went on into Pulaski, Virginia [in western Virginia]. We went to a hospital and they couldn't take him in there some way—I don't know why. We went on into Bluefield [just across the line to the north], and I took him to see a doctor and they put him in the hospital there [Bluefield Sanitarium]. So then they come back to me and told me he had about three days to live. I went to calling all his people, got his wife to come on up there from Nashville [on a Greyhound bus].
>
> He's a fellow who really loved watermelon and I asked him what he'd like to have that day and he said, "Some watermelon." So I went and got him some watermelon and brought it back to him. He went to eating some and liked it, and then I told him that watermelon was from Kentucky. You know, we used to kid each other about Kentucky and Texas. [When] I told him that watermelon was from Kentucky, he laughed and said, "That's the best kind, ain't it?"

Bill recalled that a local preacher, a Brother Lambert, had phoned him to offer his help:

> So I taken him on to the hospital and I introduced Edd to him, and then I went out, and he asked Edd could he pray for him, and it was all right with him. So, [the next day] on the Fourth of July, [the preacher] went with me [to a show Bill played while Mayfield was in the hospital] and all that day, Edd was askin' for this preacher. So when we got back, he wanted the preacher to pray for him. When [Lambert] came out that time, Edd told him that he could see the big gates opening up, and he must have knowed that time was really gettin' close or somethin'.

Bill called Mauldin in Nashville, and she drove Mayfield's young sons to the hospital. "They were there about fifteen minutes before he closed his eyes," Bill said. "He told everybody he wanted to go to sleep. But he spoke to [his sons] and called them his darling little boys, Freddie and Carl. And that was the last he ever said to anybody."[189]

On August 11, Bill's gospel album *I Saw the Light* was released (finally giving Bill two albums like Flatt and Scruggs and Reno and Smiley). Through the years, it would be considered one of Bill's best albums, even though it lacks banjo and fiddle. Only later would there be recognition for the contributions a Texas cowboy had made to it. In 1958 Edd Mayfield's name wasn't mentioned in its liner notes. Instead, Bill's supposed accompaniment was praised: "He is ably assisted by some fine banjo playing that makes one feel as though he were seated by the campfire just after dusk."[190]

Little is known of Bill's activities from July 7 through August 11, other than playing the *Opry*, with Charlie Smith on guitar. Red Cravens, who cheered for the band two years earlier, traveled to Crawfordsville (near Indianapolis), Indiana, in mid-July 1958, to see Bill at the Montgomery County Fair. Cravens said Bill was alone, and he wasn't sure how Bill got there. Bill recognized Cravens from his visits to the Brown County Jamboree; Cravens volunteered to play guitar. They sat down backstage to rehearse, and Bill told him about Mayfield. "Instead of rehearsing, we talked about birth and death and philosophy and religion, and he was like my guru," said Cravens (today a Hindu), "only he said, 'You'd better get saved,' and all this." Bill's show lasted an hour and he did all the singing, mainly older songs. Afterward, Cravens said he told Bill he ought to do the old songs more often, but that Bill said, "That's in the past. You gotta keep looking forward. . . . Don't look back."[191]

By mid-August, Bill and Mauldin had made up and she was again playing bass. Bill called Roger Smith in Indiana (Red Taylor had left), asking him to fiddle on a tour that included Bill's first appearance on Carlton Haney's *New Dominion Barn Dance* in Richmond, Virginia. Smith said Bill was having financial problems, judging by the inexperienced fill-in he had on guitar, a non-union musician who was paid whatever Bill could afford to pay. At the *Barn Dance*, Smith fiddled, then switched to banjo on "Molly and Tenbrooks," due, he said, to Bill's not wanting to pay union scale to banjo players there. The next day, at New River Ranch, Smith said Bill had Bill Emerson (then with the Country Gentlemen) fill in on banjo because he was not yet in the musicians' union. During the next two days, Don Reno guested on guitar at shows in Virginia, and Smith thinks Bill had to borrow money from him to get back to Nashville.[192]

Bill continued to minimize expenses at the *Opry*, using union musicians paid by WSM (including Jackie Phelps on guitar). Soon, a talented group of regulars formed: Charlie Smith on fiddle, Joe Drumright on banjo, and lead singer-guitarist Connie Gately, playing together locally as Connie and Joe and the Backwoods Boys. They couldn't play the road—Smith was a student at Vanderbilt; Drumright and Gately had high-level jobs in local industry—so they were happy to be able to play with Bill and rub elbows with other *Opry* favorites. "At the Ryman," Gately said, "Bill had a room where we would rehearse and then, right around the corner, Flatt and Scruggs, who didn't have a room, rehearsed out in the hall. And Joe and I would sneak out there and listen to 'em and chat with 'em, and Bill would say, 'That's not your corner. Get back in the room here.'" Gately added humorously, "Bill didn't beat on us much. I guess he knew we didn't have to do it and, in a way, we were doing him a favor since he didn't have a [full-time] band, and we were adequate. It was very enjoyable for us, however."[193]

Bobby Hicks returned from the army in early October, played with Bill on the road, and twinned with Smith at the *Opry*. Gately recalled the brief return of Charlie Cline, just out of the navy. Cline played guitar on the road, but on the *Opry* he had to play bass while Gately played guitar. "He didn't particularly like that," said Gately, so Cline didn't stay long.[194]

On a Saturday afternoon, November 1, Charlie Smith and Bill went to Hank Snow's music store at Eighth Avenue North and Church Street in Nashville, and Bill arranged for his F-5 to be sent back to Gibson again, this time to have several worn frets replaced, instead of the entire fingerboard. On the *Opry* that night, Bill began playing Gately's Gibson F-4, a mellower-sounding mandolin than the F-5. Two days later, on November 3, "Scotland" appeared in *Billboard*'s "Hot C&W Sides" chart at number 27 (of 30). It only lasted a week, but sales may have eased financial burdens somewhat.[195]

On the road that month, Bill was approached by guitarist-singer Jack Cooke, a twenty-one-year-old western Virginia native then playing bass with the Stanley Brothers. Cooke auditioned singing "Live and Let Live" (which Bill had still not recorded), and Bill called him about two weeks later. According to modest Cooke, "I think—in fact, I'm convinced—it was my guitar playin' that got me my job with Bill."[196]

Near the end of November, Bill brought Cooke and eighteen-year-old banjo player Robert "Buddy" Pennington, also from western Virginia, to the *Opry*. They had been working with him on the road but didn't belong to the local musicians' union yet. "They couldn't play [their instruments] on the *Opry*," Gately said, "so Joe [Drumright] and I played and they sung with him." Bill was ready to have a full-time band again, and Gately recalled how he broke the news: "Bill told Joe and me that he wasn't going to be using us for awhile and that he would call us when the opportunity arose." The next stop for Cooke and Pennington was the headquarters of the American Federation of Musicians, Local 257, in Nashville.[197]

Bill's next session, on December 1, 1958, was probably due to his chart success with "Scotland." Cooke and Pennington had joined the union, and Hicks fiddled solo (twin fiddling partner Smith was at officer-training school in Florida). Recorded first was "Gotta Travel On," appearing to accommodate the current popularity of commercial folk music. (The Kingston Trio's "Tom Dooley" had arrived on *Billboard*'s "Hot 100 Chart" at the end of September.) But Gately (whose F-4 mandolin Bill used on the session) remembered Bill singing "Gotta Travel On" when Billy Grammer's hit recording was released in October (on Monument), suggesting it was simply a song he liked. "No One But My Darlin'," based on a song banjoman Hubert Davis had given to Bill, was almost completely reworked over the course of several years. "Big Mon," which Bill composed in 1955, not long after the "Used To Be" session, was resurrected due to a recent reunion of Hicks and Cline (in the band when it was composed). Last was "Monroe's Hornpipe," which Charlie Smith recalled learning several months before it was recorded: "I was amazed that [Bill] recorded it on Connie's F-4, since it sounded so much better on his F-5."[198]

A single of "Gotta Travel On" and "No One But My Darlin'" was released quickly, on December 28 ("Big Mon" and "Monroe's Hornpipe" would not be released for seven years). That month, Ralph Rinzler had returned to the United States to enroll in pre-med studies at Columbia University in New York City.[199]

Decca, sensing a hit in "Gotta Travel On," probably wanted to have a follow-up ready, so they scheduled another session for January 30, 1959. Needing an instrumental but possibly busy writing a new song, Bill delegated Smith, just back from Florida, to compose a tune around an idea he'd had. "See what you can do with this," he said, strumming all of the strings on his mandolin down and up twice with a quick final downstroke.[200]

Just before the session, Bill called for a January 28 rehearsal in Studio D of the National Life building. But they worked on only two numbers, the as-yet-unnamed fiddle tune Smith had devised and the new song Bill had written, "Dark As the Night, Blue As the Day." On the latter, Smith recalled that Hicks suggested the intricate fiddle harmonies and double-time passages, and that he and Hicks often retreated to a corner of the room to work them out. With Bill's F-5 still at the Gibson factory, Smith borrowed a Gibson F-12 mandolin from local musician Bill Thomas for Bill to play, an instrument that sounded remarkably like the F-5.[201]

The session of Friday, January 30, ran about thirty minutes over the three-hour limit (for which the musicians were paid overtime), probably due to the time it took to rehearse two songs the band had never heard before. The first was "When the Phone Rang," written by Joe Hudgins, then driving

Opry star Marty Robbins's bus in exchange for singing on his shows. Second was "Tomorrow I'll Be Gone," written by Wilma Lee Cooper, who was there to hear her song recorded. These were followed by the two the band had rehearsed, Bill's "Dark As the Night" and the fiddle tune (Bill later titled it "Stoney Lonesome," the name of a small community between Columbus and Nashville, Indiana, just off State Route 46, the road he often took to Bean Blossom).[202]

"Folksong '59"

Bill's F-5 was returned to him in February or March 1959, and around that time, he was asked to be part of "Folksong '59," a concert to be presented in April at Carnegie Hall by folklorist Alan Lomax, co-producer of *Smoky Mountain Ballads*, the album that introduced the Monroe Brothers to folk music enthusiasts in 1941. The concert would demonstrate his then-novel view that authentic folk music existed in many contemporary forms, including blues, rock and roll, and bluegrass. Recently repatriated to the United States, Lomax had left the country after his involvement with the left-leaning Progressive Party in the presidential campaign of 1948. As his friend Ralph Rinzler later revealed, "Alan asked Bill Monroe to come to ["Folksong '59"] and Bill associated Alan with radical politics and told me later that he didn't accept the invitation to play at that concert because he distrusted Alan's politics." Instead, on April 3, 1959, a regional band Mike Seeger recommended to Lomax, Earl Taylor and the Stoney Mountain Boys, became the first bluegrass band to play Carnegie Hall, thrilling the urban audience with their music, much of it derived from Bill.[203]

At the time, Bill was enjoying success in mainstream country music. His "Gotta Travel On" appeared in *Billboard*'s "Hot C&W Sides" chart at number 24 on March 2, climbing to number 15 by mid-April, his most impressive performance ever in a *Billboard* country-singles chart (and his last appearance there). He was also on the road a lot, including a third trip to California in April. One show there was especially memorable: at Rose Maddox's "101 Club" in Oceanside (near San Diego), Bill met the White brothers—mandolinist Roland, age twenty, bassist Eric, eighteen, and guitarist Clarence, fourteen. Once the "Three Little Country Boys," a novelty act, they were now the "Country Boys," a bluegrass band with Billy Ray Lathum, twenty-one, on banjo. Maddox invited them to play a guest set, and afterward, Bill paid them a high compliment, saying, "That's mighty fine, boys."[204]

Mountain Music Bluegrass Style

In May 1959, Folkways released the *Mountain Music Bluegrass Style* album, the first attempt to explain bluegrass music, produced by Mike Seeger. In its accompanying booklet, Seeger provided a history of the music and was the first to praise Bill's band of 1946–48 in print: "But not until Bill Monroe, Earl Scruggs, Lester Flatt, and Chubby Wise came together after World War II did the Bluegrass band take its classic and most competent form." Seeger was also the first to acknowledge the growing public perception of Bill, noting that he was "called the father of bluegrass" (which, he later told the author, he recalled seeing on a poster advertising one of Bill's shows).[205]

Bobby Hicks left in late May 1959. Now married, with a daughter, he took a job with one of the busier *Opry* stars, Porter Wagoner. "[Bill] just said he understood that I had to leave," Hicks said later, "'cause I wasn't making no money with him" (not enough to support a family). Charlie Smith was suddenly Bill's only fiddler, and a summer break at Vanderbilt allowed him to play the *Opry* and the road for a couple of weeks in June.[206]

On July 12 Earl Scruggs appeared without Lester Flatt or the Foggy Mountain Boys at the first Newport Folk Festival. Recordings from that day were released on a *Folk Festival at Newport* album (Vanguard), and promotional efforts by Flatt and Scruggs's agent, Scruggs's wife Louise Scruggs, clearly had an effect on the writer of its liner notes: "This fabled banjo picker, whose style has influenced so many others, has been responsible, more than any other single artist, perhaps, for the upsurge in the interest in Bluegrass music."[207]

Bill, meanwhile, lost the services of Charlie Smith in July 1959, when Smith went on a navy cruise. Dale Potter and Kenny Baker each fiddled for brief spells, Potter becoming a full-fledged member of the Blue Grass Boys on the road. Buddy Pennington left, and Joe Stuart returned to pick banjo.[208]

In August, the Brown County Jamboree property was finally paid off. Fifty-eight-year-old Birch, who, as its manager since 1952, had survived Carlton Haney, a bout of pneumonia, and a fire, was formally designated its owner (to avoid Bill's liability during tough financial times or, as Adler suggested in *Bean Blossom*, to prevent Bill from losing it in a divorce settlement).[209]

The *Esquire* Article

Bill celebrated his forty-eighth birthday on Sunday, September 13, 1959. Later that month, the October issue of *Esquire* contained a brief (one-page) and oft-cited article by "Folksong '59" producer Alan Lomax, "Bluegrass Background: Folk Music with Overdrive." Louise Scruggs's influence was apparent here as well:

> Bluegrass style began in 1945 when Bill Monroe, of the Monroe Brothers, recruited a quintet that included Earl Scruggs (who had perfected a three-finger banjo style now known as "picking scruggs") and Lester Flatt (a Tennessee guitar picker and singer); Bill led the group with mandolin and a countertenor voice that hits high notes with the impact of a Louis Armstrong trumpet. Playing the old-time mountain tunes, which most hillbilly pros had abandoned, he orchestrated them so brilliantly that the name of the outfit, "Bill Monroe and his Bluegrass Boys," became the permanent hallmark of this field.

Lomax, although well-meaning, knew little about bluegrass music and drew several false conclusions about it: that it had begun in 1945, that it featured "old-time mountain tunes," that Bill was simply an arranger, and that the name of his band was somehow directly related to the name of the music.[210]

Bill had no spokesman or publicist to reveal the truth about him or his music, and even though he'd just been recognized in a national publication, he continued to avoid promoting himself in any way. Instead, it would take someone who was given complete authority to act as his manager to enlighten listeners about him. This enlightenment was still three or four years in the future, but an important step toward it came in the fall of 1959, when Ralph Rinzler joined the Greenbriar Boys on mandolin in New York City.[211]

In Nashville that fall, Joe Stuart left the band again, leaving Bill in need of a banjo picker. Charlie Smith, back from his cruise, fiddled with Bill and other bands, and introduced Bill to the lead singer-guitarist of one, Tennessee native Jimmy Maynard. Bill began using Maynard on the road and, through him, met banjoist Curtis McPeake. A fellow native Tennessean, McPeake had filled in for Earl Scruggs with Lester Flatt when Scruggs was seriously injured in a 1955 car accident and, by 1959, was freelancing full time with several bands in Nashville.[212]

Decca released the "Gotta Travel On" follow-up single, "Tomorrow I'll Be Gone" / "Dark As the Night, Blue As the Day," on October 19, but it went nowhere (and neither song would ever be released on a Decca album). Two weeks later, Saturday, October 31, was Bill's twentieth anniversary on the *Opry* (where Alabama native Ottis "Ott" Devine had recently replaced D. Kilpatrick as manager).[213]

Twenty-year-old Paul Anthony "Tony" Ellis arrived in Nashville in November to audition for the banjo job, yet another picker Reno recommended from Virginia (Ellis, born in North Carolina, was raised in Virginia). That morning, reaching into his shaving kit, he sliced open the tip of his left middle finger on the blade of his safety razor. It was bleeding as he picked with Bill and Cooke in Studio A of the National Life building. Bill's reaction when told of the injury: "'Hmm,'" Ellis said, "That was it. No sympathy at all." However, he did have compassion for a youngster who was "scared to death."

> [Bill] could see that I was nervous. He gave me a chance to calm down. He [and Mauldin, who was there but didn't play] went to lunch for about two hours and he told Jack Cooke to go over some tunes with me, to show me the way he wanted them played. Jack worked with me a long time, with backup, breaks, phrasing. I wouldn't have made it if Jack Cooke hadn't helped me like he did. . . . Just everything, right down to the finest detail.

When Bill returned, they picked again and he said, "Now, that's the way I want it played." Earlier, Ellis had been courteous with Mauldin (opening a door for her, finding her a chair). After they picked, Bill told him two others had already auditioned, but that Mauldin liked him best, so he could have the job. However, Ellis wouldn't hear from him for several weeks, and except for a brief visit to see his grandmother in Knoxville, Ellis remained at the Clarkston Hotel, waiting for Bill's call.[214]

Joe Drumright had been filling in on banjo prior to McPeake and Ellis, so he played on Bill's session of November 25, 1959, another "end of the year" outing for Decca. Benny Martin played twin fiddles with Potter on the first song of the session, Martin's only recording with Bill; Cooke played guitar, and Mauldin played bass. They recorded three songs, all vocal solos by Bill: "Lonesome Wind Blues," written by Wayne Raney, who recorded it for King in 1947; "Thinking About You," co-written by Bill with Lee Fikes (who later wrote "Milwaukee, Here I Come," a hit for George Jones in 1968); and "Come Go with Me," written by country singer Marty Robbins, who never recorded it. Cooke left the band afterward.[215]

Bill finally called Ellis at the Clarkston in December. He said they'd be going out on a tour after the first of the year, so Ellis hung on.[216]

CHAPTER SIX
1960-1969

The Country Music Association

By 1960, country music had survived the rock and roll it helped to foster. But to survive, it adopted the standards of mainstream pop, with saccharine background vocals and instrumental accompaniments, creating a style so prevalent it was given a name, the "Nashville Sound." The recently formed Country Music Association (CMA) was promoting the style, which typically excluded fiddle, banjo, or other "hillbilly" elements. As a result, bluegrass suddenly seemed more out of step than ever before.[1]

It was good to have friends in high places, especially country stars not reliant on the Nashville Sound like Johnny Cash, now a major star. He invited Bill on one of his tours in late January 1960 that began in Winnipeg, capital of Manitoba province in central Canada. Bill and the band (Ellis, Mauldin, Potter, and fill-in guitarist Jimmy Byrd) drove through a blizzard in Mauldin's 1959 Oldsmobile station wagon to get there. During the first night, Potter suffered a stroke and was taken to a local hospital. Gordon Terry was part of Cash's show then, so Bill still had a capable fiddler during the rest of the two-week tour to Saskatchewan province, Montana, Iowa, Nebraska, and Kansas.[2]

Maude and Bertha

On the way back to Nashville, Bill told Ellis about a place where he could get a room cheap, a rooming house where his sisters Maude and Bertha lived.

Bill dropped him off at 16 Academy Place, near General Hospital, and for the next year or so, Ellis would be treated like the son neither Maude, sixty-one, nor Bertha, fifty-one, ever had. "They were two very sweet, old, country ladies, just as sweet as they could be," Ellis said. Bertha would make breakfast every morning with duck and goose eggs that Bill supplied, fried potatoes, and toast. Both sisters had worked at the hospital, but now Maude was "very feeble" and not able to work. She and Ellis became "close buddies," he said. Bill seldom spent time with his sisters, Ellis said. "He was always in a hurry."[3]

At that point, the door of mainstream country music was closing on bluegrass, but another was opening. The folk music revival, with its college-aged devotees, was now keenly interested in "the first clear-cut orchestral style to appear in the British-American folk tradition in five hundred years," as Lomax referred to bluegrass in *Esquire*, and "city bands" were proliferating. On March 5, the first college concert featuring bluegrass was held at Antioch College in Yellow Springs (near Dayton), Ohio, promoted by Jeremy Foster, who had taped Bill's shows in 1956, and starring the Osborne Brothers, then living in Dayton and recording for MGM Records. Then, in April, the Greenbriar Boys journeyed to the Old-Time Fiddlers' Convention in Union Grove, North Carolina. During the convention, Ralph Rinzler's first trip to the South, he happened to meet Clarence Ashley, who'd recorded in the 1920s, and Rinzler made plans to return in September to make new recordings of him.[4]

That summer, Bill's music also inspired two rockabillies to climb high in the *Billboard* charts. The Fendermen, a duo from Minnesota (Phil Humphrey, lead singer, and Jim Sundquist, lead guitarist) recorded Bill's arrangement of "Mule Skinner Blues" for the Minneapolis label Soma. In their version, the water boy is told to bring his "buck-buck-bucket down" and the yodel becomes a "hee-haw" laugh (later heard in the *Hee Haw* TV show theme). Released in May 1960, it peaked at number 5 in "The *Billboard* Hot 100" on July 11 and soon appeared in the "Hot C&W Sides" chart, reaching number 16 (of 30), almost as high as Bill's "Gotta Travel On." But Bill would not profit from its success; arrangements can't be copyrighted.[5]

For Bill and the band that summer of 1960 "there was enough work to stay reasonably busy," Ellis recalled. "It was two or three nights a week, usually weekends." They often played a square dance in Murfreesboro (hosted by Carl Tipton) on Friday night, plus the *Opry* on Saturday night, and "that was about it," said Ellis. Sometimes, they'd play a movie theater on Tuesday or Wednesday in a neighboring state: "I liked that 'cause I'd get to see a movie and eat popcorn." Potter had recovered from his stroke and was again fiddling with Bill on the *Opry*. Others fiddled on the road, including Billy Baker, a cousin of Kenny Baker from western Virginia, and Joe Stuart. Ellis recalled that during this time, Bill turned down lucrative offers from WSM's Artist Service Bureau for *Opry* package shows because he was unwilling to pay the Bureau's 15 percent commission. Eventually, due to the scarcity of work, Ellis took a leave of absence in August, interrupted by Bill's asking him to play bass on a few shows with Tennessee native Porter Church picking banjo.[6]

On Sundays that summer, Bill often drove up to the Brown County Jamboree by himself. If he wanted to play, he knew good musicians were there to back him up: Red Cravens and the Bray Brothers from Champaign, Illinois (Cravens, guitar; Francis Bray, bass; Harley Bray, banjo; and Nate Bray, mandolin). Now the house band, they backed Bill up many times, but were never paid extra for it. According to Cravens, "If you want to be an accountant or a lawyer, you gotta go to a university and learn, and you gotta pay tuition. We felt like we were going to the University of Bill Monroe, and whatever expenses there were and whatever we could do for him, that was our tuition."[7]

Aside from the folk music revival's interest in bluegrass, recognition of it as a separate genre was growing among country music fans in the Washington, D.C., area. Many credit this to deejay, musician, record label owner, and "walking encyclopedia" of country music Don Owens, a New York City native. On Sunday, August 14, Owens co-produced the first-ever "Blue Grass Day," held at Watermelon Park in Berryville, Virginia, near D.C., with its performers booked by none other than Bill's former manager, Carlton Haney (who said later that Blue Grass Day was the idea of park owner John U. Miller). Mac Wiseman and the Osborne Brothers headlined, with Bill and the Blue Grass Boys, Reno and Smiley, and others as also-rans. (Bill and Joe Stuart, who fiddled, were flown in from Alabama, and filling in, all from the D.C. area: Rudy Lyle, banjo; Porter Church, guitar; and Charlie Cline's nephew, Danny Cline, on bass). According to some who were there, a "tremendous crowd" witnessed and was moved by the first reunion of Bill, Don Reno, and Mac Wiseman (with Mack Magaha, fiddle). They played together for about thirty minutes, doing the songs Wiseman had recorded with Bill, and a quartet they had not recorded, "When He Reached Down His Hand for Me." Bill, once fiercely angered by those who copied his music, now expressed a changed outlook just before the reunion:

> I would like to say it's a pleasure to be up here with Don Reno, Red Smiley, and all the gang, Mac Wiseman, the Osborne Brothers—most of the boys that worked on the *Grand Ole Opry* for me down there as Blue Grass Boys. . . . There's nothing

in the world like bluegrass music, I'm tellin' ya. I'm really proud of it. . . . I started
bluegrass music about twenty years ago and there's been a lot of groups follered in
and play bluegrass music today. I couldn't name all of 'em, all over the country.[8]

Bill and Carolyn

The end of Bill and Carolyn's marriage came a few days later. Bill and Mauldin
had lived together for several years, and Bill made no effort to hide it. Carolyn
sued for divorce, and it was decreed on August 21, 1960. It would take a year
for details of the financial settlement to be finalized, but until then, Bill had
to pay $262.50 (the equivalent today of about $1,900) a month in alimony.
(Melissa, twenty-three, and James, nineteen, were still living at home.) By
July 1961 Bill was ordered to pay about half that amount per month, but he
had to sell the Dickerson Road farm, appraised at $32,500 ($235,000), from
which he received only $4,000 ($29,000), with the rest going to lawyers and
to Carolyn, *and* he was to give his ex-wife $4,500 to pay off various loans. He
was also "enjoined from marrying Bessie Mauldin during the life time of the
petitioner, Carolyn Monroe." But in spite of all this, Carolyn continued to
serve as Bill's personal secretary. Even in the early 1970s, Nashville journalist
Jack Hurst noted that "to get in touch with Monroe, one calls Mrs. Monroe."
Bill was said to be without a phone on his Goodlettsville farm, but he actually
had one in the old log cabin, a well-kept secret. (America's TV "sweethearts,"
Lucille Ball and Desi Arnaz, also divorced in 1960.)[9]

In September 1960 Ralph Rinzler returned to North Carolina to record
old-time musician Clarence Ashley, who, unbeknownst to Rinzler, had arranged for thirty-seven-year-old blind musician Arthel "Doc" Watson to back
him up on electric guitar. Diehard traditionalist Rinzler refused to record
anything that included electric guitar, and he and Watson argued about it.
Rinzler later said he "would never have talked to Doc again if he hadn't come
up with an acoustic guitar the next day."[10]

After Ellis returned from his leave of absence that September, Bill sent
him to North Carolina to pick up Frank Buchanan, a lead singer-guitarist
who had previously filled in with Bill at the *New Dominion Barn Dance* in
Richmond, Virginia. But once Buchanan found out how little work there
was, he went back to Richmond to restart the band he had there, the Cripple
Creek Boys. His replacement with Bill on the road was Tennessean Bobby
Smith, a cousin of Lester Flatt. Too shy to speak for himself, he asked Ellis
to arrange an audition. "He did the rest," Ellis said. Still, work was sparse.
"Bill didn't have anything booked, not even the *Opry*," said Ellis. So, with

Thanksgiving coming up, he decided to take another leave. He informed Bill of his plans and left town.[11]

Bill hadn't said much when Ellis "informed" him—not a word about three sessions set to begin on November 30 that would result in his next album. Possibly aggravated with his leave-taking, Bill just decided he'd get Curtis McPeake to pick banjo. He had probably already planned to use country singer-songwriter Carl Butler, a longtime friend from Knoxville, on guitar. Butler, it's said, was down on his luck and needed the session pay (then about $60 per session for a sideman). Potter fiddled and Mauldin played bass.[12]

The first song recorded on Wednesday, November 30, was "Sold Down the River," written by George Vaughn Horton, lyricist of "New Mule Skinner Blues." The melody of Horton's song is similar to Lester Flatt's "I'll Never Shed Another Tear." Next was "Linda Lou," written by session guitarist Butler, whose Capitol recording of it was released in 1951. Third was "You Live in a World All Your Own," originally recorded by Cowboy Copas in 1945 and credited to him on the King release. Last was "Little Joe," one of the last songs recorded by the Monroe Brothers, and the third of theirs rerecorded by Bill.[13]

The next day, Thursday, December 1, they recorded four more songs: "Put My Rubber Doll Away," an old-time tearjerker; "Seven Year Blues," written by the Louvin Brothers with friend Eddie Hill and recorded by the Louvins for Decca in 1949; "Time Changes Everything," written by Bob Wills's lead singer Tommy Duncan and recorded by Wills in 1940; and "Lonesome Road Blues," another old-timer that McPeake suggested when they lacked a song to complete the session. Afterward, there was some discussion about what Bill wanted to do at the December 3 session, and he said he'd like to sing a Johnny Cash song called "Big River," but he didn't have the lyrics. McPeake had Cash's album (*Johnny Cash Sings the Songs that Made Him Famous*, released by Sun in 1957) and volunteered to write them out for him.[14]

Ellis arrived back in Nashville on Friday, December 2. "I'd made up my mind to go on home. There wasn't any work. I was just about ready to hang it up." The next morning, he ran into Bill and Mauldin in Linebaugh's Restaurant, on Broadway near the Ryman. Mauldin said they had been recording and her fingers were blistered and sore. Bill knew Ellis was a capable bass player, so he asked if he'd be willing to play for Mauldin at that day's session. Of course he would, he said, and they headed to the studio.[15]

The session of December 3 began shortly after McPeake handed Bill the words of "Big River." Bill sang the four stanzas Cash had recorded, but there is a fifth stanza Cash was unable to record because, he was told, it would make his recording too long.

> I pulled into Natchez the next day down the river
> And there wasn't much there to make a rounder stay (very long).
> And when I left it was rainin' so nobody saw me cry.
> Big River, why's she doin' me that way?

Next was "Flowers of Love," written by Ellen Martin, a lady who helped out occasionally on Bill's farm, Ellis recalled. Third was "It's Mighty Dark to Travel," the third song by "the classic bluegrass band" to be rerecorded by Bill. In this version, a chord change to the subdominant (in the key of G: C) is used in the verses for the first time. And last was "Blue Grass Part 1," a twelve-bar blues in G by a band that had nothing else planned that day. Bill's mandolin needed repair again, confirmed by an E string catching under the fret wire (at the fifteenth fret) at the beginning of his second break (the binding on the neck had come off and the edge of the fret wire was uncovered). But Bill knew it might happen, and he incorporated it into his break. After the session, Bill asked Ellis to stay around Nashville for a while.[16]

Bill had a definite need for work now, if only to be able to pay his alimony, but it would take some time to set up the dates. The schedule in January and February 1961 was like November and December 1960: slow. But when March arrived, it was as busy as it had been in the early 1950s.[17]

Bill and the band (Ellis, Mauldin, Smith, and various fiddlers) were playing theaters and schools in Virginia, Kentucky, and South Carolina in March, when Columbia Records (Harmony) released *The Great Bill Monroe*, an album of recordings from 1945 to 1949. Its ten selections included four by "the classic band" of 1946–47 ("Blue Moon of Kentucky," "Mother's Only Sleeping," "My Rose of Old Kentucky," and "Blue Grass Breakdown"), now available to a new generation of listeners.[18]

Bill's third Decca album, *Mr. Blue Grass*, was released in May. Its cover was the first to feature a photo of him, taken in May 1960 by Decca staff photographer Marc Brody. When it was released, Bill was playing in eastern Kentucky a lot, alternating shows at drive-ins with those at high schools, probably including the high school in Martha, Kentucky. There, he first met Ricky Skaggs, who was six years old at the time. As Skaggs recalled,

> The place was packed, the high school gymnasium, and people started . . . hollering out between Bill's songs to "Let little Ricky Skaggs get up," "Hobert and Dorothy's little boy, Ricky, let him get up and sing." And so Bill put up with about twenty minutes of that, you know, and then finally he just said, "Well, where is this little Ricky Skaggs?" . . . So I come walking up to the front of the stage and . . .

Bill looks down at me . . . and reaches down and . . . grabs me by the arm and sets me up on the stage and said, "What do you play, boy?"

And I said, "Well, I play the mandolin."

He said, "Oh, you do?"

And I said, "Well, yeah." And so he takes his mandolin off, and puts it on me . . . and I said, "I sing, too."

And he said, "Oh, you do?"

And I said, "Yeah . . . I wanna sing 'Ruby' [the still-new Osborne Brothers hit]. And of course the crowd went nuts.

Bill, ever the subtle showman, pretended to be flustered by this prodigy's performance, trying to get a laugh or, at least, a smile from the audience. "Soon as I got finished," Skaggs said, "he comes and grabs the mandolin . . . unleashes the strap, puts it back on himself and hits it about three times and says, 'Now we're gonna do "Mule Skinner Blues."'" (In January 1962 little Ricky Skaggs would appear on Flatt and Scruggs's TV show, again singing "Ruby.")[19]

On June 25, 1961, Bill and the band (with Shorty Shehan filling in on fiddle) headlined the Brown County Jamboree in Bean Blossom. There to see Bill for the first time was Berkeley, California, native Neil Rosenberg, a grad student in folklore at Indiana University in nearby Bloomington. He went backstage after the show, picked a tune on Ellis's banjo, and was overheard by Shehan and wife Juanita Shehan, the new leaders of the Jamboree's house band. Within a few weeks, he would be invited to join the band (which included local musician Jim Bessire on bass). "On several occasions," Rosenberg wrote later, "I filled in on banjo with [Bill and the band], and it was after the first of these that I, embarrassed about my lack of knowledge of Monroe's repertoire, began actively purchasing his recordings."[20]

About a week after the Jamboree, on the Fourth of July, Bill and the band (with Billy Baker on fiddle) were at Oak Leaf Park in Luray, Virginia (also near Washington, D.C.), for the country music park's "All Blue Grass Show," the third forerunner of the bluegrass festival (a second "Blue Grass Day" had been held at Watermelon Park in 1961 without Bill). This time Bill was the headliner, followed by Mac Wiseman; the Stanley Brothers; park producer Bill Clifton and his Dixie Mountain Boys; the Country Gentlemen (with former Blue Grass Boy Eddie Adcock on banjo); and Jim and Jesse. As at Watermelon Park in 1960, Bill was reunited with Wiseman, then Jack Cooke and Carter Stanley.

Revealed that day was Flatt and Scruggs's refusal to be a part of the show, the first hint of "a feud" between them and Bill (which was really just rivalry between competitors). Carter Stanley first mentioned it in a humorous way when he joined Bill for a couple of songs: "I understand that they was a group that some of the folks asked to come here today. They said no, they didn't want to play here because Bill Monroe and the Stanley Brothers was gonna be here. And that was Flatt and Scruggs. You know, we missed 'em a heck of a lot, ain't we?" To which Bill remarked, also humorously: "Well, you're talking about Lester and Earl. Now, I started the two boys on the *Grand Ole Opry*, and they shouldn't be ashamed to come on the show and work with us. And I'm sure I wouldn't hurt either one of 'em."

Carlton Haney, talent agent for the first "Blue Grass Day" in 1960, there to observe, noted the large crowd the show attracted and the enthusiastic response to reunion performances with Bill. Following the show, Ellis left and went to Richmond to work with the Cripple Creek Boys on Haney's *New Dominion Barn Dance*.[21]

Ellis's replacement was Bobby Atkins. A western North Carolina native, he had picked banjo with Charlie Monroe in 1956. "We stayed on the road most of the time," said Atkins, who recalled traveling in a station wagon with four men, two dogs, all the clothes and instruments, and Mauldin, who now usually rode shotgun. "Bessie would sleep in the front seat. Whoever was driving, she would lay her pillow on their right leg and she would sleep with her legs curled up on the other side." As in the 1940s and 1950s, her bass rode in a rack on top of the wagon and was brought inside only when it rained. "Bill kept a spare tire on top of the thing, too, but he didn't tie it down. One time, going down a hill, it flew off and passed us. We stopped and like to have never found it." Billy Baker fiddled for another month, replaced by Vassar Clements, back in Nashville after working with Jim and Jesse.[22]

By the fall of 1961, the Greenbriar Boys had come a long way since Ralph Rinzler joined them in the fall of 1959. They'd made their initial recordings for Vanguard Records (five, including "Raw Hide," were about to be released on a sampler album, *New Folks*), on which Rinzler demonstrated he'd studied Bill's mandolin picking very carefully. (And in its liner notes, Bill's band was named as "the first band that played" bluegrass.) These recordings were heard by labelmate Joan Baez, who used the Greenbriars to back her on her second album (*Joan Baez, Volume 2*) and arranged for them to tour with her that fall. Herald, Rinzler, and Yellin, playing without a bass or fiddle, provided a striking contrast to Baez's serious balladry, exposing many young folk music fans to bluegrass for the first time.[23]

For record buyers looking for bluegrass that fall, there was an album with liner notes recommending it that were signed "Sincerely, BILL MONROE." Starday Records devised the ploy to help sell the first album by The Lonesome Pine Fiddlers, released in October. Band founders Ezra Cline and nephew Curly Ray Cline had recently re-formed the band with Melvin and Ray Goins, and Bill, even if he hadn't been compensated for it, would have been glad to have his name attached to ghost-written notes to help his old friends.[24]

Bill's next Decca sessions were scheduled for November 9 and 10, 1961. Atkins had left, so McPeake returned to pick banjo. Smith had left, so Jimmy Maynard played guitar and sang on the first duets Bill had recorded since 1954. Fiddling on November 9, Clements played lead and newcomer Norman "Buddy" Spicher, a freelance session musician, played second (harmony) fiddle. Fiddling on November 10, Tennessean Horace "Benny" Williams, a veteran of several bands, played solo on his first session with Bill.[25]

At these sessions, Bill, now age fifty, recorded songs he'd performed since his thirties, folk songs and "classic bluegrass band" standards known to be appealing to folk music fans. In the folk song category were three recorded by others who probably learned them from Bill's live performances: "Little Maggie," "Shady Grove," and "Nine Pound Hammer" (the fourth Monroe Brothers recording Bill had rerecorded). From "the classic band" came "I'm Going Back to Old Kentucky" and "Toy Heart" (the fourth and fifth to be rerecorded). From neither category was "Live and Let Live," recorded by composers Wiley Walker and Gene Sullivan in 1941, and one that Bill was finally able to record. It was the first bluegrass-style recording of the song.[26]

Bill at Carnegie Hall

By this time, Bill had been invited to play Carnegie Hall on November 29, 1961, with an *Opry* package show that included Patsy Cline, Grandpa Jones, the Jordanaires, Minnie Pearl, Jim Reeves, Marty Robbins, and Faron Young. Bill accepted the invitation, presumably willing to overlook the Artist Service Bureau's percentage for it. Decca had scheduled another recording session for November 30, but WSM was flying the entire troupe to and from New York, so Bill knew he could be back in Nashville in time for it.[27]

Bill called Ellis in Richmond and asked him to play banjo at Carnegie Hall, but by the time Ellis arrived in Nashville (with fiddler Bobby Joe Lester of the Cripple Creek Boys), the musicians' union had already completed the paperwork for the show, designating McPeake as Bill's banjoist. McPeake and Maynard, meanwhile, decided to make an outing of the event and drive to New York City with their wives in Maynard's car. So, rather than disrupt their plans, Bill told Ellis and Lester to stay in town, that they would help him record the session when he got back.[28]

Bill's portion of the Carnegie Hall show lasted about fifteen minutes. Aside from McPeake and Maynard, the band included new fiddlers Spicher and Williams, and Mauldin. "We did four tunes," recalled McPeake. "We were all really nervous—we could have threaded a sewing machine and it runnin', you know?" Bill wanted McPeake to pick one on the banjo. "I didn't want to," he said. "I think it might have been 'Cripple Creek.' I tore into it and encored."[29]

The next morning McPeake and Maynard and their wives got in the car for the long drive home and the rest of the troupe headed for the airport. After the plane arrived in Nashville, Bill called Ellis and Lester to tell them the session was that afternoon.

Three songs were recorded on November 30 (Mauldin, Spicher, and Williams had flown back with Bill, so with Ellis on banjo and Lester and Spicher on fiddles, Williams switched to guitar). First was "Danny Boy," a pop music standard Decca had undoubtedly suggested. Bill's understated vocal benefits greatly from Williams's guitar playing. Then Bill and the band breezed through another Decca suggestion, "Cotton Fields," a current folk favorite written by Huddie "Lead Belly" Ledbetter, with a nicely blending trio vocal by Ellis, Lester, and Bill. And the session ended with "Journey's End," an Ernest Tubb favorite of Bill's. All were the original bluegrass recordings of the songs.[30]

Four days later, on December 4, with the same band minus Spicher, Bill completed his fourth album by recording three instrumentals. All three featured the banjo, picked by Ellis, who said they were "just some tunes I had been playing and Bill chose to record them." They had all been recorded recently in bluegrass style: "John Hardy" by Reno and Smiley earlier in 1961; "Bugle Call Rag" by Flatt and Scruggs in 1960; and "Old Joe Clark" by Mike Seeger and Bob Yellin in 1959 for *Mountain Music Bluegrass Style*. But Ellis had known them for several years and gave them his own interpretation.[31]

Ellis and Lester left after the session and returned to Richmond. "When I'd leave," Ellis said, "I'd miss it. There's just no way you can describe to anybody who's never worked with Bill the magic that happened when he started whomping that mandolin. It would lift you up to a level you had never been in."[32]

The Death of Maude Monroe

About three weeks later, Bill's oldest sister, Maude Bell, died on the day after Christmas, 1961, probably of heart failure. She was only sixty-three. She had recovered from TB in 1919, when she was twenty-one, but she had been frail from then on.[33]

Hearing of Maude's passing, Ellis called Bill to offer his condolences. Bill told him that after he'd left the band, "Maude had just cried and cried and cried." Then Bill asked him to be a pallbearer on Sunday, December 31. Ellis had decided not to return to the band, but he came back to Nashville, played the *Friday Night Frolics* (the Friday version of the *Opry*, then broadcast from the National Life building) and the *Opry*, went with Bill to Rosine for Maude's funeral, and rejoined the Blue Grass Boys shortly thereafter. (He moved into Delia "Mom" Upchurch's now-famous boardinghouse on Boscobel Street, just east of downtown Nashville, with fellow roomers Buddy Spicher and Benny Williams. Bill's sister Bertha soon went to Martinsville, Indiana, to live with Birch.)[34]

On New Year's Day 1962, Decca released "Blue Grass Part 1" / "Flowers of Love" seven months after they appeared on the *Mr. Blue Grass* album—a little late to promote the album, if that was Decca's intent. At the time, the rock and roll dance called "the Twist" was popular, and it's likely that a young Decca executive noticed the dance could be done to "Blue Grass Part 1." After such things as "Peppermint Twist—Part 1" by Joey Dee and the Starliters reached number 1 in *Billboard*, Bill's blues instrumental was officially retitled "Blue Grass Twist" when it was released on a Decca EP.[35]

The Death of John Monroe

Little more than a month after sister Maude died, Bill's brother John, already in the hospital with double pneumonia, died of a heart attack on February 1. He was only sixty-four. One of Bill's firmest advocates in the family, John was living in the Monroe homeplace's house in the 1940s when he told a neighbor that because of Bill's achievements, "Someday they'll come and look at this house." (The neighbor thought he was crazy.) There was little time for Bill to mourn. After the funeral on February 4, he had a series of shows to play that began on February 7 at high schools in Missouri and Arkansas.[36]

Soon, Carlton Haney was calling to ask a big favor. The band he managed, Reno and Smiley, had successfully backed up country singer Rose Maddox at a show, and he had talked her label, Capitol, into recording an album of them together, a bluegrass album. Haney knew Maddox was a favorite singer of Bill's, and he wanted Bill to play on it too. Bill said he would have to have Decca's permission to record for another label, but, with the sessions happening soon, he agreed to participate prior to being given permission.

As it turned out, Bill only played on half of the album's four sessions. Seven of his best-known songs had been chosen for the album, but only five were recorded at two sessions on March 19: "Uncle Pen," "Footprints in the Snow," "Blue Moon of Kentucky," "My Rose of Old Kentucky," and "Molly and Tenbrooks." Haney said later that a lot of time was wasted wrangling over the use of drums and steel guitar. He said Bill refused to play with drums, so, eventually, the drummer was paid not to play. Then Haney and Reno questioned the inclusion of a steel guitar, but Maddox insisted on some, so it would be permitted on "Footprints" and "Uncle Pen." When the sessions finally began, Bill did his best to adjust to the keys Maddox sang in, even tuning his mandolin up a half-step to play "Blue Moon" and "Molly and Tenbrooks" in C#. But after all the squabbling, there wasn't enough time to record two more songs. Bill had a show to play in Greensboro, North Carolina, the next day, March 20, and could not participate further.

The other Monroe songs, "I'll Meet You in Church Sunday Morning" and "The Old Crossroads Is Waitin'," plus five other songs, were cut at two sessions on March 20 with Donna Stoneman on mandolin. Ultimately, Decca would not give Bill permission to record for Capitol, so he was not credited in the liner notes of *Rose Maddox Sings Bluegrass*. Fans knew he'd played on the album, however, making it all the more intriguing. Released in December 1962, the first bluegrass album on a major label to feature a female vocalist was also, according to critic Dave Samuelson, the bestselling album of Maddox's career.[37]

Not long after the sessions with Maddox, in the spring of 1962, Frank Buchanan came back to the Blue Grass Boys. He was not yet in the musicians' union, so Jim Maynard or Benny Williams played guitar for him on the *Opry*. During this time, Williams brought fiddler "Red" Stanley of northeastern Tennessee into the band. They had been friends since the 1950s, and when both were available, Bill had a close-knit twin fiddling team. One time, Williams, Stanley, and Ellis took a leave of absence together to play a tour with Mac Wiseman. Buchanan recalled that while they were gone, he, Bill, and Mauldin carried on: "We went up into the coal mining country and Kenny Baker . . . came out of the mines [where he worked] and played some shows with us."[38]

Earl Scruggs: "Master of Bluegrass Music"

A world away in New York City, the April/May 1962 issue of the folk music magazine *Sing Out!* appeared with a cover story on Earl Scruggs. Its author, blues authority Pete Welding, began by declaring that "Scruggs has become the undisputed master of Bluegrass music." Ralph Rinzler would soon react, but at the time, he was busy serving as manager and booking agent for the Clarence Ashley Group (with Doc Watson) and playing with the Greenbriar Boys, whose first album, *The Greenbriar Boys*, had just been released; they were still touring with Joan Baez. In April, after Baez and the Greenbriars played a concert with Flatt and Scruggs at Vanderbilt University in Nashville, Louise Scruggs arranged for them to make a guest appearance on the *Opry*. Mrs. Scruggs knew of Rinzler's partiality for Bill Monroe (he had credited Bill as "the main-spring" of bluegrass in their album's liner notes), and she asked him not to mention Bill in any remarks he might make while on the *Opry*.[39]

Late April to mid-May 1962 was a time of intense recording activity for Bill and the Blue Grass Boys, now with the voice of Frank Buchanan. Decca scheduled six sessions, three for secular songs and three for gospel quartets, conceivably recording enough material for two albums. Eighteen songs would be recorded, more than in any similar period in Bill's recording career. The Bradley Film and Recording Studio had recently been sold to Columbia Records, but Bill would continue to record for Decca there. Just before the sessions, Bill arranged for Buchanan to join the musicians' union.[40]

Present at the first session on April 25, aside from Bill, Buchanan, Ellis, Mauldin, Stanley, and Williams, was the singer-songwriter Bill had met in Minnesota in 1955, Chuck Carson (born Charles Krenz in Anoka in 1925 and raised in Minneapolis). He was there to help the band learn the songs he had written or co-written with Bill: "There Was Nothing We Could Do," "I Was Left on the Street," and "Cheap Love Affair." Bill had written a verse and the chorus of "I Was Left on the Street" when he first showed it to Carson ("I told him if he'd finish it, I'd give him half of it," Bill said later), so Bill was familiar with one of them. Otherwise, there wasn't much certainty in the studio that day, according to Buchanan: "I said, 'Bill, I can't record these songs. I don't know 'em.' He said, 'You know 'em as good as I do. I don't know 'em either.'" Remarkably, the resulting recordings were among Bill's best.[41]

Decca may have asked Bill to record some older songs for folk music fans, and the next day he obliged, again confronting the band with songs they'd never heard before. The first was "When the Bees Are in the Hive," a Tin Pan Alley relic from 1904 recorded by country artists in the 1920s, including WLS star Hugh Cross (from whom Bill had learned "Footprints in the Snow"). Bill sang the first stanza only, while the original sheet music included a second:

> By the old mill sits a lonely maid repining,
> And her fancy like the stream roams far away;
> As she looks down in the silv'ry waters shining,
> And sees her golden locks are tinged with gray.
> Long years she's waited there for his returning,
> In vain she's thinking he'll come back someday;
> For the lamp of hope still in her heart is burning,
> As the old mill wheel turns 'round it seems to say:
> When the bees are in the hive and the honey's in the comb,
> When the golden sunbeams bend to kiss the dew,
> While the old mill wheel turns 'round I'll love you, Mary,
> When the bees are in the hive I'll come to you.

Bill's timing was off in his part of the instrumental break, but the band instinctively adjusted for it. The mistake was ignored and the recording would be issued as is. The second stranger was "Big Ball in Brooklyn" (sung "Big Ball's in Brooklyn"), which Bill told Buchanan was a song the Monroe Brothers used to sing. Third was a song the band knew, for a change—"Columbus Stockade Blues"—which the Shenandoah Valley Trio (Buchanan, Ellis, and Mauldin) had been featuring at shows. Ellis later credited Rudy Lyle as the source of his distinctive break on it. Lyle had visited Mom Upchurch's boardinghouse one night and picked Ellis's banjo. "Rudy played something very similar to that," Ellis said, "and I watched him like a chicken watches a June bug."[42]

The final secular session, on May 3, marked the debut of Cincinnati, Ohio, native Harry Silverstein as Bill's producer. Previously Owen Bradley's assistant, Silverstein would rely on Bradley for some help with Bill's sessions for the next two years. Recorded first was "Blue Ridge Mountain Blues," which

Buchanan suggested; he'd learned the song from the original 1924 recording by Riley Puckett. Next was "How Will I Explain About You?," the sixth song from "the classic band" to be rerecorded. "Foggy River" was discovered in WSM's record library in the National Life building after Bill sent Buchanan and Ellis there to look for songs. "Tony said this song 'Foggy River' would be a good song for Bill," Buchanan recalled, "and we copied the words down out of a Red Foley record" (a 1947 Decca release).[43]

The first gospel session was held on May 10, after a week of rehearsals. With banjo and fiddle excluded, Buchanan sang lead and played guitar, studio sideman Ray Edenton was contracted to sing baritone, Culley Holt again sang bass, and Mauldin played bass. First was "The Old Country Baptizing," written by former Blue Grass Boy Jim Shumate (a friend, Verlon Bryontt, was listed as co-writer in exchange for Shumate's name appearing on one of Bryontt's songs) and first heard in 1960 on Alan Lomax's *White Spirituals* album (Atlantic), sung by the Mountain Ramblers. Following it were quartet versions of two songs the Monroe Brothers had recorded, "I (Have) Found the Way" and "This World Is Not My Home," the original bluegrass recordings of both.[44]

During the week that followed it was decided that Ellis would play banjo on the remaining six gospel songs, probably encouraged by new producer Silverstein, hoping to enliven (and sell) Bill's recordings. Bill had used banjo sparingly on religious recordings before (only on 1947's "The Old Cross Road" and 1952's not-yet-released "Don't Put Off 'Til Tomorrow"). During rehearsals, Red Stanley was found to be a capable baritone singer, and he would replace Edenton on the forthcoming sessions.

First recorded on Wednesday, May 16, was "Way Down in My Soul," previously recorded in 1953 by Carl Story. Bill, apparently distracted, stopped singing in the middle of the second chorus; producer Silverstein overlooked the mistake, and the recording would be released anyway. "Drifting Too Far from the Shore" was next, the seventh Monroe Brothers song to be redone by Bill. And the last was "Going Home," written by Bill's Murfreesboro friend Carl Tipton and not previously recorded. Bill came in late with his tenor vocal at the start of the second chorus, and the tape was stopped. To save what they had, they recorded the second chorus again, a "turn-around," and the final chorus. Studio technicians later cut and spliced the tape (as they had in 1951 and 1952), cleanly joining the end of the second verse with the new finish.[45]

On Thursday May 17, splicing was used again, this time intentionally, on the first song, "On the Jericho Road." It created a half-step key change, from G to G# (A♭), possibly, in Silverstein's view, to enhance the performance. The tape was stopped after the first verse and chorus, guitar and banjo capos were installed at the first fret, and the tape was started again, with the pause later removed by splicing. It was the original bluegrass recording of the song, popularized by the Chuck Wagon Gang's 1941 waxing. Next was the original bluegrass recording of "We'll Understand It Better," first recorded by the Smiling Rangers (Wiley and Zeke Morris and Homer "Pappy" Sherrill) in 1937. And the last song of Bill's fiftieth Decca session was "Somebody Touched Me," originally recorded in 1949 and covered in 1961 by the Stanley Brothers.[46]

Three days later, on Sunday, May 20, 1962, Bill and the band drove up to Rosine to play a show at the town's ballpark, now located near the center of town. They all ate dinner at Charlie and Betty's house, then headed to the ballpark, where Bill and the Blue Grass Boys played on a flatbed trailer. The crowd clamored for Charlie to get up and sing with Bill, but Charlie, who had been retired from music for about five years, wouldn't do it, telling them, "No, I don't want to."[47]

Ralph Rinzler and the Scruggs Article

By then Ralph Rinzler had seen the April/May *Sing Out!* cover story declaring Earl Scruggs to be "the undisputed master" of bluegrass music. "I was furious," he said later. He knew, based on what he'd learned and observed, that Bill was the true master of the genre: he'd started it; he was responsible for Scruggs's renown; and, as a singer, player, and songwriter, he was still its most capable practitioner. While Scruggs was certainly the master of bluegrass banjo, Bill was much more qualified to be called "the master of bluegrass music." Later, Rinzler wrote, "There was reason for dispute, and I felt confident that Earl himself would be embarrassed by the *Sing Out!* statement. Editor Irwin Silber agreed to do a cover story on Bill Monroe if I would write it." But biographical information was limited, and to write an in-depth portrait, Rinzler realized he would have to interview Bill. "None of us had ever talked to him," he said. "He was very aloof."[48]

Unbeknownst to Rinzler, trouble had been brewing between Bill and him since the All Blue Grass Show of July 1961. A fan who taped the show had sent a copy of Carter Stanley and Bill's comments about Flatt and Scruggs to Louise Scruggs. According to Neil Rosenberg in *Bluegrass: A History*, "Monroe knew about the tape . . . because [reportedly] it was used by Louise as a pretext for threats of a lawsuit and attempts to have Monroe removed from the *Opry*." Bill had been aware that Mike Seeger and Rinzler taped his shows and was convinced that they sent the tape to her. To make matters worse, it's likely he also knew about the appearance of the Greenbriar Boys on the *Opry*, which Louise Scruggs had arranged.[49]

On Sunday, June 24, 1962, Bill and the band were appearing at Sunset Park, near Philadelphia. Bill's fourth Decca album, *Bluegrass Ramble*, with recordings from November and December 1961, had been out about two weeks. Rinzler decided the time was right to talk to Bill, and he drove to "Sunset" from his New Jersey home, knowing Mike Seeger and other friends (including Jeremy and Alice Foster and singer Hazel Dickens) would be there. He paid the one dollar admission and watched the first show with them. "During an intermission," he wrote later, "when I approached Bill about an interview, he merely said he knew Mike and me from years back and had seen us recording at the side of the stage, and then he suggested: 'If you want to know about bluegrass music, ask Louise Scruggs.'" "And," Rinzler later told Jim Rooney, "he turned and walked away."[50]

Shocked by this snub, Rinzler met with his friends at one of the park's picnic tables to discuss what to do next. No one seemed to know why Bill was so upset with Rinzler, but it was clear he needed someone to speak in his favor. Seeger suggested the Stanley Brothers might be willing to help. He had become friends with them over the years while taping their shows, and Rinzler had arranged for their first concert appearance in New York City in June 1961, sponsored by the Friends of Old Time Music, a nonprofit he co-founded to present traditional performers to city audiences. The Stanleys happened to be appearing at New River Ranch, about fifteen miles away, so Rinzler and Seeger headed there.[51]

The Stanley Brothers returned with them to Sunset that June afternoon. At a meeting that included Bill, Mauldin, Seeger, and Rinzler, the first to speak in favor of Seeger and Rinzler was former Blue Grass Boy Carter Stanley. Then it was up to Rinzler to convince Bill and "manager" Mauldin of the value of an article in *Sing Out!* "Ralph made them aware of the doors that it would open," Dickens said. And, ultimately, he promised to open the first few doors himself, using connections he'd made working with Baez and booking Clarence Ashley, to arrange for Bill to play several prestigious folk music venues. That sold Mauldin, and she encouraged Bill to go along with it. Bill, who had never really "opened up" to any writer, agreed to think about it. Negotiations continued for several weeks until Bill finally agreed to an interview in August.[52]

After Bill and the band returned to Nashville, Ellis left, this time for good. In July another twenty-year-old banjo picker from western North Carolina, David Deese, arrived. Like Ellis, Deese auditioned in the morning at WSM, but this time it was while Bill read his mail: "I don't remember what I played. I was so nervous. All that time, he was just sitting there, opening his mail with his pocket knife, not really paying any attention to me." They headed out that night to play a firemen's carnival in Roxana, Illinois, near St. Louis. As Deese recalled,

> When we got to Roxana, Bessie got out first and looked around. There didn't appear to be any bathhouses. We carried a wash pan in the back of the station wagon. Everybody had their own towel, soap, and wash cloth. She found a water spigot and filled the pan with cold water. Then she said, "Come with me. You're my guard. Don't let anybody in that curtain [covering the back of the makeshift stage]." She had to take a bath and change clothes right there behind the stage. After washing out the pan and running fresh water, she stood guard for me. I thought to myself, "Damn, this is the big time!"

Deese remembered this show as Red Stanley's last. Charlie Smith had returned from active duty and fiddled on the road some thereafter. After Smith moved to Virginia at summer's end, Benny Williams rejoined the band.[53]

"The Father of Blue Grass Music"

By then, Mike Seeger's mention in 1959's *Mountain Music Bluegrass Style* that Bill was "called the father of bluegrass" had caught the eye of Linnell Gentry, a professor at Martin College in Tennessee, who was compiling data for *A History and Encyclopedia of Country, Western, and Gospel Music*. A "just the facts" reference book, published in Nashville in 1961, its numerous artist profiles included one for Bill that began: "Monroe, Bill, called 'The Father of Blue Grass Music.'" RCA Victor, about to cash in on the interest in bluegrass with an album of Bill's 1940–41 recordings on its reissue label, RCA Camden, evidently noticed the entry; thus the album's title, *The Father of Blue Grass Music*, released on August 4, 1962, seemingly confirmed the appellation. But the writer of its liner notes was still reluctant to give Bill full credit: "Blue Grass Music, to the vast audience who know and love it, is not the invention of any one man but rather the logical development of string band music. If no one man is its creator, Bill Monroe has certainly earned the title of 'The Father of Blue Grass Music' for he has contributed more to it than anyone else."[54]

Meanwhile, Bill and the band rolled on, mainly to drive-ins in August, where the band usually played on top of the concession stands. "There was an awful lot of riding in between, and an awful lot of bologna sandwiches," according to Deese.

> You had to stop at a mom and pop grocery store by the roadside. You didn't have the luxury of mayonnaise or mustard or a Case knife to spread it with. You had no refrigeration. You'd get a loaf of bread, a dozen slices of hoop cheese, rag bologna [bologna in a waxed cloth casing], and you'd peel it. You'd take a slice of bread, a piece of bologna, and a slice of cheese and make a sandwich, and you handed it up to the driver. He always got the first one. Bessie got the next one. Bill was just one of the boys.

The band would be hungry again after they played, but this was long before the eateries that fill the interstates today (and the interstate system itself was far from complete). "It was always hard to find something to eat after a show," Deese said.[55]

Rinzler's First Interview with Bill

On Friday, August 24, came a change of pace—the Galax Agricultural Fair at Felts Park in Galax, Virginia. Meeting Bill and the band there were Ralph Rinzler and younger cousin Richard Rinzler, who had just made the long drive across Virginia before Interstate 81. Bill had agreed to be interviewed; the rendezvous was to occur in Galax, the closest he would come to the Northeast for several months. But it appears he wasn't in the mood to talk before his show that day. "Bill avoided me assiduously," Ralph Rinzler wrote later, "but Bessie reassured me." To kill time, the Rinzlers explored the midway, where Richard Rinzler recalled they were "suckered into a game of chance that started out well, but ended up with $30 or $40 lost, each." Later, during the show at the grandstand, Buchanan broke a string and Ralph Rinzler offered his guitar as a substitute, which seemed to "ease things" between Bill and him, his cousin said. After the show, it was settled—they would do the interview at the local bowling alley. It was the only place in town open that late *and* it served the latest Italian taste sensation, "pizza pie."[56]

So, while Mauldin and the Blue Grass Boys ate pizza, Bill and the Rinzlers sat down together elsewhere at Gala Lanes. "Ralph told him about our mishap on the midway," Richard Rinzler said. "Bill immediately was so nice, offered us money, was just so friendly and interested. The ice was broken and the interview went famously." Ralph Rinzler asked the questions and Richard Rinzler took notes (using a tape recorder wasn't feasible in the noisy bowling alley), and, as Ralph Rinzler remembered it, "He answered my questions unenthusiastically, but accurately and precisely." His cousin filled five pages of a standard-size, spiral-bound notebook with details of Bill's early life and career, punctuated by direct quotes ranging from boastful ("No man in the world ever taught me anything") to insightful ("If you're singing a song to satisfy your heart and feeling, you won't sing it the same way every time"). Ralph Rinzler was fascinated with the complexity of Bill's life story, but more impressed by his musical ideology: "The one thing [Bill] was extremely aware of was that he had fashioned his music. His music didn't just happen and it wasn't intuitive. He consciously did it."[57]

David Deese left "the big time" after that August 24, 1962, weekend. Without a replacement, Bill relied on familiar faces to fill in. The following Friday and Saturday (August 31 and September 1, Labor Day weekend), he was booked to play two shows and a dance in Hazard, Kentucky, so he asked Ray Goins, then living nearby, to pick banjo (brother Melvin came with him, both on leave from the Lonesome Pine Fiddlers). Also in Hazard that weekend was another co-founder of New York's Friends of Old Time Music, John Cohen (one of the original New Lost City Ramblers). Cohen was putting the finishing touches on a film documentary that featured his discovery, folksinger Roscoe Holcomb, who also lived nearby. To provide a visual example of modern music heard in the region, Cohen filmed Bill and the band (Buchanan, Williams, and Ray Goins, with Mauldin and, occasionally, Melvin Goins, on bass) without sound, playing in Hazard on September 1. Later, Cohen's documentary, *The High Lonesome Sound*, released in 1963, was the first film of its kind to include bluegrass music (the music heard while Bill and the band are shown playing was not recorded on September 1, however). Its title was also the first to associate the phrase "high lonesome sound" with bluegrass, although when the Cohen-produced Folkways album *Roscoe Holcomb: The High Lonesome Sound* was released in 1965, it was clear that the film's title referred only to Holcomb's singing.[58]

The following Saturday, September 8, 1962, twenty-two-year-old Bill Keith from Brockton (near Boston), Massachusetts, won the banjo contest at the first Philadelphia Folk Festival, playing a medley of "Devil's Dream" and "Sailor's Hornpipe." He had devised a method of playing fiddle tune melodies note-for-note that was already being copied and recorded. He would soon be playing full time with Red Allen and Frank Wakefield in the bars of Washington, D.C., and nearby Baltimore, Maryland. And three weeks after the folk festival, on September 26, *The Beverly Hillbillies* debuted on CBS-TV, with its theme song, "The Ballad of Jed Clampett," played by Flatt and Scruggs, featuring Scruggs's banjo picking. Within a few months, it would become the first bluegrass recording to reach number 1 on the *Billboard* country singles chart.[59]

On September 28, Bill, Buchanan, Mauldin, and Williams arrived in Omaha, Nebraska ("New Braska," as Bill called it; familiar territory since 1934). A seven-day tour would start there the next day, a package show that included Ray Price and Pee Wee King, and Bill was hoping to find a banjo player. Answering the call was Missouri native Lonnie Hoppers, then living near Kansas City, about 185 miles from Omaha. He had filled in before, and Bill had kept track of him; on September 30, after the package show played in Kansas City, Bill offered him the banjo job again. Hoppers had turned him down in 1957, and military service had kept him from taking it in 1960 when Ellis was absent, "and I didn't think I would ever get a third chance," Hoppers said. This time he accepted the offer, leaving a good job at Western Electric to do it.[60]

Benny Williams and Frank Buchanan left the band after the tour, Williams to work with Porter Wagoner, Buchanan to escape the 1959 Olds station wagon:

> That old car broke down wherever we were at. We had it in the garage or were late for about every showdate, and the promoter was fussin' with Bill, and I made up my mind. I'd seen a lot of 'em come and go and I said, "Bill, when we get back to Nashville, I'm going back to North Carolina." He said, "Naw, you can't quit me, Frank. You'll never quit me." We weren't making much money, and if he'd got a bus or something decent to travel in, I wouldn't have left at all.[61]

To replace Buchanan, Bill alternated between Jimmy Maynard and Joe Stuart. To replace Williams, Bill contacted Kenny Baker, who began his second stint with Bill at the annual Burley Tobacco Growers Festival in Abingdon, Virginia, on October 18. Recently, while Baker was working in a mine, a rock had crushed his right ankle. "He came to play with a cast halfway to his knee and on crutches," recalled Hoppers. "We'd carry his fiddle and help him up on the stage. He'd get set, up in front of the mike, then we'd take his crutches and lay 'em somewhere, hand him his fiddle, and there he was."[62]

On Monday, October 22, 1962, President Kennedy appeared on television to reveal that missiles from the Soviet Union were in Cuba. The "crisis" ended on Sunday, October 28, when Soviet Premier Nikita Khrushchev agreed to remove the missiles if the United States would end a blockade of Cuba and not invade the country. That same Sunday, Bill and the Blue Grass Boys (with Hoppers and Maynard plus fill-ins Roger Smith on fiddle and Birch on bass) appeared at the Brown County Jamboree, leased and managed that season by Harry Weger, a deejay and record store owner from Terre Haute, Indiana. He'd set up record racks with the latest albums in the Jamboree Barn, attracting the attention of Indiana University student Neil Rosenberg.

> That Sunday I found a copy of a new Decca LP by Monroe, *My All Time Country Favorites*. I bought it and after the first show, took it backstage and handed it to Monroe, asking him to autograph it. It was at once obvious that he had never seen this particular album before. He put on his glasses, read the list of titles and the notes on the back of the jacket; he turned it over and looked at the front picture, and then, shaking his head, carefully turned the cover back over and signed it so that the autograph was upside down in relation to the printing on the back.

Probably without consulting Bill, Decca had released a "greatest hits of the 1950s" album in response to RCA Victor's *The Father of Blue Grass Music* (a "greatest hits of the 1940s" album). Among Decca's "hits" was "Plant Some Flowers by My Grave," which the label had been sitting on for eight years, included as a "country favorite" because it was once recorded by country singer Jimmie Davis.[63]

Bill's end-of-year sessions would complete work begun in April and May on two albums, one secular and one gospel. Bill's solo voice was again spotlighted on all of the songs recorded at four sessions, with Joe Stuart, guitar; Hoppers, banjo; Baker (off crutches by then), fiddle; and Mauldin, bass. The first of two sessions on Friday, November 23, began with the folk song "Careless Love." Baker later said his fiddling on it was inspired by the piano playing of pop singer Nat "King" Cole: "[T]he idea of the tune [to accompany Bill's singing] come to me in a movie [*St. Louis Blues*, with Cole as W. C. Handy, "the Father of the Blues"] . . . every note I hit, this man had it on the piano." The song had been recorded in bluegrass style previously by Harry and Jeanie West in 1956. Next was the Hank Williams standard "I'm So Lonesome I Could Cry," written with Bill's help, according to Mac Wiseman. "Jimmy Brown the Newsboy" followed, a Carter Family song recently popularized by Flatt and Scruggs and probably suggested to Bill by Decca.

The second session began with "Pass Me Not," with Stuart switching to second fiddle and Hoppers playing guitar. "They got to messing with some twin fiddles on this old tune," Hoppers said. "[Bill] handed me that old herringbone guitar. . . . He [had] never heard me hit a lick on guitar. But I'm sure he thought, 'You're a Blue Grass Boy—you're gonna be able to do whatever I need.'" (The Stanley Brothers had recorded "Pass Me Not" in 1959, possibly causing Bill's recording to be withheld until 1973.) The next two songs, "The Glory Land Way" and "Farther Along," both gospel standards, had not previously been recorded in bluegrass style. "Farther Along," which Charlie had recorded as a trio in 1938, was the first quartet Bill and the band sang on the *Opry* in 1939.[64]

Kenny Baker recorded the first of his original fiddle tunes to kick off the session of Thursday, December 6. Hoppers recalled the band hadn't played "Big Sandy River" or "Baker's Breakdown" onstage before, but he had a few days to work out a banjo break for the former. Not so the latter, which was new to him. Then Bill sang "Darling Corey," the eighth Monroe Brothers song he'd redone. Bill was the first to record the song in bluegrass style, but many fans heard it first from competitors Flatt and Scruggs. They played the song, titled "Dig a Hole in the Meadow," at Carnegie Hall on December 8, 1962, and a recording of the show was released as an album in 1963. Bill's recording would not be released until 1964, and then only as a single.[65]

On the evening of December 9, Flatt and Scruggs appeared at Johns Hopkins University in Baltimore, opening for Merle Travis. After the show, its promoter, talent agent Manuel "Manny" Greenhill, introduced Scruggs to Bill Keith. Greenhill had booked Keith and a fellow Amherst College student, singer-guitarist Jim Rooney, in the Boston area and knew Keith had written out, in music notation and tablature, many of Scruggs's banjo tunes and breaks. Keith showed Scruggs his workbook of transcriptions, and Scruggs, already making plans for a banjo instruction book, was eager to include these tablatures in it. He invited Keith to come to Nashville so they could work on the "tabs" together.[66]

On the morning of December 10, Bill and the band reconvened in the studio to record another folk music favorite, "Cindy." It had been recorded in bluegrass style for the *American Banjo* album, and possibly knowing that, Decca producer Silverstein encouraged Bill to record a cover. A new religious song, "Master Builder," was next, followed by "Let Me Rest at the End of My

Journey," credited to brother Birch when waxed by the Shenandoah Valley Trio in 1950.[67]

Bill's first show of 1963 was the first bluegrass show ever advertised as a "Blue Grass Festival." Held at the National Guard Armory in Roanoke, Virginia, on January 1, with the Stanley Brothers, Reno and Smiley, Hylo Brown, and several local bands, it was promoted by Bill's former manager Carlton Haney, already aware of the current trend for "festivals"—folk, jazz, and otherwise. It foreshadowed the multiday event he would later pioneer, the kind of gathering that would become the lifeblood of bluegrass.[68]

Hoppers left the band a short time later. "Things were slow—Bill wasn't playing that much," he said. Stuart also found work elsewhere, so, near the end of January, Bill recruited two musicians who had filled in before: banjo player Rual Yarbrough, age thirty-two, and singer-guitarist Jacob "Jake" Landers, twenty-three. Already in a band together in Alabama (the Dixie Gentlemen), they were glad to have an opportunity to work with Bill, even if it was temporary.[69]

The Bill Monroe Article in *Sing Out!*

By then, the February–March 1963 issue of *Sing Out!* magazine had appeared, with a John Cohen photo of Bill on the cover, and inside, "Bill Monroe—'The Daddy of Blue Grass Music'" by Ralph Rinzler. The first in-depth biographical portrait in Bill's twenty-eight-year career, it introduced an estimated fifteen thousand folk music fans to J. B. and Malissa Monroe, Uncle Pen, and Arnold Shultz, and summarized the early years of Bill's life as a professional musician. Rinzler made no mention of "the classic band," choosing instead to delve into the heart of Bill's relationship with music.

> In conversation as well as in performance, Bill Monroe's respect for and belief in his music are immediately apparent. It is this conviction, as profound as a religious belief, which has enabled Monroe to resist the trends of Nashville and to retain his remarkably unique musical style throughout more than twenty years of constant exposure. This same conviction, imparted to other musicians and to audiences, is responsible for the endurance and significance of the traditional folk strain in commercial country music.

Rinzler's goal was to "revive" the career of someone he considered a great American artist. "But," he told an interviewer, "it took getting the folksong audience to understand that he was as folk as he was Nashville. And to give them the actual facts of who he learned from and how and what his philosophy was." All that audience needed was an opportunity to see and hear him in action.[70]

Bill and the band (Baker, Landers, Mauldin, and Yarbrough) played for a folk revival audience for the first time at the University of Chicago Folk Festival on the weekend of February 1, 1963. Rinzler recalled that this first attempt to book Bill took some extra effort: "We argued the Chicago kids into asking him to come and argued Jim Denny, who was his booking agent at the time, into having him come for a reasonable price and not skinning the hell out of them." Landers said the trip from Nashville, through bitter cold and snow, without the benefit of interstates, took about twenty hours. When they arrived, Rinzler gave Bill a copy of the new *Sing Out!* and the liner notes of the first Greenbriar Boys album, crediting him as "the originator and continuing force in bluegrass music." After Bill read them, "our relationship became one of unquestioning confidence and trust," Rinzler said. That weekend, Bill discovered Rinzler's ability to sing bass and pressed him into service with the Blue Grass Quartet.[71]

Virtually a visitor from another world at that point, Bill answered questions about bluegrass for Chicago Folk Festival-goers at a discussion session on Saturday afternoon, surprising everyone with his forthright explanations and amusing recollections. Rinzler later observed, "He never thought of expressing himself in words, in a way that was as important as his musical expression, or at least almost as important. And I think that was a big breakthrough for Bill."[72]

A few days later, Bill was on his way to the second show Rinzler had booked, a concert for the Friends of Old Time Music (FOTM) in New York City on Friday, February 8. Landers's and Yarbrough's jobs wouldn't let them off on a weekday, so Bill had to find other fill-ins. He called Jack Cooke, then playing at a small bar in Baltimore with his Virginia Mountain Boys, and Cooke assured him he had a banjo picker who could "cut it," twenty-three-year-old Del McCoury of nearby York, Pennsylvania. McCoury recalled Bill's arrival at the Chapel Café bar on the day before the concert: "There was a side door to the place that come right in front of the stage. Here this guy walked in and set down right there while we was pickin'—he wasn't ten feet from the stage. I thought, 'Man, that looks like Bill Monroe!' Then I thought, 'Nah, that wouldn't be Bill Monroe.'" But it was, and the next day McCoury was on his way to New York, sitting in the backseat of the 1959 Olds station wagon between Bill and Baker while Cooke drove and Mauldin rode shotgun.[73]

An enthusiastic crowd greeted them at New York University's School of Education auditorium (used at no cost to the FOTM, thanks to Richard Rinzler, founder of the university's folk song club). Cooke was in fine form on guitar, and the rest of the band melded with him. Applause followed almost every one of McCoury's banjo breaks, and after the show, McCoury said Bill told him, "If you ever quit Jack, come to Nashville and I'll give you a job."[74]

Two Banjo Players Offered the Job

The next day, February 9, Bill Keith arrived in Nashville with Red Allen and Frank Wakefield, Keith to work with Scruggs on his banjo instruction book, and they to discuss a recording contract with Starday. Flatt and Scruggs were out of town, so Allen and Wakefield took Keith to the *Opry* and, while picking a little backstage, Keith caught the ear of former Blue Grass Boy Connie Gately. Bill wandered into the room at one point and Gately told him, "This is a guy that you need to hear!" Keith played a little more and Bill listened briefly but "showed no reaction that I could measure," Gately said. The following week, Keith got together with Scruggs and worked on the book, then Flatt and Scruggs left town (and Allen and Wakefield rode home with them). When Flatt and Scruggs returned on February 16, they were scheduled to play the *Opry*, so Scruggs took Keith with him. Keith played in a jam session, and this time Roy Acuff heard him play. Yarbrough, playing with Bill that night, recalled the scene: "Roy Acuff was there and he started going down the hall and gettin' guys. He said, 'You gotta come down here and hear this guy on the banjo!' He said, 'He's playin' notes on the banjo that they play on the fiddle!'" Then Kenny Baker happened by.

> I heard this banjo belting out this "Sailor's Hornpipe," "Devil's Dream"—several numbers, you know? I believe he was in Acuff's dressing room at that time. Boy, I heard that and I could not believe my ears! So I went to Monroe and I told him, I said, "You must come over here and listen to this boy." Well, Bill, he never went in the room, but he heard this banjo. He said, "That's not my kind of music." So, I said to him, I said, "Bill, your kind of music—I believe that banjo would help you" or "help us," I think is the way I put it. He said, "Well, go talk to the boy."

Baker did more than just talk to him. "Later that evening as I was leaving the building," Keith said, "Kenny came up and asked me if I would like a job with Bill Monroe. Of course, I accepted." Two people had now been offered the banjo spot with the Blue Grass Boys.[75]

During the next few days, Keith continued working with Scruggs on the book. He called Bill, explaining he had an air force reserve meeting in Massachusetts coming up and saying he would call him when it was over. Bill continued to use Yarbrough and Landers, and one night backstage at the *Opry*, Landers said Bill sang the chorus of a song for him that he had just started writing:

> Walk softly on this heart of mine, love.
> Don't treat it mean and so unkind.
> Let it rest in peace and quiet, love.
> Walk softly on this heart of mine.

Bill hadn't written any verses yet, so Landers went home and wrote two. The following week, he sang them for Bill, "but it wasn't what he wanted," Landers said.[76]

Keith returned home for his reserve meeting. By Monday, March 4, after it was over, he wasn't sure if the job with Bill would still be available. "[O]nce back in Brockton . . . I called Ralph Rinzler, who I knew to be in contact with Bill Monroe, to ask him if the offer was real, and whether I should relocate to Nashville." Rinzler, aware of Keith's ability on banjo, phoned Bill: "I called him up . . . and asked him to hire Bill Keith and he said he'd already [offered the banjo job to] Del McCoury, and I said, well, let Del do something else and put Keith on the banjo because he'll make a new sound in bluegrass . . . and [have] a different impact." This suggestion was "rejected" by Bill, Rinzler said. However, he was able to convince Bill to give Keith another listen, arranging an audition in Nashville on March 15. "[Rinzler] called me back after he'd spoken with Bill," Keith said, "to tell me the job was available."[77]

Keith arrived in town on the morning of Friday, March 15, and checked into the Clarkston Hotel as directed. He couldn't help noticing another guy carrying a banjo case checking in at the same time, and after he and McCoury introduced themselves, they discovered they were both there to audition for Bill Monroe. McCoury had not set a date with Bill for his audition, but in a "cosmic coincidence" (as Keith later called it), he too had come to Nashville on the 15th.[78]

That evening Bill came to the hotel. Saying, "Come on, boys. Follow me," he took Keith and McCoury to the National Life building next door and they watched as he played the *Friday Night Frolics* with Landers and Yarbrough. After the broadcast ended at 9:00 P.M., Bill took the two prospective banjo pickers to a small studio where his Martin guitar was waiting in a brown

Gibson case. Keith remembered that both he and McCoury demonstrated their abilities to play guitar with Bill, then Keith picked banjo. McCoury did not recall taking his banjo out of its case. "It was clear to all of us that Del could play guitar much better than I," Keith said, "and I believe I had the edge in banjo playing." Bill hired them both that night, Keith to play banjo and McCoury to play guitar, telling McCoury that if his playing improved in a few weeks, he would pay to get him in the musicians' union. "I had no idea what I was doing," McCoury admitted later, "but for some reason, he figured I could do it. He told me I'd like it. . . . He was right, of course. I did like it."

Keith and McCoury debuted with Bill on the *Opry* the next night (March 16). Live recordings include several whoops and shouts of joy from the audience for the banjo picking. McCoury, not yet in the local union, sang only (Landers played guitar). He would soon be a regular visitor to WSM's music library in the National Life building, learning the words to Bill's songs.[79]

In the end, the situation was resolved as Rinzler had suggested. This, combined with the *Sing Out!* article and the successful shows of February, may have caused Bill to see him in a new light. Perhaps there *was* a man who could manage him. According to Rinzler, by the end of March 1963, "we had worked out an agreement for me to move to Nashville and serve as a manager and booking agent in coordination with Jim Denny's agency and Decca Records."[80]

Bill was soon calling Keith "Brad" instead of "Bill," and Keith's friend Rooney asked him to explain.

> He said, "Well, when I came to work with Bill, he asked me what my name was. I said, 'Bill Keith.' Then he said, 'Well, what do people call you?' I said, 'Bill.' Then he said, 'What's your real name?' I told him, 'William Bradford Keith.' So he said, 'I'll call you Brad, because there's just one Bill in Bill Monroe's band, and that's Bill Monroe,'" and Keith smiled one of his Keith smiles.

A recording session was hastily arranged for Wednesday, March 20, and rehearsals were held on the 18th and 19th. McCoury was still not in the union, nor skilled enough, so Benny Williams filled in on guitar while Baker fiddled and Mauldin played bass. They recorded three banjo-driven instrumentals in quick order, all of which fiddlers had recorded in the 1920s: "Salt Creek," originally "Salt River," was retitled to avoid confusion with the soon-to-be-released "Big Sandy River"; "Devil's Dream" had been recorded by the Tommy Dandurand band with Rube Tronson (who fiddled while the Monroe brothers danced in the 1930s); and "Sailor's Hornpipe," which Baker wanted to play in the key of B♭, so Keith tuned his banjo up a half-step and played out of A. With the instrumentals "out of the way," as Bill used to say, there was time for him to cut a solo rendition of a song he and the band recorded as a quartet in 1941, "Were You There?" It would not be released for four years.[81]

On Wednesday, March 27, they held another session. This time, Jackie Phelps played guitar, ending his eight-year absence from Bill's recordings. Keith, yet to play a show on the road, was again the featured player. The first of three more banjo instrumentals was a remake of "Pike County Breakdown," with Keith alternating breaks in "Scruggs style" and "Keith style." Next was "Shenandoah Breakdown," a tune originally played by Rudy Lyle, who taught it to Joe Drumright in 1951. "When they decided to cut the tune," Drumright recalled, "Bill called me and I played it for him over the phone. He had forgotten the melody. It is my opinion that Rudy actually put the tune together." Last was an instrumental similar to the song "I Don't Love Nobody" titled "Santa Claus." Rinzler later wrote that Bill learned it from a fiddler "who lived in the area of northern Kentucky and southern Indiana," possibly in the town of Santa Claus, Indiana.[82]

The folk music revival had arrived in mainstream America, evidenced by the debut on April 6 of a show called *Hootenanny* on ABC-TV, broadcast from a different college campus each week. Near the end of April, Decca released a single of two recordings from 1962: "There Was Nothing We Could Do" and the aforementioned "Big Sandy River."[83]

As April 1963 was ending, Bill and the band headed west for the first tour Rinzler had arranged, Bill's fourth visit to California, his first of the 1960s. He and the band appeared at the first UCLA Folk Festival on the weekend of May 3, then drove four hundred miles north to the San Francisco Bay Area to play at Napredak Hall in Santa Clara on Friday, May 10, followed by a "Folk Bluegrass Festival" at Garfield Junior High School in Berkeley on Saturday, May 11. By then, "the boy from Boston, Massachusetts" (as Bill referred to Keith) was turning heads with "Devil's Dream" and "Salt Creek," and his driving picking was breathing new life into standards like "Raw Hide." "You give him about three more years on that five-string," Bill told the festival audience, "and every banjo picker in the country will be behind him—they'll all be following him."[84]

Bay Area bluegrass enthusiast Sandy Rothman, seventeen, had been studying Bill's music and went to the shows in Santa Clara and Berkeley. "It was fascinating to see Bill put on two quite different kinds of shows, one in a dance hall for down-home folks, and the other a bit more formal, for urban folk music enthusiasts. I met him backstage at the Berkeley show, introduced by Keith who was instantly friendly."[85]

Rinzler Teams Bill with Doc Watson

Bill and the band returned to Los Angeles on May 12, with a day or two to rest before the start of a six-night stand (May 14–19) at the Ash Grove, a folk music club in Hollywood. The Clarence Ashley Group was just finishing up a week there on May 12. Rinzler, in town to interview group member Doc Watson for an article published later in *Sing Out!*, discovered Watson had not only grown up listening to Monroe Brothers radio broadcasts, he was also was a longtime fan of Bill.

> Along with his younger brother David, Doc cut four truckloads of wood the sum-mer he was seventeen years old. With his share of the money, Doc bought a Sil-vertone guitar from Sears and Roebuck. That year [1940], he made his first public appearance on the stage at a fiddler's convention in Boone [North Carolina], and his song was the tune which a newcomer to the *Grand Ole Opry* was featuring as his theme, "The Mule Skinner Blues," as sung and played on guitar by Bill Monroe.

Before the Ashley Group left Los Angeles, Rinzler had an idea, one he thought would appeal to both old-time and bluegrass fans.

> I asked Bill if he would develop some repertoire that he and Doc could perform as duets. At the first rehearsal [probably on Monday, May 13], Doc suggested start-ing with tunes that Charlie and Bill had recorded. After rehearsing two or three of these, Bill suggested trying fresh repertoire that he had never performed or recorded with anyone else. . . . Bill made it clear that he was delighted to perform with Doc, but he wanted to make a distinction between the Monroe Brothers' sound and the Monroe-Watson sound. Nonetheless Bill was open to a thoroughly even exchange, incorporating Doc's ideas and his own.

The duo of Bill and Doc debuted at the Ash Grove on Tuesday, May 14, between sets by Bill and the Blue Grass Boys, and was an instant hit with audiences. Word traveled fast and, within a few days, they were booked to appear at the first Monterey Folk Festival, 325 miles to the north. On Sunday morning, May 19, the two flew to the festival ("I slept all the way up," Bill jokingly told the audience, "and Doc brought the plane in hisself"), then were flown back to L.A. to finish out the engagement at the Ash Grove.[86]

After the West Coast tour, Rinzler moved to Nashville, establishing his "Bill Monroe Associates" agency there. But, always on the go, "Nashville was never his permanent abode," according to Keith. After the tour, Baker left again, returning to the coal mines of eastern Kentucky as a safety inspector. Bill kept his spot open for a while, relying on the fiddling of fill-ins Buddy Pendleton of Virginia (who had recorded with the Greenbriar Boys in 1961) and Bill Sage of West Virginia (whom McCoury met in Baltimore). But Baker would not return until 1968.[87]

Bill, Keith, and McCoury played without a fiddle at the Brown County Jamboree on June 2 (with Jim Bessire filling in on bass). Before Keith picked "Salt Creek," Bill spoke of a forthcoming album: "Everybody that's interested in some new-type of bluegrass banjo pickin', you want to be sure that you get this banjo album. We've got six of the numbers already made [at the sessions of March 20 and 27] and we're tryin' to round up six more that nobody's heard, around over the country—some real old numbers—and we'll have it in shape in two or three months."[88]

Rinzler Meets Haney

Rinzler occasionally served as "chauffeur" for the band and, a week or so later, during a long drive back to Nashville from the East Coast, Bill decided Rinzler needed a break and directed him to a house in the Roanoke, Virginia, area. There Rinzler met Carlton Haney, and they had a "long and interesting talk," Rinzler said, with Haney telling him "he wanted to do a history of Bill Monroe's role in bluegrass. And he said, maybe it would be interesting to do it as a festival." Haney recalled that "Rinzler started telling me things about the music that I would have never known."[89]

Two new albums featuring Bill were released that month. The first, in early June, was his latest for Decca, *Bluegrass Special*, with recordings from 1962. According to its liner notes, Bill was now the academically approved "king" of bluegrass: "Folklorists, musicologists and millions of record collectors testify to this fact." Then, the deceptively titled *Early Blue Grass Music by the Monroe Brothers* was released in late June on RCA Victor's Camden label. Not bluegrass, early or otherwise, only half of its twelve selections were by the Monroe Brothers (the others were by Charlie from 1938–49). Its liner notes claimed that Bill "often referred to" his birthday on the 13th of September by saying he was "lucky from Kentucky."[90]

Near the end of June 1963, Keith's friends from Boston, folksingers Robert
Jones and Geoff Muldaur, and picking partner Jim Rooney, visited him in
Nashville. Keith, McCoury, and Rinzler had recently moved into an old house
near Centennial Park at 3324 Fairmont Avenue (later demolished), a large,
upstairs apartment that doubled as the "office" of Bill Monroe Associates.
As Rooney recalled:

> The day after we got there, Jones and Muldaur and the rest of us were all sitting
> around playing when the door flew open and in came Bill Monroe and Bessie
> Lee, his woman and bass player at the time. Bessie had her arms full of pies and
> homemade mayonnaise and all sorts of food that she had made, and she went
> into the kitchen. Bill just sort of stood there, grinning at us through his thick
> glasses. . . .
>
>   There was a guitar lying around. [Bill] picked it up and started picking on it. I
> don't know why, but I was amazed that he could play the guitar. I only knew that he
> could play the mandolin. I could see Geoffrey's jaw drop, as he watched Monroe's
> fingers dance on that guitar. It was the most natural thing in the world for him to
> be playing like that, and we were just sitting there with our faces hanging out. Then
> he just stopped right in the middle of what he was playing and handed the guitar
> to me. I panicked. I broke out in a sweat. I had to do something. All I remember
> was that I played something in D. I felt totally stupid and scared. After what he had
> just done, my little upside-down, left-handed style seemed really dumb [Rooney, a
> lefty, plays a standard-strung guitar turned "upside-down"]. When I got through
> he said, "That's good. You've got your own lick on that. Keep that up. That's good."
> That meant a lot to me. I'd never really thought of what I did as being "my own" or
> original, but it was, and he made me aware of that and made me want to keep at it
> and improve what I was doing, instead of being ashamed of it.[91]

This pleasant scene contrasts with the events of Sunday, June 23, when
Rinzler's plans to boost Bill's career finally collided with Birch's management
of the Brown County Jamboree. Rinzler had booked Bill and the band at the
Jamboree with an extra added attraction, the *Opry*'s star piano player, Del
Wood; Rinzler had called Birch, who told him that, yes, there was a piano on
the stage of the Jamboree Barn. But Birch didn't tell him it was out of tune
with several keys that didn't work (which, it was later suspected, he knew
but spitefully didn't tell, based on dealings Rinzler and other "outsiders" had
previously had with him). When Rinzler arrived on the 23rd to find the piano
unacceptable, a desperate search for another followed, ending with Bill and
several helpers hoisting a substitute onto the stage just before the afternoon
show. After the evening show, Rinzler confronted Bill, informing him that

he and Mauldin agreed—Birch had to be replaced. Rooney was there and later recalled what he observed that night.

> "Miss Del" [Wood] was going back with us [in Keith's car], as was Barry [Murphy, an English friend of Rinzler's, also visiting Nashville]. Keith was waiting for Monroe to pay him before we left. Monroe and Ralph were over in the [Jamboree Barn] talking. As we sat there we could hear snatches of the conversation. Ralph had a tendency to huff and puff when he got excited, and he was huffing and puffing a lot. He was talking to Bill about brother Birch and how slow he was and how the park needed a live wire to run it and build it into something. Ralph was treading on dangerous ground. Before we knew it, Monroe materialized at [Keith's] car. "Miss Del, you're going to stay up here tonight and go back with Bessie tomorrow [in the station wagon]. I'm going now." That was that. He didn't ask. He just told her. She was great. She just got out, and he got in. He closed the door and said, "I'm aggravated. Let's go." He didn't say another word until we got to Nashville.

Bill wasn't exactly angry, but he was extremely upset about being told what was going to happen, something no other person who served as his manager had ever done. The Monroes had chosen the Brown County Jamboree managers in the past. This time, Rinzler would choose.[92]

The next day (Monday, June 24), Rinzler called Neil Rosenberg. They'd first met at the Jamboree on June 2 and talked about the situation there. Rosenberg had written to him thereafter, mainly about booking Joan Baez at Indiana University, but also about improving attendance at the Jamboree. Based on all this, Rinzler thought he'd found the right man to be the new manager, and he called to ask Rosenberg to do it. But he passed, recommending longtime Jamboree enthusiast Marvin Hedrick (who'd made the first live recording there in 1954). Rinzler called Hedrick, who said he was too busy, but he offered to help Rosenberg in any way he could. When Rinzler called Rosenberg back, he was encouraged by Hedrick's offer and agreed to take the job. Birch would continue to direct the Saturday night square dances, and Rosenberg would begin managing the Brown County Jamboree the following Sunday, June 30.[93]

A Visit to Rosine

There don't appear to have been any hard feelings about replacing Birch by mid-July 1963, when Bill invited Rinzler and McCoury to go to Rosine with him for their first visit there. Rinzler recalled meeting Bill in a parking lot near his Goodlettsville farm: "We had difficulty finding him because, though he was standing nearby clad in baggy bib overalls and a baseball cap, he looked nothing like the dapper Bill Monroe we were used to as a performer." They went in Bill's pickup truck, with two piglets for brother Speed and two hunting dogs for brother Charlie in the back. "And that night, Bill and Charlie and Del and I went out, all of us, to the woods and listened to those dogs bay, and Bill could tell which one was which." Rinzler was surprised at how well Bill and Charlie got along: "There was no trace of the often overemphasized animosity between them. Del and I were regaled with jokes and stories about the old days."

The next morning Bill took them to the Rosine Cemetery to see the inscriptions on his parents' tombstones, mentioned in "Memories of Mother and Dad." Then they went to the old homeplace. As they walked up the ridge, Bill told them about coming there in 1949, seeing no light in the window of the house, and writing "I'm On My Way Back to the Old Home." He revealed his cross-eyed condition and told of hiding in the barn to keep strangers from laughing at him. "He then took us down to the barn," Rinzler wrote, "where we discovered that a trunk full of his father's papers, correspondence, and farm transaction logs had been scattered out across the floor."

> We spent an hour gathering all the papers and replacing them in the trunk, which we then took back to Nashville. At my request, Bill gave me two of the numerous log books his father so meticulously kept. He described his pride at the care and precision of his father's documentation and noted his sense of satisfaction that his family was both literate and highly competent in basic mathematics. The message that I derived from that experience with Bill was that his music was only one aspect of the deep commitment he felt to his family and regional culture.[94]

By July 23, Bill and the band, with Billy Baker on fiddle, were in New York City to tape Oscar Brand's *Folksong Festival* radio show. Then on the 26th, they were the opening act at the Newport Folk Festival, not held in 1961 or 1962 due to rioting at its sister jazz festival. Bill's brief set that Friday evening was given a lukewarm reception by a crowd of about fifteen thousand waiting to hear headliners like Joan Baez and Peter, Paul, and Mary. Vanguard Records recorded it all (including a set by Bill and Doc that night), but Decca, as usual, refused to allow Bill's music to be issued by another label.[95]

One week after Newport, an announcement appeared in *Billboard*:

> Decca is planning a two-record volume on Bill Monroe and His Blue Grass Boys to be released this winter. Titled "The Bill Monroe Story," it will include extensive notes and photos [of the] Bluegrassers back to 1939, when Bill made his debut

on the *Grand Ole Opry*. Volume will also feature all of Monroe's old favorites, some of which have been out of print on old Columbia and Decca issues for as many as twenty years.

The concept for this album probably originated with Rinzler. Two months earlier, Bill had spoken with some certainty of a banjo album. Neither album would be made right away, which suggests there may have been an impasse over how to proceed, possibly the reason Bill did not record again in 1963.[96]

On Saturday night, August 10, sixteen-year-old Tom Ewing of Columbus, Ohio, went to his first Bill Monroe show at a high school in nearby Delaware, Ohio. The future Blue Grass Boy had been playing guitar about two years: "I distinctly remember that whenever McCoury played a G-run, the rest of the Blue Grass Boys would smile or laugh—as if he'd been told by Bill to 'play 'em louder.' He was really booming them out there."[97]

Bill's son James, now twenty-two, and Brenda Faye Harris, nineteen, were married by a justice of the peace in Livingston, Tennessee, on August 15, 1963. Harris had graduated from Litton High School in the Nashville suburb of Madison in 1962, and James was working nights loading trucks at the Sunbeam bakery in Nashville.[98] A few days later, Bobby and Sonny Osborne, affiliated with MGM Records since the mid-1950s, recorded their first session for Decca Records on August 21. Their first single release would be available in October. Decca was now the label of Bill Monroe, Jimmy Martin, and the Osborne Brothers.[99]

Rinzler moved his base of operations back to New York in September 1963, after only three months in Nashville. With the 10 or 15 percent commission he was earning booking Bill or Doc Watson (now a solo act), he was having trouble paying his bills, causing him to again play with the Greenbriar Boys. (Their last album with him, *Ragged but Right* [Vanguard] was released in 1964.) He continued to handle Bill's bookings and traveled with him whenever he could, and he left behind a representative in Nashville, Alabama native Ken Marvin (né Lloyd George; formerly "Lonzo" of Lonzo and Oscar). On September 23 (ten days after Bill's fifty-second birthday), Decca released the first of Bill's records featuring Bill Keith, "Devil's Dream," backed with 1954's "New John Henry Blues." Rinzler has been credited with allaying Decca's fears concerning Bill's reference to John Henry as "a little colored boy."[100]

Not long after he returned to New York, Rinzler joined the board of directors of the Newport Folk Foundation, to help choose the festival's performers. He also became an employee of the foundation as head of its Field Research Programs, earning $5,000 for a three-month effort to find undiscovered talent for the festival. Busier now than ever, he still found time to visit Decca's New York office to investigate Bill's unreleased recordings.[101]

It was "Monroe Family Day" for the first time at the Brown County Jamboree on Sunday, October 13, with Bill and the band (Joe Stuart fiddling) plus brother Birch, who fiddled on the afternoon show, and daughter Melissa, now twenty-six, who sang on the evening show. It was also to have been a Monroe Brothers reunion. But, reportedly, Bill, who had the Blue Grass Boys to pay, couldn't convince Charlie to perform gratis. Nonetheless, Bill seemed in a good mood that afternoon, joking with the audience after Keith picked "Devil's Dream": "Brad Keith is the only banjo picker that I ever had down at the *Grand Ole Opry* that could be playin', just standin' around some place, then, after he got through, all the *Grand Ole Opry* players would give him a hand. They'll do that for him, though they never would do that for me."[102]

The last show of the Jamboree's 1963 season came four weeks later, on Sunday, November 10. Bill and the band were featured, as usual, with Melissa returning as a special guest. According to Keith, she was traveling with the band full time so Bill could keep her away from Martin Haerle, a Starday Records executive who, Bill was convinced, was courting her solely to influence her father to leave Decca for Starday. Meanwhile, Rosenberg had been dealing directly with Bill about the Jamboree's management, and he recalled later that whatever ill feelings there might have been between Bill and him earlier were now gone: "[Bill] asked me to stay on for the following year as manager—an offer I declined because of the negative impact the job had on my performance as a graduate student at I.U., where I was finishing up my M.A. and about to start on a Ph.D." Birch would again manage the Brown County Jamboree in 1964.[103]

Six days later, on Saturday, November 16, Bill and the band with Melissa appeared at Mechanics Hall in Worcester, Massachusetts, with Grandpa Jones and the Lilly Brothers. Bill's show that evening was recorded by eighteen-year-old David Grisman, a New Jersey protégé of Rinzler who had inspired him to begin playing mandolin while in junior high school.[104]

Six days after that, on Friday, November 22, 1963, President Kennedy was assassinated in Dallas, Texas. The nation was in shock with sorrow abounding, but there was no respite for Bill and the band (or Melissa). Bill had purchased Johnnie and Jack's old bus, a GMC 3703, and its "maiden voyage" as the "Blue Grass Special" began on November 22, en route to shows in Miami on November 23 and Tampa on November 24. On the 25th, as the band returned to Nashville, the president's funeral ceremonies were broadcast all day on television and radio.[105]

Melissa Breaks Down

Following two days off, Bill and the band and Melissa crisscrossed the eastern United States, playing in Warrenton, Virginia, on November 28, New York City, on the 29th, and Wheeling, West Virginia, at the *WWVA Jamboree* on the 30th. During the Jamboree broadcast, Melissa's emotional problems first became evident. Shortly after she began singing her featured song, she burst into tears and was inconsolable the rest of that evening. Rinzler, who had joined them for the broadcast, tried to convince her father that she might need professional help. But Bill angrily rebuffed him, insulted by the suggestion that Melissa might have some sort of mental problem.[106]

On they went. In three days, they were due back in Hollywood for a return engagement at the Ash Grove with Doc Watson, from Tuesday, December 3, through Sunday, December 8. They picked up Tex Watson in Bean Blossom to help drive the bus. It took them most of the way without a problem but finally broke down near Las Vegas on December 2. Bill, Melissa, and Mauldin flew on to L.A., and the rest (Keith, McCoury, Stuart, and Watson) were left to get the bus fixed. Bill played a set on December 3 with a young local guitarist, Al Ross, then finished the night playing with Doc Watson. The Blue Grass Boys, Tex Watson, and the bus arrived on December 4.[107]

During that week at the Ash Grove, Georgia-born Dobro player Robert "Tut" Taylor surprised Bill by presenting him with a new case for his mandolin. Taylor, in Hollywood to record an album for World-Pacific Records, had known Bill since the 1940s. "In the early sixties," he said, "I noticed what a crummy case he was carrying his mandolin in," an old contour case held together with black electrician's tape. A sign painter by trade, Taylor painted Bill's name, a silhouette of an F-5 with a king's crown in its center, and a scroll beneath his name declaring "Original Bluegrass Since 1927" on the top of a new brown, rectangular Gibson case. He had asked Bill what year he began playing with Charlie and Birch, thinking that was the year that bluegrass started, and Bill had estimated 1927.[108]

Before the week was over, the band scheduled to play the following week (December 10–15) had cancelled. Ash Grove owner Ed Pearl asked Bill to play in their place, and Bill agreed. Unfortunately, Keith was due at an air force reserve meeting in Nashville that weekend and would be in trouble if he didn't show up. The band had already been told they were playing the *Hootenanny* TV show in January, and Keith had informed Bill he would not play it, due to the show's blacklisting of Pete Seeger, his inspiration for playing the five-string banjo. With growing doubt about what to do next,

Keith recorded a session with "Tut" Taylor without Bill's permission (which could have caused him to be fired). Then, on December 7, Keith's uncertainty was resolved. A clearly disturbed Melissa lashed out at Mauldin, smearing lipstick on her white ermine coat. Afterward, she told her father that Keith and McCoury had made improper advances toward her, which Bill angrily accused them of and they vehemently denied. "If she was going to be on the road with him," Keith said later, "there's no way that I could have stayed." On December 9, he flew back to Nashville, his days as a Blue Grass Boy over.[109]

Keith had worked with Bill for nine months, longer than most of Bill's banjo pickers after Lyle's departure in 1954. Regardless of how his tenure ended, whenever Keith and Bill encountered each other in the years that followed, their relationship was always warm and cordial. As Bill said later,

> At a time when I needed a boost, I think that Brad gave it to me. I think it just came in when I needed it. Before he came along, no banjo player could play those old fiddle numbers right. You have to play like Brad could play or you would be faking your way through a number. It's learned a lot of banjo players what to do and how to do it to where they can come along and fill that bill today.[110]

Ash Grove owner Pearl quickly arranged for local musician Ryland "Ry" Cooder, seventeen, to fill in on banjo during the second week (Keith tutored him briefly concerning kickoffs and tempos before he left). Cooder was soon replaced by Maryland native Bobby Diamond, a friend of McCoury's from Baltimore, who flew to California immediately after being summoned. "I got there before I left," he said later. This new edition of the band worked well enough to be held over at the Ash Grove for yet another week, from December 17 to the 22nd.[111]

The Beatles: Four Young Men

A new kind of rock and roll from England had just invaded the United States about that time. Bootleg copies of "I Want to Hold Your Hand" by the Beatles were being played on American radio stations, forcing Capitol Records to move the release date of their album up from January 13, 1964, to December 26, 1963. By February 1, 1964, the song would zoom to number 1 in *Billboard*'s "Hot 100" chart. "The Fab Four" appeared on *The Ed Sullivan Show* on February 9, seen by 73 million viewers. By then, it appears likely that, based on what actually happened during the next few years, Rinzler advised Bill that to survive the onslaught and attract young people to bluegrass, his Blue Grass Boys should include four young men. Bill's bands had always included musicians younger than he was, but now it was imperative that they all be young *and* all be male, like The Fab Four.[112]

Meanwhile, Bill and the band finally appeared on *Hootenanny* on Saturday, January 25, 1964 (nine months after its debut), taped that afternoon at the University of Tennessee in Knoxville (with McCoury, guitar; Joe Stuart, banjo; Billy Baker and Benny Williams, fiddles; and Mauldin, bass), then returned to Nashville to play the *Opry* that night. For some reason, McCoury didn't get the word that a recording session was scheduled for Monday, January 27. "Billy [Baker] and me figured we didn't have nothin' to do for a few days," he said, "so we went to Knoxville and got on the Cas Walker [TV] show [the *Farm and Home Hour*], just to have somethin' to do."[113]

Joe Stuart played guitar in place of McCoury at the session on the evening of the 27th, with Joe Drumright (banjo), Benny Williams (fiddle), and Mauldin (bass). Bill sang three vocal solos: a remake of his "I'll Meet You in Church Sunday Morning," originally recorded in 1950 with a quartet chorus; "Mary at the Homeplace," written to the tune of "East Virginia Blues" by Ken Clark, a Georgia native who recorded for Starday; and a remake of Pete Pyle's "Highway of Sorrow," originally cut in 1951.[114]

Mauldin called McCoury the next day, telling him about the session that evening, his first as one of the Blue Grass Boys and, as it turned out, his last. Stuart played twin fiddles with Benny Williams, with Drumright and Mauldin again on banjo and bass, respectively. Bill first sang another solo, "One of God's Sheep," by gospel star Wally Fowler. "Roll On, Buddy, Roll On" followed, the ninth Monroe Brothers song to be reprised. Bill and McCoury sang the duet chorus into one mike, and McCoury showed off his improved guitar playing throughout. He later said he learned the song at the session. He also said that only Bill seemed familiar with the last song, "Legend of the Blue Ridge Mountains," written by musician Robert Horace Scarlett of Putnam County, Tennessee, just east of Nashville. McCoury recalled Bill asking him the meaning of the word "rendezvous" in its second verse.[115]

Six days later, on Monday, February 3, another session was held, and by that time, McCoury was gone, picking banjo in the L.A. area with the Golden State Boys. Bill persevered, of course, calling Jimmy Maynard in to play guitar, moving Stuart to banjo, and arranging for Buddy Spicher to fiddle with Williams. The first of only two songs recorded was "Last Old Dollar," from the repertoire of Lonzo and Oscar, via Bill's current manager, Ken Marvin. According to Marvin, "I claim I wrote it. Actually, I've been hearing it since

I was about six years old. I 'stole it' is the way to put it." The second was the instrumental "Bill's Dream," with a melody Bill said he'd heard in his sleep, dreaming he was pulling dogs out of a well.[116]

The Birth of James William Monroe II

Bill's first (and only) grandchild, James William Monroe II, was born to James and Brenda Monroe on February 11, 1964, in Nashville. Bill was on a tour in London, Ontario, Canada, on the day "Jimbo" was born, followed by shows in five Michigan cities, ending in Saginaw on February 16. And shortly after the tour started, Bill told Mauldin that it was her last road trip with him.[117]

Mauldin's Dismissal

Bill may have been acting on Rinzler's advice regarding the need for four young male Blue Grass Boys, or he may have hoped to cure Melissa's emotional problems by eliminating an old source of unhappiness. Whatever the case, it's clear that Bill was no longer worried about Mauldin retaliating for her dismissal by informing the *Opry* of their supposed "love child." But Mauldin was not going without some form of retaliation. On Valentine's Day she wrote a letter to Rinzler from a hotel in Grand Rapids, expressing her dismay at losing her livelihood, but primarily telling him of Bill's attentiveness to Melissa while on the road, twisting it into something ugly by suggesting that their relationship was incestuous. But if she was hoping to turn Rinzler against Bill, it obviously didn't work.[118]

Rinzler's investigation into Bill's unreleased Decca material was about to yield results, beginning with the appearance on March 2 of *Bill Monroe Sings Country Songs* on Vocalion, Decca's label for less-than-new recordings. The album included "Peach Pickin' Time in Georgia," "Used To Be," and "When the Phone Rang," recordings that had been waiting since 1951, 1955, and 1959, respectively, to be released. Among the other selections on Bill's tenth LP were several old favorites undoubtedly chosen by Rinzler, including "I'm on My Way (Back) to the Old Home," "The Little Girl and the Dreadful Snake," "Close By," and "No One But My Darlin.'" Coincidentally, also on March 2, Jim and Jesse joined the *Grand Ole Opry*, signed that day by *Opry* manager Ott Devine. Jesse McReynolds later recalled Bill's encouragement: "Bill was always positive about anything we done at the *Opry*. In fact, the first time we went to Nashville to record [in 1952], he took us backstage at the *Opry*. He was always nice to us."[119]

Aside from his involvement with Bill's recordings, Rinzler continued to write about Bill and his music. "The Roots of Bluegrass," an update of his 1963 *Sing Out!* article, appeared in the March 1964 issue of *Hootenanny* magazine, a spin-off of the TV show.

> Now a part of the national folk music revival, bluegrass no longer belongs to "country music" alone; it stands on its own, apart from the commercially oriented industry, as a development from traditional vocal and instrumental music of the rural South.
>
> This development has been championed and almost consciously directed by one man: Bill Monroe. Of the currently successful bluegrass bands, all but one or two are headed by musicians who got their start as members of Bill's "Blue Grass Boys."

Rinzler went on to outline, for the first time in print, the major players in Bill's band from 1945 through 1954, a very useful explanation for readers just developing an interest in Bill's music.[120]

Mauldin's rancorous feelings toward Bill don't show in her playing at Bill's sixtieth Decca recording session, on Thursday evening, April 9. But she probably didn't know that this session, her thirty-sixth with him, was also her last. (Bill would soon ask her to stay home and take care of the Good-lettsville farm.) Phelps returned to play guitar and, as in February, Stuart picked banjo while Williams and Spicher played twin fiddles. They started with the newest first, "Louisville Breakdown," an original fiddle tune by Bill (who always pronounced the city's name as "Louis-ville"). Then Bill sang lead on the verses, switching to tenor when Williams sang lead on the choruses of a song Williams wrote, "Never Again." Next, Bill sang an impassioned solo on "(We're Going) Just Over in the Glory Land," originally recorded as early as 1925. Then an old standard show closer, "Fire on the Mountain," was probably chosen at the last minute to end the session. Stuart's timing is off when he comes in for his break, but the other players quickly adjust and save the take. It was, however, the last time he picked banjo on a Bill Monroe session.[121]

Out in California, Sandy Rothman was playing guitar and singing lead in a Bay Area band called the Black Mountain Boys, with twenty-one-year-old Jerry Garcia on banjo. Rothman had visited the East in 1963 and, intent on returning, tried to get everyone he knew to go with him. "The only one game enough was Jerry," he said. There were several reasons for going, but most exciting was the remote possibility of getting a job with Bill Monroe. So, in May, they headed out in Garcia's 1961 Corvair.[122]

On Saturday and Sunday, May 16 and 17, Bill and the band (with Bobby Smith [possibly] on guitar; Joe Stuart, banjo; Benny Williams, fiddle; and Ken Marvin filling in on bass) were part of the first country music show at Madison Square Garden in New York City, with a host of stars, including George Jones. Told beforehand that he could do only two songs, Jones was determined to do more. By the fifth song, Bill had volunteered to help: "In front of thousands of people," Jones later wrote, "Monroe and a member of his band [possibly Marvin] slipped out of the shadows, into the spotlight, and put an arm under each of my arms. They physically lifted me off the floor. My voice trailed to silence as I was pulled from the microphone's reach." Jones said there were two reasons why he wasn't angry with Bill: "First, he was much bigger than me, and second, he was my hero."[123]

Bill played the Jamboree in Bean Blossom on May 24, with Jimmy Maynard on guitar, Bruce Weathers (a member of Maynard's Cumberland Mountain Boys) on banjo, Williams fiddling, and Marvin on bass. California hopefuls Rothman and Garcia were there, letting Bill know they were musicians by standing around on the grounds of the Jamboree, leaning on their instrument cases. "Neither one of us had the courage or the slightest idea, or plan of action, how to tell him we wanted to play with him or ask him for a job," said Rothman. "We were petrified. We never said a word."[124]

As in June of the previous year, a new Decca album and a reissue album were released in June 1964. First to appear this time, on June 6, was the reissue album, *Bill Monroe's Best* on Harmony-Columbia, with seven of its ten cuts by "the classic band." Now, eleven of the twenty-eight recordings the band made were available on LP. The new Decca album, *I'll Meet You in Church Sunday Morning*, was released about a week later, most of its recordings from 1962.[125]

In mid-June 1964, Jerry Garcia decided to return to California (where, in 1965, he would found the Grateful Dead). Rothman stayed on with an old friend from California, Neil Rosenberg, and the next time they went to the Jamboree, Bill happened to be there on a Sunday off. This time, he approached Rothman, saying he remembered meeting him in Berkeley and asking what he was doing there. "I told him I just wanted to hear a lot of his music," Rothman said. Bill invited him to "come along with us on the bus sometime and go around to some shows," then gave the surprised youngster his phone number. A few days later, Rothman called to find out his location from Carolyn, and caught a ride to North Carolina to meet up with him. Bill readily recalled his offer, telling the eighteen-year-old carrying only a guitar and a small suitcase, "Put your things on the bus." After traveling to several showdates with the band (Jimmy Elrod, banjo; Maynard, guitar; Williams, fiddle; and possibly Marvin on bass), Rothman rode back to Nashville with them.[126]

Bill may have been recruiting another young man for the Blue Grass Boys. It appears that earlier in June, Bill had already tried to involve his twenty-three-year-old son James, starting him off on upright bass in much the same way as Mauldin.

> He said, "Go with me and if you can play the bass, keep time with it with your right hand, it will fulfill my contract." He had a five-man contract to do a show in Atlanta, to open up a big shopping center there. I said, "You know I can't play. I don't know where the chord change is." He said, "Well, don't worry about that, just play your timing, if you can, with your right hand, and stand behind me." He was a pretty good-sized man, so he gave me a pretty good shield, you see? On the stage there were various mikes and he would move from one to sing out of . . . to another to play out of. I would follow behind him with that bass and try to hide, you know, from the audience. That was my introduction to bluegrass music.

In late June, after Rothman was in Nashville a few days, Bill asked if he would play a few shows with him (he said yes, of course), then took him to a western shop to buy him a hat. Shortly thereafter, James would become a regular member of his father's band, learning to play bass.[127]

Banjo pickers were in scarce supply at the time. When Bill heard Rothman pick a banjo "that lived on the bus," he asked him to pick it on shows while fiddler Williams switched to guitar for a few numbers. Rinzler, meanwhile, recruited his first young man for the band, twenty-year-old New York City native Steve Arkin, a "melodic" banjo picker (who won second place in the Philadelphia Folk Festival banjo contest Keith won in 1962). On summer break from Marlboro College in Vermont, Arkin took a bus to Nashville, made his way to the *Friday Night Frolics*, introduced himself to Bill, and told him he was his new banjo player. "He just looked right through me," Arkin said.[128]

Bill might have been put off by Arkin's directness. He may have also been disgruntled because, by this time, he was using another young banjo player, Gene Roberts of Richmond, Virginia, to fill in occasionally, but felt obligated to accept Rinzler's choice. He hired Arkin and eventually wrote a banjo tune for him, but Arkin described it as "a miserably embarrassing tune . . . which I never wanted to play." It was never given a name.[129]

Melissa reappeared about this time, traveling with the band occasionally. Rothman recalled she was very withdrawn.

> When I first encountered her, it was a surprise. One day, the bus pulled up at the Y [where he was staying], and when I got in, there was this perfect, doll-like, youngish woman sitting stiffly in about the third seat back from the door, all dressed up, wearing heavy makeup, and propped slightly forward in her seat by a big head of stiff-sprayed hair. Melissa was silent most of the time, as I recall.[130]

Near the end of July 1964, Carlton Haney visited the Newport Folk Festival, invited by one of its directors, Ralph Rinzler. Rinzler said later that Haney wanted to do a multiday event like the Newport festival, so he told him to come and see it for himself (even though Bill wasn't there that year). As an observer, Haney noticed the workshops in particular, later a part of his festival. His involvement with the *New Dominion Barn Dance* was nearly over, and his management of Reno and Smiley would end when they broke up in late 1964, so he would soon have the time to make his ideas a reality.[131]

On August 7 President Lyndon Johnson asked Congress for, and was granted, unlimited authority to wage war against North Vietnam. And on August 8 the Osborne Brothers joined the cast of the *Grand Ole Opry*. But Bill never protested the membership of the *Opry*'s fourth bluegrass band. "He never did question the fact at all that we came there," said Bobby Osborne. One night shortly after they joined, Osborne sang "Mule Skinner Blues," playing guitar when their regular guitarist was absent and singing it in B♭ (the Osbornes had recorded their 1963 rendition in A, a whole step higher than Bill's key of G). "Bill met me when I come off the stage. He said, 'That's the way that number ought to go, right there.'"[132]

Arkin stuck with it until mid-August. Money was a major problem: both he and Rothman were musicians' union members in New York and California, respectively, but neither joined the Nashville local (and, as a result, neither played the *Opry*). As such, it appears that Bill viewed them as nonunion musicians and, as usual, he paid them less.[133]

Bill replaced Arkin with Don Lineberger, another young (age twenty-five) melodic-style banjo picker from Georgia. A protegé not of Bill Keith's but of the other pioneer of melodic picking, Bobby Thompson, Lineberger was the first (and only) left-handed banjo picker with the Blue Grass Boys. Rinzler hadn't been the one to find Lineberger: he had approached Bill for the job in mid-July when the band played close to where he was living in Georgia.[134]

Bill and the band were in New York City in late August, meeting up with Doc Watson at Ralph Rinzler's Greenwich Village apartment on the day before they were to appear together at Sunset Park, Sunday, August 23. Former Blue Grass Boys Jack Cooke and Bill Keith were there to greet them, and among the local bluegrass aficionados "dropping by" for the jam session that afternoon was New York musician and photographer Artie Rose, bringing with him Richard "Richie" Brown, a young black man learning to play bluegrass guitar. Keith had picked with Brown at Washington Square and he introduced the nineteen-year-old to Bill. Told that Brown hadn't brought his guitar, Bill quickly solved the problem. "Bill gets up and takes the guitar from Doc Watson and gives it to me!" Brown said later with a laugh. Then they sang "Sittin' on Top of the World" together. (Brown would later concentrate on playing mandolin, becoming a leading exponent of Monroe-style picking.)[135]

Rothman left at the end of August. His departure had more to do with guitar playing than with pay: "Our duet singing was good, but he and I both knew my rhythm guitar playing needed to be, in his words, 'more stout.'" Several guitarists filled in afterwards, including Jack Cooke, Kelly McCormick of the McCormick Brothers, Ken Marvin, Jimmy Maynard, and a young Alabamian, Garry Thurmond. Then *Opry* veteran Jimmy Elrod, twenty-five years old, was hired to play guitar. He had recorded with Bill on banjo about seven years earlier.[136]

By mid-September, Rinzler had booked several concerts in the North in October. Flying to two was necessary, but paying for airline tickets for the entire band would have eaten up the profits, so Rinzler arranged for several local young men to substitute, also providing Bill with an opportunity to audition some potential Blue Grass Boys. For the first show, in Plainfield, Vermont (near Barre), on Friday, October 9, Rinzler enlisted twenty-one-year-old New Jersey native Gene Lowinger, fiddler with the up-and-coming New York Ramblers, and twenty-four-year-old Californian Roger Bush, bass player with the Kentucky Colonels, formerly the Country Boys (staying with Rinzler in New York while playing shows in the area). Rinzler asked Bill Keith to pick banjo and bring a lead singer-guitarist with him. Keith chose twenty-two-year-old fellow Massachusetts native Peter Rowan.[137]

Rowan had recently left Colgate University in upstate New York and was playing mandolin with Keith and Rooney's band around Boston.

> Here he was—the master—walking fifteen feet off to the left of the band, chopping rhythm and watching the band from over there! . . . His rhythm was so

magnetizing, you felt there was a direct electrical current running through this man. . . . I had learned "Up along the Ohio River" ["On the Old Kentucky Shore"], which was the first duet I ever sang with him. . . . We sang that, and after the show we were sitting there and he said, "You pick pretty good. You ought to come to Nashville. I could help you."

Bill flew back to Nashville the next day (October 10), arriving in time to play the *Opry*. His twenty-fifth anniversary on the show was celebrated early, on October 24, with *Opry* officials knowing he would be absent on the 31st, the last Saturday night of the month, his actual anniversary date.[138]

Second Fiddle to a Steel Guitar

It appears that during this time in October, Bill and the Blue Grass Boys (Jimmy Elrod, guitar; Don Lineberger, banjo; James Monroe, bass; Benny Williams, fiddle) were involved with the making of the first (and only) motion picture to feature Bill: *Second Fiddle to a Steel Guitar*. Categorized as a comedy starring Leo Gorcey, Huntz Hall, and Arnold Stang, it is notable only for the musical performances of numerous "Nashville heavyweights of the time," as Charles Wolfe described them. Most sang their recent hits, recorded and filmed at Owen Bradley's new "Bradley's Barn," in Mt. Juliet, Tennessee, near Nashville. Bill sang the songs that helped make him a "heavyweight": "Mule Skinner Blues" and "Blue Moon of Kentucky." Benny Williams wasn't available when the soundtrack was recorded, so Buddy Spicher fiddled in his place. As a result, when Williams was available for the filming, his movements didn't match the soundtrack.[139]

Bill and the band then traveled to Chicago to appear with Doc Watson at Orchestra Hall on Friday, October 30. An ad for the show in the *Chicago Tribune*, using promotional info Rinzler provided, was the first to use the phrase "high lonesome sound" to describe Bill's music.[140]

The next morning (October 31), Watson and Bill flew to Boston to play Jordan Hall, then the city's biggest concert venue. With not enough money to include the Blue Grass Boys, Rinzler arranged for Bill's old friend Tex Logan to fiddle, Gene Lowinger to twin fiddle, and Bill Keith to pick banjo. Rinzler tried to get Del McCoury or Jack Cooke to play guitar, but they weren't available, so Peter Rowan again served as lead singer-guitarist and Everett Alan Lilly, Everett Lilly's twenty-year-old son, played bass. That night, Rowan talked to Bill again about working for him: "He asked me about school and the army. I didn't tell him that I was due to go for a physical. Vietnam was getting hot and I was twenty-two."[141]

The current Blue Grass Boys (Elrod, Lineberger, James Monroe, and Williams), meanwhile, left Chicago and went to Bean Blossom to play the Brown County Jamboree without Bill on Sunday, November 1. Neil Rosenberg was there, expecting to see Bill, but what he saw was, nonetheless, "a revelation."

> I realized when I saw this group the extent to which Bill himself made the Blue Grass sound in the band. Not everyone in the band knew all of his songs—breaks, keys, parts—so Bill made sure they did what they were expected to do. Also, the band members would get out of synch with each other sometimes, and he'd stamp his foot to get everyone on the same time. Often he would lay back on the mandolin rhythm at the start of a song or tune and then up his volume and attack to pull everyone together. Those things were missing from this show.[142]

Keith brought Rowan to Nashville that week, with Rowan expecting to go to work. But Bill still had Elrod on guitar. "He didn't want to just drop the guy," Rowan said (but he eventually let him go, according to Rowan). Bill invited Rowan to play the Brown County Jamboree with him, on Sunday, November 8 (making amends for his absence the previous Sunday). A tape of the afternoon show reveals their voices blended well on "True Life Blues," but they couldn't answer a request for "Memories of You" because Rowan didn't know it yet. He returned home to continue learning Bill's songs and, to be available whenever Bill called, he deliberately flunked his physical exam for the draft.[143]

Charlie and Betty

By this time (late 1964) Charlie and Betty Monroe were living in Martinsville, Indiana. They had mortgaged the Monroe property to finance their coal business and were unable to repay the loans, and they'd had no success leasing the property to an Owensboro, Kentucky, coal company. Eventually, two Ohio County businessmen, pharmacist brothers Hayward and Jack Spinks, bought Charlie and Betty out, leaving them with enough money to buy a home elsewhere. They chose Martinsville, near Birch and Bertha.[144]

By February 1965 Bill's banjo man, Don Lineberger, appears to have suffered from the temporary self-doubt that afflicts many professional musicians (but particularly Blue Grass Boys, since their leader seldom told them outright how they were doing). As Lineberger later said,

When I'd been playing with Bill about six months, I asked him what I could do to improve my banjo playing. . . . He'd never said a word to me about my banjo playing up until then. But when I asked him that, he turned to me and said, "Don, your playing is sounding like a machine gun. You got to give a note a chance to *do* something."[145]

Bill had begun consulting with Rinzler, Decca producer Silverstein, and a representative from Jim Denny's Cedarwood Publishing Company before sessions. So, the session of Tuesday, March 16, began with a Cedarwood property, "Long Black Veil." Already closely associated with the Country Gentlemen, Bill might have avoided it otherwise. Next was "I Live in the Past," written by Virginia Stauffer, a Michigan native who had lived in Nashville since 1960. Then twenty-four, she was fifty-four-year-old Bill's newest love interest. Third was "There's an Old, Old House." Sandy Rothman heard Bill sing this George Jones song during his tenure in 1964 and, when he later played briefly with the New York Ramblers, he sang it with them. Their recording of it (on Silver-Belle, without Rothman) would be released eight months before Bill's December 1965 release. Lineberger had no banjo solos on any of these songs, but they all benefited from his backup. He and James (playing their first official session) were joined by the rest of the band seen in *Second Fiddle*, including the unseen fiddler playing on Bill's segment, Buddy Spicher, this time actually playing second fiddle.[146]

Two more Rinzler-arranged concerts using substitutes followed, the first a folk festival at Rinzler's alma mater, Swarthmore, on April 2. Lowinger again fiddled, and Julian "Winnie" Winston picked banjo (both from the New York Ramblers), with Del McCoury returning to play guitar and brother Jerry McCoury on bass. Then Bill appeared at Dartmouth College in New Hampshire, with Lowinger fiddling, Keith on banjo, and Rowan on guitar. Lowinger recalled, "At the Dartmouth gig, as we were warming up [before the show], Peter Rowan told me that Monroe had asked him to return to Nashville to work with him. I was jealous and determined to get the same invitation." After the show, he got it, but he told Bill he needed to finish his last semester at Rutgers University in New Jersey. "He said that was fine, that he'd be glad to have me."[147]

The first major anti–Vietnam War protest was held in Washington, D.C., on Saturday, April 17, with an estimated fifteen thousand protesters. Then, on April 18, the Brown County Jamboree opened under the management of the Brown County Music Corporation: TV-store owner Marvin Hedrick, school teacher Carroll D. "CD" McClary, Indiana State Police officer Jim Peva, and former Blue Grass Boy Roger Smith. The four men, helped by their families and others (including former staff band bassist Jim Bessire), made many improvements to the Jamboree Barn prior to the opening, completely remodeling the kitchen and food service area. Headlining at the season opener were Bill and the band, with Lineberger, James on bass, Rowan, and Williams.[148]

Lowinger graduated in May 1965 with a bachelor's degree in political science and promptly made plans to go to Nashville. He'd gotten to know Jim and Jesse when the New York Ramblers opened some shows for them, and when the brothers played at Sunset Park on May 30, he asked them for a ride to "Music City" on their bus. He auditioned at the *Opry* on June 5 and played on the show that night, managing somehow to do it before joining the local union. Bill introduced him in a joking kind of way, possibly to indicate his uniqueness in the South: "He's a Jewish boy from New York City, and if you folks really like the way he plays, I'll give him the job." Years later Lowinger said, "I didn't feel any insult, but I was surprised by his referencing me that way." Without elaborating, he said the prejudice he experienced from those who heard the introduction was more disturbing to him.[149]

Album Impasse Resolved

By June 14, it was apparent that the impasse over "banjo album" versus "Bill Monroe Story" album had been resolved. The solution, which Rinzler guided, was to release both albums, beginning with *Bluegrass Instrumentals*. Not a banjo album, it did, however, include two new banjo-driven tunes recorded with Keith, "Sailor's Hornpipe" and "Santa Claus." There were also five never-before-released fiddle tunes, two of which had been waiting ten years to be heard: "Tall Timber" and "Brown County Breakdown." The rest had only been released as singles, including "Get Up John" in 1954 and "Raw Hide" in 1952. Rinzler wrote the liner notes, based largely on his first taped interview with Bill in 1964, explaining the origins of the tunes and listing the session date and musicians for each one. Neil Rosenberg, who wrote in his *Bluegrass: A History* that it was "the first historically-oriented collection of Monroe's recordings," agrees that it was the first such collection of *any* bluegrass artist's recordings. (Bill is pictured on the album's cover with a small price tag on his mandolin's headstock. It came from a package of socks Bill

Keith bought on the way to the Brown County Jamboree in 1963. Keith put the socks on in the dressing room while Bill was gone, then stuck the price tag on the headstock. "When he returned he got a laugh out of it," Keith said. "But what surprised me the most was that he left it there for years!")[150]

As usual, Columbia was eager to checkmate Decca, also releasing in June an album with nine recordings by the "classic band" on *The Original Blue Grass Sound* on Harmony-Columbia. Available on LP for the first time were "Will You Be Loving Another Man," "Little Cabin Home on the Hill," "Molly and Tenbrooks," and six others plus "Travellin' This Lonesome Road" from 1949. Twenty of the twenty-eight recordings made by Bill's band in 1946–47 were now available on three albums.[151]

First Party at Tex Logan's

Bill and the band were soon on their way to the first New York Folk Festival, held at Carnegie Hall in New York City, where they were to play on June 18. They arrived on the 17th, welcomed by Rinzler, who then called Tex Logan at his home in nearby Madison, New Jersey.

> He called up and said Bill wasn't doing anything, how about them coming out to the house, and I said, "Fine." When I learned they was coming, I decided, well, let's just make a good party out of it. I rushed around there and cooked some barbecue and beans, made a salad, and a twenty gallon crock of iced tea. We invited some friends from around Madison there that had never heard this music and we had this party and played all night after we had this big supper. We started then, carrying those on.

Parties for Bill, sometimes twice a year, would be held at Tex's through 1974.[152]

Ira Louvin's Funeral

On June 20, 1965, Ira Louvin, tenor voice of the Louvin Brothers, died in a car crash following a show in Missouri. He and his brother Charlie had parted, recording their last song, "What Would You Give in Exchange?," in September 1963. In 1964, after Ira Louvin borrowed Bill's mandolin to sing a song with his brother on the *Midnite Jamboree*, he was overheard to joke with Bill that he wanted him to sing "Swing Low, Sweet Chariot" at his funeral, to which Bill had laughingly agreed. According to Louvins biographer Charles Wolfe, "As it turned out, Bill kept his word. He was working in Pennsylvania [after the New York Folk Festival] when he learned that Ira had died. He dropped his entire schedule, returned to Nashville, and sang at the funeral, as he had promised."[153]

It appears the writing of the song "Walls of Time" began after Bill rejoined the band following Ira Louvin's funeral, as they were en route to play the Brown County Jamboree on June 27. Bill's bus, now dubbed "the Bluegrass Breakdown," had broken down, and they were traveling in cars. As Rowan recalled later:

> We were driving through Kentucky. The sun was just coming up. He [Bill] was in one car. I was in another. He pulled over and signaled me to stop. I got out and he said, "Listen to this and don't forget it," and he sang the whole melody. I got back in the car, singing it over and over, and by the time we got to Bean Blossom, I had some words for it. We were writing all over napkins in the restaurant where we stopped for breakfast.

Asked thirty years later about the song, Rowan said it originally began with the first two lines of the first verse ("The wind is blowing across the mountain and down o'er the valley way below"). He said the song's writing was a collaborative effort that continued for weeks thereafter, verified by Lowinger: "The song was a work in progress over several road trips. Bill and Peter would sit across from each other and talk about the poetry of the lines, how the phrasing should be sung, the chord progression, when to get soft or loud. And I sat there and watched the whole thing take shape."[154]

The Brown County Music Corporation called it quits at the Brown County Jamboree at the end of June (after two months). "As Birch may have told you," Jim Peva wrote to Bill earlier, "we have not had a really good crowd at the Jamboree so far this season." The largest, 258, paid one dollar each on May 16 to see the first appearance there by the Osborne Brothers, but the band was paid $300. Management of the Jamboree again reverted to Birch.[155]

On July 24, Bill and the band were again featured at the Newport Folk Festival. There Bill met fiddler Byron Berline, whose *Pickin' and Fiddlin'* ("the first bluegrass fiddle album," Elektra) had been out about five months. Rinzler had invited Berline and his father to perform at the festival, and Jim Rooney and Bill Keith backed them onstage. As Rooney recalled, "[Lue Berline] was a champion fiddler and so was Byron. Lue was a crusty old son of a bitch. . . . Monroe really liked Byron's fiddling, and he liked Byron's old man a lot, too." Bill asked the younger Berline to guest with the Blue Grass Boys onstage, later offering him the fiddle spot whenever it might be open.

A student at Oklahoma State University, he promised to contact Bill after he graduated in a year and a half.[156]

On the main stage at Newport, with an audience of thousands, Bill introduced the band as he had at smaller venues. Thinking it clever, he referred to Lowinger as "the only Jewish bluegrass cowboy in the country." "I had never taken offense at Bill's introduction," Lowinger wrote in *I Hear a Voice Calling.* "I knew that he was proud that, coming from a background that was so unfamiliar to him, I loved his music so much that I'd worked hard to learn it." This time, however, Bill went a little too far—he told Lowinger to "say something in Jewish to the audience." Defusing an embarrassing moment, Lowinger managed to say "Oy vey" (a Yiddish expression of exasperation), to the amusement of the crowd. Afterward, he asked Bill not to do this again and he agreed not to. But he continued to introduce him as a "Jewish bluegrass cowboy" for several months.[157]

After leaving Newport, they arrived at Sunset Park on July 25. There, Rowan ran into twenty-seven-year-old Lamar Grier, a banjo-picking native of the Washington, D.C., area where they had met at a picking party. Rowan arranged for him to pick a couple of tunes with the band that day, and after August 7, when Lineberger quit, Grier started filling in. Bill soon offered him the banjo spot, but Grier was married with two children, had a good job with Western Electric (like Lonnie Hoppers), knew the pay would be less, and didn't know whether to accept the offer or not: "I hemmed and hawed and was wishy-washy, and that went on for a couple of weeks."[158]

In late August 1965, "Blue Moon of Kentucky" was included on the newest album by Ray Charles, *Country and Western Meets Rhythm and Blues* (ABC-Paramount), the third collection of country songs interpreted by the pop music great. In *Billboard*'s "Top LPs" (pop) chart in September and October, it only reached number 116 of 150, and Charles's rendition owed more to Presley than to Monroe, but the royalties it earned went to Bill and must have improved his financial situation.[159]

The First Multiday Bluegrass Festival

Preparations for Carlton Haney's multiday bluegrass festival—bluegrass music's first—were nearly complete by then. Rinzler, Haney's collaborator, wrote an announcement about the "First Annual Roanoke Blue Grass Music Festival" for *Billboard* and placed ads in folk music magazines. Haney typed up, mimeographed, and mailed a flier to contacts all over the country advertising "3 Big Days" (September 3, 4, and 5) at Cantrell's Horse Farm, near the town of Fincastle, "12 miles north of Roanoke, Va., on 240 acres of beautiful blue grass" (the location Bill had chosen). Headliners mentioned were "the originiator [*sic*] of the music, Bill Monroe," plus Jimmy Martin, Clyde Moody, Ronnie Reno, Don Reno, Red Smiley, the Stanley Brothers, Mac Wiseman, Howdy Forrester (who did not appear), and Doc Watson. Workshops and instrumental contests filled the mornings and afternoons on Friday and Saturday, with shows in the evenings, and on Sunday, a "Gospel Singing" followed by a banjo contest. After the contest, from 3:30 to 7:00, came the culmination of Haney's efforts, "The Blue Grass Music Story," told by reuniting Bill with former Blue Grass Boys. "My only reason to put on a bluegrass festival was to let the world know that it all came from Bill Monroe," Haney said later.[160]

Mayne Smith arrived at the festival grounds from California on Thursday morning, September 2. He was working for the John Edwards Memorial Foundation, a new organization dedicated to the study of traditional music, which had sent him to "observe" this historical event. The scholarly *Journal of American Folklore* had recently published his "An Introduction to Bluegrass," a detailed explanation of the genre in which he wrote that "Bill Monroe and his Blue Grass Boys played the first bluegrass music in 1945" (when Earl Scruggs joined the band). Smith brought a copy with him to the festival, and it was passed to Bill. Later that evening, after Rinzler warned him of Bill's unhappiness with it, Smith found himself in a room with Bill and a few others.

> As soon as there was a lull in the conversation, I said to Bill I'd heard that there were things in my article that he didn't like, and that I would appreciate his telling me about them. Bill replied to the effect that he hadn't planned on bringing it up, because he knew I meant well, but since I asked. . . . Then followed quite a long statement, with me sitting down, looking directly at him and listening very intently, and him standing, moving around on his feet and looking in different directions.

Bill was understandably upset at Smith's notions of when and how bluegrass began. In effect, Smith gave Scruggs the credit for it. These were "damn lies" Bill told him, and he challenged Smith to correct them. Not long after, in his report on the festival for *Sing Out!*, Smith wrote, "Bluegrass is the intimate, personal music of a single man, Bill Monroe."[161]

Lamar Grier was still hemming and hawing, so, while he went to his regular job on Friday, September 3, former Blue Grass Boy David Deese picked banjo with Bill on the first day of the first bluegrass festival (Deese was already there to play with Red Smiley's new band, the Bluegrass Cut-Ups). Grier arrived on Saturday to play the rest of the festival with Bill, with a Scruggs-inspired style that was distinctly different from the melodic picking of the previous two years.[162]

Carlton Haney emceed "The Story of Blue Grass Music" on Sunday, using humor to relax the famous participants and provoke intriguing comments from them. In one from Bill, concerning the many musicians who had worked with him over the years, he tried to make amends for his flippant comments about Flatt and Scruggs.

> People like Mac Wiseman, Carter Stanley, Clyde Moody, plumb on back to when bluegrass music first started—they have really been just old warhorses, stayed right in there, and helped me all the way through. I haven't done everything for bluegrass. I don't claim that. I just claim that I started it. And a lot of fellers has helped me right on down the road with it—people like Earl Scruggs, Don Reno, Lester Flatt—boys like that. And I could just keep on namin' 'em off. . . .

The musical highlight was another reunion of Bill with Don Reno and Mac Wiseman, joined this time by Benny Martin.[163]

Grier was hired that weekend, but he had to work off a two-weeks' notice with Western Electric. Filling in at the fairgrounds in Irvine, Kentucky, on Saturday, September 11, was J. D. Crowe (who told biographer Marty Godbey he "had a ball"). The next day, on the eve of Bill's fifty-fourth birthday, Neil Rosenberg filled in at the Brown County Jamboree. Grier finally met up with the band the next Sunday, September 19, at Elicker's Grove Park in Spring Grove, Pennsylvania, and he would soon get a taste of what life was like in "the big time." On the way back to Nashville, the bus's brakes (operated by a compressed air system) needed attention, bringing things to a halt in Ozone, Tennessee, just west of Knoxville. As Grier recalled:

> It was due to a rubber air-brake hose that split apart. We waited for hours for a replacement, which couldn't be found, so a guy [patched the hose], and Bill decided that we needed to shove off to get back to Nashville. I didn't know how to drive the bus yet, so Pete Rowan drove off. The first encounter with a problem was driving the bus down off the mountain, using the gears to slow it down. The bus had a history of jumping out of gear and popping back into neutral . . . so Lowinger assigned himself to kneel on the floor by the transmission shift lever and hold it into whichever gear it was in.[164]

Work thinned out in October and November. Grier took a part-time job at a grocery store (which Jimmy Martin helped him get), after his family moved to Nashville. Suddenly, the few dollars he could earn playing shows at the Brown County Jamboree (on October 3 and November 7) were welcome. At the afternoon show on November 7, Bill again introduced Lowinger as a "Jewish bluegrass cowboy." The audience laughed, but by then, it was no longer funny to Lowinger. After the show, he again asked Bill to stop referring to him that way. "He said, 'Okay.' That was the last I heard of it," Lowinger said.[165]

Lowinger had begun attending services at a synagogue on West End Avenue in Nashville, telling Bill that, because of it, he might be a little late for a *Friday Night Opry* (formerly *Friday Night Frolics*, now held at the Ryman). A few days after the band returned from Bean Blossom, Lowinger got a phone call from Bill.

> It was usual for the Blue Grass Boys to get a call from Bessie when Bill got bookings, and I got a call directly from Bill only once in my tenure with him. He wanted to join me at a service at the synagogue. We went together, and it was a strange feeling sitting in an environment in which I had been raised with a man who had never experienced it before. I glanced at Bill several times. He had his eyes closed, his chin raised, and he looked as though he was just absorbing the atmosphere around him. At the end of the service, Bill and I greeted the rabbi and shook hands. Bill thanked him for the music and said, "I really liked the songs, and I'm gonna find a way to use some of those notes in my music."

This seems to have been Bill's attempt to atone for whatever hurt he might have caused, by openly demonstrating his tolerance and appreciation for the Jewish faith.[166]

With the air-brake hose replaced, Bill and the band headed west in the Bluegrass Breakdown in early December to play first in Oregon, then California. Arriving in Hollywood, they had nothing to do during the week before Christmas while they waited to play the Ash Grove the week after Christmas. Lowinger, already taking violin lessons, stayed with relatives in L.A. and met a classical violinist friend of theirs, took some long walks, and arrived at a decision: he was going to leave Bill to study classical violin. Two weeks later, after the *Opry* on January 8, 1966, Bill and James took Lowinger to the airport for the flight home to New Jersey. "[Bill] let me know that I would always be welcome to play with him and that he wanted me to stay in touch."[167]

If you tuned your radio to a country music station during this time, you might have heard George Jones and Melba Montgomery singing a duet rendition of "Blue Moon of Kentucky" (United Artists). Their recording, with former Blue Grass Boy Curtis McPeake on banjo, didn't appear in *Billboard* for some reason, but reached number 25 in the "Country Top 50" of *Cash Box* and number 33 of 50 in the "Top Country Singles" of *Record World* in January 1966.[168]

After Lowinger left, Bill and the band were returning home after a few days on the road, with the Bluegrass Breakdown's air-brake system again in need of maintenance. "You could stand up on the brake pedal and the bus would slowly crawl to a stop," Grier recalled. "As we drove into Nashville, Pete was unable to stop at a red traffic light, resulting in a broadside crash into a car driven by a young woman [who] went into near-hysterics. The police arrived and had the bus towed back to its usual parking place, on the grounds of the Nashville Transit Company, and work on it began."[169]

It was still being worked on at the end of January, and Bill was booked to play at McGill University in Montreal, Canada, so Grier, Rowan, and he drove the one-thousand-plus miles in the station wagon in the dead of winter (James was ill and unable to go). "Two people sat in the front seat, Bill always in the passenger's seat," said Grier, "while the other tried to sleep in the back seat." Rinzler had arranged for a fiddler to meet them in Montreal, twenty-three-year-old Californian Richard Greene. Classically trained, he had "dabbled" with old-time music until he heard the fiddling of Scott Stoneman. He then played electric bass and occasional fiddle with the Greenbriar Boys, recorded with Red Allen (*Bluegrass Country*, County), and was familiar with some of Bill's recordings when he arrived by plane in Montreal on Thursday, January 27, but he still didn't know what Bill looked like.

> [When] I first met him, I didn't even know it was him. I asked somebody, "Where is he?" because here was this heavy, big guy and I thought of him as a little guy because of his high voice—I know these are ridiculous associations I had—and he was dressed very casually. They had made a long road trip the previous day, and he was tired and sullen. And it was a tremendous shock to first meet him.

Filling in on bass that evening was Canadian musician Dick Miller, and on Friday, Saturday, and Sunday, in the bar of the Hotel des Chenaux, in the Montreal suburb of Vaudreuil, it appears the band played without bass.[170]

Greene was unable to join the band when the weekend in Montreal ended, due to a two-months' notice he had to work off with the Greenbriar Boys. But he visited Nashville on March 11 and 12, 1966, to play the *Opry* with Bill, then joined the Blue Grass Boys full-time on April 1.[171]

In early 1966, after the bus was repaired, Bill wrote "Crossing the Cumberlands." As Grier recalled:

> We were riding back home to Nashville in the bus and Bill said, "It's about time we made you a banjo tune." I immediately thought, "Oh, boy!—another 'Blue Grass Breakdown'. . . ." So Bill took my banjo and played some rudimentary notes and patterns and gave the banjo to me to duplicate. After I did the verse portion, or A part, Bill said he would take one of his fiddle tunes and change it around somewhat to make the B part, or the chorus of the tune. He hummed the tune he wanted me to duplicate. Later he asked, "Where are we?" and he answered himself that we were crossing the Cumberland Mountains [in eastern Tennessee]—hence the tune title. . . . It developed that I really didn't enjoy playing that tune onstage because it had a very slow pace, plus it was difficult to play.[172]

After Greene joined the band, Bill began to mentor to his young bandsmen. He noticed Greene rushing when soloing and took steps to correct it. "My rhythm was uneven in those days," Greene said. "For six months, Bill had me play rhythm chops on each backbeat and nothing else. He wouldn't let me do background licks until I learned how to stop rushing." Grier, under the influence of guitarist Clarence White (of the Kentucky Colonels), was trying to incorporate White's "syncopated syncopations" into his banjo picking. "Bill got on me in a nice but firm way to straighten up my act," Grier said. "Pull it together, and don't be so loose and disjointed. And he was right—because I was experimenting with what I was doing."[173]

Bill's First Trip Overseas

For three nights in early May 1966 (Wednesday the 4th through Friday the 6th), the band played at the Gaslight Café, a tiny folk music "coffeehouse" in New York's Greenwich Village, just a few blocks from Rinzler's apartment, where they all stayed during the engagement. Then, on Monday, May 23, the band flew to England for Bill's first trip overseas. For the next three weeks, they toured throughout the country, playing at nine different venues (including Philharmonic Hall in Liverpool, Town Hall in Birmingham, and the Stevenage Folk Festival in Kent), traveling in a bus owned by Bill Clifton, then living in Kent. The high point came on Friday, June 10: London's equivalent of Carnegie Hall, the Royal Albert Hall, with Clifton and American folk singer Hedy West the opening acts. Bill "got standing ovations after many songs he did," Grier recalled.[174]

The tour included an unpleasant interlude: during it, Bill heard folk-style songwriter Tom Paxton's "The Last Thing on My Mind" and mentioned his interest in recording it to Rowan. Rowan told this to Greene, who thought the song was inappropriate for Bill, and when Rowan repeated this to Bill, he reportedly told him, "You have ruined it for me," ending the possibility of it being recorded by him. Rowan later said Bill "took it like I had really crossed him," and he didn't speak to him for about three months. It appears Bill believed that what he'd told Rowan was confidential.[175]

Bill and the band returned to the United States in mid-June 1966, during the time Decca released *The High, Lonesome Sound of Bill Monroe and His Blue Grass Boys*, the album that began life as "The Bill Monroe Story." A comma distinguished it from 1965's Roscoe Holcomb album *The High Lonesome Sound*, subtly indicating its contents were both high in pitch *and* lonesome in sound, rather than just extremely lonesome (the original meaning of "high lonesome"). On the front cover, Bill indeed looks lonesome, holding his battle-scarred F-5 with the price tag Bill Keith stuck on its headstock still firmly in place. On the back cover were more of Rinzler's detailed notes with extended comments by Bill, gleaned from interviews in February 1966. *The High, Lonesome Sound* gave renewed life to Bill's recordings of 1950–54, and released, for the first time anywhere, 1952's "My Dying Bed" and the 1954 version of "My Little Georgia Rose" with three fiddles. Neither Columbia nor RCA Victor offered a competing album this time.[176]

While Bill was overseas, Rinzler booked the band into Nashville's Black Poodle night club in Printer's Alley, then one of the city's seedier areas, between Third and Fourth Avenues North. The club had called Rinzler, encouraged by Greene's girlfriend, a waitress there, agreeing to pay $1,200 for a six-night stand in late July. So, in late June–early July 1966, James and Rowan decided to check it out. The Blue Grass Boys (without Bill) had played that night at King Henry's Lodge, a bar near Nashville, earning a few dollars on a Wednesday night. Afterward, James put his bass in his car and Rowan laid Bill's guitar (which he'd been playing instead of his own) underneath it, behind the front seat, and they drove to the Black Poodle, parking in a lot nearby. "That was a mistake," James said, "because it was darker down there." They were in the club about an hour, listening to the Stoneman Family, and when they returned to the car, it had been broken into and Bill's fine old herringbone guitar was gone. According to Rowan, when he told Bill, he was greeted with "a massive silence," followed by, "Pete, why don't you quit?" Rowan said later that Bill owed him about four hundred dollars, so he decided to stay. (The guitar remains missing to this day.)[177]

In July 1966 five avid bluegrass fans (including Pete Kuykendall and Richard Spottswood) published the first issue of *Bluegrass Unlimited*. Not yet a magazine, its eight mimeographed, legal-sized pages were a godsend for underinformed bluegrass fans in the D.C. area, with reviews of the latest records and listings of upcoming appearances. Its first regular article, in the August issue, was a report by musician Fred Geiger on a one-day "festival" at Whippoorwill Lake Park in Warrenton, Virginia, on July 10, with Flatt and Scruggs, Jim and Jesse, Jimmy Martin, the Osborne Brothers, and Bill.

> All the "big names" in bluegrass were there, but Monroe's band was the biggest, and as usual he proved it. His bands have changed countless times over the years—banjo pickers, fiddlers, and guitar men have come and gone—but it doesn't really matter. The individual brilliance (or incompetence) of Monroe's musicians is irrelevant when it comes to Monroe himself, for he transcends those struggling around him and projects a creative honesty which could no more be changed than could the path of the earth around the sun or the law of gravity. He projects himself.

On the way to the Park, Grier recalled that Bill had stepped to the front of the bus to make an announcement: "Before arriving, Bill announced to us all to not go to suck up with any other musicians that were there [particularly Flatt, Scruggs, or the Foggy Mountain Boys]. He said to let them come to you, don't you go to them."[178]

Bill and the band went through with their engagement at the Black Poodle (July 25–30), in spite of the loss of Bill's guitar. Bill seemed to relish the extra time he had, playing near home: "I think we did six sets a night and finished at 2:00 A.M. every night," Greene said, "then Bill would drive home and get up every morning at 5:00 A.M. to tend to farming. I don't think he knew what sleep deprivation was—he sang and played brilliantly every night." Bill told an interviewer he was making up for lost time.

> I like to do a lot of things on the farm that maybe, down through the busy years of music, why, I missed, you know? In the spring, I farm and raise cattle and hogs; and I have a pack of foxhounds that I enjoy going out a couple of nights a week, if I'm around Nashville, and listen to them run—I enjoy that kind of life. When I'm doing that . . . I work, you know, and play music on the side. . . . But I have always been a feller, I guess, could work twenty-four hours if I had to do it, you know, and stand up pretty good under it.

Bill was also growing tobacco on his Goodlettsville farm, a crop that requires constant tending if grown the old-fashioned way. His cattle were Black Angus, a breed that derives from his ancestors' native Scotland.[179]

Bill and the band were due to play the one-day "First Annual Pennsylvania Bluegrass Festival" in New Tripoli (near Allentown) on August 28, reason enough for another party at Tex Logan's in nearby Madison, New Jersey, on Friday the 26th. Doc Watson was there, and, during a jam session, he and Bill were recorded playing some of their last commercially released music together. Rinzler had tried to convince Decca to record them as a duo, but the label refused to budge for anyone not affiliated with it. Watson would record an album for Columbia Records with Flatt and Scruggs in December.[180]

The Bill Monroe Fan Club

Carlton Haney's second multiday bluegrass festival, still the only one of its kind, was again held on Labor Day weekend (September 2–4) in Fincastle, near Roanoke, Virginia. This time, the stage was decorated with a banner calling for Bill's election to the Country Music Hall of Fame (established by the CMA in 1961, its inductees already included Roy Acuff, Tex Ritter, Jimmie Rodgers, Ernest Tubb, and Hank Williams). On Saturday, Bill's first fan club was organized, suggested by West Virginia native Marvine Johnson (now Marvine Loving), later its first president. Bill asked her what a fan club was and why she thought he needed one.

> So I said, "Well, you have been kindly shunnin' your admirers and you're gonna have to quit that." I knew he was bashful, so I said, "You're gonna have to buck up. Them people out there loves you and loves your music. You're gonna have to shake hands with 'em, talk to 'em, have pictures made." He said, "What would I say to 'em?" I said, "Just ask 'em if they like your music and if they play music. You can lead it on from there."

Also on Saturday, David Grisman hosted a mandolin workshop with himself, John Duffey (of the Country Gentlemen), Bobby Osborne, Ronnie Reno (Don Reno's eighteen-year-old son), and Bill—all of them at one point playing "Sally Goodin." "All tried their hardest to project their personal style in the tune," Neil Rosenberg wrote later in his first *Bluegrass Unlimited* article, "and they all played good things. But Monroe, with a gracefulness the others lacked, showed his command of the whole tune. It didn't have to be far-out to be good; it was merely 'Sally Goodin' played right with Bill Monroe's personal stamp of beauty on it." On Sunday, "The Story of Blue Grass Music Part 2" benefited from the presence of former Blue Grass Boys not present in 1965, including Kenny Baker, Jim Eanes, Rudy Lyle, Sonny Osborne, and "Tater" Tate. Sonny and Bobby Osborne, joining Bill to sing "I Hear a Sweet Voice Calling," brought down the house. "That song alone was worth the trip," wrote Rosenberg.[181]

In early October 1966 Bill and the band were recruited to attract crowds to a series of campaign speeches by U.S. Senator John Sparkman, an Alabama Democrat who had served in the senate since 1946. As Grier recalled:

> We performed on a flatbed trailer and the sound system came with the trailer. During one of the jaunts from town to town, Bill asked, "Where's my mandolin?" No one knew, and it couldn't be located. We all traveled by car to the next town and met up with the truck, usually in parking lots around shopping centers. Bill mentioned that if the mandolin was gone, he wouldn't be playing anymore—it was that mandolin or nothing. Everyone got nervous about it. It all ended up well though, because the mandolin was found [in its case] . . . just laying on the trailer—not held down or secured in any way.

Returning to Nashville afterward, with James behind the wheel, his father told him to pull over to the side of the road, and Bill stepped to the front of the bus to make another announcement—they were going to record that week. Grier later said, "I remember asking Bill, 'What are we going to record?' Bill said don't worry about it. You all play well enough to come in and do it."[182]

On Friday, October 14, 1966, Bill ended a nineteen-month absence from the recording studio, the longest "dry spell" since 1955–57. After warming up on the renamed *Friday Night Opry*, he and the current band began recording the first of two sessions that began at 10 P.M. and ended early the next day. Bill had probably already decided that James, not Rowan, would sing lead on the choruses of the songs (James had been singing lead on gospel quartets at shows). Others have speculated that Bill was penalizing Rowan for past mistakes, but it seems more likely that he was primarily intent on furthering his son's musical career. Also, the two songs had choruses with trio harmony, and Bill knew Rowan had the best voice for the baritone part. Both songs had been country music standards since the 1940s: "When My Blue Moon Turns to Gold Again" was recorded in 1941 by composers Wiley Walker and Gene Sullivan. Bill had sung "I Wonder Where You Are Tonight" with former Blue Grass Boy Jim Eanes a few weeks earlier at Fincastle. Grier, meanwhile, had gotten wind that they were to record "Turkey in the Straw" (which Doc Watson and Bill had played at Tex Logan's on August 26).

> So I went home and practiced it. I told Bill I was having trouble with it and he replied, "Just play the melody." . . . A few days later, in the recording studio, Bill started the [tune] at around three times faster than I had done at home. Hence, I could not get all of the notes into the [tune] that I had in mind to do. I had to deliberately omit some notes to be able to handle the increased speed.[183]

Three days later, Bill and the band were back at the Black Poodle for six more nights (October 17–22). The annual Disc Jockey Convention was held during this time (October 19–22), and the Stanley Brothers were in town on Thursday the 20th for a luncheon sponsored by their fan club, where they were presented with an award for twenty years in the music business. That night, Carter Stanley visited the Black Poodle and sang a few songs with Bill. It was the last time Bill would see him alive.[184]

Bill and the band returned to the studio on Thursday, November 3, at 10 P.M., joined by Buddy Spicher on second fiddle. Spicher and Greene had already worked together successfully at the *Opry*: "He was incredibly fast at finding two- and three-part harmonies to any part I played," said Greene. "I'd show him the way I was going to do it and he would just do perfect harmony." This session's selections were all aimed at the folk music audience. First was a ballad Bill learned from his mother, "Pretty Fair Maiden in the Garden," which Bill sang publicly for the first time at the Newport Folk Festival in 1963 in the key of G. On November 3, "Bill was in less-than-perfect voice," according to Greene, so he chose to sing it a half-step lower, in F#. Bill and Greene played in standard tuning, while Grier and Spicher tuned down a half-step. Second was "Log Cabin in the Lane," an old-timer recorded recently (1959) by Jim Eanes (Starday). Last was "Paddy on the Turnpike," with Greene fiddling solo, another mandolin-driven traditional fiddle tune. Bill had played it at the first bluegrass festival's mandolin workshop in 1965 (and Rinzler had taken note). The recording lacks a banjo break because, according to Grier, he'd had no advance notice that it was to be recorded.[185]

They soon left for Canada, returning to Montreal for a week (November 7–13) at the Country Palace, a nightclub near McGill University. During the week, Doug Benson, president of McGill's Folk Music Society, who had arranged for Bill's appearance at the university in January (and was responsible for the banner urging Bill's election to the Hall of Fame at Roanoke in September) interviewed first Rowan and Greene, then Bill. In the interviews,

Rowan—in spite of everything—and Greene had only highly complimentary things to say about Bill. Asked about Greene, Bill, who had become an arbiter of what was and what was not bluegrass, thanks to the current band, made a classic comment: "Richard is adding a lot to bluegrass—it's hard to keep him from adding too much. . . . The biggest job of bluegrass is to keep out what don't belong in it." (The taped interviews were edited into a four-part series of radio programs, broadcast on McGill University's CFCF in February 1967.)[186]

The Death of Carter Stanley

Bill and the band were back in Nashville, preparing to leave for a show on Saturday, December 3, in Ponchatoula, Louisiana (near New Orleans), when word came that Carter Stanley had died on December 1 (of liver disease at age forty-one). After the show in Louisiana, Bill flew to Bristol, Virginia. The next morning, he was driven to the funeral, which was held in the gymnasium of Ervinton Elementary School in Nora, Virginia, to accommodate the crowd of mourners. Formerly the high school where the Stanleys were once students, it was also the place they first saw Bill perform in 1940. As Ralph Stanley recalled:

> The coffin was laid out in the middle of the gym floor. It was dead silent when Bill walked out by himself, his footsteps echoing up to the rafters. He held his hat in his hand and sang the old hymn "Swing Low, Sweet Chariot" a cappella, like we do it in the Primitive Baptist Church. Then he put his hand on the coffin and he said, "We'll meet again."[187]

Two days later, Bill was back in the studio, recording on Tuesday evening, December 6. He sang two more solos, beginning with "That's All Right," written by Autry Inman, who also wrote "You Rule My Heart," recorded by Melissa Monroe in 1950. (Inman also served briefly as Bill's manager in 1964–65, in association with Rinzler.) Next was "It Makes No Difference Now," penned by Floyd Tillman and sold to Jimmie Davis in 1938. In 1962 Ray Charles had included it in his first album of country songs, *Modern Sounds in Country Music* (ABC-Paramount). The session's traditional fiddle tune was "Dusty Miller," again led by Bill's mandolin. "Bill taught me the tune one-on-one," Greene said. He was not shown a third part, which fiddlers from the Southwest often played, and Bill may have learned it that way from southeasterner Arthur Smith.[188]

Ten days later, on the night of Friday, December 16, Bill and the band recorded again. They started with the duet "Midnight on the Stormy Deep," with Rowan singing lead for the first (and only) time, a folk song that Doc Watson and Bill had revived. Bill probably learned it from the original 1926 recording by Mac and Bob. (Comparing their recording with his, there are only slight differences of wording, most significantly in the last stanza, in which Mac and Bob sang, "Than to trust *in* love so false as thine.") Then came "All the Good Times Are Past and Gone," already a bluegrass standard thanks to the Monroe Brothers, the tenth song of theirs Bill would redo. Last was "Soldier's Joy," one of the first tunes Bill heard played by a string band and one of the few instrumentals he was permitted to play with the Monroe Brothers. It ended ineffectively, so a flourish by mandolin and fiddle was recorded separately and spliced onto the end of the take.[189]

The Deaths of Betty Monroe and Speed Monroe

The old year ended with the death of Charlie's wife Betty, on New Year's Eve at age fifty-six. The new year began with the death of Bill's brother Speed, a heavy smoker like Betty, of lung cancer, on January 14, 1967, at age seventy-one. That night on the *Opry*, Bill dedicated "Wayfaring Stranger" to him, a song he and the band had been featuring as a vocal, this time played as a mandolin solo with the band backing him up. "That was a very moving experience," Grier said. "I almost stopped playing to hear and feel the mood that Bill was generating."[190]

Bill, as usual, had little time to grieve. A recording session was scheduled for Monday, January 23, a week after Speed's funeral. It was the last for this particular bunch of Blue Grass Boys and the least productive, with only two numbers recorded. First was Bill's solo vocal of Kirk McGee's "Blue Night," another unfamiliar song for the band and more of the "stuff the producer said to record," according to Rowan. Bill modified McGee's song slightly, changing from tonic (I) to subdominant (IV) chords on the *third* beat in each stanza's third line, rather than on the fifth beat, as in the original. The second number, the traditional fiddle tune "Grey Eagle," featured some un-orthodox fiddling that Greene said Bill was O.K. with at the time: "He and I worked together. He would show me some ideas and then I'd show him; he accepted some pretty far-out stuff on that tune." (However, "Soldier's Joy" and "Grey Eagle" would not be released until 1976 in Japan and the 1990s in the United States.)[191]

In February 1967 fiddler Byron Berline drove from Oklahoma to Nashville to tell Bill he'd graduated from college and was ready to go to work. During this usually slow time, workwise, Grier flew to Washington, D.C., to record a Folkways album with Bill's old friends Hazel (Dickens) and Alice (Foster). One of the songs they waxed was "The One I Love Is Gone," which Bill said he wrote in 1955 but never recorded. The album (*Won't You Come and Sing for Me?*) would not be released until 1973.[192]

Rowan played his last with the band on March 1, 1967. He said he left without a studio recording of "Walls of Time" being made "because Bill knew that he would have to deal with the fact that I was [one of] the writer[s] of that song when he recorded it. So, he was holding it back until I was out of the picture." As we have seen, however, Bill had long operated with the belief that a bandleader could claim a song as his own if he had the original idea for it.[193]

Greene departed the band after March 5. Later, he commented on the experience of playing with Bill:

> I was very fortunate to work for Bill because of the way we focused on his music. It was always easy to get the "truth" about what we were involved in, which was his way of playing music. If he liked it, it was right. If he didn't, it was wrong. Everything was very black and white. . . . Since that time, I've learned that that approach to music was unique. . . . Even today I still long for that convenient source of the "truth" we had in those days. It was never again like that for me.[194]

Although Bill hated to see any member of his Blue Grass Boys leave him, he developed a philosophical outlook about it:

> If you were a Blue Grass Boy, you knew your name would be called [announced] on the *Grand Ole Opry*, and that helped you, whoever you were. So, if you worked for me a year and a half, up to three years, then you were ready to get out on your own. And that was all right with me, because by that time, I needed somebody else in the music. . . . I think it's better that way than it would've been if I'd kept four of the same players all the way through, you see? It's given people a chance to hear all kinds of banjo playing, and singing, and fiddle players.[195]

When Bill called Berline to tell him the fiddle spot was available, Berline told him he had received his draft notice and could be called to duty at any time. "Bill told me to play with him as long as I could," Berline said. Bill began to feature him fiddling a tune on almost every *Opry* appearance.[196]

Several capable lead singers came and went during March and early April 1967, including Curtis Blackwell from South Carolina and two Texas natives,

Mitchell Land and Mylos "Myles" Sonka. By the second week in April, fiddler Benny Williams was filling in as lead singer-guitarist.[197]

By this time, Ralph Rinzler had been hired by the Smithsonian Institution in Washington, D.C., and would help found its annual Folklife Festival, combining traditional music and traditional crafts. Still involved with the production of Bill's recordings, he wasn't able to handle his folk-music-related bookings. These (as well as Doc Watson's) he turned over to Manny Greenhill's Folklore Productions, which also handled bookings for Flatt and Scruggs.[198]

The Denny agency, however, probably booked a black-tie stag dinner celebrating the thirtieth anniversary of the Evans family as publishers of the *Nashville Tennessean*, held at the Municipal Auditorium on April 6. Bill and the band, wearing tuxedos (which Bill rented), played on a riser four feet off the floor, alternating five-minute sets with the Nashville Symphony Quartet, also on a riser in another corner of the banquet hall, while a thousand guests feasted on "gourmet-cut roast prime rib eye au jus." When the speeches began, Bill and the band sat down on folding chairs at the back of the riser, and Berline, sitting next to Bill, recalled what happened next.

> And he scoots his chair back and off he goes, and as he's going, he grabbed me with his left hand. He knocked the bridge off my fiddle—almost tore the fiddle out of my hand. As he did, I turned to my right and I watched him, and all I could see was just the soles of his shoes going down. And the noise he made, falling on a concrete floor with a chair underneath him! . . . I remember Benny Williams with tears in his eyes, from laughter. . . . I asked Bill, "Are you O.K.?" He said, "Get down here and help me. I think I broke my mandolin."

Sure enough, the impact, combined with the pressure of Bill's right arm holding on to it, cracked apart the seam in the middle of the mandolin's back (and a small section of binding was also knocked off). But Bill appeared to be all right. "After this loud crash of chair and Monroe," Grier said, "Bill got up without a scratch! No following moaning or groaning either. Just another example of his excellent physical condition."[199]

Bill may have stoically willed himself to be OK. He and the band were about to embark on a twelve-day tour, playing every day, April 8–19. Before leaving town, Bill turned his F-5 over to Benny Martin's brother Gene Martin, former guitarist with Roy Acuff, who would glue it back together at his workplace, the Grammer Guitar factory in Nashville. (*Opry* star Billy Grammer began producing his line of guitars there in 1965.)[200]

Bill was still looking for a lead singer when Red Allen arrived in Nashville shortly after Bill and the Blue Grass Boys got back to town. Well known as a bandleader, Allen had decided to try out for the lead-singing spot again (he had reportedly failed once in the 1950s, due to drinking). Grier recalled Allen playing the *Opry* with the band, and the next weekend he was supposed to play with them in Waverly, Ohio, on Saturday, April 29, and at the Brown County Jamboree on Sunday the 30th. Between sets in Waverly, however, Allen told Grier he thought he was having a heart attack. "Word got back to Bill," said Grier, "and Bill asked me to run him over to the hospital. [But] that ended up being a case of nerves, the effects of alcohol abuse." Allen stayed in Ohio "under a doctor's care," according to biographer Dennis Satterlee, and would not get to Bean Blossom until midway through Bill's first set.[201]

Earlier that Sunday, twenty-one-year-old Doug Green, an English major who was between semesters at the University of Michigan, arrived at the Jamboree to audition as lead singer. He'd been playing bluegrass in Ann Arbor and had promoted one of Bill's shows at the university in March, getting acquainted by phone with Carolyn Monroe, who later told him Bill was looking for a guitar player. So, on the 30th, Green played most of the first set, and he believes his knowledge of Bill's repertoire helped: "Not that I was the best singer he ever had or even probably the third-to-worst, but, boy, did I know the material!" He even knew the words to "Walls of Time," not yet released on record. By the end of the evening, Allen would go home and Green would board the Blue Grass Special, filling in as lead singer for the next four weeks.[202]

Those weeks would include Bill's seventh trip to the West Coast, which began almost immediately, and en route, the "Bluegrass Breakdown" broke down again, this time near Dallas, Texas. Berline, Grier, Virginia Stauffer (traveling with the band), and James waited there for former fill-in Mitchell Land to repair its transmission, while Bill and Green flew to Washington state for shows on May 5 and 6 with local musicians Paul Wiley (banjo), Phil Williams (bass), and wife Vivian Williams (fiddle). Then Bill and Green took a Trailways bus to Los Angeles, a thousand miles to the south, arriving there several days before the rest of the band.[203]

Members of the Dillards and the Kentucky Colonels filled in at the Ash Grove on May 12 and 13, respectively, then the Blue Grass Boys and Stauffer arrived on the 14th. Roland White of the Colonels kept coming to the shows, and Bill would always ask him to sit in on guitar. Grier, an old friend of White's, was soon urging him to join the band. Struggling to make a living after brother Clarence White left the Colonels to play electric guitar (soon to join the Byrds), White was playing electric bass with a dance band. By the end of Bill's West Coast sojourn, on May 21, he'd borrowed brother Eric White's guitar and joined the Blue Grass Boys.[204]

The band returned to Nashville at the end of May, after shows in Texas and Alabama. Stauffer, wanting to visit her parents in Michigan, drove Green home to Ann Arbor. "She was from Michigan, so she felt we had a bond," he said. "To me," he said, speaking of his experience with Bill, "it was a fantasy come true."[205]

Decca released Bill's tenth album for the label, *Blue Grass Time*, on June 12, 1967. Greene, Grier, James Monroe, and Rowan were featured on ten of its twelve cuts, more by one group of Blue Grass Boys than on any of Bill's previous Decca albums, and many of the album's recordings (including 1964's "Roll On, Buddy, Roll On" with Del McCoury) became instant standards in the bluegrass repertoire. The cover photo, probably taken in April 1967, featured new member Berline (who isn't heard on the album). Bill, as usual, looks older than his actual age (fifty-five), emphasized by the youthful Berline and son James on either side of him.[206]

Bill's First Festival—1967

That June, Bill quietly held his first multiday bluegrass festival, inside the Brown County Jamboree Barn in Bean Blossom, Indiana, on Saturday and Sunday of the last weekend of the month (June 24–25). The first to follow Carlton Haney's groundbreaking Roanoke gatherings, it was a somewhat tentative affair, a test of the multiday concept "way out west." Bill, likely not convinced that Northeasterners who came to Haney's festivals would travel all the way to Indiana, spent nothing on national advertising (only a brief listing in *Bluegrass Unlimited*) or on building an outdoor stage. There were no workshops either. So, rather than call it a "festival," Bill advertised it as a "Big Blue Grass Celebration."[207]

Headliners of the festival (which is what everyone called it anyway) were few: Bill and the Blue Grass Boys; Ralph Stanley and the Clinch Mountain Boys; Benny Martin (teamed temporarily with Rudy Lyle playing electric guitar); plus Red Allen and Hylo Brown. The Country Gentlemen were advertised, but leader John Duffey and Bill disagreed on the band's fee, and they did not appear (and would not appear at a Bean Blossom festival until 1969, after Duffey left the band). Several lesser-known bands filled out the schedule, including the McCormick Brothers from Tennessee; the Moore Brothers, eastern Kentucky natives living in northern Indiana; and the Stone Mountain Boys (with Mitchell Land) from Texas.[208]

Just prior to the festival, Bill honored a promise he'd made at Haney's festival in 1965 to Calvin Robins, a friend of Haney's, to hire his banjo-picking son, "Butch" Robins, after he graduated from high school. Eighteen-year-old Robins was hired and picked with the Blue Grass Boys both days at the festival (with Grier temporarily laid off). Afterward, Bill, James, and White, plus Robins *and* Grier went to Canada to tape three episodes (on Friday, June 30) of the CTV network's *Country Music Hall*, hosted by former *Opry* star Carl Smith (with Grier picking banjo because Robins wasn't in the musicians' union). Berline was absent, taking his army physical, and Canadian fiddler Paul Menard filled in. Robins was to play the *Opry* the next night, but after an unsuccessful rehearsal, the disillusioned teenager suddenly went home to Virginia.[209]

Grier left about a month later, after a show on July 23. His replacement, twenty-eight-year-old Vic Jordan, had offered Bill his services while working with *Opry* stars Wilma Lee and Stoney Cooper in 1965–66. Thereafter, he picked banjo with Jimmy Martin and had just given Martin his notice when James called, offering the job with Bill. "So I was out of work for thirty minutes," Jordan said.[210]

The film *Bonnie and Clyde* was released a few weeks later (on August 13), with Flatt and Scruggs's "Foggy Mountain Breakdown" used as "traveling music," and interest in bluegrass banjo playing was suddenly reignited.[211]

Berline was due to report for active duty soon, so Bill arranged for a recording session before he had to leave. On Wednesday, August 23, the band (with Berline, Jordan, White, and James) recorded three fiddle tunes: "The Gold Rush," a new original by Bill, so new it had no title yet (listed as "Fiddle Time" in session records); the traditional "Sally Goodin," introducing the multiple variations of Berline's southwestern-style fiddling to bluegrass; and "Virginia Darlin'," another original by Bill, named for Virginia Stauffer, then traveling with the band full-time. Jordan recalled she was "pretty easy-going" and "got along with everybody, except Bill, at times."

> Goin' down the road in the bus, I'm drivin' in the middle of the night. Bill would get mad at Virginia over something. He'd come up front, get the mandolin out of the case, and sit in the front seat and take it out on that mandolin. He would play some aggressive stuff I've never heard him play at any other time. It wasn't just one tune—he'd start one, and stop, and start another.[212]

Two weeks after the session, Bill and the band played at Carlton Haney's third Labor Day weekend festival, held in 1967 at Watermelon Park in Berryville, Virginia (site of the first "Blue Grass Day" in 1960). Then they raced westward to Hugo, Oklahoma, due there on September 5 to perform at the annual meeting of the Choctaw Electric Co-operative, booked by Bill Grant, a local bluegrass and country singer-songwriter. He was seventeen in 1947 when he first met Bill, on the trip to Oklahoma with Benny Martin filling in, and they had renewed their acquaintance in May when Bill and the band played in Ft. Worth, Texas, on the way back from California.[213]

This September 5 show was the last for Berline, now conveniently back in his home territory just before his army service. Years later, asked about his time with Bill, he too recalled Bill picking his mandolin on the bus, but not "taking it out" on the instrument: "I remember those days and nights travelling with Bill . . . he would spend hours playing Uncle Pen's fiddle tunes on the mandolin." Bill had spoken to Rinzler about these tunes in a 1966 interview, expressing his goal to preserve them: "That's something I want to do," he said. "I want all of 'em put on record and as near the way that he played 'em as I can . . . so they won't be just throwed away and forgot about." On Wednesday, September 13, 1967, Bill turned fifty-six. Four of his seven siblings had died, three in their early sixties, and he may have felt he was running out of time.[214]

October brought the sixteenth annual Deejay Convention in Nashville. Bill's old friend Tut Taylor rented two rooms in the Clarkston Hotel and, moving the furniture from one to the other, created a picking room for visiting bluegrass musicians. There Bill met Taylor's new friend, fellow Georgia native and stringed instrument repairman Randy Wood. During the convention, the CMA again overlooked Bill when choosing its inductees for the Country Music Hall of Fame. Instead, they chose Red Foley, Jim Reeves, RCA Victor executive Stephen H. Sholes, and the man who arranged for Charlie and Bill's burlesque show audition in 1933, Joseph Lee "Joe" Frank. Sadly, Frank's induction was posthumous; he had died in 1952 at age fifty-two.[215]

At the end of October 1967, the November *Bluegrass Unlimited* appeared with the first installment of "Bill Monroe: King of Blue Grass Music," transcribed versions of radio show interviews by Doug Benson of a year previous in Montreal. Comments Bill made in Rinzler's earlier interviews were used sparingly or were cobbled together to form an extended statement, but this was the first time his answers were published verbatim. Unfortunately, it permitted inaccurate generalizations, as in Bill's explanation that "the process of elimination" caused him to play mandolin (Birch had the fiddle, Charlie the guitar, "So I got the mandolin. I wound up with that") or in his guesstimate of when he found his F-5 in Miami ("about 25 years ago").[216]

Benny Williams had replaced Berline on fiddle when Bill returned to the recording studio on the evening of Thursday, November 9. For this session, Williams played second fiddle to Vassar Clements, recently back in Nashville after a five-year struggle with alcoholism. First up was "Is the Blue Moon Still Shining?," written by Bill's daughter Melissa, then age thirty-one. The second number, "Train 45 (Heading South)," was a bluegrass instrumental that Flatt and Scruggs and others had already made popular. Bill's vocal, derived from recordings by Grayson and Whitter and Wade Mainer, gave it new life. After it, Clements had to leave, to be on time for his regular job playing tenor banjo at a Nashville nightclub, and Williams was less than successful at soloing on Bill's "Kentucky Mandolin," a tune Doc Watson named when Bill and he first played it in 1964.

By the end of 1967, the Blue Grass Boys had begun wearing matching outfits—sport jackets and coordinating slacks—that Carolyn Monroe picked out.[217]

Early in January 1968, Williams went hunting with Jimmy Martin, and Martin accidently shot him, luckily from a distance. After his buckshot wounds healed, Williams returned to work with Bill but called it quits by mid-March. The emphasis on youth in the music business appears to have lessened, so Bill contacted forty-one-year-old Kenny Baker. Once again musically active, Baker would release his first album, *High Country*, for the independent County label in April, a cooperative effort with fiddler Joe Green. Roland White, who had not yet heard Baker, recalled Bill saying he was "a classy fiddler." "That was a good way to put it," White said later. "I couldn't believe how good he was." Baker began his third stint with Bill on March 23. His first, in 1957, lasted about ten months and his second, in 1962–63, about eight months. This time he would stay for sixteen years.[218]

Two weeks later, on Thursday, April 4, 1968, Dr. Martin Luther King Jr., leader of the civil rights movement in America, was assassinated by James Earl Ray in Memphis, Tennessee. Violent riots erupted in more than a hundred cities, and in Nashville, the *Opry* was cancelled for the second time in its history (a tape of a previous show was broadcast). It was E. W. "Bud" Wendell's initial weekend as manager of the *Opry*, and one of his first duties was arranging for the Ryman's windows to be covered with mesh, to protect them from rioters.[219]

The Stage at Bean Blossom

On Sunday, April 21, Bill and the band opened the season at the Brown County Jamboree. Between then and the festival in June, Bill and a work crew (the Blue Grass Boys among them) made significant changes to the property, including the building of a new stage in the natural amphitheater of its woods. During this time, they all "camped out" in the tourist cabins, James and Jordan in one, Baker and White in another, and Bill and Stauffer in the third, a slightly larger cabin with electricity. "The one they stayed in had a kitchen and a stove," Jordan said, "and she would make us breakfast in the morning, lunch at midday, and supper in the evening." "Bill was training her to cook," White said, remembering the meals they all ate together in Bill and Stauffer's kitchen.[220]

Mealtimes, it appears, were some of the more pleasurable times. Lots of trees had to be cut down to open up the amphitheater area and Bill, of course, wanted to use a two-man crosscut saw. Early on, he and Baker used one to cut down a hollow tree with a bee hive in it, providing honey for the crew. "It took us forever to talk him into getting a chain saw," Jordan said. After they did, Baker "came close to taking a leg off with it, while up in a tree, trimming branches" (inflicting a nasty gash). Then the logs went to a local sawmill, to provide inexpensive lumber for the stage. As White recalled,

> We loaded those trees onto this truck—I can't even remember how we did that. Bill had one truck, and I mean, those things weren't light. And we did it with ropes and all that kind of stuff, you know? There weren't any mules up there—we were the mules! And the hardest part was when you got back with the planks, inch-thick planks, green, heavy stuff, and we had to load 'em on our shoulders, and they were every bit of ten feet long. And I remember . . . shouldering the first one off the truck, I almost fell to the ground. "Well," I told myself, "I'm gonna do this!"

The planks had to be carried about a quarter of a mile, across a steep dip in the path that's still there (then "a swamp," White said), to an area where a temporary stage had once stood and the new one was built. "Bill wanted it put back in the same place."[221]

They built the new stage—thirty feet wide with two tune-up rooms behind it and covered with a tin roof about fifteen feet overhead—without a drawing or plan of any kind. "Bill never wrote anything down," according to White. "It was all in his head. Him and Kenny kind of worked that out—and what they told me to do, I did." It would be used for the next twenty-four years at annual Bean Blossom festivals.[222]

At the end of May, Brenda Monroe filed for divorce from James after less than five years of marriage (they had separated in February, the month their son "Jimbo" turned four). James was enjoined from having any contact with her.[223]

Decca, meanwhile, achieved a new low in its handling of Bill's recordings with the release on June 17 of a second "greatest hits" album. This time actually titled *Bill Monroe's Greatest Hits*, it duplicated most (eight) of the titles on the first "greatest hits" album, 1962's *My All Time Country Favorites*. (Its new "hits" were "In the Pines," "Molly and Tenbrooks," and "Danny Boy.") In February Rinzler and producer Silverstein had discussed the possibility of an all-gospel reissue album, but presumably Decca executives saw more sales potential in *Greatest Hits*. Regrettably, it was Bill's only album release of 1968.[224]

"Bill Monroe's Blue Grass Festival" (as Bill's second Bean Blossom festival was advertised in *Bluegrass Unlimited*) began on Friday, June 21. With workers still building plank benches for seating in the woods, an amateur band contest was held in the Jamboree Barn that afternoon. At sunset near the park entrance, a gathering of amateurs and professionals playing together with Bill at the helm established the "Sunset Jam Session" tradition, repeated every June thereafter. A square dance in the barn followed, with Bill and the band providing the music at first; then Bill and White joined the dancers, and the band contest winners, Mitchell Land and the Stone Mountain Boys, took over. As Land recalled: "There was one time during the dance that we got so tickled we could hardly play. Somehow Roland White would go the wrong way every time. While going the wrong way, he met up with Bill face-to-face! Bill just grabbed and spanked him, sending him the right way." Years later, a laughing White explained, "I never could square dance. If they said go left, I'd go right. I could never follow directions."[225]

Workshops were held for the first time the next morning, all of them in the barn. That afternoon and evening, the scene shifted to the woods for the first performances on the new stage. In the audience were Oklahomans Bill Grant of Hugo, and the new president of the Bill Monroe Fan Club, Glen Mowrey of Strang (the former Oklahoma representative, he took over when the club became too big for Marvine Johnson). "It was Heaven to us," said Grant. "We saw and heard all the bluegrass pickers we'd always admired." With Bill's encouragement, Grant would promote the first multiday bluegrass festival west of the Mississippi, at Salt Creek Park, near Hugo, in August 1969.[226]

On Sunday morning, June 23, 1968, the barn was used again, this time for the "gospel sing." Making an unadvertised appearance was the Sullivan

Family, a bluegrass gospel group from southern Alabama that Bill had discovered while playing for church organizations there. As he had anticipated, the Sullivans were a success, and with Bill as their unofficial agent, they would begin playing bluegrass festivals on a regular basis. After "Brother" Tim Hardison of Tennessee preached the "service," fiddlers Kenny Baker, Jim Buchanan, and Joe Stuart played "Pass Me Not" and "Precious Memories" as a collection was taken up for Hardison.[227]

The Osborne Brothers were featured on Sunday afternoon, flush from their success with Felice and Boudleaux Bryant's "Rocky Top" (it had peaked at number 33 on *Billboard*'s "Top 40" in March). They had played with an electric bass for more than a year, on the *Opry* and elsewhere, so when newest member Ronnie Reno plugged his bass guitar into an amplifier, it does not appear to have been a problem for Bill. But the band's new Decca album, *Yesterday, Today, and the Osborne Brothers*, on which they played in "traditional" style (including a rendition of "Molly and Tenbrooks") on side one and a more "contemporary" style on side two (with steel guitar and piano), seemed to suggest they thought Bill's style was "yesterday."[228]

Bluegrass Festival Movement Under Way

At this point, nearly three years after the first multiday bluegrass festival of 1965, there were still only two such events in the entire country—Haney's festival in Virginia and Bill's in Indiana. But this was soon to change, aided by the availability of advertising in *Bluegrass Unlimited*, with ads for a Haney festival in Norwalk, Ohio, in July; the International Bluegrass Festival in Warrenton, Virginia, in August; and the Chautauqua Bluegrass Festival in Franklin, Ohio, in September. The bluegrass festival movement was finally underway.[229]

Carlton Haney's fourth Labor Day weekend festival, held at Watermelon Park in Berryville, Virginia, was preceded by a "Summer Music Camp" from Monday, August 26, through Thursday, August 29. According to its ad, "Your favorite bluegrass pickers will be on hand for daily workshops and seminars, from 10 in the morning to 10 at night. There will be *no charge!*" Bill and the band arrived on the 29th, and Bill invited all comers to pick or sing with him. Among them was nineteen-year-old Charles "Skip" Gorman, who had asked Bill how to play "Blue Grass Breakdown" at Newport in 1963. ("He just stared through me and played the tune fast and with lots of rhythm. 'Thanks a lot,' Bill said, and he walked away, attempting to contain a smile.") Gorman showed him what he'd learned, playing both "Blue Grass Breakdown" and "Big Mon." Singing with Bill on the 29th was Jim Rooney, the left-handed guitar player Bill had encouraged in 1963. Rooney, a former manager of Club 47, the well-known Cambridge, Massachusetts, folk music venue (where Bill had played many times), was then working for Newport Jazz Festival founder George Wein's Festival Productions as a tour manager for jazz musicians in the United States and Europe.[230]

Haney's Labor Day festival proper got underway on Friday, August 30, and the Blue Grass Boys had the day off. Taking advantage of the lull, Baker arranged to record his first solo album on that day with Jordan, banjo; White, mandolin; and former Blue Grass Boy Del McCoury, guitar. At the "Music Camp," Baker had asked Doug Green to play bass, and even borrowed one for him to play. (Not asking James to play bass ensured that Bill would not find out about it and object, since Baker had not asked for his permission.)

The album was recorded at a motel in Winchester, Virginia, about ten miles west of the festival. Engineer Charlie Faurot set up four mikes, mixing them into a single-track Nagra tape recorder as each tune was played. Between 8:30 A.M. and 2:30 P.M., a dozen tunes were recorded. One of the visitors to the session was Fred Bartenstein, Carlton Haney's seventeen-year-old festival assistant and emcee. He loaned McCoury his Martin D-28 guitar when McCoury decided the strings on his guitar were dead. (The album, *Portrait of a Bluegrass Fiddler*, released in July 1969, would be the bestselling County LP for more than fifteen years. And, as it turned out, Bill did not object. Between 1970 and 1984, Baker would record nine more solo fiddle albums.)[231]

Meanwhile, at Haney's festival, the "Bluegrass Story" was told again on Sunday, September 1, and during it, Bill sang "Close By" accompanied by six fiddlers—Baker, Joe Green, Curly Ray Cline, "Tater" Tate, Vernon Derrick, and Charlie Smith—and the same six later played a fifteen-minute version of "Sally Goodin" with him. Regarding "Close By," Charlie Smith recalled it was already "a tradition" at the *Opry* that every fiddler on or near the stage would come out and do multiple fiddles" with Bill on it. Haney may have been aware of this and caused it to happen at his festival. Bill would later adopt the idea at his festival, with a "roll call" of fiddlers.[232]

At this point in 1968, Charlie Monroe had left Indiana and moved back to Ohio County, Kentucky, taking Bertha with him. Sixty-five-year-old Charlie and his sixty-year-old sister rented a small house about two miles north of Rosine, on Salem Road. Bill visited them on September 26 and may have brought Charlie news of a forthcoming Decca album that featured the two of them.[233]

Three days after Bill's visit, he and the band were back at Sunset Park on Sunday, September 29. James was due in court that week for a divorce hearing, so Doug Green filled in for him on bass. On October 3, custody of four-year-old James William "Jimbo" Monroe II was awarded to Brenda Monroe, and his father was ordered to pay child support and the balance due on a color TV.[234]

Former vice president Richard Nixon was elected president on November 5, 1968, narrowly defeating Democrat Hubert Humphrey. Nine days later, on November 14, Bill recorded the last session with the threesome of Jordan, White, and James. It was, however, the first session with Baker since 1963.[235]

The session began with one of Bill's new songs, "I Want to Go with You," the first by him to be recorded since 1958's "No One But My Darlin'." In a rare trio, James again sang lead and White baritone. The other two items were remnants from 1965–66: "Walls of Time" and "Crossing the Cumberlands." White sang lead on "Walls" standing on an empty wooden Coke case, to sing into the same microphone with Bill.[236]

At the beginning of 1969 the Osborne Brothers went all-electric, fitting their acoustic instruments with pickups and plugging into amplifiers—necessary, according to Sonny Osborne, because they were having problems being heard at country music package shows, where other bands were using electric instruments. He recalled Bill calling early in the year to book them at his festival (where they didn't have to amplify their sound), asking them not to use electrification:

> He wanted us to come play his bluegrass festival in Bean Blossom and he wanted us to leave our amps at home and I told our agent to tell him not only that I said, "No," but that I said, "Hell, no." And I told him, in fact, that me and Bobby wants to book him and for him to leave his pick at home, because it's all a matter of volume, one way or the other.

The Osborne Brothers would not play at Bill's Bean Blossom festival until 1976, two years after they stopped using electrified banjo, guitar, and mandolin.[237]

Bill took his second trip overseas with the Blue Grass Boys in February 1969, playing at U.S. military bases in Italy and Germany from the 12th through the 23rd. While they were gone, Flatt and Scruggs ended their twenty-year partnership on the night of February 22, after the first of two shows on the *Opry*. It seems Flatt had anticipated it: when Roland White spoke to him around Thanksgiving of 1968 about someday playing man-dolin with the Foggy Mountain Boys, Flatt told him, "There's gonna be some big changes in this band after the first of the year." Still, White said he was shocked when he heard the news, after calling his wife when the band landed in the States: "I remember dropping the phone and thinking, 'There's been a Flatt and Scruggs my whole life—they can't do that!'" He'd already turned in his notice to Bill, but Bill asked him to stay until he found someone else. Flatt wasn't ready to form his new band yet, so White stayed a little longer.[238]

Decca Records, meanwhile, released *Bill Monroe and Charlie Monroe* on February 24, an album that looks like a gift for Rinzler, a consolation for 1968's *Greatest Hits*. It provided him with an opportunity to promote, with-out actually mentioning, the Smithsonian's salute to the Monroe family, to be held that summer at the Institution's third annual Festival of American Folklife in Washington, D.C. The album, the first of Bill's Decca LPs with eleven selections instead of the usual twelve, had five by Bill—four from the 1950s plus the previously unissued "Louisville Breakdown" of 1964—alternat-ing with six by Charlie from 1952 and 1956. RCA Victor would follow suit in March 1969, releasing ten Charlie Monroe recordings from 1946–50 on *Who's Calling You Sweetheart Tonight?* (Camden).[239]

By March 1969, both White and Jordan were gone. Before they left, the two agreed to help Bill out by driving up to Indiana to pick up the "new" bus, a used GMC Scenicruiser. Both joined Lester Flatt's band and thought Bill would resent it, but he would only give them "the silent treatment" until he and Flatt renewed their friendship in 1971.[240]

James Monroe on Guitar

If Bill was upset by White and Jordan's defection, he was probably molli-fied by the opportunity to further the musical career of his handsome son James, who'd just turned twenty-eight years old. Bill gave James the guitar spot straightaway, in spite of the fact that he was the least experienced gui-tarist Bill had ever had. Four years later, James admitted to his deficiency in *Bluegrass Unlimited*: "Back when Roland left to go to work with Lester, I wasn't ready for the guitar job. I never had done much with the guitar. Oh, I had done one number as part of the show [he and White traded instruments for "When My Blue Moon Turns to Gold Again"], but that was all. I knew that job was going to be hard." It tended to weaken Bill's music, but Bill, as usual, was determined to make the best of it.[241]

Former fill-in Doug Green was living in Nashville by then, going to graduate school at Vanderbilt. Next-door neighbor White tipped him off to the latest developments with the band, and Green soon replaced James on bass. Green played his first show on Friday, March 21, the day after his twenty-third birthday, at the Astro Inn in Columbus, Ohio. The "Inn" was actually a bar, but James needed all the experience he could get, so Bill had agreed to play there. Howard Aldridge of nearby Springfield, who filled in on banjo after Ellis left in 1962, filled in again.[242]

That weekend, former fill-in Rual Yarbrough was filling in on banjo with former Blue Grass Boy, Bobby Smith, and his band, the Boys from Shiloh. They were on their way from Nashville to play the Wheeling Jamboree on March 21 and stopped by Columbus to visit with Bill at the Astro. Yarbrough, finding Jordan gone and Bill using a fill-in, told Baker he'd like to have the banjo job. "Kenny told me he thought I could get the job if I wanted it. So he went back to the dressing room and told Bill. Bill came out and talked to me and told me to call him on my way back from Wheeling on Monday." During that call, Yarbrough was hired, and on Tuesday, March 25, he met with Baker "to run over a few things." Bill's seventieth Decca recording session was the next day.[243]

First recorded on March 26, 1969, was "I Haven't Seen Mary in Years," written by Missouri native Damon Black, then a staff writer at country star Mel Tillis's Sawgrass Music (with offices on Music Row in Nashville). Black "pitched" it to James and gave him a copy of Tillis's recording (released in 1968 on *Something Special* [Kapp]). Porter Wagoner was actually the first to record it, in March 1968, but he evidently delayed its release (on *Porter Wagoner Country* [RCA Victor]) until after Bill and James released their recording. Next, Bill revived "Fireball Mail," written by Fred Rose and originally popularized in the 1940s by publishing partner Roy Acuff. Last was "The Dead March," the first of Uncle Pen's tunes to be recorded. Twinning with Baker on it and the others that day was legendary country music fiddler Joseph "Red" Hayes (1926–1973), co-writer of "Satisfied Mind." Substituting for the less-experienced Green, to provide extra rhythmic support for inexperienced James, was legendary Nashville session bassist Joe Zinkan.[244]

Around this time, in early spring, Ralph Rinzler and three other Smithsonian fieldworkers were injured when a large truck broadsided their rented van in western Pennsylvania while on the way to a folk festival there. James R.

Morris, then the director of the Smithsonian's Division of Performing Arts, recalled the circumstances:

> Ralph had been driving the van and he was the most severely injured—one leg crushed, ribs broken, concussion. He was transferred to George Washington University Hospital in Washington, D.C., where he underwent several operations to repair his leg. . . . I was in New York City, attending a conference, when news of his accident reached me. I left New York immediately and met his ambulance in Washington. I was in his room every day for several days, and we thought he might lose his leg. Eventually, he recovered.

Morris arranged for a private telephone line for Rinzler in his hospital room, and within a couple of weeks he was back at work on the Folklife festival, making preparations by phone from the hospital.[245]

With the recording of "The Dead March," an album of Uncle Pen's tunes was finally begun and more frequent sessions were held during the next two years to complete it. On April 29, Bill recorded with the same band as on March 26, except that Hayes was replaced by another legendary fiddler, Tommy Williams, a Florida native who'd filled in with Bill in 1956, and would join the staff band of the *Hee Haw* TV show when it debuted in June. He fiddled solo on the session's first recording, "Cripple Creek." It was an opportunity to show off James's improvement on guitar, and his playing was clearly better. Next, James sang the old Johnnie and Jack favorite, "What About You?" The first solo vocal a member of the Blue Grass Boys would attempt since Cousin Wilbur's "Coupon Song" in 1941, it would not be released by Decca. Bill sang solo next on "With Body and Soul," a new song by Virginia Stauffer, who had stopped traveling regularly with the band, according to Doug Green. Released in October 1969, it would quickly become a standard in the bluegrass repertoire. And, with the session's recordings going quickly, there was time to record Uncle Pen's "Methodist Preacher," with Baker fiddling solo.[246]

Bill and the band accomplished more than usual at this session because they had rehearsed beforehand. Yarbrough recalled that later they tried recording without any preparation: "We did a session one time and got zero out of a three-hour session. They didn't get a thing they could salvage out of it, and it was just because we hadn't rehearsed." Bill paid the cost of this "lost" session as a deduction from his royalties. They would not try this again.[247]

Decca quickly released a single of "I Haven't Seen Mary in Years" (b/w "Crossing the Cumberlands") on May 19, 1969, crediting "Bill Monroe &

James Monroe" as the song's performers on its label, a distinct departure from the past, when either Bill "and his Blue Grass Boys" or just "Bill Monroe" were named. Decca seemed to be aware of the sales potential of this new father-and-son team, but, inexplicably, their first album together would not appear for four years.[248]

Cleo Davis, the first Blue Grass Boy, came to Nashville in June and visited with Bill. Davis said later that Bill had proposed that the original band (with Garren and Wooten) reunite for a recording session in June 1970. But Davis's wife was ill at that time and he couldn't leave her, so plans for this reunion recording were put on hold.[249]

Bill's third annual Bean Blossom Bluegrass Festival ran four days in 1969, beginning on Thursday, June 19. Visiting a bluegrass festival for the first time was *Grand Ole Opry* manager Bud Wendell. A newcomer to country music when he took over the *Opry* in 1968, he had developed an interest in bluegrass that helped further its success in the mainstream. And on Sunday morning, Wade Mainer, then performing primarily in churches, was part of the gospel music program for the first time. Apparently, peace had been made between Bill and the Monroe Brothers' old nemesis.[250]

Calvin Robins, father of former Blue Grass Boy Butch Robins, was then one of Bill's most ardent helpers at Bean Blossom, and his son won the banjo contest there on June 19. After the festival they traveled to central Ohio, where Bill and the band were due to play a festival on Saturday and Sunday, June 28 and 29, at the Buckeye Lake amusement park. Meanwhile, Bill and the band, with former fill-in Jake Landers riding with them, were en route to the festival from Nashville when the bus broke down in Kentucky. Yarbrough and Landers stayed with the bus while it was worked on, and a *hearse* was located to carry the rest of the band (Baker, Green, James, and Bill) to Buckeye Lake. The younger Robins was there to fill in on Saturday afternoon, and Yarbrough, Landers, and the bus arrived for the evening show. (Butch Robins would continue to travel with the band that summer, prior to being drafted.)[251]

After the evening show, as Landers and Bill sat talking on the bus, Bill again sang the chorus he'd written back in 1963 that began "Walk softly on this heart of mine, love." Landers then sang the two verses he'd written that Bill had rejected six years earlier. This time, Bill said, "That's just exactly what I'm lookin' for!"[252]

On June 30, Decca released *A Voice from On High*, an album of some of Bill's finest religious recordings from 1950–55. All had appeared before on

78s or 45s except Pete Pyle's "Don't Put Off 'Til Tomorrow," a recording from 1952 that Decca had withheld for seventeen years. Rinzler, in his liner notes, tried to lessen the blame somewhat, explaining that it had been "forgotten" for only twelve years—the remaining five were the years it took to get the album out. He quoted Bill saying, with considerable understatement, "It's really a good song and I'm glad they're going to release it."[253]

The Smithsonian's "Monroe Family Tribute"

The Smithsonian Institution's third annual Festival of American Folklife had already been underway on the National Mall for two days when Bill and the band arrived in Washington, D.C., on July 3. That afternoon, amid sheep-shearing demonstrations and a Seminole Indian crafts show, there was an unscheduled onstage session of reminiscing by Bill, Birch, and Charlie, hosted by Alice Foster, Rinzler (still on crutches), and Mike Seeger. But the main event was a show that evening in the center of the Mall, with a "Monroe Family Tribute" at its midpoint. Proclamations were read from the governor of Kentucky and the secretary of the Smithsonian honoring "the sons of James Buchanan and Malissa Vandiver Monroe . . . for their outstanding contribution . . . to the living culture of the United States of America." Birch fiddled, then he, Bill, and Charlie (playing Doug Green's guitar) sang a gospel song, Bill and Charlie sang two together, followed by brief sets by Charlie and the Kentucky Pardners (Tex Logan, fiddle; Don Stover, banjo; Mike Seeger, mandolin; Doug Green, bass) and Bill and the Blue Grass Boys. When no one else spoke up at the end, Bill did his best to express their gratitude: "To be up here in Washington, D.C., in honor of Kentucky, [and] our folks that was born and raised in Kentucky, our father and mother, it's really wonderful."[254]

Charlie Remarries

Charlie, who turned sixty-six the next day, and his forty-four-year-old lady friend, "Martha" (Draper, Gammon) Winecoff, were "honeymooning" during the festival. (Born Myrtha Draper on August 6, 1924, she was called "Martha" or "Mert." Her mother married a Gammon when Martha was a child, and Martha's first husband was a Winecoff.) On Friday, July 11, Charlie and Martha went to the Ohio County Courthouse in Hartford, Kentucky, and made their union official. It's been said that she and Bill "dated" previously, to what extent is not certain. What *is* certain is that the union of

Martha and Charlie resulted in the complete disunion of Bill and Charlie. (After Charlie and Martha married, they settled in Cross Plains, Tennessee, about twenty-five miles north of Nashville. When Charlie revived his musical career, Martha, like Betty, handled his bookings. Bertha left Rosine and moved back to Martinsville, Indiana, to live with Birch.)[255]

July 12 at the *Opry* was Doug Green's last with the Blue Grass Boys. According to Green, "[M]uch like baseball, it was a swap arranged by the owners, specifically Bill and Jimmy [Martin]. I had no say in the matter. . . . I was to play for Jimmy, and his bassist, Bill Yates, was to play for Bill." When it was known that the more experienced Yates was leaving Martin, James had offered him the bass-playing job, and it was arranged for Green to join Martin's band. Green said there were no hard feelings, and that Bill was an inspiration for the band he formed later, Riders in the Sky: "His commitment to his style was irresolute and unwavering, and although Riders work in a different tradition, I drew from the example of his determination to present his music his way . . . to keep true to our tradition and our style."[256]

Bill had played at the Newport Folk Festival every other year since 1963 and, as planned, he and the band were there on July 19, 1969, along with Don Reno, his new partner, Bill Harrell, and Mac Wiseman. They all worked together to present a version of "The Story of Bluegrass" on that Saturday. Supplementing their performances was the festival program article "My Life in Blue Grass," assembled using quotes from Alice Foster's interviews with Bill.

> When I started trying to originate the music, or get it the way I wanted it, I was going to be sure there was a lonesome sound to it, because I do know that the country people love the lonesome sound of music. . . . After we [Charlie and Bill] broke up, I knew I was going to have to come up with some kind of a group. I figured on four men, and I didn't know what it would really be like. . . . I wanted to advance old-time music, and it leads back to where people who played and sung in a low key couldn't do much to advance it. . . . When I started here in Nashville, nobody played in B flat or B natural, so that has been one thing which has give bluegrass such a brilliant tone and it's put the music up where the singing's at. . . . There's been different people with their ideas and their way of playing that's helped bluegrass music. For my kind of playing, each year we've added something to bluegrass and it makes it more interesting. . . . It's not altogether just notes and to run through a number that suits me, that I get any enjoyment out of; I listen for the tones and try to make them satisfy me and please me, and people that understands music like that, they please them too.[257]

The following evening, July 20, 1969, astronauts Neil Armstrong and Edwin "Buzz" Aldrin Jr. became the first human beings to walk on the Moon. The once-mysterious orb that had inspired so many love songs, including "Blue Moon of Kentucky," would never be looked at in exactly the same way again.[258]

Three weeks later, on the weekend of August 8, Bill and the band appeared at the fourth annual Pennsylvania Bluegrass Festival with several regional bands, including former Blue Grass Boy Del McCoury and his Dixie Pals. McCoury visited with Bill on the bus between shows, and Bill sang a chorus he'd just written that lacked verses. McCoury later sang the chorus for one of the Dixie Pals, mandolinist Dick Staber: "Del had a big 1959 Cadillac at the time. . . . We drove back [home to York, Pennsylvania] together, just the two of us in the Caddy. I just made up two verses for the song while we were driving along and I sang them for Del. He learned them right there while we were in the car. We started performing ["Bluest Man in Town"] from then on."

That August 8, 1969, weekend, the "family" of sociopath Charles Manson committed its horrific murders in California, and a week later, the Woodstock Music and Art Fair was held near Bethel, New York, with an estimated five hundred thousand revelers.[259]

During the Woodstock weekend of August 15, Bill was about as far away from it as one could get: the Salt Creek Bluegrass Festival in Hugo, Oklahoma, the first such gathering west of the Mississippi. The Goins Brothers band and the Country Gentlemen traveled there on Bill's bus, then in top form. (Bass player Yates had taken the Blue Grass Special home in Nashville to work on it. He built a separate compartment for Bill in the middle of the GMC, with the help of Butch Robins. It was the first time Bill had a space of his own on a bus. Yarbrough built bunk beds for the rest of the band at his music store in Muscle Shoals, Alabama, with help from Randy Wood, then working at the store, and Joe Stuart.) At the festival, fan club president Mowrey presented Bill with an outrageously large rattlesnake rattle ("twenty-nine rattles [segments] and a button," Bill said later), made by combining two rattles, which Bill put inside his mandolin, never suspecting it wasn't real. The practice of placing a rattlesnake rattle in an instrument is said to have started with Southern fiddlers, supposedly to improve the tone of their fiddles or prevent rodents from nesting in them. (Mowrey served as Bill's fan-club president for the next six years, replaced in 1975 by Bettie Leonard of Murfreesboro, Tennessee.)[260]

Randy Wood, thanks to his connection with Yarbrough and his work on the bus, took several trips with Bill and the band that summer. By then, it appears Bill's late-night routine wasn't very popular with all of his band members.

> Bill was bad to sit up in the front of the bus at night and distract whoever was driving, 'cause he'd wanna talk, or he was working on a tune. Nothing was said about it, but I was kind of unofficially appointed by the band to sit up there and keep Bill company, so that they could sleep—which was fine with me. We'd talk if he wanted to, or if he wanted to pick, I'd play guitar with him.

Wood would move to Nashville in January 1970, helping New York City–born George Gruhn and old friend Tut Taylor to found "GTR Inc.," one of the first companies to specialize in vintage instrument sales and repair.[261]

After the trip out west, Bill headed east to play Carlton Haney's fifth annual Labor Day weekend festival, held at the end of August 1969 at yet another location: Camp Springs, North Carolina, near Haney's Reidsville hometown. Haney included a program for the festival in the first issue of a new magazine he published, *Muleskinner News*, with a photo of Bill on its cover, taken in the early 1950s. Country music historian Richard Spottswood reviewed the festival for *Bluegrass Unlimited*. "Monroe," he wrote, "didn't come off this time as well as in the past because he is still breaking in his new band [Baker, James Monroe, Yarbrough, and Yates]. But the difficulties were minor; with practice and stage experience they should become as tightly knit as some of Bill's better past units." Spottswood was among the first to comment on a new characteristic of Bill's music: "Kenny Baker and Bill play together as one man and their work together is worth the price of admission anywhere you can hear them."[262]

Signs of the growing mainstream acceptance of bluegrass in general, and Bill in particular, followed in September and October. Shortly after his fifty-eighth birthday, on September 22, Bill taped an appearance on the TV game show *To Tell the Truth* (then in its first year of syndication after twelve years on CBS). Bill and two imposters claiming to be him answered the questions of a panel of four showbiz celebrities, who then voted for the one they thought was really Bill Monroe. (Unfortunately, tapes of the show's 1969–70 season have been lost.)

Then, October 18, 1969, was proclaimed "Bill Monroe Day" in Kentucky by Governor Louie B. Nunn, celebrated in Madisonville, Kentucky, county seat of Hopkins County (twenty-five miles west of Ohio County). Bill in one car and the Blue Grass Boys in another, the band rode in a parade through town that Saturday afternoon, and a banquet followed at a local restaurant. That evening, at the annual Police and Firemen's Benefit Show—the event that helped make Madisonville the place for the celebration—"Pee Wee" King, standing in for the governor, presented Bill with a plaque bearing a copy of Nunn's proclamation. Bill and the band played a few for the crowd of three thousand, there to be entertained by "Boots" Randolph and country-gospel singer Martha Carson, then left to play the *Opry*, escorted to Nashville by a squad of Tennessee State Troopers. At the *Opry*, Bill was filmed singing "With Body and Soul" for a documentary called *The Nashville Sound*, released in 1970 (and reused in Rachel Liebling's *High Lonesome* in 1991).[263]

The *Ohio County Times* (one of Bill's home county weeklies) almost completely ignored "Bill Monroe Day," except for a brief mention on October 2, buried in the "Rosine Personals" column: "The city of Madisonville . . . has announced it will hold a 'Bill Monroe Day' honoring our own Bill Monroe." Three pages later, Charlie received more coverage, with an uncredited article titled "Charlie Monroe Making Come-Back in Music Field." It included some surprising news: "This past week (Friday, September 26th), Charlie went to Nashville, Tenn., and completed the transaction for Decca Records to release two albums by him. Mr. Silverstein of Decca says one album will be an all-gospel album and the other will be of country songs and they hope to release them on the market within six weeks."[264]

Mr. Silverstein, meanwhile, was busy producing two sessions with Bill and the band. On Tuesday, October 28, 1969, just a few days after his thirtieth anniversary on the *Opry*, Bill recorded "Walk Softly on My Heart" first, the song with verses by Jake Landers that had taken six years to come to fruition. Then a new Damon Black song, "Tall Pines," was completed (but shelved, inexplicably, for more than two years). And third was "Candy Gal"—the third Uncle Pen tune to be recorded, the second with Red Hayes playing second fiddle. (This was Bill's first regular session at "Bradley's Barn" in Mt. Juliet, Tennessee, just outside Nashville, where he continued to record throughout the 1970s. In 1964, Bill had recorded and filmed his two-song segment of the "Second Fiddle" movie there.)[265]

Back in the Barn on Tuesday, November 25, they first recorded a new fiddle tune by Bill, "Land of Lincoln," which would be shelved in favor of material for the Uncle Pen album, but which Decca would later lose. Two of Uncle Pen's tunes followed, fiddled solo by Baker: "Going Up Caney" and "The Lee Weddin Tune." According to Monroe-family lore, the former is associated with Harry Monroe's visits to Caneyville (about fifteen miles east of Rosine) to court Nola "Nolie" Goff. Singing the chorus was Bill's idea, and when James had trouble with the high notes, Bill asked Yates to sing lead. "I learned the melody while driving the bus," he said. "The Lee Weddin Tune" was next, possibly connected in some way to the marriage of sixty-eight-year-old Alfred T. Lee and the much younger divorcée Minnie Renfrow Wedding, in Hartford, Kentucky, in November 1919. Mrs. Lee filed for divorce six months later.[266]

Yates left the band after the session. Former Blue Grass Boy Earl Snead filled in on bass briefly, then Bill called William "Skip" Payne. Bill had known Payne since 1967–68, when he played with Georgia fiddler Randall Collins and his Carolina Buddies, the first band to record "Little Georgia Rose" with a trio chorus (on the Rally label). Payne had just turned twenty-one, bringing out the paternal instincts of the band's older members. "Bill and Kenny Baker—they hovered over me like two hawks," Payne said. They didn't know until after they hired him that Payne was a trained diesel mechanic. After that, he said, "I got to drive most of the time and I worked on the bus."[267]

Jim Rooney's Bossmen

Jim Rooney, meanwhile, was out of a job. Expenses at the Newport Jazz and Folk festivals had temporarily put George Wein's Festival Productions out of business. Rooney said his thoughts turned to his days at Club 47 and the acts he'd booked there, like Bill and Chicago blues bandleader Muddy Waters.

> I woke up one night with this idea about Bill and Muddy. The more I thought about it, the more it seemed true—how similar they were as people and also what they'd done with music—taking it out of a rural setting and bringing it to a commercially viable place, like Nashville or Chicago, and changing the music to make it work as a commercial music. And they both attracted the best players—people were just attracted to them 'cause they were so good—and they were willing to put up with really bad working conditions because the music was so good. And then those people went on and started their own bands.

Rooney wrote a proposal for a book about these two "bossmen" (used later in the book's introduction), and Dial Press of New York agreed to publish it. Rinzler wasn't consulted because Rooney didn't think it would be as in-depth as "the real biography" Rinzler planned to write. He said later that Rinzler had told him he was going to write his book after Bill died, so it wouldn't jeopardize their friendship, and Rooney felt his book was needed then.[268]

Bill held his last recording session of the 1960s on the evening of December 17, but officially it was a James Monroe session. Forsaking his father's long-established practice of recording "live," James decided to use the then-new technology of overdubbing to record the vocals for "Bonny" (by Juanita Southern) and the third of three solo songs recorded by a member of the Blue Grass Boys, "Sweet Mary and the Miles in Between" (by Damon Black). Decca would release them on a single credited to James Monroe, without mention of Bill or the Blue Grass Boys.[269]

The year and the decade ended with the release on December 30 of *Blue Grass Style*, an album on Vocalion, Decca's discount-priced label. It contained ten of the fourteen recordings Bill made in 1957 (excluding "A Fallen Star," "Four Walls," "Molly and Tenbrooks," and "A Lonesome Road"), all recorded "live" in the studio with a limited number of takes. Suddenly, the recent past seemed like a long time ago.[270]

CHAPTER SEVEN
1970–1979

The Deaths of Harry Silverstein and Howard Watts

The 1970s began with the deaths of Harry Silverstein and Howard Watts, both victims of heart attacks. Bill's Decca producer since 1962, Silverstein died at age thirty-nine on January 8. Decca would provide Bill with an unnamed temporary replacement for a session on January 19. It began with rerecording the vocals on "Bonny" and "Sweet Mary" by overdubbing, preceded by Bill announcing, "William Smith Monroe does not wear headphones" (normally worn when overdubbing). So Bill recorded his tenor on "Bonny" without them, while James used them to overdub his lead vocals. Two of Pen Vandiver's tunes, "McKinley's March" and "Texas Gallop," were then recorded "live," the only ones waxed during the rest of 1970 for the *Uncle Pen* album project, temporarily derailed after Silverstein's passing. Permanently derailed was whatever agreement Charlie Monroe had with Silverstein to record two albums for Decca. Two days after Bill's first session of the decade, Howard Watts, bassist of "the classic bluegrass band," died at age fifty-six on January 21.[1]

Bill and the Scruggs Revue

After the breakup of Bill's archrivals Flatt and Scruggs in February 1969, Bill contacted Scruggs and arranged for his new band, the Earl Scruggs Revue, to play at the 1970 Bean Blossom festival. Then, from February 1970 on, Bill took the new band under his wing, arranging for the Revue to appear with him on a majority of his *Opry* shows through October. Scruggs, returning the favor, arranged for Bill and the Blue Grass Boys to appear in the documentary *Earl Scruggs: His Family and Friends*, in a segment filmed at the Ryman during two or three of their joint appearances there. (The film aired on National Educational Television stations in January 1971, and the Scruggs Revue continued to appear on Bill's *Opry* shows throughout that year.)[2]

On March 26, 1970, at Bill's seventy-fifth session for Decca, the band recorded four new gospel songs: "Road of Life" by Virginia Stauffer; "It's Me Again, Lord" by Dottie Rambo; "Beyond the Gate" by Jake Landers and Bill; and "I Will Sing for the Glory of God," credited to Tex Logan. Just before the session, Skip Payne's father had a heart attack, and Payne wanted to go home to be with him. "Bill told me to go on," he said. As a result, the songs were recorded without a bass; otherwise, Bill would have owed Decca for another session with nothing to show for it.[3]

Jim Rooney had been traveling with Bill and the band since January but hadn't had much luck interviewing him for his book. "The times when I tried to interview him, he was pretty stiff: 'Yes, sir.' 'No, I don't think so,' and so on." Inevitably, a bus breakdown happened on a trip to the Northeast in early April, and they all spent the night in a bus garage near Troutville, Virginia. Rooney recalled that most of the band had gone to bed.

> Kenny and Bill were sitting up front and they just started chatting about the past. They knew I was there, and I had a little hand-held cassette recorder, and I'm sure they were aware that I was listening and taping. But they just felt like doing it. I might have asked one or two questions, but I tried not to get in their way because they were just flowing. That was a real gold mine—I got eighty percent [of the quotes in the book] right there.

Rooney's groundbreaking *Bossmen: Bill Monroe and Muddy Waters* would be published in early 1971 and serve as the primary biographical source about Bill for nearly thirty years.[4]

On Monday, May 4, 1970—the same day four Kent State University students died while protesting the decision to send American forces to Cambodia—Dolly Parton recorded Bill's arrangement of "Mule Skinner Blues." She had been urged to record it by her singing partner at the time, Porter Wagoner, who said he "felt she needed something exciting, almost outrageous, to grab attention," after six of her previous releases failed to reach the Top Ten. It worked—the RCA Victor single entered the charts in June and quickly went to number 1 in *Record World*, number 2 in *Cash Box*, and number 3 in *Billboard*. It was Parton's first "megahit."[5]

Bill and the Festival Business

Bill was usually busy during the first months of the year, working behind the scenes to prepare for his June festival, but this year he was twice as busy, preparing for both Bean Blossom and his second festival, the first in Kentucky, in September. Festivals were rapidly proliferating, with one or two held every month from May to September that year, and Bill had decided that if Carlton Haney could have two, and festival promoter Jim Clark could have two (in Maryland and Pennsylvania), he should be able to have two as well. It was the beginning of Bill's involvement in the festival business, peaking in 1974 with thirteen events from Delaware to California with his name on them (some endorsed by Bill and run by others), including two with Ralph Stanley and one with the Sullivan Family.[6]

Bill's fourth Bean Blossom fest (June 17–21, 1970) was deluged with more than twenty thousand attendees (with minimal advertising). Many were "hippies" in search of a Woodstock-like experience, but many more were serious "bluegrassers" from outside the Midwest, visiting Bill's festival for the first time. It began on Wednesday and "was by Saturday night a thrumming mass of fans, pickers, artists, vendors, instrument dealers, and camping families," wrote Tom Adler in his *Bean Blossom*. Eighteen-year-old Doug Hutchens, a banjo picker from Stuart, Virginia, had been recruited by Calvin Robins to help with the myriad tasks required. In the evenings, Robins would get out his guitar and they would jam with fellow campers Eddie "Slick" Bush on mandolin and his singing wife, "Peanuts." "Usually Bill would come by and take Eddie's mandolin and play and sing a few with us," Hutchens recalled. "Then he would go on and do the same thing until he had covered a good amount of the grounds."[7]

By Sunday afternoon, the crowd had thinned considerably, and many missed the appearance of the Earl Scruggs Revue, whose music was very different from the "traditional" fare that had come before. A team of reporters from *Newsweek* magazine, on the lookout for Woodstock-like events, covered the festival. In their story, the first by a mainstream magazine to acknowledge Bill's existence, a quote from him sounded remarkably openminded.

[T]here's room in bluegrass for differences. You know, I intended this music for country people, but it's growed and gone all over. The mountain people have been with me 30 years. But my hippie fans know when the music is played right. And the college kids are my biggest audience. People have learned that bluegrass has a wonderful feeling. If you play it right, people know you got your heart in it.

Newsweek, with this article, was the first nationally distributed publication to say, unequivocally, that "Bill Monroe is 'the father of bluegrass,'" and one of the first widely read publications to mention that "Blue Moon of Kentucky" was one of Elvis Presley's first recordings.[8]

Released the same day *Newsweek* was published (June 29, 1970) was Bill's newest Decca album, *Kentucky Blue Grass*, which should have been released in time to sell at the Bean Blossom festival. Its tardiness may have been due to Rinzler's late completion of its liner notes, not mailed to Decca until May 16. In the resulting rush to get the album out, session data that Rinzler had provided were not included. Five of its eleven selections had been waiting since 1964–65: "Last Old Dollar," "Never Again," "Fire on the Mountain," "The Long Black Veil," and "I Live in the Past." Columbia Records' response was *Sixteen All-Time Greatest Hits*, released in August, near the time of Haney's Labor Day festival. Its "Hits" were reissues of previous reissues: eight from *The Great Bill Monroe* (1961) and eight from *Bill Monroe's Best* (1964).[9]

Haney's Big Ideas

Haney, meanwhile, had big ideas. He wanted to build, on the 160-acre farm he had purchased for his Camp Springs festival, a "Blue Grass Museum and Archives," a "Hall of Fame," and a "School of Music" (with dormitories) where musicians could study and learn to play bluegrass. At the beginning of 1970 he'd also put forth his proposals for organizing the bluegrass festival business, which he believed was out of control. In an editorial in the second issue of his *Muleskinner News*, he offered to establish an office to provide several services, including: "1) Clear all Festival dates and sanction all Festivals" and "2) Clear all artist bookings for 5% of artist fee." Then he said he had another idea involving the eight major bands of the time: the Country Gentlemen, Lester Flatt, Jim and Jesse, Jimmy Martin, Bill Monroe, Don Reno, Red Smiley, and Ralph Stanley. According to Butch Robins in his *What I Know 'Bout What I Know*, "[Haney] wanted to divide the major acts . . . into two touring groups and have them be like a package show. He wanted to hold two festivals at each venue [location]. He proposed working a circuit around the country so that every major act could get exposure to all festival audiences."

It's not difficult to imagine Bill's reaction, especially when he was about to get involved in the festival business. Haney said later, "I got to talkin' onstage and announced that I was going to build a hall of fame museum for this music. And [Bill] thought I was tryin' to take it over." But it was more likely Haney's designs on the business of festivals that convinced Bill he had to be stopped, and the only way was to sever all ties with him. Bill arrived at Haney's sixth festival on Saturday, September 5, and the next day, at the beginning of yet another "Blue Grass Music Story," Haney announced, choking back tears, "There'll be no more Stories after today. . . . Today will be the last time we'll do this." Bill carried on as if nothing had happened.[10]

Bill wasn't the only one upset with Haney. The leaders of the major bands at the festival convened an impromptu meeting with Haney during "the Story," in the warmup room under the Camp Springs stage. There, with Don Reno as the main speaker, the bandleaders expressed their dissatisfaction with Haney's ideas, declaring they would join together in a union of their own to oppose his proposed control of them. Fred Bartenstein, Haney's assistant, recalled, "I'll never forget Don saying, 'Carlton, if you don't like it, that's the way the pickle squirts.' And everybody had a big laugh." Neither the union of musicians or Haney's proposals ever happened, undoubtedly nullified by the meeting, but Bill's conviction to disassociate himself from Haney was bolstered. The resulting split (including the end of all communication between them) was reportedly heartbreaking for the festival pioneer. Ronnie Reno recalled, "I know in later years, Carlton would swell up just talking about it."[11]

Bill and Virginia Stauffer

At the same time Bill was severing ties with Haney, he was also cutting the cord with Mauldin. She had been living with him on the Goodlettsville farm, staying there while he was on the road, for about six years. But she would say in a lawsuit that in September 1970 he "abandoned" her, providing her with only enough money to buy food. Bill had been a frequent guest of Virginia Stauffer's in the trailer park she managed on Murfreesboro Road, southeast of downtown Nashville, and it could have been then that he moved in with her.[12]

Bill's Kentucky bluegrass festival, the first in the Blue Grass State, was held on the weekend of September 18 at the Rockdale Jamboree, a country music park near Ashland and the Ohio River. Aside from Bill, its lineup included Jim and Jesse, Jimmy Martin, Reno and Harrell, and Ralph Stanley. Jack Hicks (not related to Bobby), then an eighteen-year-old banjo picker who'd grown up in the Ashland area, remembered "a pretty good crowd" at the festival, even though it wasn't advertised in either *Bluegrass Unlimited* or *Muleskinner News*. Bill had featured Hicks on his shows at the Bean Blossom festival, and at Ashland he called him up onstage to pick a tune. (After the festival, Skip Payne left the band, and Joe Stuart, already back to twin with Baker, switched to bass.)[13]

On Saturday, October 3, Bill and the band played an all-gospel show at the National Guard Armory in Jackson, Alabama. Twelve-year-old Marty Stuart, a budding mandolin player, came with his family from Philadelphia, Mississippi, to see Bill there. "He was the very first country artist I ever saw in concert," Stuart wrote.

> After the concert, I bought one of his records and went backstage to get his autograph. He signed the album for me. When he handed it back, I told him I had just gotten a mandolin and wanted to learn to play like him. Monroe reached in his pocket, pulled out a mandolin pick, and gave it to me. "Go home, and learn to use it," he said.

Stuart's professional career would begin the following summer, playing mandolin with the Sullivan Family.[14]

The Country Music Hall of Fame

Two weeks later, on October 14, 1970, the Country Music Association finally inducted Bill into the Country Music Hall of Fame. Faced with the ever-increasing popularity of bluegrass music, it appears the CMA was willing to admit it might have been wrong. At the televised awards ceremony, Bill gave what may have been the briefest acceptance speech on record: "This is a great honor and I thank every one of you. Thank you." The bronze plaque commemorating his membership reads:

> The "Father of Bluegrass Music," Bill Monroe developed and perfected this music form, and taught it to many great names in the industry. Even-tempered and a possessor of spiritual values, this direct descendant of the fifth president of the

United States is a composer and recording artist. He helped stimulate interest in this form of down-to-earth music in colleges long after its initial popularity.

The "great names," if mentioned by name, would undoubtedly include Flatt and Scruggs and the Osborne Brothers, star pupils who'd had commercial success with bluegrass, thereby helping Bill win this recognition. He acknowledged this in a letter published in the next issue of the fan club newsletter: "My Blue Grass Boys, past and present . . . deserve so much praise and credit for their part in this great honor which was bestowed on me." A distant cousin of President James Monroe, Bill would continue to be incorrectly called "a direct descendent" throughout his life, thanks to this plaque.[15]

Bill was scheduled to appear all three days of the Thanksgiving weekend at the South Carolina State Bluegrass Festival, the first three-day *indoor* festival, to be held at the Myrtle Beach Convention Center. Advertised with a two-page center spread in the November issue of *Bluegrass Unlimited* (the first to be published in its present size, previously an $8^{1}/{2}"$ by $7"$ booklet), it caught the eye of Doug Hutchens, and during his Thanksgiving break at Berea College in Kentucky, he went. Bill called him up onstage to pick a tune every day. "As I got ready to leave on Sunday afternoon," Hutchens said, "I went by the bus to tell Bill I was leaving, and he asked if I'd like to work for him next summer. I asked him what I would be doing and he said he didn't know, but he would guarantee me a job. I was to call him in the spring."[16]

By then, Rual Yarbrough had turned in his two-weeks' notice, telling Bill he would stay longer if a replacement couldn't be found. Yarbrough was busier than ever with his music store in Muscle Shoals, and he was thinking about re-forming his old band, the Dixie Gentlemen, with a less demanding itinerary. Bill, distracted by festival planning, had begun to let some things slide, and this was wearing thin on Yarbrough: "Like he'd let the bus sit out there on an old dusty lot [on Dickerson Road in Goodlettsville] all week, knowin' that there was somethin' wrong with it. We'd get in that thing and drive out as far as Lebanon [about thirty miles east of Nashville] and pull into a truck stop and start havin' it worked on, when it should have been worked on while it was in town."[17]

Year-end recording sessions were held on December 2 and 3, the first with Bill's new producer, Walter Haynes. A steel guitar player in Nashville since the 1950s, Haynes had been Owen Bradley's assistant for several years before Bradley appointed him staff producer in 1969 (he would eventually be Jimmy Martin's producer also). Haynes's first album project with Bill celebrated his Hall of Fame membership, with Bill rerecording some of his most popular numbers. On December 2: "Kentucky Waltz" (with three fiddles: Baker, Red Hayes, and Gordon Terry), "The Girl in the Blue Velvet Band" (with Baker and Hayes on fiddles and Terry playing guitar), and "My Little Georgia Rose" (ultimately rejected, possibly due to a too-recent release on *The High, Lonesome Sound*). With Yarbrough on his way out the door, Bobby Thompson was recruited by Baker to pick banjo. Thompson, co-pioneer of melodic banjo, was being heard every week on CBS television, picking the *Hee Haw* theme, an adaption of Bill's "Mule Skinner Blues."[18]

The band recorded instrumentals on December 3, beginning with Bill's minor-keyed masterpiece "Lonesome Moonlight Waltz," called simply "Moonlight Waltz" when played with Doc Watson in the 1960s. Next was a new tune by Bill called "Tallahassee," named for the capital of Florida (where the capitol building is located on Monroe Street). Both featured three fiddles by Baker, Hayes, and Terry. Last was a rerecording of 1953's "Get Up John," with Baker and Hayes twin fiddling and Terry again on guitar.[19]

As Yarbrough had promised North Carolinian Roby Carter "R. C." Harris (who'd picked banjo with Skip Payne in the Carolina Buddies), he called to let him know he was leaving. Harris debuted with the band on the *Friday Night Opry* on Christmas Night 1970. But the former bank manager began having second thoughts about supporting his family after realizing he would only be paid union scale of $15 per *Opry* show and $35 per day on the road. "I had no idea what I was gonna make," he said. "It didn't ever cross my mind." He quit after about a week.[20]

It was a lucky break for former Blue Grass Boy Earl Snead, who hadn't been able to record with Bill back in 1958. On the January 13, 1971, session (with Baker, fiddle; James, guitar; Snead, banjo; and Stuart, bass), work continued on the *Hall of Fame* album with a redo of "Summertime Is Past and Gone," a trio with a somewhat less-than-good blend of voices (the seventh "classic band" song). They loosened up a bit on "Rocky Road Blues," with Stuart adding a jazzy ending with his bass. Then James solidly kicked off "Mule Skinner Blues" and Bill included for the first time the "Workin' on the railroad" stanza he had been singing at shows since the early 1950s. "Katy Hill," another number from Bill's 1940 session, was attempted but ultimately rejected, possibly because Snead couldn't manage a melodic-style break. He continued to play with Bill on shows but would be replaced at future sessions by Thompson.[21]

It appears, however, that Thompson had worked out his breaks on the tunes recorded at these sessions long beforehand, possibly prior to the sessions of December 1970. On January 15, three of Uncle Pen's were recorded: "Poor White Folks" (full title: "Poor White Folks Ain't Treatin' Me Right"); "The Old Gray Mare Came Tearing Out of the Wilderness" (reminiscent of the gray mare Pat, given to Bill after his father died); and "Kiss Me Waltz," originally recorded in the early 1920s as "Kiss Waltz." And on January 20, two more from Uncle Pen: "Jenny Lynn," mentioned in the song "Uncle Pen" as "the greatest of all," named for Swedish songstress Jenny Lind of the mid-1850s, and "Heel and Toe Polka," played not only by Pen but also by Bill's mother, and by Sally Ann Forrester in the 1940s. And with these five, the *Uncle Pen* album was completed. As if to celebrate, the band recorded "Milenburg Joy," a jazz tune from the 1920s (originally "Milneburg Joys," credited to Jelly Roll Morton) that Bill likely heard the Hoosier Hot Shots play in the 1930s. Buddy Spicher joined the group to twin on the last three.[22]

During this time in January 1971, RCA Victor released Elvis Presley's *Elvis Country* album. It included a tip of the hat to Bill—a brief (1:45) "Little Cabin Home on the Hill," recorded on June 4, 1970 (with banjo and fiddle overdubbed later by Bobby Thompson and Buddy Spicher).

Shortly after Bill's January 20 session, R. C. Harris asked for his job back. "I came home and I couldn't stand it," Harris said. "I thought, 'Man, I've made a mistake.' So . . . Bill hired me back, but he was aggravated at me" (probably because he had to let Snead go).[23]

In the February 1971 *Bluegrass Unlimited*, in its "Notes & Queries" column, a reader in England had written to ask what Bill ate for breakfast. Columnist Marion Kuykendall (first wife of editor Pete Kuykendall), consulted with Bill, then answered: "Fried pork shoulder, eggs, fried potatoes, blackberry jam, and rolls. He also eats peanut butter on donuts. Try that and see if it improves your tenor singing."[24]

Rooney's *Bossmen: Bill Monroe & Muddy Waters* was published in April, and by then, banjo player Harris experienced renewed concerns about his pay. When asking Bill for a salary didn't work, he said he had to quit again. He was replaced on the weekend of April 23 by Jack Hicks, still eighteen. On Monday the 26th, Bill's fifteenth Decca album, *Bill Monroe's Country Music Hall of Fame*, was released.[25]

Also in April, officials of WSM and its owner, the National Life and Accident Insurance Company, announced their plan to tear down the Ryman Auditorium ("The Grand Ole Opry House"). Its dilapidated condition and the expense of renovating it had prompted the decision to build a new Opry House, and that decision ultimately resulted in the concept of the "Opryland USA" theme park, under construction north of downtown Nashville. Bricks from the Ryman were to be used to build a chapel in the nearly completed park. Chosen as a "board of advisors" for the chapel project were Roy Acuff, Tennessee Ernie Ford, Reverend Billy Graham, Tex Ritter, Ernest Tubb, and Bill, who all gave their approval for the plan. Tired of dealing with the inadequacies of the Ryman, *Opry* veterans had few sentimental feelings for it. But opposition to the demolition would put the plan on hold and ultimately save "The Mother Church of Country Music."[26]

James Forms a Band

By then, thirty-year-old James Monroe had decided to form his own band, after nearly five years on bass (June 1964–March 1969) and two years on guitar (March 1969–April 1971) with his father. "I felt that I was ready," James said later. "I had some new material and wanted to get a different sound from a lot of the bands. It also gave me a chance to sing more." To replace him, Bill called thirty-six-year-old Louisiana native Travis Stewart, who had played with the Country Cut-Ups in Texas and the Southern Bluegrass Boys in Louisiana. When he joined in early April, Bill asked Stewart to play bass until James departed (with Stuart again playing twin fiddle). After James left, Stewart recalled a night at the *Opry* when Roy Acuff had just finished his spot: "As he was comin' off, we were goin' on, and Bill walked up to him and said, 'Go out and do a number with us.' Acuff said, 'I'd love to.' So, me and him and Bill did 'Sittin' on Top of the World'—I would do the verses, Acuff took the lead on the chorus and I'd drop down and do baritone, and Bill tenored."[27]

Doug Hutchens finished his first year at Berea College that spring and, after contacting Bill, he reported to Bean Blossom on May 11 to help Birch get the park ready for the June festival. Bertha helped, too, Hutchens said: "She came over during the day and cleaned around in the kitchen there in the barn." Joe Stuart and Bill usually arrived on Tuesdays to pitch in, sometimes bringing Virginia Stauffer with them. Hutchens's biggest task was cutting the grass in the huge parking areas with a push mower—there was no expensive riding mower for frugal Birch. Hutchens was at the Jamboree on Sunday, May 30, for James Monroe's first show with his own band, the Midnight Ramblers (its name borrowed from Joe Stuart's 1940s band). Bill and the band, meanwhile, were at Ralph Stanley's first festival (May 28–30), in the Clinch Mountains of Virginia, at the Stanley homeplace near McClure. Stanley's first featured a fox hunt, an event after Bill's heart. It was called a "race" in the *Bluegrass Unlimited* ad: "Anyone having hounds and wants to enter the race is welcome. Bring on the dogs. There will be a red fox turned loose."[28]

Bill's fifth Bean Blossom festival followed, now extended to six days: Tuesday, June 15, through Sunday, June 20, 1971. Robert Cantwell (later author of *Bluegrass Breakdown*) arrived on Tuesday afternoon: "I got my money's worth right at the gate, where Bill Monroe, who had never seen me before in his life, said, 'Howdy!' and smiled like a senator." His impression of the Sunset Jam appeared later in the *Atlantic Monthly*:

> Everyone who dreams of playing bluegrass with Bill Monroe here found his opportunity. In the confines of a small grassy area defined by a clothesline hung across temporary posts, Bill had gathered with upwards of one hundred and twenty guitar, banjo, and mandolin pickers, fiddlers, and singers to play and sing, into three widely spaced mikes wired to a sound truck, songs and tunes from the Bill Monroe canon which *everyone* knew by heart. Knew, that is, in an absolute, liturgical sense. Clustered around Bill in his gleaming white jacket and white cowboy hat were the very young, amateurs and professionals, musicians who had learned under Monroe, played in his band, and had gone off to make their own reputations, and those who hoped eventually to record and carry on Bill Monroe's music themselves. Bill administered each number, singing and playing into one of the mikes, dropping behind and inviting a stranger or a friend to sing or play a bit, or with the palm of his hand gently prodding a shy and thrilled youngster to play a hesitating but thoroughly satisfying instrumental solo. "I call you all my children," Bill said, and suddenly it became clear that this bluegrass festival was nothing more or less than an old-time camp meeting, an evangelical retreat of the very kind that rural folk a century ago waited all summer for, yet now somehow enlightened beyond dogma, hellfire, and exploitation. And here was Bill Monroe the teacher, founder of the brotherhood and sisterhood, standing among all the picking and singing like John Wesley on the green of an eighteenth-century English village. That night, when someone in the audience asked the highly talented mandolin picker for the Brown County Boys to play "Raw Hide," an instrumental created by Bill Monroe and requiring incredible dexterity in both hands, the young man drawled, "Naw, let's leave that one for the Master."

According to Doug Hutchens, however, *he* was the one who spoke those words. Filling in on bass with the band-contest-winning Brown County

Boys, he didn't know how to play "Raw Hide" on the bass and was trying to avoid playing it.[29]

Bill and Lester Flatt

The festival's most memorable moments, however, occurred on Sunday, June 20, 1971: many of the featured bands were playing brief, fifteen-minute sets that afternoon, and Lester Flatt and his Nashville Grass, whom James had booked for the festival, had just finished theirs. Flatt was backstage when he felt a tap on his shoulder. He turned around to see Bill, with his hand extended, saying, "Welcome to Bean Blossom." They shook hands, a bear hug followed, and after years of silence, as Flatt's biographer Jake Lambert put it, "the two famous bluegrass giants were once again friends." A "Bluegrass Music Story" was scheduled next, hosted by Ralph Rinzler, and Bill invited Flatt to sing with him. As Flatt recalled:

> When I came out on stage with Bill, the crowd gave us a standing ovation as soon as we shook hands. It was the greatest thing I had ever seen since I have been in show business. Even a lot of the other entertainers were crying. I didn't think that anyone would even remember that I had played with Bill.

First they sang "Roll in My Sweet Baby's Arms," the Monroe Brothers favorite, then "Little Cabin Home on the Hill," their co-written classic, recently recorded by Elvis (royalties may have helped melt, if not break, the ice). The surprised crowd—most of whom knew of the rift—was beside itself with joy. Hutchens was among them, listening carefully: "While Bill was taking a mandolin break, Lester looked over and said, 'It's been a long time, Bill.' Bill, in mid-break, nodded. Few heard this—it's not on the tape of that reunion—but I was sitting at the corner of the stage and heard it." Afterward, as the crowd called for more, Bill echoed Flatt, saying, "It has been a long, long time since Lester Flatt and me have sung together."[30]

That day was Travis Stewart's last, and the word was out that Bill might be wanting another lead singer-guitarist. "I heard that he was lookin' for someone," said Kentuckian Danny Jones, "so I asked Bill and he gave me a specified time to be at the bus" to audition. Jones had previously played mandolin and recorded with the original Bluegrass Alliance. Raised in Ohio County, he was in the army in 1959 when the rest of his family lived in the house at the Monroe homeplace, renting it from Charlie. But Bill wouldn't know of this until a month later, during a conversation on the side of a western Kentucky road, waiting on a tow truck for the broken-down bus.[31]

After the festival, cleanup started on Monday morning, June 21. Between loads of trash trucked to the landfill, Bill invited Hutchens "to travel around with the band for the summer, sell records, and keep gas in the bus's air-conditioning generator." He readily accepted. That evening, it was time to "settle up," and all of the helpers came on the bus, one at a time, for Bill to pay them. "It was then," Hutchens said, "that he asked me what it would cost to go to school for the next year. I told him eight or nine hundred dollars. He counted out nine one-hundred-dollar bills and said, 'Take this home and put it in the bank and meet me at the truck stop on 11W, south of Roanoke, on Friday afternoon.'" They would be heading to Lancaster, Pennsylvania, for a show on Saturday, June 26, at "The Shindig at Cripple Creek" country music park.[32]

Bill's recording of "Tallahassee" had been released on May 3 (with "Going Up Caney") and several boxes of the new 45 rpm record had been brought to the Shindig. As Hutchens recalled,

> Bill asked me an hour or so before the show if I had "ever played any bass," to which I replied, "No, not really." [Bill probably noticed him playing with the Brown County Boys.] Then he said, "Go out there and let Joe Stuart show you how to play 'Tallahassee.' . . . [Y]ou can play that number, then go set up the record table." Joe was happy to show me the notes on the bass because that would mean that he would play twin fiddles with Kenny Baker, and Joe loved to play fiddle.
>
> After "Tallahassee" [the show opener], I started to take Joe's fiddle, give him the bass, and go set up the records. Bill said, "Just stay with us." After a second tune, "Footprints in the Snow," again I started to take Joe's fiddle and give him the bass when Bill turned around and said, "Are you determined to leave us?" I said, "Well, no, not really." He said, "You stay right here until I tell you to go."

Bill never did tell him to go; Hutchens was a full-fledged band member from then on.[33]

The next day, Sunday, June 27, they played a one-day festival at Frontier Ranch, a country music park near Columbus, Ohio. Hutchens was sitting on the bus with Bill when Lester Flatt knocked on the door and came aboard. Hutchens recalled,

> I only wish I could have had the presence of mind to make a few notes of what they talked about. I remember the conversation began with Lester asking, "Where did y'all work last night?" For the next two hours, they talked about all sorts of

things. The only thing I remember well was the idea came up of working some together. Bill said we could "go right across the country, all the buses together." Lester said we could call it "the Bluegrass Caravan." As Lester was getting ready to leave, to get dressed for the show, Bill asked him, "Do you think we could do a couple of numbers together this afternoon?" to which Lester said, "It would be my pleasure, Bill." My chill bumps were plentiful and it was in the high 90s outside.

The crowd was large and many had heard of Bill and Lester's reunion the week before in Bean Blossom. Anticipation was in the air—Would they do it again? Then, when Lester and his group came out at the end of Bill's show and "Little Cabin Home on the Hill" was kicked off, the crowd came unglued.[34]

After Frontier Ranch, Jones was dropped off near his home in Louisville. At that point, he was sporting a moustache and long hair. Hutchens decided to camp out on the bus after it arrived at the Goodlettsville lot. Years later, at a Blue Grass Boys reunion, Hutchens and Jones recalled what happened next:

HUTCHENS: One morning, Bill came out to the bus where I was staying and said, "Danny is coming down this morning. I was supposed to meet him at eleven o'clock to transfer his paperwork from Louisville to the [musicians'] union down here. I've got another meeting." Bill handed me some money and said, "Give this to Danny. Tell him I think he will be a good, strong guitar man and we'll have a good duet, but he will have to shave his moustache, and he will have to cut his hair. There has never been a Blue Grass Boy with a moustache. If he wants the job, that's just the way it will have to be." Then Bill left. (*laughter*) I don't mind telling you that I didn't know how I was going to say it. I had only known Dan for a week or so.

JONES: That was quite a predicament that Bill put you in. When I got there, you just said, "Dan, Bill said for you to cut your hair and shave your moustache." (*laughter*) . . . I said . . . "Well, I'll do it. . . . I want the job and I won't let that stand between me and the job."

Later that day, after Jones shaved off his moustache at a nearby motel, Bill returned. Jones recalled him saying, "My Uncle Pen, you know, he had a moustache, and I love a moustache, but I think you'll look better on the *Opry* with me if you shave that moustache." The haircut, however, wouldn't happen for awhile.[35]

James put on his first festival that weekend (July 2–4) in Cosby (near Gatlinburg), Tennessee, the first multiday bluegrass festival in that state. Bill and the band were there, as well as Lester Flatt and the Nashville Grass, including Josh Graves and his Dobro. Bill had refused to accept the Dobro as a bluegrass instrument, as much for his dislike of its sound ("A Dobro, to me, sounds like a tin bucket," he once told Rinzler) as for its role in popularizing Flatt and Scruggs's music. Now that he had "buried the hatchet" with both Flatt and Scruggs, it appears he wanted to make amends by inviting Graves to play an entire set with him. During the set, it appears Bill rediscovered an old favorite, "Evening Prayer Blues" (originally a harmonica solo DeFord Bailey recorded in 1927). Hutchens said later, "I remember Bill told the audience to imagine a colored meeting house and they would be praying, and, every now and then, saying 'Praise the Lord.'" Dave Samuelson, future record producer, was there: "Bill and Josh traded licks on it for five or six minutes—or maybe longer. I had never before seen two musicians so naturally in synch with each other—two master bluesmen on a totally harmonious wavelength. After forty years, I still remember the magic."[36]

As summer began to wane, Bill and the band spent seven days (August 2–8) at the Ohio National Blue Grass Festival in Ottawa, Ohio, and Jones still needed a haircut. On the seventh day, Bill finally "laid down the law," according to Jones:

> Bill said, among other things, "Your hair is too long, and you get to a barber shop today!" I said, "Bill, this is Sunday. There are no barber shops open." He said, "Well, Don Reno, he cuts hair." Don, Red [Smiley], and Bill [Harrell] were there [then working together], so I went over to Don and just said, "Would you cut my hair?" So, I got an old shirt and we went out there on a picnic table and he cut my hair.[37]

During the rest of August, Bill and the band were on the run. Near the end of it, Jones decided to call it quits, finally facing the fact that he wasn't making enough money. After a county fair in Pennsylvania on the 24th and a party at Tex Logan's in New Jersey on the 26th, he was replaced on guitar by Joe Stuart. Hutchens played his last at the Philadelphia Folk Festival on the 28th and returned to college. "Bill told me," he said later, "'I think you need to go back and finish school. Your folks want you to do that. Then, if you ever want a job and I have an opening, it's yours.' It was some of the best advice anyone ever gave me."[38]

Labor Day weekend followed, during which Bill became the first promoter of a multiday festival to challenge Carlton Haney's "ownership" of the weekend. The "Lone Star Bluegrass Festival" (Bill's third festival of 1971), held at Garland (near Dallas), Texas, September 3–5, was about a thousand miles west of Camp Springs, making it less than a head-to-head challenge. But it still defied Haney's supposed dominance of the holiday weekend. Several musicians filled in on bass with the Blue Grass Boys, including Bill's fan club president Glen Mowrey.[39]

After the festival, Bill contacted a bluegrass veteran, forty-two-year-old Alabama native Monroe Fields, to fill the bass spot. Fields had worked with Carl Sauceman's Green Valley Boys in the 1950s (with Joe Stuart), then with Jim and Jesse (on bass) and Flatt and Scruggs (on mandolin) in the early 1960s.[40]

Songwriter's Hall of Fame and the First Early Bird

October of 1971 brought the twentieth annual Deejay Convention in Nashville, from Friday the 8th through Sunday the 16th. James published the first issue of his new magazine, *The Bluegrass Star*, just in time for it. Included was the first of three installments of the biographical "Bill Monroe: From a Farm Boy to a Legend," which James himself had written. (*The Bluegrass Star* would be published through February 1973, providing more coverage to Bill than Haney's *Muleskinner News*.) On October 11, the Nashville Songwriters Association elected Bill to its Hall of Fame, inducting him with nineteen others, including Vaughn Horton (lyricist of "New Mule Skinner Blues"). The best part of the week for Bill, however, was the first "Early Bird Bluegrass Show," his and *Opry* manager Bud Wendell's brainchild, held at the Ryman on the evening of October 13, with almost all of the top bands.[41]

The season closer at the Brown County Jamboree was "a three-day mini bluegrass festival" held November 3–5 in the Barn, with Bill, Ralph Stanley, the Goins Brothers, and James. In the crowd was sixteen-year-old Glen Duncan, then seriously "into" rock, but there with his father Carlton Duncan from nearby Columbus, Indiana, "to see Ralph Stanley sing 'Little Maggie.'" The young Duncan had recently heard the 1960 Stanley Brothers recording; "I thought that was the greatest thing I'd ever heard," he said. The elder Duncan had played at the Jamboree in the 1940s, and his son had been there many times with him, but Glen Duncan hadn't paid attention to Bill since 1967.

> Ralph had a great band [Duncan wrote], with Roy Lee Centers and Curly Ray Cline, and they just wrecked the place—encored three or four times. Bill followed and Dad said, "Do you want to stay and see Bill?" and I replied, "No, I've seen him a lot of times. Let's just go." So, we're walking out of the Barn and we've made it as far as the refreshment stand [near the back exit] when Bill and the boys tear

into "Uncle Pen." I stopped dead in my tracks and whirled around. I said to Dad, "What is that?!?" Dad said, "That's 'Uncle Pen.' You've heard that one a hundred times." I said, "Not like that!!!" Dad said, "Well, do you want to go back and watch them?" Needless to say, we did. Most of the crowd had flocked to Ralph's record table, or left, so there were a lot of empty seats. We went right down front, and I stared up at Kenny Baker for the rest of the show.

Hearing Baker for the first time was the beginning of a love affair with the fiddle for future Blue Grass Boy Duncan. "We didn't have a fiddle in the house, so I went home and tuned a ukulele up to violin tuning. I had to keep gluing the bridge back on because [the uke] didn't like being tuned that high." He would get his first fiddle a few months later.[42]

At the beginning of 1972 the idea of "working some together," which Bill and Lester Flatt had discussed the previous June, came to fruition. Flatt and Bill and their bands, joined by James and the Midnight Ramblers, appeared in a series of concerts together as "The Bluegrass Express." During the last two weekends of January they played three shows in Ohio (Akron, Dayton, Toledo) and one each in Mississippi (Hattiesburg) and Louisiana (Monroe), with Jim and Jesse added on two of the shows in Ohio. It proved to be an excellent way to encourage bookings during an otherwise slow month.[43]

Work continued to be limited, however, even into March 1972. With little else to do, Bill accepted a weekend-long engagement (March 10–12) at a new nightclub in Columbus, Ohio, the Country Palace. Former Blue Grass Boy Sandy Rothman, recently moved to Columbus, was there all three nights, along with new friend Tom Ewing. Bill called Rothman up to the stage and they sang "Little Cabin Home on the Hill," then, while still onstage, Rothman convinced Bill to let his friend sit in. As Ewing recalled, "I took Joe Stuart's guitar, which ended up near my knees [due to portly Stuart's long strap], and suggested 'Blue Ridge Mountain Blues.' When it was over, Monroe Fields said, 'Good job, buddy,' an offhand remark that meant the world to me at the time." That night, after the show, Bill called a new lady friend, Jewell Breeding, in Prestonsburg, Kentucky, and he and the band played her a new song he'd written about her, "My Old Kentucky and You."[44]

Two days later, Bill returned to Bradley's Barn to begin recording an album to promote his son's career: *Bill Monroe & James Monroe: Father & Son*. Nine of its eleven songs were recorded in three sessions (the others, "I Haven't Seen Mary in Years" and "Bonny," were recorded in 1969), with James continuing to overdub most of his lead vocals and Bill singing all of his vocals "live." Otherwise, James was given full rein to achieve the "different sound" he favored: a softer, more contemporary sound combining less-aggressive guitar playing with Hicks's melodic banjo picking. Recorded on March 14: "Sweetheart, You Done Me Wrong" (the eighth "classic band" song, later credited correctly to Lester Flatt–Bill Monroe), "Banks of the Ohio" (the eleventh Monroe Brothers song), and "Tall Pines" (with a new lead vocal dubbed into the unreleased 1969 recording). Recorded on March 15, James's thirty-first birthday: "Mother's Only Sleeping" (the ninth "classic band" song), "Foggy Mountain Top" (the twelfth Monroe Brothers song), "Love, Please Come Home" (the Reno and Smiley song Bill had sung since 1963, recorded just two months after the death of Arthur Lee "Red" Smiley), and the duet "What Would You Give in Exchange?" (the thirteenth Monroe Brothers song).

Things were different on the session of March 21. Instead of "classic band" or Monroe Brothers songs, it began with a redo of "When the Golden Leaves Begin to Fall." Then came a new version of "Walls of Time." Hicks recalled the background of its then-remarkable banjo break: "One night [at a show], Bill broke a string, so he pushed me up there to take a break. I took a break like that before, I thought, and he liked it. He had me do it over and over, like three times. He liked it, so I just stuck with it." Then Joe Stuart, there to play third fiddle with Baker and Tommy Williams, tuned up his guitar and replaced James on Bill's latest, "My Old Kentucky and You." According to Neil Rosenberg, "Monroe featured the song at nearly every show that summer, and whenever [Jewell] Breeding was present he invited her onto the stage." (During this time, Bill also wrote an instrumental he called "Kentucky Jewel," remembered by Hicks, but, as yet, not recorded.)[45]

Randy Wood and the Picking Parlor

After the sessions, Bill went to see luthier Randy Wood. Wood, Tut Taylor, and musician Grant Boatwright had formed a new partnership and opened the Old Time Picking Parlor, with vintage instruments, instrument repair, and live music four nights a week at 105 Second Avenue North in Nashville. The metal fret wires on Bill's F-5 were "completely worn out," Wood said, and even though he told Bill he could simply replace them, Bill insisted he replace the entire fingerboard (and wires), as Gibson had always done in the past. Wood explained:

That meant that I had to keep it three or four days, so I could work on it, and when I told Bill that, he asked me if I wouldn't mind taking it home with me every night and not leave it at the Parlor after hours. Well, actually, he asked me if I wouldn't mind taking it home with me and sleeping with it every night, so I'd be sure and not let anything happen to it.

Bill often visited the Parlor in 1972, usually sitting with regulars Ken and Della Streeter, former Minnesota fan club representatives who had recently moved to Nashville. Regular performers at the Parlor were Buck White and the Down Home Folks, also newcomers in town from Oklahoma. One of their instrumentals was an original minor-keyed mandolin number called "Indian Blood," which may have inspired Bill's well-known "Jerusalem Ridge."[46]

Photographing Rosine

Neil Rosenberg, former Brown County Jamboree manager, was teaching folklore at the Memorial University of Newfoundland, Canada, and had been commissioned by the University of Illinois Press to write a book about bluegrass. Wanting to include the best possible visual images, he contacted Carl Fleischhauer, filmmaker and photographer teaching at West Virginia University, whose photos of Bill had recently appeared in Rooney's *Bossmen*. As a result, in early 1972, Fleischhauer decided to visit Rosine, Kentucky, to photograph whatever was left of Bill's early life there, particularly the house on the Monroe homeplace. He asked former Blue Grass Boy Sandy Rothman, whom he'd met through Rosenberg, to go with him. "He said it was because he wanted somebody along who could talk to country folks," Rothman said, "something he said was difficult for him."

Arriving on the morning of April 20, they were directed to the home of Darrel and Rosetta Dukes (Rosetta, daughter of Speed Monroe) and found Speed's widow, Geanie, living with them. The ladies assured them "the old home" still stood, sending them down the road to Charlie's house, where one of Geanie's grandsons, David Raley (older brother of Jill Raley of "The Little Girl and the Dreadful Snake"), was living. Raley "directed us back through the woods to the old Monroe house," Fleischhauer wrote later. The land around it was relatively clear at the time, but there were deep ruts in the ground, where Charlie had strip-mined. "The (ugly) strip mine . . . comes right up to the house itself," Fleischhauer noted. "The house was used as a coal company office for a while—maybe this fact saved it from destruction." As Rothman remembered,

Reaching the house was a revelation and a shock, due to its deteriorated condition. Windows were broken and gone, doors were missing. I just couldn't believe it had been treated this way. Going inside definitely felt like being on hallowed ground, as I tried to picture Bill and his family living there. Remembering his stories of hiding under the porch or in the barn and going out to sing in the fields [he'd heard Rinzler's taped interviews with Bill], I walked around those places while Carl documented the scene with his camera.

Thoroughly documented, the house and environs are seen in nearly half of 180 exposures made that day (and among the others, Charlie's house and the tombstones in Rosine Cemetery). That evening, Rothman and Fleischhauer introduced themselves to Rosine historian Wendell Allen. Allen, an avid booster for Charlie (and the likely author of the article about him signing with Silverstein), shared information he'd collected about the Monroes and invited them to stay overnight. Allen's father, Stanley Allen, happened to think of Uncle Pen's cabin (where Pen and Bill lived together), so, although the cabin now featured extensive additions, Fleischhauer photographed it the next day, along with a fiddle that may have once belonged to Pen. (It was decided that Rosenberg's book, *Bluegrass: A History*, should have a variety of older photos. So, Fleischhauer's photos were known to a few researchers, but none would be published for more than twenty years.)[47]

On May 15 Decca released "Lonesome Moonlight Waltz" / "My Old Kentucky and You." Only the latter would appear on a Decca album, four years later. On May 27 the 110-acre Opryland USA theme park opened. Construction of the new Opry House there had not yet begun but was expected to be completed in two years.[48]

June 1972: A Red-Letter Month

June 1972 was a red-letter month for Bill, beginning with the release of the *Bill Monroe's Uncle Pen* album on the 1st, the accomplishment of a goal he'd dreamed of for many years. In his words about it at the time, it's clear he was grateful to have lived long enough to do it:

> I don't think he wrote any of them [his fiddle tunes]. I think they were just tunes that he played. But I've kept about thirty of them in my head since then [the 1920s], and he died when I was nineteen or twenty. I been meaning to record them for a long time and I've finally got around to it. I'm sixty years old now, and you don't ever know what will happen.

June 1972 was also the start of Bill's third year as a bluegrass festival entrepreneur, with the number of "Bill Monroe festivals" growing to seven: four in his name only (Bean Blossom; McKinney, Texas; Jackson, Kentucky; Chatom, Alabama), two in partnership with Lester Flatt (in Arkansas and Mississippi), and one with Ralph Stanley (in Delaware). Auspiciously, Bill's eight-day Bean Blossom festival (June 11–18), was a tremendous success, with crowd estimates as high as forty thousand. And, on Friday, June 16, according to Jim Rooney, Bill was introduced to a very special mandolin:

> A couple from Detroit had inherited it and brought it down to Bill. They told him that it had belonged to the wife's mother. She left it to them to pay them back for taking care of her in her last years. . . . When he opened the case he could smell the must of forty years of lying in an attic unused. . . . Touched by the couple's story and knowing full well the worth of the instrument, Bill bought it from them.

It was another Lloyd Loar F-5, serial number 72214, which dated it to February 26, 1923, making it about five months older than his main mandolin. But it had been played a lot less and was, as a result, much less "powerful." Bill would keep it in alternative tunings, using it otherwise only when 73987 was being worked on.[49]

The renewed friendship of Lester Flatt and Bill was further strengthened on August 10, when Flatt recorded one of Bill's new songs, "It's Sad to Be Alone" (released later in 1972 on Flatt's *Foggy Mountain Breakdown* album [RCA Victor]). Reminiscent of "Little Cabin Home on the Hill," the setting this time was urban.

> There's a cold, drizzling rain outside my window.
> There's a sad and lonesome feeling in my heart.
> In this cold, windy city my tears keep falling,
> And it's all because that we're so far apart.[50]

Bill's friendship with Flatt would be mentioned later in *Bluegrass: A History* as a probable reason Bill turned down the Nitty Gritty Dirt Band's invitation to help record their *Will the Circle Be Unbroken* album in August 1972, with Earl Scruggs involved and "Flatt . . . estranged from Scruggs." Another probability: Bill was simply not familiar with the Dirt Band. Primarily aware of the bluegrass world, he knew only what others told him about them—mainly, that they played "rock and roll" (country rock). "I ain't got nothin' against it," he said, "but it's not bluegrass. All the way through, I've had to be careful how I done my music and who I worked for." Aside from this, he was also busy with his relocated Kentucky bluegrass festival, moved, due to land development, from Ashland to Jackson (still in eastern Kentucky), and held August 11–13.[51]

Appearing for the first time together at the Brown County Jamboree on Sunday, September 24, were Bill and fellow Country Music Hall of Famers Roy Acuff and Ernest Tubb. This "Hall of Fame Show" would be repeated in 1973 and 1974.[52]

President Nixon was reelected by a landslide on November 7, 1972, losing only the state of Massachusetts and the District of Columbia to Senator George McGovern of South Dakota.[53]

Charlie Coaxed Out of Retirement

A few days later, on Saturday, November 11, at Bill and Flatt's "Mississippi Delta Bluegrass Festival" at Runnellstown (near Hattiesburg), the audience was treated to a unique rendition of "Roll in My Sweet Baby's Arms," with Bill and Flatt on guitars and Jimmy Martin on mandolin. (Martin had recently [in August] coaxed Charlie out of retirement to appear in tandem with him at a few shows and a couple of festivals. Bill apparently did not react negatively.)[54]

Bill and Flatt teamed up again at the beginning of 1973 for the second (and last) Bluegrass Express tour, during the last two weekends of January (18–21, 26–28). This time they were joined by James and the Midnight Ramblers *and* Jim and Jesse for six concerts in West Virginia, Ohio, Georgia, and Louisiana, which James coordinated with the help of Carolyn Monroe, from her home at 1206 Bell Grimes Lane in Nashville, a familiar address in Monroe festival ads as the place to write for more information. During the tour's second weekend, on January 27, the war in Vietnam ended.[55]

Bill and the Blue Grass Boys were soon headed for California—their first visit since the 1960s—due in Los Angeles on Tuesday, February 13. That day a ninety-minute salute to Bill was to be videotaped with an audience in the studios of KCET in Hollywood, a production promoted by fiddler Richard Greene. According to plan, Greene and two other 1960s Blue Grass Boys, Bill Keith and Peter Rowan, joined by mandolinist David Grisman, bassist Stuart Schulman, and lead guitarist Clarence White, would play the first set, then Bill and the current Blue Grass Boys (Baker, Fields, Hicks, Stuart) would play a set, and they would all play together to close the show. But the inevitable happened: Bill's bus broke down in Stockton, about four hundred miles to the north. So, Greene and friends carried on, taping a set that would air later in 1973 on public television stations, titled *Bluegrass Country*.[56]

By the time Bill and the band returned from California, in March 1973, the Music Corporation of America, owner of Decca Records since 1962, had changed the label's name to the contemporary-sounding acronym "MCA." Bill's first MCA album, *Bill Monroe & James Monroe: Father & Son*, was released on the day the change became official: March 1, 1973.[57]

The California tour was the last road trip with Bill for Joe Stuart, who turned forty-five during it. His friendship with Bill remained strong, and he would record with him from time to time, but for now, Stuart chose the less demanding road schedule of the Sullivan Family. Replacing him on March 12 as lead singer-guitarist was Alabama native Bob Fowler.

Fowler was tending bar at the Ash Grove in 1966 when he first heard Bill and the band with Rowan. He came to Nashville in 1972 and became friends with Buck White of the Down Home Folks. White had been filling in for Monroe Fields on bass, and when he couldn't make a trip to the Northeast, he called Fowler. During the tour, Fowler played guitar and sang some with Bill, and after Bill found out Stuart was leaving, Fowler was hired.[58]

Monroe Fields left the Blue Grass Boys in early April. Guy Stevenson, age forty-three, of southeastern Missouri, and a bass player with a band there, had offered his services to Bill and James several times over the years. Set to fill in with James at the Mississippi Delta Bluegrass Festival on the weekend of April 13, Stevenson instead played with Bill at the University of Nebraska in Lincoln on Friday the 13th after James called and asked him to. Hired that night, he would play with Bill the next day at the Mississippi Delta festival, the first of nine "Bill Monroe festivals" Bill was promoting in 1973.[59]

Recording at Bean Blossom

The second of Bill's nine festivals was Bean Blossom, scheduled to run nine days (Saturday, June 9, through Sunday, June 17) for the first time. An MCA Records mobile unit arrived to record a live album during the second weekend, probably encouraged by the recent success of the *Deliverance* movie and album (Warner Brothers). Bill knew about it (and is said to have suggested it), but didn't tell the band until the last minute. "He didn't say anything about it to me until the day before we were going to record," Fowler said. Bill and the band were the first of several groups recorded on the afternoon of June 16, and one song, "You Won't Be Satisfied That Way," which Bill had sung as a duet with Doc Watson in the 1960s, was a surprise for Stevenson: "He got up there and announced it and I'd never heard it before!"[60]

There were several young banjo players in the bands at Bean Blossom that weekend: Jack Hicks with Bill; Marc Pruett with James; and Kenny Ingram with Jimmy Martin, but, during the recording, Bill chose to feature nineteen-year-old Carl Jackson, a visitor to the festival, whom Bill introduces as "a good friend of mine" and "a great banjo player from the state of Mississippi." Bill first encountered Jackson in the late 1960s when he was picking with Jim and Jesse and the Sullivan Family, and recently he'd "hit the big time," joining the band of superstar Glen Campbell. And it appears that Bill simply wanted to celebrate his success.[61]

Bill needed a big finish for the album, so Haney's multiple-fiddles idea came in handy, with the help of every fiddler in sight that June 17, a Sunday afternoon. Naming all twelve in a "roll call," he set them to playing three old-time favorites, the evergreen "Down Yonder" and two tunes he recorded in 1966–67 that had not been released, "Soldier's Joy" and "Grey Eagle." Bill also used them to good advantage on "Swing Low, Sweet Chariot," his usual end-of-show singalong by then, given new life with an "orchestral" accompaniment.[62]

Aside from the honor of helping Bill record his first live album, Fowler was dissatisfied—the Father of Bluegrass wasn't working with his musicians as he had in 1966–67. "He really didn't pay much attention to being a bandleader," Fowler said. Lead singer-guitarist Bill Box had spoken to Bill at a festival in Box's native Missouri in mid-July, and Bill, suspecting Fowler was going to quit, asked if Box was willing to leave his band, the Dixie Drifters, to join the Blue Grass Boys. He was willing, so when Fowler quit, "Billy" Box (as Bill called him) started on July 19. (After Box moved to Nashville, he found a job driving a truck to help support his family. He said that neither Bill nor the rest of the band ever knew about this "side job.")[63]

Stevenson had taken a leave of absence from his regular job as an auditor with the Missouri State Department of Revenue to work with Bill. By mid-July 1973, his time off had run out. He would be replaced by twenty-one-year-old Gregg Kennedy from Oklahoma, joining when Box did. Kennedy was studying classical music at North Texas State University in Denton and had been playing bluegrass for about six months when Bill played there in May, shortly after Stevenson started.[64]

Box arrived at the Ryman to play his first *Opry* on August 4, finding Charlie Collins, guitarist with Roy Acuff's Smoky Mountain Boys, in the dressing room with Bill, playing guitar on a new tune called "Jerusalem Ridge." Bill had just written it and, with Box not there yet, he collared Collins, one of the *Opry*'s best rhythm guitarists. Collins would play with Bill and the Blue Grass Boys when they debuted the tune on the *Opry* that night (while Box "played along" in the background).[65]

Bill's seventh of nine "Bill Monroe festivals" in 1973 was the second Dixie Bluegrass Festival in Chatom, Alabama (September 7–9). At the end of this unsuccessful weekend, Bill split the profits with the Blue Grass Boys, paying each about $650. Jack Hicks had already turned in his two-weeks' notice, and this was his last weekend with Bill. "I was just a kid when I went to work with him and he was just so good to me," Hicks said. "He taught me about life—even more than pickin'. Just the way he did things for people. He'd do it and nobody'd ever know about it." Hicks and Sharon White of Buck White and the Down Home Folks were about to be married, and Hicks was planning to pick with the Down Home Folks, so he encouraged their regular banjoist, Ben Pedigo, to audition for Bill that weekend. Pedigo played with the band onstage but wasn't hired. "I think Bill was looking at other banjo players," he said.[66]

The First "Monroe Homecoming Festival"

The eighth of nine "Bill Monroe festivals" was the inaugural "Monroe Homecoming Bluegrass Festival," in Rosine from September 13 through 16, probably inspired by Ralph Stanley's festival at his Virginia homeplace, begun in 1971. Among those appearing with Bill were James and the Midnight Ramblers, Wilma Lee and Stoney Cooper, Lester Flatt, and Ralph Stanley. Aside from Bill and James, however, the only other Monroes "coming home" that weekend were Birch and Bertha (from Indiana). Rosine also celebrated its centennial that weekend, regardless of the festival, with an arts-and-crafts show, the Ohio County High School marching band parading through town, and an old-fashioned square dance in the street. And, in spite of the possibility of large crowds with festival and centennial combined, attendance at the festival was estimated at only about six thousand. Everett Park in Rosine, then the home of the Rosine Redlegs baseball team, was the site of the festival, its use offered to Bill in exchange for a donation to the team. Reportedly, he later sent $50, which some felt was "pitiful" (but, after all expenses were paid, it may have been a reasonable percentage of the profits).[67]

Bill was still without a regular banjoman when the festival started. But Harley Carpenter was there, lead singer with West Virginia's young traditional band, the Black Mountain Bluegrass Boys, and he volunteered the services of the band's banjo picker, Richard Hefner, to Bill. After Carpenter called him, Hefner drove from West Virginia on Friday morning and played with Bill that night, then Saturday and Sunday. It was reported that he was "auditioning for the position of banjo player," but Hefner disagrees, saying he already had a spot with the Black Mountain Boys. Still, Bill admonished the moustachioed Hefner, telling him he'd never had a Blue Grass Boy with a moustache, to which Hefner had said, "I really don't want to cut my moustache off." This and the dismal festival attendance may have caused Bill to feel less than obligated to pay him. "I wasn't really expecting anything," Hefner said. "I sorta thought he would pay me gas money. But it was worth it, just gettin' to be around him."[68]

For Bill, the weekend was saved by including his sixty-second birthday. On Thursday, September 13, James gave him the two-and-a-half acre property where he and his Uncle Pen "bached" during 1928–30. Others had lived there since, including carpenter Bill Rafferty, who built an addition onto the log cabin in the mid-1930s, complete with front porch; James Hohimer had added gray, brick-patterned siding in the 1950s. But the gift on the 13th complemented perfectly the gifts Bill gave on Sunday the 16th in Rosine Cemetery: a tombstone for Pen's son Cecil and, next to it, a six-foot, four-inch-tall monument dedicated to "Pendleton Vandiver." (Bill had remembered the location of Cecil's grave but was uncertain of where Pen's grave was located.) The monument was to be unveiled "late in the evening, about sundown," so about then, Bill and the band (Baker, Box, and Kennedy plus Hefner) rode the short distance from the festival grounds in the bus, then stood around the covered stone, placing their hats on the ground before it. Telling the large crowd around him that he was "too filled up and choked up to even talk to you," Bill said the monument was "for the most wonderful uncle in the world." Then he and the band played "Uncle Pen." The unveiling followed, and when the applause died down, Bill spoke briefly of his childhood, saying that back in the days when they had square dances in Rosine, "this was the man here that they would call."[69]

After the band returned to Nashville, Baker called Ben Pedigo (Bill had asked Baker to do the hiring of new band members), and Pedigo played his first show with Bill on September 18. Just turned twenty and a student at Vanderbilt, he was torn between playing banjo and finishing college, so he left school for a semester to decide. Following trips to Florida and to California (for Bill's ninth of nine festivals and the state's first major multiday event, at Corona, October 26–28), Pedigo played his last at the Brown County

Jamboree on November 4 and went back to school. Texan Jim Moratto, in Nashville during Pedigo's last weeks, auditioned by playing shows with Bill during that time.[70]

Three days before Pedigo's last, on November 1, 1973, MCA released the two-record *Bean Blossom* album. Capitol Records simultaneously released a single that sang Bill's praises, "Daddy Bluegrass," written by "Rocky Top" co-writers Felice and Boudleaux Bryant and sung by Stoney Edwards, Capitol's answer to Charley Pride.

> There's a fella down in Nashville, a super country name.
> He's got to be the top brass in the Bluegrass Hall of Fame.
> He needs no introduction to any country fan.
> I call him "Daddy Bluegrass," the father of the clan.

It lasted only seven weeks on the country singles charts, peaking at number 85 in *Billboard* and number 72 in *Record World* (both with 100 entries). The *Bean Blossom* album, on the other hand, was Bill's most commercially successful album ever, remaining in the country albums charts for more than three months, peaking at number 17 in *Billboard* (of 50) and *Cash Box* (of 45), and at number 27 in *Record World* (of 75). But, possibly due to the cost of its production, Bill would not record during 1974. It would be the first time in eighteen years that he did not record for Decca-MCA.[71]

The Deaths of the Akemans

About a week after "Daddy Bluegrass" was released, Bill's first banjo player, David "Stringbean" Akeman, fifty-seven, and his wife Estelle, fifty-nine, were murdered by thieves upon returning home from the *Opry* on November 10. Bill and the band were playing at the State University of New York in New Paltz that night, and were in Washington, D.C., on the 11th, getting ready to play at the Smithsonian, when Bill told the band about the Akemans with tears in his eyes.[72]

Several banjo players besides Jim Moratto filled in or auditioned after Pedigo left. In mid-December 1973, Bill and the band taped a Johnny Cash TV special at Radio City Music Hall with Moratto on banjo, and two days later, he was hired. While in New York, Bill was interviewed for the first issue of *Pickin'* magazine, published in nearby New Jersey. It seems he took the opportunity to slyly chide Jack Hicks when asked about problems finding musicians:

You have more trouble today than you ever had, I think. I don't have no trouble with the fiddler or the guitarman or the bass, right today, but the banjo pickers are gettin' maybe a little bit lazy and they want to stay at home, stay nice. When someone's got wives, of course, their wives is the boss and they have to stay at home.

Rumors were circulating that Bill was going to retire, but they were quieted after the interviewer asked, "What's the thing you're after now?"

What I'd like to do now is keep my health, go . . . if I can, as long as possible, and help people in bluegrass music. That gives me a good feeling that I'm doing something good every day through my life, especially now, you know? I want to do something in that day if I can. I don't want to retire.[73]

Bill certainly wasn't going to retire at the height of his money-making capabilities. In 1974, aside from a full road schedule, he would be involved with a peak number of festivals (thirteen) from coast to coast and would partner with James in the lucrative business of booking others via "Monroe's Bluegrass Talent Agency." Its initial clients included the Bluegrass Alliance (led by fiddler Lonnie Peerce), Jimmy Martin, Bobby Smith and the Boys from Shiloh, Ralph Stanley, and the Sullivan Family. They established the agency's office on the top floor of a reconfigured house at 726 Sixteenth Avenue South on Music Row in Nashville, and hired the Bluegrass Alliance's former manager, Kentucky native Chuck Campbell, as its director.[74]

Bill played his last *Opry* show at the Ryman on Friday, March 8, 1974, after nearly thirty-one years of broadcasts from the now-venerated building. As the host of the ten o'clock portion, he opened with "Mule Skinner Blues" and closed with "Working on a Building" (with new bus driver, Travis Lee, singing bass in a suit and hat that matched those of the Blue Grass Boys). Bill would not be in Nashville the following weekend for the last performance from the Ryman on March 15, nor on March 16 for the first from the new Opryland Opry House, now remembered for the visit of President and Mrs. Nixon. Instead, he was touring with Lester Flatt.[75]

Recording with Flatt

The tour began on Wednesday, March 13, in New Jersey. That night, the Blue Grass Special broke down, so Flatt invited Bill and the Blue Grass Boys to ride with him, and they took up residence in the front section of his bus for the next three days. After they returned to Nashville, RCA Victor had arranged for them to make a live recording together, and for it, the label promoted a free concert on Monday, March 18, at Vanderbilt's Neely Auditorium. *Lester Flatt Live! Bluegrass Festival with Guest Bill Monroe* was released in June 1974, with Bill and Flatt singing "Will You Be Loving Another Man" and "Little Cabin Home on the Hill." The year before, Flatt and the Nashville Grass had recorded for MCA on Bill's *Bean Blossom* album, and this recording appears to have been in exchange for it.[76]

During this time, Charlie and Martha moved to North Carolina and settled into a mobile home on Carlton Haney's Camp Springs festival grounds. Haney paired Charlie with a band from Virginia, the Dominion Bluegrass Boys (led by Cecil Hall), and in the fall of 1973 they played a "jamboree" together every other Saturday evening on the grounds. By the spring of 1974, with Hall booking shows in the tri-state area and Haney booking festivals, Charlie Monroe and the Dominion Bluegrass Boys were playing somewhere nearly every weekend.[77]

Bill took his second trip to England during the second weekend of April 1974, making his first appearance at the International Festival of Country Music, the sixth of twenty-three annual extravaganzas held at London's Wembley Arena. Among many others appearing there were George Jones and Tammy Wynette, the Oak Ridge Boys, Kitty Wells, and Mac Wiseman. Bill and the band played on April 13, and Wiseman, backed by the Blue Grass Boys (minus Box), played on the 14th. Box, with the day off, was the only band member able to go sightseeing. (Bill Monroe and the Blue Grass Boys would return to Wembley in 1980 and 1983.)[78]

Former Blue Grass Boy Bob Fowler and wife Ingrid had begun getting together with friends in Nashville (including Jim and Wilma Bornstein, Marty and Charmaine Lanham, Red and Birdie Smith, and former Blue Grass Boy Roland White) for an onstage bluegrass jam session once a week at Bobby Green's Dusty Road Tavern. "Bobby wanted to have country music," Fowler recalled, "so we said, 'Why don't we open our own place?'" At first, they hoped to get a room in Nashville's Union Station train depot and planned to call it "The Station Inn." The deal fell through, but the name stuck, given to a space they renovated at the corner of Twenty-Eighth and West End Avenues, near Vanderbilt, where it opened in May 1974. Bill visited shortly thereafter and "sat in" with its founders, who had become the house band. (The Station Inn moved to 402 Twelfth Avenue South in Nashville in 1978 and was purchased by current owner J. T. Gray in 1981.)[79]

James's first solo album was released in May 1974, not on MCA, but on independent Atteiram of Marietta, Georgia (Marietta spelled backwards).

Between 1972 and 1974, independent labels began taking over the bluegrass record market. By the end of 1974, MCA would drop both Jimmy Martin and the Osborne Brothers (and it was seemingly not interested in James). So, the only option for him was an independent label. Bill didn't play on James's *Something New! Something Different! Something Good!*, but, continuing to believe in his son, he wrote one of the endorsements on its back cover, saying in part, "He has a wonderful voice, a Monroe bluegrass voice. I think his album is fine."[80]

The release of James's album was well-timed for sales at his father's eighth annual Bean Blossom festival (June 8–16). A few weeks later, Bill told *Cash Box* magazine that every state in the union and several foreign countries were represented at the festival and "more than 75 thousand" attended during its nine days.[81]

Released in June on the County label, *Charlie Monroe on the Noonday Jamboree* featured two of Charlie's 1944 radio broadcasts, with a group of Kentucky Pardners that included Lester Flatt playing mandolin and singing tenor before he joined the Blue Grass Boys. Charlie had saved several shows recorded on fragile sixteen-inch glass discs, which radio stations played when the band wasn't able to broadcast live.

> Around the time that Decca put out that *Bill Monroe and Charlie Monroe* LP, [County founder David Freeman recalled], someone at Decca heard that Charlie had those old radio shows from 1944 and said Decca would be interested in putting out some of that material. So, Charlie loaned Decca all of the 1944 shows—I think there were fifty-two of them. Decca kept the best-conditioned electrical transcriptions and returned the other half of them to Charlie. But Decca never did anything with the shows, and when Charlie got tired of waiting, he asked for the electrical transcriptions back. But, in the meantime, they had lost them.

The two broadcasts released by County, rejected by Decca, were scrupulously cleaned up, Freeman said ("Many hours were spent in editing out clicks and 'pops'"), and he wrote the album's detailed liner notes.[82]

In July 1974, Atteiram released *Take a Look and Listen to the Pinnacle Boys*, the first album by this group of bluegrass veterans. Among its selections was "Six Feet Under," a new song credited to Bill. Franklin D. "Bud" Brewster, lead singer-guitarist for the band, recalled that Bill wrote a verse and a chorus for it in the early 1960s, when Brewster had filled in with him on banjo or guitar, and Bill made him an offer: 'If you and your brother [fiddler Willie Brewster] write the other verse and record it, I'll give you half.'" When the Pinnacle Boys were recording in 1973, Brewster wrote a second verse, and the

Pinnacles recorded the song without Bill's approval. (Later, in 1978, Brewster contacted Bill to see if the original deal still stood. Bill had just recorded the song [made aware of the Pinnacle Boys' recording by Atteiram labelmate James], changing the third line of Brewster's verse from "I'd rather be laid down in some dark coffin" to "I'd rather be in my dark grave, dear." At any rate, a stipulation of Bill's offer had not been followed and the deal was off.)[83]

Replacing a Band

For reasons unknown, in mid-July, shortly after Bill's fourth annual Lone Star festival in McKinney, Texas, Bill was suddenly without a band (except for Baker). Rumor has it he fired them for some minor infraction, but two say they'd already quit and one isn't talking. Whatever the cause, Box, Kennedy, and Moratto were gone, all at once. So, Bill called on Baker to find replacements as soon as possible. Baker contacted forty-six-year-old Ralph Lewis of Asheville, North Carolina, a favorite guitarist of his in-festival jam sessions (whose musical family had known Bill since the days of the Monroe Brothers), and Baker urged him to become the new lead singer. "I said, 'I don't know any of his damn songs!'" recalled Lewis, a diehard Reno and Smiley fan. But he agreed to get together with Bill and bring along two musicians from his band, the Piney Mountain Boys: banjoist Marc Pruett, age twenty-two, and bassist Randy Davis, twenty. Their get-together at James's house was successful, and Lewis and Davis were hired, but Pruett had recently opened a music store in Asheville and decided he couldn't leave it.[84]

The following week, eighteen-year-old Dwight Dillman was passing through Nashville on his way home to Peru, Indiana, after a visit to Florida. He'd been to the Bean Blossom festival in the past and jammed with Baker a few times. "I had my banjo with me, so I went to a phone booth and called 'Monroe Talent.' Bill was there and I asked him if I could audition." Dillman found the office on Sixteenth Avenue South, picked "Blue Grass Breakdown" and another he doesn't recall, and was hired.[85]

Thanks to Baker and some good fortune, Bill had been able to find replacements in plenty of time before his next showdate, at a festival in Lavonia, Georgia, on Saturday, July 27. On Thursday the 25th, however, he was at the office when he got another unexpected phone call: Tom Ewing was asking for an audition. A friend in Texas had called to tell him what happened at McKinney, and Ewing decided that now was his chance. He had driven from Columbus, Ohio, to Nashville, and called Monroe Talent.

I remember Bill asking, "Do you know our material?" to which I replied that I'd let him be the judge of that. When I got to Monroe Talent on Music Row, we went in his office, he sat down behind his desk and said, "Let me hear something." So, I got out my guitar and began to sing "Come Back to Me in My Dreams." He joined me on the chorus. Then we sang "I Hope You Have Learned" as a duet, all the way through. He asked if I knew any hymns, and he sang tenor again on the chorus of "Build Me a Cabin in Gloryland." He didn't have his mandolin with him, so he tapped the stub of a pencil on the desk.

Only then did Bill tell Ewing that Ralph Lewis had already been hired. But he invited him to go to Lavonia with the band, to see "who worked the best." The next morning, Ewing met Bill at the bus and told him he didn't want to interfere with Lewis's hiring. He thanked Bill, asked him to call when the job was available, and went home.[86]

President Nixon announced his resignation on August 8, 1974. He would be succeeded by Gerald Ford, whom Nixon had appointed vice president after the resignation of Vice President Spiro Agnew, found guilty of tax evasion.[87]

That August, Charlie began including former Kentucky Pardners James "Slim" Martin and bass-playing wife Wilma Ann on shows with the Dominion Bluegrass Boys. ("Slim" Martin played fiddle and harmonica on Charlie's 1947 recording of "Bringin' in the Georgia Mail.") According to Dominion Bluegrass Boys leader Cecil Hall, Charlie soon tried to convince him to change the name of his band to Kentucky Pardners and talked about going to Nashville: "He said, 'I can get on the *Opry.*'" After Hall turned him down, Charlie blew up at him when two band members were late for a show. "He talked the hatefulest that I ever seen since I ever been around," said Hall. Breaking with the Dominion Bluegrass Boys, Charlie started re-forming the Kentucky Pardners in September 1974, with the Martins, Dominions' bassist Grady Bullins (who played lead guitar), and other North Carolinians. Charlie and Martha moved into a little house they rented cheaply from a fan, halfway between Camp Springs and Reidsville.[88]

Neil Rosenberg's Illustrated Discography

Also in September, detailed information about Bill's recordings became available for the first time with the publication of *Bill Monroe and His Blue Grass Boys: An Illustrated Discography*, compiled by Neil Rosenberg. Rosenberg was already working on *Bluegrass: A History* when he was asked to write another book about bluegrass by Bill Ivey, newly appointed director of the Country Music Foundation (a nonprofit branch of the Country Music Association, which operates the Country Music Hall of Fame and Museum in Nashville). Rosenberg suggested a Bill Monroe discography: "[Ivey] agreed this was feasible and appropriate, given Monroe's recent induction into the Hall of Fame and the popularity of bluegrass festivals, and so the project began." Data came from a variety of sources, and twenty-one hundred copies of the small, 122-page book, with many band photos, were printed, selling for $3.50. For Rosenberg, it was a labor of love.

> Although I didn't see Monroe until some six or seven years after it appeared, his comment to my friends, acquaintances, and relatives who mentioned my name to him was, on more than one occasion, to ask how much money I'd made on the book. I'd made none—it was done without a contract.[89]

The First "Big Plan"

Finances (including whatever profits Rosenberg was supposedly making) probably weighed more heavily on Bill's mind after September 9, 1974. On that date, a few days before the second Homecoming festival in Rosine, he and James paid $50,000 for fifty acres of farmland in Ohio County, Kentucky, to realize the first of several "Big Plans" they would dream up together: a large-scale amusement and music venue, to be called Monroe's Bluegrass Musicland Park. Located six miles west of Rosine and two miles east of Beaver Dam, at the intersection of Highway 62 and Rob Roy Road, the park, as they envisioned it, would be a mini-Opryland, with monthly shows and at least two annual festivals, an open-air amphitheater and a two-thousand-seat auditorium, kiddie rides, boat rentals on the property's lake, and both Uncle Pen's cabin and the Monroe homeplace's house relocated there.[90]

Dillman gave Bill his two-weeks' notice during the Homecoming weekend (September 11–15), after only two months with the band. Jimmy Martin had offered him a job, and Dillman decided his style of banjo picking was better suited to Martin's music.[91]

Not long afterward, banjo player Bob Black was visiting a longtime friend of Bill's, fiddler Smokey McKinnis, in St. Louis, Missouri. Black, age twenty-five and from Iowa, was another favorite of Baker's at festival jam sessions and had already played on his fourth County LP, *Dry & Dusty*, in 1973. He had just quit a band, and McKinnis was encouraging him to try out for the banjo spot with Bill. McKinnis even called "the Old Man" (his name for Bill) and, to his and Black's surprise, Bill was looking for a banjo player. By September 19, Black was in Nashville to audition, and the next day he was on his way to his first show with Bill, in Asheville, North Carolina (where Ralph Lewis and Randy Davis continued to live during their tenures with Bill).[92]

Bill and the band returned to Nashville on Saturday morning, September 21. That afternoon they headed out again to play an outdoor concert at Middle Tennessee State University in nearby Murfreesboro. Before the show, Bill was interviewed on the university's radio station by Charles K. Wolfe, a professor of English at the university, then working on a book about the early *Grand Ole Opry*. The interview (transcribed later for the Spring 1975 issue of *Old Time Music* magazine) dealt primarily with one of Bill's favorite subjects, "the old days." Appearing in it was an aphorism now intimately associated with Bill: "I like to sing from the heart, and in singing that way I hope it will touch the man that's listening to me, that he will get the meaning of what I'm doing, and it will touch his heart too."[93]

Charlie Diagnosed with Lung Cancer

In October, Charlie, at age seventy-one, was diagnosed with lung cancer. By the end of November, he was in a hospital in Greensboro, North Carolina. It appears preliminary surgery determined the cancer was too extensive for further surgery to be effective. He continued to play shows when he was able.[94]

MCA Records, meanwhile, may have been taking inventory. After discovering that eight of Bill's unissued recordings were songs of a religious nature, the company released an all-gospel album, *Road of Life*, on November 4. Four had waited for more than a decade: "The Old Country Baptizing," "Somebody Touched Me," "Pass Me Not," and "(We're Going) Just Over in the Glory Land." The other four were from the session of March 26, 1970, recorded without a bass (including the title song, written by Virginia Stauffer). To fill out the album, MCA reissued three: "This World Is Not My Home," "Were You There?," and a song having no connection with religious music whatsoever, "Out in the Cold World."[95]

By mid-November 1974, after the season of thirteen "Bill Monroe festivals" was over, Bill's ex-wife and secretary Carolyn had studied the financial results. James later recalled her conclusion:

My mother called me and Daddy into the den. She said, "I want to show y'all somethin.'" So, she showed us numbers where we lost on every festival except Bean Blossom and Cosby [James's Tennessee festival in July, in which Bill had invested]. She said, "All y'all are doin' is supportin' the bluegrass festivals."

From 1975 to 1978, Bill would promote an average of only seven festivals per year.[96]

Bill's First Trip to Japan

At the end of 1974, Bill paid his first visit to Japan, already home to thousands of bluegrass fans. Preceding him were Flatt and Scruggs (1968), Ralph Stanley (1971), the Country Gentlemen (1972), and the Lilly Brothers (1973); Everett Lilly would serve as road manager and guide for Bill and the band, introducing them in Tokyo, Osaka, and Kyoto, December 10–14. Bob Black, who wrote about the tour in his memoir *Come Hither to Go Yonder* and eventually played with Bill throughout the world, recalled that "nowhere was there a greater outpouring of affection for him than in Japan."[97]

Within a few weeks of returning to the United States, Bill and the band were headed back to California for their first shows of 1975, a concert at UCLA on January 10 and a night at the Palomino Club, a North Hollywood country music venue, on Saturday the 11th. (The Ash Grove, Bill's usual Hollywood destination, had burned to the ground in November 1973.) In the audience at the Palomino was Bob Dylan, who came backstage to pay his respects. Black wrote, "I overheard him talking to Bill about possibly traveling around with the Blue Grass Boys at some future date." But their paths would not cross again.[98]

At that point it had been nearly three years since Bill had been in a studio—his only longer absence had been from 1941 to 1945. Finally, he recorded a series of sessions on March 10, 11, and 12, and, beginning with these sessions, his close business relationship with James would include a musical aspect, with his son playing second guitar on all of his MCA recordings from 1975 to 1978.[99]

The session of Monday, March 10, began with the religious-themed "Clinging to a Saving Hand." It and others at these sessions suggest that Bill, nearing sixty-five and knowing that three of his siblings had died in their sixties, was giving serious thought to his own mortality, particularly after learning of Charlie's cancer. Next was another religious-themed song, "Show Me the Way," in which the singer consults a gypsy fortune-teller instead of seeking divine guidance. It was written by "Gypsy"—Bill's nickname for Virginia Stauffer. Third was the original recording of "Jerusalem Ridge," composed in 1973. According to Ralph Lewis, he and James, not Joe Stuart, played guitars on it (contrary to *The Music of Bill Monroe*). And last was "Ashland Breakdown," which Bill wrote in 1971 during his second and final Kentucky festival in Ashland, featuring twin fiddles by Baker and Stuart.[100]

On the March 11 session, they began with Bill's "Mary Jane, Won't You Be Mine," a derivative of "Say, Won't You Be Mine" and "Let Me Be Your Friend" (both by the Stanley Brothers), which derived from Bill's "It's Mighty Dark to Travel." Next—attempted but rejected—was "Farther On," one of Bill's favorite gospel solos, concerning what's waiting on the other side. Another solo followed, a redo of "There's an Old, Old House," which Bill first recorded in 1965. Back then, possibly on the "first take," he'd accidentally sung the wrong words, and according to him, it was that take that was released: "They come out with one—the words didn't even rhyme on it. We picked out the one we wanted, but this sorry engineer, he picked out another one." Last was again an instrumental: "Watson Blues," with Stuart laying his fiddle down to play the distinctive guitar lick that begins each section.[101]

Bill and the band were unfamiliar with the first song recorded on the evening of March 12: Hazel Smith's "Thank God for Kentucky." Ralph Lewis recalled that when Smith tried to teach it to them in the studio, she was singing it to the tune of "My Old Kentucky and You." According to Lewis, "I said right away, 'Now, that ain't gonna work.' Bill said, 'How about gettin' in the corner and we'll work it out?' He said to me, 'I want you to put the tune to it.'" So, he did, without credit as co-writer. The second song, "Reasons Why," was written by Juanita Southern, who also wrote "Bonny." And last was "Weary Traveler," which Bill later said he bought from Cliff Carlisle for five dollars, with a melody similar to "The Girl in the Blue Velvet Band." Not a religious song, its final verse revisited the subject that the sessions began with.

> I'm growing feeble. My hair is like the snow.
> I'm on my pathway leading home. I know that I must go.
> And you will follow after. No one with you can be.
> You'll cross the great divide of life into eternity.[102]

The first two books written about bluegrass music were published that spring: Steven D. Price's *Old as the Hills: The Story of Bluegrass* (Viking) in

March and Bob Artis's *Bluegrass* (Hawthorn) in May. Their chapters on Bill included a few significant errors: in the former, that Uncle Pen's full name was "Pennoyer Vanderver" and that Bill wrote "Footprints in the Snow," "Mule Skinner Blues," and "Molly and Tenbrooks"; in the latter, based on Bill's off-the-cuff comment, that when he was a child, the mandolin "was left to Bill—the last choice of the last chooser."[103]

Music City News visited Bill at that time, asking him to explain bluegrass, which he did at length for "Monroe Talks," a feature article that would appear in its May 1975 issue. Bluegrass, he said, is "good, clean, pure music" with "no smut." This led to an observation about current country songs:

> There is just one thing that I wish about the people of today . . . that every song they write wouldn't have to be on sex. I think that is taking it too far, and I can't see that.
>
> Sex is meant for behind closed doors where you have a bed. I think that's where it should be kept. I don't think it should be brought out and sung in front of little boys and girls growing into their teens. . . . I don't believe in writing [a] filthy song to make a million dollars. . . . I don't think it should be dug into that far.

Bill had clearly been paying attention. There was, indeed, a trend in mainstream country for "suggestive" songs, some reaching number 1 in *Billboard*: Freddie Hart's "Easy Loving" (1971), Don Gibson's "Woman (Sensuous Woman)" (1972), Charlie Rich's "Behind Closed Doors" (1973), Tanya Tucker's "Would You Lay with Me?" (1974), and Conway Twitty's "Linda on My Mind" (1975).[104]

Bob Black was the only Blue Grass Boy living in Nashville then, so to him went the "honor" of early-morning phone calls from Bill that began with "Are you awake?" (Bill also never said goodbye on the phone, hanging up when he was done talking.) He was needing help on his Goodlettsville farm. So, after they ate hearty breakfasts at Mason's, Bill's favorite Goodlettsville restaurant, Black learned all about "old-fashioned farm work," including planting potatoes with a team of mules, digging holes for fence posts, and stringing the posts with "high-quality woven wire."

> I looked on Bill as a parent figure in those days—and not always in an amiable way. I disliked the early morning phone calls and the daily injunctions to come and help him on the farm. I misinterpreted his motives. I thought he wanted me to prove myself by showing him what a good worker I was. In reality, he was just giving me an opportunity to improve my self-confidence and assurance. He was treating me exactly like a father would treat his son.

Black was also elected to drive Bill and a truckload of posts up to the Blue-grass Musicland property, near Beaver Dam, and they worked together there on the fences. The park's grand opening was scheduled for May 9 with a Spring Bluegrass Festival, but Bill would be out of the country, on a European tour promoted by Bill Clifton.[105]

On April 22, the band gathered at Nashville's International Airport, ready to begin their longest overseas tour: fourteen performances in Scotland, Ireland, England, Holland, and Germany through May 17. Their leader passed the time before the flight to New York by studying the "fine print" of the tour's contract and discovered it stipulated the band must include twin fiddles. Ralph Lewis recalled that an upset Bill approached Baker with the news.

> Kenny said, "Why, hell, Chief [his nickname for Bill]. Ralph can play the god-damned second fiddle." Bill said, "Surely not." Baker said, "You're goddamned right he can." Right there in the airport, we got over in the corner [with Lewis playing one of two fiddles Baker carried], and Bill wanted us to do "Roanoke," and we got that, and Bill started dancing. . . . He actually hollered!

They played their first show in Britain on April 25 at the Greyfriars Monas-tery near Glasgow, Scotland, their only show in the Monroe family's native land. At that show, Baker and Lewis were featured playing twin fiddles on Bill's "Scotland."[106]

Some of the last days of the tour were in Germany, and German banjo picker Rolf Sieker drove them in a van to four different cities within the then-divided country (including West Berlin in East Germany). He also shared a room with Bill each night after the shows.

> Late at night we got into long conversations about bluegrass music. . . . Sometimes we got out our instruments and played in the hotel rooms. Bill played some of his mandolin tunes and I played some tunes on the banjo. He encouraged me to write my own songs and play my original banjo tunes. First thing in the morn-ing, he took his mandolin, looked out of the window, and played a tune in his favorite key of A minor.[107]

MCA released an album especially for Bill's tour, *Best of Bill Monroe and His Blue Grass Boys*, available only in Europe. It contained an unusually large number of selections (twenty) for a single LP, chosen by John Atkins, an Eng-lish authority on American country music. Included were "Devil's Dream" and "McKinley's March," available on an album for the first time. Atkins also wrote about Bill for a souvenir program sold at the shows, concluding with:

Here before you is a man who has no musical equals in what he has achieved. He has created and, at times almost single-handed, preserved and evolved a style of music copied by thousands and enjoyed by millions the world over. Bill Monroe's music is an expression of his life and emotions, so each performance is a little different from the last. The only thing common to each one is that they are all good . . . enjoy the experience.

MCA soon (June 1975) released *The Best of Bill Monroe* in the United States, Bill's twentieth album for the label. It was a twenty-selection collection as well, but this time in a two-record set, and all twenty had been released on albums previously.[108]

MCA finally ended, about this time, Decca's policy prohibiting its artists from recording for other labels, and Bill quickly used his newfound freedom. At the end of May, a short time after he returned to the States, he recorded two songs with Ralph Stanley and the Clinch Mountain Boys for Rebel, at Stanley's fifth annual festival in McClure, Virginia (released in April 1976 on *Live at McClure*). Then, in early June, Bill and three of the Blue Grass Boys (Black, Davis, and Lewis) helped Birch record a long-overdue album of his fiddling, *Brother Birch Monroe Plays Old Time Fiddle Favorites* for Atteiram (released in December 1975).[109]

Celebrity endorsements by bluegrass artists had begun appearing in *Bluegrass Unlimited* in early 1974 with the sometime-team of Lester Flatt and Mac Wiseman endorsing Black Diamond Strings, "The Official Strings of Opryland U.S.A." This presumably encouraged Bill to join in; the first ad proclaiming "Bill Monroe plays Black Diamond Strings" appeared in the July 1975 issue (even though it was common knowledge that he preferred Gibson strings). That summer Bill also sang the praises of Dr. Pepper. Like other country notables, he and the band recorded a radio jingle for it, which Bill and the Blue Grass Boys learned from a recording by Maybelle Carter and the Carter Sisters. "Bill himself was fonder of RC Cola in those days," Black recalled. "He sometimes drank Coca-Cola too. (Bill pronounced it 'Co-Cola.')."[110]

Stars of Country Music and Mauldin's Lawsuit

Many country music fans made their first acquaintance with the University of Illinois Press in July 1975, after the publication of its *Stars of Country Music*. The book's scholarly monographs on a host of influential performers included "Bill Monroe" by Ralph Rinzler. Briefly recapping Bill's life, Rinzler discussed his vision problems as a child, relating them for the first time to his tendency to be a loner. Rinzler's mention of "gathering data for a biography" included an endnote: "to be published by the University of Illinois Press in 1978." Meanwhile, Bill was dealing with a lawsuit brought by Bessie Lee Mauldin, seeking a divorce as his common-law wife on the grounds he had "completely abandoned" her. The State of Tennessee did not recognize common-law marriages, so the suit was clearly intended to embarrass Bill into reaching a financial settlement. (Mauldin reportedly settled for $75,000 and left the Goodlettsville farm shortly thereafter. She lived and worked in Hendersonville for several years, then returned to her Norwood, North Carolina, hometown in 1982.)[111]

Also that July, RCA Victor released *Feast Here Tonight*, a two-record set containing thirty-two of the Monroe Brothers' sixty recordings. Near the end of the month, Charlie and the Kentucky Pardners played in Rosine, and that day, July 26, was declared "Charlie Monroe Day in Ohio County" by Judge-Executive C. B. Embry Jr. According to an uncredited report in the *Ohio County Times* (probably written by Wendell Allen), "It was an emotional evening for Charlie Monroe, who has been very ill in recent months, coming home, seeing so many folks he had known down through the years."[112]

Bill's Kentucky bluegrass festival, which had been moved from Ashland to nearby Jackson (county seat of Breathitt County) in 1972, ended its run there unpleasantly in August 1975. Bill had tried to establish friendly relations with Breathitt County, playing a benefit show for the Jackson police department in March, but it didn't seem to matter when it came to enforcing the county's dry laws. As Bob Black recalled,

> On Saturday evening [August 9], while people were watching the show, local law-enforcement officials sent a young boy around to the various campsites to peek into coolers, checking for beer and other alcoholic beverages. Later, when people had retired for the night, the police moved in and arrested those with coolers of beer by forcibly removing them from their tents. One young man was dragged out of his van by the hair and struck with a billy club. Bill tried to reason with the lawmen, but they were unmoved by his protests and closed down the festival then and there.

Bill would move his Kentucky bluegrass festival to Sanders (1976), about sixty miles northeast of Louisville, and then to Pendleton (1977–78), about thirty miles northeast of Louisville.[113]

Cecil Hall and the Dominion Bluegrass Boys had the weekend of August 28 off, so he and his wife drove down from Virginia to the Camp Springs festival. To get there, they had to pass Charlie's little house and, in spite of the unpleasantness of a year earlier, Hall decided to stop and say hello. "He come to the door and that fella hugged my neck and cried like a baby," Hall said. After Charlie admitted he'd been wrong, Hall told him, "I ought to have took a ball bat and flailed you one to help set you straight." They laughed and were friends again.[114]

Two weeks before Bill's sixty-fourth birthday, the September 1 issue of the new *People Weekly* magazine featured him with a cleverly worded story by staff writer Frank W. Martin. "At 63," Martin wrote, "the gentleman hillbilly is still as musically prolific and lustily alive as when he originated the sound [of bluegrass] back in the 1930s." Emphasizing the "lustily alive" angle, he quoted Bill giving a odd explanation for the breakup of his marriage to Carolyn ("Some outside folks got to messing in our lives and by the time we got things straightened out, it was too late") and an overly frank answer to a "what-if" question ("I guess if I hadn't left Rosine and gone up north [to Indiana], I'd probably be just like the other folks who live here now, farming and raising a family. I probably wouldn't have gone through seven, 10, 15 women"). Bill probably thought the magazine would never print this remark, but its editors were quick to recognize an opportunity to titillate inquiring minds.[115]

Charlie's Last Days

Charlie was seriously ailing by then, but a return show in Rosine, promised in July, was coming up on Friday, September 19, 1975, and Rosine friend Wendell Allen had arranged for "The Charlie Monroe Blue Grass Festival" on Saturday and Sunday, the 20th and 21st, at Windy Hollow Park, a popular place for camping getaways near Owensboro. On Monday, September 15, Allen called Charlie at the hospital in North Carolina and Charlie reportedly told him, "If my doctor lets me go by Thursday [the 18th], and by the grace of God, I'll be on a plane to Nashville and on to Rosine for the show. Folks there mean too much to me."[116]

He made it to Rosine, but cold and rainy weather forced the show there to be moved to the Horse Branch elementary school (formerly the high school), where he and the Kentucky Pardners shared the night with Carl Story and the Rambling Mountaineers. Charlie and Story also headlined the Charlie Monroe festival, held under cloudy skies, with Louisville's Bluegrass Generation (with former Blue Grass Boy Danny Jones), North Carolina's Conrad Hinson Family, the Rosine Band (with Wendell Allen on autoharp), and

"Fiddlin' Tex" Atchison (formerly of the Prairie Ramblers, recently moved back to his native Rosine). Local singer and guitarist Floyd Stewart was there, too. He'd met Charlie in 1959 and played a few shows with him in the area back then. At the festival, Charlie asked him to join him onstage for one of his shows. "He was gettin' old," Stewart said, "but he looked good and he sung pretty good, but he didn't have as much energy as he used to have."[117]

Charlie had managed to pull it off, even "with one lung completely eaten away," as Bill Vernon wrote later in *Pickin'*. Wendell Allen told readers of the *Ohio County Times*, "I think he sensed this would be the last." Charlie and Martha stayed around Rosine a couple of days, then flew back to North Carolina on Wednesday, September 24, and checked into the Reidsville hospital. On Saturday night, September 27, 1975, Charlie died there, alone with Martha.[118]

Bill was playing the *Opry* that night and didn't get the news until the next day. He and the band were appearing in Memphis on September 28, and Black remembered Bill being irritable for no apparent reason. Black later realized it was due to Charlie's death: "He hadn't talked about it at all, but his behavior on that day spoke volumes." Eventually, Bill asked all of the Blue Grass Boys to go with him to the second funeral, held in Rosine at the Methodist Church on Thursday, October 2 (the first was held in Reidsville on Tuesday, September 30). The band traveled to Rosine in separate cars, wearing their matching dark-green suits.[119]

The visitation was at Danks Funeral Home in Beaver Dam on the evening of October 1 and the morning of the 2nd, but Bill wouldn't go because Martha was there (and had reportedly spent the night in the funeral home). At the funeral, Black sat behind Bill: "[W]henever he turned his head sideways, I saw tears on his cheeks. It was the only time I had ever seen him cry. It was obvious to me that Bill cared very deeply for his brother." Cecil Hall was there, Martha having asked him to be a pallbearer, and he recalled the Blue Grass Boys helped Bill say farewell: "About ten minutes before they closed the casket, Kenny and all of 'em come down the aisle around Bill, and he bent over the coffin to get close to Charlie."[120]

Bill and the band left that night to play the weekend at the Florida State Bluegrass Convention in Lawtey. The next time Bill returned to the Opry House, for the *Friday Night Opry* of October 10, he spoke of Charlie and sang "Weary Traveler," dedicating it to him.[121]

As in December 1974, Bill and the band were again in Japan in December of 1975. During the two-week visit (December 7–19), they conducted business, including signing an agreement with the Hoshino Music Company for Bill to promote their Ibanez mandolin (and Black, their Ibanez banjo). Japanese Victor (under contract with MCA) celebrated Bill's visit, releasing in October a three-LP boxed set, *Bill Monroe and His Blue Grass Boys, Vol. II, 1950–1972*. Among its thirty-eight selections were seven never issued in the States: "My Carolina Sunshine Girl," "Ben Dewberry's Final Run," and "Those Gambler's Blues" (1951); "Soldier's Joy" and "Grey Eagle" (1966–67); "Walls of Time" (1968); and "What About You?" (1969). (Also in the box was a 20" × 28" poster of Bill playing an Ibanez mandolin.) On the trip home, Bill surprised the band by arranging for a brief vacation for them at a fancy hotel in Honolulu, Hawaii. Once back at the *Opry*, Bill surprised Ralph Lewis's ten-year-old son, Don, presenting him with one of the Ibanez mandolins he'd received for his endorsement. (The first full-page ad with a photo of Bill playing an Ibanez mandolin appeared in the June 1976 *Pickin'* magazine.)[122]

At the beginning of 1976, twenty years after Jimmy Martin's first Decca release, Bill was the only bluegrass artist on a major record label. The first of his albums to appear after he achieved this status was *The Weary Traveler*, released on January 5, with recordings from the recent March 1975 sessions. Wrote former producer Owen Bradley in its liner notes: "Bill Monroe knows HIS music. He is not looking for, experimenting, or searching for something different, as he found it long ago; however, Bill is still perfecting it."[123]

Bill and James and their bands toured together in early January, playing a series of gospel music shows in the Deep South with the Sullivan Family. James was planning to record a tribute album to his Uncle Charlie, and Bill was going to help him, so the tour gave them a chance to rehearse. Uncle Birch had loaned James recordings of Charlie from his collection so he could learn them, and Birch came down from Madisonville, Indiana, to be at the Nashville sessions. With Jim Brock (formerly with Jim and Jesse) and Joe Stuart fiddling on February 9; Kenny Baker and Stuart fiddling on the 10th and 11th; former Blue Grass Boy Vic Jordan on banjo; and Gerald Sullivan on bass, James recorded his third Atteiram album, *James Monroe Sings Songs of "Memory Lane" of His Uncle Charlie Monroe*, released in June 1976.[124]

Ralph Lewis had let Bill know he was leaving the band shortly after they returned from Japan. But he told him, "I don't want to get you in no tight place," promising to stay until Bill found a replacement. Bill tried calling Tom Ewing in Columbus, Ohio, but was unable to reach him. Then Bob Jones arrived in Nashville. The Seattle, Washington, native had known Bill since the

1960s when Jones had written about bluegrass in Boston, Massachusetts, for the folk music magazine *Broadside*. By the end of February, the left-handed guitar player would be Bill's lead singer.[125]

There were then two Bobs in the band, but it wasn't a problem—Bill already had a nickname for Black ("the Dark Cloud," for his seriousness). But, as Jones recalled, he was given one anyway: "One time, when Mr. Bill asked one of us a question as we were cruising along in his station wagon, I replied—wanting to clarify whom Mr. Bill was addressing—with the query, 'Me, Bob?'" After that, Bill called him "Me-Bob."[126]

On March 29 and 30, 1976, Baker recorded his sixth County album, book-ending James's tribute to Charlie Monroe with an instrumental tribute to Bill Monroe. It's said that Bill surprised everyone, most of all Baker, by showing up, ready to play. Bill proceeded to play breaks on eleven of twelve tunes recorded, even taking a partial break on "Jerusalem Ridge" (which he hadn't done on the original recording). Three not recorded previously—"Road to Columbus," "Fiddler's Pastime," and "Mississippi Waltz"—were, according to former Blue Grass Boy Doug Green's liner notes, "written by Monroe years ago." Old friend Joe Stuart played guitar. Picking banjo were Vic Jordan on the 29th, then Bob Black on the 30th, and Randy Davis on bass throughout. The album, *Kenny Baker Plays Bill Monroe*, was released in November 1976.[127]

An unusually slow April, with only three road dates, gave Bill lots of time on his Goodlettsville farm (which Mauldin had left the year before), and that's where reporter Kelly Delaney of *Music City News* found the "man of rural eloquence" for a feature story, "The Father of Bluegrass Is at Home on the Farm," published in its May 1976 issue.

> Monroe has said that bluegrass is the "kind of music you have to work hard at." He applies that same philosophy of hard work to his farm. . . .
>
> "There's always somethin' to do on a farm," he says. "It's just settin' there waitin' on ya."
>
> "To me, there is nothing like Mother Nature," Monroe said while walking across a pasture on his farm.
>
> He walks quickly, standing tall and straight, never huffing and puffing as he climbs up steep hills [there were several on his farm].
>
> Occasionally, he stops and points out different types of trees, like he would point out old friends on a crowded city street. "There's a poplar, and over there's a hackleberry, and that yonder is a sycamore."
>
> As he strolls across his land, he also points out fox dens. Monroe is an avid fox hunter and has a kennel of walker dogs to help in the hunts. . . .

> Monroe's farm is not a "gentleman's farm." The buildings are not painted and the grounds are not manicured. The only flowers that grow there are the ones that grow wild.
>
> The barns are old but still functional.
>
> "A lot of people think that to be with the world today, everything they have has to be all fancied up," Monroe explains. "I guess they forgot we're all still just human beings, that's all." . . .
>
> As he walks through a herd of his cattle grazing peacefully in a meadow, Monroe approaches an Angus bull and then ever so gently swings up on his back. The bull makes no attempt to throw him off.
>
> "I started training that bull to let me ride him since he was six months old," Monroe says proudly.

The article included a photo of Bill sitting on back of the four- or five-year-old "Bo Bo." Obviously, to train him, Bill was not completely absent from the farm during the last few years, as Mauldin's divorce suit had suggested.[128]

Bill was also featured in the May 1976 issue of *Country Music* magazine, with a full-color photo of him smiling (one of the first) on the cover. Inside was "Daddy Bluegrass and His Blues" by managing editor Martha Hume, a thoughtful review of his life and career. It included Bill's admission that he "handled" the people who worked for him: "I've planned ahead in the way of . . . how I thought this man was, how to keep him under control and keep him in his place." Hume suggested that by isolating himself in this way, Bill was naturally inclined to have the blues.[129]

On May 4, at a studio in Nashville, Bill and the band (and James) taped a guest appearance on a new Canadian Broadcasting Company radio show, *Country Road.* Unfortunately, as an LP of the show released later showed, Bill had developed a tendency to sing flat on his solos. There are many possible causes for it, but in this case, as Bill neared age sixty-five, it was probably due to a decreased level of energy (which Bill would never have admitted to anyone, including himself).[130]

The weekend of May 7 followed—Bob Jones's last, as it turned out. On Saturday the 8th, Bill and the band played the Paramount Theatre in downtown Ashland, Kentucky, and singer-guitarist Wayne Lewis guested on a couple of songs. Born in Kentucky and raised just across the river in New Boston, Ohio, Lewis had played and recorded with the Kentuckians (on Jalyn) and with Lillimae and the Dixie Gospelaires (on Gloryland). Jones left a few days later, and according to Baker, Bill told him to call "that boy up in Ohio" (referring to Tom Ewing). More familiar with Wayne Lewis up in Ohio, however, Baker called Lewis. He auditioned at Bill's Goodlettsville farm on Saturday, May 22, and played his first show the following weekend (May 28–30) at Ralph Stanley's McClure festival.[131]

That May 28 weekend, Birch transferred ownership of the Brown County Jamboree property, which he'd held since 1959, to his brother Bill. Birch turned seventy-five on May 16, and, with the recent passing of Charlie at age seventy-two, he may have felt it was time to settle his business affairs. The upcoming festival, advertised as a celebration of "The 200th birthday of the United States 1776–1976 and the 10th Anniversary of Bill Monroe's Bluegrass Festival at Bean Blossom, Indiana, June 16–20, 1976," was also the first held there with Bill as the formal owner.[132]

Country singer-songwriter and Kentuckian Tom T. Hall had, by then, recorded a string of number 1 hits, so his record label, Mercury, was probably agreeable to the former bluegrass musician's idea of recording a bluegrass album. Reportedly afraid to ask fellow *Opry* member Bill to play on it, Hall arranged for songwriter Harlan Howard to ask him to play mandolin on "Molly and Tenbrooks." Bill of course said yes, but, according to Hall, he seemed somewhat apprehensive at the July 13 session: "He was over in the corner picking for about five or six minutes and I asked him if all was well. He said, 'I've never played the lead part on this song before.'" Actually, he had, with Rose Maddox in 1962, tuning up a half-step to play it in C#. However, he rarely took a break on the song otherwise, especially in the key Hall sang it in—F—and figuring it out may have caused him to appear apprehensive.[133]

Bill Meets Julia LaBella

A couple of weeks later, Julia Anne LaBella, about to turn twenty-one, was headed to the first Berkshire Mountains Blue Grass Festival, near Hillsdale, New York. Born in Lubbock, Texas, she had moved with her family to Boston, Massachusetts, in 1967, and first heard bluegrass on the Harvard University radio station's "Hillbilly at Harvard" show (briefly co-hosted by Carlton Haney's assistant, Fred Bartenstein, when he was a student there). By the summer of 1976, she was playing guitar and taking fiddle lessons when she bought a copy of Peter Wernick's new *Bluegrass Songbook*, which included quotations from a variety of performers about bluegrass. She said she was particularly taken with one by Peter Rowan that urged the serious fan to "go to one of the masters" and say "you're there because you think he embodies a great tradition." Then musician friend David Nelson (later a member of the New Riders of the Purple Sage) encouraged her to go and see Bill at the Berkshire festival.

On Sunday morning, August 1, Bill and the band (Baker, Black, Wayne Lewis, and Davis) had just finished playing the gospel show when LaBella noticed the crowd gathered around the bus to get Bill's autograph.

> I thought, I've got to tell him how much the music means to me, but I was nervous and didn't really know what to say. So, I asked him to sign my songbook and he signed it and wrote his address and phone number down and asked me for my phone number. He asked me if I loved bluegrass and I said, "Oh, yes!" He asked if I liked animals and I told him I was working at an animal hospital. He said, "Well, I'm so glad to have met you," and that was it. I went on my merry way and went back home.[134]

After a busy August and the Homecoming festival at Bluegrass Musicland Park in September, Bill called LaBella, and her mother answered the phone. "My mother said, 'There's a man on the phone and he's asked my permission for you to come to Nashville.' So, he talked to me and said he wanted me to come down." At this point, she thought it was a job offer: "He wanted me to help him on the farm—'cause he knew I worked at an animal hospital. He probably had other things in mind, but I wasn't thinking in those terms."[135]

About this time, two bootleg albums of Bill's 1950s and 1960s recordings, imported from Germany, were available in the United States, both titled *Bill Monroe Blue Grass Special* (BS 1 had a black cover, BS 3 a red cover). Almost all of BS 1's recordings were also on the first Japanese boxed set, released in 1973, and almost all of BS 3's selections were either on it or 1975's *Vol. II*—including three unissued songs from 1951. Unconnected with these bootlegs, the original 1946 recording of "Why Did You Wander?" was also made available, released by New World Records in a series of albums devoted to traditional American music, *Hills & Home*, originally available to libraries only. Neil Rosenberg, who wrote its liner notes, picked its eighteen selections, including the unreleased gem by the classic band. Seven of the band's twenty-eight recordings had yet to be released on LP.[136]

By then, Bill was apparently concerned with Bob Black's health. He had been misdiagnosed with epilepsy, "but what it really was," Black said, "was the stress of playing with Monroe." Bill consulted with Baker and, years later, Baker told Black about their conversation: "Kenny said Bill would talk to him about letting me go and said he had tears in his eyes." At that point, it appears that banjo player Bill Holden stopped in Nashville on his way home to Texas and called Bill to offer his services. Holden had worked with James in 1974 and told Bill then he wanted to pick with him someday. He'd just left the Country Gentlemen after two years and was available. So, in mid-September, Bill let Black go, trying to put the blame on himself rather than admit his concern for Black's well-being: "Bob, I'm changin' the style of my music," he told him, "and I've got to get me a new banjo player."[137]

Within a month of Black's departure, Bill was in the studio to record with Holden on banjo, Wayne Lewis and James on guitars, and Davis on bass, plus triple fiddles by Baker, Joe Stuart, and Baker's nineteen-year-old protégé Blaine Sprouse. The October 20 session began with the previously unthinkable—Bill recording one of Flatt and Scruggs's signature songs, "Cabin in Caroline." Then he sang the verses, with Lewis on the chorus, of the World War I tear-jerker "No Place to Pillow My Head" (then recently recorded by Lester Flatt). Last was a new song by Bill, "My Sweet Blue-Eyed Darling," with Lewis singing the verses. Bill may have written it in anticipation of blue-green-eyed LaBella's arrival. "He always said it was for me," she said later. (Brown-eyed Stauffer's reaction isn't known.)[138]

They returned to the studio the following day, recording first a new mandolin-driven instrumental, "Monroe's Blues." Bob Black had named it, after hearing Bill noodling around with the tune one night on the bus. Its distinctive bridge, with chords sliding from F to F# to G, was something Bill added later. They then made an unsuccessful attempt to turn "The First Whippoorwill," the duet from 1951, into a trio, with James singing lead. Evidently realizing it wasn't working, they moved on to "Lucky Lady," another mandolin-driven tune Bill said was "about a Texas lady named Luckie." A longtime Texas friend of Bill's, "Tootie" Williams, said "Luckie" was the surname of a woman in her thirties whom Bill courted briefly. He added that Bill never owned a ranch in Texas named "Lucky Lady"—it was just a story Bill made up to avoid telling about her. The inspiration for the session's last, "My Louisiana Love," was a singer-guitarist from Baton Rouge in her twenties (who wishes to be anonymous). Bill flirted with her and wrote the song for her, but she refused his advances.[139]

James Earl "Jimmy" Carter Jr. was elected president twelve days later (on November 2, 1976), the first man from the Deep South to win the office in more than 125 years.[140]

Julia LaBella arrived in Nashville on December 9, after a long drive from Massachusetts in her blue 1971 Volkswagen Fastback. Bill paid for her room at the Holiday Inn on Trinity Lane and they went out for supper. After they returned to the room, LaBella said Bill read the newspaper for a while, then pulled a piece of paper out of his pocket with a song he'd written on it, and sang "Beautiful Julia LaBella" for her.

> Beautiful Julia LaBella stood there in her young maidenhood. In her eyes,
>   through her tears, she said I love you,
> And there before me she stood,
> Like an angel from Heaven she was sent there.
> In her eyes the light of Heaven shone through.
> Beautiful Julia LaBella.
> Julia, you know I love you.

Taken aback, LaBella said she was suddenly scared. She recalled Bill saying, "I don't want you to be afraid—in time you will learn to love me." Then, telling her he would pick her up in the morning and take her to the farm, he abruptly left.[141]

The next morning, the first stop on the tour of the farm was a visit to the cabin. After Bill opened the padlocked door, LaBella said he asked, "Do you think you could help me fix up this old place?" She said she answered yes. Later, they walked to the top of one of the hills that surround the property on three sides. "Bill asked me if I could be happy there with him," she said, "and I told him I would."

LaBella, Bill, and several male helpers were soon loading and hauling hay bales from the Bluegrass Musicland site near Beaver Dam to the Goodlettsville farm. Bill, meanwhile, arranged for a room for her on a weekly rate at the Monterey Motel on Dickerson Road, just north of Nashville. (Bill had recently met the motel's head cleaning lady, Armolee Green, and her husband, Clarence Green. They had convinced him to attend their church, Shallow Ford Pentecostal Church in White House, Tennessee, after he told them he hadn't gone to church regularly in more than twenty years.) Bill was still living with Virginia Stauffer at the Murfreesboro Road trailer park and drove from there to pick up LaBella each morning before the day's work began.[142]

Writing "My Last Days on Earth"

On a wintry night about that time, Bill arose from the recliner at Stauffer's place, where he usually slept, and began writing a new instrumental tune. Ten years later, he recalled the beginnings of "My Last Days on Earth":

Well, one night, way along in the morning around two or three o'clock, I couldn't sleep, and it was cold as it could be, boy. So I thought I'd get up and I'd get my mandolin and I'd just see what I could come up with. I'd see what different style I could tune. Something new. So I got my mandolin and I went to comin' up with tuning a different style, where it would harmonize—you could play two strings and one would be harmony for the other string, you see? So I got it tuned up the way that I wanted it, and then I went to playin' some on it, you know, seein' how the one sound would play along with the other sound and add what notes, or the tune, I wanted to go with. But it seemed like when I started on it, [it] just wrote itself, like it was there already. I was going along with it, and it was really sad.[143]

Shortly after the release of Bill's *Sings Bluegrass, Body and Soul* album on January 10, 1977, he and the band left for a quick, unannounced third visit to Japan, arriving on January 17 and staying through the 26th. After they returned to Nashville, they (along with LaBella) again headed out west by bus, playing, among other places, San Francisco's Great American Music Hall for the first time, on February 7.[144]

Bill returned to the Southeast to tour with James. Bill Holden left in mid-March 1977, dissatisfied with the pay, he said, during a slow February. A member of James's Midnight Ramblers, Alan O'Bryant, filled in on banjo until a replacement could be found.[145]

The opening was soon filled by Kentuckian Larry Beasley, twenty-four, a six-year veteran of Carl Story's Rambling Mountaineers. Planning to get married and settle down, he had just given Story his two-weeks' notice. When word of it got around, Bill called to offer him the spot. Beasley, considering it "the ultimate job for a banjo player," couldn't refuse.[146]

Biography? Autobiography?

Ralph Rinzler was committed to writing a biography of Bill, but his work-load at the Smithsonian made completing it by 1978 an impossibility. At the American Folklore Society conference in October 1976, Judith McCulloh of the University of Illinois Press had introduced him to Robert Cantwell, writer of the 1971 article "Believing in Bluegrass," and they decided to collaborate on the biography, with Cantwell doing the writing based on data Rinzler would provide. After Rinzler introduced Cantwell to Bill, he traveled with the band to a few showdates on the weekend of April 17, 1977. (At least one of his observations, made during this brief sojourn, would be included in his *Bluegrass Breakdown*, published in 1984.) But Bill would soon decide he preferred to tell the story himself, in his own words, possibly advised by James, who would have been aware of the success of Loretta Lynn's autobiography, *Coal Miner's Daughter*, published in 1976.[147]

Near the end of May 1977, Bill and the band were again on their way to Ralph Stanley's Memorial Festival, the seventh annual, to play every day, from Wednesday through Sunday, May 25–29. They went in separate vehicles, to make travel to and from a nearby motel easier. Beasley volunteered to drive Bill in Bill's station wagon, and they left Nashville on Tuesday night. By the time they got into the hills of western Virginia, Beasley was tired.

> It was the dead hours of the mornin' and I could just barely hold my eyes open. I slipped off the edge of the road just enough so the gravels kindly got to zinging there and it woke Mr. Monroe up. He looked up at me and said, "Don't you think we need to pull over and rest a little?" Then he grinned and said, "You don't want to be responsible for the death of the Father of Bluegrass Music." I pulled over.

It was no laughing matter about two weeks later, when James's bass player, Tommy Franks, fell asleep at the wheel of the Midnight Ramblers' camper van and died after rear-ending a truck on I-65. James, the only other person in the van, was asleep in the back and wasn't seriously injured. They were on the way to the Bean Blossom festival, set to begin that Saturday morning, June 11.[148]

Bill was in Oklahoma that weekend at the first Sanders Family Festival in McAlester. He phoned Jim Peva to ask him to take over James's ticket-selling job at Bean Blossom's front gate. Peva later wrote, "When Bill arrived . . . he insisted on paying me. . . . I refused payment, telling him I was glad to do him a favor. Several days later at the festival, I was sitting by my campfire, and Bill and all of the Blue Grass Boys walked up, with their instruments. They played a song, and then Bill had a framed certificate in his hand, which he handed me." It was a pass for Peva and his family to the festival "for as long as I live," signed "Bill Monroe."[149]

Larry Beasley turned in his notice at the Sanders Family Festival. "I had wedding plans and was in the process of building a house *and* I was 'road-beaten,'" he said. Visiting the festival was his predecessor, Bill Holden, who had driven up from Texas just to say hello. Once there, friends encouraged him to rejoin the band. "Before the festival was over," Holden said, "I was on the bus and Larry was driving my car back to Nashville." Beasley picked until the end of June, then Holden was back "in the saddle," but only briefly.[150]

In July, during a lull in the schedule, Baker drove to Lexington, Kentucky, to visit old friend and fellow fiddler Bobby Slone. Baker later told Bobby Osborne that he and Slone went to see "an old man" who had some fiddles they wanted to check out (and it appears they may have been drinking). Baker had a new hunting knife a fan made for him and, while showing it to them, he accidently lost his grip on it. He reflexively made a grab for it, missed the handle, and the razor-sharp blade cut deep into the palm of his left hand. "Baker told me that Slone got him in his car and headed for the hospital," Osborne said, "and had it not been for [Slone] knowing where the hospital was, he would have bled to death." Emergency microsurgery followed. Baker would not return to full-time playing until October.[151]

With recording sessions coming up on July 25, 27, and 28, Bill called on Buddy Spicher, a veteran of his sessions since 1961, to substitute for Baker. The album that resulted, *Bluegrass Memories*, would be released in October, just before the holidays, with a new Christmas song by Virginia Stauffer ("That's Christmas Time to Me") and a new recording of "Christmas Time's A-Comin." Bill was still living with Stauffer, but hints of his relationship with Texas native LaBella are apparent on the album: "Texas Blue Bonnet" (the state flower), recorded on the 25th, and "She's Young (and I'm Growing Old)" and "Blue Goose" (Bill's nickname for LaBella's blue Volkswagen) on the 27th. Also recorded on the 27th was "My Sweet Memory," for which Bill unintentionally plagiarized lyrics from "My Favorite Memory," written by songwriter Darrell Statler and recorded by the Osborne Brothers in 1967. Used almost word for word to make a chorus for "My Sweet Memory" was the second stanza of "My Favorite Memory":

> You gave me something time can never take from me,
> A light that guides me when life's dark and I can't see.
> When I'm cold, a hand to hold will comfort me,
> 'Cause you'll be there, my favorite memory.

The Osborne Brothers' recording was on the flipside of "Rocky Top" in 1968, and Bill may have heard it on a hundred jukeboxes, absorbing lyrics that came to him several years later, from where he didn't know. MCA recording executives failed to notice the similarities and, surprisingly, few others did either.[152]

The July 28 session began with Stauffer's "That's Christmas Time to Me," her last contribution to Bill's repertoire. A new banjo tune followed: Holden's "Pinewood Valley," named for a country music park owned by Buddy Spicher, its publisher. Another new love song by Bill was next, "My Florida Sunshine," inspired by an unknown resident of the Sunshine State. And the session ended with "Wabash Cannon Ball," long associated with Roy Acuff. At the time, some of Bill's bookings were handled by the Acuff-Rose Artists Corporation, with former Blue Grass Boy Howdy Forrester, then of the Smoky Mountain Boys, as his agent.[153]

Holden left again in early August, and Bill was without a regular banjo player for the rest of the month. Before he left, Holden called Butch Robins to tell him he was leaving. Since 1975, Robins had picked banjo with Wilma Lee and Stoney Cooper on the *Opry* (staying on after Stoney died in March 1977) and had just given Wilma Lee Cooper notice when Holden called. On September 2, he would begin his second stint as one of the Blue Grass Boys.[154]

Bill's New Compositions

Bill used several fill-in fiddlers before choosing James Bryan in mid-August 1977 to temporarily replace Baker. The twenty-three-year-old Alabaman had studied with Baker since high school and wanted to play like him, but Baker insisted he find his own style. "He gave me a big lecture—I shouldn't just try to copy him," Bryan said. "He was really adamant about that." One aspect of Bryan's style, a perfect match for Bill, was his respect for melody.

Bill, in recent years, had "composed" many new instrumental tunes, more than he could interest MCA in recording. Baker had recorded a few on his County albums ("Roxanna Waltz" and "White Horse Breakdown" in 1972, "Road to Columbus" and "Mississippi Waltz" in 1976), but Bill's output caused Bryan to bring along a cassette tape recorder to preserve them and, with Bill's encouragement, to learn them. "He liked to show 'em to me," Bryan said, "'cause I'd try to play 'em just like he did on the mandolin."[155]

Music City News came back in August for another "At Home on the Farm" feature story for its September 1977 issue. It included an inventory of his farm's animals, an indication of the workload: "80 cattle, four mules, one pony, two pigs and a passel of bellering foxhound pups." And among the article's photos was Bill, soon to be sixty-six, sitting on a porch swing with a smiling twenty-two-year-old identified as "Julie."[156]

The young man who apologized to Bill in 1954 for changing his song was, at age forty-two, still a young man when he died on August 16, 1977. Reportedly, doctors determined that Elvis Presley's death was caused by cardiac arrhythmia (irregular heartbeat).[157]

Bluegrass: For the Common Man?

The fifth annual Homecoming Festival at Monroe's Musicland Park was held on Labor Day weekend, September 2–4. The day before it began, twenty-one-year-old Donald Evans, a deaf-mute from nearby Mt. Pleasant, was killed when he pulled the car he was driving (without a license) out of the Rosine general store parking lot onto Highway 62 and was hit by a westbound coal truck. Reverend Mike Taylor, then pastor of both the Rosine and Mt. Pleasant Methodist Churches, went to the visitation on Saturday and talked with the young man's father, Nelson Evans. He asked Taylor to conduct the funeral on Sunday, and Taylor asked him if there were any particular recordings he wanted him to play. "He said, 'No, I'll have somebody to sing.'"

> Bill was having his festival [Taylor recalled]. So, Nelson, the morning of the funeral, went to Bill's bus before daylight and knocked on the door, and Bill came to the door. Nelson said, "My son got killed in a car wreck and his funeral's this evenin'." Said, "Would you kindly sing at his funeral?" Bill said, "What time is the funeral?" Nelson told him two o'clock and Bill said, "We'll be there."

Bill shut down the festival for a couple of hours and brought the whole band with him to the funeral home. "Bill always said his music was for the common man," Taylor said. "He lived up to that, I thought." After the service, Taylor said Nelson Evans told him, "Donald's never ever heard Bill Monroe, but he heard him today."[158]

Since Bill originally intended bluegrass for the common man (or, "for country people," as he actually put it), it's no wonder he was skeptical about those who wanted to "modify" the music. It was only natural that, by the mid-1970s, his festivals featured mainly "traditional" performers, with an occasional "contemporary" band. At the time, there seemed to be a trend for festivals to be either "traditional" or "contemporary," so the *Louisville Times* sent feature writer Becky Homan to Nashville to ask Bill about the apparent rift in the genre. She found him shortly after the 1977 Homecoming festival, troubled not by contemporary bluegrass per se, but by its most "progressive" band, the New Grass Revival, a group that fused bluegrass with rock music, particularly the rock of the 1970s drug culture, to create "newgrass."

> What I set out to do all my life—and somebody come along and try to tear it all up, or make it into a bluegrass rock, you know? That's sickening to think about. . . . These people that are trying to change bluegrass—they're trying to show off with their music, you know? They finally learned how to play a mandolin a little bit, and then they're playing the banjo, but they're keeping the banjo more in line

and the fiddle more in line. But the mandolin's what's putting a lot of hot stuff in it, you know?

Without mentioning his name, bluegrass fans knew Bill had indicted Kentuckian Sam Bush, the mandolin-playing leader of the Revival (once welcome at the 1968 Bean Blossom fest when he played with the Bluegrass Alliance). Bill had lately refused to speak to him, according to Homan, who also interviewed Bush. "I like Monroe," he said then. "Nobody can play the mandolin like him, and it used to bother me that he didn't like me. But it doesn't kill me anymore."[159]

Ralph Rinzler wrote to Bill on September 13, 1977 (Bill's sixty-sixth birthday), inviting him to meet with Cantwell and himself in October, to work on his autobiography. Rinzler had chosen an idyllic setting, an island off the coast of Massachusetts owned by his wife Kate's family. "There are four thousand acres of wilderness with no way of getting around except on horseback or in a buggy," he wrote. "It takes a few days to wind down from the pace we live today, and then, after a day or so, I think you might remember things from your early youth that you might be less likely to think about in the pressured life of the mainland." But it was not to be. Bill was involved with an "Autumn Bluegrass Festival" at Bean Blossom (September 16–18), and his schedule in October was full. Cantwell didn't recall further attempts to get together with him, and Rinzler was soon informed that a contract with another publisher had been signed and that his and Cantwell's services would not be needed.[160]

Meanwhile, Bill had found a small apartment for LaBella in Madison. After a few suppers at her place, LaBella said he asked her to marry him and she told him yes. But, naturally, she was troubled by the uncertainty of where he went when he left her apartment. So, one night she followed him (made easier by his poor eyesight: "It was dark and he didn't see the best at night"), going all the way to Murfreesboro Road and Virginia Stauffer's small house in the center of Fulton's Trailer Park. She went to the front door and knocked. "[Stauffer] came to the door and I asked, 'Is Bill here?' and she just cursed me out." . . . "She said, 'Get your blankety-blank outta here or I'll call the police on you.' I said, 'I'm not trying to cause any problems. I just would like to speak with him.' She said, 'Get outta here,' and slammed the door. LaBella went home.

The next day, Bill "was so apologetic," according to LaBella. "He said, 'I've been trying to get away from her. She's threatened me—that she will contact the *Tennessean*, sue me, make things really rough on me. And I can't have that.' He said, 'If you'll just give me some time. . . .' He said, 'I don't sleep with her. I sleep in the chair.'" Not sure if she believed him, she went back again: "I waited and watched and, sure enough, she went to the other end of the house and he would stay there reading the paper and turn out the lights and go to sleep in that recliner. So I knew he was telling me the truth, and when he asked me to wait, I told him I would."[161]

Kenny Baker returned to full-time fiddling with Bill about that time, and James Bryan joined James Monroe's Midnight Ramblers. By October 3, the day *Bluegrass Memories* was released, Bill and the band were in San Francisco, reappearing at the Great American Music Hall. Former protégé David Grisman, living in the area, took the opportunity to interview Bill for his new publication, *Mandolin World News*. Asked about the tunings he used over the years, Bill mentioned the tune he'd written in the middle of the night the previous winter (1976–77), and it's clear he'd already shown it to MCA producer Walter Haynes.

> I've got a tuning now that I really want to do, and MCA wants me to put it on a record. It goes back . . . the sound, the tone, the tune of this number would go back 150 years, and there's nothing played today like that. You wouldn't need no fiddle in it . . . you wouldn't need a banjo . . . you would use a guitar if he was careful and be quiet with it, and a bass. But that's all you would need . . . you wouldn't need another thing.[162]

By then, Bill had achieved "living legend" status, and most people treated him with the greatest respect. Not so John Duffey, who left the Country Gentlemen in 1969 and helped found the contemporary band Seldom Scene in the early 1970s. A match for Bill physically, Duffey openly decided to confront him. According to Tom Gray, bassist with "the Scene" throughout the 1970s, "I remember John saying, 'It seems like everyone bows down and treats Monroe like some kind of god; I'll try acting like I'm his equal and tease him.'" The first widely publicized incident involving this resolve came on November 12 during the finale of a bluegrass package show at the University of Maryland, with eight bands on the stage. When it came time for someone to sing tenor for Ralph Stanley on the second chorus of "Can't You Hear Me Calling?," Duffey decided he should do it, and as he sang, he reached out his hand to cover Bill's mouth, to stop him from singing. A photo of it soon appeared in *Bluegrass Unlimited* and the photographer, Winnie Willard-Richardson, recalled that Bill "shook his head 'no' and swatted Duffey's hand away like a bothersome fly." Naturally, the audience roared with laughter.[163]

At the end of 1977 the Monroe Talent Agency moved from Music Row in downtown Nashville to 3819 Dickerson Road, a small lot on the outskirts of town, just south of the intersection of Old Hickory Boulevard and Dickerson Road, where Bill's first farm in Nashville once stood. The lot would contain a small, two-room modular cabin that served as an office, a house trailer, and room to park a bus and the band's cars when they were on the road.[164]

In January 1978, it had been fifty years since the *WSM Barn Dance* became the *Grand Ole Opry*, celebrated with an NBC television special, "Fifty Years of Country Music," taped at the new Opry House with a huge cast of country stars. Bill sang the obligatory "Blue Moon of Kentucky" with the Blue Grass Boys (Baker, Davis, Lewis, and Robins) stationed separately on risers of various heights. Then the show's producers paired two singers who'd had success with "Mule Skinner Blues," Dolly Parton and Bill, to sing the song together. Robert Cantwell was watching, writing later in *Bluegrass Breakdown*: "Here is Bill—dignified, aloof, gazing into the distance as he always does, splendidly handsome and venerable as a Supreme Court justice, his awareness of the glamorous and ebullient Dolly betrayed only by a grin—you can hardly see it—gathering at the corner of his mouth."[165]

The *Father & Son* album, released in 1973, had probably sold well enough by 1978 that MCA decided to produce a sequel. The songs on *Father & Son* were mainly older redos; this time there would be an equal mix of old and new. There would also be a somewhat bigger sound, with two of James's Midnight Ramblers added (James Bryan and Alan O'Bryant), with two banjos and two fiddles on all three sessions. The first, on Tuesday, January 24, began with the new "Hard Times Have Been Here," written by Damon Black, whose popular "I Haven't Seen Mary in Years" was on *Father & Son*. This was followed by "Six Feet under the Ground," which Bill had started in the early 1960s. And the session ended with "Who's Gonna Shoe Your Pretty Little Feet?," a remake of "Little Red Shoes," the fourteenth Monroe Brothers song rerecorded.[166]

The session of Monday, January 30, began with another new Damon Black song, "Jake Satterfield," then "Muddy Waters," written by Phil Rosenthal and previously released by the Seldom Scene on *Act 3* in 1973. And last was "Corrina, Corrina," originally recorded in 1929 by Hugh Cross, from whom Bill first heard "Footprints in the Snow."[167]

The final session for the sequel (later titled *Together Again*, released that June), on Wednesday, February 8, was also the last session Bill recorded at Bradley's Barn (destroyed by fire in 1980) and the last session James recorded with his dad for MCA. This end-of-an-era session began with the fifteenth Monroe Brothers song rerecorded by Bill, "Have a Feast Here Tonight." Next was "Golden River," originally recorded by its writer, Stuart Hamblen, for Bluebird in 1931. It was followed by "I'm Going Back to Old Kentucky," the second time Bill rerecorded this "classic band" standard. Then came banjoist O'Bryant's new "Those Memories of You," a song that would find widespread popularity in 1987, as sung by Emmylou Harris, Dolly Parton, and Linda Ronstadt on their *Trio* album (Warner Brothers).[168]

At this time in 1978, syndicated columnist Joe Edwards asked sixty-six-year-old Bill about retirement. "Some day, it'll have to happen," Bill said. "As long as my health's good, I'd hate to quit. I like to travel and play to crowds and build up to the point where we like to see each other." Which achievements was he proudest of? "To have a family and raise kids, to originate this music, and be on the *Opry*," he said. Concerning that music, he made an observation he would repeat often in the coming years: "Bluegrass has brought more people together and made more friends than any music in the world. You meet people at festivals and renew acquaintances year after year."[169]

Also during this time, James was planning to release his fourth album on the "Monroe Recording Company" label. Bill agreed to help him, of course. The first session was held on March 17 at Hilltop Studios in Madison with Bryan and O'Bryant, *Opry* bassist Billy Linneman, and Buddy Spicher playing second fiddle. Bill joined them two days later (contrary to the account in *The Music of Bill Monroe*), recording seven songs, including new versions of "I Haven't Seen Mary in Years" and "Bonny." Advertisements for the Monroe Recording Company were soon offering record-production services to all comers, but James quickly realized the record business, on top of the Monroe Talent Agency and his band, was more than he wanted to handle. "I was spread too thin," he said recently. "I was just tryin' to do too much." James's album, titled *Satisfied Mind*, would eventually be released in 1984 by Atteiram. Bill's participation would not be credited in its liner notes.[170]

By the spring of 1978, Bill and LaBella were doing some serious gardening at the Goodlettsville farm. As LaBella recalled:

The gardens were first plowed under with his International tractor. Ground was disked up, then dirt clods smoothed out with a big log chained to the back of the tractor. [It seems Bill had changed his mind since the 1950s, when James said he "didn't believe in having a tractor."] We loved the rich smell of the newly-plowed earth. Bill plowed with mules to "lay the rows by" and also used a special double-shovel plow for the sweet potatoes.

We plowed and planted three vegetable gardens. The one up the hollow [a distance from the old cabin] was one acre of sweet potatoes, bush beans, Kentucky Wonder beans growing up the Silver Queen corn, yellow squash, zucchini, cucumbers, cantaloupe, watermelon, okra, peppers, and eggplants. The garden between the cabin and the outhouse [then in use, because there was still no running water available] had one hundred tomato plants, and in the one directly behind the cabin, we planted potatoes, corn, onions, peas, lettuce, carrots, beets, cabbage, and half-runner beans.[171]

Bill's twelfth annual Bean Blossom festival ran nine days that year, from Saturday, June 10, through Sunday, June 18. Among the featured bands was Don Reno and his Tennessee Cut-ups (Reno and Harrell had separated in 1976), and Reno's youngest son, Don Wayne, then fifteen, asked to come along. He told his father he wanted to meet Bill Monroe. But after they arrived and he saw him, he was "frightened to death."

> On the next day, Dad and I were sitting in our motor home, thinking about getting some breakfast, when we spied the Father coming in our direction. Boy, did I get nervous when he came up to the door and knocked. "Don, let's go get some breakfast," he said. . . . During breakfast, all my fears of Bill just melted away. I didn't say much, but I sure did listen. It seemed like those guys could remember everything that ever happened to them. They talked about the old days and how hard they had to work. They used to go from town to town, setting up the big tent for the show. After the shows, they would play baseball. Dad said he never worked harder in his life. . . . Bill told Dad that his hair was getting out of control. He raised his hat, and it was very long in the back. Dad said, "Come in the motor home and I'll give you a trim." . . . Watching those two together reminds me now of a couple of kids—best friends that hadn't seen each other in awhile. It had probably happened many times before and I was just lucky enough to be a part of it. Bill told me, "Play this good bluegrass, as it is the best." I told him not to worry, because I already had my sights set on playing the banjo. Bill grinned and said, "That's good."

Don Wayne Reno joined the Tennessee Cut-ups the following year, playing bass, but would be featured regularly picking twin banjos with his dad.[172]

Bill Comes to Gibson

The Gibson Musical Instrument Company, meanwhile, had begun making small improvements in its acoustic instruments after consulting with luthier Roger Siminoff, one of the founders of *Pickin'* magazine. In 1977, Siminoff convinced Gibson to make a large improvement—to again build mandolins based on the specifications of the 1920s Lloyd Loar F-5, the kind Bill played. In effect, Gibson would be attempting to make an instrument "as good as" Bill's (which he'd told them in 1953 they couldn't do). On the weekend of June 23, 1978, a prototype of it, designated as the F-5L ("L" for Loar), was displayed for the first time at the National Association of Music Merchants (NAMM) convention in Chicago. Siminoff was manning the Gibson booth on Saturday the 24th when a surprise visitor appeared.

> As if by magic [Siminoff wrote], the one person least expected to be at NAMM came by the Gibson booth to see what mandolins were on display. Bill Monroe, who just happened to be in Chicago at the time of NAMM [probably playing the night in town]—with his F-5 in hand—came into the booth and picked up the F-5L. Yes, he played it. And, yes, he liked it. We talked for awhile about the comparison between the F-5L and his mandolin, and the work Gibson did to bring back this instrument. I remember standing there holding his mandolin while he played the F-5L, then we swapped back, only for him to ask to play the F-5L again—that was a good sign!
>
> Soon, a huge crowd had gathered around us, with a lot of people wanting to see who this old geezer was, playing the heck out of a mandolin.

Bill had discovered that Gibson might be able to build a mandolin almost as good as his after all. In the process, he helped heighten awareness of their new product, and the company received a flood of orders from dealers during that weekend. "All of a sudden, Gibson was back in the mandolin business—big time!" Siminoff said.[173]

That summer of 1978, more than thirty years after "the classic bluegrass band" recorded together, the first album devoted exclusively to their recordings was *finally* released. It was not released by Columbia, owner of the musical treasures, but was licensed by them for release on independent Rounder Records. All twelve selections on *Bill Monroe with Lester Flatt and Earl Scruggs: "The Original Bluegrass Band"* had already been released on three Harmony-Columbia albums in the 1960s, but this album made it possible for a new generation to hear them all in one place. Unfortunately, the album's title and its liner notes (in which Neil Rosenberg wrote: "Bluegrass music began with Bill Monroe and his famous Blue Grass Boys of 1945–48") would not have been approved by Bill or those who believed that bluegrass began in 1939.[174]

In June 1978, former Blue Grass Boy Doug Hutchens had graduated from Berea College, gotten his master's degree from Eastern Kentucky University, and was teaching at Alice Lloyd College in Pippa Passes, Kentucky. By then, he was considering a special project—documenting all of the former Blue Grass Boys. Inspired by the identification of those who had recorded with Bill in Neil Rosenberg's *Discography*, he knew there were many others who had not recorded with Bill. A notice appeared in the October 1978 *Bluegrass Unlimited* ("If you can contribute information to the project, please contact Doug c/o Alice Lloyd College. . . .") and a questionnaire was sent to former band members. Among its questions: "How did you get the job with Bill?" and "How did working with the Blue Grass Boys influence your life?" By early 1979, twenty-five had been completed.[175]

The Death of Lester Flatt

Former Blue Grass Boy Lester Flatt's health had deteriorated since open-heart surgery in July 1975. In November 1978, after a stroke, he spent several weeks at Nashville's Baptist Hospital, visited there by Scruggs and by Bill and James. He recovered, and he and his Nashville Grass played the *Opry* several times in March 1979. But after he returned to Baptist on April 23 for a "reevaluation of his heart condition," he died there on May 11, 1979, at age sixty-four.[176]

A month after Flatt's death, while recording a second live album at the thirteenth annual Bean Blossom festival (June 9–17), Bill spoke in praise of him on Saturday the 16th, finally telling the world who wrote a song long credited to the two of them:

> You know, when Lester Flatt passed away, we lost a mighty good bluegrass man because he'd worked with Bill Monroe and the Blue Grass Boys and was a wonderful singer, and he is really gonna be missed. He wrote a number that we used to feature a lot. He wrote a number that we wanna do in memory of Lester Flatt, entitled "The Little Cabin Home on the Hill."

Bill or producer Haynes may not have been satisfied with the music that followed. The song would be rerecorded in a studio later without banjo or bass (the tenth "classic band" song redone; Bill's one hundredth session for Decca-MCA), then added to Bill's twenty-fifth Decca-MCA album, *Bill Monroe: Bean Blossom '79*, blended in with crowd noise. All of the album's selections had been waxed previously by Bill except "The Old Mountaineer," a fiddle tune James Bryan recalled Bill writing in 1977. (As with Bill's first live album, it appears production costs again caused MCA to cut back on its budget for Bill. For the first time in eighteen years, an annual Bill Monroe album would not be released in 1979—*Bean Blossom '79* would not be released until February 1980—and Bill would not record in a studio again until 1981.)[177]

After the Bean Blossom festival ended on June 17, Randy Davis left the band. Raymond Huffmaster of Mississippi, a Bean Blossom regular since 1969, was a helper at the festival, and when it was over, Bill asked the singer-guitarist to help further by playing bass with the band until a replacement could be found.

> We were going to a show in Missouri and got off on a very small dirt road. [We] drove for several miles and came up on an old metal suspension bridge, one of them rattlin' kind. Bill had the driver stop the bus. He got out and looked the bridge over and walked across. On the other side, he motioned for us to walk across. . . . Then he told the driver . . . to come on across, slowly. He eased that old bus up on that old iron bridge and it was squeaking and popping and singing as he came across it, scared to death. When he got across and we all got back aboard, Monroe said, "It'd be bad for the Blue Grass Boys to fall in a river."[178]

A few days later, Bill and the band arrived at the Southeastern Wisconsin Bluegrass Festival, near Muckwonago, for Saturday and Sunday, June 23–24. There from nearby Milwaukee was twenty-three-year-old Mark Hembree. He'd played bass with several bands, notably Colorado's Monroe Doctrine, and the festival's promoters, the Piper Road Spring Band (featured at Bean Blossom since 1976), encouraged him to ask Bill for the job. With hair he described as "to the middle of my back," Hembree asked, but was doubtful. On June 24, after a quick haircut and a successful audition backstage, Bill took his phone number. About a week later, Bill called, telling Hembree to report to Nashville on Monday, July 16.[179]

Renovation of Bill's Cabin

At that time, renovation of the old log cabin on Bill's farm had just begun, guided by contractor "Cotton" Williams from Portland, Tennessee (in northern Sumner County, near the Kentucky line). First, the one-hundred-year-old structure was completely dismantled. "We numbered the logs," LaBella recalled, "and we kept the ones that were in decent shape and replaced the other ones. There was a sawmill near Cottontown [also in Sumner County, closer to the farm], and the logs we needed to replace were cut up there." A half-basement was dug for storage, giving the cabin a solid foundation for the first time. Originally one large room with a kitchen, the first floor was divided up into living room, two bedrooms, bathroom, and kitchen, and a second floor was added, with two guest bedrooms and a half-bath. Flooring throughout was replaced with the maple floor of a roller skating rink being torn down in Portland. The cabin's overall size could have been increased even more, but "Bill just wanted it humble," LaBella said. She estimated the project took about a year to complete.

At the same time, former Blue Grass Boy Carlos Brock and older brother Lonnie Brock, carpenters and housebuilders by trade, made extensive improvements to "the little house up the holler" (including adding a second floor). Birch and Bertha were making regular trips to Nashville by then, for Bertha to see a doctor at Vanderbilt Hospital, and this would give them a place to stay when in town. "It was hard to remodel, much harder than a modern home," Carlos Brock said. "The walls were out of plumb." The Brock brothers (including youngest brother Bobby Brock) were simultaneously helping to build a house for James at 3699 Dickerson Road, just south of the office, where he would live throughout the 1980s.[180]

On August 18, 1979, Doug Hutchens went to the first McLain Family festival, near Berea, Kentucky, mainly to talk to Bill about his project to document the Blue Grass Boys. He wanted to ask him about some of the lesser-knowns he was looking for, and he was hoping Bill had liked an article in the July *Bluegrass Unlimited*—"Blue Grass Boy Turns Detective," written by friend Marty Godbey to help draw attention to his quest. Bill suggested meeting in a little while, on a hill away from the crowd, not giving any indication of a problem; he then "lit into him" as soon as they met. Godbey had written in her article, with tongue somewhat in cheek, that "detective" Hutchens was going to "probe" into people's "private lives." Bill didn't see the humor and obviously misunderstood Hutchens's intent, based on this. "He was stern about the fact that it didn't need to be done" and that "it was nobody's business," Hutchens said. Respecting Bill's wishes, he dropped the project but would put the contact information he'd gathered to good use later.[181]

Mary Starkey of Columbus, Ohio

Tom Ewing went to see Bill and the band (Baker, Hembree, Lewis, Robins) at the Mountain Lake bluegrass festival near Bellefontaine, Ohio, on Saturday, September 22, about a week after Bill's sixty-eighth birthday. He went by the bus to say howdy and ended up singing a song with Bill on his second set. Afterward, he hung around to thank him and walked back to the bus with him. On the way, Bill asked if he knew a lady in Columbus, Ohio, named Mary Starkey. "I didn't know Mary then," Ewing said later, "but I made it a point to meet her after that."[182]

Born in eastern Kentucky in 1938, Mary Blevins moved to Columbus in 1959. She'd grown up listening to Bill on a battery-powered radio but didn't see him until June 1960, at a country music show he played without the Blue Grass Boys at the fairgrounds in Columbus. In 1961 she married Mr. Starkey, who didn't like bluegrass, so in the mid-1960s she went to see Bill in a bar, telling her husband she'd gone to get milk and there was a long line at the checkout. "When Bill would see me after that," Starkey said, "he'd ask, 'Can you stay for the show or do you have to take milk back to the kids?'" She divorced in 1970, and "when he'd be coming close to Ohio, he'd always call me," she said. Starkey believes "Road to Columbus" was written when Bill was on his way to play at Frontier Ranch, near Columbus, where he would see her.[183]

Playing for a President

On September 30, 1979, Bill played for a president of the United States for the first time, joining many other stars for "A Celebration of Country Music," videotaped by NBC at Ford's Theatre in Washington, D.C., and broadcast nationally on October 16. Butch Robins, in his *What I Know*, writes of events leading up to what he says "was basically a political fundraiser. The cheap seats in the back of the balcony were in the neighborhood of $5,000 a pop and seats near President Carter required a donation of $40,000 to $50,000." *Time* magazine, however, reported it was "two hours of pickin' and singin' to benefit Washington's Ford's Theatre." Unfortunately, with more than a dozen stars, there was only time for Bill to sing "Blue Moon of Kentucky."[184]

Bill celebrated his fortieth anniversary on the *Grand Ole Opry* on October 27. By a sad coincidence, his old friend and fellow Kentuckian, country singer-songwriter Jimmie Skinner, suffered a heart attack and died that night at age seventy. Two years earlier, Bill's *Bluegrass Memories* album featured Skinner's "He Knew" on the back cover:

> He knew the world needed music that was different,
> Even when he was a boy.
> With the bluebirds he'd sing 'til the whole world would ring,

And Mother Nature would shout from pure joy.

He knew that in music there was sadness, too,
That the good old time-tested songs
Often told of lovers, a broken romance,
Of a friend or loved one gone on.

Oft times in the cool of the evening,
When summer was turning to fall,
A sweet and mellow mandolin to the song "Uncle Pen"
Would blend with the nightbird's call.

He knew long before he became a man,
He was destined to follow a dream,
That the music he'd make, he'd change and reshape
And take it far from the town of Rosine.

He never patterned himself after anyone else.
He laid a new brand of music down.
When it won wide acclaim, it acquired a name.
Some called it the high, lonesome sound.

Today it proudly bears a title known to all,
That's bluegrass wherever you go,
All started by the man from Blue Grass land,
Kentucky's own Bill Monroe.[185]

Gibson Comes to Bill

Bill played the *Opry* every weekend in December 1979. During that time, he met Rendal "Ren" Wall, Research and Development Department manager for the Gibson company, introduced backstage by *Opry* star Billy Grammer, a longtime mutual friend (whose hit recording of "Gotta Travel On" Bill recorded in 1958). Both Grammer and Wall wanted to end Bill's feud with Gibson, telling him the company was willing to make whatever repairs he wanted at no charge to achieve that goal. The price was certainly right for Bill, and Wall's words helped: "I told him one of my dreams was for Gibson and him to make up." Bill quickly agreed to have the work done, later commenting on Wall's reaction: "I don't think it would be lying to say that I saw tears in that man's eyes."[186]

CHAPTER EIGHT
1980-1989

Bill and James: Together Again

The first year of the 1980s began with weekend tours in the South from January through April, featuring Bill and James and their bands (sometimes with Carl Story and his band or the Sullivan Family). This schedule was interrupted during April 2–5, when Bill and the Blue Grass Boys (Baker, Hembree, Lewis, Robins) flew to London for the second visit to Wembley.[1]

Picking Sessions at the Farm

Work continued on the cabin that spring. Helping was twenty-seven-year-old Illinois native Larry Sledge, mandolinist with James in the late 1970s who'd worked on Bill's farm, off and on, since then. This time, he helped cut down several poplar trees on the property, to use in the top beams of the cabin. "Bill had me handle the wedge," Sledge said, explaining that the wedge, used to fell the tree in a particular place, was pounded in with a *sledge*hammer. "That was the right job for me, according to Bill's sense of humor." After work, Sledge and friends—musicians Norman and Nancy Blake (guitar and cello, respectively) and former Blue Grass Boy James Bryan—were occasionally invited for supper, which LaBella fixed in "the little house up the holler," where picking sessions followed. It gave Bill an opportunity to play the instrumentals he'd written lately, among them the unnamed tune in the odd tuning that came to him one night in 1976. "When we would go out there," recalled Norman Blake, "he had a mandolin under the bed that he had in that tuning, 'cause he was kind of afraid he would lose the tuning."[2]

Music City News was the first publication to report that Bill had agreed to allow Gibson to restore his main mandolin ("serial number 73987"). He was quoted in its April 1980 edition, saying, "I'm glad that it's come down to this, that things can be right between me and Gibson. You don't gain anything by being on the outs." But he still didn't believe the company could top serial number 73987: "There's not a mandolin I've ever had that could touch it in any way. I never played a better mandolin in my life."[3]

After sputtering ominously for months, the Mount St. Helens volcano in Washington finally erupted on Monday, May 19. The explosion was felt a hundred miles away, and a cloud of ash extended 60,000 feet into the sky. But compared to the Krakatoa volcano of a hundred years earlier that made the moon look blue, author Simon Winchester observed, "Krakatoa was a monster, Saint Helens was a pussycat."[4]

Butch Robins's father, Calvin Coolidge Robins, died on Wednesday, May 21, 1980, after a long battle with cancer. Bill and the band were playing at Ralph Stanley's festival (May 22–25), so Bill was able to attend a memorial service for him in nearby Lebanon, Virginia. "He seemed to be emotionally upset with the whole thing," Butch Robins wrote of Bill. "He sang 'Wayfaring Stranger,' 'Swing Low, Sweet Chariot,' and 'It's Me Again, Lord.'"[5]

Bill and James's $50,000 investment of 1974, Bluegrass Musicland Park, had not yet been especially successful, and it appeared they needed to try something new. That June, Birch started coming down from Martinsville to be the host of monthly shows at the park that headlined local talent. Also that June, the fourteenth annual Bean Blossom festival was hit by tornado-like weather that knocked down several trees, but with the help of festival attendees, the show went on.[6]

In July, Bill met with members of the Ohio County, Kentucky, Chamber of Commerce to discuss the possibility of a bluegrass music museum at the new Ohio County Park (site of the county's fair), on Route 69, just outside Hartford. He told the *Ohio County Times* he was being "pressured" to have it built in eastern Kentucky, but, he said, "I was born here and I think it should be located in Ohio County." They also discussed moving the Monroe homeplace's house and Uncle Pen's cabin to the Park. But the Chamber of Commerce, along with Ohio County's fiscal court and Industrial Foundation, would soon commission an Owensboro planning and development specialist to do a feasibility study, and a bluegrass museum in Ohio County was judged to be not feasible.[7]

James, meanwhile, lent his name to "James Monroe's Bluegrass Club," a bar-restaurant that opened on July 30 (paid for by an investor who prefers anonymity) in Nashville's Vanderbilt University area (1929 Division Street). Bill, Roy Acuff, and Wilma Lee Cooper played for its grand opening, but the club closed about the time it was mentioned in the September *Bluegrass Unlimited*. "I didn't get anything out of it," James said later, "and it wasn't a good deal" (but, he said, he didn't lose any money doing it).[8]

Bluegrass Unlimited noted Bill was playing a Gibson F-5L that summer. "He is quite happy with the sound," Marion Kuykendall reported in her "General Store" column. One of three prototypes built before the 1978 NAMM convention, it was loaned to Bill by Gibson *before* he turned over his 1923 F-5 to them. They would later give it to him.[9]

The eighth Homecoming festival at Bluegrass Musicland Park was held on the August 29 weekend. Aside from Bill and the Blue Grass Boys, James and his band, and Birch, only lesser-known acts were featured. Bill and James were determined not to lose money.[10]

Bill's Mandolin Restored

Bill returned to Nashville on Monday, September 1, and handed over his main mandolin to Rendal Wall for the trip to the plant in Kalamazoo. "I flew it back first-class, and I sat in coach," said Wall. "Back then, instruments could fly one-half off the ticket price." A team of expert luthiers repaired the headstock, inlayed a new "Gibson" in its veneer, replaced the fingerboard, and installed new tuning machines. Then, they added a custom-made tension rod cover engraved with Bill's name. After about five weeks, on October 8, 1980, it was returned to its owner, who declared it "one of the greatest days of my life." He picked a little "Sally Goodin," then stopped to say,

> Listen to how it rings and keeps on ringing. I've been offered $40,000 for this mandolin, but I don't think I would sell it, even if they went up to $500,000. It's meant so much to me and what I wanted to do, . . . I wouldn't put a price on it. Everything with Gibson is 100 percent. They've done a good job and we've made up and forgiven each other, which I guess is the way it should be.[11]

Bill and the band soon began a demanding tour of the West Coast, playing eleven showdates between November 1 and 15. It started in Portland,

Oregon, near the site of the Mount St. Helens eruption. Then the band played in Seattle, Washington, Vancouver (Canada), and Medford, Oregon, before traveling the length of California and back again. In San Jose on November 14, a local reporter asked Bill about retirement: "I don't see any use to it. I've got too many fans to forget about them and if I stopped, I'd never see 'em again. And I don't want it to end that way."[12]

While Bill and the band were on tour, California's former governor Ronald Reagan was elected president of the United States, defeating incumbent Jimmy Carter on November 4. Republican Reagan and Democrat Bill Monroe were both born in 1911, but the Republican was seven months older, born on February 6. Sixty-nine-year-old Reagan was then the oldest man ever elected to the highest office in the land.[13]

On the way home, Bill and the band stopped in Austin, Texas, on Wednesday, November 19, to tape their first appearance on *Austin City Limits*, the Public Broadcasting Service (PBS) television series that had debuted in 1976. Bill's renovated mandolin would make its national debut when the show aired in early 1981.[14]

The band was in New York City by December 5 for "Bluegrass Festival 3" at the Lincoln Center, with the gospel-singing Lewis Family, former Blue Grass Boy Byron Berline with Dan Crary and John Hickman, and former Blue Grass Boy Del McCoury and his Dixie Pals. Three days later, former founding member of the Beatles John Lennon, age forty, was gunned down outside his New York City apartment building by Mark David Chapman, a twenty-five-year-old deranged fan.[15]

Bill Signs with Buddy Lee

The year 1980 ended with Bill signing with one of country music's top booking agencies, Buddy Lee Attractions, founded in the 1960s by former wrestler Buddy Lioce. Bill would remain with the Buddy Lee agency during the rest of his performing career.[16]

Bill and the band spent January 1981 preparing to record a mandolin album (*Master of Bluegrass*, recalling the *Sing Out!* article), encouraged by the many tunes Bill had written. Robins purchased "a fairly expensive portable tape recorder" and used it to record the prospective inclusions, in order to learn them. (Robins also happened to capture Bill and Baker being silly, singing W. C. Handy's "St. Louis Blues" together and "mimicking black folks"; reportedly, his tape recorder was temporarily banned from the bus.)[17]

It had been nearly two years since Bill had recorded for MCA when he arrived at Nashville's Music Mill Studio on Tuesday, February 3, 1981. His band was the same as then, except for Hembree, recording the first of more than a dozen sessions with Bill. LaBella remembered Bill writing the first tune, "Old Ebenezer Scrooge," after he watched *A Christmas Carol* for the first time on a motel TV. The title for the next tune, "Come Hither to Go Yonder," was a phrase Bill noticed in a Louis L'Amour western novel, which Lewis had brought on the bus. (MCA, attempting to outdo itself in the gaffe department, listed it as "Go Hither to Go Yonder" when the album was released.) And Bill had been picking "Right, Right On" since before his last MCA studio session (February 1979), its title from then-current slang.

The next day (Wednesday, February 4), the band recorded "Lochwood" first, named for the park near Chatom, Alabama, where the Dixie Bluegrass Festival had been held since 1972. LaBella recalled Bill writing the next tune, "Old Dangerfield," as she drove him back to Nashville from Bean Blossom one late night. She insisted he write three parts for it, to help keep her awake. Its title comes from the town of Daingerfield in eastern Texas, near where her grandmother lived. The title of the third tune, "Fair Play," also comes from a town: Fair Play, South Carolina, not far from Lavonia, Georgia, site of several bluegrass festivals. LaBella, present when it was mixed, said Bill insisted on the removal of the second half of Robins's banjo break: "I remember Bill wanting to drown that out and Walter [Haynes] turning to him and asking, 'Are you sure?' Bill said yes, and I don't know why."

Two weeks later, they were back in the studio on Thursday, February 19, with Norman Blake (guitar) and Larry Sledge and Jesse McReynolds (of Jim and Jesse) on mandolins. The first two tunes, "Melissa's Waltz for J.B." and "Lady of the Blue Ridge," were recorded with the three mandolins playing in harmony, waltzes Blake and Sledge had played with Bill on the farm. Sledge found out they were to be recorded, so he figured out harmonies before the session; McReynolds worked out his harmonies in the studio. The third tune, with five distinct parts and as yet untitled, was also a waltz that only Sledge and Blake were familiar with. For it, all the musicians except Bill, Blake, and Hembree left the room so that Bill could record it as he envisioned back in 1976, with just guitar and bass. Hembree and Blake had to tune their instruments a half-step below standard to match the tuning of Bill's alternate F-5 Loar (lowest to highest: AA/DD/AC/DF, all lowered a half-step, resulting in "a C# minor tuning"). After the first run-through, Blake noticed something was wrong. "Bill had gone out of the studio, and he didn't have [the tuning] quite right. Nancy [his wife, present at the session] had written it down, so we tuned the mandolin while he was out, back to where he originally had it." In spite of this, some of the strings continued to slip out of tune, particularly noticeable in the third part. Then, all of the other musicians returned to record Bill's adaption of DeFord Bailey's "Evening Prayer Blues," said to have been a favorite of *Opry* founder George D. Hay.[18]

LaBella Leaves

After the sessions, while Bill was on the road, twenty-five-year-old Julia La-Bella decided to leave. She said later she'd lost hope that they would marry, due to Bill's affairs with other women and because James didn't approve of their union. She had already lived apart from Bill twice and had met forty-nine-year-old former Blue Grass Boy Benny Williams during one of those times. They were married on February 25 (for "six terrible and tumultuous days," she said).[19]

Bill Diagnosed with Colon Cancer

Bill collapsed, whether due to ongoing health problems or upset over La-Bella is not clear (possibly a combination of both). He was taken by his farm helpers to Nashville Memorial Hospital in Madison, and, after a thorough physical exam, he was found to have colon cancer.

When the new Mrs. Williams heard Bill had cancer, she told her husband. She said he'd been drinking and reacted violently, threatening to harm her because he thought she'd been in contact with Bill "behind his back." She said she realized then the mistake she'd made in marrying him, and she left him that night, taking refuge with church and motel friends Clarence and Armolee Green. With the help of the Buddy Lee agency, a divorce was granted, and LaBella was soon reunited with Bill at the hospital. "He told me he loved me and I told him he was gonna be alright," she said.

Bill would have welcomed the reassurance. In 1981 a cancer diagnosis was much more likely to be a death sentence than it is today. During the days before and after his March 9 cancer operation, it appears he faced the fact that they might be his last, and thus, the title given to the untitled tune he'd recently recorded—"My Last Days on Earth." Thankfully, he was physically fit and could withstand the demands of an operation. Years later, after the fear of recurrence was gone, he bragged about it a little: "They operated on me and I was up walkin' that day. They said, 'Anybody else, it would have been the next day before they would have got up.'"

That March, County Records, authorized by CBS Records (Columbia), issued the first of two albums with classic bluegrass band recordings that had never been released on LP. *Bill Monroe: The Classic Recordings—Vol. 1* included "How Will I Explain About You?" from 1946 and "I'm Travelin' On and On" from 1947. Available in May, *Bill Monroe: The Classic Recordings—Vol. 2* contained "That Home Above," "Remember the Cross," and "Shine, Hallelujah, Shine," all from 1947. At that point, after more than thirty years, two of the band's twenty-eight recordings had still not been released on an LP.[20]

Following his release from the hospital in mid-March, Bill stayed briefly at son James's new house on Dickerson Road, but he did most of his recuperating at the Hendersonville home of former Blue Grass Boy Clarence "Tater" Tate (then fiddling with Wilma Lee Cooper) and Tater's wife Lois, whose down-home cooking was second to none. Bill reappeared on the *Opry* on March 28, and, after a few more weeks, he moved out of Virginia Stauffer's place (with help from daughter Melissa, then forty-four and still living with her mother). He and LaBella moved into the restored cabin, and LaBella started traveling with the band, singing and playing guitar as a guest at every show.[21]

The Second "Big Plan"

Shortly after Bill was released from the hospital, he and James announced their second Big Plan—a combination restaurant and museum in Nashville: "Monroe Manor." They renovated an old Southern-style mansion with a tall-columned front porch, just north of the Monroe Talent office, at 4411 Dickerson Road (later torn down), and they actually operated a restaurant there for about a year. The museum never happened.[22]

Bill had played a half-dozen showdates by April 28, when he met with producer Haynes at the Music Mill Studio to mix the *Master of Bluegrass* album. Haynes, with Bill's OK, had already added the sound of a trio of background singers to "My Last Days on Earth," and, with Bill's approval that day, he would dub in sound effects and record symphonic strings to further "sweeten" it. The strings arrangement had already been written by William McElhiney, old friend of Owen Bradley, so it appears that Haynes didn't expect Bill to disapprove. When asked later about the strings, Bill justified them in his own way.

They was so far back in the background that they didn't hurt anything. The mandolin was up front and so, I [wouldn't] have let them take it over, you see? That's . . .
controlling it, keeping it like it should be. . . . I was down there when [the six
string players] was fillin' in, you know . . . and they'd go through that, then they'd
come out there and set down and cry. It was so sad, the number was to them.

By the time Bill said this (October 1981), the initial release of "My Last Days
on Earth" as a single on June 12 (with "Come Hither to Go Yonder") had
attracted a lot of attention, particularly from FM country-radio stations.[23]

The single had just been released when the fifteenth annual Bean Blossom
festival began on Friday, June 12, and Bill, clearly proud and excited, wanted
festivalgoers to be among the first to hear "My Last Days." Future Blue Grass
Boy Glen Duncan remembers Bill coming out on stage one afternoon, unannounced, with a cassette tape copy of it and a tape player (possibly Butch
Robins's). As Duncan recalled, "[Bill] said, 'You gotta hear this. This is the
most powerful thing I've ever heard in my life.'" Then he played it for the
crowd, holding the tape player up to one of the mikes.[24]

By the time Bean Blossom was over, on Sunday, June 21, Robins was unhappy. As detailed in his autobiography, he was struggling financially, the
Blue Grass Boys had not been paid for television shows taped the previous
fall, *and* Bill had misplaced his tape recorder. Bill was seeming more and
more inept to him: "His feet of clay had become a little bit more than I was
willing to tolerate." Then, when Bill did pay band members for their work
at the festival, he didn't pay a bonus for extra work they'd done, as he had
previously. It was union scale, $80 a day times ten ($800) and nothing more.
When Robins returned home to Virginia, the Nashville musicians' union
called, telling him the television money had gone to Monroe Talent, and no
one there knew the band needed to be paid from it. By the time he returned
to Nashville, on Friday, June 26, he was very unhappy. After a loud confrontation with Bill backstage at the Opry House, it was decided that Thursday,
July 2, in Chautauqua, New York, would be Robins's last engagement. When
Bill and the band returned to Nashville from it, they left right out to play a
festival in the same general area (Geneva, Ohio) on July 5. Once there, Bill
asked soundman Jerry Williamson to recommend a banjo picker, and local
musician Paul Kovac, playing with a band at the festival, filled in.[25]

Bill contacted former Blue Grass Boy banjoist R. C. Harris, who filled
in for a while. Twenty-four-year-old Blake Williams, formerly with Lester
Flatt's Nashville Grass, was picking banjo with James at the time. At a festival

with Bill on July 25, and knowing Harris was just filling in, Williams took the direct approach: "I went straight to Bill's bus and said, 'I want to come down tonight and play with you onstage,' and all he said was, 'O.K. Be ready.'" The following week, Bill called, asking him to play a few shows. "Does this mean I've got the job?" Williams asked. "Bill just said, 'Well, I guess so. . . .'" Born and living in Sparta, Tennessee, Flatt's hometown, Williams would be dubbed "the Sparta Flash" by Bill, possibly for his readiness to arrive quickly in Nashville on short notice.[26]

In August 1981 rare live recordings of the classic bluegrass band first became widely available on the bootleg LP *Bluegrass Classics Radio Shows 1946–1948*, offered for sale only in the *County Sales Newsletter*. It wouldn't be known until later that these recordings derived from Earl Scruggs, who, in the 1940s, paid a dollar for each of several *Opry* shows to be recorded on a disc-cutting machine hooked up to a radio in a private Nashville residence. In the 1950s, it appears Scruggs allowed someone to copy the discs onto tape, and the recordings began to circulate among private collectors. Eventually, one of them had the album made.[27]

On September 10, Bill and the band (Baker, Hembree, Lewis, Williams) played at the Dixie Bluegrass Festival in Chatom, Alabama, then "flew" (in the bus) to the "Bluegrass Festival of the United States" in Louisville, Kentucky, for Friday and Saturday, September 11 and 12. On the 12th, the day before Bill turned seventy, one of the sponsors of the free event, Kentucky Fried Chicken, arranged for Claudia Sanders, widow of Col. Harland Sanders (who died in December 1980), to present Bill with a huge birthday cake shaped like an F-5 mandolin. (According to Bill, Col. Sanders once told him, "Me and you have done more for the state of Kentucky than any two men.")[28]

In 1981 Bill's brother Birch turned eighty (in May), and his sister Bertha turned seventy-three (in July). Birch was still actively involved in three festivals at Bluegrass Musicland Park on the May 29, July 24, and September 4 (Homecoming) weekends. But the number of shows at the Brown County Jamboree may have been cut back to lighten his workload (other than the April 19 opener and the November 15 closer, there's no record of other shows). When the Jamboree season ended, Bill invited Birch and Bertha to spend the winter on his Goodlettsville farm, and they left Martinsville, Indiana, to move into the little house up the holler.[29]

Shortly before the Jamboree closer, on November 4, Bill taped his first appearance on *Hee Haw* (then in syndication after CBS dropped it in 1971).

First, he and the band played a medley of "My Rose of Old Kentucky" and "Blue Moon of Kentucky," then later they did "I'm on My Way Back to the Old Home." In between, Bill took part in one of the show's regular "bits," announcing a salute to his hometown, stumbling on the word "approximately" when giving the population of Rosine ("300"). The show would air nationwide on January 23, 1982.[30]

James, meanwhile, was now looking for someone to write his father's biography, instead of an autobiography. Thinking songwriter Damon Black ("I Haven't Seen Mary in Years," "Tall Pines") might be the perfect storyteller, James mentioned it to him, and he eagerly offered to try. Black visited Rosine in early February 1982, interviewed folks, and took photographs, and, when he returned home to Missouri, wrote to Ralph Rinzler, asking him to "forward copies of any documented information or photos" that he might have "on file" (an indication he was unaware of the extent of Rinzler's research).[31]

Bill, Bertha, and Birch were in Rosine themselves a short time later, attending the funeral of brother Speed's widow, Geanie Monroe, who had passed away on March 5, at age eighty-six. Not long after, Bertha and Birch decided to move back to Rosine, invited by a childhood friend, Mary Fanny Rogers, to live with her until they found a place of their own.[32]

The Death of Birch Monroe

Bertha and Birch were still living with Rogers on Saturday, May 1, when the three of them, driven by Darrel Dukes, spent the day putting out fliers advertising the Bean Blossom festival. That evening, Dukes was taking them back to Rosine for supper at his and Rosetta's house. "We got back up here to Beaver Dam," he recalled, "and Birch started takin' on with his heart" [it was hurting]. The pain eased when they reached the hospital in Hartford, so they didn't stop there, but it returned on the way to the Dukes's house. "He said, 'Oh, it's on me again,' so I didn't go back to Hartford. I just headed for Owensboro." There, at the Owensboro-Daviess County Hospital, it was verified that Birch was having a heart attack. Bill and the Blue Grass Boys, along with President Reagan, were in Knoxville on Saturday, May 1, at the opening of the 1982 World's Fair (the only known occurrence of Bill "playing for" Reagan). Bill arrived at the hospital the next morning.

He stayed through Tuesday, May 4, but when Birch's condition stabilized, he returned to Nashville. Eleven days later, on Saturday, May 15, Birch died of a "massive myocardial infarction" in the hospital (one day before his eighty-first birthday). Bill managed to perform as advertised at a Musicland Park festival that weekend, and he attended Birch's funeral on the 18th. Pallbearers included Jim and Jesse McReynolds, Bobby Osborne, Joe Stuart, and nephew James. (Bertha would move in with Darrel and Rosetta Dukes in Rosine.)[33]

An obituary for Birch appeared in the June 1982 *Bluegrass Unlimited*, so when the sixteenth annual Bean Blossom festival began on June 11, longtime fans arrived knowing of his passing. "Regulars at Bean Blossom," Tom Adler wrote, "all felt as if they had lost a quirky, irreplaceable uncle of their own." Adler also noted that Birch's departure would bring an end to "predictable seasons of Brown County Jamboree shows."[34]

Del McCoury was back at Bean Blossom that June, and his Dixie Pals now included his fifteen-year-old son, Ronnie McCoury, on mandolin. He had only been playing a couple of years, so watching Bill play was an important part of learning.

> It was Sunday [June 20], the last day of the ten-day fest. Bill and the Blue Grass Boys were doing their last set and I was watching from around the corner of the old stage doorway. I was really shy and was basically peeking around, watching and listening. Bill was the reason I played mandolin—my hero. I watched the whole set and towards the end, they played "Uncle Pen," and after the kickoff, he walked back and took his mandolin off and put it around my neck! He had me join the band and I took the solo where he always did with THE mandolin. After it was over, he told me to stay up there and he did a medley of his songs in B!
>
> That evening we went in town to eat with him at a diner. When the check came, Bill said, "Me and this feller will pay for it—us mandolin pickers have got to stick together." Of course, he paid. I doubt I had two dollars in my pocket at that age.[35]

A couple of weeks later, on July 3, Bill was one of the first to receive the National Heritage Fellowship Award from the National Endowment for the Arts, one of his highest governmental honors. He and LaBella flew to the awards ceremony in Washington, D.C., from Alvorado, Texas (near Dallas), where the band played on July 2. The next morning, they flew to Alabama for a recording session, an ill-fated attempt to record a live gospel album at Cathedral Caverns, near Huntsville (which Rosenberg and Wolfe discuss at length in *The Music of Bill Monroe*).[36]

Prostate Problems

After Bill's colon cancer in 1981, other health problems began catching up with him in 1982. An enlarged prostate (a common condition of older men) had made urinating difficult for several months, but, by the end of July, it would completely block his bladder's normal drainage. He and the band were due to play three days at a festival in Nova Scotia, beginning July 27—a trip that required a long bus ride to Portland, Maine (with new bus driver Alan Phelps, who was also playing Dobro with James), then an overnight ferryboat voyage, carrying the bus to the port of Yarmouth, Nova Scotia. After the crossing, they had about 135 more miles to travel to the festival, at the fairgrounds in Bridgewater. As Hembree recalled,

> It might have been near Barrington [about 30 miles outside of Yarmouth] when Bill began experiencing extreme pain. We got off the highway to a little hospital, and they were taking their own sweet time while Bill was in a waiting room screaming in pain. I collared a nurse and said, "You don't know this man—he is famous for his high tolerance for pain. If he's yelling like that, he is about to die!"

Bill's bladder had ruptured. Doctors performed emergency surgery, installing a catheter to allow his bladder to drain; he then traveled by ambulance to a hospital in Bridgewater. The band was ready to play without him that evening, but the show's promoter came to see Bill, hoping to talk him into making an appearance. As might be expected, it took very little encouragement for Bill to want to go, especially with morphine dulling his pain. So, a nurse helped him get dressed and she and a doctor went along to the fairgrounds, where he surprised everyone, including Hembree:

> We're getting set to go on and here comes an ambulance and out comes Bill, in a wheelchair, wearing his suit and hat. Wayne and I jumped all over the nurse and doctor, saying, "What the hell is he doing here?" They couldn't keep him from doing it, the nurse said. He was going to call a cab.
>   They wheeled him out there and he said, "I come all the way here and I mean to play for you folks tonight" and he sang "Little Georgia Rose" as if in his sleep. He got a nice hand, and Wayne hollered, "Thank you very much!" and we grabbed the wheelchair and got him the hell out of there.

But Bill would be back, for one song on each of the next two nights. WSM got word and sent their corporate jet to bring him back to Nashville on July 30, allowing Bill to avoid a bumpy bus ride. At Nashville Memorial Hospital in Madison, it's possible Bill underwent "transurethral resection of the prostate," a delicate procedure to remove the prostatic tissue blocking the bladder outlet.[37]

LaBella Leaves Again

A few weeks later, in August 1982, a year and a half after she first left the Goodlettsville farm, LaBella left again. She said later that she wanted to visit her grandmother in Mt. Vernon, Texas (near Daingerfield), and Alan Phelps offered to drive her there. She said she hadn't intended to leave for good, but when she tried to contact Bill, she was told she was not to return. She and Phelps would soon be married, but they would divorce seven-and-a-half years later.[38]

Hutchens's First Birthday Surprise

Bill's spirits may have been low by September, considering all he'd been through since May, but they were given a boost at the Kentucky Fried Chicken Festival (formerly "the Bluegrass Festival of the United States") on Saturday, September 11. That afternoon, in keeping with the festival's tradition of recognizing Bill's birthday, former Blue Grass Boys member Doug Hutchens, using the contact information of other former Blue Grass Boys musicians he'd gathered, organized the first of several birthday commemorations, surprising Bill with band members he wasn't expecting to see and special gifts paid for by all the former members—partially, Hutchens later admitted: "I'd ask for a donation of five or ten dollars, if they could, knowing full well that some weren't in a financial condition to send anything. I don't think we ever really got enough funds to cover whatever the gifts were, but I'd take care of the remainder. I was just happy that I was at a place in my life where I could take care of it."

The first gift was a cream-colored western hat, custom made from beaver-fur felt by hatter Randy Priest of Donnelly, Idaho (presented by Hembree, Lewis, and Williams). Next was a new mandolin case, custom made by mandolin builder John Paganoni of Manassas, Virginia, and leather craftsman Nick Boone of Louisville, Kentucky, engraved on its top with "Bill Monroe" and "Father of Bluegrass Music" (presented by Kenny Baker, Byron Berline, Red Taylor, and Gordon Terry). Last was a "birthday card," its front and back covers crafted by Hutchens of rosewood with "Happy Birthday Bill Monroe" inlaid in ivory on the front, and inside, seventy-two handwritten birthday greetings on blank pages sent by Hutchens, mainly from former Blue Grass Boys (presented by Cleo Davis).[39]

For the serious Bill Monroe fan, September 1982 brought the availability of two of the three unreleased Decca recordings: "Legend of the Blue Ridge Mountains," with Del McCoury singing on the chorus, and the instrumental "Bill's Dream," both from 1964. They were issued in Japan in November 1981 on the third *Bill Monroe Singles Collection* album (Japanese Victor). Imported by County Sales, it was offered for sale in limited numbers.[40]

By the end of September, Damon Black had given James a sample of his work on Bill's biography, but James was not happy with it. "He made things into rhymes, using song titles," James said. "It turned out to be like a nursery rhyme." With no other prospective writers in sight, Ralph Rinzler was again asked to help Bill write an autobiography. So, he spent some time traveling with Bill in October. After a show in West Virginia, Rinzler opened his portable typewriter in Nashville the next morning and wrote himself a letter, admitting the situation was "somewhat disorienting."

> Part of the disorientation results from the strangeness of the experience or the feeling of going back to a 1963 of having traveled and lived this way, and part of it from the sheer weariness of living on a bus, of being immersed in this kind of performance situation day after day. At the same time, it's intriguing, because there are so many ideas about how to approach the matter of treating Bill's life, and the whole subject and project is so vast, as treating anyone's life would be. But treating seventy-one years in the life of [an] extremely odd person—an impressive and miraculous person, but odd—it is overwhelming at times.

Clearly, he wasn't sure about how to proceed, and he wasn't sure that Bill was capable of helping him.

> At times, I think he has a completely holistic view of how to deal with his life story and at other times, I think he has no idea of what is involved, and that when he understands the depth of the interviewing I would find essential, why, he'll shy away from it, or become fractious at the thought of penetrating at the memories in his mind to the degree it would be essential for a proper book of this kind, at least one that I would do. Perhaps it's not possible for us to do it together, but I have to try to at least get started.

But that, unfortunately, seems to be as far as it went. Rinzler may have returned to his plan of writing a biography after Bill died.[41]

That fall in 1982, Bill met Kathy Chiavola [Key-avo-la], a thirty-year-old Chicago-born singer who was raised in Kansas City, Missouri, and had recently come to Nashville after studying classical singing at Oberlin College and Indiana University. New to bluegrass, she taught herself to play electric bass and was working with the newly formed Doug Dillard Band. One Saturday night, she was filling in with Hubert Davis's band when John Hartford brought Bill to the club and introduced her to him. Bill complimented her singing and said he was looking for "a lady singer." He wanted to hear her recordings and asked her to meet him the next night at a Shoney's restaurant on Dickerson Road. "I'd heard about his reputation," she said, "so I figured there was 'a clincher.' But I thought maybe he *is* serious."

> So, we met at Shoney's and went out to his Cadillac with my tapes in the parking lot. He listened and said, "You've got a fine voice; it's a true voice" (which I think meant I sang in tune). Then we sang six or seven of his songs and it sounded good! So he asked, "How much money would you have to have?" I picked an outrageous sum—twenty thousand dollars. He said, "That won't be no problem." Then I mentioned the added expense of an extra room, saying I couldn't sleep with the band. He said, "No, you couldn't very well do that." Then he said, "What would you do if I was to learn to care for you?" I said, "Mr. Monroe, I couldn't do that. I don't mix my personal life with my business." And he said, "Well, I guess you're not the girl I'm looking for." I said, "I guess I'm not." He said, "I wish you'd change your mind." I said, "No, I'm not gonna change my mind."

Thereafter, Bill called a few times, again saying he wished she'd change her mind; eventually, he stopped talking to her whenever they were at the same Nashville nightspot. Unhappy with this, Chiavola soon confronted him at the Monroe Talent office and, on the spur of the moment, suggested they bow their heads and pray on the matter. "I don't know what I said," she said, "but when heads came back up, I was his best friend in the world."[42]

On November 19, Bill and the band played in the Chicago suburb of Evanston, Illinois, and were visited that night by Evanston resident Kenneth Burns, better known as "Jethro," the mandolin-playing half of the famous Homer and Jethro comedy team (that had ended with the passing of Henry "Homer" Haynes in 1971). Invited onstage, Burns told the audience, "For a long time I've heard people say, 'Bill and Jethro really have a feud going.' Heck, I just wish I was that important." Then they picked "Roanoke" together, and when it ended, Burns (then sixty-two) quipped, "That's a little hard to do when you're touching 39." Later that night, he assured *Chicago Tribune* reporter Jack Hurst there never was a feud: "That was one of those things that everybody was in on except me and Bill." This may have inspired Burns to write "'Cept Old Bill," a song he recorded a few months later with fellow mandolinist Red Rector.

> The folks outside of Tennessee, they never even heard of old Red and me
> And the chances are, they prob'ly never will.
> I'm a mandolin-pickin' son of a gun and old Red Rector's number one
> And we can beat 'em all a-pickin', 'cept old Bill.[43]

Bill would soon be interacting with other country music stars. Reportedly, when Jim Foglesong took over as head of MCA Nashville in 1979, he was "distressed" with Bill's sagging album sales. So, word came down from above that Bill needed to tap into the contemporary country music field. Thus, *Bill Monroe and Friends*, an album (mainly) of Bill redoing songs he'd already recorded, with popular country music performers of the day. One-song sessions began in December 1982 at the Burns Station Sound Studio (partly owned by producer Walter Haynes) in Burns, Tennessee, about thirty miles west of Nashville, with Mel Tillis, the Gatlin Brothers, and new *Grand Ole Opry* member Ricky Skaggs. Sessions continued in January and February 1983, with John Hartford, Waylon Jennings, Johnny Cash, the Oak Ridge Boys, and Willie Nelson.[44]

Meanwhile, back in Ohio County, Kentucky: although the 1980 feasibility study nixed a bluegrass museum, it endorsed an annual Bill Monroe festival. So, to prepare for such a county-sponsored event (regardless of the lack of success at Bill's Musicland Park), the county's judge-executive, C. B. Embry Jr., issued a proclamation on January 24, 1983, honoring Bill and declaring "that Ohio County be proclaimed the Bluegrass Music Capitol [*sic*] of the World."[45]

The Death of Bessie Lee Mauldin

By then, Bessie Lee Mauldin had left the Nashville area, due to poor health, and moved back to Norwood, North Carolina, to be cared for by her family. She died there "of heart trouble" at age sixty-two on February 8, 1983.[46]

Significant changes had come to the business of entertainment in Nashville. In 1981 the National Life and Accident Insurance Company sold its television station, WSM-TV, to Gillett Broadcasting of Wausau, Wisconsin. In 1982 National Life sold the rest of its holdings, including the *Grand Ole Opry* and Opryland USA, to American General Corporation of Houston, Texas. In 1983 the $40 million that National Life made from the sale of WSM-TV reportedly went to help finance a cable TV venture, The Nashville Network (TNN). It debuted on March 7, 1983, with a "coast-to-coast party" hosted by Ralph Emery that included Emmylou Harris singing a couple of songs with Bill and the Blue Grass Boys via satellite from the set of *Austin City Limits*. (The Gaylord Entertainment Company of Oklahoma, which already owned *Hee Haw*, would acquire the *Grand Ole Opry*, Opryland USA, and TNN in July 1983.)[47]

On April Fool's Day, Bill left the United States for his sixth trip across the Atlantic, taking him to Wembley (April 2), Ireland (Cork, April 3; Belfast, April 5–6), Germany (Essen, April 8; Frankfort, April 9), and ending with his first visit to Switzerland (Zurich, April 10). Returning to Burns, Tennessee, on April 20, Bill recorded "Kentucky Waltz" with Emmylou Harris for *Bill Monroe and Friends*. Then, near the end of April, Bill served as grand marshal of the Pegasus Parade in Louisville, Kentucky, one of several annual events leading up to the Kentucky Derby. It appears to have been an attempt by city officials to court Bill's endorsement of a bluegrass museum in Louisville.[48]

The last session for *Bill Monroe and Friends* was held on May 4 with Bill and Barbara Mandrell singing "My Rose of Old Kentucky," the eleventh "classic band" song rerecorded. Originally due out on June 1, 1983, the album would not be released until January 12, 1984. It was Walter Haynes's last as Bill's producer. (Probably due to the expense involved in making the album, Bill would not record for MCA in 1984.)[49]

DeFord Bailey, star of Bill's tent shows in the 1940s, died in July 1982, and in June 1983, Bill was asked by Bailey's biographer, David C. Morton, to help dedicate his tombstone. On Wednesday, June 23, Bill, Roy Acuff, several *Opry* old-timers, WSM executives, state and local government officials, and Bailey's large family gathered at Greenwood, Nashville's black cemetery on the near-east side of town. Morton recalled that after the invocation, Bill played Bailey's "Evening Prayer Blues," then said, "DeFord was the best harmonica player, when it came to playing the blues, of any man, I thought, that ever lived."[50]

By the weekend of June 25, Bill was in Colorado, appearing with the New Grass Revival and playing for "hippies" at the tenth annual Telluride Bluegrass Festival. Clearly, the animosities of the 1970s had lessened. As he'd already told an interviewer:

> Well, now, you know yourself that bluegrass is different people playing it. They're going to play it their own way, the way they think it should be. If they want to

put blues in it or jazz it up like that, or however they want to go, people will still know that it is a copy off of bluegrass music.

The weather in Colorado that weekend was cold and rainy, but when the sunshine suddenly appeared during a gospel set by Bill and the band, he reportedly told the crowd, "That's the way the Lord wanted it to be."[51]

The Trip to Israel

By mid-June 1983, the time was drawing near for a "Tour to Israel," featuring Mac Wiseman and Bill. Arranged by Reverend Jimmie Snow, son of Hank and host of "Grand Ole Gospel Time," the *Friday Night Opry*'s new last segment, the tour had been advertised in *Bluegrass Unlimited* since April— "You will be [Wiseman and Bill's] special guest at two great bluegrass music concerts . . . ten full days [July 17 to 26, 1983] of travel and sightseeing and tickets to the concerts." With less than three weeks to go, it had become clear that the price was too high for most bluegrass fans ($1,596 first class, $1,796 deluxe)—only a handful had signed up, and not enough money was available to pay the entertainers. With arrangements already made, Wiseman and Bill were offered all-expense-paid trips if they would forego their pay and go anyway. Wiseman backed out, but Bill, eager to be baptized in the Jordan River, convinced the Blue Grass Boys to go with him, even though they wouldn't be paid either. Accompanying Bill on the trip, and making her debut as "a lady singer" with the band, was Dee Dee Prestige.[52]

Born Deloris Bacon in Brainerd, Minnesota, in 1944, she, like Bill, was the youngest of eight children. She married Dennis Prestidge in 1961, and they had five children before divorcing in 1976. A talent scout paid for her first record, a single released in 1964 for Gold Standard Records, one of many Nashville labels catering to hopefuls. She remarried in 1978 and moved to Nashville to pursue her career (divorcing again in 1982). Her first album, *Dee Dee Prestige Sings Country with Love*, was released by Look Records in 1980, produced by an old friend of Bill's, Hillous Butram, one of the original Drifting Cowboys, who also played on the album. A lifelong Bill Monroe fan, the "raven-haired" Prestige recalled that when she met him in 1983, backstage at the *Opry*, he asked if she thought he should do all gospel music in the Holy Land. "I said, 'Oh, no, Bill. All of your songs are spiritual and they would love them all, and I betcha they would really love "Jerusalem Ridge."'"[53]

The two concerts in Israel, one at Tiberias, on the banks of the Sea of Galilee, and the other at Tel Aviv, in the Hilton Hotel, came early and late in the tour. The rest of the time was spent traveling, musicians and tourists together in one small bus, seeing the sights. "It was cool to see things from the Bible that I'd read about my whole life," Williams said. Everyone watched as Rev. Snow immersed Bill in the River of Jordan, "no bigger than an average creek around home," according to Williams. Hembree recalled the scene at the airport in Nashville after it was all over: "When we got back, Bill shook the hand of everyone in the band and said, 'Boys, you never done no one a bigger favor than this.' 'That's for goddamn sure,' said Baker, [who] then stalked off."[54]

There were barely two days before they were due at "Ohio County's first Bill Monroe Bluegrass Festival," inspired by a feasibility study, with Bill and the band there on Saturday, July 30. Interviewed by local press shortly after he arrived at Ohio County Park, and probably tired, Bill openly expressed his frustration with the lack of success of his own festivals: "It's hard to make it in your home town. Ohio County has never done what they should have for this music and they've never tried to help me get anything started here." His remarks would appear the following week with the headline "Monroe unhappy with Ohio County."

The festival was judged a success, however, by then–Ohio County Park director David Johnston, who told a reporter it was "less than $5,000 in the red." The number of attendees on Saturday was estimated to be two thousand, the best of the three-day event. (Later that Saturday, Bill and the band, with son James and grandson "Jimbo" Monroe, now nineteen, dedicated the tombstone of Birch Monroe, who had died in May 1982. They sang several songs, including "Precious Memories" and "A Beautiful Life.")[55]

The eleventh and last of Bill's Homecoming festivals was held six weeks later, on the weekend of September 9 at Monroe's Musicland Park. The talent lineup included familiar names at Bill's festivals: Wilma Lee Cooper, Clyde Moody, Bobby Smith's Boys from Shiloh, the Sullivan Family, and a new name, Dee Dee Prestige, as she began to travel full time with Bill. Attendance at the festival was probably poor, as usual, and after Bill's remarks in the *Ohio County Times-News*, it wasn't likely to improve.[56]

Doug Hutchens held his second birthday salute to Bill at Mason's Restaurant in Goodlettsville, on the evening of Bill's seventy-second birthday (Monday, September 13, 1983). "I thought they were planning a dinner," Bill said. "And I expected a present or something, nothing like this." "This" included 180 friends, fans, and musicians, among them fourteen former Blue Grass Boys. Bill was presented with two hats this time, a white Stetson from the owners of Mason's and another custom-made one by Randy Priest. Bill could be heard shouting, "Oh, boy! Oh, boy!" when he saw his next gift—a custom-made saddle by Nick Boone (who helped make Bill's mandolin case). He also received another birthday card containing more than sixty birthday greetings.[57]

A week later, former fill-in lead singer-guitarist Garry Thurmond of Alabama, and his band, the Warrior River Boys, came to Nashville on September 21 to record a tribute album to Bill, and Thurmond invited Bill to come to the session at the Hilltop Studio. The band's young mandolinist, David Davis, Cleo Davis's nephew, hadn't been picking long and didn't feel ready for the session's first tune, "Roanoke." After it was recorded, Davis recalled, Bill approached him.

> He said, "Can I show you a few notes that you're not puttin' in there?" And I said, "Certainly." I knew the notes I wasn't putting in there. I knew his stuff inside and out—I just couldn't do it. He took my mandolin and he played the break and then he handed it back to me and said, "Now, do you think you can do that?" I said, "Well, I'll try." So, I played it again, just like I did a few minutes before, and he said, "That's fine."

But Davis had gotten the message. "I remember thinking, I *will* show you," he said. He worked hard to improve his picking and returned to overdub a better break about a month later.[58]

The Third "Big Plan"

Bill and James's third Big Plan began to take form about that time (October 1983). After lots of talk about a bluegrass museum in Kentucky, Bill and James decided to create one in Nashville, with the added attraction of a Bluegrass Hall of Fame (reminiscent of 1973's "Daddy Bluegrass"). Father and son formed a corporation, bought four acres of land on Music Valley Drive, near Opryland, for $87,500 per acre ($350 thousand), and planned to extensively remodel a restaurant already on the property into a museum. Reportedly, they also envisioned a walkway taking visitors up a nearby hillside to a bronze statue of Bill.[59]

One of the last showdates of 1983 was in New York City's Greenwich Village at the Bottom Line. The second set on that Thursday night, December

15, was recorded and would be broadcast in January 1984 as part of an FM-radio series called the *Silver Eagle Cross Country Music Show*.[60]

On Saturday, January 28, 1984, Bill was the first inductee named to "The Preservation Hall of Greats" by the Society for the Preservation of Bluegrass Music in America (SPBGMA, a fan-based organization founded in Missouri in 1974) at its first convention held in Nashville.[61]

At some uncertain time in the early months of 1984, Bill overdubbed a mandolin break on Ricky Skaggs's jazzed-up rendition of "Wheel Hoss" for CBS-Epic Records. Rosenberg and Wolfe, able to provide dates for most of Bill's studio recordings in *The Music of Bill Monroe*, noted, "It is not known when Monroe did his overdub."[62]

The Bill Monroe Museum and Bluegrass Hall of Fame, advertised as opening in April 1984, actually opened in late May, with its grand opening on June 4 (coinciding with the new gathering of fans in Nashville: "Fan Fair"). It would be managed by Jim Bessire, the Brown County, Indiana, native who played bass in the Jamboree house band and served as road manager for James, and co-managed by Dee Dee Prestige. The museum's stylish glass-and-brick exterior, with a large parking lot, looked like a potentially successful tourist attraction, but the location at 2620 Music Valley Drive, about a mile from Opryland, seemed a little too remote for most country music fans. (Later called the Bill Monroe Bluegrass Hall of Fame and Museum, it closed in late 1985, shortly after its ticket booth was robbed. The museum's contents were relocated in June 1986 to a building in the Music Village entertainment complex ["Twitty City"] in Hendersonville, Tennessee, then moved to Monroe's Festival Campground in Bean Blossom, Indiana, in 1992.)[63]

Mark Hembree left the band after the eighteenth annual Bean Blossom festival (held June 13–17, 1984). Former Blue Grass Boy Clarence "Tater" Tate, then fiddling with Wilma Lee Cooper, was playing at the festival with her when he heard Hembree was leaving. Kenny Baker's son Johnnie Baker filled in with the band briefly, but Bill hired Tate to play bass, starting the weekend of June 29.[64]

The Death of Carolyn Monroe

In July, James's fourth album, *Satisfied Mind* (Atteiram), recorded back in 1978, was released, with uncredited performances by Bill. Near the end of the month, Dee Dee Prestige quit her job at the museum due to phlebitis, which she said she developed while working there. Her involvement with

Bill cooled and she stopped performing. Then, on Monday, July 30, Bill's ex-wife Carolyn died at age seventy-one.[65]

If there was grieving on Bill's part, there was, as usual, little time for it. He was due in Milwaukee, Wisconsin, on August 1; Flint, Michigan, on the 3rd; and Hartford, Kentucky, for the second annual Bill Monroe Bluegrass Festival at Ohio County Park, on Saturday, August 4. At the latter, rain kept attendance down to the same as the previous year, in spite of a lineup that included Ralph Stanley, Jimmy Martin, and a popular new band, the Boys from Indiana. Bill, interviewed again by the local paper, couldn't resist giving Ohio County another zinger: "I've always been in hopes for the music to grow here, but it's been more accepted in foreign countries and in the North than it has right here at home." Before the end of August, the last of the classic band's twenty-eight recordings were finally reissued on LP: "Shining Path" and "Along About Daybreak" were released on the *Bill Monroe: Columbia Historic Edition* album. It had taken nearly forty years for all twenty-eight to be reissued.[66]

The *Grand Ole Opry*'s great triumvirate of the twentieth century—Acuff, Monroe, and Tubb—came to an end when Ernest Dale Tubb died on Thursday, September 6, 1984, at age seventy. At the funeral on September 10, Bill sang "Swing Low, Sweet Chariot" and served as a pallbearer with ten others, including Carl Butler, Porter Wagoner, and Hank Williams Jr.[67]

The new leaders of the Bill Monroe International Fan Club hailed from North Carolina: President Hazel "Libby" Ramsey from Asheville and Vice President Mary Ruth Stamey from nearby Brevard. Their twenty-five-page, mimeographed Newsletter #1 of mid-September 1984 was filled with letters telling of recent sightings of Bill. Member Bonnie Powell of Falls Church, Virginia, saw the band at the Birchmere nightclub in Alexandria. Bill was having sinus problems and was unable to sing, so he asked John Duffey to sing for him. "John was very cooperative," she wrote, "and kept asking if there was anything else he could do. Bill said, 'No, he didn't want him to do too much because he was only planning to pay him a dollar, and he was afraid he would get to expecting more.'"[68]

Baker Quits

By then, the friendship of Bill and Kenny Baker had lasted a long time, and their expression of it onstage always made a live performance more special. There were problems, of course, as in any long-standing relationship. One, according to Baker, was Bill's unwillingness to give him a schedule of upcoming showdates. Baker said it was "somethin' he'd never do, for some cause" (possibly Bill's way of controlling the fiercely independent fiddler). In the past, he'd "gone on strike" a few times, leaving Bill without a fiddler, because he hadn't been given an itinerary. In September, Baker said he found out the band was going to Japan, and he asked Bill for a list of the showdates, telling him his oldest brother was terminally ill and he needed to know where he was going to be, in case he passed away. When an itinerary wasn't forthcoming, he said he told Bill he would not go to Japan without one. On Friday, October 12, 1984, at the "World Series of Bluegrass" festival in Jemison, Alabama, Bill still had not given Baker an itinerary, and the trip to Japan was the following week.

> So I went down and I played the first show [Baker said], and they was gonna pull out, drivin' to California to make that Japan trip. And they put him on early for his second show, and we hit the stage. And my itinerary had not been mentioned to me. So, I'd already made up my mind, if I didn't get it during this second show, I's just gonna go and leave Bill there. I didn't care. I had transportation waitin' on me [a friend willing to take him home].
>
> So, we got onstage . . . and the people kept hollerin', wantin' to hear "Jerusalem Ridge." Bill, he steps up to the mike [and] he said, "Why, I'm sure Kenny wants to play 'Jerusalem Ridge' for you good folks, don't you, Kenny?" And I was mad as hell, I'll just tell you the truth . . . I held my fiddle out to the audience and, right over the mike, I said, "I don't care a damn thing about it," and I turned around and walked off the stage.

After the show ended, Bill tried to make amends—he delegated Wayne Lewis to take an itinerary to Baker. "They brought me an itinerary three times," Baker said, "and the last time they brought it to me, I said, 'By God, you can take it back to him. I don't need it. I've quit.'"

It was the end of a wonderful musical partnership. The man Bill often introduced as "the greatest fiddler in bluegrass" would never play onstage with him again, except for a brief guest appearance many years later, when they finally "buried the hatchet."[69]

The next day, October 13, *Billboard* rated Ricky Skaggs's recording of Bill's "Uncle Pen" at number 1 in its country singles chart (where it would remain for a week). It was the eighth number 1 for Skaggs.[70]

The trip to Japan, Bill's fourth, went on as scheduled. Tater Tate fiddled and fill-ins played bass. Fiddler Jerry Rivers, another of the original Drifting Cowboys, was then an agent with Buddy Lee and served as road manager, occasionally twinning with Tate. En route, Bill and the band played a show in Honolulu, Hawaii. A band there, the Harvest Time Bluegrass Band, greeted the group at the airport on Thursday, October 18, and its banjo player, Paul Sato, played bass that night. The next evening, Bill and the band arrived in Japan. Saburo "Sab" Watanabe (banjoist with the Bluegrass 45, the first Japanese band to play in the United States in 1971) arranged for Tatsuya Imai to play bass on five of the six shows (October 20–24), and Watanabe himself played bass on the sixth (October 27). The group traveled by train to three different cities, and Imai remembered one incident at a station in particular: "When we got off the train and I was walking with my big bass and bag on the platform, Bill gently smiled and took my bag."[71]

Shortly after Bill and the band left the United States, Betty McInturff, secretary at the Monroe Talent office since 1981, called teenaged fiddler Randy Franks. The Georgia native first met Bill at the Cathedral Caverns in 1982 and had come to Nashville in 1984 to help with the museum. Asked by Wayne Lewis, shortly after Baker quit, if he could go to Japan, Franks told him he didn't have a passport. So, Franks would take his first airplane ride to Yakima, Washington, to rendezvous with Bill and the band on October 30. Bill, uncertain that Franks knew the repertoire well enough, told him he would start out playing "the big fiddle." Tate took him backstage, put adhesive tape on his fingers, showed him how to play bass in the usual keys, and advised him to "smile a lot."

Thereafter, for five more shows in the West (October 31–November 4) and a night in Ann Arbor, Michigan (November 7), Franks played bass, and occasionally fiddle. "When Bill wanted to kick up his heels, I usually played 'Liberty,'" he said. Bill knew he was due to return to Georgia State University, so when they returned to Nashville, "he thanked me for working with him and I went on my merry way back home."[72]

The day before Ann Arbor, on November 6, the then-oldest man ever elected president was reelected. Incumbents Ronald Reagan and Vice President George H. W. Bush overwhelmingly defeated Democratic challengers Walter Mondale, a former vice president, and Rep. Geraldine Ferraro, the first woman from a major political party to run for vice president.[73]

Fiddler Dale Morris was backstage at the *Opry* on November 17, waiting to play with someone (he doesn't remember whom), possibly Ray Price, whom he'd worked with since 1981. He'd also been playing with James Monroe lately, and was approached by Bill that night, asking if he would like to work for him. Morris, a native of the Ft. Worth, Texas, area, took the job, initially intimidated by following "the greatest fiddler in bluegrass." So he was glad when Bill expressed approval of his fiddling. "Bill didn't really want me to play just like Kenny," Morris said. "He liked the Texas style that I did."[74]

A slow January 1985 may have been the time of the filming of Ricky Skaggs's "Country Boy" music video. Then a new marketing tool, the video was used to promote his *Country Boy* album (Columbia-Epic) and "Country Boy" single (Epic), later a number 1 hit. Filmed in a cold New York City, the shooting schedule was intense, according to Bill: "We were there twenty-four hours, and out of the twenty-four hours, I worked twenty-two." Skaggs commented in his *Kentucky Traveler* autobiography that Bill "stole the show."

> I mean, I had fun hamming it up, but the real star was Mr. Monroe as Uncle Pen. He laid down his Kentucky backstep like a pro, and it really impressed those break dancers. They said, "Man, that is a cold-blooded step!" Same with the female dancers on the set. They were classically trained, but Mr. Bill really showed 'em a thing or two! In between the filming, he was throwing 'em over his shoulder and dancing up a storm with these gals. They loved him![75]

In February 1985, Skaggs's rendition of "Wheel Hoss" was awarded a Grammy by the National Academy of Recording Arts and Sciences (NARAS) for "Best Country Instrumental Performance" of 1984. Skaggs gave his award to Bill. "I gave my Grammy to Mr. Monroe because he hadn't yet won a Grammy, and I thought he deserved one," he told autobiography ghostwriter Eddie Dean.[76]

Bill and the Blue Grass Boys returned to the road in February. Dale Morris, a former member of the Sons of the Pioneers, remembered an incident he observed in a truck-stop restaurant:

> Bill came in and a table full of people recognized him. They were telling how much they loved his music. He said, "I'll go out to the bus and get my mandolin and pick a few for you." And he sat there for an hour, entertaining those people. Other people I'd worked with would never have done something like that. It would be too far beneath them.

Morris left the band in mid-March 1985. He said he was unable to make an adequate living for his family: "I just had to give it up and I hated it [having to leave]."[77]

His successor was Glen Duncan of Indiana, inspired to fiddle by Baker back in 1971. By March 1985, he was fiddling with the Kendalls, the popular father-daughter country duo, when Kathy Chiavola called to tell him about the opening. (When she was a student at Indiana University, they'd played together in a short-lived band.) Chiavola and Bill were at a jam session at luthier George Chestnut's house when Bill said he was in need of a fiddler, so she called Duncan. When he wondered how to contact Bill, she told him, "He's standing right here!" Bill arranged to meet them at Mason's Restaurant the next day and, after lunch, they played together at the Monroe office. One tune was enough, according to Chiavola.[78]

Bill Marries Della Streeter

Trips to Wembley and Japan in April and May 1985 were cancelled at the last minute, so Bill and the band mainly played the *Opry* during this time. The slow schedule encouraged seventy-three-year-old Bill and forty-four-year-old Della Streeter to take full advantage of the lull and proceed quickly with their plans—to get married.

Back in 1972, Streeter and first husband Ken, former fan club reps from Minnesota, had just moved to Nashville. She had been aware of Bill Monroe, country music star, since childhood, when her father booked him on shows in the 1950s. Their wedding, on Wednesday, April 24, 1985, was a very private affair. Only the Blue Grass Boys, their wives, Bill's children, Della's children (two teenaged daughters), and a few close friends attended the ceremony at the "Evangel Temple" of Holy Land tour organizer Rev. Jimmie Snow, across Dickerson Road from the Monroe Talent office. Afterward, guests followed Bill and Della's rented limo to the previously unannounced location of the reception, the Opryland Hotel.[79]

Meanwhile, Bill's new MCA producer, Georgia native Emory Gordy Jr., had listened to the *Friends* album and decided he needed "to get [Bill] back to being himself." A Monroe fan, Gordy suggested an album to Bill featuring bluegrass artists Bill had influenced, an idea that coincided with Bill's new Bluegrass Hall of Fame and Museum. Right after the wedding, they held sessions (May 2–June 17) to record remakes of some of Bill's best-known songs featuring Bluegrass Hall of Famers Bill chose in 1984 and 1985: the Osborne Brothers (with "I Hear a Sweet Voice Calling," the twelfth "classic band" song), Carl Story, the Country Gentlemen, Mac Wiseman, Jim and Jesse, the Seldom Scene (with "Remember the Cross," the thirteenth "classic band" song), Ralph Stanley, and Del McCoury. (Hall of Famers not participating: Lester Flatt and Reno and Smiley were deceased; Earl Scruggs was ill.)

Bill and the Blue Grass Boys recorded new material for the album on June 10 and 17, during and after the nineteenth annual Bean Blossom festival (June 7–16). Producer Gordy had heard Bill's "Let the Gates Swing Wide" on a *Friday Night Opry* broadcast when the autobiographical gospel song was new and only had one verse ("We'd go to church . . ."), and he immediately encouraged Bill to record it. Bill and Della wrote additional verses in the studio on Monday, June 10. On Monday, June 17, Duncan and guest fiddler Bobby Hicks worked up the twin fiddle harmonies for two tunes in the studio: "The Golden West," which Bill wrote during a visit to California to play his "Golden West" festival in 1974, then forgot and only recently remembered. Bill wrote "The Old Brown County Barn" three days before the session, just prior to the square dance in the Barn that followed the Sunset Jam on June 14. Duncan suggested the title, but said Bill preferred "The Old Brown County *Jamboree* Barn." (MCA chose the shorter title when it released the tune later.)

The resulting album, *Bill Monroe and Stars of the Bluegrass Hall of Fame*, features the first of Bill's recordings to use digital technology, then new to Nashville. The digital process begins with musicians recording each song or tune several times, aiming for the best take each time. All of the sounds they make are converted into a series of electronic "frames," as in a movie, with each frame assigned a number [digit] recorded on a multitrack digital recorder. Identified by its digits, a section of one take can then replace the same, but less desirable, section in another take, eventually creating a "perfect" recording with no noticeable sign of editing. The technology eliminated the need for overdubbing, but producer Gordy didn't like using overdubs anyway: "Having played bluegrass myself, I realized my primary job was capturing the special excitement of a true bluegrass experience. You can't do that with the clinical use of overdubs—you have to do it all in a single take, or you can do several takes in a row and combine the best parts of each performance later."[80]

A very busy July followed. Bill and the band traveled to thirteen states, from Oklahoma in the west to New Jersey in the east. On Sunday, July 28, at Sunset Park in eastern Pennsylvania, owner Lawrence Waltman presented Bill with a framed poster advertising his first appearance at the park thirty-nine years earlier, a five-day stand from Sunday, July 21, through Thursday, July 25, 1946, with Flatt, Scruggs, Watts, and Wise.[81]

The third annual Bill Monroe Bluegrass Festival, sponsored by Ohio County, Kentucky, was held from August 9 through 11, 1985. Bill was again the headliner, but the local paper didn't seek him out for comment. He would not appear at the fourth and last Bill Monroe Bluegrass Festival in 1986.[82]

"Bad Words"

After Bill's autumn festival at Bean Blossom (September 19–22), in the early morning of September 23, the bus carrying Bill and the band pulled into the Monroe Talent lot in Nashville, where they'd parked their cars. Duncan said when he woke up and looked out a bus window, something looked odd about Bill's black 1976 Cadillac Sedan Deville. Sure enough, someone had written all over it using orange spray paint, words so hateful, Duncan later refused to repeat them, but "You knew it was a woman who had written it," he said. Williams recalled "something like 'Dirty Old Man' or words to that effect." (Bill told a reporter from the *Tennessean* they were "bad words.") Duncan remembered Bill's reaction when he first saw it: "Bill wasn't mad—he was worried." And he noticed a decline in his well-being: "The minute the trouble started, Bill's health just went down like a flat tire."[83]

The Bill Monroe Bluegrass Hall of Fame and Museum was robbed in October, the cashier assaulted, and the day's receipts taken. It may have been due to the museum's out-of-the-way location, where there would have been few witnesses. A connection with the hate crimes in September and later was never verified.[84]

Bill's Mandolins Vandalized

Bill should have been on his guard, but he probably wasn't expecting anything worse. On Wednesday, November 13, he and Della left the cabin, he to go to the office and she to shop. When they returned in the early afternoon, something much worse was waiting. Someone had broken in, removed Bill's two F-5 mandolins from their cases, laid them in the fireplace, and pierced them repeatedly with a fireplace poker. And there was more, which Bill's longtime friend, Hazel Smith, described in her *Country Music* column: "Also damaged in the incident was a huge photograph of Monroe taken from the living room wall and poked through the face with the poker. Various awards and mementos also on the walls of his home were thrown into a pile with the other items and Monroe's name pried off each one."

Blake Williams, second-in-command on the road, was the first person Bill called: "He said, 'I can't believe anybody would have done this.' He said,

'I don't know what to do.' And I said, 'Well, for one thing, you need to get a box or sack and put every piece of the mandolins in it and sweep up the splinters. Salvage every piece you can.'" Following his directions, Bill and Della picked up hundreds of bits and pieces and put them into two black trash bags.

Bill and the band had to leave town the next day for shows in the Northeast. Before they left, Bill got a call from Charlie Derrington, a young luthier in the Research and Development Department of Gibson, then recently relocated to Nashville. He told Bill that Gibson would do its best to repair the mandolins and, before Bill left town, he brought him his own 1925 F-5 to play. While Bill was gone, old friend Bill Hawkins, then with the Sumner County Sheriff's Department, followed Bill's directions and took the shattered F-5s and trash bags to the Bank of Goodlettsville, where they were placed in a vault. When Bill returned, he gave the broken instruments to Derrington, and he and a team of craftsmen at Gibson began piecing them back together.

Publicly, Bill claimed he didn't know anything about who was responsible. On November 15, he told the crowd at the Nightstage club in Cambridge, Massachusetts, "Nobody knows who it was or anything about it. Bound to have been somebody who was really against me, but I don't know who it could've been." On December 1, in spite of all, Bill agreed to appear as Santa Claus, wearing a fluffy white beard and Saint Nick's tasseled hat over the crown of his Stetson, during the caroling and tree-lighting ceremonies at the Country Music Hall of Fame's "Country Christmas Celebration."[85]

Troubles returned a few weeks later when Bill's "Blue Grass Special" bus, parked in the lot of the Monroe Talent office, was broken into and a two-hundred-pound safe taken from it. Inside the safe, later found empty, were photographs and jewelry valued at ten thousand dollars, and three hundred dollars in cash. "You just never know what they might try next," Bill told the *Tennessean* on December 17. "I think there is more than one person involved in this and I hope the law catches them and they end up serving some time." He also said he might hire a bodyguard but didn't say he thought an attempt on his life was possible. However, Duncan recalled, "Bill was going out on the *Opry* stage wearing a bulletproof vest" (after a phone call, warning that someone was gunning for him).[86]

With the coming of 1986, tensions remained high over what "they might try next." "I remember it being scary on several different levels," Williams said. Wayne Lewis decided to take a vacation, and he and his wife went to Hawaii during the first full week of January. He arranged for Joe Stuart to fill in for him on the weekend of January 10, which included Friday and Saturday *Oprys* and the taping of Bill's second appearance on *Austin City Limits*, on Sunday, January 12.[87]

Tate and Stuart drove the recently burglarized bus the nearly nine hundred miles from Nashville to Austin as fast as they could, but the band arrived just before they were scheduled to play, and there was no time for a sound check (to adjust the levels of their microphones). Duncan remembered being surprised by Stuart as they were about to be introduced to the studio audience: "Joe leans over to me and says, 'Hey, Duncan—can you sing lead?' I said, 'Yeah, I guess. Why?' He said, 'I can't sing that high anymore. You're gonna have to sing lead on this show.' I said, 'Here?' He said, 'Yeah, I can't do it.' So, Bill's fiddler would sing lead on this nationally aired program (and Bill didn't show much reaction, Duncan added).

During their portion of the show (shared with Jim and Jesse and Ralph Stanley), Bill told the audience his lead singer had gone to (as he pronounced it) "Hi-wa-ya." Not missing a beat, Williams recalled, "Joe Stuart said, 'Fine, thank you.' And Bill just looked at him."

Both Duncan and Williams remembered Stuart's antics when Ralph Stanley joined Bill to sing "Can't You Hear Me Callin'?" A thirty-year veteran with Bill, Stuart was sure there was no subdominant (IV) chord in the chorus (as there may not have been originally) and he didn't hesitate to tell Tate, audibly, while the videotape was rolling, "That C ain't in there. Never was. Never will be."[88]

The "reign of terror" appeared to be over by February. Glen Duncan, citing requests by other artists to record sessions, played his last with Bill at the *Opry* on Valentine's Day weekend. He was replaced by fifty-two-year-old Kentuckian Art Stamper, best known for his work with the Stanleys and the Osbornes in the 1950s.[89]

Main Mandolin Returned

Bill's main mandolin (#73987) was returned to him on Tuesday, February 25, after fourteen weeks of painstaking work by Derrington and his team at Gibson. Surrounded by newsmen and photographers at Gibson's Nashville plant, Derrington handed the mandolin back to Bill, who held it in his arms as if giving it a bear hug. After picking "Wheel Hoss," backed by Chet Atkins on guitar (with Derrington telling him the chord changes), Bill reportedly said, "It sounds good! It's awful close to the old sound! Time will take it back to what it was." That weekend on the *Friday Night Opry*, Bill used it to play a new tune he'd written, "The Lloyd Loar," its title provided by Derrington.[90]

Art Stamper's tenure with Bill was very brief, lasting only about four weeks. Williams remembered him backstage at a festival in March, casually playing along with whomever was onstage, and Bill telling him, "You need to keep your mind on *our* music." Stamper's response, according to Williams: "Bill, I just don't think this is gonna work out. I don't want to mess up our friendship. I'll just give my notice and you can get somebody else." During the show that followed, Bill mocked Stamper's habit of stamping his right foot to keep time by stamping his own right foot. But Stamper insisted later that he and Bill remained friends. "Bill was a hard man to understand," he said. "I think it took me the whole time he was living to understand him."[91]

Tater Tate switched to fiddle on the following (March 14) weekend at the *Opry*, but for four recording sessions scheduled on Monday and Tuesday, March 17 and 18, Bill again called on Buddy Spicher to substitute on fiddle, and Tate played bass. Before Duncan left the band, he gave producer Gordy a tape of tunes Bill wrote during 1985, and from it Spicher learned the first of two tunes recorded at the afternoon session on the 17th, "Dancin' in Branson" (MCA titled it "Dancin' in Brancin'"). Duncan recalled it was written on a night off (October 18, 1985) before a show in the Missouri showplace and that he suggested the title to Bill. (Then Bill said, "How about we call it 'Dancin' in Branson?" to which Duncan said, "Oh, that's a great idea!") Also recorded on the afternoon of the 17th was "Jekyll Island," featuring Bill's recently restored mandolin. A first cousin of 1981's "Old Ebenezer Scrooge," the tune may have been written to commemorate Bill's first appearance at the Georgia island's indoor festival in 1983. At the evening session on the 17th, Bill recorded two new vocal solos, "Stay Away from Me," which he'd written but hesitated to record because he thought it was "too country," and "Music Valley Waltz," written with John Hartford, using the name of the area where the then-closed Hall of Fame and Museum was located. For this session and the next two, Spicher teamed with Bobby Hicks on second fiddle for the first time.[92]

The afternoon session on the 18th was completely unsuccessful, beginning with the complex first number, "Texas Lone Star," another tune on Duncan's tape. Written at Rockefeller's nightclub in Houston, its name came from the local band opening on June 1, 1985 (Larry Brockett, bass; Paul Brummer, guitar; Don Eggers, Dobro; Chris Hirsch, banjo). According to Hirsch, "Brockett and I were standing backstage listening to [Bill and] the band playing a new instrumental tune. Bill turned to us and asked, 'What's the name?' Larry thought he was asking what the name of our band was, so he told him 'Lonestar.' Bill said, 'Texas Lone Star—I like it.'" The second number seems to have failed due to a general lack of enthusiasm by all concerned, except Bill. He had written a new love song, "I Love the State of Virginia," and wanted to record it. Its chorus:

> Oh, I love the state of Virginia.
> On the old Blue Ridge I have roamed.
> Say yes to me, my darling.
> We'll make the Shenandoah Valley our home.

It would never see the light of day. (A song with a similar melody, "The Days Gone By," would be recorded in 1988.)[93]

The evening session on the 18th was a success, beginning with a revisit to the gospel quartet "Angels, Rock Me to Sleep," which Bill first recorded almost exactly thirty-five years earlier (March 17, 1951). And the session ended with "The Long Bow," another tune from Duncan's tape, similar to the traditional "Lost John."

That spring in 1986, bluegrass music first appeared on compact disc (CD), and MCA Records announced it was going to release several of Bill's "classic" LPs in the new format. It never did.[94]

Tate returned to the fiddle after the sessions but insisted it only be until they could find another fiddler (openly expressing dissatisfaction with his ability to play Bill's newer material). Called to fill in on bass was fifty-seven-year-old Johnny Montgomery, a former member of Lester Flatt's Nashville Grass, like Tate and Williams. He had filled in with Bill in the 1950s: "He used to be kindly aggravating in his younger days; he'd cut you pretty sharp. But when I went back with him, he had changed a whole lot. Me and him got along just fine, 'cause I'd pick at him on that bus." Montgomery would be hired full-time when another fiddler couldn't be found.[95]

In May 1986 Wayne Lewis decided to leave the band after ten years, the longest tenure of any of Bill's lead singers. Bill called Tom Ewing, who formally auditioned on Monday, May 18. The next day, he was elected to drive Bill to Bean Blossom in the 1976 Cadillac defaced in 1985, now painted baby blue, to meet with county officials to discuss improvements needed at the park. During the return trip, Bill took the classified section of the newspaper he was reading, turned it upside down, and wrote a song on it. (Its melody was similar to "I Love the State of Virginia" and to "The Days Gone By," recorded in 1988.)[96]

The Deaths of Cleo Davis and Art Wooten

Cleo Davis, the first of Bill's Blue Grass Boys, died of cancer at age sixty-seven on Thursday, July 17, 1986. On that day, Bill played a show at Music Village in Hendersonville, Tennessee (to promote the relocation of his museum there), then traveled to Missouri for a festival on the 18th. He was back at Music Village on the 19th, where he learned of Davis's passing, but there was no time to attend the funeral in Florida—he was due in New Mexico in two days. But on July 26, after a show at Winston-Salem, North Carolina, Bill went out of his way to visit another of his original Blue Grass Boys, eighty-year-old Art Wooten, hospitalized with emphysema and heart disease. Wooten died less than three months later, on October 6, 1986.[97]

By August 1986, MCA producer Gordy had nine selections "in the can" for Bill's next album: three from sessions in May and June 1985 and six recorded in March 1986. One more would make MCA's usual ten, and Gordy hoped that one of three religious songs Bill and the band (Ewing, Tate, Williams, Montgomery, with Buddy Spicher) would record on Tuesday, August 19, would be it. The first, "God Holds the Future in His Hands," was originally recorded by the Riley Quartette in 1927, then the Monroe Brothers in 1936. This attempt, sung in four-part harmony throughout, suffered from a lack of rehearsal and was judged unworthy of release. Second was "Farther On," recorded by the Carter Family for Decca in 1938. Bill had attempted to cut it back in 1975, without luck. Producer Gordy recalled that this time, Bill wanted the *Opry*'s Carole Lee Singers to sing harmonies (as on the *Opry*), which was rejected, possibly influencing its ultimate shelving. Third was "The Old Crossroads," originally recorded by the classic bluegrass band in 1947 as "The Old Cross Road" (and the fourteenth song of theirs to be rerecorded). The current band had played it often, so it was the easiest of the three to record, and was the one chosen to complete Bill's album (*Bluegrass '87*). But Bill would not record for MCA again until January 1988.[98]

Three days after the session, Bill and the band were in Owensboro, Kentucky, at the second "Bluegrass with Class," now sponsored in partnership with the International Bluegrass Music Association (IBMA)—its "first-ever bluegrass industry trade show," held during the festival.[99]

"Carlton Haney's 22nd Annual Original Blue Grass Music Festival" began on August 28 in Camp Springs, North Carolina. It was not the twenty-second consecutive year Haney promoted the Labor Day weekend festival—for a few years, a partnership ran it for him—but this year, he was back in charge. One of those drawn to it was fiddler Mark Squires, age twenty-seven, from South Carolina. On Saturday he filled in successfully with a local band, and Haney arranged for him to back up Jim Eanes on Sunday. After Haney told him Bill Monroe was looking for a fiddle player, Squires found out Bill would be at the Kentucky Fried Chicken Festival in Louisville the next weekend and he decided to go there.[100]

As Bill's seventy-fifth birthday drew near, two national magazines featured articles about him. The September 1, 1986, issue of *People* devoted five pages to a cleverly worded review of Bill's career, with observations on current events by senior writer Roger Wolmuth. He and legendary photographer David Gahr had visited Bill at the *Opry*, Bean Blossom, and the Goodletts-ville farm in June, and when the article was published, Gahr's photos nearly stole the show. In one, a smiling Della hugs "her hubby" of one year, and in its caption she says, "Sometimes he'll say something that sounds so stern, but in his heart he's really teasing." The September *Frets* put Bill on its cover, reenacting the "bear hug" he gave #73987 back in February. Inside were another review of his career, a separate feature on #73987, five mandolin solos in standard notation and tablature, a transcription of "Happy Birthday Bill Monroe" (a tune by David Grisman), and a July interview. About playing the mandolin (in bluegrass), Bill stated emphatically, "Everybody's got a right to play it the way they want to play it."[101]

The pre-birthday hoopla continued at the Kentucky Fried Chicken Festival on Saturday, September 6. The KFC Corporation presented Bill with a huge cake decorated with sparklers (which, Bill learned, couldn't be blown out like candles). That day was the last for Johnny Montgomery, who needed to work full time on his dairy farm. With Tate ready to reclaim the job playing bass, Bill was feeling some pressure to find a fiddler, and at that point, Squires approached him at the festival. Squires told him Haney encouraged him to ask for the job, and he said later that he didn't detect a negative reaction from Bill. He auditioned in Nashville on September 11, and Bill, in a hurry, only asked him to play a few standards. Squires had to give his employer in South Carolina notice and couldn't start until the end of September, so Tate continued to fiddle and several bassists (Kenny Jones, Roy Huskey Jr., and Forrest Rose) filled in.[102]

Bill was supposed to spend his birthday (Saturday, September 13) at the fourteenth semi-annual Gettysburg Bluegrass Camporee in Pennsylvania, but first, he had to get there. After playing the *Friday Night Opry*, Bill and the band boarded the bus (a 1978 Silver Eagle, the last Blue Grass Special Bill would own), planning to arrive at the festival the next morning. But the bus had a flat tire in the middle of the night in the middle of nowhere, and the only way to get to the festival on time was to charter a private plane. So, shortly after daylight, a "puddle-jumper" carried the band across the Appalachian Mountains to York, Pennsylvania, where festival promoter Joe Cornett met them, then drove the group some thirty miles west to the Camporee. (Ewing, like David Deese back in 1962, recalls thinking, "Damn, this is the big time!") At the festival, Bill received a letter dated September 10, 1986:

> Dear Bill,
>
> I am delighted to send my heartfelt congratulations as you celebrate your 75th birthday and the 50th anniversary of your first recording, "Mule Skinner Blues." Little did you know that this recording would be the start of a truly American art form, Bluegrass Music.
>
> Since that time, you have thrilled Americans with your music and you have inspired countless others to follow in your footsteps down this path of traditional American music. Today, I join with your many friends and fans in saying thank you for all you have given us.
>
> Nancy and I send our best wishes for continued success. God bless you.
>
> > Sincerely,
> >
> > Ronald Reagan

The president was wrong about the anniversary of "Mule Skinner Blues," but he was certainly correct about its effect. Bill later proudly presented a copy of this letter to each of his Blue Grass Boys, advising them to frame it and hang it in their living rooms. The California band High Country was playing at the Gettysburg festival, and its fiddler, Jack Leiderman, auditioned for Bill (who told him Squires had already been hired). Ewing recalls Bill advising him, "Your right hand and your left hand have to work together, and you have to be thinking in between them."[103]

Yet another fiddler auditioned before Squires started. Billy Joe Foster of Oklahoma came to Bill's show at the Municipal Auditorium in Ottawa, Kansas, on September 26, the day before his twenty-fifth birthday. A multi-instrumentalist, he was playing electric bass with the Country Gazette, and the Gazette's Roland White had spoken to Bill about him. His ability with a fiddle was also known to Sonny Osborne, who recommended him to Bill. As a result, Bill called Foster and asked him to come to Ottawa to audition. The farmer-turned-musician said Bill told him, "You've got the job," but he'd have to wait until after Squires had a chance to play.[104]

The Brown County Jamboree Barn

Bill's meeting with Brown County, Indiana, officials back in May had ultimately resulted in the cancellation of events at the park after the June festival *and* the demolition of the forty-plus-year-old Jamboree Barn. As James told *Bean Blossom* author Adler, "[T]he county said that, you know, 'You gonna have to take this down. It's dangerous for the folks to be up under there [its sagging roof].'" In mid-October 1986, the old wooden structure was bulldozed down and hauled away, and whatever remained was burned. Fans were shocked and saddened ("We feel we have lost an old and valued friend," one wrote to *Bluegrass Unlimited*), but Bill and James may have been glad to be rid of it, if it hindered future events being held there.[105]

Mark Squires, meanwhile, had reported for work at the end of September. But the talented beginner was not as familiar with Bill's music as he should have been, and Bill eventually gave him notice. He played his last on Tuesday, November 11, smiling bravely while twinning with Buddy Spicher on a "New Country" taping at Nashville's Cannery club. Billy Joe Foster's first with Bill was the *Friday Night Opry* of November 14.

> I went out there and I remember when it come my break, he turned around and . . . when he would turn around, kinda toward you, his [right] shoulder would go up and he'd really start "countin' that timing off." I just remember thinking, I could hear every note that I might be rushing a little bit—just [a] tiny [bit], you know?[106]

A disturbing time on the road followed, as Bill lost, in rapid succession, an electric shaver, his keys, a raincoat, and then, worst of all, his wedding ring. It appeared his thoughts were elsewhere, and by the end of December, this was confirmed—there was trouble at home. At the *Friday Night Opry* on December 26, 1986, Tate told Ewing, Foster, and Williams that Della left home on Christmas Eve and hadn't returned. For the first show that night, Bill wanted to open with "Love, Please Come Home."[107]

The Fourth "Big Plan"

A possible cause of the discord was the fourth Big Plan, which James announced during a visit to the *Opry* soon after: they would convert the former Hall of Fame and Museum building on Music Valley Drive into a nightclub. The projected cost involved may have been a major concern for accountant Della. And, at that time, according to longtime Monroe Enterprises secretary Betty McInturff, Bill was about to allow James to take control of all of his business affairs. As a result, the first week of 1987 would be the last for the efficient and personable McInturff. She had openly disagreed with Bill about the advisability of such a "takeover," so he fired her. (She would return in 1992.)[108]

Rachel Liebling and *High Lonesome*

On Tuesday, January 13, 1987, Bill and the band played at New York City's Lone Star Café. In the audience that night was a young art student, Rachel Liebling.

> At the time [Liebling wrote], I knew very little about the music, but when [Bill Monroe] and the Blue Grass Boys began to play, I was riveted. Looking down from the balcony, all I could see were their cowboy hats, the tips of their boots, and their stringed instruments. As each band member stepped up for their solo break, I was mesmerized. Suddenly a piercing gospel harmony arose from below. Monroe's high tenor voice cut through, sending a shiver up my spine—the "high lonesome" sound Monroe is famous for.
>
> That moving experience inspired me to produce *High Lonesome* [a documentary about bluegrass, released in 1991]. I was surprised to find that few films explored the rich cultural heritage of bluegrass music, and [I] undertook the project with a sense of urgency. [109]

After Bill returned to Nashville, a thirty-two-page commemorative booklet, *Bill Monroe: 50 Years of Music*, was published, celebrating the fiftieth anniversary of Bill's first session in 1936, only a little belatedly. James had compiled it, including a brief biography, eighteen photos of Bill, and more than thirty *paid* congratulatory ads from celebrities like Johnny Cash, Jerry Reed, and Conway Twitty. At the *Friday Night Opry* of January 16, after it arrived from the printer, Ewing recalled: "Bill raced around backstage with childlike excitement, carrying a handful of booklets to give to his *Opry* friends, returning long enough to sing tenor on the chorus of a song the band was rehearsing, then leaving again with another handful."[110]

The recent trip to New York City had been the final run for the last Blue Grass Special Bill owned. When he and the band left Nashville on January 24, bound for Florida, it was in a maroon, early 1980s Silver Eagle leased from the Hemphill Brothers Coach Company. Leasing a bus, with drivers provided by the company, was becoming the way to go for many country music entertainers, glad to eliminate costly repairs on buses they owned. Bill's "new" bus had bunks for the band in its middle section with a separate "stateroom" for Bill in the back, just the opposite of the old bus. The stateroom, where Bill slept, was directly over the engine, the noisiest place on the bus when underway.[111]

Following a trip to North Carolina in early March 1987, Bill began crafting new words to fit the melody he'd used to write a song back in May 1986, writing two verses and a chorus of a song about an old romance, set in the Tar Heel State. He taught it to Ewing and, between shows on March 6 and 7 in Brevard and Burnsville, North Carolina, they sang it for the rest of the band on the bus. Williams suggested a change to the subdominant chord at the beginning of the chorus, a modification Bill readily accepted. A couple of days later, while driving home to Columbus, Ohio, Ewing wrote a first verse for it:

> In Asheville, North Carolina,
> Many a mile ago,
> I met a beautiful lady,
> But then I had to go.

He called Bill the next morning and sang it for him, and, much to his surprise, Bill approved. For the next nine months, however, "The Days Gone By" would not be mentioned again.

Meanwhile, *Bluegrass '87*, Bill's twenty-ninth Decca-Vocalion-MCA album, was released in March. A smiling seventy-five-year-old Bill was pictured on its front cover, sitting in a wagon with the reins in his hand and a dog, later identified as "Stormy," on his lap. Bill later revealed he'd raised the dog "since she was a pup."[112]

Bill and Della Divorce

It appears a song about an old romance was set aside because a current relationship was on Bill's mind. The first official word of the end of his and Della's marriage appeared in the "Divorces Filed" listings in the April 6, 1987, edition of Sumner County's *News-Examiner*. Surprisingly, Bill had filed for the divorce, not Della. (Legal wrangling continued for another year and a half, not ending until late 1988.)[113]

Even marital discord couldn't keep Bill from spring planting. He planted a hundred pounds of potatoes a few days after Good Friday (April 17 in 1987), the traditional time for potato planting, then got on the bus on April 21 to go to Missouri and Iowa for a four-day tour. He'd plowed with a mule, he told Foster: "He said, 'I got blisters all over my feet from follerin' that mule,' and the longer we went on that trip, the worse his feet was a-hurtin' him." Bill's ankles and feet were already swollen before he plowed (due, it was learned later, to a blood clot), and the shoes he'd worn didn't fit properly, resulting in the blisters. Eventually, Foster spotted a sign for a foot doctor from a bus window, and Bill's wounds were treated.[114]

Bill's discomfort didn't prevent him from writing new tunes, especially with a fiddler he trusted. During this time, he often wrote a new tune before every show, a way to confirm his creativity *and* a stunt that never failed to charm an audience. The tunes were usually named for the city he was playing in or a local landmark (in Strawberry Point, Iowa, he wrote "Strawberry Point" and in Hannibal, Missouri, "Monroe City Breakdown," for a nearby town). Varying widely in quality, they were always played with a promise to be recorded someday. Foster was particularly adept at learning them. But remembering them, to play them effectively at mid-show, was very stressful. Ewing recorded several with a portable tape recorder after shows but stopped when it didn't appear they would ever be recorded.[115]

Kentucky's State Bluegrass Song Proposed

That spring of 1987, Kentucky State Representative Willard C. "Woody" Allen submitted a bill to be considered by the General Assembly in 1988, urging the adoption of "Blue Moon of Kentucky" as the state's bluegrass song. Allen said later it was never his intention to replace Kentucky's official state song, Stephen Foster's "My Old Kentucky Home." Instead, he recalled he and other legislators were still trying to get "a bluegrass museum and festival park" established in Kentucky: "I thought this would enhance those efforts."[116]

Roland White offered his services as bus driver for Bill and the band at the beginning of May 1987, while the *Country Gazette* was disbanding. Bill had given White his first bus-driving lesson twenty years earlier, showing him how to double-clutch when shifting the gears of the Bluegrass Breakdown.

Since then, he had gained considerable experience driving for Lester Flatt from 1969 to 1973, and James and Bill were glad to hire someone willing to drive for less than lease companies charged for a driver. White drove through mid-August, giving much-needed encouragement to newer band members.[117]

Returning from the road on May 12, Bill found Della's furniture removed from the cabin and a wedding photo burned in the fireplace. The following weekend, Bill was certain he heard someone shooting at the cabin. He called Ewing, who stayed with him that night and the next, then cabin-sat while Bill made his annual pre-festival visit to Bean Blossom.

The twenty-first annual Bean Blossom festival followed (June 12–21), a haphazard affair that Tom Adler described kindly in *Bean Blossom* as having "lapses in management and planning." He correctly credited Joe Stuart, then suffering with terminal cancer, and several amateur bands, with saving it, filling gaps in the schedule. Also worthy of mention were Blue Grass Boys Foster and Williams, who backed up a host of performers, and bus driver White, who tried to get things organized. The "lapses" were probably due to nightclub plans or divorce troubles, not to mention the fear instilled by possible potshots. By the second weekend of the festival, Bill was again wearing a bulletproof vest, which WSM provided after someone phoned in a death threat to the station.[118]

The high-mileage bus Bill leased began having mechanical problems by July. It broke down in the *Opry* parking lot on Friday, July 17, just before a trip to Ft. Worth, Texas, to play Billy Bob's nightclub on the 18th, forcing the band to cram into Bill's Cadillac to get there. Tate, fearing lack of sleep and resulting headaches, declined to go, and White volunteered to play bass. A trip to the West Coast was already planned to start on the 21st, so, instead of returning to Nashville after Billy Bob's, the band drove to the home of Joe Foster, Billy Joe Foster's father, near Duncan, Oklahoma, to wait there while the bus was being repaired (with Tate bringing it to them when it was ready).

For the next two days, Bill and band were treated like long-lost kinfolks. Foster's mother, Carrie Foster, divorced from Joe Foster, came to the house and prepared a feast on Sunday, July 19, while friends from miles around came to "welcome them home." Foster recalled, "Bill said, 'We're gonna have to get our antiques out and play for our supper for these folks.'" So, the band stood on the concrete roof of a backyard storm cellar and played without a sound system. "At one point," Ewing said, "I was taking a guitar break, turned toward the band. In a flash, Bill came up behind me, grabbed me by my shoulders, and physically turned me toward the audience. They laughed, of course. But he'd taught me a valuable lesson in showmanship without saying a word."[119]

A couple of weeks later, the band was back on the bus, returning from shows in Washington, Idaho, Oregon, California, and Missouri, when Bill woke up feeling bad, with severe chills, on the morning of August 6. An emergency squad took him to a hospital in Indianapolis, Indiana. Four hours later, the diagnosis was dehydration, a simple case of not enough liquids. For all concerned it was a revelation: the once-invincible Bill Monroe was now capable of being felled by the lack of fluids.[120]

After they returned to Nashville on August 10, Foster learned his father was having health problems and knew he was needed at home. "Me and him had bached since I was seventeen," he said, "and I knew how to take care of Dad." He fiddled for Bill until the end of August, then took a leave of absence, due to return in the spring of 1988. His replacement was Kentuckian Mike Feagan, age twenty-nine (and at six foot, six inches, the tallest Blue Grass Boy), then fiddling with the Boys from Indiana. He had given Bill a cassette tape of his fiddling shortly after Foster joined.[121]

Feagan's formal audition was his first show, an afternoon performance on Thursday, September 3, at the Park Place Retirement Center in Hendersonville. In the audience was Bill's daughter, Melissa, then fifty years old, a resident at the assisted-living facility since her mother died in 1984. Afflicted with diabetes, she had recently recovered from a heart attack. After this show, encouraged by Park Place staff, Melissa would travel with her dad on several road trips in 1988.[122]

Two days later, Bill and the band flew to Burbank, California, for a recording session (with producer Emory Gordy) and a show at the Starlight Amphitheater on Monday, September 7, 1987. The session attempted to record Bill and comedian John Candy singing "Blue Moon of Kentucky" together (in unison), for the soundtrack of the movie *Planes, Trains, and Automobiles*. But, according to Ewing, "It didn't work out too well. Bill wasn't thrilled with the idea of 'goofing around' with his signature song." Recorded anyway, but never used, the song was sung solo by Candy in the movie. That evening, the band played to a small crowd at the amphitheater and flew home the next morning.[123]

Belt Buckles for Bill and His Blue Grass Boys

Among the birthday gifts Doug Hutchens gave Bill for his seventy-sixth birthday was one that honored both Bill and his Blue Grass Boys, a limited-edition belt buckle. Inspired by one Ernest Tubb gave his Texas Troubadors, Bill's buckle featured an engraved portrait of him framed by smaller depictions of Uncle Pen and the Ryman Auditorium. On the back was an inscription:

> Since 1939, Bill Monroe's Blue Grass Boys have set the standards for aspiring musicians around the globe. On this, the occasion of Bill Monroe's 76th birthday, September 13, 1987, *Bluegrass Unlimited* and the *Grand Ole Opry* [corporate sponsors of the buckle] proudly honor Bill Monroe and the Blue Grass Boys for their contributions to the American way of life through music.

On the September eleventh airing of the Nashville Network's popular *Now* show, Bill was presented with a set of three buckles—one each of brass, gold-silver plate, and solid silver, and all numbered "1" on the back. He was later given another set of three, all numbered "2," for his museum. *Bluegrass Unlimited* and the *Grand Ole Opry* received sets "3" and "4," respectively. A brass buckle was eventually given to every member of the Blue Grass Boys past and present (and a few fill-ins, including Tatsuya Imai and Sab Watanabe, who played bass in Japan). The number on these buckles indicated (generally) the order in which Hutchens received a page for Bill's birthday card.[124]

The Death of Joe Stuart

Sadly, coinciding with Bill's birthday was the passing of Joe Stuart at age fifty-nine on September 13, 1987. The most versatile of the Blue Grass Boys, Stuart played guitar, fiddle, bass, or banjo on more than twenty-five of Bill's Decca-MCA sessions between 1955 and 1983. "He had a good heart," Bill said at the time. "He would do things for people. I'm sorry we lost him—he was one of my best friends."[125]

Perhaps it was the loss of fiddlers (Stuart and Foster) who knew exactly what Bill wanted musically. Perhaps it was the frustration of having to tell a fiddler what to do. Whatever it was, beginning in October, "Bill started coming down hard on Mike [Feagan]," Ewing said, "correcting him on every note sometimes. It was painful." Feagan later summed up his feelings by saying, "It was like I was on pins and needles all the time around him."[126]

The Ploy

In late October, band members (Ewing, Feagan, Tate, Williams) were told of a ploy to increase the price of booking Bill for a show, then ranging between

$5,000 and $7,000. It would be announced he was retiring and would play a "farewell tour" in 1988. When demand increased for "one last show," his price would go up to between $12,000 and $15,000 (and band members would get a raise), even though he would not retire after all. Bill actually went along with the ruse (never very convincingly); ultimately, however, the ploy failed, mainly because those who'd booked him over the years balked at the inflated price, causing him to lose many bookings.[127]

Bill flew to New York City on November 4, accompanied by his Buddy Lee agent Tony Conway, to attend the Grammy Lifetime Achievement Awards show. The awards, given to "performers who, during their lifetimes, have made creative contributions of outstanding artistic significance to the field of recording," went that year to Roy Acuff and Hank Williams.[128]

On New Year's Eve 1987, before leaving for shows in Tampa, Florida, and Jekyll Island, Georgia (on Friday and Saturday, January 1–2), Bill invited the current Blue Grass Boys to a special service at his new church, Holiday Heights Baptist Church, in Hendersonville, located close to the Park Place Retirement Center, where Melissa lived, and to the Bell Cove, where Bill often sat in with the house band on Wednesday nights after church. That Thursday night at the church, Bill and the band provided backup for songs by Clarence and Armolee Green, Ferlin Huskey, Wayne Lewis, and Buck White. That weekend, Melissa went along with her father on the trip to Florida and Georgia; Ewing remembered her as being very quiet but having a ready sense of humor.[129]

Two days later, the recording of Bill's thirtieth (and last) Decca-MCA album, *Southern Flavor*, began on Monday, January 4, at the Sound Stage studio in Nashville, with guest fiddlers Bobby Hicks and Buddy Spicher joining Feagan. The title tune, "Southern Flavor," recorded that afternoon, began life as a minor-keyed love song Bill wrote a verse for in November 1987, then may have forgotten.

> Soon I'll be comin' back to you.
> Oh, you know I love you so.
> Meet me at the door with a smile on your face.
> Put your arms around me, darlin', once more.

By January 1988, it had become an instrumental, one that had to be learned and arranged before the band could record it, and, as a result, was the only thing recorded that day. (Later, in live performance, "Southern Flavor" provided a little comedy in Bill's shows with a routine that developed onstage. At one point, Bill would lower his microphone as low as it would go and, crouching down, play the tune softly into it. After band members wondered aloud about what he was doing, Tate would finally explain, "He's gettin' down!")[130]

The band recorded two more instrumentals the next afternoon (Tuesday, January 5): "Stone Coal" and "Texas Lone Star." The first was new to the band, but easy to learn, played on mandolin with a new tuning Bill had devised. When asked about it later, he said, "It's something like what I used on 'My Last Days on Earth,' but it's different." In other words, in the tunings for "My Last Days" (AA/DD/AC/DF) and "Stone Coal" (GG/CC/EG/GC), the two sets of lower strings are tuned in unison; otherwise, the strings are different. Bill recorded it using former fill-in Raymond Huffmaster's mandolin, a 1939 Gibson A50 that Randy Wood had converted to an A5, because Bill's mandolin (#72214) "wouldn't stay in tune." "Texas Lone Star," attempted the previous year, was familiar to all except Ewing and Feagan. They learned it from the 1987 recording, played for them in the studio's control room.[131]

On the afternoon of January 8, before the *Friday Night Opry*, the group returned to the Sound Stage studio to record the first vocal for the *Southern Flavor* album, "What a Wonderful Life," written by Huffmaster. The phrasing of the lyrics on this quartet, which Bill and the others had never sung before, did not jell on this day and would be tried again later. Next was "Sugar Loaf Mountain," named for a ski resort in Maine, near Ellsworth, where the band played in 1987, featuring Blake Williams on banjo. As Williams recalled: "When we recorded the *Southern Flavor* album, Emory Gordy said, 'We need a banjo tune.' I started playing 'Sugar Loaf Mountain' and Bill said, 'Who wrote that?' and I said, 'You did!' Emory said, 'Let's do it.'"[132]

The rest of the three *Southern Flavor* sessions took place in the evenings, the first just four days later, on Tuesday, January 12. It began with another surprise: "Blue Savannah Waltz," a new song written by west Tennessee fiddler Wayne Jerrolds. Jerrolds had gifted Bill with a couple of mules, and Bill was repaying the favor. But he was not really familiar with the song, so it was attempted and ultimately scrapped. More successful was the trio-chorused song Ewing had written a verse for, "The Days Gone By." "I wasn't happy with the tempo," Ewing said, "but Bill wanted it that way, so if the boss wants it slow, you do it slow!" This was followed by yet another surprise, "White Rose," written by Bill's old friend Carl Butler, who recorded it first for Capitol Records in 1950. Sung solo by Bill, it was his most personal musical expression of the sessions.[133]

The next evening, Wednesday, January 13, began with the much more upbeat "Life's Highway," written by former Blue Grass Boy Bobby Smith, who had sung it with the Boys of Shiloh (which included Blake Williams) in the 1970s. The second item, contrasting with the new gospel songs, was an old one, "Take Courage Un' Tomorrow," which Bill remembered after hearing it at the graveside service for Uncle Pen's son Cecil in 1925. It was new to Tate, so he asked producer Gordy (a bassist) to play bass while he concentrated on singing bass. But the recording was ruled unacceptable and it would have to be tried again. (When tried again, the second line of the first verse was recorded as "And your heart was free from care," based on Bill's memory. But Ewing now believes it should be "And your heart was filled with care.")[134]

The sixth and last *Southern Flavor* session was held the following evening, Thursday, January 14. Emory Gordy, producing his last of three Bill Monroe albums, played bass throughout as Tate focused on his singing. His bass lead voice was featured on "Give Me Wings," another new gospel song, written by bluegrass musician Gerald Evans, once a worker on Bill's farm. The rest of the session was devoted to redos of "What a Wonderful Life" and "Take Courage Un' Tomorrow."[135]

Less than three weeks later, Bill was suddenly hospitalized, "a drug reaction" the only reason given. Years later, James speculated it could have been caused by the wrong balance of medicines used to treat a blood pressure problem, which he had experienced too. If so, the proper combination continued to be elusive; Bill would frequently complain of feeling weak and tired, or of not feeling well, throughout the rest of 1988.[136]

A Return to Carnegie Hall

February 19–29 (of a leap year) Bill and the band played a tour taking them to a different location almost every day, including Carnegie Hall on Tuesday the 23rd. Tate's wife, Lois Tate, was undergoing a medical exam on the 22nd, so he arranged for a fill-in on bass (until the 25th): Billy Rose, then picking banjo with the Wayne Lewis Band. Bill shared the Carnegie Hall evening with the popular Celtic band the Boys of the Lough, but many bluegrass fans were in the audience. Answering requests at the end of his set, Bill ran over the 11:00 P.M. end time specified in the stage crew's union contract, and the sound system was abruptly turned off. All the band could do was wave as they left the stage.[137]

Ewing, after about two years with Bill, decided he'd had enough: "I was disillusioned—by the ploy to increase Bill's price, by the way Bill was treating Mike, by my playing." He turned in his two-week notice and said goodbye to Bill on Sunday morning, March 27, after a trip to Missouri. One week later, he realized he was "hooked" and rejoined the band on April 15. At a show that night in Yanceyville, North Carolina, Bill introduced him as "the newest member of the Blue Grass Boys." (Wayne Lewis filled in during his absence.) Meanwhile, on March 31, the Kentucky General Assembly approved House Bill 7, naming "Blue Moon of Kentucky" the state bluegrass song. Governor Wallace Wilkinson signed the bill, and it became official on July 14, 1988.[138]

During this time, the April *Bluegrass Unlimited* appeared, with a small (2^1/$_2$" x 5") ad declaring, "Bill Monroe's Brown County Jamboree Park and Annual Bean Blossom Bluegrass Festival are For Sale." In spite of the ad's size, word spread like wildfire in the bluegrass community. But it was only part of the ploy, "proof" that Bill really was getting out of the business.[139]

Southern Flavor, Bill's last Decca-MCA LP, was released on May 2, 1988. Billy Joe Foster's father was better by then, and his son was overdue to return. According to Foster, "I called Bill and he said, 'You need to be here yesterday. Why ain't you down here? Come right on, boy!'" Bill informed Feagan the weekend of May 27 would be his last. It had been a difficult time for Feagan, but years later, he was remarkably positive about it: "Even though it was hard to tell what he wanted, he taught me a lot about music just by watchin' him and listenin' to him."[140]

Bill Monroe's Bluegrass Country

Bill Monroe's Bluegrass Country, the two-million-dollar conversion of Bill Monroe's Bluegrass Hall of Fame and Museum into a supper club that took two years to complete, opened at 2620 Music Valley Drive in Nashville on June 6, during Fan Fair. Called "the Club" by those who worked there, it featured a cavernous 450-seat dining room with a spacious area for dancing, a separate VIP dining room, a small "Bluegrass Lounge" (bar) near the front entrance, and, initially, a four-seat shoeshine "parlor." Bill and the band (Ewing, Foster, Tate, Williams) usually played two sets there on Tuesday and Thursday nights, to small crowds on Tuesdays and slightly larger ones on Thursdays, when tourists arrived in town. Between sets, Bill sometimes napped in the Club's office.[141]

Dee Dee Returns as Diana

Among the first Nashvillians to visit the Club was Dee Dee Prestige, recovered from phlebitis and reincarnated at age forty-four as "Diana Christian" (a name she saw in a dream on a theater marquee for a big show). Now, dressed in fancy cowgirl garb, she would become an occasional guest on the stage of Bluegrass Country, backed by Bill and his band, her relationship with him rekindled.[142]

The band was back on the road by Friday, June 10, playing Fitzgerald's in Houston, Texas, then the Sanders Family festival, near McAlester, Oklahoma, on June 11. Between shows at the festival, one of Foster's friends came looking for him at the bus and found Bill sitting alone in the shotgun seat. The friend asked, "Is this Billy Joe Foster's bus?" To which Bill answered without hesitation, "Yes, sir, and I play mandolin for him." Foster's friend told Bill he was doing a good job and Bill, of course, thanked him.[143]

The twenty-second annual Bean Blossom festival was next, cut back to four days (June 16–19, 1988) and advertised as the "LAST," in keeping with the ploy. A story published in *Bluegrass Unlimited*, depicting the festival's end, included the following:

> His voice cracking with emotion, Monroe said, "We've all stayed right here together and I really enjoyed this. There's a lot of good memories here at Bean Blossom, Indiana," a sentiment which echoed through the crowd as one fan stood up and yelled, "Don't let it end, Bill!" To that the audience cheered wildly in agreement while Monroe swallowed the lump in his throat and regained the rigid composure for which he is so well known.[144]

A week later, Bill and the band were backstage on June 26 at the one-day Frontier Ranch festival near Columbus, Ohio, when inspiration struck and Bill started writing a new tune in the key of E. He showed it to the band, and they were putting the finishing touches on it as they were being introduced. Played without a name, its title would come three days later, on the way to Liberty, New York. Bill, again in the shotgun seat and looking out at a northern sky full of huge cumulus clouds, remarked on their beauty and declared he had his title: "Northern White Clouds." (Bill would record the tune three times between 1989 and 1993, but, oddly, never for MCA.)[145]

On Tuesday night, August 2, Diana Christian was at the Club, ready to sing with the band. Also there, probably making a surprise visit, was one of Bill's other lady friends, fifty-year-old Wanda Huff from Birmingham, Alabama.

No connection was ever found, but two weeks later, threats on Bill's life were received at the Jemison, Alabama, festival, and he again wore a bulletproof vest onstage. A week after the festival, someone called in a bomb threat to the Club.[146]

It was a good time to get as far away as possible, and, luckily, that's exactly what happened. Bill and the Blue Grass Boys left the United States on August 25 for a quick, four-day return to Switzerland to play a music festival in Mollis, near Zurich. The European love of things American was clearly evident here: before the show, Bill and the band were driven around in a convoy of restored Detroit masterpieces of the 1950s and 1960s, treated to a meal of steak and French fries, then greeted by enthusiastic festivalgoers, many decked out like Wild West cowboys and cowgirls.

Back home on August 29, the band zigzagged between Midwest and Northeast, playing in six locations through September 5, seemingly testing the roadworthiness of the bus. On the way back to Nashville, early on the 6th, the left-rear dual tires separated from the main axle and went careening across the median to the opposite side of Route 65. Thankfully, there was no traffic in those lanes at that hour. (The repair would cost Bill $3,200; the bus returned to service on October 1.)[147]

A few days later at the Club, Foster told Bill he had to go home again to take care of his dad, and he'd already asked former fill-in Blaine Sprouse and studio regular Buddy Spicher to fill in "indefinitely." Bill managed to joke, "You're the first Blue Grass Boy that's ever replaced hisself." Foster played his last in Branson, Missouri, on September 19.[148]

Sprouse filled in the next weekend: Friday in Connecticut, Saturday in Massachusetts, and Sunday, September 25, in Owensboro, Kentucky, at IBMA's "Bluegrass Fan Fest," a descendant of "Bluegrass with Class." (On that Sunday, photographer MaryE Yeomans took the photo used later on the cover of *The Bill Monroe Reader*.) Then Spicher fiddled during October and November, the longest stint he'd ever worked with Bill. "I wish I had never done it," he said later, explaining that the regard stars have for a studio musician is diminished when he goes on the road with them: "They just lose the respect—you're just a road musician to them." By the end of October, Bill was complaining about both substitute fiddlers, saying Sprouse had fiddled "some crazy stuff" and Spicher "don't play like he used to."[149]

In the interim, Bill Monroe's Bluegrass Country closed for the season on October 22. On a November 3–6 tour of the Northeast that Spicher couldn't make, Tate fiddled and Billy Rose again filled in on bass. On November 8,

Vice President George H. W. Bush defeated Massachusetts Governor Michael Dukakis in the presidential election. And on November 11 Bill and Della's divorce was final, with Bill ordered to pay her attorney's $1,500 fee and alimony of $1,000 a month for thirty months (until 1991).[150]

It appears Bill was intent on repaying Wayne Jerrolds for the mules he'd given him, especially after the failed recording of his song. On October 28, Bill and the band played at Cedars of Lebanon State Park, about thirty miles east of Nashville, and Jerrolds came to the show. Bill told him he'd be playing in Ripley, Mississippi (just south of Jerrolds's Savannah, Tennessee, home), on Saturday, December 3, and encouraged him to audition then for the fiddle spot. Forty-nine-year-old Jerrolds would start on December 9 at the *Friday Night Opry*.[151]

Ewing gave Bill his second notice at the end of the night on December 9. Many issues were troubling him, but foremost were finances. He would stay until the end of December and meet his replacement, twenty-eight-year-old Scottie Baugus, former banjo picker in a band with Jerrolds in Savannah. Baugus and Jerrolds would commute to and from Nashville together, continuing to live in Savannah.[152]

The ploy had already fizzled by December, with Bill saying things like "I've got too many fans from all over the world. It would be bad not to ever see 'em again." But confirmation of its demise came in a 2¹/₂"-square ad in the January 1989 issue of *Bluegrass Unlimited*: "Bill Monroe has changed his mind there will be Bean Blossom Festivals in 1989 [sic]." That month Bill's *Southern Flavor* album was nominated for a Grammy for "Best Bluegrass Recording," then a subcategory of NARAS's "Country" category.[153]

Bill's Last LP Wins Grammy

At the thirty-first Grammy Awards ceremony in Los Angeles on February 22, with Bill not in attendance, the Grammy was awarded to *Southern Flavor*. Three days later, Bill and the band (Baugus, Jerrolds, Tate, Williams) were appearing in Ewing's Columbus, Ohio, hometown at the venerable Valley Dale Ballroom. Ewing led them to Valley Dale (directions were seldom provided for the band), and by the end of the evening (after conferring with his wife), Ewing asked Bill if he could come back. He called Bill a few days later to get his decision and Bill said he wanted him back, but he was reluctant to let Baugus go, creating a hardship for Jerrolds to commute without him.[154]

Meanwhile, Bill and the band played in Las Vegas, Nevada, on March 3. After their show, Baugus told Bill he was going to try the casino's slot machines.

> Mr. Monroe said, "Let me take my mandolin to the room. I'm going with you." In a few minutes, I was out of quarters—I was done. I walked back to where he was and asked, "How're you doin'?" He said, "Look in that bucket," and he had a bucket full of quarters! The next day, he'd put those quarters in the other mandolin [72214] case. I'll bet that thing weighed a ton.[155]

During that busy March, Bill still visited the Bell Cove club on Wednesday nights after church, sitting in with a house band that included former fill-in Billy Rose on bass. Tate began sitting in as well, to twin with the band's fiddler, former Blue Grass Boy Glen Duncan. Tate soon came up with a plan to resolve Bill's indecision about rehiring Ewing, resulting in both Baugus and Jerrolds being let go: Tate would return to playing the fiddle and Ohio native Rose would take over the bass spot. Rose, then twenty-five, recalled that "Bill said, 'I need a man that can stay right there on top of the beat.' And I said, 'Well, I think you got your man.'" Bill called Ewing on March 26, telling him to report to the *Friday Night Opry* on the 31st, and letting him know the usual springtime switch from felt hats to straw hats would be made that night.[156]

A Disturbance at Bill's Farm

April 1989 was almost as busy as March, ending with a four-day weekend in Kentucky and North Carolina. By Monday, May 1, Bill was probably ready for some peace and quiet, but instead he received a visit from Wanda Huff. "I was leaving him," she told a newspaper reporter, "and I wanted my things back. I was just getting my things out of his house." Tony Conway, then an executive with Buddy Lee, spoke to the reporter for Bill:

> Supposedly this woman drove up from Birmingham, came to his house, and caused a major disturbance; she started destroying property. He asked her to leave several times and she refused to leave. Mr. Monroe called the police, the police came to the house, took statements from both parties, and I guess she filed charges against him.

Bill calling the police on Huff appears to have encouraged her to even the score by accusing him of assault. She said he "knocked her down, kicked her in the face," he "held her neck, stating he was going to break her neck," and most tantalizing of all, he "hit her in the face with a Bible" (on which she wanted him to swear he was not "running around" with other women). After the Nashville press published the story, the national media had a field day. The *San Francisco Chronicle* ran a photo of Bill with the caption "Bible Belter."[157]

Bill's next recording for MCA, celebrating his upcoming fiftieth anniversary at the *Grand Ole Opry*, was already in the works, and regardless of the recent uproar, it would proceed on schedule. Steve Buchanan, recently hired as the *Opry*'s first marketing manager, was given the task of producing *Live at the Opry*. It required several "sessions" during May and June to capture the best performances, but an accurate record of when each recording was made wasn't maintained. As a result, *The Music of Bill Monroe* lists the first session as Friday, May 5, 1989, when Bill and the band (Ewing, Rose, Tate, Williams) were in Ann Arbor, Michigan. They *did* play the *Grand Ole Opry* on Saturday, May 6, however, and this was likely the project's first session. After that, due to a busy festival season when Bill was out of town on Saturdays, the band recorded the other sessions at *Friday Night Oprys* or *Opry Matinees* (on Tuesdays or Thursdays).[158]

Bill appeared at a hearing in Sumner County General Sessions Court in Gallatin on the morning of Wednesday, May 10. His attorney, Bob Ingrum, requested that Wanda Huff and her vehicle be searched before the hearing, and a loaded .25-caliber automatic pistol was found in her pickup truck. Ingrum revealed it was Huff who had called Bill at the *Opry* back in December 1985, telling him someone was gunning for him, and they had met thereafter under these questionable circumstances. Assistant District Attorney Dee Gay had already interviewed Huff and others involved in the case, and told Judge Jane Wheatcraft he "had serious problems with the credibility and mental condition of the victim [Huff]" and: "In my opinion, the state of Tennessee cannot carry the burden of proof and we ask that this case be dismissed." Judge Wheatcraft granted his request, telling Bill at hearing's end, "You leave here totally exonerated."[159]

That night, Bill and the band played the recently reopened Bluegrass Country, sharing the evening with the *Opry*'s pop-country Four Guys. It was Bill's last time to appear there. James soon arranged with the Four Guys, experienced Nashville cabaret owners, to host the Club for the rest of the season. Thereafter, it was sold, reportedly for $650,000, considerably less than the amount invested in it.[160]

Between *Live at the Opry* "sessions," Bill and the band appeared on the *Mountain Stage* radio show, broadcast live from the packed Capitol Plaza Theatre in Charleston, West Virginia, on May 21, and their performance was recorded. Diana Christian joined them, becoming a regular guest after the sale of the Club.[161]

Filming at the Monroe Homeplace

The twenty-third annual Bean Blossom festival was four days long (June 15–18), like "the last one." During it, Bill announced from the stage that he had "just made the decision to continue the festival," forced to do this to end doubts about it (caused by the ploy). After the festival, Bill asked Rose to drive him up to Rosine on the morning of the 19th. Rachel Liebling, working on her *High Lonesome* documentary, had shot some footage at the festival and now she wanted to film Bill at the Monroe homeplace's house, which was in a very dilapidated condition at the time. Arriving in Rosine, Bill and Rose met Liebling and her crew at the Rosine Volunteer Fire House. Fire Chief Stoy Geary, then one of Bill's biggest boosters in the area, had offered to drive them to the site in his four-wheel-drive pickup truck. Geary and Bill rode in the cab, while Liebling, her crew, and Rose were in the cap-covered bed of the truck. Liebling later recalled the journey:

> We had an accident on the way up in the mudslide that was supposed to be a road—the pickup truck slammed into a mud hole—the cameraman, soundman, and myself were in the back and got thrown against the [cap]. I whacked my head and it was a dizzying challenge—finally making it up there and capturing all that amazing footage while seeing stars!

After the filming (which included Bill playing a tune inside the house, one he'd learned from his Uncle Pen: "Going Across the Sea"), a catered lunch was served at the firehouse. After everyone said their goodbyes, Bill told Rose to drive him to the Rosine Cemetery. While there, Bill pointed out his family's graves to Rose, telling him, "It won't be long 'til I'm layin' here with 'em."[162]

Bill undoubtedly knew he actually was "Going Across the Sea" soon. He took his fifth trip to Europe at the end of July, playing a festival near Basel, Switzerland, on Saturday the 29th and a concert the next day at a "gasthaus" (a combination beer hall and hotel) in the village of Streekermoor, near the town of Oldenburg, Germany, with the Osborne Brothers and the German band GroundSpeed (then with former Blue Grass Boy Bob Black on banjo). The three bands traveled nearly five hundred miles between Basel and Streekermoor during the night, "crammed together into two Volkswagen vans," Black recalled, adding: "The van I rode in was leading the way much of the time, and it seemed as though every time I looked back toward the other van, I could see Bill napping in the passenger seat; the top of his white hat bobbing up and down as his head drooped in slumber." Due to the hectic schedule of the tour, this may have been the only sleep Bill had. Bear Family Records of Germany would later release audio and video recordings of the next day's show, and in its booklet notes Bill is described as "so old and in frail health." Indeed, he was old (nearly seventy-eight), and the demands of the trip had severely challenged his health.[163]

Within a few weeks, around mid-August 1989, Bear Family released its first Bill Monroe boxed set: *Bill Monroe—Bluegrass 1950–1958*. It was also the fourteen-year-old company's first boxed set of bluegrass music *and* its first CD release—four CDs in this case, containing 109 songs and tunes in the order they were recorded, from 1950's "Blue Grass Ramble" to 1958's "Monroe's Hornpipe." Enclosed with them in a 12 1/2" x 12 1/2" box was a booklet with detailed notes by Charles Wolfe, rare photographs from the 1950s, and a discography by Neil Rosenberg, fiddling deejay Eddie Stubbs, and Bear Family founder Richard Weize.[164]

Rachel Liebling and her *High Lonesome* crew came to Nashville on September 13 to film Bill and the band playing at Bill's seventy-eighth birthday party, held at the Bell Cove for the first time. Liebling also wanted to film them riding around in the "Blue Grass Special" before the party started. The Blue Grass Boys, dressed in their stage clothes and playing gin rummy, appear to be having a great time in the finished film (but minutes before boarding the bus, were all complaining about doing such a silly thing as riding around town).[165]

A week later, Bill was going across another sea, to Japan, with the band and grandson "Jimbo," then twenty-five. Bill's fifth (and last) visit to Japan was also his briefest (September 20–23), but he was to play only one show on the 23rd, the "Country Gold International Country Music Festival," near the city of Kumamoto, with headliners Roger Miller, Hank Thompson, and Wanda Jackson. The pace of this trip was much more relaxed, with days of sightseeing and an informal rehearsal preceding the show, so no one was expecting Bill to suffer another bout of dehydration, just before showtime. Temporarily out of his head, he insisted on seeing his doctor in Tennessee until Blake Williams reminded him he was in Japan. During a brief hospital visit, Jimbo stayed with his grandpa, watching over him. Then, after Bill was hydrated and returned to the venue, his way to the stage was made easier: an audience of twelve thousand at Japan's first outdoor country music festival watched as Bill Monroe and his Blue Grass Boys rose from beneath the stage on a hydraulic lift, never suspecting that a medical emergency had just been averted.[166]

Bill's Fiftieth Anniversary on the *Opry*

MCA released *Live at the Opry—Celebrating 50 Years on the Grand Ole Opry* in early October on cassette and CD only, and a very busy month followed. On October 28, 1989, fifty years to the day after his *Opry* debut, Bill was honored by the Nashville Network, replacing its usual primetime *Opry Live* program with *Bill Monroe's 50th Anniversary*. During the show the Blue Grass Man sang three of his most famous songs of the Blue Grass State, "Kentucky Waltz," "My Rose of Old Kentucky," and "Blue Moon of Kentucky," all with country star Emmylou Harris singing harmony. Then WSM presented Bill with a custom-made mandolin, his likeness carved in the headstock. Clearly delighted, Bill said (in the third-person) that it had "his picture and everything right up here on top!"

Capping the show, Larry Cordle and Lonesome Standard Time (from the Bell Cove) played a new song of tribute to Bill, "Kentucky King."

> He gave us "Blue Moon of Kentucky"
> And we'll follow his footprints in the snow.
> For the music that he fathered, let us stand and sing:
> Long live the old Kentucky King.

Regrettably, "the King" looked very old on the night of his fiftieth anniversary. Anemic. Nervous. Uncertain of what was happening next. The demands of October had worn him out, and making matters worse was the blood-thinning medication he was taking (for the clot causing his ankles and feet to swell).[167]

About a week after the anniversary broadcast, sometime in early November with absolutely no fanfare, Bill traveled to Washington, D.C., invited to the White House for a private congratulatory meeting with President George H. W. Bush. "I went into his office and talked with him awhile," Bill told country music writer Don Rhodes. "He knows all about bluegrass music, and he knows it belongs to America. He gave me a little present to keep: a little pen knife with the presidential seal on it."[168]

At year's end, the state of Bill's health continued to be troubling. On December 23, at the *Opry*, he was suddenly unsteady on his feet, possibly due to the blood thinners. The Blue Grass Boys rushed to him and convinced him to sit down (which he never did in the wings of the *Opry*). They summoned Opryland's paramedic unit, but Bill refused to go to a hospital for a checkup until after he sang "Christmas Time's A-Comin.'"[169]

CHAPTER NINE

1990-1996

No Grammy for *Live at the Opry*

Live at the Opry was nominated for a Grammy for "Best Bluegrass Recording" at the beginning of 1990. This time, Bill attended the awards ceremony in Los Angeles on February 21, but the Grammy went to "The Valley Road," a song done in "bluegrass style" by pop singer Bruce Hornsby with the Nitty Gritty Dirt Band on its *Will the Circle Be Unbroken, Vol. II* album (Universal).[1]

On Saturday, April 7, Bill was one of many stars donating their time for Farm Aid IV, a benefit for family farmers in financial trouble, broadcast live by the Nashville Network from the Hoosier Dome in Indianapolis, Indiana. Bill most welcomed the chance to pay back one of Farm Aid's co-founders, Willie Nelson, for taking part in 1984's *Friends* album. Immediately after, Bill and the band raced southward to play the ten o'clock *Opry*. Even though *Opry* manager (since 1974) Hal Durham had completely relaxed attendance requirements for members, Bill still wanted to be there whenever possible. (Due to an increase in bookings, a result of the failed ploy, he would only play the Saturday night show seven times in 1990.)[2]

Melissa Moves to the Farm

Bill arranged for Diana Christian to appear on the *Friday Night Opry* of May 4, and she sang the soon-to-be-widely-popular "Walk Softly on My Heart." Christian had become friends with Melissa during visits with Bill to Park

Place, and Melissa had urged her father to make the *Opry* appearance possible. That May, Melissa moved in with him on his Goodlettsville farm, due to his inability to pay for assisted living. Bill hired Javonda Charlene "Charlene" Smith, thirty-six, a sometime-ceramicist from Mobile, Alabama, to take care of Melissa. Smith said she'd originally come to Nashville in 1987 "to be with Bill" but had lived elsewhere. (She said she was with him in June 1989, the night he came home after visiting the Monroe homeplace for *High Lonesome*. "It tore him up," she said. "One of the few times I saw the man cry.") In spite of the surreptitious nature of their relationship, Smith had gotten to know Melissa too and was familiar with the medicines she needed to take daily.[3]

Bill's Last for Decca-MCA

Bill recorded what would be his last regular release for MCA, *Cryin' Holy Unto the Lord*, during May, June, and July of 1990. He had reportedly initiated the project, telling MCA, "I want to do a gospel album with Steve [Buchanan, producer of *Live at the Opry*]." Several of its ten selections were familiar, among them remakes sixteen and seventeen (the last) of items previously recorded in a studio for Decca-MCA ("Just Over in the Glory Land" and "You're Drifting Away"); the fifteenth and last Decca-MCA remake of a recording by the classic bluegrass band ("Shine, Hallelujah, Shine"); and the seventeenth and last Decca-MCA remake of a song recorded by the Monroe Brothers ("This World Is Not My Home").[4]

In exchange for help Rosine Fire Chief Geary had given the *High Lonesome* film crew the previous June, Bill agreed to give a free performance in Rosine on June 2, which Geary promoted as the "17th Annual Rosine Bluegrass Festival" (seventeen years since the first homecoming festival there in 1973). In May, before Bill came to town, Geary hit upon an idea to honor and surprise Bill when he arrived: Using his authority as fire chief, he temporarily changed the names of the streets in Rosine to Monroe-related monikers. New street signs were installed changing McLeod ["McCloud"] Street to Bill Monroe Avenue, First Street to Blue Grass Place, Front Street to Uncle Pen Boulevard, and so forth. This went over like the proverbial lead balloon with residents, some of whom thought the change was permanent. Afterward, the "Rosine Happenings" column in the *Ohio County Times-News* reported the event "drew several thousand, many from bordering states," and that Bill wrote a tune called "Rosine," telling the crowd he was going to record it. (Unfortunately, the tune was lost.) The columnist (probably Wendell Allen) observed that "Bill Monroe fans weren't disappointed."[5]

Steve Gebhardt's Documentary

The twenty-fourth annual Bean Blossom festival again spanned four days
(June 14–17). On Friday the 15th, everyone in the band except Bill was surprised to see another documentary film crew there. This crew, led by professional filmmaker Steve Gebhardt, had come to film the band's afternoon and
evening shows on both the 15th and 16th. Gebhardt, age fifty-three, had only
recently returned to his native Ohio after twenty years of living in New York
City, L.A., and Berkeley, making films with John Lennon and Yoko Ono and
the Rolling Stones. His interest in bluegrass had begun in the 1960s, while
a student at the University of Cincinnati, and one of his first films was shot
at Bean Blossom festivals in 1968 and 1969.[6]

Liebling's film would tell "the story of bluegrass music" (its subtitle) and
include Bill prominently, but Gebhardt, long before hearing of her work,
wanted to make a film about Bill Monroe. "I wanted to do the definitive work
on Bill and, in so doing, bluegrass in general," he said later. So, after Bean
Blossom, he shot a lot of footage of Bill in several locations that summer: at
the Frontier Ranch festival on June 24 (including a "reunion" with Bill Keith,
Del McCoury, and Chubby Wise, already arranged for by festival promoter
Darrel Adkins); at an *Opry* matinee and the *Grand Ole Opry* on July 7; and at
Bill's farm in Goodlettsville in early July (a front-porch interview with John
Hartford, recommended to Gebhardt by longtime friend Jacky Christian, a
flatfoot dancer featured at Bean Blossom festivals since 1984).[7]

On August 11, Bill and the band left Nashville early, on the way to a five-
day tour of the West Coast, stopping to play a small festival in Greenup,
Kentucky, before heading west. At the end of the day, Bill told Rose to come
to his "office" in the back of the bus so Bill could pay him ($125 per day be-
fore taxes), giving him spending money for the trip. But to Rose's surprise,
after Bill paid him, he gave Rose a two-weeks' notice. At that moment, Rose
recalled, he didn't know what to say.

> I waited 'til we got on the trip and we were way out west somewhere. We'd stopped
> at a truck stop. He wandered off alone, the way he used to, way out in the park-
> ing lot, and I thought this would be a good time to ask him. So I said, "Bill, did I
> do anything wrong, for you to be lettin' me go?" And he said, "No, we just gotta
> make some changes in the band."

The "changes," Rose learned later, involved hiring twenty-six-year-old
fiddler Jimmy Campbell, former protégé of Kenny Baker from Michigan

who came to Nashville in 1987 to play with Jim and Jesse. Campbell had cultivated a friendship with Bill, who asked him to twin with Tate on his fiftieth-anniversary night at the *Opry,* as well as on his final MCA sessions. Then, after a disagreement with Jim McReynolds, Campbell asked Bill for a job. Bill unhesitatingly said yes, causing Tate to return to the bass and Rose, with the least seniority, to lose his job. This, according to Campbell's friend Rose, didn't trouble Campbell: "He was for hisself when it came to that stuff [the music business]."[8]

One of Rose's last appearances was the *Nashville Now* show of August 23. On the show with Bill that night was a newly popular country rock band, the Kentucky Headhunters, whose first album, *Pickin' on Nashville* (Mercury), included a cover of Bill's "Walk Softly on My Heart." It brought the band its first success on the country charts in late 1989, causing their album to be designated a Gold Record by the Recording Industry Association of America in April 1990. So, during the show, "the Headhunters" presented Bill with a framed copy of the Gold Record. He would repay them for this (and for the royalties involved) by inviting them to appear at his Bean Blossom festival in 1991.[9]

A few weeks later, Diana Christian learned of the end of her touring with Bill while on the road with the band (Campbell, Ewing, Tate, Williams) in her native Minnesota. "I'd heard rumors that James wanted the money I was making [$100 a day] to spend on a new pickup truck," she said, "and he didn't think Bill needed me either." She and Bill would continue seeing each other for awhile, going to church and the Bell Cove together on Wednesday nights.[10]

The Death of Melissa Monroe

On September 27, while Bill was on a four-day tour in Texas, Melissa developed a fever and was taken by Charlene Smith to a doctor who diagnosed a urinary tract infection. She was allergic to penicillin, so another antibiotic was prescribed, but was ineffective. Her condition worsened that night and an ambulance took her to a hospital, where she had a stroke, common among people with severe diabetes. Convinced she was dying, Melissa withdrew, and her willingness to communicate became minimal. That same September 27, while Bill and the band were in Dallas at Poor David's Pub, thirty-five-year-old Julia LaBella reappeared after nearly eight years. Then in the process of divorcing Alan Phelps, she brought Bill the 1939 Martin 00–18 guitar he'd given her, asking him to have the bridge reglued in Nashville.

In mid-October, Bill contacted fans and friends from Ohio, Fred and Denise Painter, and asked them to visit Melissa while he was on tour. He had seen their cheerful interaction with her during visits to the farm and hoped they might bring her out of her withdrawal. At first, Denise Painter said, Melissa didn't respond, but then she showed her a photo she'd taken of Melissa with her father: "She said, 'Me! Daddy! Daddy! Me!' And all the nurses came running in the room—she hadn't talked until then."

Melissa was moved out of intensive care the next day, and hopes were high that she would soon be talking to her father. She still wasn't eating, so a feeding tube was installed, but before Bill returned to town, she accidently dislodged it and material from her stomach, including stomach acid, entered her lungs, causing "aspiration pneumonia." In a coma-like state, she lingered for six weeks, never speaking again, and died on Monday, December 3, 1990.[11]

On Tuesday, at the visitation at the Madison Funeral Home, Bill was seen guiding Earl and Louise Scruggs to the casket. On Wednesday, Melissa was buried next to her mother in Nashville's Spring Hill Cemetery, not far from Opryland.[12]

Bill was devastated but couldn't let it show. Contracts had been signed, tickets had been sold, and money had to keep rolling in to pay creditors. Bill and the band were due in Knoxville on Friday, December 6, for a weekend tour with Ralph Stanley. Later, in his autobiography, Stanley recalled that Bill called to tell him of Melissa's death: "She was young, only fifty-four, and Bill took it real hard. No parent wants to survive their children." Asked how Bill handled the loss, Charlene Smith said, "He just went on with his life. Diana [Christian] made a wreath she painted black, to go on Melissa's bedroom door. He put it on there and shut the door and, pretty much, that was the end of it. The room wasn't messed with for years."[13]

By the beginning of the new year, 1991, Ewing had helped Bill remember lyrics many times, "feeding" them to him with a whisper and not being concerned about it. But that changed on the *Friday Night Opry* of February 15, 1991, when seventy-nine-year-old Bill forgot the words of "Blue Moon of Kentucky," a song he'd sung at nearly every show for more than forty years. "I fed him the first few lines, then he had it," Ewing said. "But it was a shocker—another reminder that Bill was not invincible, that he was going to have memory problems like any other oldster."[14]

Julia LaBella, recently divorced, came to Nashville in late February to retrieve her repaired guitar and went out to Bill's farm to get it. There she found him with a visitor, Sue Smith of upstate New York, a Monroe-style mandolin player and off-and-on companion on the road since 1986. LaBella and Bill had already talked: "He wanted me to come back. So, of course, I was surprised that there was someone else there." LaBella took her guitar and left, telling Bill that if he ever needed her, to let her know.[15]

On April 30, 1991, the last surviving member of Bill's original Blue Grass Boys, Tommy "Snowball" Millard, died at age seventy-nine. Bill had outlived them all: Cleo Davis (1919–1986), Amos Garren (1914–1977), Art Wooten (1906–1986), and Millard (1911–1991). Undoubtedly informed of Millard's passing, he was again reminded of his own mortality. He had outlived his five brothers too, three of whom had died of heart attacks, and he was already taking time-released nitroglycerin pills for chest pains (angina).[16]

Of the twenty-fifth annual Bean Blossom festival (June 13–16), Tom Adler wrote only that "Bill's enthusiasm for the park seemed high," but that the festival "seemed almost routine." The event was marred by the deaths of two Indiana couples, friends sleeping in the same motorhome who died of carbon monoxide poisoning, due to a faulty air conditioner. Their bodies were discovered on Sunday after most festivalgoers had left the park.[17]

Lowinger and His Camera

Former Blue Grass Boy Gene Lowinger hadn't played bluegrass for more than twenty years when he went to see Bill at Sunset Park, on July 14. He'd developed an interest in photography and was looking for an opportunity "to play with" his camera, but he wondered if Bill would be "welcoming." He'd grown a beard and his long hair was in a ponytail, so Bill didn't recognize him when he started photographing him talking to some fans.

> Then I said, "Hey Bill, remember that Jewish Blue Grass Boy from New York City?" He broke into a wide grin and put his hand out for me to shake. He had an old routine when greeting someone of whom he was fond: when I took his hand, he pulled me off balance towards him, as if to say, "I may be the old man, but I'm still stronger than you." He put his arm around my shoulder and gave me a squeeze. I felt a warm glow spread through me, and all the tension dissipated.[18]

Bill's Bypass Surgery

As the festival season began to wind down, Bill's angina worsened. "The pain was comin' more frequent," Charlene Smith said, "and it was stayin' on him longer." She said she insisted Bill have a thorough checkup at Baptist Hospital in Nashville on August 8, and it was then that he learned that his coronary arteries had blockages of 90, 80, 70, and 10 percent, indicating the need for immediate triple-bypass surgery. Still, Bill wondered aloud if he could play the *Opry* first. Smith said a doctor told him, "You could bend over and have a heart attack and die." The surgery was performed the next morning.[19]

Charlene Smith, Bill's Caregiver

Bill spent the next ten days recovering, registered under the name of Charlene Smith's father, "Ira Smith," and James decided to strictly limit access to him. Ewing and Rose tried to visit but were turned away. On August 20 Bill returned to the farm and, shortly thereafter, received a visit from former Blue Grass Boy Butch Robins, "rekindling musical relationships" after a ten-year absence from Nashville.

> I listened as he told me of the excruciating pain and discomfort he had endured. He also told me of hallucinations he incurred as a result of medication. He told me at one point, while he was sitting at his kitchen table playing his mandolin, he saw before him an audience of thousands. I told him I had taken enough drugs to kill a mule and had never seen anything such as that. In response to my response, he said, "Well, that ain't no part of nothin'."

Initially, male nurses cared for Bill, another of James's decisions, according to Smith. This decision was not popular with Bill. Within a short time, at Bill's insistence, Smith became his sole caregiver and "for the next three or four months, he didn't go anywhere without me," she said.[20]

On September 9, Blake Williams called his fellow band members to say he'd turned in his notice, and his ten-year tenure would end on September 21 at the *Opry*. He'd conferred with Bill, then called Dana Cupp of Michigan to offer the banjo spot and "he said immediately that he wanted the job." Cupp, age thirty-two, was a regular at Bean Blossom festivals, his Detroit Bluegrass Band featured there in 1985 and 1990. While with Bill, he would maintain a full-time job in Detroit and fly to Nashville each weekend. Jim Bessire, former manager of the museum and road manager for James, was hired to handle Williams's "other jobs," selling merchandise and serving as Bill's road manager. Bessire's sense of humor would be invaluable to band members in the difficult times to come.[21]

The Bean Blossom autumn festival in 1991 (September 12–14) began five weeks after Bill's bypass surgery, and, naturally, he insisted on being there, long before he had completely recovered. He had not played a show and was still pale and weak, so substitutes filled in for him in the 95-degree heat of afternoon shows (Terry Eldredge on the 12th and *Bluegrass Unlimited* editor Pete Kuykendall on the 13th and 14th). But each evening, when temperatures moderated, the now-eighty-year-old Bill joined the band for a few numbers and "improved, little by little, each time," according to Ewing. He even managed to sit in with the plugged-in and loud Kentucky Headhunters on the evening of the 14th, playing "Walk Softly" and a few others (with Jimmy Campbell joining them on fiddle, disguised in white overalls, ball cap, and hippie wig).

On September 26, the first three members of the International Bluegrass Music Association's "Hall of Honor" were announced: Bill and two of his former employees, Lester Flatt and Earl Scruggs. Also, at the end of September, Lois Tate was injured in a car wreck, and thereafter Tater Tate would sometimes be absent from the band, staying home to take care of her.[22]

The Fifth "Big Plan"

While Bill continued to recuperate, James took the lead in their business partnership and arranged for extensive changes at Bean Blossom (the fifth Big Plan, without Bill's direct involvement, but with his blessing). After the September festival, construction began on a large structure near the entrance, the new home of the Bill Monroe Bluegrass Hall of Fame and Museum. Then James had an idea for an added attraction for it—a reconstruction of the cabin his father and Uncle Pen "bached" in during 1928–30. At the end of October 1991, a few logs from the original that hadn't rotted were transported from Rosine to Bean Blossom, much to the consternation of a few Ohio County Kentuckians. (One told the *Times-News*, "Except for a lot of pride and history, Rosine doesn't have a lot. Now we have even less.") The reconstruction was accurate except for its chimney and front porch, which the original didn't have. Meanwhile, underway in early 1992 was the building of a stylish, state-of-the-art stage in the woods to replace 1968's "homemade" stage. Complete with heated/air-conditioned dressing rooms and a large back porch, it was built by a contractor James had met at a Bean Blossom festival, Kenny Baker (no relation to the fiddler), from Madisonville, Indiana. There were also plans to build a motel on the grounds, but they "never got beyond the talking stage," according to James.[23]

From mid-September 1991 to the end of January 1992, Bill and the Blue Grass Boys (Campbell, fiddle; Cupp, banjo; Ewing, guitar; Tate, bass) played mainly at the Opry House in Nashville on Friday and Saturday nights. In February, it was decided that Bill was well enough to tour again, but it soon became clear that he was really not yet ready. Like others who underwent bypass operations, he had memory problems and seemed to be "out of it" when offstage. His physical well-being was questionable as well; having lost a lot of weight from dietary restrictions, his clothes hung on him. Musically, he seemed to be losing his sense of rhythm, and his tendency to sing flat became much more noticeable. But, as his old Bean Blossom compadre Jim Peva observed (with some exaggeration), a change often came over him at showtime:

> His complexion was sometimes pale and ashen. But to the last, he could still pull himself together just before stepping onstage and have the appearance, complexion, and actions of the young Bill Monroe of the 1940s. . . . Whether it was self-hypnosis or divine inspiration, Bill could do it. He could transform a sick old man into a young vigorous performer in a very short time.[24]

The Instructional Video

Bill tried hard to make the transformation on March 3, 1992, taping an instructional video for his style of mandolin playing. Only a few days after a long weekend in Michigan and Illinois, he gave it everything he had. Homespun Tapes produced the video at a studio in Nashville; the Kaman Music Corporation, makers of Ovation guitars sponsored the effort through a grant to the Smithsonian Institution. Thus, Bill and Ewing are seen playing Ovation guitars at various times. One of the video's two executive producers was Ralph Rinzler, and Bill undoubtedly gave his all for him.

The finished product makes it clear that, in spite of other problems, Bill's memory for instrumental tunes was undiminished. Included were several wonderfully quirky pieces he had been playing for years, heard here for the first time: "Frog on the Lily Pad," "Galley Nipper," "Smoky Mountain Schottische," "Tombstone Junction," and "Never Leave the A String."[25]

By the spring of 1992, Bill's affiliation with MCA was at an end. His first full session thereafter was with Ralph Stanley and the Clinch Mountain Boys, recorded sometime in May for the Charles R. Freeland Recording Company (CRFRC), a new independent label owned by the founder of Rebel Records. Remakes of "Letter from My Darling" and "I'll Meet You in Church Sunday Morning" were successful, but an attempt to record another "Can't You Hear Me Callin'" was rejected.[26]

LaBella Returns to Nashville

Julia LaBella, then age thirty-six, returned to Nashville in mid-May, this time to be a deejay on WSM radio. She had been working in "small market" FM radio in east Texas for about five years and decided "the time was right to step up to a 'large market' station." She sent recordings of her shows to several stations in the Nashville area but didn't ask Bill for help. "I wanted to get it on my own merits," she said. After she was hired, she visited *Opry* manager Hal Durham, and he expressed concern for Bill's health. She said she promised him she would look into it.[27]

Advertised in the June *Bluegrass Unlimited*, the June 20 grand opening of Bill Monroe's Bluegrass Hall of Fame and Museum at Bean Blossom didn't happen. The museum's displays were not ready (during the twenty-sixth annual festival, June 18–21), and to make matters worse, the backstage area of the new stage had not been completed either. Still, the show went on. Few probably noticed the new name of the festival's location in the *Bluegrass Unlimited* ad: "Bill and James Monroe's Festival Park and Campground"—a clear indication that father and son had made formal the joint ownership of the site.[28]

On July 5, Gene Lowinger returned to Sunset Park, this time to discuss with Bill a plan to photograph him on the road. Lowinger still had a beard and long hair, and hadn't played, but Bill called him out of the audience to play a tune on Campbell's fiddle. "I didn't play too well," he wrote later, "and as I shook hands with Monroe during the applause, he said to me, 'You need to practice, shave, and get a haircut.'" (The next time he went to see Bill, he'd shaved off his beard and practiced on a friend's fiddle. "Two out of three ain't bad," Lowinger told him.)[29]

At the end of July, Bill took what would be his last trip overseas, a three-day visit to southern France to play a small country music festival near Dore-l'Eglise on Sunday, July 26. On that day, a pink-colored facsimile of a one-dollar bill, with a photo of Bill replacing George Washington's portrait, was the only currency accepted at the festival. Surprising Bill by stopping by was former Blue Grass Boy Bill Keith, a frequent visitor to France after marrying a native, Claire Liret, in 1976. Keith guested, picking "Roanoke" with the band.[30]

One of Bill's oldest friends, country music star Carl Butler, died of a heart attack on September 4, 1992, at age sixty-seven. Bill had recorded his "White Rose" in 1988. At his funeral, Bill placed a white rose in his casket.[31]

Bill Sings "Mule Skinner Blues" and Plays Guitar

Earlier that year, at the instructional videotaping, Bill had demonstrated the guitar kickoff and "lick" he used when he sang "Mule Skinner Blues" in the late 1930s and early 1940s. At the *Opry* on October 17,while rehearsing in Dressing Room 2 (the dressing room for all of the *Opry*'s bluegrass bands), Cupp encouraged Bill to sing the song while playing Ewing's guitar, and that night on the 6:30 show, with Ewing playing Bill's mandolin, Bill sang and played "Mule Skinner Blues" as he had originally, for the first time in nearly fifty years.[32]

During the first years of Bill's life, a "William" was president of the United States (William Howard Taft, 1909–13) and a "William" would be president during his last: William "Bill" Clinton defeated incumbent George H. W. Bush on November 4, 1992.[33]

About three weeks later, another of Bill's oldest friends, Roy Acuff, died at age eighty-nine on November 28. Acuff's biographer, Elizabeth Schlappi, briefly but memorably recalled the two *Opry* stars in the 1970s, exemplifying the dedication *Opry* members have to their craft: "when Roy Acuff and Bill Monroe sing their hearts out together in a dressing room to practically no audience." Now only Bill remained of the *Opry*'s great triumvirate.[34]

At the *Opry* on January 2, 1993, fiddler Campbell arrived in an obviously inebriated state. Bill was willing to overlook it. But *Opry* officials noticed and contacted Bill on Monday, January 4, asking him not to let it happen again. Campbell was let go that day.[35]

During the 1990s Bill's weekend bookings declined and appearances on the *Grand Ole Opry* outnumbered his showdates, peaking in 1993: Of the year's fifty-two Saturdays, Bill appeared on the *Opry* thirty-three times. (The number would decrease in 1994, then increase to thirty in 1995.)[36]

Tate fiddled for about a week until Bill found Campbell's replacement: Robert Bowlin, age thirty-seven, a veteran sideman who'd played several instruments with various country stars. When Bowlin first came to Nashville in 1983–84, he fiddled briefly with James Monroe's Midnight Ramblers. Bessire, then James's road manager, hadn't seen him since then, but called and encouraged him to audition for Bill. After the audition on Friday afternoon, January 15, Bessire took Bowlin to get a hat. There was no time to waste—he was due to play the *Friday Night Opry* with Bill that night.[37]

Bill Plays for President Clinton

Three days later, on January 18, 1993, Bill and the Blue Grass Boys were in Washington, D.C., one of several bands playing in a huge, heated tent at "America's Reunion on the Mall," a festival celebrating the inauguration of President Clinton. First Daughter Chelsea Clinton was in the audience that day to hear Bill and the band, then Peter, Paul, and Mary. "I was still having to ask Dana [Cupp] what key the next song was in," Bowlin recalled.[38]

Chet Atkins and Bill, together when Bill's mandolin was returned to him in 1986, were together again on February 24 when the National Academy of Recording Arts and Sciences presented them with Lifetime Achievement Awards, recognizing them as "performers, who, during their lifetimes, have made creative contributions of outstanding significance to the field of recording." Only three country artists had previously been so honored: Roy Acuff and Hank Williams (1987) and Kitty Wells (1991).[39]

The Sixth "Big Plan"

Meanwhile, it appears James was thinking about the possibility of increased revenues at a refurbished Bean Blossom, and to that end, the sixth Big Plan was hatched (with Bill's blessing). Announced with full-page ads in the March 1993 *Bill Monroe Fan Club Newsletter* and the April 1993 *Bluegrass Unlimited* were festivals at Bean Blossom every month, from May to September. The May, July, and August events would feature country music, and a weekend in September, after the bluegrass festival, would feature an all-gospel music festival. But the May festival was cancelled (for reasons unknown) and the July festival was poorly attended, as was the all-gospel weekend. A second season of May-to-September festivals would not be attempted.[40]

Meanwhile, Bill appears to have been thinking about the future—about who would carry traditional bluegrass on at the *Grand Ole Opry* after he was gone. And he may have let *Opry* management know his choice, Ralph Stanley, about this time. Stanley, in his autobiography, credited Bill with doing the most to encourage his eventual membership in 2000.

> Bill made the loudest noise. It was all his doing. I didn't have to say a word to him. Bill told them they needed me on the *Opry* and that was all it would have took. This was 1993. Hal Durham was running it back then, and Harold [possibly

announcer Hairl Hensley] told me, "You're the only man that Bill's ever asked for them to put on the *Opry*." Bill wouldn't even put in a word for his own son, James, to get on the *Opry*.[41]

The June 1993 schedule was hectic, as usual, taking Bill and the band from Telluride, Colorado (June 17) to the twenty-seventh annual Bean Blossom fest (cut back to three days, June 18–20), then to festivals in Canton, Texas (June 22), Charlotte, Michigan (June 25), and Summersville, West Virginia (June 26), followed by a long jump to Long Island, New York, and the town of Huntington, for a concert on June 27. At the Summersville festival, Ernie Sykes, a Long Island native, asked Bill if he could "bum a ride" to Huntington. A bassist and singer Bill had seen with several bands since the 1980s, Sykes was welcome on the bus, Bill said. Also heading to Huntington, driving there from his apartment in Parsippany, New Jersey, was Gene Lowinger, proceeding with his plan of taking "informal nonperformance shots" of Bill.[42]

Later, Lowinger traveled to Nashville twice in July to go on trips with Bill and the band, taking many memorable photos. Then, on August 24, Bill came to "Lowinger's country" for a show in New York City at the Lincoln Center's Damrosch Park (with Ernie Sykes filling in for Tate, suffering with shingles). Bill, as usual, called on Lowinger to fiddle, and, anticipating this, Lowinger had prepared by practicing "Big Mon." He wrote in his memoir that everyone in the band knew he was going to play it, but that Ewing "must have been feeling a bit mischievous" when Bill asked him what was next and he suggested "Uncle Pen." Ewing insists he didn't know of the plan to play "Big Mon" and that he thought "Uncle Pen" would be easy for Lowinger. But Lowinger hadn't played it in a long time and wasn't happy with his performance. He would, however, practice it the following week and play it well at Sunset Park on August 29, the last time he saw Bill.[43]

On September 2, Bill and the band appeared on *Nashville Now* for the last time. The Nashville Network, soon to go out of business, dropped the popular program on October 15, 1993, eliminating a primary source of national exposure for Bill.[44]

A True Believer

With the loss of MCA, a decline in bookings, and the end of *Nashville Now*, it was the time for Bill to reach out for the help of a true believer. West Virginian Vic Gabany was working as an engineer at Bradley's Barn in the early 1970s when Bill met him, and he would serve as a consultant on all of Bill's MCA recordings thereafter. Hired by WSM in 1976, Gabany handled the complicated Opry House sound system for all of Bill's radio performances. Eventually he offered his services as a producer if Bill ever wanted to record on his own—but a long time had passed without a word about the offer. One night, Gabany was visiting in Dressing Room 2 and finally heard the decision: "Bill said, 'Boys, Vic is going to start producing my recordings.'" Only then did they talk about financing the venture, with Gabany offering to cover expenses (including studio time and session pay for the Blue Grass Boys), to be recouped after the project was sold. They scheduled a session for Monday, September 19, six days after Bill's eighty-second birthday.[45]

The September 19 session was cancelled and rescheduled for October 10. It too was cancelled and rescheduled for November 9, which was also cancelled. Finally, the band entered Imagine Studios in Nashville on Sunday, November 14, 1993, with Bill wearing a jaunty, new dark-blue felt hat. Gabany was convinced that indifference by MCA could be overcome with another collection of Bill's instrumentals, so the session began with one of the newest, "Friday Night at the *Opry*," a banjo tune Bill had composed at the *Friday Night Opry* of August 20. This was followed by "Tombstone Junction" and "Northern White Clouds," recorded in live performances in 1989 and 1990, but not yet available on CD. Last was "Slow and Easy Blues," so named, Bill explained, "because you play it slow and easy."[46]

The second session was scheduled for (and actually happened on) Sunday, January 9, 1994. That afternoon, everyone was surprised to see Jimmy Campbell arrive at the studio. Bowlin had a flat tire on the way into town, and Campbell was called to substitute. But Bowlin made it to the session sooner than expected, so Bill put the two of them to work on a twin fiddle rendition of "Tombstone Junction." After Campbell departed, Bowlin fiddled solo on the next six tunes, including 1987's "Jack Across the Way" (a title Bill once said he liked because it could be about a man or a male donkey). The older "Frog on the Lily Pad" and "Smoky Mountain Schottische" were already familiar, thanks to the 1992 video *The Mandolin of Bill Monroe*. Also from the past came the seldom-heard "Boston Boy," a tune Uncle Pen used to play, which David Grisman had originally recorded in 1976 on *The David Grisman Rounder Album*, and Bill's "Roxanna Waltz," which Kenny Baker had recorded in 1972 for *Kenny Baker Country* (County). The session ended with a redo of "Slow and Easy Blues."[47]

The number of Bill's showdates increased to sixty in 1994, after an all-time low of thirty-eight in 1993. Helping to up the total was "Bill and James Monroe's Father and Son 1994 Winter Tour," ten shows in eight states during January and February, a few including the Sullivan Family and Gary Brewer and his Kentucky Ramblers. James recalled that Brewer booked several of the dates first, then Bill and he were added to create the tour. Also affecting the increase was the possibility that 1994 might be the last year to book the Father of Bluegrass. No ploy was needed, even though his price was now between $10,000 and $15,000 a day. But Bill was always willing to agree to a lesser amount for smaller venues, according to Jimmy Zmudka, Bill's longtime agent at Buddy Lee.[48]

Charlene Smith decided to end her relationship with Bill at the end of January. With LaBella back in Nashville, Bill had been alternating his affections between the two of them, Smith said. She also said she'd just become a grandmother and needed to return to Alabama to help with the baby.[49]

Falls and Fractures

After a long weekend on the Father and Son tour, Bill was back home on the farm on Sunday, February 6, when he fractured his right wrist. How it happened isn't known, but it was likely the result of Bill being unsteady on his feet, trying to stop a fall with his hand. The fracture was immobilized with a splint and, although he had little flexibility in his wrist, he continued to play.[50]

Bill removed the splint when he appeared at the first "Wintergrass" festival, held in a downtown Tacoma, Washington, hotel on the weekend of February 25, three weeks after an injury that normally takes six to heal. He made quite an impression that weekend, as reported in *Bluegrass Unlimited*:

[T]he most notable feature for many in attendance was the continued, energetic, and enthusiastic participation by the Father of Bluegrass Music. From the time Bill Monroe arrived at the hotel on Friday afternoon, he spent his non-entertaining hours singing, playing, laughing, and visiting with the adults and children who had come for the sole purpose of hearing him play.

By Sunday, everyone had a Bill Monroe story. One fan observed the white-hatted hero walking stealthily up behind a mandolin player absorbed in his break. Bill stood and watched over the picker's shoulder, motioning to the other players not to say anything. When the break was over, Bill tapped the mandolin player on the shoulder and graciously asked if he might borrow the instrument.[51]

Following a comparatively easy weekend playing the *Friday Night Opry* and the *Grand Ole Opry*, Bill was on the farm on Monday, March 7, when he fell again and fractured his right hip. According to witnesses, he was not feeling well but walked out of the cabin to say goodbye to a couple of visitors, and lost his footing in some gravel. That night, he underwent hip-replacement surgery at Baptist Hospital and would be out of action for nearly five weeks.[52]

Mary Starkey, Bill's Caregiver

Bill was back home by the end of March, using a walker to get around. It was then that road manager Bessire called Bill's longtime lady friend Mary Starkey in Columbus, Ohio. First he asked if she knew anyone who might be willing to take care of Bill, which she said she didn't.

> Then he told me, flat out, "Well, it's you or the nursing home." He said that Bill was running caregivers off faster than James could hire 'em—that he ran three off in one week. He said, "Frankly, James is just fed up." So, I told him, "O.K. I'll be there."

Straightaway, she quit her job and arrived in Goodlettsville within a few days. (Bill greeted her with "Where you been? You're late.") She would live on the farm through the end of April, not only taking care of Bill and doing all the housework, but also feeding the horses, dogs, and chickens for $225 a week. After a brief visit to Columbus in May, Starkey moved into a house she bought in nearby Bethpage, Tennessee, in June, with LaBella filling in for her until July. Then Starkey arranged with James to visit the farm and "hang out with Bill" two or three times a week, mainly serving as a housekeeper for five dollars an hour. This arrangement would continue for about a year, through August 1995.[53]

Selling the Farm

Bill returned to performing on April 8, at the *Friday Night Opry*. That weekend, in the classified section of Nashville's Sunday *Tennessean*, a large ad began appearing for an "Absolute Auction—Sat., Apr. 23, 10:30 A.M., 244 Scenic Rolling Acres, Rustic Two Story Log Home, Plus 3 Bedroom 2 Bath 2 Story Home ["the little house up the holler"], The Legendary Bill Monroe Farm, Father of Bluegrass Music." A description of the log cabin followed and, beneath it, a list of "personal property," including horses, farm machinery, a 1968 Cadillac Eldorado [once spray-painted with "bad words"], pickup trucks, and a horse-drawn wagon. At first glance, it appeared that Bill's farm and everything on it would be sold to the highest bidder. But the ad's "fine print" revealed otherwise: "Although [Bill] is reserving the log home, barn, and approximately 10 acres for a lifetime estate, he is selling the farm, affording you the opportunity of a lifetime."

Bill would be able to live out his life in his cabin on (actually) fourteen acres of the farm. Still, it was a sad outcome for a man for whom having a farm meant so much, the final result of the failure of the Big Plans; of large sums of money borrowed and lost during the last twenty years, now due to be repaid. Starkey said Bill was in denial: "He said that he wasn't the one that created the bills, that he shouldn't have to sell his farm to pay off James's bills." She said she reminded him that he was an equal partner in most of the Big Plans and was equally responsible for the debts. Evidently, James would later feel it necessary to say this publicly, paying for a full-page "Advertorial" in *Bluegrass Unlimited* to explain the financial realities involved. In it, he also noted: "James Monroe advised his father that if he was going to sell the farm by auction, he should retain the rights to his home and some acreage as a lifetime estate."[54]

On Saturday morning, April 23, the farm was "packed," recalled Glen Duncan, the only Blue Grass Boy, former or current, at the auction. Once there, he went straight to Bill. "I was worried that he would be so sad and distraught," Duncan said, "but he absolutely wasn't. I think he loved the fact that he drew a crowd!" Duncan hadn't read the ad's fine print and thought the worst was about to happen, but Bill knew better.

Bidding on the farm came first. The auctioneer briefly introduced Bill, seated on the cabin's porch, and he waved to the crowd. Then the auctioneer asked if there was anything he wanted to say. Bill stood up, removed his hat, sang "Blue Moon of Kentucky," and disappeared inside the cabin. The old master showman, though hurting, went out on top, Duncan thought: "He made sure that every one of those people knew who Bill Monroe was and he demonstrated that 'Blue Moon of Kentucky' was a 'powerful' song, and *that* meant more to him than fifteen farms."

In the bidding that followed, a representative of the Gaylord Entertainment Company (owners of WSM and the *Opry*), Tony Conway of Buddy Lee, and "a couple of others," James recalled, bid as high as they could go. Surprising everyone, Gaylord was the highest bidder: $375,000.[55]

Almost exactly one month later, on Sunday, May 22, Bill and the band recorded the third and final session Vic Gabany would produce. It began with a new tune Bill titled "Pocahontas," the name of both the Native American "Indian princess" and the Arkansas hometown of fiddler Bowlin. The next tune was also new, memorializing recent events: "Old Farm Blues." Third was "Two Finger Waltz," which Bill may have amused himself with for years, a tune played by fretting the mandolin with only two fingers of the left hand. It was followed by a resurrected "Land of Lincoln," first recorded in 1969, but lost by Decca. "Watermelon on the Vine," as if closing an *Opry* show, ended the session.[56]

The First Bluegrass Night

After a $9 million renovation of the Ryman Auditorium was completed in May 1994, the first "Martha White Bluegrass Night" was held there on June 14, appropriately starring Bill (who agreed the Ryman should be torn down in 1971) and his Blue Grass Boys. Also appearing was new *Opry* member Alison Krauss and Union Station. Bill's reviews were mixed: in the morning edition of the *Tennessean*, Tom Roland wrote that Bill "struggled with pitch when he took vocal solos, painfully evident on 'Wayfaring Stranger.'" Jay Orr, in the evening edition of the *Banner*, thought Bill was in "a jovial mood and looking fit" and his mandolin playing was "sure and vibrant."[57]

Three days later, Bill was welcoming crowds to his twenty-eighth annual Bean Blossom Festival (June 17–19). Vic Gabany, hoping to interest MCA Records in a sequel to the live Bean Blossom albums of 1973 and 1979, recorded all of Bill's sets that weekend.[58]

The Death of Ralph Rinzler

On July 2, Ralph Rinzler, the man who renewed Bill's musical career, died of AIDS at age fifty-nine, during the 1994 edition of the Festival of American Folklife that he helped to found. That evening, a choral group from the Bahamas was about to sing in a large tent on the National Mall in Washington, D.C., when a thunderstorm struck. As Richard Kurin of the Smithsonian recalled,

> Some of the folks from the Bahamas noted how it was God that was talking through the thunder and lightning and that it was not appropriate to perform until he'd finished. Kayla Edwards, the presenter and the Deputy Director of Culture for the Bahamas, explained [to the audience] how some people thought that such strong storms signified that a great person had died—that the storm

was nature's way of making room for a new, ascending spirit. She did not know that Ralph had passed away just at that time.

In the same tent, on July 7, a memorial service was held, with several speakers and singers, including the Bahamian group. Bill, just back from a trip to Montana, flew there, guided by LaBella. Mike Seeger picked them up at the airport and played guitar for Bill when he sang "Wayfaring Stranger" (with no noticeable pitch problems). Then Bill spoke:

> Ralph Rinzler was such a wonderful friend of mine and he done so much for me. . . . [H]e was the first man to ever put me in the colleges all over the United States and I really appreciate all that, everything he done for me. He was just a wonderful friend and I really appreciate everything, and I hate that we have lost him, but I'm glad [that I was] invited to come up here and bring my mandolin along and sing.[59]

Two weeks later, Bill and Earl Scruggs were reunited at the Ryman, part of Ricky Skaggs's "Bluegrass Night" on Tuesday, July 19. With Skaggs on guitar, Benny Martin, fiddle, and Roy Huskey Jr., bass, they played a thirty-minute set that received several standing ovations. Bill and the band were due at the Turning Point club in Piermont, New York, the next night, so, while most of the band left Nashville that night and traveled to Piermont by bus, Bill flew to Newark, New Jersey, the next morning, with Ewing as his escort (and with tickets Skaggs had paid for). Bill was late arriving at the Nashville airport, causing them to nearly miss the flight, and by the time they got to the club, after several hours of Bill's disorientation, Ewing was "fit to be tied," he said. Drinks were on the house at the club's bar, and Ewing's condition that night was obvious. But Bill never said a word to him about it, and, by the next day, it was as if it had never happened.[60]

In the summer of 1994, Kathy Chiavola asked Bill to be a part of her first bluegrass project. At his suggestion, Vic Gabany set up recording equipment in the living room of Bill's cabin and, with just Bill and Chiavola playing and singing, they recorded duet renditions of "Stay Away from Me" and "Old, Old House" on the afternoon of Wednesday, July 27. Added a few months later were banjo (Butch Robins), fiddle (Randy Howard), and bass (Kurt Storey).[61]

Bill's birthday parties, from 1989 to 1992, were held at the Bell Cove in Hendersonville, then were moved to the farm; Charlene Smith hosted the first, on Sunday, September 12, 1993. The 1994 party, which Julia LaBella organized, was on Bill's eighty-third birthday, Tuesday, September 13, 1994. Invitations for the party read "Come Help Me Celebrate My 83rd Birthday in a Powerful Pickin' and Picnicin' Way!—Bring your instrument and covered dish." Former Blue Grass Boy Sandy Rothman, who came in from California, recalled the arrival of Earl Scruggs as the Del McCoury Band played on the cabin's porch:

> At one point during the proceedings, Earl Scruggs drove up, alone. He sat for awhile at the same picnic table I was sitting at, watching the music. He didn't play. Later, after the cake-cutting, Bill and Earl sat side-by-side in the yard in two rocking chairs, receiving friends and fans. It was truly heartwarming to see the two old lions sitting together like that, after all the years and all the history.[62]

Former Blue Grass Boy Butch Robins was the next to ask Bill to record with him. Robins scheduled sessions on Friday, October 28, and Sunday, October 30, to record four of Bill's instrumentals, with Lamar Grier's son, David Grier, on guitar, Jimmy Campbell on fiddle (with Buddy Spicher twinning on one tune), and Marvin Cockram or Mike Bub on bass. Monroe-style mandolinist Mike Compton was there also; Robins asked him to help Bill remember the tunes. On the two Bill played lead on, "The Golden West" and the new "Old Lonesome Waltz," Compton played rhythm only, but, uniquely, he played harmonies to Bill's picking on the new "I'd Like to Be Over Yonder" and on a tune Robins recorded for Rounder in 1980, "My Father's Footsteps." Robins remembered Bill cutting up, shuffling his feet like a dancer while playing sitting down, flirting with the wives and girlfriends present, and blowing them kisses.[63]

In between sessions with Robins, on Saturday, October 29, 1994, Bill celebrated his fifty-fifth anniversary on the *Grand Ole Opry*. He played Ewing's guitar and sang "Mule Skinner Blues" on the 7:30 portion. Visiting Bill backstage was thirty-year-old grandson "Jimbo," then a deputy sheriff with the Sumner County Sheriff's Department. Just before the 10:15 portion, someone suggested Jimbo ought to sing a song on the show and, of course, Bill's reply was, "That'll be fine, right there." That night on the *Opry*, Jimbo sang lead on "My Sweet Blue-Eyed Darling," one he'd often sung with "granddaddy" when he'd traveled with him that year. "This was a huge deal for me," he said later, "to stand in the circle where Bill Monroe, Hank Williams, and Elvis Presley stood and sang was just an otherworldly experience."[64]

Former Blue Grass Boy Byron Berline was next to solicit Bill's help in recording a new CD and, in the process, he reunited "the two old lions" (Earl Scruggs, seventy, and Bill, eighty-three) in a recording studio for the first time in nearly fifty years. On Tuesday, November 8, they rerecorded "Sally Goodin," with Bill singing four of its seldom-recorded stanzas. Sadly, he seemed to be having timing problems, particularly on the second stanza. Ewing recalled Bill's increasing inability to play rhythm during this time, but said there were usually no timing problems when Bill sang or took a break.[65]

Gary Brewer, who arranged showdates for Bill and James at the beginning of 1994, asked Bill to record via overdubbing at the end of the year. On December 8, Brewer brought a multitrack tape to the Fox Farm Studio in Mt. Juliet (near Nashville), Tennessee, that he and his Kentucky Ramblers had recorded in Louisville a week earlier. They left tracks open on Bill's guitar specialty "Ozark Rag" (which Brewer played on guitar) and a new tune, "The Old Kentucky Blues," which Bill had shown to Brewer back in January. Bill added a mandolin chop to "Ozark Rag" and dubbed in a full mandolin break on "The Old Kentucky Blues." Listening to the playback, Brewer asked Bill if it needed something, and Bill suggested "Uncle Josh" Graves's Dobro picking. Brewer said later that they called Graves and he "came right over" from his nearby Madison, Tennessee, home.[66]

Bill's road schedule evaporated during the first two months of 1995, limiting him to appearances on the *Friday Night Opry* and the *Grand Ole Opry*. Finally, he and the band flew to Tacoma, Washington, for a return engagement at "Wintergrass" on February 25. When he was there before, Bill had circulated among festivalgoers in the hotel and played with some, "jamming" in the hallways. This time, after two months of inactivity, the long trip, and two performances (including one that began at 11:00 P.M.), he was completely exhausted. Unfortunately, when he tried to circulate, he was observed by a writer who would later portray him in this condition.[67]

"Bill Monroe and the Boys"

Trying to stay in shape musically with a limited schedule, Bill had become a regular at a Tuesday night jam session at Goodlettsville's Long Hollow Jamboree, a storefront converted into a showplace, close to his farm. In March 1995 he played some shows with a guitar player and singer he'd met there, Lonnie Jones, and his band, Fast Forward (Gary Reece, banjo; cousin Ricky Reece, mandolin and electric bass; and then-wife Shirley Jones, upright bass). Joined by Tater Tate on fiddle and billed as "Bill Monroe and the Boys," they played three or four shows on Thursday nights, from March 16 through the end of May, in an old high school gym dubbed "Monroe Music's Little *Opry*," sponsored by Monroe Music, a music store in Tompkinsville (Monroe County), Kentucky. "We'd pack the house," said Jones.[68]

Bill recorded an all-instrumental session with Jimmy Campbell on March 20 at the same small studio where he'd recorded with Robins about six months earlier (the "Top of the Hill" studio, in the basement of a Nashville duplex). Three musicians from Robins's sessions reappeared: Mike Compton played rhythm mandolin, soloed on one, and twinned with Bill again on one; Buddy Spicher twin-fiddled on one, and Mike Bub played bass. All of the musicians involved were sensitive to Bill's abilities at this point, playing at slower-than-normal tempos to accommodate him—even slowing completely in mid-tune ("Fiddlers Blues") to match him.[69]

Bill and Jimmy Martin

That spring, in his ongoing attempt to reconcile with everyone during his last days, Bill tried to make peace with Jimmy Martin. They had been estranged for many years, as much for Bill's opinion of Martin's drinking as for Martin's knowledge that Bill had opposed his *Opry* membership. Vic Gabany was standing with Bill at the side of the *Opry* stage one night when Martin came to visit and stood in the darkened area just offstage.

> When Bill noticed Jimmy, he slowly started walking over to where he was standing. Just prior to reaching him, Bill stuck out his hand, as if to offer Jimmy a handshake. Jimmy looked down at Bill's extended hand and said, "What's that for?" Bill replied, "I want to shake your hand." Jimmy then said, "Well, I don't want to shake yours!" Bill didn't say anything, and slowly turned around and walked back to where he was earlier.[70]

Also that spring, Kentucky Governor Brereton C. Jones issued a proclamation designating April 30, 1995, as "Bill Monroe Appreciation Day." It appears to have been prompted by Bill's willingness to play benefits, prominently mentioning that he had "used his God-given talents to benefit those in need." The Kentucky House of Representatives quickly followed suit, issuing a thoughtfully worded declaration to honor him:

> Kentucky's own native son and the "Father of Bluegrass Music," for his phenomenal contribution to the nourishment and preservation of traditional music. Let it be known from this day forth that music creates the heart and soul of an individual; and that music makes a despairing heart soar and the smallest child smile; therefore Bill Monroe, being truly an artist who has produced such grand musical moments for Kentuckians and the world, must be praised for his brilliant interpretation of bluegrass music and recognized by this prestigious body

for that gift, which will be listened to and appreciated by music lovers now and for decades to come.[71]

Blue Grass Boys Boycott Benefits

Meanwhile, the Blue Grass Boys (Bowlin, Cupp, Ewing, and Tate) had recently declared their unwillingness to play benefit shows with Bill. For months, Bill had accepted any invitation to play a benefit, sometimes two or three a week, and he refused to pay the Blue Grass Boys to play them with him. This was contrary to musicians' union regulations, which required they be paid *something*. So, they let him know, as a group, that he would have to play benefits without them. Unfortunately, as far as Bill was concerned, this included *any* show he played for no pay. As a result, there were a few shows they would later regret not playing with him.[72]

One was Bill's first appearance at the Ole Barn Jamboree on Highway 62 in Rosine, Kentucky (later "the Rosine Barn Jamboree"), on Saturday, May 20. Ohio County natives Hoyt and Eleanor Bratcher were managing a general store in Rosine in 1992 when they renovated the adjacent barn as a showplace for local performers. At that time, they were also regular visitors to the Long Hollow Jamboree on Tuesday nights and the Bell Cove on Wednesday nights, sometimes taking Bill's sister Bertha and niece Rosetta with them. Ohio County officials heard about this, and, hoping to improve Bill's relationship with the county that "has never done what they should have," they asked the Bratchers to ask Bill what the county could do to honor him. Bill said he would like a memorial or plaque, like one for Rosine's war hero, Wesley Phelps, then standing near the renovated barn.

At this juncture, the Bratchers asked Bill to play at the Ole Barn Jamboree, but told him they couldn't afford to pay him. So, Hoyt Bratcher called local musicians Ralph Goodwine, Jim Hunt, and Doug Morris to play bass, fiddle, and guitar, respectively, with Bill. After Bill invited Butch Robins and Mike Compton to meet him, LaBella drove him there on May 20. During the fifty-minute show, he played the new tune he'd recorded with Robins last October, calling it "I Would Love to Be over Yonder."[73]

Bill and Baker

Vic Gabany once again brought his recording equipment to the Bean Blossom festival, the twenty-ninth annual, restored in 1995 to four days (June

15–18). Still believing that MCA might be interested in a live album, Gabany recorded all of Bill's shows, including one with a long-overdue reconciliation.

On Sunday afternoon, June 18, Gabany and Bill were alone together in one of the backstage dressing rooms, just before Bill's last set of the weekend. Through the door, they could hear the sounds of Baker and musical partner Josh Graves finishing their set, and Bill suddenly asked who was playing. Gabany told him, then decided to do something he said he'd never done before—he offered Bill advice: "Bill, if you and Kenny ever play together again, it should be here at Bean Blossom, your festival." After a long pause, Bill asked, "Would you go ask him if he would come out and play with me if I invited him out on stage?" Gabany said he left the room immediately and, as Baker was leaving the stage, he asked him Bill's question. "I no longer than got the words out of my mouth before Kenny said, 'If that's what the old man wants, then that's what I want.'"

Bill's set began as usual, with "My Sweet Blue-Eyed Darlin'," then Bill introduced "Mule Skinner Blues," saying, "Now we're gettin' ready to do a number for you right here, was the first one I ever sung on the *Grand Ole Opry*, and there's one of the greatest fiddlers comin' out on the stage and play with me on that that's ever been in the country. Let's give him a nice hand. His name is Kenny Baker." After the surprised crowd's applause died down, Bill asked, "Kenny, are you ready?" With his salty eastern Kentucky twang, Baker, last onstage with Bill in 1984, replied, "Ready? I been ready for this since '84!"[74]

Another grueling round of June festivals followed, from the 20th through the 25th (including Canton, Texas; Dahlonega, Georgia; Summersville, West Virginia; and Porterfield, Wisconsin). On Tuesday the 27th, Bill played a 3:30 *Opry* matinee, with Tate fiddling for an absent Bowlin, Mike Bub on banjo filling in for an absent Cupp, and Ernie Sykes filling in for Tate on bass. (Sykes, age twenty-four, would be the last of the Blue Grass Boys Bill would hire. Beginning in November 1995, Sykes would frequently replace Tate on bass at the *Opry* and on the road, as Tate's wife's health continued to deteriorate.) On the June 29, Bill was taken to Nashville Memorial Hospital with pneumonia. Released from Baptist Hospital on July 5 with a doctor's order for eight to ten days' rest, he was kept out of action until July 21.[75]

Mary Starkey quit "hanging out" with Bill on Monday, August 7, two days before she married Frank Elkins, a Bethpage, Tennessee, contractor. After she and her first husband divorced in 1970, she said she had hoped Bill would ask her to marry him. "I told Bill I was tired of waitin' for him and he had refused to get rid of Julia. He said that it was my place to tell her not to show up. I said, 'It's your house—it's your place [to tell her].'" After Starkey left, LaBella took over the housekeeping duties.[76]

Meanwhile, during July and August 1995, Wilma Hutchings, granddaughter of Caroline Goff (Malissa Monroe's friend of the early 1900s), with the help of her son, Aaron Hutchings, formed a nonprofit organization to encourage tourism in Rosine. The plans of The Rosine Association (TRA) included a museum with a life-size bronze statue of Bill on a large granite pedestal. According to Aaron Hutchings, Bill told a sculptor how he wanted to be depicted: wearing riding britches with his mandolin in one hand and his hat, raised high above his head, in the other. "He loved [the concept of] the statue because it was dressed the way he thought of himself," Hutchings said. (The TRA attempted to raise funds for this project, offering to inscribe a donor's name and message on a brick in the statue's pedestal for a donation of fifty dollars for a forty-character inscription. They didn't raise enough money, but donations amounting to about $5,000 were saved in a Beaver Dam, Kentucky, bank.)[77]

The Plaque

LaBella again drove Bill to the Ole Barn in Rosine on Thursday, September 21, for the ceremonial unveiling of Ohio County's honor to him—a large (41¼" in diameter), round, brass plaque, crafted at the nearby McHenry Brass Company by Bill Wallace and son Bill Wallace Jr. When it was unveiled, the honoree was quoted as saying, "I'm proud of that and the folks in Rosine should be too. I've played for four presidents, and they all told me the same thing: Bluegrass music belongs to all Americans. It originated right here in Rosine. I'm really proud of Rosine, Kentucky."

Engraved on the plaque, above and below a portrait of Bill's face (sculpted by Wallace Jr.), was its message: "The Great Legendary Father of Bluegrass Music Welcomes You To The Birthplace Of The Monroe Family—Rosine, KY." In between were the words "Bill Monroe Day" and "September 13," included before plans for the presentation on Bill's eighty-fourth birthday fell through. (The plaque was later attached to the front of the Ole Barn, where it's still located today.)

Five bluegrass musicians from the U.S. Navy's "Country Current" band, then appearing at the Executive Inn in Owensboro, provided music at the ceremony. A reporter from Owensboro's *Messenger-Inquirer*, Steve Vied, noted that Bill was walking with the help of a cane (due to hardening of the arteries, LaBella said later). So, it wasn't certain if he would feel like playing. But, after the band began to play, Bill called for his mandolin and temporarily took over the show, singing "Blue Moon of Kentucky," "Uncle Pen," and even doing a little dancing. "I thought once the music got started, he couldn't resist," Eleanor Bratcher told Vied.[78]

That afternoon, LaBella drove Bill the thirty miles north to Owensboro to visit the IBMA Convention at the Executive Inn. That evening, they attended the awards ceremony, Bill dressed in a white-coated tuxedo. Ronnie McCoury, accepting the Mandolin Player of the Year award for the third year in a row, told the audience, "I think there is someone here who deserves this award a lot more than I do." With that, he walked into the audience and handed it to Bill. After he thanked McCoury, Bill was photographed lifting the award toward Heaven.[79]

The National Medal of Arts

Two weeks later, on October 4, Bill flew to Washington, D.C., once more, accompanied by LaBella, and the next day he received from President Clinton one of the nation's highest civilian honors.

> The President of the United States awards this National Medal of Arts to William Smith Monroe for a brilliant and innovative musical career in an all-American style. Fusing traditional and gospel styles with country music and the blues, he originated the "high lonesome" sound of bluegrass and profoundly influenced 20th century American music.

The eighteen recipients were not scheduled to speak at the presentation ceremony, but Bill insisted on making a statement: "I have played for the last four presidents of the United States—President Carter, President Reagan, President Bush, President Clinton here—and they all tell me that the music I originated belongs to America, and I'm really proud of that. It's a great honor."[80]

After the ceremony, a black-tie dinner was held that evening in the State Dining Room, followed by orchestral music in the East Room, classical "fiddling" that may have inspired an unscheduled performance: after whispering to LaBella that he wanted to say something, Bill walked to the stage using his cane and announced he'd like to sing "Blue Moon of Kentucky." Unfortunately, no one in the orchestra knew it. But Bill persevered, singing it a cappella and asking everybody to join him. (It was the first time Bill actually sang *in* the White House.)[81]

An unusually busy October followed, taking the band to Louisiana, then Tennessee, North Carolina, and Florida during the second weekend, then on to Indiana for the third. Shortly thereafter, Bill was back in the hospital with another round of pneumonia. He was too ill on October 28 to play the *Opry* on his fifty-sixth anniversary, but he was back the following weekend and almost every Friday and Saturday after that during November and December of 1995.[82]

A Fan Meets Bill

During this time, a young bluegrass fan and mother of two in Springfield, Tennessee, heard Bill Monroe was playing at the Long Hollow Jamboree nearly every Tuesday night, so she drove the twenty miles to Goodlettsville, with her youngsters in tow, to see him. Kathy Seibel, recreation director of the Beverly Healthcare and Rehabilitation Center in Springfield, had grown up listening to bluegrass, so she relished an opportunity to see "the King," as she called him. As luck would have it, she was introduced to him that night and, not surprisingly, he tried to kiss her. "He went for the lips and I turned my head real quick," she said. Her admiration undiminished, she recalled observing, based on her experience at the nursing home, that he seemed very lonely. She said she wrote in her journal that night, "I don't think he will be here by Christmas next year." But she would become a regular at the Jamboree and soon be friends with Bill's driver, farmhand Lincoln Hastings, a struggling songwriter.[83]

Blood Pressure Problems

Bill's blood pressure problems seemed to reappear as soon as the new year began. Before his appearance on the *Friday Night Opry* of January 12, 1996, he complained of pains in his arms. *Opry* paramedics found his blood pressure to be dangerously high and, as a result, he would not play that weekend. But he played the next, after the dosage of his medication was adjusted. When the pains came back the following weekend (January 26), another adjustment was made, and the problem seemed to be solved during February. But it was only temporary.[84]

The *Bluegrass Unlimited* Article

Meanwhile, in the midst of this blood pressure upset, the February 1996 issue of *Bluegrass Unlimited* appeared in late January, featuring an article titled "With Body and Soul—notes from Wintergrass '95." It depicted Bill during his return visit to the indoor festival, beginning with a description of him as he attempted to circulate after a late night show:

> A very old man stood alone in a dim hallway. He was tired, confused, and not well. Slowly he struggled toward a bench and sat down near some standing musicians who were playing songs. A woman from the group who was a nurse stopped her playing to attend [to] the old man's health. He had traveled a long distance that day and the food he had eaten didn't agree with the dozen or so pills he had taken. The group played another song while the old man stared blankly into the crowd of curious passersby. Someone yelled, "Hi, Bill!," but what he saw was far away, and he said little to the nurse who worried about the old man's heart and kidneys. A pin that spelled JESUS was attached to the old man's lapel.[85]

Although "accurate," Bill was portrayed at his worst, and many readers were outraged. *Bluegrass Unlimited* received numerous letters of protest, but only three were published in its next issue. Significantly, the three included a forceful statement (excerpted here) from Tony Conway, future CEO of Buddy Lee Attractions.

> Where is the humanity when some writer dissects a person the way this writer did in his article regarding Mr. Monroe? . . . [F]or someone of Mr. Monroe's age to still have the passion, desire, and the need to perform live at the age of 84 years old, I would assume your readers would wonder in amazement how he does it, instead of how he could barely do it, according to your article.
>
>   I am very aware of the freedom of the press and its rights. However, such a special person with such extraordinary talent should not be depicted the way your magazine most recently did. In the true art of reporting, you should report on the outstanding shows, the standing ovations, the fire in the eye, the speed in the hand that still exists when Bill Monroe does what he loves to do: perform live bluegrass music.

Editor Pete Kuykendall replied by writing he believed the article "reported a bittersweet emotional occasion," and he offered a qualified apology: "I apologize to those who did not share my vision of the message the writer meant to convey." The next issue of *Bluegrass Unlimited* (April 1996) included a photo of a smiling Bill on its cover and a much more positive article about him inside.[86]

During this time, in mid-February 1996, Julia LaBella decided she couldn't continue being Bill's caregiver. She had filled in beginning in early 1994, when Mary Starkey couldn't be there, then took on the job full-time in August 1995 after Starkey left. She said that James refused to pay her, so to make ends meet, she waitressed nights at the Cherokee Steak House in Gallatin. "After two years of that," she said, "it was just too much."[87]

What would be Bill's last studio recordings were made a few days after La-Bella's departure. On Wednesday, February 21, 1996, Bill revisited three of his better-known songs with the duo of Billy and Terry Smith, sons of Hazel Smith, recording an album of tribute to him. He played two full breaks on "Mule Skinner Blues," a song he usually didn't take a break on, while Billy Smith did the singing. Then, on "Walk Softly on This Heart of Mine," which Bill usually took a break on, he didn't take one, and his tenor singing isn't heard until the third of three choruses. "He'd got sort of feeble during that time, so we didn't work him too hard. We used him sparingly," Billy Smith said later. A brief (two-minute) rendition of "Blue Moon of Kentucky" followed, also lacking his usual mandolin break. Notably, there was a slight change in the lyrics, with Bill singing "keep on *a*-shinin'" several times, instead of the usual "keep on shinin'." Sadly, on this fourth and last studio recording of his signature song, his singing was tremulous and often noticeably flat in pitch.[88]

Bill's blood pressure troubles returned that weekend. On February 24, between *Opry* shows, he again complained of pains in his arms, but when *Opry* medics checked, they found his pressure normal. The pains returned on the 28th at the Bell Cove; former Blue Grass Boy Wayne Lewis took him to the Hendersonville Hospital. Thereafter, James let it be known that doctors had told him they could not solve his father's blood pressure irregularities with an operation. Reducing stress might help, his doctors said, so Bill's upcoming *Opry* appearances were cancelled for March 1 and 2. The following weekend, he played three *Opry* shows without a problem. But to further reduce stress, James arranged for his father to be taken to Destin, Florida, for a week-long "vacation," accompanied by now-caregiver Lincoln Hastings.[89]

Bill's Last Show

Bill returned to Nashville for one show on the *Friday Night Opry* of March 15, a show that would turn out to be his last anywhere. He and the Blue Grass Boys (Bowlin and Tate, fiddles; Cupp, banjo; Ewing, guitar; Sykes, bass) opened the eight o'clock portion with the uptempo instrumental standard "Down Yon-der." Disconcertingly, Bill had trouble keeping up when he took a break, and his picking was uncharacteristically choppy (signs that he may have already suffered another minor stroke). A short time later, he sang "Stay Away from Me," and his singing, although on pitch, was weak. Several minutes later, the show's closer was the duet "True Life Blues" and for it, Bill seemed to rally—his singing was stronger and his mandolin picking was much smoother when he took a break. "Ah, that's a fine song right there," he said when the applause died down. Then a mumbled comment that Bill somehow managed to make humorous: "We're gonna be back here again tomorrow night with some of the same songs that we've already sung here for you tonight and we're gonna do 'em again for ya." As the audience chuckled, he seemed lost, asking: "Have you enjoyed it?" (*applause*) "Will you let us come back again?" (*laughter and applause*) "You got to hang in there with us now, hear?" he said sincerely. Then, mechanically, "And speakin' for the Blue Grass Boys and yours truly, we're just gonna say so long and we'll see you a little bit later on and we love you." Not certain he'd said the last three words loudly enough, he said them again. And as the band played the "Watermelon" theme, announcer Hairl Hensley credited Bill with "fifty-seven years at the *Grand Ole Opry*," anticipating that he would still be there in October 1996. But he would not.[90]

Bill complained to Hastings of having a headache as they drove home that night. The next morning Bill told him he was feeling worse, so Hastings took him straight to Baptist Hospital. Doctors determined he had, indeed, suffered a minor stroke, and, although he'd not been seriously affected by it, they decided to keep him at the hospital for observation. That night, the Blue Grass Boys played the *Grand Ole Opry* without him, allotted one song on the 6:30 portion. Ernie Sykes sang a moving rendition of "Kentucky Waltz."[91]

For the next three weeks, Bill remained at Baptist. Frustrated with this prolonged confinement, he had to be restrained and tranquilized after re-portedly pushing nurses away. He was formally admitted to the hospital on April 5, and a few days later, he suffered a major stroke. It robbed him of his ability to talk intelligibly and to walk. (At this point, it appears that Bill's mandolins were quietly put away for safekeeping.)[92]

Bill at the Medical Center

On April 12 Bill was transferred to the Tennessee Christian Medical Center in Madison. A pacemaker was installed on the 24th, standard procedure to boost a slow heart rate caused by high blood pressure and to prevent a heart attack. Then a visit was arranged on the 26th for four of the Blue Grass Boys (Cupp, Ewing, Sykes, and Tate), road manager Jim Bessire, and Terry Eldredge, a fill-in for Bill, all of whom were unprepared to see him in the condition he was in when they shuffled into room 408. "I'd been told he was having trouble talking," Ewing recalled, "but it really didn't hit me 'til I heard him mumble something and it didn't make sense. I tried to be cheerful, pinching his toes under the covers at the end of the bed, not realizing 'til later that he couldn't walk." "He knew what was going on," Sykes observed, "but he couldn't talk." Still, Bill tried to make contact: "I'll never forget that day," Sykes added, "because he grabbed my hand and he just held it right on his chest for, like, five minutes."[93]

Bill would remain at the Medical Center throughout May and June. Many old friends visited him during that time, including Jim Peva and his wife. Peva wrote of their first visit in his *Bean Blossom: Its People and Its Music*:

> He was sitting in a wheelchair, his head down, but with the white Stetson hat on his head. Ailene bent down and greeted him and he responded, but his speech, affected by the stroke, was unintelligible. His eyes showed that he recognized us, and Ailene managed to coax a smile out of him. But his eyes reminded me so much of the eyes of my own father who had suffered a fatal stroke several years earlier—eyes that expressed a loss of the will to live. Here was this man, so strong, proud, and independent all of his life, reduced to near helplessness, having to be dressed and undressed, helped in and out of bed by others, and unable to speak an intelligible sentence. The situation rendered me nearly speechless. What can you say in a situation like that? Ailene is much better than I in handling those situations. As a fellow Christian, I should have held Bill by the hand and said a prayer, but I couldn't bring myself to do it. Instead, I mumbled some nonsense about how he would come out of this like he had many illnesses before, but I knew, and I think Bill knew, they were just words. It was one of the saddest days of my life.

Fred and Denise Painter of Ohio visited Bill several times and developed the ability to understand a few words. Denise Painter recalled one time in particular:

> We went to see him and he wanted us to take him outside. They had a little picnic-type area outside the hospital and we rolled him out there in a wheelchair. He couldn't talk hardly at all, but we knew him well enough that we could communicate with him without having to talk—he could say enough words for us to know what he meant. We would say what we thought it was and he would nod his head. And, this time, he wanted us to take his slippers off and let him walk

in the grass one more time, and we did. We took his slippers off and helped him walk barefoot in the grass.

Bill was outside that summer when Julia LaBella made an unauthorized visit, seeing him for the last time. "They had wheeled him out to a hill under some trees, and he looked up, grabbed my hand and said, 'Farm! Home!'"[94]

Bill at the Nursing Home

But going home to the farm was not an option at the end of June, when Bill was about to be discharged from the Tennessee Christian Medical Center. It was then that caretaker Hastings remembered his friend Kathy Seibel, recreation director at a nursing home. And on July 2, she was there to greet Bill when he arrived at the Beverly Healthcare and Rehabilitation Center in Springfield, Tennessee, about twenty-five miles north of Nashville, where he would spend most of the last ten weeks of his life. (Shortly after arriving, he developed a kidney infection and went to the nearby Northcrest Medical Center for a short time, causing the confusion concerning his location.)[95]

Seibel recalled Bill was "sullen and sad" when he arrived at the Beverly Center. "There was nothing gleeful about his arrival. He was like a beaten man." Her job, she said, was "to make sure that people enjoyed life," and, in this case, she had her work cut out for her. Busy with all of the center's ninety-five residents, working with fifteen to twenty on a one-to-one basis, two or three times a week, she began by taking the time to visit Bill every day. "What I did was I just took care of what I could take care of. He wanted soft Kleenex, soft socks—I made sure he had 'em." He didn't like the food very much—"Sometimes he would take a spoonful of it and slap it on the floor"—so she started making him peach pie and fried chicken.[96]

"Bill gave me more trouble than five husbands," Seibel said, "but, at the same time, he never gave me a minute of trouble." Every bit was eliminated when she reminded herself of who he was: "This is the most amazing musician we will ever know in our lives!"[97]

Among the first to visit him, in early July, were Bill and Wilma Millsaps, a traditional bluegrass music husband-and-wife team from western North Carolina. During their brief visit, Bill Millsaps realized Bill had no mandolin. When the Millsapses returned later that month, they brought their band, the Snowbird Mountain Boys, and a mandolin Bill Millsaps had built, a copy of Bill's F-5. He presented it to Bill in his room; then the band (Bill Millsaps, mandolin; Wilma Millsaps, guitar; her sister Joan Lovelace, bass; Robert Jenkins, fiddle) played for a group of residents in the cafeteria. Bill was taken there in a wheelchair, clutching the mandolin in his arms. Afterward, Millsaps told Seibel to "make sure he has access to it at all times."[98]

Was Bill capable of playing it? "It was very choppy and very loud, but yes, he could play it," said Seibel. "Did he feel it, did he hold it, did he love it? Absolutely." She played guitar with him a few times: "If anybody struck a note that was wrong, did he know it? Oh, hell, yeah!"[99]

Seibel also sang with Bill on several occasions: "I would prompt him— once you started singing, he would chime right in." Seibel recalled that when Bill sang, every word was clearly understandable, unlike the slurred speech he was afflicted with. When they sang together, she said it was sometimes "old-time church stuff," rather than Monroe material. Bill's voice may have been a little weak, but "although it wasn't as powerful in volume as it used to be, it was in soul."[100]

The second band to play for Bill was the Melvin Goins band (then still known as "the Goins Brothers"). Heading back to eastern Kentucky after playing the Hugo, Oklahoma, festival (which Bill and the Goins Brothers helped start in 1969), Goins decided to stop by and see Bill on Monday, August 9. He'd spoken to James and, as an old friend, he was cleared for a visit, but not so the rest of the band (Dave Baker, bass; Buddy Griffin, fiddle and banjo, filling in for semi-retired brother Ray Goins on a few numbers; John Keith, mandolin; and John McNeely, guitar). Not being allowed to see him "was understandable, but disappointing nonetheless," mandolinist Keith said later. Sensing the band's disappointment, Seibel suggested they play for Bill (without official clearance, jeopardizing her job), and she directed them to the yard outside the window of his room. "She pointed to an open window and told us to 'casually' make our way in that direction," Keith explained. "As we peered in the window, they had Bill sitting up and were giving him his glasses." Goins and his band would play for Bill for about a half hour, doing several Bill Monroe favorites, including "I'm on My Way Back to the Old Home," "Blue Moon of Kentucky," "Raw Hide," "My Rose of Old Kentucky," and "Uncle Pen." Goins said later he could hear Bill humming along.[101]

As the End Neared

James visited every other day and Lincoln Hastings almost as often. But in spite of all this attention, Bill "was givin' up," Seibel said, and one of the toughest things to deal with was reminiscent of Bill of the past:

He had a tendency to shut everyone off from time to time. . . . In a room with one hundred people, he could shut everyone out, but know everything that was going on. . . . "You had to screw with him to get him going. I'd say, 'Come on, you old crapper. Let's go!' Then he would giggle, wink an eye, or play a tune."[102]

Their relationship had deepened, but, as the end neared, Seibel wasn't always sure Bill knew who she was:

We sang, we played, we laughed, we cried, we prayed. Sometimes Bill knew me, and I reckon sometimes he knew me as someone even more special to him—maybe Melissa or Julia. I don't know. But I do know he always responded to me with sincere gentleness, respect, and love. So, no matter who I was, he felt loved back.[103]

Bill's death certificate would list the cause of death as a "probable" heart attack due to hardening of the arteries, but Seibel believes he willed himself to death: "He just said to himself, 'I'm done. I've done my time. I'm done.'" She was with him when the end came, four days before his eighty-fifth birthday: "On Monday, September 9, 1996, at 9:40 A.M., he closed those precious blue eyes and traveled on—not a struggle, no strife; he simply left this world as we know it." And, just before he left: "The very last soft, sweet words spoken into Bill's so-keen ears were 'Make a joyful noise unto the Lord.'"[104]

EPILOGUE

Readers of this book have undoubtedly noticed Bill Monroe's ongoing involvement with women who were younger than he, and they may consider it his worst fault. It should be noted, however, that those relationships helped Bill continue to feel young and vital throughout the years we knew him, and they inspired some great love songs. Commenting on this latter aspect of relationships, Bill once said, "If you've got something to write about, you can write good songs."

It should also be noted that Bill's life was filled with fortunate circumstances. Readers have probably noticed a few, but just in case, I'll mention some of the most prominent ones here:

He had a mother who cared about him, sympathized with his struggles to play music, and provided him with an instrument that was ideally suited to him.

He grew up knowing and playing with two master musicians.

Suffering with appendicitis, he was carried by six men for over five miles and put on a train to a hospital, and, if he'd arrived less than an hour later, he might have died.

One of his older brothers eventually gave him the opportunity to shine vocally and instrumentally, resulting in the first widespread notice of his musical abilities.

His first wife gave him two children and stood by him, helping him with his career for many years, in spite of his infidelity and their divorce.

I speculated that Bill learned of his older brother's appointment to audition for the *Opry* and went there ahead of him as a result. But his decision to go to Nashville when he did may have just been a whim.

While strolling around Miami, window-shopping, he just happened to find his first F-5 mandolin, a remarkable instrument that was exactly what he needed.

He was able to form "the classic bluegrass band" with four extremely talented young men who, for the most part, came to him, rather than him having to find them.

He was involved in a serious car accident, a head-on collision he stubbornly helped cause, which could have ended his career or killed him, but he survived and recovered.

When his career was sagging, he was approached by a young scholar who, in spite of Bill's initial rejection of him, was determined to help (and did famously).

I speculated that he was advised to include four young men in his band in the 1960s, due to the popularity of the Beatles. But young men may have wanted to play with him simply because of their interest in folk music or their rejection of rock and roll.

He was diagnosed with colon cancer, an enlarged prostate, and heart problems, but underwent surgeries and survived them all.

And, at the end of his life, he was cared for by a woman younger than he who knew who he was and made an effort to actually get to know him.

Two funerals were held for Bill: the first in Nashville on September 11, 1996; the second, the next day in Rosine, just prior to his burial in Rosine Cemetery, to rest there with his mother and dad and, eventually, all of his brothers and sisters (Bertha died on April 1, 1997).

I didn't attend either service for Bill. I was on the way to, or playing in, Salem, Illinois, with another band, David Davis and the Warrior River Boys, which I'd joined when it was clear that Bill would never play again. But even if I hadn't joined another band, I wouldn't have attended his services because I did not want to accept the fact that he was dead. Writing this book has helped me realize that all of us, including the great Bill Monroe, must have a last chapter, and that as long as he's remembered, he will continue to be alive.

APPENDIX:

BLUE GRASS BOYS

Edward Windsor "Eddie" Adcock: born in Scottsville, Va., June 21, 1938

David "Stringbean" Akeman: born in Annville, Ky., June 17, 1916, died Nov. 10, 1973

James "Jim" Andrews: born in Elkmont, Ala., further information not available

Steve Arkin: born in New York, N.Y., May 1, 1944

Bobby Lee Atkins: born in Shoals, N.C., May 22, 1933

Billy Baker: born in Pound, Va., July 5, 1936

Kenneth Clayton "Kenny" Baker: born in Burdine (near Jenkins), Ky., June 26, 1926, died July 8, 2011

Scottie Brian Baugus: born in Savannah, Tenn., Sept. 16, 1960

Larry Wayne Beasley: born in Casey Co., Ky., Jan. 29, 1953

Byron Berline: born in Caldwell, Kan., July 6, 1944

Robert Wilson "Bob" Black: born in Des Moines, Iowa, June 14, 1949

James Garfield "Gar" Bowers: born in Winston-Salem, N.C., Mar. 21, 1927, died Nov. 6, 2003

Robert Ray Bowlin: born in Pocahontas, Arkansas, Sept. 22, 1955

Billy Joe "Bill" or "Billy" Box: born in Seymour, Mo., Feb. 3, 1937

James Andrew "Andy" Boyett: born in Miami, Fla. (date unknown), died 1989

Elliott Thurman "Curley" Bradshaw: born in Green Co., Ky., Dec. 27, 1911, died Oct. 27, 1958

Carlos Ray Brock: born in Hyden, Ky., Mar. 18, 1934, died May 17, 2016

James Earl Bryan: born in Gadsden, Ala., Nov. 24, 1953

Franklin Glenn "Frank" Buchanan: born near Penland, N.C., Mar. 25, 1934, died July 4, 2012

James Robert "Jimmy" Campbell: born in Bellville, Mich., Apr. 28, 1963, died Oct. 24, 2003

Mack Louis Carger: born in Bryant, Ark., May 31, 1919, died Mar. 28, 2014

Gene Christian: born in Mt. Pleasant, Tenn., Feb. 22, 1926, died Oct. 4, 2013

Porter Church: born in Bristol, Tenn., Apr. 17, 1934, died Aug. 18, 1995

Vassar Clements: born in Kinard, Fla., Apr. 25, 1928, died Aug. 16, 2005

Charlie Cline: born in Baisden, W.Va., June 6, 1931, died Nov. 19, 2004

Vernon Crawford "Jack" Cooke: born in Bear Branch, Va., Dec. 6, 1936, died Dec. 1, 2009

Noah Crase: born in Barwick, Ky., Dec. 10, 1934, died Apr. 13, 2010

Dana Cupp Jr.: born in Detroit, Mich., July 11, 1959

Vic Ray Daniels: born in Independence, Va., Jan. 4, 1925, died in 1988

Johnnie Cleo "Cleo" Davis: born in Antioch, near Cedartown, Ga., Mar. 9, 1919, died July 17, 1986

Stephen Randall "Randy" Davis: born in Asheville, N.C., June 20, 1954

Clonnie David "David" Deese Jr.: born near Faith, N.C., July 9, 1941, died Mar. 13, 2011

Myron Dwight "Dwight" Dillman: born in Peru, Ind., Feb. 9, 1956

Joseph Dudley "Joe" Drumright: born in Fort Worth, Tex., Jan. 31, 1929, died Mar. 29, 1996

Glen Carlton Duncan: born in Columbus, Ind., May 5, 1955

William "Bill" or "Chum" Duncan: born near Charleston, W.Va., Feb. 1, 1929, died Oct. 19, 2013

Homer Robert "Jim" Eanes Jr.: born in Mountain Valley, Va., Dec. 6, 1923, died Nov. 21, 1993

Paul Anthony "Tony" Ellis: born in Sylva, N.C., July 29, 1939

James W. "Jimmy" Elrod: born in Morristown, Tenn., in 1939, died Oct. 15, 2009

Thomas Dollison "Tom" Ewing: born in Columbus, Ohio, Sept. 1, 1946

John Michael "Mike" Feagan: born in Augusta, Ky., Sept. 29, 1957

Monroe Fields: born in Berry, Ala., Dec. 31, 1928, died Feb. 21, 2015

Lester Raymond Flatt: born in Overton Co., Tenn., June 19, 1914, died May 11, 1979

Goldie Sue Wilene (Russell) "Sally Ann" Forrester: born in Raton, N.M., Dec. 20, 1922, died Nov. 17, 1999

Howard "Howdy" Forrester: born in Hickman Co., Tenn., Mar. 31, 1922, died Aug. 1, 1987

Joseph "Joe" Forrester: born in Hickman Co., Tenn., Mar. 21, 1919, died Jan. 16, 2011

Billy Joe Foster: born in Duncan, Okla., Sept. 27, 1961, died Jan. 23, 2013

Robert "Bob" Fowler: born in Birmingham, Ala., Sept. 18, 1939

Walter Franklin "Amos" Garren: born in Hendersonville, N.C., May 10, 1914, died May 10, 1977

Connie Marvin Gately Jr.: born in St. Louis, Mo., May 31, 1929, died Oct. 15, 2012

Ernest Edward "Ernie" Graves: born in Speedwell, Tenn., June 4, 1932

Douglas Bruce Green: born in Great Lakes, Ill., Mar. 20, 1946

Yates Alvin Green: born in Lattimore, N.C., Sept. 2, 1923, died May 9, 2016

Richard Sanders Greene: born in Los Angeles, Calif., Nov. 9, 1942

Philip Lamar Grier: born in Washington, D.C., Apr. 15, 1938

Roby Carter "R. C." Harris: born in Statesville, N.C., Feb. 20, 1940

Mark Gilbert Hembree: born in Chicago, Ill., Sept. 11, 1955

Bobby Hicks: born in Newton, N.C., July 21, 1933

Jack Lee Hicks: born in Louisa, Ky., Aug. 1, 1952

William O'Neal "Bill" Holden: born in Ft. Worth, Texas, July 25, 1950

Lonnie George Hoppers: born in Goodson, Mo., July 25, 1935

Douglas Michael "Doug" Hutchens: born in Stuart, Va., Jan. 26, 1952

Clennon Wayne "Wayne" Jerrolds: born in Savannah, Tenn., Apr. 15, 1939

Enos Johnson: born in Del Rio, Tenn., Aug. 17, 1928, died Jan. 26, 2009

Danny Lee Jones: born near Oscar, Ky., June 3, 1939, died Feb. 3, 2017

Robert Charles "Bob" Jones: born in Seattle, Wash., Sept. 30, 1944

Victor Howard "Vic" Jordan: born in Washington, D.C., Oct. 19, 1938, died Aug. 26, 2016

William Bradford "Bill" or "Brad" Keith: born in Brockton, Mass., Dec. 20, 1939, died Oct. 23, 2015

Marion Gregg "Gregg" Kennedy: born in Shawnee, Okla., Mar. 28, 1952

Ralph Lewis: born near Asheville, N.C., Apr. 25, 1928, died Aug. 5, 2017

Wayne Lewis: born in Sandy Hook, Ky., Mar. 17, 1943

Don Gray Lineberger: born in Columbia, Tenn., Jan. 25, 1939, died Dec. 5, 2010

Eugene Norman "Gene" Lowinger: born in Newark, N.J., Nov. 10, 1942

Rudy Richard Lyle: born in Rocky Mount, Va., Mar. 17, 1930, died Feb. 11, 1985

Tommy Magness: born in Mineral Bluff, Ga., Oct. 21, 1916, died Oct. 5, 1972

Benny Edward Martin: born in Sparta, Tenn., May 8, 1928, died Mar. 13, 2001

James Henry "Jimmy" Martin: born in Sneedville, Tenn., Aug. 10, 1927, died May 14, 2005

Bessie Lee Mauldin: born in Norwood, N.C., Dec. 28, 1920, died Feb. 8, 1983

Thomas Edward "Edd" Mayfield: born near Dawn, Tex., Apr. 12, 1926, died July 7, 1958

James H. "Jimmy" Maynard: born in Temperance Hall, Tenn., Apr. 22, 1928, died Dec. 15, 2015

Delano Floyd "Del" McCoury: born in Bakersville, N.C., Feb. 1, 1939

Curtis McPeake: born in Scott's Hill, Tenn., Oct. 9, 1927

Ralph "Joe" Meadows: born in Basin, W.Va., Dec. 31, 1931, died Feb. 8, 2003

Thomas Arthur "Tommy" or "Snowball" Millard Sr.: born in Chattanooga, Tenn., May 19, 1911, died Apr. 30, 1991

Birch Monroe: born in Rosine, Ky., May 16, 1901, died May 15, 1982

James William Monroe: born in Nashville, Tenn., Mar. 15, 1941

Johnny Thelbert Montgomery: born near Cookeville, Tenn., July 22, 1928, died Sept. 4, 2015

Clyde Leonard Moody: born in Cherokee, N.C., Sept. 19, 1915, died Apr. 7, 1989

Jim Moratto: born in Lamarque, Tex., Aug. 3, 1953

Vernon Dale "Dale" Morris: born in Sanger, Tex., Nov. 25, 1944

Sonny Roland Osborne: born in Hyden, Ky., Oct. 29, 1937

William Howard "Skip" Payne: born in Detroit, Mich., Nov. 25, 1948

Benjamin Harrison Pedigo: born in Little Rock, Ark., Aug. 1, 1953

Robert Lee "Buddy" Pennington: born in Tazewell, Va., June 9, 1940, died Nov. 6, 1977

Claude Jackson "Jackie" Phelps: born in Suffolk, Va., in 1925, died Apr. 22, 1990

Dale Potter: born near Puxico, Mo., Apr. 28, 1929, died Mar. 14, 1996

Billy Jack "Bill" Price: born in Monroe, N.C., May 8, 1934, died Sept. 11, 2000

Joel Price: born in Gumlog, Ga., Nov. 27, 1910, died May 3, 1999

Raymond Harold "Pete" Pyle: born in Burnsville, Miss., Apr. 18, 1920, died Mar. 11, 1995

Donald Wesley "Don" Reno: born in Spartanburg, S.C., Feb. 21, 1927, died Oct. 16, 1984

Larry Richardson: born near Galax, Va., Aug. 9, 1927, died June 17, 2007

Joseph Calvin "Butch" Robins: born in Lebanon, Va., May 12, 1949

William Paul "Billy" Rose: born in Orrville, Ohio, Sept. 22, 1963

Sandy Rothman: born in Miami, Fla., Jan. 30, 1946

Peter "Pete" Rowan: born in Boston, Mass., July 4, 1942

South Salyer: born in Tip Top, Ky., Feb. 18, 1927, died Oct. 22, 2000

Leslie Matheson "Les" Sandy: born near Raeford, N.C., Aug. 8, 1928

Lucky Eugene Saylor: born in Rose Hill, Va., May 23, 1925, died July 7, 2010

Earl Eugene Scruggs: born in Cleveland Co., N.C., Jan. 6, 1924, died Mar. 28, 2012

Oscar "Shorty" Shehan: born near Erwin, Tenn., Oct. 26, 1923, died Aug. 1983

James Fred "Jim" Shumate: born in Wilkes Co., N.C., Oct. 21, 1921, died Oct. 10, 2013

Bobby Smith: born near Algood, Tenn., Jan. 23, 1937, died June 24, 1992

Charles Morehead "Charlie" Smith III: born in Nashville, Tenn., Sept. 6, 1938

James Harrell "Hal" Smith: born in Fairview, Ala., Nov. 21, 1923, died Sept. 13, 2008

Roger Jesse Smith: born in Amelia, Va., July 11, 1926, died May 21, 2013

James Benjamin "Jim" Smoak: born in Round O, S.C., July 7, 1934

Earl T. Snead Sr.: born in Danville, Va., Oct. 29, 1939, died Sept. 8, 2002

Norman Keith "Buddy" Spicher: born in Dubois, Pa., July 28, 1938

Mark Ruben Squires: born in Anderson, S.C., Aug. 13, 1959

Art Stamper: born near Hindman (Knott Co.), Ky., Nov. 1, 1933, died
    Jan. 23, 2005

Carter Glen Stanley: born in McClure, Va., Aug. 27, 1925, died Dec. 1,
    1966

Harold "Red" Stanley: born in Jamestown, Tenn., May 4, 1922, died Feb.
    8, 1967

Guy Benton Stevenson: born near Vulcan, Mo., Dec. 16, 1929

Obie Travis "Travis" Stewart: born in Florien, La., Apr. 19, 1935

Carl Moore Story: born in Lenoir, N.C., May 29, 1916, died Mar. 31,
    1995

Don Stover: born in White Oak, W.Va., Mar. 26, 1928, died Nov. 11, 1996

James Wilson "Chick" Stripling: born in Tifton, Ga., Mar. 4, 1917, died
    Nov. 19, 1970

Joe Earl Stuart Jr.: born in Knoxville, Tenn., Feb. 7, 1928, died Sept. 13,
    1987

Ernest Claude "Ernie" Sykes II: born in Long Island, N.Y., Nov. 13, 1960

Clarence Eli "Tater" Tate: born in Gate City, Va., Feb. 4, 1931, died Oct.
    17, 2007

Merle "Red" Taylor: born in Saltillo, Miss., May 19, 1927, died May 3,
    1987

Esmond Arnold Terry: born in Patrick Co., Va., June 22, 1933

Gordon Terry: born in Decatur, Ala., Oct. 7, 1931, died Apr. 9, 2006

Jack Thompson: Birth and death date information not available

Carl Eugene Vanover: born in Pound, Va., Dec. 25, 1934

Howard Staton "Cedric Rainwater" Watts: born in Monticello, Fla., Feb.
    19, 1913, died Jan. 21, 1970

Willie Egbert "Bill" or "Cousin Wilbur" Wesbrooks: born in Gibson
    County, Tenn., Mar. 5, 1911, died Aug. 13, 1984

Luther Elmer "LE" White: born in Knoxville, Tenn., May 27, 1931, died
    Aug. 13, 1984

Roland Joseph (LeBlanc) White: born in Madawaska, Me., Apr. 23, 1938

Blake Williams: born in Sparta, Tenn., Oct. 8, 1956

Horace "Benny" Williams: born in Bledsoe Co., Tenn., Mar. 28, 1931,
    died Oct. 11, 2007

James "Tex" Willis: Birth and death date information not available

Robert Russell "Chubby" Wise (né Dees): born in Lake City, Fla., Oct.
    2, 1915, died Jan. 6, 1996

Malcom B. "Mac" Wiseman: born near Waynesboro, Va., May 23, 1925

Art Wooten: born in Sparta, N.C., Feb. 4, 1906, died Oct. 6, 1986

Doyle Wright: born in Holmes Co., Fla., July 13, 1928, died May 9, 2006

Rual Holt Yarbrough: born in Lawrence Co., Tenn., Jan. 13, 1930, died Sept. 21, 2010

Robert Billy "Bill" Yates Sr.: born in Big Rock, Va., Apr. 30, 1936, died Jan. 26, 2015

A. E. "Jack" Youngblood: born in Oneonta, Ala., Feb. 15, 1922, died Apr. 24, 2007

NOTES

ABBREVIATIONS

BAH	Bluegrass: A History
BU	Bluegrass Unlimited
CMR	Country Music Records: A Discography, 1921–1942
DC	Definitive Country
GN	Greenville News
G-NR	A Good-Natured Riot
HH	Hartford Herald
HT	Hammond Times
JCM	The Journal of Country Music
MN	Muleskinner News
N&O	News and Observer
NH	A New History of Kentucky
NM	Nashville Musician
OCM	Ohio County Messenger
OCN	Ohio County News
OCT	Ohio County Times
OCT-N	Ohio County Times-News
SO	Sing Out!
TBS	The Bluegrass Star
TE	The Encyclopedia of Country Music (2012)
TE (98)	The Encyclopedia of Country Music (1998)
TMBM	The Music of Bill Monroe
TMBM (36 to 94)	The Music of Bill Monroe from 1936 to 1994

PROLOGUE

1. Bill Monroe, interviewed by Alice (Gerrard) Foster, Nashville, Tenn., May 16, 1969.

2. **The early Monroes**: Helen McKeown (genealogist), Ohio County, Ky. **John Monroe's Revolutionary War record**: Emma Dunn Masters et al., comp., *The Ancestors Honor Roll of General Evan Shelby, 1925–30* (Daughters of the American Revolution, unpublished), pages not numbered; Virgil D. White, abstractor, *Genealogical Abstracts of Revolutionary War Pension Files* 2: *F–M* (Waynesboro, Tenn.: National Historical Publishing, 1991), 2388; Documents from the National Society, Sons of the American Revolution (SAR) Library, Louisville, Ky. The SAR reported that John Monroe was awarded a "bounty land warrant" of one hundred acres in 1788 for his military service, but according to records in the Land Office of the Kentucky Secretary of State, Frankfort, Ky., this warrant was never used. **Family of John Monroe and Kentucky history**: Lynn Miller, "Monroe Family—Ohio County, Kentucky," *Kentucky Family Records* 22 (1998), 95–96; Lowell H. Harrison and James C. Klotter, *A New History of Kentucky* [hereafter *NH*] (Lexington: University Press of Kentucky, 1997), 53–61.

3. **Date of arrival in Kentucky and John Monroe's children**: Masters et al., *Ancestors Honor Roll*; Document from the National Society, Sons of the American Revolution (a letter from Executive Assistant A. D. Hiller to Mrs. Thomas W. Staley, Dec. 21, 1937); Miller, "Monroe Family," 96–98. **Route to Kentucky**: Harrison and Klotter, *NH*, 48–52. **Early days of Monroe family in Kentucky**: Miller, "Monroe Family," 95; Masters et al., comp., *The Ancestors Honor Roll*, pages not numbered; Virgil D. White, abstractor, *Genealogical Abstracts of Revolutionary War Pension Files* 2: *FM–M* (Waynesboro, Tenn.: National Historical Publishing, 1991), 2388.

4. **James Monroe and John Monroe**: H. McKeown (genealogist), Ohio County, Ky.; Harry Ammon, *James Monroe: The Quest for National Identity* (Charlottesville: University of Virginia Press, 1990), 1–4.

5. **Andrew Monroe and Ailsey Q. Harris**: U.S. Census of 1820, Ohio Co., Ky.; Ohio Co., Ky., Marriage Bonds, A:178. **Western Coalfield region**: Harrison and Klotter, *NH*, 22–23. The Western Coalfield region is surrounded on all sides by the Pennyroyal (or Pennyrile) region.

6. **John Jesse Monroe**: Birthdate: Miller, "Monroe Family," 98; birthplace: Ohio Co., Ky., Marriage Bonds, 5:516; middle name: Joe Taylor (genealogist), email, July 18, 2006; U.S. Census of 1830, Woodford Co., Ky. **John Monroe and family in Ohio County**: Miller, "Monroe Family," 96–98. John Monroe died on May 25, 1837, at age eighty-seven (Miller, "Monroe Family," 95). **John Jesse Monroe and Lydia Charlotte Stevens**: Anna Lea Barry (genealogist), Columbus, Ohio. **Monroe farm near Elm Lick**: *Hartford Herald* [hereafter *HH*], June 15, 1881, 3; June 22, 1921, 5. **Renaming**: *HH*, Oct. 12, 1881, 3. This edition reported that Elm Lick was recently renamed Horton "in honor of Mr. B. J. Horton, General Agent on the P. & E. Railroad." Horton is about five miles east of the town of Beaver Dam via US 62 (Uncredited, *Kentucky Atlas and Gazetteer* [Yarmouth, Me.: DeLorme, 1997], 46.) Note: The distance from Hartford to Elm Lick-Horton and all subsequent distances in the text are "as the crow flies," unless otherwise stated.

7. Miller, "Monroe Family," 98. Additional information found on tombstones at Old Bethel United Methodist Church cemetery and at Mt. Pleasant cemetery, Ohio Co., Ky.

Data for the children of John J. and Lydia Monroe were verified at the Kentucky Office of Vital Statistics and the Department of Libraries and Archives, Frankfort, Ky.

8. **Monroe family as slave owners**: H. McKeown (genealogist), Ohio County, Ky.; U.S. Censuses, 1820 and 1830, Woodford Co., Ky., and 1840 and 1850, Ohio Co., Ky. **John J. and Lydia Monroe as slave owners**: Ohio Co., Ky., Circuit Court Equity file 2665, case 111. In 1860, John J. Monroe used his slaves as collateral in securing a loan. Named in this document were Lucretia, Aaron, George, Frances, Sam, Sanferd, and "a little negro girl child about one year old." **Slave owners in Kentucky**: Harrison and Klotter, *NH*, 168.

9. **Slavery in Kentucky**: Harrison and Klotter, *NH*, 168, 170. **George Monroe**: Bill Monroe, interviewed by Ralph Rinzler, Ralph Rinzler Folklife Archives and Collections, Smithsonian Institution (hereafter Rinzler Archives), tape RINZ-RR-0006. In the U.S. Census of 1900 for Ohio County, Ky., George Monroe's birthdate is given as August 1843; he was sixty-eight years old when Bill was born.

10. **The Civil War in Kentucky**: Harrison and Klotter, *NH*, 209–10; Beth Chinn Harp, *Torn Asunder: The Civil War in Ohio County and the Green River Country* (self-published, 2003), 78–79, 116–19. **J. B. Monroe's education**: Alice Foster, ed., "Growing Up in Rosine, Kentucky: An Interview with Bill Monroe," *Sing Out!* [hereafter *SO*], July/Aug. 1969, 7.

11. Harrison and Klotter, *NH*, 134; Virginia S. Thatcher, ed., *The New Webster Encyclopedic Dictionary of the English Language* (Chicago: Consolidated, 1970), 352.

12. **Louisville Jockey Club and Richard Ten Broeck**: Samuel W. Thomas, *Churchill Downs: A Documentary History of America's Most Legendary Race Track* (Louisville: Kentucky Derby Museum, 1995), 32, 54. **Ten Broeck's speed record**: *HH*, June 13, 1877, 1. **Pre-race details**: Bill Wagner, "Molly and Tenbrooks: The Race," *Bluegrass Unlimited* [hereafter *BU*], Dec. 2003, 38–39; D. K. Wilgus, "Ten Broeck and Mollie: A Race and a Ballad," *Kentucky Folklore Record* 2, July–Sept. 1956, 77; "Ten Broeck Beats McCarthy," *New York Times*, July 5, 1878.

13. *HH*, July 10, 1878, 2.

14. Ibid., 2.

15. **Rumor and folk song**: Wagner, "Molly and Tenbrooks," 39. **"Molly and Tenbrooks"**: Wilgus, "Ten Broeck and Mollie," 79, 84. **Quote**: Bill Monroe, onstage interview, Feb. 2, 1863, by Ralph Rinzler, Mike Seeger, and others, University of Chicago Folk Festival (hereafter "B. Monroe, onstage interview, 1963").

16. **Depression**: Thomas J. Schlereth, *Victorian Life: Transformations in Everyday Life, 1876–1915* (New York: HarperCollins, 1992), 34–35. **J. B. and Andrew Monroe**: U.S. Census of 1880, Ohio Co., Ky. **Lydia Charlotte Monroe**: *HH*, June 15, 1881, 3.

17. **Krakatoa**: Simon Winchester, *Krakatoa: The Day the World Exploded: August 27, 1883* (New York: Perennial, HarperCollins, 2003), 286. **Blue Moon**: Rudolph Brasch, *How Did It Begin?* (New York: Pocket, 1969), 272–73; Philip Hiscock, "Once in a Blue Moon," *Sky and Telescope*, Mar. 1999, 52–55; Philip Hiscock, email, Sept. 7, 2007.

18. *HH*, Sept. 26, 1883, 3.

19. **Jack Monroe**: J. H. Battle (with W. H. Perrin and G. C. Kniffin), *Kentucky, a History of the State* (Louisville: Battey, 1885), 170. **Businessmen**: Ohio County, Ky., Circuit Court Equity File 3966, Case 2503.

20. **The store's inventory**: Ohio County, Ky., Circuit Court Equity file 3966, case 2503. Derived from lists of goods supplied by the companies. **Jack as clerk**: Ibid. Derived from

the claim filed by J. H. Monroe. **Mollie Walla**: *HH*, Apr. 29, 1885, 3, and May 13, 1885, 1. These announcements of Miss Walla's hiring were the only mentions of the store in the *Hartford Herald*.

21. **Weather in 1884**: *HH*, 1884: Jan. 9, 2; Jan. 16, 2; Feb. 6, 1; Feb. 20, 2; Mar. 5, 2; Mar. 12, 3; May 7, 2; May 14, 2; June 11, 1; July 30, 2; Sept. 9, 3. **Weather in 1885**: *HH*, 1885: Feb. 11, 3; Feb. 18, 3; Mar. 18, 1; Apr. 1, 3; Apr. 8, 3; May 27, 3; June 3, 3; June 24, 3; July 22, 3; July 29, 3; Aug. 18, 2; Aug. 26, 1. **J. B. and Andrew**: *HH*, May 13, 1885, 2. **Jack**: Ibid., June 10, 1885, 1.

22. **Goods total, Jack's suit**: Ohio County, Ky., Circuit Court Equity file 3966, case 2503. **Auction**: *HH*, Dec. 23, 1885, 4; Jan. 6, 1886, 3; Jan. 13, 1886, 3; Jan. 20, 1886, 3.

23. **Vandiver family**: Larry Warren (great-grandson of William J. Vandiver, brother of Malissa Vandiver Monroe), Vandiver family genealogist, Lexington, Ky.

24. Harrison and Klotter, *NH*, 182.

25. Muhlenberg Co., Ky., Grantee Deeds, 23:52 (1867), and Grantor Deeds, 23:231 (1868); U.S. Census of 1870, Muhlenberg Co., South Carrollton, Ky., p. 10. The birthdate for Malissa given here contradicts the widely published birthdate of July 12, 1870, which derives from her tombstone. Her birthplace and that of brother James Pendleton, often cited as Ohio County, appears to have actually been Muhlenberg County.

26. **Railroad in Ohio County**: McDowell A. Fogle, *Fogle's Papers: A History of Ohio County, Kentucky* (Hartford, Ky.: Ohio County Historical Society, 1981), 240. **The E&P**: Bobby O. Wallace, "A Lady from Rosine" (excerpts from unpublished manuscript), *Blue Moon News*, Dec. 2005–Mar. 2006, 9. **The route of the E&P**: Fogle, *Fogle's Papers*, 240.

27. **Coal importation**: *Hartford Republican*, "Industrial Edition," Sept. 22, 1911, 11. **Ohio County and coal production**: Harrison and Klotter, *NH*, 307.

28. **Henry Davis McHenry**: Battle, *Kentucky: A History of the State*, 162–63; J. M. Armstrong, ed., *The Biographical Encyclopedia of Kentucky* (Cincinnati, Ohio: Armstrong, 1878), 48–49. **Martha Jane "Jennie" Taylor McHenry**: "Taylor Family Papers," Currituck Co., N.C., http://www.rootsweb.com/~nccurrit/bibles/taylorfam.html. Jennie T. McHenry was born on Oct. 4, 1832, the youngest of the six children of Rev. James W. Taylor and Sarah "Sally" (Morris) Taylor. **"Home Again"**: *Louisville Daily Journal*, June 30, 1858, 2. **Rosa Vertner Jeffrey**: Identified by reference specialist Pen Bogert at the Filson Historical Society, Louisville, Ky. **Called "the Queen"**: *Louisville Daily Journal*, June 28, 1856, 2.

29. Armstrong, ed., *Biographical Encyclopedia*, 48–49.

30. **Completion of E&P**: Wallace, "Lady from Rosine," 4. **Pigeon Roost**: Wallace, "Lady from Rosine," 4; Robert M. Rennick, *Kentucky Place Names* (Lexington: University Press of Kentucky, 1984), 256.

31. **McHenry claim to land**: Ohio Co., Ky., Deeds, R:1. In this document from 1859, John H. McHenry granted power of attorney to his son Henry D. McHenry "for over 40,000 acres which I claim . . ." in Ohio County. **"Plat of the Town of Rosine"**: Ohio County, Ky., Deeds, book X, 164–66. Rosine was incorporated by the Kentucky legislature on Mar. 16, 1878. **McHenry Coal Mine and town of McHenry**: Rennick, *Kentucky Place Names*, 183–84.

32. U.S. Census of 1880, Butler Co., Ky.

33. **Arnold Shultz**: Keith Lawrence, "The Greatest (?) Guitar Picker's Life Ended before Promise Realized," *John Edwards Memorial Foundation Quarterly* 17, no. 61 (Spring 1981), 3; William Lightfoot, "A Regional Musical Style: The Legacy of Arnold Shultz" in *Sense of Place: American Regional Cultures*, eds. Barbara Allen and Thomas J. Schlereth (Lexington: University Press of Kentucky, 1990), 128–29. **Shultz family**: U.S. Census of 1900, Ohio Co., Ky.

34. **Malissa Vandiver and family**: U.S. Census of 1880, Butler Co., Ky.; L. Warren, Vandiver family genealogist, Lexington, Ky. **Instruments played**: Ralph Rinzler, "Bill Monroe," in *Stars of Country Music: Uncle Dave Macon to Johnny Rodriguez*, eds. Bill C. Malone and Judith McCulloh (Urbana: University of Illinois Press, 1975), 206. **Type of accordion**: Rob Howard (author of *An A to Z of the Accordion and Related Instruments*), emails, Aug. 6–7, 2006. **Quotation**: Foster, "Growing Up," 7.

35. **Quotation**: Bill Monroe, Rinzler Archives, tape FP-1994-CT-0520. **Malissa's physical features**: Alanna Nash, *Behind Closed Doors* (New York: Knopf, 1988), 340; L. Warren, Vandiver family genealogist, Lexington, Ky. **J. B.'s physical features**: Noble Stewart, interview, Dec. 4, 2006; Bill Monroe, interviewed by Alice (Gerrard) Foster, Nashville, Tenn., May 16, 1969. **Their personalities and descriptions**: L. Warren, Vandiver family genealogist, Lexington, Ky., as told to him by Bertha Monroe Kurth and Rosetta Monroe Kiper. **Dancing styles**: Foster, "Growing Up," 7.

36. Jack Hurst, "Mellowing Father of Bluegrass," *Tennessean*, June 25, 1972, 3S.

37. **Separation and relocation**: L. Warren, Vandiver family genealogist, Lexington, Ky.; Ohio Co., Ky., Quarterly Court, case 2168; 1890 Tax List for the Rosine Precinct, Ohio Co., Ky. **William Vandiver**: *HH*, Aug. 20, 1890, 3.

38. **Jack's work**: U.S. Census of 1900, Ohio Co., Ky. **Jack's land purchases**: Ohio Co., Ky., Deeds, 23:359 (lot in Rosine, 1896); 20:437 (36.4 acres near Rosine, 1900); 23:617 (lot in Rosine, 1900); 24:590 (lot in Rosine, 1900); 25:464 (house and lot in Rosine, 1902); and 26:367 (246 acres near Rosine, 1902).

39. **John J. Monroe's second marriage**: Ohio Co., Ky., Marriage License and Bonds, 5:516. **Mary and John Renfrow**: U.S. Census of 1880, Ohio Co., Ky.; Joe Taylor (genealogist), email, July 8, 2006.

40. **Initial announcement**: *HH*, Dec. 17, 1890, insert. **John Hardin McHenry Jr.**: *History of Daviess County, Kentucky* (Chicago: Inter-State, 1883), 135. **Obituary**: *HH*, Dec. 24, 1890, 3. **Jennie McHenry's move to Louisville**: *HH*, May 12, 1897, 3. **Summer visits**: *HH*, May 18, 1904, 3; Aug. 21, 1907, 5; Mar. 15, 1911, 1; June 21, 1911, 5.

CHAPTER ONE. 1892–1919

1. *HH*, Aug. 3, 1892, 3.

2. **Southern weddings:** David Freeman Hawke, *Everyday Life in Early America* (New York: Harper and Row, 1988), 42. **The wedding:** Ohio Co., Ky., Marriage License and Bonds, 7:330–31; License file 26 (1891–92); Larry Warren, email, June 12, 2013.

3. **Pledge of Allegiance**: Richard J. Ellis, *To the Flag: The Unlikely History of the Pledge of Allegiance* (Lawrence: University Press of Kansas, 2005), 16–20, 228n40. **Union Gospel Tabernacle**: William U. Eiland, *Nashville's Mother Church: The History of the Ryman Auditorium* (Nashville: Opryland, 1992), 19.

4. **Location**: Based on a comparison of 1900 and 1910 U.S. Censuses, Ohio Co., Ky.; B. Monroe, Rinzler Archives, FP-1994-CT-0520. In the latter, Bill says that all of his brothers and sisters except Bertha and himself were born in a log cabin. **Elevation**: Kentucky Geological Survey (Map), series 6, 1925.

5. **First four children**: Kentucky Office of Vital Statistics, Frankfort. **James Speed**: Harrison and Klotter, *NH*, 246. **"Speed"**: *Webster's Ninth New Collegiate Dictionary* (Springfield, Mass., 1985), 1133. **John Jesse's death**: Miller, "Monroe Family," 98. **The Monroes of Beaver Dam**: *HH*, Aug. 21, 1895, 2. According to genealogist Helen McKeown, "This Monroe family . . . came [to America] 100 years after your group" (email to author, June 8, 2006.)

6. **1893**: *HH*, May 3, 3; June 14, 3. **1894**: *HH*, Mar. 21, 2; June 20, 2; Sept. 12, 3; Oct. 17, 3. **1895**: *HH*, Mar. 6, 2; Apr. 10, 3; May 1, 3; May 15, 2. **Quotation**: *HH*, Nov. 13, 1895, 3. **Rail line ownership**: *HH*, Dec. 12, 1894, 2.

7. **1896**: *HH*, Apr. 1, 1; May 6, 3; May 13, 2. **1897**: *HH*, Feb. 24, 2; Mar. 17, 3; Apr. 14, 3; Sept. 1, 2; Oct. 6, 3. **1898**: *HH*, Aug. 3, 2; Oct. 5, 2; Oct. 12, 3. **War with Spain**: W. A. Swanberg, *Citizen Hearst: A Biography of William Randolph Hearst* (New York: Scribner's, 1961), 136.

8. **Ohio County forest**: S. K. Hill (Bureau of Agriculture), "Our Own Ohio County," *HH*, Apr. 18, 1894, 1. **Logging camp**: "An Ohio County Trip," *HH*, Oct. 12, 1898, 1.

9. Eliot Wigginton, ed., *Foxfire 4* (New York: Anchor, 1977), 268–81.

10. **Quotation**: Ralph Rinzler, liner notes for *Bill Monroe and the Blue Grass Boys, Bluegrass Instrumentals*, Decca, DL 4601. **Recording**: Rosenberg and Wolfe, *The Music of Bill Monroe* (Urbana: University of Illinois Press, 2007), 111. **Bill's preference**: Bill Monroe, personal communication with the author.

11. Rinzler, *Stars*, 206.

12. **Charles M. Schwab**: *Encyclopedia of World Biography* (New York: McGraw-Hill, 1973), 9:475–76. Charles M. Schwab is not related to Charles R. Schwab, founder of the brokerage firm that bears his name.

13. **Election officer**: *HH*, Apr. 24, 1901, 2 (re: 1900); Feb. 19, 1902, 1; June 28, 1911, 4; July 31, 1912, 4; Oct. 4, 1916, 4; Oct. 3, 1917, 5; Oct. 8, 1919; *Hartford Republican*, Feb. 25, 1921, 3 (re: 1920). **William Monroe**: age: Miller, "Monroe Family," 98; marriage: Ohio Co., Ky., Marriage License and Bonds, 10:454. **Pen and Anna Belle Vandiver**: Ohio Co., Ky., Marriage License and Bonds, 14:460; *HH*, July 24, 1901, 3. **Susan Monroe**: *HH*, July 23, 1902, 2; Ohio Co., Ky., Deeds, 27:250. **Jack and "Eldamary" Monroe**: Ohio Co., Ky., Marriage License and Bonds, 15:620; U. S. Census of 1900, Ohio Co., Ky.; Jerry Long, comp., *Ohio County, Ky., Obituary Index (1920–80)* (Utica, Ky.: McDowell, 2004), 294. **Cecil E. Vandiver**: U. S. Census of 1910, Ohio Co., Ky. **Wright brothers**: Clifton Daniel et al., *20th Century Day by Day* (London: Dorling Kindersley, 2000), 59; David McCullough, *The Wright Brothers* (New York: Simon and Shuster, 2015), 6.

14. **Purchases**: Ohio Co., Ky., Deeds, 26:449–53; 27:252; 35:458; 3:483; and 44:427. **Equivalent value**: "Seven Ways to Compute the Relative Value of a U.S. Dollar Amount—1774 to Present," http://www.measuringworth.com/UScompare. **Location of Jerusalem Ridge**: Darrel Dukes (Rosine, Ky., native), conversation, 2006. **House**: *HH*, Sept. 14, 1904, 2. **Quote**: Robert Cantwell, *Bluegrass Breakdown* (Urbana: University of Illinois Press, 1984),

23. Between 1919 and 1925, J. B. Monroe sold about 150 acres to brother Jack and bought back about 30 from him. J. B. has been credited elsewhere with owning 655 acres (Ohio Co., Ky., Deeds, 62:471, and book 67:584; Rinzler, *Stars*, 206).

15. **Lots purchased**: Ohio Co., Ky., Deeds, 26:449–53; 36:406; 37:599; 42:531; and 44:430. **Lots Sold**: Ohio Co., Ky., Deeds, 50:447; 60:471; and 67:15.

16. **William and Joseph Vandiver**: L. Warren, Vandiver family genealogist, Lexington, Ky. **J. B. Monroe's notation**: J. B. Monroe, ledger ("D. E. Ledger"), Rinzler Archives, RR343, box 9. **Lena B. Vandiver**: U.S. Census of 1910, Ohio Co., Ky.; Sara Jane McNulty, "Uncle Pen's Fiddle," *BU*, July 1992, 60. **Pen and Anna Vandiver's farm**: L. Warren, Vandiver family genealogist, Lexington, Ky.; Ohio Co., Ky., Deeds, 40:92.

17. **Electricity**: *HH*, Jan. 11, 1905, 3; Harrison and Klotter, *NH*, 222, 298. **Roads**: *HH*, Jan. 28, 1903, 4; Harrison and Klotter, *NH*, 314. **The first Model T**: Daniel et al., *20th Century*, 115. **Travel**: Harrison and Klotter, *NH*, 314. **Indoor plumbing**: Ibid., 298.

18. **Rosine, decline in population**: *HH*, May 7, 1879, 3; Apr. 19, 1911, 8. **Reputation**: *HH*, Oct. 7, 1903, 3; Sept. 27, 1905, 3. **Kentucky's declining population growth**: Harrison and Klotter, *NH*, 221–22; *HH*, May 23, 1900, 2, and May 7, 1902, 2.

19. **Bertha Vandiver**: L. Warren, Vandiver family genealogist, Lexington, Ky. **Lees in Butler and Ohio Counties**: U. S. Census of 1910, Butler Co. and Ohio Co., Ky.

20. **Caroline and Robert Goff**: Frances Harvey, interview, Mar. 20, 2006. **Goff family move to Ohio County**: U. S. Census of 1910, Butler Co., Ky.

21. Charlie Monroe, interviewed by Douglas B. Green: Frist Library and Archive (hereafter Frist Library), Country Music Hall of Fame and Museum, tapes designated OH347-LC (1 of 4).

22. Daniel C. Scullin Jr., MD, email, June 6, 2011.

23. **Economic conditions (1907–10)**: Schlereth, *Victorian*, 34; Harrison and Klotter, *NH*, 301; C. Daniel et al., *20th Century*, 127. **Purchase of house**: B. Monroe, Rinzler Archives, FP-1994-CT-0520. In this interview Bill said, "There was an old log house there that I guess they all lived in, and all of 'em was born there but me and Bertha, and we was borned in another house up the road."

24. **Heat wave and end of drought**: *HH*, 1911: June 14, 8; July 12, 3; Aug. 9, 4; Aug. 16, 1; Aug. 23, 1; Aug. 30, 8. **Quote**: F. Harvey, interview, 2006, and conversation, Oct. 31, 2006.

25. **Vital Statistics Law**: *HH*, Jan. 11, 1911, 1. **Midwife**: B. Monroe, Rinzler Archives, FP-1994-CT-0520. **Birth Certificate**: Commonwealth of Kentucky Certificate of Birth, file 46054. Birth weight not indicated. **Women in Ohio County**: Author's survey, 1910 U.S. Census, Ohio Co., Ky. The population of Ohio County in 1910 was 27,642 (*HH*, Dec. 14, 1910, 3).

26. **Horton School**: Doug Green, "Charlie Monroe Story" (part 1), *MN*, no. 1 (Jan. 1973). In Mar. 2007, the author measured the distance to the former location of the school. **The Monroe children**: *Census Report for School Purposes, Year 1911–12*, Ohio Co., Ky., Board of Education, Hartford.

27. **William Monroe**: *HH*, May 6, 1903, 3, and Sept. 4, 1918, 2. **Smith**: B. Monroe, Rinzler Archives, FP-1994-CT-0520. **Monroe family history**: Miller, "Monroe Family," 95; H. McKeown (genealogist), Ohio Co., Ky.

28. **Strabismus and esotropia**: Robert Berkow, ed., *Merck Manual of Medical Information* (Home Edition) (Whitehouse Station, N.J.: Merck Research Laboratories, 1997), 1314–15. **Farsightedness and night blindness**: Dr. Richard A Eiferman, clinical professor of ophthalmology, University of Louisville, emails, Mar. 22–Apr. 2, 2007. **Quote**: Bill Monroe, Rinzler Archives, tape RINZ-RR-0005.

29. Bill Monroe, from *High Lonesome: The Story of Bluegrass Music*, a film produced by Rachel Liebling, Shanachie 604.

30. **"Old Joe Clark"**: Neil V. Rosenberg, "A Front Porch Visit with Birch Monroe," *BU*, Sept. 1982, 59. **"Heel and Toe Polka" and Malissa's voice**: Rinzler, *Stars*, 206. **"How Old Are You?"**: Ralph Rinzler, booklet notes for *Bill Monroe and the Bluegrass Boys: Live Recordings 1956–1969, Off the Record, Vol. 1*, Smithsonian Folkways, SF CD 40063, 18–19. **"The Butcher Boy"**: Rinzler, *Stars*, 206. **Lyrics**: "The Butcher Boy" as sung by Sairey Garland Ogan, Pikeville, Ky., Dec. 3, 1939, from the Mary Elizabeth Barnicle–Tillman Cadle Collection (BC-520), Archives of Appalachia, East Tennessee State University, Johnson City (used by permission). A "butcher boy" was a young man who rode the railroad lines and sold a variety of items to passengers, including reading materials, snacks, and tobacco products (Stewart H. Holbrook, *The Story of American Railroads* [New York: American Legacy, 1981], 399–412).

31. **"Ancient tones"**: Cantwell, *Breakdown*, 15. **Quote**: Ralph Rinzler, "The Daddy of Blue Grass Music," *SO*, Feb.-Mar. 1963, 8.

32. **Malissa and religion**: Noble Stewart, interview, Dec. 4, 2006. **Methodist church**: Wendell Allen, speaking on the occasion of the one hundredth anniversary of the Rosine Methodist Church, Apr. 2, 1989, via Merlene Austin and Geraldean Jones, conversations, 2006–07. **Quote**: Dix Bruce, "An Interview with Bill Monroe: 'Bluegrass—There's Not a Prettier Name in the World,'" *Frets*, May 1979, 21. **John as bass singer**: Nash, *Behind*, 351.

33. **First quote**: Bill Monroe, Rinzler Archives, tape FP-1993-CT-0262. **Second quote**: Bill Monroe, onstage interview, 1963.

34. **Older sons playing fiddle**: Rosenberg, "Front Porch Visit," 59. **Pen as teacher**: Ibid., 58. **First quote**: Ibid., 59. **Second quote**: Foster, "Growing Up," 7. **Third quote**: Charles Wolfe, "Bluegrass Touches: An Interview with Bill Monroe," *Old Time Music*, Spring 1975, 8. **Fourth quote**: Bruce, "Interview with Bill Monroe," 21. **Fifth quote**: Wolfe, "Bluegrass Touches," 10.

35. **Candy**: D. Green, "Charlie Monroe Story" (part 1), 5. **Quote**: Rinzler, *Stars*, 206.

36. **Equivalence of acreage**: Joshua Johnston, Ohio Co., Ky., agronomist, email, Apr. 24, 2007. **Crops planted**: Roger Wolmuth, "Bio: Bill Monroe," *People Weekly*, Sept. 1, 1986, 50. **Tobacco**: Harrison and Klotter, *NH*, 294–95. **Mining coal**: Nash, *Behind*, 340. **Supplying the church**: Eloise Ragland Howell, ed., *Shouts and Hosannas: A History of Methodism in Ohio County, Kentucky* (self-published, 1994), 179. **The Monroe mine**: James Monroe, "Bill Monroe: From a Farm Boy to a Legend" (part 1), *The Bluegrass Star* [hereafter *TBS*], Oct. 1971, 5. **Timber**: Rinzler, *Stars*, 206. **Quote**: D. Green, "Charlie Monroe Story" (part 1), 4. **Otherwise**: Monroe, "Bill Monroe" (part 1), 4. **Income taxes**: Schlereth, *Victorian*, 78–79.

37. **Charlie re: his father**: D. Green, "Charlie Monroe Story" (part 1), 4, 6. **Charlie re: his mother**: C. Monroe, Frist Library, OH347-LC (no. 1).

38. C. Monroe, Frist Library, OH347-LC (no. 1).

39. **Family tradition**: Nash, *Behind*, 340. **Harry Monroe and Nola Goff**: Ohio County, Ky., Marriage Bonds, 26:110. **Jennie Taylor McHenry**: *HH*, Nov. 18, 1914, 5. Reportedly, Mrs. McHenry was buried next to her husband in Oakwood Cemetery in Hartford. The location of their graves is not known. **Buck as subscriber**: *HH*, Aug. 1, 1917, 5.

40. **First quote**: J. Monroe, "Bill Monroe" (part 1), 4. **Mothers as disciplinarians**: Schlereth, *Victorian*, 276. **Second quote**: Foster, "Growing Up," 7.

41. **Bill around home**: J. Monroe, "Bill Monroe" (part 1), 4; B. Monroe, Rinzler Archives, FP-1994-CT-0520. **Quote re: hunting**: Nash, *Behind*, 352. **Quote re: Jerusalem Ridge**: Don Rhodes, "Monroe, the Father—Monroe, the Son," *BU*, Feb. 1978, 15.

42. Foster, "Growing Up," 7; L. Warren, Vandiver family genealogist.

43. **Shultz Family Band**: Lawrence, "Greatest (?) Guitar Picker's Life," 3–4. **Shultz, 1914–15**: Lightfoot, *Sense*, 133.

44. **Singing conventions in Ohio County**: *Hartford Republican*, June 3, 1910, 5. The first mention of a singing convention in the county was found here. **Singing conventions**: Wallace, "Lady from Rosine," 12–13; Glenn C. Wilcox, ed., *The Southern Harmony and Musical Companion* (Lexington: University Press of Kentucky, 1987), reprint p. xxxi; Charles Reagan Wilson et al., eds., *Encyclopedia of Southern Culture* (Chapel Hill: University of North Carolina Press, 1989), 1039–40; Hattie B. Bradley, "My Memories of Walnut Grove" (unpublished family memoir, ca. 1982), 4.

45. *HH*, Aug. 11, 1915, 5.

46. **Corn crib size**: J. Monroe, "Bill Monroe" (part 1), 4. **Quote**: B. Monroe, Rinzler Archives, FP-1994-CT-0520.

47. B. Monroe, Rinzler Archives, FP-1994-CT-0520.

48. **The "musical"**: Rebecca Morris, "Mt. Pleasant Community," *Ohio County News* [hereafter *OCN*], Dec. 26, 1974, 13. **Quotes re: musicals**: Rinzler, *Stars*, 206–7; Foster, "Growing Up," 10.

49. James Rooney, *Bossmen: Bill Monroe and Muddy Waters* (New York: Dial, 1971), 22.

50. **Bertha playing guitar**: Rosenberg, "Front Porch Visit," 59. **Burch's gift to Birch**: Jan Otteson, "Birch Monroe Is Bean Blossom's Fiddler," *Music City News*, May 1977, 9. **First quote**: Rosenberg, "Front Porch Visit," 59. **Second quote**: B. Monroe, Rinzler Archives, RINZ-RR-0005.

51. **Declaration of war**: C. Daniel et al., *20th Century*, 217. **The draft**: Martin Gilbert, *The First World War: A Complete History* (New York: Holt, 1994), 336; *HH*, 1917: Apr. 11, 4; May 2, 1; May 30, 1. **Harry and Speed register**: *HH*, Aug. 29, 1917, 1. **Speed's enlistment**: Ohio County, Ky., Veteran's Discharges, 1:187. **Oct. 6, 1917**: *HH*, Oct. 10, 1917, 1.

52. B. Monroe, Rinzler Archives, FP-1994-CT-0520; Rich Mensing, "Charlie Monroe Visits Rosine for Unveiling of Welcome Sign," *OCT*, June 3, 1971, 14.

53. **Cruciform plan**: Schlereth, *Victorian*, 88. **Exterior measurements and architectural details**: Leatherwood, Inc. (Fairview, Tenn.), undated assessment published prior to the company's restoration of the structure in 2001, unnumbered pages 1, 9, and 24. **Room assignments**: Bill Monroe and James Monroe via Merlene Austin, conversation, Apr. 10, 2007. **Interior measurements**: T. Ewing, Feb. 2007. **Quote**: Bill Monroe,

remarks recorded Aug. 1983, West Tennessee Bluegrass Festival, Waynesboro, author's collection.

54. **Survey:** Matthew E. Prybylski, *An Archaeological Assessment of a Portion of the Bill Monroe Homestead in Ohio County, Kentucky* (Lexington: Kentucky Archaeological Survey, 2001), 17. Additionally, no evidence of burning was found at the site, suggesting a story of an older house destroyed by fire may not be true. **Trees:**"'I'm On My Way to the Old Home'—Bill Monroe," *OCN*, Dec. 31, 1970, 8.

55. **School year:** Harrison and Klotter, *NH*, 378; Anna Laura Duncan and Betty Martin, conversations, Dec. 2006. **Enrollment records:** Based on an examination of documents at the Ohio Co., Ky., Board of Education, Hartford, 2007. **Class photo:** Ohio County Times [hereafter *OCT*], Sept. 14, 1967, 3.

56. **"Double Pneumonia":** "Definition of double pneumonia," http://www.Medicine Net.com. **Quote:** B. Monroe, Rinzler Archives, FP-1994-CT-0520.

57. **First quote:** John W. Rumble, booklet notes for *The Music of Bill Monroe from 1936 to 1994*, MCA, MCAD4-11048, 15. **Second quote:** Nash, *Behind*, 349. **Third quote:** Bruce, "An Interview with Bill Monroe," 21.

58. **Speed's rank and training:** Ohio County, Ky., Veteran's Discharge Documents, 1:187. **The *Tuscania*:** Gilbert, *First World War*, 397. **Hoboken:** "Camp Merrit," Kevin Wright, Bergen County (N.J.) Historical Society, http://www.bergencountyhistory.org.

59. **John's registration:** *HH*, Aug. 21, 1918, 1. **American forces and influenza:** Gilbert, *First World War*, 428, 437. **Influenza in the U.S.:** Harvey Green, *The Uncertainty of Everyday Life: 1915–1945* (New York: Harper Collins, 1992), 181. **Cancelled draft calls:** *HH*, Nov. 6, 1918, 3.

60. **Start date:** *HH*, July 10, 1918, 5. **Enrolled at Horton School:** Ohio Co., Ky., Board of Education, Hartford. **During school year:** Anna Laura Duncan and Betty Martin, conversations, Dec. 2006.

61. Lightfoot, *Sense*, 130–35; Lawrence, "Greatest (?) Guitar Picker's Life," 4–5; Bill Monroe, Rinzler Archives, tape RINZ-RR-0002. Bill told Rinzler that Shultz sang blues songs but could not identify the songs by name.

62. **End of war:** C. Daniel et al., *20th Century*, 241–44. **Number of soldiers:** H. Green, *Uncertainty*, 143. **Speed's arrival:** Ohio County, Ky., Veteran's Discharge Documents, 1:187. **Bill's recollection:** James Monroe, "Bill Monroe: From a Farm Boy to a Legend" (part 2), *TBS*, Nov. 1971, 6. **Hymn:** *Church Hymnal* (Cleveland, Tenn.: Tennessee Music and Printing, 1951), 251. **Rosetta's remembrance:** Rosetta Kiper via Merlene Austin, conversation, Feb. 2007.

63. **Pen helping Bill with guitar and fiddle:** *Official WSM Grand Ole Opry History-Picture Book* (Nashville: WSM, 1961), 85. It is stated herein that Pen "taught" Bill to play guitar, fiddle, and mandolin. **Quote:** Wolfe, "Bluegrass Touches," 6.

64. **First quote:** Cantwell, *Breakdown*, 221. **Hubert Stringfield:** Rinzler, *Stars*, 207; U. S. Census of 1910, Ohio Co., Ky. **Second quote:** Rinzler, *Stars*, 207. **Third quote and first mandolin:** David Grisman, "Bill Monroe Interview," *Mandolin World News*, Winter 1977–78, 4. **Place of manufacture:** Frank Ford, Gryphon Stringed Instruments, emails, May 6–7, 2007. **Fourth quote:** B. Monroe, Rinzler Archives, RINZ-RR-0005.

65. **Maude Monroe and T. B.**: Richard D. Smith, *Can't You Hear Me Callin'* (Boston: Little, Brown, 2000), 29n98); **Hazelwood Sanatorium**: "Tuberculosis History Archives," http://chfs.ky.gov/dph/epi/tbhistoryphotos.htm.

CHAPTER TWO. 1920–1929

1. **Pen and chords**: Author unknown, *Official Grand Ole Opry*, 85. **First quote**: Foster, "Growing Up," 10. **Second quote**: Wolmuth, "Bio," 50.

2. **First quote**: B. Monroe, onstage interview, 1963. **Second quote**: Rosenberg, "Front Porch Visit," 61.

3. **First quote**: Rinzler, *Stars*, 207. **Second quote**: Nash, *Behind*, 332.

4. J. Monroe, "Bill Monroe" (Part 2), 6.

5. **Favorite sport**: Gene Dudley (agent for Bill Monroe), "Testimonials," in *Bill Monroe's WSM Grand Ole Opry Song Folio No. 1* (New York: Peer International, 1947), 4. **First and second quotes**: Smith, *Can't You Hear*, 12. **Eyeglasses**: *HH*, May 4, 1921, 3. J. B. and Malissa would have complied with the new requirements of the State Board of Health reported here, that "any [vision] defects [in school age children] must be corrected by glasses." **Bill's childhood ball playing**: Elvis Hines, interview, Sept. 12, 2007. **Third quote**: Rooney, *Bossmen*, 80–81. **Fourth quote**: Nash, *Behind*, 348.

6. C. Daniel et al., *20th Century*, 273; *HH*, Oct. 4, 1920, 1. Quoted is part of the first line of "I'm Blue, I'm Lonesome," written by Hank Williams and Bill.

7. **Snowfall**: *HH*, Feb. 23, 1921, 5. **Fruit crop**: *HH*, Apr. 6, 1921, 2. **Prices for produce**: H. Green, *Uncertainty*, 7. **Coal production and strikes**: *HH*, May 11, 1921, 1. **Fire**: *HH*, June 22, 1921, 5. **House**: Ohio Co., Ky., Deeds, 27:250. **Susan**: *HH*, Sept. 8, 1920, 2; Sept. 7, 1921, 4. In Columbia, Susan was working for the law firm of Lyles and Lyles.

8. **Malissa**: Commonwealth of Kentucky Certificate of Death, vol. 21 (22), file 10054; Recollections of Rosetta Kiper via Merlene Austin, conversation, Apr. 2007; Daniel C. Scullin Jr., MD, emails, Apr. 22–May 21, 2007; Berkow, ed., *Merck Manual*, 246–47. **"There Was Nothing We Could Do"**: Rosenberg and Wolfe, *TMBM*, 141, 305.

9. Rosenberg and Wolfe, *TMBM*, 107, 301.

10. Frank J. Sulloway, *Born to Rebel: Birth Order, Family Dynamics, and Creative Lives* (New York: Pantheon, 1996), 173–94.

11. **Previous obituaries**: (for Lydia Monroe) *HH*, July 27, 1881, 1, and (for Ida Monroe) *HH*, July 17, 1907, 7. **Pen staying with family**: J. Monroe, "Bill Monroe" (part 2), 6.

12. J. Monroe, "Bill Monroe" (part 1), 5; Rooney, *Bossmen*, 21.

13. **Pen and Annie's separation**: L. Warren, Vandiver family genealogist, Lexington, Ky.; Ohio Co., Ky., Deeds, 70:379. **Land purchased by Pen**: Ohio Co., Ky., Deeds, 63:240.

14. Mildred (Austin) Leach, interview, Aug. 28, 2006.

15. **First quote**: J. Monroe, "Bill Monroe" (part 1), 5. **Game**: Kentucky Dept. of Fish and Wildlife, http://fw:ky.gov.deerrestoration.asp?lid=1733&NavPath=C557; Wilson et al., *Encyclopedia of Southern Culture*, 325.

16. Lawrence, "Greatest (?) Guitar Picker's Life," 4–5.

17. **Prohibition**: C. Daniel et al., *20th Century*, 262. *Herald* **report**: *HH*, Nov. 15, 1922, 4. *Republican* **report**: *Hartford Republican*, Nov. 17, 1922, 1.

18. **First quote**: Hurst, "Mellowing Father," 3-S. **Second quote and "Bill the man"**: J. Monroe, "Bill Monroe" (part 1), 5.

19. **Birch, Charlie, and Bill playing together**: Rosenberg, "Front Porch Visit," 59. **Bill playing mandolin and guitar for Uncle Pen**: Wolfe, "Bluegrass Touches," 8; Foster, "Growing Up," 11. **Quote**: B. Monroe, Rinzler Archives, RINZ-RR-0005.

20. Foster, "Growing Up," 10.

21. **Bill's appendicitis**: Keith Lawrence, "Bill Monroe Fathered His 'Own' Music," *Owensboro Messenger-Inquirer*, Sept. 27, 1987, 1A–10A; Owensboro City Hospital, receipt for medical services dated Sept. 8, 1923. **Appendicitis**: Berkow, ed., *Merck Manual*, 547–48; Daniel C. Scullin Jr., MD, email, Oct. 25, 2009. **Names of men who carried Bill**: Wilma (Johnson) Hutchings, conversation, June 22, 2007. William Johnson was then married to Mac Goff, daughter of Malissa's friend, Caroline Goff.

22. **Carrying Bill to Horse Branch**: F. Harvey, interview, 2006; Louise (Basham) Moore, conversation, June 24, 2007; Henry Leach (friend of Monroe family), conversation, July 5, 2007. Merlene Austin and the author walked the railroad track from Rosine to Horse Branch and measured the distance on July 11, 2007. **Dr. R. A. Byers**: Stanley Byers (grandson of Richard Anderson Byers), conversation, July 18, 2007. **"The Peggy"**: David Russell Sandefur Sr., *Footsteps to Follow: A Short History of the Horse Branch Community and of the Horse Branch Christian Church*, self-published, 1985, 28. **Quote**: Lawrence, "Bill Monroe Fathered 'Own' Music," 10A.

23. **First and second quotes**: B. Monroe, Rinzler Archives, RINZ-RR-0005; Rooney, *Bossmen*, 23. **Third quote**: Lawrence, "Greatest (?) Guitar Picker's Life," 3. **Fourth quote**: B. Monroe, Rinzler Archives, RINZ-RR-0005; Rooney, *Bossmen*, 24.

24. **Quote**: H. Green, *Uncertainty*, 11. **Fiddlers and Singers**: Tony Russell, *Country Music Records: A Discography, 1921–1942* (New York: Oxford University Press, 2004), 175, 241, 715, 757, 887, 954. **WBAP Barn Dance**: Paul Kingsbury and Alan Axlerod, eds., *Country: The Music and the Musicians* (New York: Abbeville, 1988), 59. **WLS Barn Dance**: James F. Evans, *Prairie Farmer and WLS: The Burridge D. Butler Years* (Urbana: University of Illinois Press, 1969), 161, 165, 214–15; Paul Kingsbury et al., eds., *The Encyclopedia of Country Music* (New York: Oxford University Press, 1998), 372–73.

25. Nash, *Behind*, 343–44; Doug Benson, "Bill Monroe: King of Blue Grass Music" (program 1, part 1), *BU*, Nov. 1967, 6; B. Monroe, Rinzler Archives, RINZ-RR-0005.

26. **Singing in choir**: J. Monroe, "Bill Monroe" (part 1), 6; Bill Monroe, from interview notes, Aug. 1982, Ralph Rinzler Folklife Archives and Collections, Smithsonian Institution: RR343, box 9. **First quote**: Nash, *Behind*, 351. **Singing convention**: *HH*, Sept. 10, 1924, 6. **Singing school**: Bradley, "My Memories," 4; Rinzler, *Stars*, 207. **Melvin Kessinger**: Norma Dell Patterson, conversation, Aug. 16, 2007.

27. C. Monroe, Frist Library, OH347-LC (#1).

28. Wolfe, "Bluegrass Touches," 6; Rinzler, "The Daddy," 6–7.

29. **Charlie and Birch go to Detroit**: C. Monroe, Frist Library, OH347-LC (#1); Rosenberg, "Front Porch Visit," 59. **Briggs**: "Briggs Manufacturing Co., 1909–1954," http://www.coachbuilt.com/bui/b/briggs/briggs.htm. **Boarding with Wallaces**: JoNell (Wallace) Patterson (daughter), conversations, Feb. 21 and June 18, 2008; Bobby Wallace (son), conversation, June 20, 2008; *1926–27 Detroit City Directory*, 2075. **"May I Sleep in Your Barn Tonight, Mister?"**: Russell, *CMR*, 698–99.

30. **Bill "yarding timber"**: J. Monroe, "Bill Monroe" (part 1), 5.

31. **Shultz living in Hartford**: *HH*, Jan. 6, 1926, 1. **Shultz's fiddling**: B. Monroe, Rinzler Archives, RINZ-RR-0005. **Playing with Shultz**: Millard, "Bill Monroe"; Benson, "King of Blue Grass" (program 1, part 1), 6. According to Millard (in 1983), "Monroe maintains that he only played publicly with Shultz one time." But, in 1966, Bill told Benson he had played "some dances" with Shultz. **Quote**: Rooney, *Bossmen*, 24. **Tunes**: B. Monroe, Rinzler Archives, RINZ-RR-0006. **Pay**: B. Monroe, Rinzler Archives, RINZ-RR-0005.

32. **First quote**: J. Monroe, "Bill Monroe" (part 1), 5. **Second quote**: Martha Hume, "Daddy Bluegrass and His Blues," *Country Music*, May 1976, 24.

33. **Buck's foxhounds**: J. Monroe, "Bill Monroe" (part 1), 4. **Johnnie Ragland**: Thelma (Ragland) Hines, interview, Sept. 12, 2007.

34. **Playing with Uncle Pen**: Wolfe, "Bluegrass Touches," 8.

35. **Death of Cecil Vandiver**: L. Warren, Vandiver family genealogist, Lexington, Ky. **Cause of Cecil's death**: McNulty, "Uncle Pen's Fiddle," 60; Sara McNulty Crowder, "Pen Vandiver," *BU*, June 1993, 52. **Three-acre plot**: Ohio Co., Ky., Deeds, 67:449. **"Take Courage Un' Tomorrow"**: Bill Monroe, personal communication with the author; Bill Monroe, interviewed by Ralph Rinzler, Feb. 6, 1966, Rinzler Archives, RINZ-RR-0004. In this interview, Bill referred to the song as "Then There'll Come a Happy Day."

36. **Pen with the Wilsons**: Crowder, "Pen Vandiver," 52. **Ages of Wilson family**: U.S. Census of 1920, Ohio Co., Ky.

37. Charles Wolfe, *A Good-Natured Riot: The Birth of the Grand Ole Opry* (Nashville: Country Music Foundation Press, 1999), 4–11, 67–85.

38. **Birch and Charlie coming home, 1925**: D. Green, "Charlie Monroe Story" (part 1), 7; Rosenberg, "Front Porch Visit," 59. **Phonograph**: Rinzler, *Stars*, 209. **Quote**: B. Monroe, Rinzler Archives, FP-1993-CT-0262. **New releases**: Russell, *CMR*, 717, 887.

39. *HH*, Jan. 6, 1926, 1.

40. **Shultz in Horton**: Lawrence, "Greatest (?) Guitar Picker's Life," 6; Crowder, "Pen Vandiver," 52–53. **Bill joining in**: E. Hines (b. 1916), interview, 2007.

41. **At Uncle Jack's**: N. Stewart, interview, 2006. **Uncle Jack's house**: E. Woosley, interview, 2007. **Bill's quote**: Wolfe, "Bluegrass Touches," 9.

42. **Birch and Leora Baize**: Edna Kathleen (Baize) Murphy (sister of Leora Baize), interview, Oct. 18, 2007. **Birch and Pen**: Flossie (Wilson) Hines, "History of Rosine" (a collection of taped interviews conducted by Sara Jane McNulty), interview of Mar. 9, 1992.

43. **Departure**: *OCN*, Aug. 20, 1926, 8. **The Calumet**: Howard H. Peckham, *Indiana: A Bicentennial History* (New York: Norton, 1978), 117–23. **Work in Whiting**: *HH*, Dec. 24, 1924, 1.

44. **Deaths of "Annie" and Lena Vandiver**: L. Warren, Vandiver family genealogist, Lexington, Ky. **Annie Vandiver and Monroe Hayes**: Muhlenberg Co., Ky., Marriage Bonds, vol. 60, 87. **Annie Vandiver and James Higgs**: Ohio Co., Ky., Deeds, 70:381. In this document, involving the sale of land Pen purchased in 1910, the two are named as husband and wife.

45. *OCN*, Dec. 31, 1926, 4.

46. **Radio debut**: Charlie Monroe, *Old Time Songs and Hymns* (self-published, 1948), unnumbered p. 1. **Crowder's Store**: Dr. Kenneth Stevens, interview, Aug. 23, 2007.

47. **Buck's health**: Wolmuth, "Bio," 50; Commonwealth of Kentucky Certificate of Death, vol. 5, file 2388. Listed as a contributory factor in Buck's death was "Senility." **Dementia**: Daniel C. Scullin Jr., MD, emails, Oct. 15 and Nov. 8, 2007. **First quote**: Hume, "Daddy Bluegrass," 24. **Second quote**: B. Monroe, Rinzler Archives, FP-1994-CT-0520.

48. **Pen's location and Dr. Willis**: Wendell Allen, letter to Ralph Rinzler, Nov. 6, 1974, Rinzler Archives, RR344, box 10. **Pen's accident and injury**: Crowder, "Pen Vandiver," 53–54; Author unknown, *The Bill Monroe Foundation Presents the Ribbon Cutting and Free Bluegrass Show, August 23, 2001* (booklet), unnumbered p. 20.

49. **Bill at Crowder's Store**: Dr. K. Stevens, interview, 2007. **"Grand Ole Opry"**: Wolfe, *Good-Natured Riot*, 21–22. **Bill, harmony singer**: B. Monroe, Rinzler Archives, FP-193-CT-0262.

50. **Mac and Bob**: Kingsbury et al., *TE* (98), 319; Russell, *CMR*, 542–50. **Darby and Tarlton**: Kingsbury et al., *TE* (98), 133–34; Russell, *CMR*, 293–95. **Jimmie Rodgers and the Carter Family**: Russell, *CMR*, 187, 799.

51. **Shultz in Rosine**: Lawrence, "Greatest (?) Guitar Picker's Life," 7. **Quote**: Rooney, *Bossmen*, 24. **Shultz in Morgantown**: Lightfoot, *Sense*, 134. **His death**: Ibid., 136; Lawrence, "Greatest (?) Guitar Picker's Life," 8.

52. Rooney, *Bossmen*, 28.

53. N. Stewart, interview, 2006.

54. Del McCoury, interview, Oct. 15, 2007.

55. *OCN*, 1927: Dec. 23, 8; Dec. 30, 4; 1928: Jan. 13, 2; Jan. 27, 1.

56. **J. B.'s illness**: Commonwealth of Kentucky Certificate of Death, Vol. 5, File No. 2388. **"Memories of Mother and Dad"**: Rosenberg and Wolfe, *TMBM*, 107, 301. **J. B.'s death**: N. Stewart, interview, 2006.

57. **J. B.'s obituary**: *OCN*, Jan. 20, 1928, 1. **Tombstones and footstones**: Don Kissil, "Rosine Revisited," *BU*, Nov. 1982, 28–29.

58. Foster, "Growing Up," 7.

59. **Appraisal and auction**: Ohio Co., Ky., Estate Papers, file 2737. **"Pat"**: J. Monroe, "Bill Monroe" (part 2), 6.

60. Foster, "Growing Up," 11. According to Bill, "My sisters, I believe, was stayin' with my uncle that I was named after, Uncle William" (Hume, "Daddy Bluegrass," 24).

61. **"I'm on My Way to the Old Home"**: Rosenberg and Wolfe, *TMBM*, 84, 101. **Living with Uncle Jack**: Peter Guralnick, "Bill Monroe: Hard-workingman's Blues," *Country Music*, May 1981, 31. **Bill farming**: J. Monroe, "Bill Monroe" (part 2), 6–7.

62. **Rain in Ohio County**: *OCN*, July 6, 1928, 3. **Measles in Rosine**: *OCN*, 1928: May 18, 2; June 22, 6; June 29, 6. **Jack's children**: B. Monroe, Rinzler Archives, FP-1994-CT-0520. **Ages**: U. S. Census of 1910, Ohio Co., Ky. **Moving in with Pen**: Hume, "Daddy Bluegrass," 24.

63. **Start of school**: *OCN*, May 11, 1928, 1. **Bill in school**: Ohio Co., Ky., Board of Education, Hartford, Ky.

64. **John's measles**: *OCN*, June 22, 1928, 6. **John's departure**: *OCN*, Aug. 3, 1928, 3.

65. **"The Cutting Incident"**: James Hines, "History of Rosine," interview of July 23, 1991. **Location of barber shop**: Roy Lindsey, "Born, Bred and Buttered in Kentucky," *Ohio County Messenger*, Mar. 1, 1985, sec. 2, p. 2. **Quote**: T. Hines (Mrs. Elvis Hines), interview, 2007.

66. *OCN*, Oct. 5, 1928, 4.

67. **Harvest**: *OCN*, Nov. 2, 1928, 5. **Corn decimated**: *OCN*, Nov. 23, 1928, 2. **Bill's cane**: J. Monroe, "Bill Monroe" (part 2), 7. **Sorghum**: Bill Monroe, liner notes for *Bill Monroe's Uncle Pen*, Decca, DL-5348. **"Hard days"**: Guralnick, "Hard-workingman's Blues," 31.

68. **Bill working for Uncle Andrew**: J. Monroe, "Bill Monroe" (part 2), 7. **Quote**: B. Monroe, tape of show, Aug. 1983, author's collection. **"Rough-lock"**: George Duvall (Beaver Dam wagoner), conversation, Dec. 4, 2007.

69. **School ends**: *OCN*, Mar. 15, 1929, 7. **Bill's school days**: Documents at the Ohio Co., Ky., Board of Education, Hartford, Ky., 2007. Teachers' Record Books, which included records of attendance and grades received, were available for the 1926–1928 school years only.

70. **Working for Jack**: J. Monroe, "Bill Monroe" (part 2), 7. **Quote**: Foster, "Growing Up," 11. **Playing every day**: Doug Benson, "Bill Monroe: King of Blue Grass Music" (program 2, part 2), *BU*, May 1968, 2.

71. **Pen and Bill**: Rinzler, "The Daddy," 6. **Quote**: Foster, "Growing Up," 11. **Dances at Dever's**: Pauline McGuiness, "History of Rosine," interview of Mar. 9, 1992 (tape 2). **Location of Dever's**: Lindsey, "Born, Bred and Buttered," Mar. 1, 1985, sec. 2, 2.

72. **House parties**: Bruce, "Interview with Bill Monroe," 21. **The money they made**: Benson, "King of Blue Grass" (program 1, part 1), 6. **Equivalence**: "Seven Ways to Compute," http://www.measuringworth.com/index.html. **Giving Bill half**: Author unknown, *Official Grand Ole Opry*, 85; Rooney, *Bossmen*, 25.

73. Foster, "Growing Up," 10.

74. **First quote**: Foster, "Growing Up," 10. **Second quote**: Grisman, "Monroe Interview," 4.

75. *OCN*, Aug. 9, 1929, 2.

76. **Mentions**: *OCN*, 1929: Apr. 12, 7; Apr. 19, 7; May 10, 6; May 24, 7 and 8; June 14, 4 and 8; July 12, 1 (sec. 2); July 19, 3; July 26, 3; Aug. 2, 3 and 8; Aug. 9, 7; Aug. 16, 2 and 7; Aug. 23, 7. **"Bached"**: Nash, *Behind*, 343. **Bill re: Uncle Pen**: Foster, "Growing Up," 10.

77. Foster, "Growing Up," 10.

78. **Four-month stay**: *OCN*, Aug. 8, 1929, 2; *OCN*, Nov. 29, 1929, 6. **Bill's quote**: Rooney, *Bossmen*, 21.

79. *OCN*, Nov. 29, 1929, 6; *OCN*, Dec. 6, 1929, 7.

CHAPTER THREE. 1930–1939

1. **Speed in Owensboro**: *OCN*, Jan. 4, 1929, 5. **Ages of Geanie (Clark)**: U.S. Census of 1920, Ohio Co., Ky. **Quote**: Rooney, *Bossmen*, 21.

2. **First quote**: B. Monroe, Rinzler Archives, FP-1994-CT-0520. **Second quote**: Guralnick, "Hard-workingman's Blues," 32.

3. Rosenberg, "Front Porch Visit," 59; Cantwell, *Breakdown*, 276–77, note 3.

4. **Bill's departure**: *OCN*, May 9, 1930, 7. From that week's report of Rosine news from the previous week: "William Monroe went to Whiting, Ind., Wednesday to seek employment." **Uncle Pen**: Foster, "Growing Up," 11. **Speed at the depot**: Rosetta Monroe (Speed Monroe's daughter) via F. Harvey, interview, 2006.

5. **First quote**: B. Monroe, Rinzler Archives, RINZ-RR-0006. **Unemployment**: Rooney, *Bossmen*, 26. **Second quote**: Doug Green, "The Charlie Monroe Story" (part 2), *MN*, Feb. 1973, 8.

6. **Jimmie Rodgers**: Nolan Porterfield, *Jimmie Rodgers* (Urbana: University of Illinois Press, 1992), 225–62, 408. **Avid record-buyers**: D. Green, "Charlie Monroe Story" (part I), 8.

7. Rooney, *Bossmen*, 26.

8. Guralnick, "Hard-workingman's Blues," 32.

9. **Maude and Bertha's arrival**: *OCN*, Aug. 15, 1930, 5. **Charlie losing job**: D. Green, "Charlie Monroe Story" (part 2), 8. **First quote**: Nash, *Behind*, 341. **Bill's salary**: Jack Hurst, "Bill Monroe: From Refined Oil to Slick Music," *Chicago Tribune*, Oct. 12, 1977. **Second quote**: Rooney, *Bossmen*, 26.

10. **"Talking pictures" in Ohio County**: *OCN*, Apr. 18, 1930, 1; May 2, 1930, 1. **WLS in 1930**: Evans, *Prairie Farmer and WLS*, 176–204, 216–17, 220. **Additional information on WLS performers**: Kingsbury et al., *TE* (98), 15, 121, 282–83; Russell, *CMR*, 482–84; *Prairie Farmer*, Mar. 7, 1931, 40.

11. **Charlie finding work**: D. Green, "Charlie Monroe Story" (part 2), 8. **Maude and Bertha at Queen Anne**: Bertha (Monroe) Kurth via Merlene Austin, 2007. **Queen Anne Candy Company**: "Company History," http://www.queenannecandy.com/go/?icontent/ About_History. **Birch**: Rosenberg, "Front Porch Visit," 60. **First quote**: Bill Monroe, from *Bill Monroe: Father of Bluegrass Music*, a film produced by Steve Gebhardt (Original Cinema, OC-1001, released 1993). **WWAE**: John Russell Ghrist, *Valley Voices: A History of Radio Broadcasting in Northern Illinois and Northwest Indiana from 1910–1992* (West Dundee, Ill.: JRG Communications, 1992), 76–80. **Second quote**: Wolfe, "Bluegrass Touches," 7.

12. **The move to East Chicago**: Rooney, *Bossmen*, 26. **The location**: *Hammond (Ind.) Numerical Telephone Directory* (Directory Survey Co., 1940), 542; Maps of the period, including one from the directory; Steven Good, email, Mar. 13, 2004. **Queen Anne Candy**: *Hammond (Ind.) City Directory* (1931), 349. **Standard Oil**: Map, *Hammond Numerical Telephone Directory* (1940), 542. **John**: *OCN*, Nov. 14, 1930, 4; June 12, 1931, 3.

13. **Quote**: Hurst, "From Refined Oil." **Co-worker's recollection**: Rickey Lamb (grandson of Roy Orvel Hatton), interview, Jan. 6, 2008.

14. **WLS's wattage increase**: Evans, *Prairie Farmer*, 183. **WSM's wattage increase**: Jack Hurst, *Nashville's Grand Ole Opry* (New York: Abrams, 1975), 104. **Mac and Bob**: Ivan Tribe, liner notes for *Mac and Bob's Great Old Songs, Vol. 1*, Old Homestead Records, OHCS-158, rel. 1985; Kingsbury et al., *TE* (98), 319. **Quote**: B. Monroe, from interview notes, Rinzler Archives: RR343, box 9. **Gene Autry**: Kingsbury et al., *TE* (98), 22–23; Russell, *CMR*, 71–76. **Hugh Cross**: *Prairie Farmer*, July 11, 1931, 4; B. Monroe, Rinzler Archives, RINZ-RR-0004. In the latter, Bill said he learned "Footprints in the Snow" from Cross. **Max Terhune**: *WLS Family Album* (1933), 32; *WLS Family Album* (1936), 45.

15. **Delmore Brothers**: Russell, *CMR*, 309; Alton Delmore, *Truth Is Stranger than Publicity* (Nashville: Country Music Foundation Press, 1977), 31–41. **Karl and Harty**: Russell, *CMR*, 470; Kingsbury et al., *TE* (98), 275.

16. **Andrew Monroe**: Commonwealth of Kentucky Certificate of Death, vol. 10, file 4538; *OCM*, Feb. 5, 1932, 1; *OCN*, Feb. 12, 1932, 3. **Susan Monroe visiting Andrew**: *OCN*, Dec. 11, 1931, 6. **John Monroe and Clara Wilson**: Ohio Co., Ky., Marriage Bonds, vol. 49, 29; *OCN*, Apr. 1, 1932, 4.

17. **Eighth Street Theater**: Evans, *Prairie Farmer and WLS*, 222. **WWAE**: Author's survey, all editions of the *Hammond (Ind.) Times*, 1931–34.

18. **Pen's last days**: Allen, letter to Rinzler, Rinzler Archives, RR344, box 10; Opal Taylor (via Wendell Allen), "Rosine Happenings," *Ohio County Times-News*, June 30, 1988, 8-B. **Bronchitis and pneumonia**: Daniel C. Scullin Jr., MD, email, Jan. 6, 2008.

19. **Burial preparations**: Allen, letter to Rinzler, Rinzler Archives, RR344, box 10. **Joseph Vandiver's grave**: L. Warren, Vandiver family genealogist. **No telephone**: Author's survey, Whiting and East Chicago telephone directories, 1930–34. **First quote**: Foster, "Growing Up," 11. **Second quote**: Wolmuth, "Bio," 50.

20. **Monroe Brothers on WWAE**: *Hammond Times*, 1932: July 16, 4; July 23, 4; Aug. 6, 4; Aug. 13, 4; Aug. 24, 11.

21. **Quotes**: Rooney, *Bossmen*, 27. **Playing at dances**: Rosenberg, "Front Porch Visit," 59.

22. **Monroes spotted by Owens**: D. Green, "Charlie Monroe Story" (part 2), 9. The date of this incident is based on a survey of the *Hammond Times*, 1932. **WLS road shows**: Author's survey of volumes 1 and 2 of the WLS weekly, *Stand By!*, 1935–36.

23. **First quote and pay for dancers**: Rooney, *Bossmen*, 27. **Second quote**: B. Monroe, Rinzler Archives, RINZ-RR-0006. **WWAE**: *HT*, Oct. 15, 1932, 6; Jan. 18, 1933, 7.

24. **Rube Tronson and his Texas Cowboys**: B. Monroe, Rinzler Archives, RINZ-RR-0006; Wayne A. Guyant, "When Then Was Now," *Waupaca (Wisconsin) Post*, June 3, 1993 (http://www.mainstreet-marketplace.com/pageswis%20gas,%20christoph,%20 hollenbeck01.htm). **Stage outfits**: *WLS Family Album* (1933), 38. **Quote**: Rosenberg, "Front Porch Visit," 59.

25. **Main acts**: B. Monroe, Rinzler Archives, RINZ-RR-0006; Kingsbury et al., *TE* (98), 204–5, 538; Evans, *Prairie Farmer and WLS*, 219. **Quote**: Rooney, *Bossmen*, 27.

26. **First quote**: Rooney, *Bossmen*, 26. **Bill playing Davis's mandolin**: Charles Wolfe, "Karl and Harty," *BU*, Oct. 1983, 29. In this article, the date of this event was incorrectly given as 1936. **Linda Parker with Cumberland Ridge Runners**: *Prairie Farmer*, Apr. 30, 1932, 9. **Red Foley with same**: *Prairie Farmer*, Oct. 1, 1932, 9; *WLS Family Album* (1933), 20. **"Snakehead" design**: George Gruhn, "Pickin' Technical Reference Manual," *Pickin'*, Oct. 1978, 66.

27. **"Chick" Hurt**: Kingsbury et al., *TE* (98), 420; Russell, *CMR*, 704–13. **Prairie Ramblers**: *HT*, Dec. 22, 1932, 8; Barry McCloud et al., *Definitive Country: The Ultimate Encyclopedia of Country Music and Its Performers* (New York: Berkley Publishing Group, 1995), 642–43; Kingsbury et al., *TE* (98), 420. **Comparison**: Russell, *CMR*, 633, 704. **"Tex" Atchison**: Wolfe, *Kentucky Country*, 112; Lilly Beatty (Tex Atchison's niece), conversation with author, 2007. Ms. Beatty said that Tex's family moved to McHenry when he was eight years old (1920).

28. **Depression**: Robert S. McElvaine, *The Great Depression: America, 1929–41* (New York: Times Books/Random House, 1984, 1993), 121–37. **RCA Victor and Bluebird**: Russell, *CMR*, 11–12; Richard Spottswood, booklet notes for *Charlie Monroe: I'm Old Kentucky Bound*, Bear Family, BCD 16808 (rel. 2008), 10; Tony Russell, email, May 8, 2008. **Montgomery Ward**: Russell, *CMR*, 20–21.

29. D. Green, "Charlie Monroe Story" (part 2), 9.

30. **Roosevelt**: C. Daniel et al., *20th Century*, 418–19. **Delmore Brothers**: Delmore, *Truth Is Stranger*, 57. **Playing at churches**: *HT*, 1933: Mar. 29, 2; Apr. 1, 4; Apr. 24, 6; Apr. 28, 15; Apr. 29, 6. **WWAE during March and April**: *HT*, 1933: Mar. 16, 6; Mar. 27, 6; Apr. 3, 10; Apr. 24, 9. **WWAE during summer 1933**: Based on a survey of the *Hammond Times*, 1933.

31. **Jimmie Rodgers**: Porterfield, *Jimmie Rodgers*, 53, 349–55. **Rodgers on Bluebird**: Guthrie T. Meade Jr., Richard K. Spottswood, and Douglas S. Meade, *Country Music Sources: A Biblio-Discography of Commercially Recorded Traditional Music* (Chapel Hill: Southern Folklife Collection, 2002), 146.

32. **Bluebird issuing new recordings**: Tony Russell, email, May 10, 2008. **The Girls of the Golden West**: Russell, *CMR*, 370–371; Kingsbury et al., *TE* (98), 204.

33. Charlie and Bill Monroe, *The Monroe Brothers: Their Life, Their Songs* (Raleigh, N.C.: by the authors, 1937), 5; B. Monroe, from interview notes, Rinzler Archives: RR343, box 9; Rinzler, *Stars*, 209.

34. **WJKS**: Ghrist, *Valley Voices*, 103–5. **Ray Pierce**: Martin Pierce (younger brother of Ray), interview, Oct. 18, 2007. Martin Pierce said Bill sold his tater bug to him in 1933–34 for $5. He later pawned it in Milwaukee, Wisconsin. **Pay at WJKS**: Wolfe, "Bluegrass Touches," 7. **WJKS-WIND**: Ghrist, *Valley Voices*, 105–6; *HT*, July 17, 1933, 9. **Monroe Brothers at WIND**: B. Monroe, from interview notes, Rinzler Archives, RR343, box 9.

35. World's Fair Archives, University of Illinois, Chicago, Ill.; *WLS Family Album* (1934).

36. *National Barn Dance*: Evans, *Prairie Farmer and WLS*, 224. **Ramblers and Delmores**: Russell, *CMR*, 309, 704. **Monroes on WWAE**: Survey of *Hammond Times*, 1934.

37. **Linda Parker**: "Sunbonnet Girl," *Stand By!* (a WLS weekly fan magazine), Aug. 24, 1935, 11. **Bill's operation**: Nash, *Behind*, 349.

38. Oliver Saks, "A Neurologist's Notebook; Stereo Sue The Blessings of Binocular Vision," *New Yorker*, July 19, 2006, 64–73.

39. **January–March 1934**: *HT*, 1934: Jan. 4, 1; Jan. 5, 1; Jan. 6, 1 (re: a revival in February); Mar. 2, 3. **Performance at home**: *HT*, Jan. 4, 1934, 1.

40. **WWAE schedule**: Author's survey of *Hammond Times*, 1934. **Bill quitting job**: Rooney, *Bossmen*, 27. **Quote**: Jack Hurst, "Bill Monroe: Still the Pick of Bluegrass Legends," *Chicago Tribune*, Sept. 20, 1984. **Red Foley**: Kingsbury et al., *TE* (98), 176; Russell, *CMR*, 350–52. **Hoosier Hotshots**: Kingsbury et al., *TE* (98), 246–47; Russell, *CMR*, 435–40.

41. **Charlie and Bill re-employed**: D. Green, "Charlie Monroe Story" (part 2), 10. **Charlie and Texas Crystals**: Rinzler, *Stars*, 209; Rosenberg, "Front Porch Visit," 60; Green, "Charlie Monroe Story" (part 2), 10. **Dollar Crystal Co.**: From Texas Crystals box in author's collection, "Copyright 1934 by Dollar Crystal Co., Inc."; "Purgatives and Politics," *Time*, Oct. 7, 1940 (www.time.com/time/printout.0,8816,802082,00.html). At the time, purgatives like Texas Crystals were promoted as medications to be taken to avoid or relieve a variety of illnesses by cleansing the bowels.

42. Rosenberg, "Front Porch Visit," 60; "Citgo," http://en.wikipedia.org/wiki/citgo. In 1965, after diversifying into the oil business, Cities Service introduced the brand name Citgo.

43. **The audition**: D. Green, "Charlie Monroe Story" (part 2), 10; Author unknown, *The Monroe Brothers: Their Life, Their Songs* (Raleigh, N.C.: Monroe Brothers, 1938),

5. **James S. Thompson**: 1935 Omaha, Nebraska, City Directory, R. L. Polk. **Pay**: Hurst, "Mellowing Father," 3-S.

44. **Speed and family at homeplace**: Merlene Austin (formerly Mrs. Scottie Monroe), conversation, 2007. **Mention in local press**: *OCM*, July 13, 1934, 2.

45. **Monroe brothers at World's Fair, 1934**: D. Green, "Charlie Monroe Story" (part 2), 9. **WLS Barn Dance at World's Fair, 1934**: World's Fair Archives, University of Illinois, Chicago.

46. **Unemployment**: McElvaine, *Great Depression*, 75, 170–95. **First quote**: Bruce, "Interview with Bill Monroe," 21. **Second quote**: B. Monroe, onstage interview, 1963.

47. **Thompson's directions**: D. Green, "Charlie Monroe Story" (part 2), 10. The "Big Four" was the Cleveland, Cincinnati, Chicago, & St. Louis Railroad. **Burlington Route**: Seth Bramson (railroad historian), emails, Apr. 19 and 20, 2008. The Burlington Route was the Chicago, Burlington, & Quincy Railroad. **Location of company**: 1935 Omaha City Directory.

48. George A. Freeman, "Sowing Seeds: Growing America's Broadcasting System," *The A.W.A. [Antique Wireless Association] Review*, vol. 15 (2002), 127–33.

49. George A. Freeman, email, Nov. 6, 2002.

50. **KFNF facility**: *Studio and Broadcasting Station KFNF, the Friendly Farmer Station*, booklet published by the Henry Field Seed Co., Shenandoah, Iowa, ca. 1928. **Wattage**: Freeman, "Sowing Seeds," 131. **Monroe Brothers broadcasts on KFNF**: B. Monroe, Rinzler Archives, RINZ-RR-0006.

51. J. Monroe, "Bill Monroe" (part 2), 6; Bob Black, *Come Hither to Go Yonder: Playing Bluegrass with Bill Monroe* (Urbana: University of Illinois Press, 2005), 15; Tennessee Dept. of Vital Records, Death Certificate, file 84-021461; James Monroe, conversation, Apr. 2, 2009.

52. **Dollar Crystal performers**: B. Monroe, Rinzler Archives, RINZ-RR-0006. In this interview, Bill mentioned the Newman Brothers, Hiram and Henry, and Cowboy Loye as three of "seven or eight different groups" who worked for Dollar Crystal. **Charlie and Bill on WAAW**: *Omaha World-Herald*, Nov. 11, 1934, 9-E; Survey of *World-Herald*, 1934–35. **WAAW**: *Omaha Chamber of Commerce Journal*, vol. 27, no. 5 (May 1939). **Charlie and Bill's address**: Omaha (Neb.) City Directory (1935).

53. D. Green, "Charlie Monroe Story" (part 2), 10; McCloud et al., *DC*, 617.

54. **Tenure at WAAW**: Survey of Omaha *World-Herald*, 1934–35. **Radio pay increase**: Hurst, "Mellowing Father," 3-S. **Parker as booking agent**: Neil V. Rosenberg, *Bluegrass: A History* (Urbana: University of Illinois Press, 1985), 33. **Meeting with Thompson**: D. Green, "Charlie Monroe Story" (part 2), 10. **Byron Parker's wife**: 1935 Omaha City Directory. **Bill taking Carolyn with him**: C. Monroe, Frist Library, OH347-LC (#1).

55. **First quote**: *OCM*, Aug. 9, 1935, 6. Also mentioned in this report, Birch, Maude, and Bertha came home for a few days. **Second quote**: *OCM*, Aug. 23, 1935, 3. **Mainer's Mountaineers**: Russell, *CMR*, 581; McCloud et al., *DC*, 497–98.

56. **WIS**: *Hill's Columbia City Directory* (1935), 576. **Columbia's newspapers**: Surveys of the *State* and the *Columbia Record* for Aug.–Sept. 1935.

57. **Loss of sponsorship**: J. Monroe, "Bill Monroe" (part 2), 7. **First quote**: D. Green, "Charlie Monroe Story" (part 2), 10. **Second quote**: Hurst, "Mellowing Father," 3-S.

58. **Crazy Water Crystals**: Gene Fowler, *Crazy Water: The Story of Mineral Wells and Other Texas Health Resorts* (Fort Worth: Texas Christian University Press, 1991), 1–42. **Quote**: Gene Fowler, "Old-Time Spas in Texas," *Texas Co-Op Power*, May 2002, 6–11. **J. W. Fincher in Charlotte**: *Charlotte Observer*, Aug. 13, 1933, sec. 4, p. 2; Pat Ahrens, "The Role of the Crazy Water Crystals Company in Promoting Hillbilly Music," *John Edward Memorial Foundation Quarterly* 6 (Autumn 1970), 107–9; Rosenberg, *BAH*, 32. **Size of Charlotte**: Thomas W. Hanchett, "Recording in Charlotte," *The Charlotte Country Music Story* (Charlotte: North Carolina Arts Council, 1985), 12.

59. **Crazy Water Crystals and WBT**: Author's survey of *Charlotte News*, Aug. 1935–Dec. 1936; Rosenberg, *BAH*, 32; Pamela Grundy, "From Il Travatore to the Crazy Mountaineers: WBT, Charlotte, and Changing Musical Culture in the Carolina Piedmont, 1922–1935" (Master's thesis, University of North Carolina, 1991), chap. 3, 60–95. **Fisher Hendley**: Grundy, "From Il Travatore," 74, 81; Kingsbury et al., *TE* (98), 236–37. **WBT location**: *Charlotte City Directory* (1936), 623. **Lesser-known acts**: Pat J. Ahrens, *The Legacy of Two Legends: Snuffy Jenkins and Pappy Sherrill* (Columbia, S. C.: self-published, 2007), 7–13. **Earl Scruggs**: Earl Scruggs, *Earl Scruggs and the 5-String Banjo*, New York: Peer, 1968), 147–50; Scott Cohen, "Pickers: They Might As Well Spell Banjo E-A-R-L S-C-R-U-G-G-S," *Country Music*, Aug. 1977, 54.

60. **WBT's signal**: Pamela Grundy, "'We Always Tried to Be Good People': Respectability, Crazy Water Crystals, and Hillbilly Music on the Air, 1933–1935," *Journal of American History*, Mar. 1995, 1593. **Pay and traveling expenses**: Grundy, "From Il Travatore," 77–79; Rosenberg, *BAH*, 32–33. According to Grundy, "Fincher paid small salaries to the most popular groups and nothing to most of the rest."

61. **Charlotte roominghouse**: Don White (North Carolina musician whose mother-in-law owned the roominghouse), interview, Sept. 21, 2004. **Playing in Greenville, 1935**: Author's survey of the *Greenville News*, 1934–36; Rooney, *Bossmen*, 30–31. The exact start date isn't known. Shows were listed in the *Greenville News* as "The Crazy Water Crystals Co. Presents 'Souvenirs.'"

62. **First quote**: Pat Ahrens, "Pioneer Radio Performers: 'Snuffy' Jenkins and 'Pappy' Sherrill," *Old Time Country* 16, no. 4 (Winter 1990): 11. **Second quote**: Della Coulter, "The Piedmont Tradition," in *The Charlotte Country Music Story* (Charlotte: North Carolina Arts Council, 1985), 10.

63. **"Financial questions"**: Grundy, "From Il Travatore," 94. **Featured performers**: *GN*, Nov. 7, 1935, 14; Nov. 8, 1935, 13; Nov. 10, 1935, C-6. **Kentucky Colonels**: "Honorable Order of Kentucky Colonels," http://kycolonels.org.

64. *GN*, Nov. 15, 1935, 3; Nov. 27, 1935, 11.

65. **Aunt Susan in Greenville**: *Hill's Greenville City Directory* (1931), 415. **Monroe address in Greenville**: As given on daughter Melissa's birth certificate: North Carolina State Board of Health, Standard Certificate of Birth, no. 1419. **Uncle Jack Monroe**: Jack Monroe, tombstone in Rosine Cemetery, Rosine, Ky.; *OCM*, Nov. 29, 1935, 1.

66. Bessie Mauldin, interviewed by Ralph Rinzler, ca. 1978, collection of Dwanna Pyle, Nashville, Tenn., 2012; Bessie Lee Mauldin, North Carolina State Board of Health, Certificate of Birth no. 29 (177).

67. **Cutback and name changes**: Author's survey, *GN*, 1934–36. **Saturday shows**: *GN*, Jan. 19, 1936, 9. **Addresses**: *Hill's Greenville, S.C., City Directory* (1935), 785, 908. **Time increase**: *GN*, Jan. 26, 1936, A-9.

68. **Signing with Bluebird**: D. Green, "Charlie Monroe Story" (part 2), 11; Guralnick, "Hard-workingman's Blues," 32; Rosenberg, *BAH*, 33; Rosenberg and Wolfe, *TMBM*, 5. **Average royalty**: Grundy, "From Il Travatore," 93. **Monroe Brothers royalty**: Rooney, *Bossmen*, 31.

69. Wilson et al., *Encyclopedia of Southern Culture*, 806; "How To Know If Your Common-Law Marriage Is Recognized," Sheri and Bob Stritof, http://marriage.about.com/od/commonlaw.

70. **Sunday shows**: *GN*, 1936: Feb. 2, A-9; Feb. 9, C-6; Feb. 16, C-5. **Location of recording session**: Rosenberg and Wolfe, *TMBM*, 18. **Acts recording**: Russell, *CMR*, 310 (Delmores), 581 (both Mainers), 632 (Monroes), 841 (Smith). **Events of Feb. 17**: Wolfe, "Bluegrass Touches," 7–8; Rosenberg, *BAH*, 33; Hanchett, *Charlotte Story*, 12–15; Wolfe, notes for *Blue Moon*, 9–10.

71. **Quote from Charlie**: D. Green, "Charlie Monroe Story" (part 2), 10. **Two of nine**: Bill Monroe, remarks recorded July 3, 1969, Smithsonian Institution's Folklife Festival, author's collection.

72. **"What Would You Give"**: Rosenberg and Wolfe, *TMBM*, 7; Tony Russell, email, Apr. 24, 2008. **Montgomery Ward release**: Spottswood, booklet for *C. Monroe: I'm Old Kentucky Bound*, 9.

73. **Monroe Brothers and others on WGST**: Wayne W. Daniel, *Pickin' on Peachtree* (Urbana: University of Illinois Press, 1990, 2001), 155–61; *Atlanta Constitution*, 1936: Feb. 25, 5; Feb. 26, 19; Feb. 29, 9; Mar. 3, 12; *Atlanta Journal*, 1936: Feb. 26, 25; Feb. 27, 27; Mar. 1, 7D; Mar. 2, 21.

74. **WFBC at noon**: *GN*, Mar. 4, 1936, 12. **WFBC on Sunday**: *GN*, Mar. 8, 1936, 9. **Marriage of Charlie Monroe and Betty Miller**: South Carolina Marriage License, Oconee Co., no. 9766. **Betty's background**: Bill Vernon, liner notes for *The Songs of Charlie Monroe*, County Records, 539, rel. 1974; Betty Monroe, scrapbook, collection of Rosetta Monroe, Rosine, Ky.; U.S. Census, 1920: South Carolina, McCormick County, Sheet 3A. **Betty remembered**: Doug Green, "The Charlie Monroe Story" (part 3), *MN*, Mar. 1973, 14; Merlene Austin, conversation, Apr. 23, 2008.

75. **First songbook**: Charles and Bill Monroe, *Favorite Hymns and Mountain Songs* (Greenville, S.C.: self-published, 1936), 1–14.

76. **Gillespie as sponsor**: *GN*, Mar. 30, 1936, 10. **Three shows**: *GN*, May 16, 1936, 14. **Don Reno**: Don Reno, *The Musical History of Don Reno. His Life, His Songs* (Hyattsville, Md.: self-published, ca. 1975), 4.

77. **Bluebird release**: Ad, *MN*, Feb. 1973. On the back cover of this issue is a re-printed ad with the handwritten notation "April, 1936." According to former *Muleskinner News* managing editor Fred Bartenstein, it came from the collection of Charlie Monroe (Fred Bartenstein, email, June 17, 2008). **Quote**: Rooney, *Bossmen*, 31. **Textile mill workers**: David M. Kennedy, *Freedom from Fear: The American People in Depression and War, 1929–1945* (New York: Oxford University Press, 1999), 180–81; Grundy, "We Always Tried," 1616. **Bluebird releases**: Rosenberg and Wolfe, *TMBM*, 311–13.

78. **Songs**: Russell, *CMR*, 581–82, 632–33; Wolfe, notes for *Blue Moon*, 15. **Recording speed**: Tom Mindte, emails, Oct. 20 and 31, 2011. Although Bill apparently did not write "Just a Song of Old Kentucky," he later copyrighted it.

79. **Loss of Crazy sponsorship**: *GN*, July 4, 1936, 10; July 18, 1936, 12. **Vacation**: *GN*, Aug. 2, 1936, 7; author's survey, *OCN* and *OCM*, Aug.–Sept. 1936. **Return to Greenville**:

GN, Sept. 7, 1936, 8; Oct. 3, 1936, 6. **Regaining Crazy sponsorship**: *GN*, Sept. 23, 1936, 14.

80. **Birth of Melissa**: North Carolina Standard Certificate of Birth, no. 1419 (694). **Kathleen**: James Monroe, conversation, Sept. 27, 2008; Russell, *CMR*, 166.

81. **Mainer-Morris and Monroe Brothers sessions**: Russell, *CMR*, 583, 633. **"Roll in My Sweet Baby's Arms"**: Ibid., 181. Listed here is the 1931 recording by Buster Carter and Preston Young titled "I'll Roll in My Sweet Baby's Arms."

82. **Bill and Carolyn's marriage**: Rinzler, *Stars*, 210. **Sunday program**: *GN*, Oct. 11, 1936, 5.

83. Author's survey, *GN*, Nov. and Dec., 1936; *GN*, Dec. 25, 1936, 25.

84. *Raleigh, N. C., City Directory* (1937), 398 (Monroes), 688 (WPTF). The Parkers were not listed.

85. **WPTF wattage**: Rick Martinez (program director, WPTF), conversation, May 28, 2008. **Country music on WPTF**: Author's survey, Raleigh, N.C., *News and Observer*, January 1937. **Boyd Carpenter**: *GN*, Oct. 9, 1935; *N&O*, Jan. 31, 1937, M-4.

86. *N&O*, Feb. 7, 1937, M-4; *N&O*, Feb. 14, 1937, M-4.

87. **Hotel Charlotte**: Hanchett, *Charlotte Story*, 14; Wolfe, notes for *Blue Moon*, 69 (discography by Neil V. Rosenberg). **Sessions of Feb. 15–16, 1937**: Russell, *CMR*, 583, 633.

88. **Parker as manager**: Rosenberg, *BAH*, 33. **Quote**: D. Green, "Charlie Monroe Story" (part 2), 11.

89. **Bluebird release**: Meade et al., *Sources*, 220; Porterfield, *Jimmie Rodgers*, 294–95. **New show time**: *N&O*, Apr. 4, 1937, M-4. **Parker's departure**: Rosenberg, *BAH*, 35. **Crazy's troubles**: Grundy, "From Il Travatore," 94–95; Fowler, *Crazy Water*, 46.

90. **The Old Hired Hand**: Rosenberg, *BAH*, 35. **Carpenter as replacement**: Wolfe, notes for *Blue Moon*, 20.

91. **Songs**: Russell, *CMR*, 376, 584, 633; Wolfe, notes for *Blue Moon*, 69 (discography by Neil V. Rosenberg). **Recording speed**: Tom Mindte, emails, Oct. 20 and 31, 2011.

92. *Renfro Valley Barn Dance*: Wolfe, *Kentucky Country*, 76–78. **Roy Acuff**: Elizabeth Schlappi, *Roy Acuff: The Smoky Mountain Boy* (Gretna, La.: Pelican, 1978, 1993), 32- 36.

93. **Gibson instrument catalog**: Rosenberg and Wolfe, *TMBM*, 14. **WPTF tenure**: Author's survey, *N&O*, Apr. 1937–Jan. 1938.

94. **Swing Billies on WPTF**: Author's survey, *N&O*, Apr. 1937–Jan. 1938. **James Clay Poole**: C. Kinney Rorrer, *Rambling Blues: The Life and Songs of Charlie Poole* (London, Eng.: Old Time Music, 1982), 17, 60–62; Russell, *CMR*, 885. **Charlie singing song**: B. Monroe, Rinzler Archives, RINZ-RR-0002.

95. Russell, *CMR*, 113, 197, 224, 310–11, 322, 391, 409, 427, 445–46, 495, 578, 582, 584, 633, 643, 704, 705, 841, 908.

96. **Songbook**: Charlie and Bill Monroe, *The Monroe Brothers: Their Life, Their Songs* (Raleigh, N.C.: By the authors, 1938). In *The Bill Monroe Reader* (University of Illinois Press, 2000), the publication date of this songbook is incorrectly given as 1937. **Amos 'n' Andy**: *Tennessean*, Aug. 19, 2002, 2.

97. **Radio schedule changes**: Author's survey, *N&O*, Apr.–June, 1938. **Crazy sales**: Fowler, *Crazy Water*, 46–47; Dorothy Neville, *Carr P. Collins: Man on the Move* (Dallas: Park, 1963), 69. **Crazy as first Opry sponsor**: Craig Havighurst, *Air Castle of the South:*

WSM and the Making of Music City (Urbana, Ill.: University of Illinois Press, 2007), 72. **Victor sessions, June 1938**: Russell, *CMR*, 160, 167, 194, 451, 487, 667, 674, 746, 821. **House trailers**: D. Green, "Charlie Monroe Story" (part 2), 18. **Last on WPTF**: Author's survey, *N&O*, Apr.–June 1938.

98. **First quote**: Nash, *Behind*, 350. **Second quote**: B. Monroe, Rinzler Archives, RINZ-RR- 0005. **Extended quote**: C. Monroe, Frist Library, OH347-LC (#2).

99. Sulloway, *Born to Rebel*, 191–93.

100. **Charlie in Knoxville**: D. Green, "Charlie Monroe Story" (part 3), 10; McCloud et al., *DC*, 553. **"Lefty" McDaniel**: Mark Waters (grandson), conversations, Jan. 28 and Feb. 10, 2011. McDaniel was born in Rutherford Co., N.C., on Apr. 20, 1915. **WNOX wattage**: "History of American Broadcasting," Jeff Miller, http://jeff560.tripod.com/broadcasting. html; Jeff Miller, email, Sept. 3, 2008.

101. B. Mauldin, interviewed by R. Rinzler, ca. 1978; C. Monroe, Frist Library, OH347-LC (#2).

102. **WMC**: Wolfe, *G-NR*, 8. In 1922, when WMC first went on the air, George D. Hay made his radio debut on the station. **Bill at WMC**: Robert E. Jamieson, first and third interviews, Nov. 29, 2003, and Dec. 4, 2004.

103. R. Jamieson, first and third interviews, 2003 and 2004. Robert E. "Bob" or "Handy" Jamieson was born in Ripley, Miss., on Jan. 22, 1916, and died on June 6, 2006. Birth and death dates for Charles "Chuck" Haire are not available.

104. **Arrival in Little Rock**: James Monroe, "Bill Monroe: From a Farm Boy to a Legend" (part 3), *TBS*, Dec., 1971, 4; R. Jamieson, first and third interviews, 2003 and 2004. **KARK**: Ray Poindexter, *Arkansas Airwaves* (North Little Rock, Arkansas: self-published, 1974), 206–30. **Debut on KARK**: *Arkansas Democrat*, July, 14, 1938, 8. **Lonnie Glosson and Light Crust Doughboys**: McCloud et al., *DC*, 326–27, 473–74.

105. **Living arrangements and work during this time**: R. Jamieson, first interview, 2003, and conversation, Feb. 20, 2005. **Four more weeks on KARK**: *Arkansas Democrat*, 1938: July 21, 15; July 28, 9; Aug. 4, 15; Aug. 11, 8.

106. **Bill as bandleader**: R. Jamieson, first interview, 2003, and second interview, Dec. 12, 2003.

107. Justice of Peace Marriages, Crown Point, Lake Co., Indiana, lic. A63428, pp. 276, 307; Steven Good, email, Mar. 19, 2010.

108. **Return to KARK**: Author's survey, *Arkansas Democrat*, Sept. Nov. 1938. **Waking Bill up and name change**: R. Jamieson, first interview, 2003. **Charlie's session**: Russell, *CMR*, 632.

109. **Final broadcast on KARK**: Author's survey, *Arkansas Democrat*, Sept.–Nov. 1938. **Last days of first band**: R. Jamieson, first interview, 2003.

110. **Re: Birmingham**: J. Monroe, "Bill Monroe" (part 3), 4. **Bill's vehicle**: Wayne Erbsen, "Cleo Davis: The Original Blue Grass Boy" (conclusion), *BU*, Mar. 1982, 60. **Re: Atlanta**: W. Daniel, *Pickin' on Peachtree*, 1–14.

111. Juergen Eichermueller (vintage trailer expert), email, July 21, 2008.

112. *Atlanta Journal*, 1939, Jan. 5, 31; Jan. 6, 26; Jan. 7, 13.

113. **Cleo Davis and details of audition**: Wayne Erbsen, "Cleo Davis: The Original Blue Grass Boy" (part 1), *BU*, Feb. 1982, 28–30; J. Monroe, "Bill Monroe" (part 3), 4. **Location**

of Gallimores: Atlanta City Directory (1939), 469. William Henry Gallimore's address was 1223 Lorenzo Drive SW.

114. **The next day**: Erbsen, "Cleo Davis" (part 1), 30; Erbsen, "Cleo Davis" (conclusion), 59. **Charlie's session**: Russell, *CMR*, 632; McCloud et al., *DC*, 554.

115. **Cross Roads Follies**: W. Daniel, *Pickin' on Peachtree*, 127–51. WSB's motto: *Welcome South, Brother* (*Welcome South Brother* [Atlanta: Cox, 1974], 15). **Audition**: Cleo Davis, taped replies to interview questions of Wayne Erbsen, 1981, designated as tape 1; Erbsen, "Cleo Davis" (conclusion), 59. **Davis on Bill**: C. Davis, taped replies, tape 1.

116. Erbsen, "Cleo Davis" (conclusion), 59.

117. Erbsen, "Cleo Davis" (conclusion), 60; Delmore, *Truth Is Stranger*, 129–41; Cleo Davis, taped replies to interview questions of Wayne Erbsen, 1981, tape designated as tape 2.

118. **WWNC audition**: Erbsen, "Cleo Davis" (conclusion), 60; author's survey, *Asheville Citizen*, Jan.–June, 1939. **"Sunset Slim"**: *Asheville Citizen*, Feb. 3, 1939, 16.

119. **The return trip**: Erbsen, "Cleo Davis" (conclusion), 60. **Asheville Lunch Room**: *Asheville City Directory* (1939), 44.

120. **Cold weather**: Erbsen, "Cleo Davis" (conclusion), 60; *Asheville Citizen*, 1939: Feb. 23, 1; Feb. 24, 20. **Relocation of WWNC**: *Asheville Citizen*, Apr. 1, 1939, B-1–20; author's survey, *Asheville Citizen*, Jan.–June 1939. **Old WWNC address**: *Asheville City Directory* (1938), 547. **Bill and Davis's first broadcast**: *Asheville Citizen*, Apr. 3, 1939, 12. **"Your Family and Mine"**: Jon Foulk (old-time radio expert, OTRCAT.com), email, Aug. 1, 2008. **Radio program schedule**: Author's survey, *Asheville Citizen*, Jan.–June, 1939.

121. **Art Wooten**: James Lindsay, "Art Wooten Remembered," *BU*, Apr. 1988, 55; Erbsen, "Cleo Davis" (conclusion), 60–61. **Galax**: Booklet from the 32nd Annual Old Fiddlers' Convention, Aug. 1967, 2. **Tommy Millard**: Wayne Erbsen, "Tommy Millard: Blackface Comedian and Blue Grass Boy," *BU*, May 1986, 22–25; Erbsen, "Cleo Davis" (conclusion), 61; Rooney, *Bossmen*, 32; C. Davis, taped replies, tape 1.

122. **Delmores leaving WFBC**: Delmore, *Truth Is Stranger*, 140–41. **Debut and the next five weeks**: GN, May 8, 1939, 10; author's survey, GN, May–Oct. 1939.

123. **Grease house**: Erbsen, "Cleo Davis" (conclusion), 62. **Bill singing solos**: Wolfe, "Bluegrass Touches," 7; B. Monroe, Rinzler Archives, RINZ-RR-0004. **"Blue Eyes"**: Erbsen, "Cleo Davis" (conclusion), 63; C. Davis, taped replies, tape 1.

124. **First quote**: B. Monroe, Rinzler Archives, RINZ-RR-0006. **Second quote**: Erbsen, "Cleo Davis" (conclusion), 61. A cassette tape Wooten recorded in the 1980s, *One Man Band* (HRC-1324), released by Heritage Records of Galax, Va., features him playing six tunes with his one-man band. The sound is reminiscent of Charlie Poole and the North Carolina Ramblers.

125. **First quote**: Bruce, "An Interview with Bill Monroe," 21. **Second quote**: B. Monroe, onstage interview, 1963. **Third quote**: Nash, *Behind*, 333.

126. **Sponsorship changes**: Author's survey of GN, May–Sept. 1939; GN, June 8–10, 1939, 6, 9, and 24 respectively; GN, July 23, 1939, C-4. **Opry move**: Eiland, *Nashville's Mother Church*, 49; Hurst, *Nashville's Opry*, 119.

127. **"Snowball" Millard**: GN, July 23, 1939, C-4; Erbsen, "Tommy Millard," 25; Haywood Co., N.C., Public Library, Medford Data Base (birth records). **"Amos" Garren**: Paul Garren (son), interviews, Apr. 16 and May 7, 2001. **Blue Grass Quartet**: Erbsen,

"Cleo Davis" (conclusion), 63; B. Monroe, Rinzler Archives, RINZ-RR-0006. **German invasion**: Kennedy, *Freedom from Fear*, 425.

128. **Charlie and Kentucky Pardners**: Bob Carlin, "Charlie Monroe," *BU*, Oct. 2003, 46; Penny Parsons, "Curly Seckler: Bluegrass Pioneer," *BU*, June 2004, 39–40; Penny Parsons, email, Aug. 14, 2008. **Bill writing to WSM**: Erbsen, "Tommy Millard," 25. **Opry vacancy**: Wolfe, *G-NR*, 259.

129. **Green Spot sponsorship**: Author's survey, *GN*, May–Oct., 1939. **Quote**: C. Davis, taped replies, tape 1.

130. **Charlie informing band**: Parsons, "Curly Seckler," 40. **Quote**: Erbsen, "Cleo Davis" (conclusion), 63.

131. **First quote**: Wolfe, "Bluegrass Touches," 11. **Second quote**: Nash, *Behind*, 334. **Third quote**: Erbsen, "Cleo Davis" (conclusion), 63. **Hay's book**: McCloud et al., *DC*, 378.

132. **Return to Greenville**: Erbsen, "Cleo Davis" (conclusion), 63. **Trailer location**: Walt Trott, booklet notes for *Johnnie and Jack and the Tennessee Mountain Boys*, Bear Family, BCD 15553 (rel. 1992), 4. **Opry debut**: *Nashville Banner*, Oct. 28, 1939, 8; Wolfe, *Good-Natured Riot*, 248–49; Erbsen, "Cleo Davis" (conclusion), 63. **Monk and Sam**: *Mountain Broadcast and Prairie Recorder*, Nov. 1939, 4; Tina Cox (granddaughter of Samuel Lane Johnson), conversations, Oct. 13 and 14, 2008. Monk and Sam (Charles Hansen Jr. and Sam L. Johnson) joined the *Opry* cast on Sept. 30, 1939, after five years at WHAS in Louisville, Ky. **"Foggy Mountain Top"**: Russell, *CMR*, 188.

133. **Seating capacity**: Wolfe, *G-NR*, 23. **First quote**: C. Davis, taped replies, tape 1. **Second quote**: Rooney, *Bossmen*, 34.

134. Parsons, "Curly Seckler," 40; Penny Parsons, email, Aug. 14, 2008.

135. **Following the 8:45 show**: *Nashville Banner*, Oct. 28, 1939, 8; Wolfe, *G-NR*, 241–65. **Quote**: Erbsen, "Cleo Davis" (conclusion), 63.

136. **First quartet sung on Opry**: Rooney, *Bossmen*, 35. **"Farther Along"**: Luther G. Presley, comp., *Heavenly Highway Hymns* (Stamps-Baxter, 1956), 208. The song, copyrighted in 1937, was recorded by Charlie Monroe in 1938 (Russell, *CMR*, 632). **Quote**: B. Monroe, Rinzler Archives, RINZ-RR-0002. **Blue Grass Quartet**: John Rumble, email, June 30, 2016.

137. **WSM's coverage**: Rosenberg, *BAH*, 50; Wolfe, *G-NR*, 245. **Prince Albert portion**: Wolfe, *G-NR*, 258–64.

138. **Trapped in Nashville**: C. Davis, taped replies, tape 1. **Record of showdates**: Hatch Show Print Co., Nashville, Tenn. (hereafter, Hatch), receipts for account of Bill Monroe and his Blue Grass Boys, 1. *Gone with the Wind*: C. Daniel et al., *20th Century*, 501. A live recording of Bill and the Blue Grass Boys performing "Mule Skinner Blues" on the *Opry* of Nov. 25, 1939, is included on *The Music of Bill Monroe from 1936 to 1994* (MCA, MCAD4-11048).

CHAPTER FOUR. 1940–1949

1. **Artist Service Bureau bookings**: Hatch, 1–2. **Artist Service Bueau**: Wolfe, *G-NR*, 24, 245; Havighurst, *Air Castle*, 73. **WSM commission**: Rumble, *TMBM (36 to 94)*, 30; John Rumble, conversation, May 13, 2009.

2. **Showdates**: Hatch, 2–3. **Lester Flatt**: Neil V. Rosenberg, "Lester Flatt and Earl Scruggs" in *Stars of Country Music: Uncle Dave Macon to Johnny Rodriguez*, ed. Bill C.

Malone and Judith McCulloh (Urbana: University of Illinois Press, 1975), 256; Pete Kuyk-endall, "Lester Flatt and the Nashville Grass," *BU*, Jan. 1971, 5; Bill Vernon, "A Conversation with Lester Flatt," *MN*, Aug. 1972, 3. **Harmonizers**: *Roanoke Times and World News*, Jan. 22, 1939, 18. The band included Flatt, guitar; leader Charlie Scott, guitar; brother Lloyd Scott, guitar; Laurence Harron, fiddle; and Wallace Spicer, banjo.

3. **Acuff's recording**: Russell, *CMR*, 50.

4. **Blue Grass Boys pay**: C. Davis, taped replies, tape 1. **Showdates**: Hatch, 3, 4; *Star* (Port St. Joe, Fla.), Apr. 19, 1940, 2. **Bailey**: David C. Morton with Charles K. Wolfe, *DeFord Bailey: A Black Star in Early Country Music* (Knoxville: University of Tennessee Press, 1991), 102; Fred Bartenstein, email, Nov. 27, 2012. **Magness replacing Wooten**: Erbsen, "Cleo Davis" (conclusion), 63–64; Hatch, 6. **Tommy Magness**: Charles Wolfe, "Fiddler in the Shadows: The Story of Tommy Magness," *BU*, May 1997, 52–55.

5. Hatch, 6; Cousin Wilbur [Wesbrooks] with Barbara M. McLean and Sandra S. Graf-ton, *Everybody's Cousin* (New York: Manor, 1979), 121–22.

6. **Moody**: "Clyde Moody (The Carolina Woodchopper)," *TBS*, Oct. 1972, 5; Ivan M. Tribe and John W. Morris, "Clyde Moody: Old-Time, Bluegrass, and Country Musician," *BU*, July 1975, 28–30. **Davis's last**: C. Davis, taped replies, tape 1. **Stanleys**: Ralph Stanley, with Eddie Dean, *Man of Constant Sorrow: My Life and Times* (New York: Gotham, 2009), 57; Gary Reid, email, June 22, 2013.

7. **First session**: Rosenberg and Wolfe, *TMBM*, 34–35; Russell, *CMR*, 114, 160, 390, 585, 631, 836, 963. **Location**: W. Daniel, *Pickin' on Peachtree*, 14. **Moody's D-18**: Wolfe, booklet for *Blue Moon*, 29–30 (photos). **Quote**: B. Monroe, Rinzler Archives, RINZ-RR-0002.

8. **Arthur Smith with Monroe**: Rosenberg, *BAH*, 52; Wolfe, *G-NR*, 284; Russell, *CMR*, 842; Charles Wolfe, *The Devil's Box: Masters of Southern Fiddling* (Nashville: Country Music Foundation Press / Vanderbilt University Press, 1997), 129–31. **Magness with Roy Hall**: Russell, *CMR*, 391; Wolfe, "Fiddler in Shadows," 56. **Pete Pyle**: Russell, *CMR*, 723; Douglas H. Green, "Pete Pyle: Bluegrass Pioneer," *BU*, Mar. 1978, 22. Of the eight songs Pyle recorded, six were written by Crowe.

9. **Road schedule**: Hatch, 9–10. **Wesbrooks's comments**: (Wesbrooks), *Everybody's Cousin*, 132–33.

10. **Roosevelt**: C. Daniel et al., *20th Century*, 517. **First release**: Rosenberg and Wolfe, *TMBM*, 313; Jeff Woodard, "Bill Monroe 'Proud' to See Growth of Bluegrass Music," *Advertiser-Journal* (Montgomery, Ala.), Sept. 19, 1980, 13.

11. **Showdates, early 1941**: Hatch, 10–12. **Melissa**: James Monroe via Merlene Austin, conversation, 2007. **Speed and family**: Merlene Austin, conversation, 2007. **James William Monroe**: James Monroe, conversation, Sept. 27, 2008.

12. **First Opry tent show**: Schlappi, *Roy Acuff*, 50. **Wilds's brainchild**: David Wilds, "The Wilds, the Innocent, and the *Grand Ole Opry*," *No Depression*, Summer 1996, 48–55. **Quotes**: Hurst, *Nashville's Opry*, 121.

13. **Moody's departure and WBBB**: Rosenberg, *BAH*, 53. **Cherokee, N. Ca.**: Hatch, 13. **Pyle**: D. Green, "Pete Pyle," 22.

14. **Magness's departure**: Wolfe, "Fiddler in Shadows," 56. **Hall recording**: Russell, *CMR*, 391.

15. Alan Axlerod and Harry Oster with Walton Rawls, *Penguin Dictionary of American Folklore* (New York: Penguin Reference, 2000), 434; Dick Spottswood, "Alan Lomax, 1915–2002," *BU*, Sept. 2002, 21; John Szwed, *Alan Lomax: The Man Who Recorded the World* (New York: Penguin, 2011), 140, 142–45; Rosenberg and Wolfe, *TMBM*, 315.

16. **Mauldin in Nashville**: B. Mauldin, interview with R. Rinzler, ca. 1978. **Tulane Hotel**: George Zepp, "Tulane Hotel Played Key Role in Developing Music City," *Tennessean*, Dec. 11, 2002, 6B. **Quotes**: B. Monroe, Rinzler Archives, RINZ-RR-0005.

17. **Hawkins**: Bill Hawkins, interview, Nov. 5, 2003. **Showdate**: Hatch, 18.

18. **Second session**: Rosenberg and Wolfe, *TMBM*, 35. **Road schedule**: Hatch, 18. **Pyle session**: Russell, *CMR*, 723. Of the eight songs Pyle recorded this time, five were written by accompanist Crowe.

19. **Tuning high**: Rosenberg, *BAH*, 54–55. **Pyle, RCA Victor soloist**: D. Green, "Pete Pyle," 22; Rosenberg and Wolfe, *TMBM*, 36, n.1. **Songs not recorded**: Russell, *CMR*, 305, 906.

20. **Recordings**: Russell, *CMR*, 585, 827.

21. **House in Nashville**: *Nashville City Directory (1942)*, 566. **Showdates**: Hatch, 20. **First time in Ohio Co.**: Survey of Hatch, sheet nos. 1–20. **Dec. 11, 1941**: Kennedy, *Freedom from Fear*, 426–515, 524.

22. **Pyle**: P. Pyle, Frist Library and Archive, Country Music Hall of Fame and Museum (hereafter, FLA-CMHOF&M), OH149-LC (#1); D. Green, "Pete Pyle," 22. **Moody**: Jake Lambert (with Curly Sechler), *A Biography of Lester Flatt: The Good Things Outweigh the Bad* (Hendersonville, Tenn.: Jay-Lyn, 1982), 6; Tribe and Morris, "Clyde Moody," 30.

23. **The Forresters**: Murphy Henry, "Sally Ann Forrester: The Original Bluegrass Girl Pulling Her Own Weight with the Blue Grass Boys," *BU*, June 2000, 55. **Tommy Thompson**: Henry, "Sally Ann Forrester," 55; Recording of "Prince Albert *Grand Ole Opry*," Feb. 7, 1942.

24. **Tent show breaks**: Hatch, 23. **DeFord Bailey**: Morton with Wolfe, *DeFord Bailey*, 108, 121–30; Rooney, *Bossmen*, 37.

25. **Recording ban**: "A Chronological Chart of Events in A.F.M.'s Two-Year Ban," *Billboard*, Mar. 3, 1945, 92; "1942–44 Musicians' Strike," http://en.wikipedia.org/wiki/1942%E2%80%9344_musicians%27_strike. **Columbia signing**: Rosenberg and Wolfe, *TMBM*, 45–46.

26. **Wooten replaced by Forrester**: Henry, "Sally Ann Forrester," 55; "Uncle Dave" Sturgill, liner notes for *A Living Legend—Fiddlin' Art Wooten*, Homestead Records, 104, rel. 1976. **Quote**: Rooney, *Bossmen*, 34. **Cleo Davis's remembrance**: C. Davis, taped replies, tape 1.

27. **Charlie's Opry audition**: Carlin, "Charlie Monroe," 49–50. **Retirement?**: C. Monroe, *Old Time Songs and Hymns*, unnumbered page 1. **Purchases**: *Ohio County, Ky., Deeds*, book 93, 104 (1942); book 109, 405 (1949); book 140, 59 (1959); book 140, 70 (1959); book 157, 443 (1963); book 158, 357 (1963).

28. **Quote**: Ray Edlund, "Bill Monroe—The Master Speaks," *Bluegrass Breakdown* (magazine), Mar./Apr. 1982, 6. **Acuff's tent show**: Schlappi, *Roy Acuff*, 50. **DeWitt "Snuffy" Jenkins**: Ahrens, *Legacy*, 3, 8; Pat Ahrens, conversation, Nov. 2, 2008.

29. **Akeman writing for job**: Charles Wolfe, "String," *BU*, June 1982, 47–48. **Akeman's illiteracy**: John Roger Simon, *Cowboy Copas and the Golden Age of Country Music* (Ashland, Ky.: Jesse Stuart Foundation, 2008), 261. **Stringbean with Charlie**: Wolfe, "String," 48; Carlin, "Charlie Monroe," 47, 49; Bob Carlin, email, Nov. 3, 2008. **First quote**: Tony Trischka and Pete Wernick, *Masters of the 5-String Banjo* (New York: Oak, 1988), 10. **Second quote**: Bruce, "Interview with Bill Monroe," 22. **String with band**: Country Music Hall of Fame and Museum Library, live recording, "*Grand Ole Opry's* Prince Albert Show," Dec. 12, 1942.

30. **Carrying the Blue Grass Boys**: Nash, *Behind*, 352–53.

31. **Howdy's draft notice**: Murphy H. Henry, "'Come Prepared to Stay. Bring Fiddle,' The Story of Sally Ann Forrester: The Original Bluegrass Girl" (Master's thesis, George Mason University, 1999), 43. **Bill's draft status**: Kennedy, *Freedom from Fear*, 632–35.

32. **William's death**: William Monroe, Kentucky State Department of Libraries and Archives, cert. 0470644, roll 7020644. **Bill's location**: Hatch, 26. **Quote**: B. Monroe, Rinzler Archives, FP-1994-CT-0520.

33. **Magness**: Rooney, *Bossmen*, 42. **Carl Story**: Carl Story, Doug Hutchens's Questionnaire (information derived from a one-page questionnaire distributed by former Blue Grass Boy Hutchens), Dec. 1978; Ivan M. Tribe, "Carl Story: Bluegrass Pioneer," *BU*, Jan. 1975, 9–10. **McGarr and Ethridge**: Rosenberg and Wolfe, *TMBM*, 39; "Mac" McGarr, signature on cover, *Minnie Pearl's Grinder's Switch Gazette*, Dec. 1944. **Quote**: Wolfe, "Bluegrass Touches," 9. **Bill's announcement**: Mike Carpenter and Don Kissil, "Chubby Wise: Sweet Fiddler from Florida," *Pickin'*, Oct. 1977, 10.

34. Carpenter and Kissil, "Chubby Wise," 10–11.

35. **Trial basis**: Ivan M. Tribe, "Chubby Wise: One of the Original Bluegrass Fiddlers," *BU*, Feb. 1977, 11. **Tubb**: Ronnie Pugh, *Ernest Tubb: The Texas Troubadour* (Durham, N.C.: Duke University Press, 1996), 84–85. **Quote**: Wayne W. Daniel, "Chubby Wise: Dean of the Bluegrass Fiddlers," *BU*, Apr. 1987, 33. **Ethridge**: A. J. Coates (friend of Ethridge), conversation, Nov. 8, 2008.

36. **Tent show route**: Hatch, 28–31. **First quote**: Guralnick, "Hard-workingman's Blues," 33. **Wehle**: Rooney, *Bossmen*, 36; Harry Rice, "Barn Dance in a Tent: John Lair's Renfro Valley Tent Shows, 1942–47" (parts 1 and 2), *JCM* 24, no. 3 (2006): 33–37, and 24, no. 4 (2007): 39. **Guest stars**: Reno, *Musical History*, 6. **"Billie" Forrester**: Henry, "Come Prepared," 50–61. **"Curley" Bradshaw**: Mrs. Billy Wayne Gumm and Mrs. Rachel Hughes (relatives), conversations, May 30, 2001. **Billed as**: Advertisement (flyer) for appearance in Lawrenceville, Va., Aug. 22, 1944, author's collection.

37. **Sally Ann and accordion**: Henry, "Come Prepared," 16–19; Henry, "Sally Ann Forrester," 57; Rinzler, *Stars*, 206; Rosenberg and Wolfe, *TMBM*, 40–41.

38. Eiland, *Nashville's Mother Church*, 49–54; *Nashville (Tenn.) City Directory* (1944), 59. "Broadway" in Nashville is neither street nor avenue; it is Broadway.

39. B. Monroe, onstage interview, 1963.

40. Hatch, 30; Reno, *Musical History*, 6; Bill Vernon, "The Don Reno Story, Part 1: The Early Years," *MN*, June 1973, 10.

41. Pete Kuykendall, "Don Reno, Red Smiley, Bill Harrell and the Tennessee Cut-Ups" (part 2), *BU*, July 1971, 12; Rooney, *Bossmen*, 50–51.

42. **Charlie's House**: James Rogers, conversation, Mar. 7, 2016. Rogers, son of contractor Archie Rogers, recalled working on the house in 1943, just before he entered the service. **Flatt with Charlie**: Rosenberg, *BAH*, 68; Carlin, "C. Monroe: 1930s and 1940s," 50. **"Will You Be Loving"**: David Freeman, liner notes for *Charlie Monroe on the Noonday Jamboree*, County Records, 538. **Charlie's first song**: Ibid. **Birch returns**: Rosenberg, "Front Porch Visit," 60.

43. **Wesbrooks quits**: Walter V. Saunders, "Notes and Queries," *BU*, Nov. 1991, 10–11; Kingsbury et al., *TE* (98), 114–15. **Howard Watts**: Tom Ewing, "Howard Watts: Better Known as Cedric Rainwater," *BU*, May 2002, 45. In this article, I incorrectly estimated the time of Wesbrooks's departure as late 1943. **Quote**: [Wesbrooks], *Everybody's Cousin*, 177. **Jubilee Hillbillies**: Walt Saunders, "Notes and Queries," *BU*, Apr. 2008, 21.

44. Ewing, "Howard Watts," 45–46.

45. Howard Watts, *C. Cedric Rainwater Souvenir Folio*, self-published booklet, ca. 1953.

46. **Baseball in wartime**: H. Green, *Uncertainty*, 222–23. **Quote**: Nash, *Behind*, 348. **Using baseball**: Rosenberg, *BAH*, 59–60; Nash, *Behind*, 348.

47. **Moody**: Tribe and Morris, "Clyde Moody," 30; Rosenberg, *BAH*, 59. **Akeman**: Wolfe, "String," 48; Rooney, *Bossmen*, 58. **Quote**: Nash, *Behind*, 348. **Watts**: Ewing, "Howard Watts," 46.

48. **1944 tent show**: Hatch, 37–40; Rooney, *Bossmen*, 36; Rice, "Barn Dance in a Tent," 33–37. **First quoted paragraph**: Rhodes, "Monroe, the Father," 15. **Second quoted paragraph**: Guralnick, "Hard-workingman's Blues," 33.

49. Jerry Paul, "James Monroe," *Acoustica Magazine*, Jan. 2003, 4.

50. Kennedy, *Freedom from Fear*, 698–718; Kingsbury et al., *TE* (98), 551–52; "Grant Turner, WSM Pioneer," *Inside WSM* 3 (3rd Q 1996), 1–2.

51. **Roosevelt elected**: C. Daniel et al., *20th Century*, 580. **End of ban**: "A Chronological Chart," 92; Kingsbury et al., *TE* (98), 6–7; "History of the AFM: 1940–1949," http://www.afm.org/about/history/1940-1949; Walt Trott, conversation, Dec. 17, 2008.

52. *Grinder's Switch Gazette*, Feb. 1945, 5, 6; Ewing, "Howard Watts," 45.

53. **Trip to Miami**: Hatch, 41–42. **Finding F-5**: Grisman, "Monroe Interview," 5. **Specifications and original price**: Jim Hatlo, "Bill Monroe's Mandolin," *Frets*, Sept. 1986, 32. Photos taken in 1944 clearly show Bill playing his F-7 mandolin. (Booklet, *Bill Monroe: Blue Moon of Kentucky*, BCD 16399, 46–48. The photos are incorrectly dated "circa 1943.")

54. John Morris, liner notes for *Moody's Blues* by Clyde Moody, Old Homestead 90013 (released 1972).

55. **Session**: Rosenberg and Wolfe, *TMBM*, 51–52, 57. **"Rocky Road Blues"**: Rosenberg, *BAH*, 62. **"Goodbye Old Pal"**: Rosenberg and Wolfe, *TMBM*, 48; Bill Monroe, personal communication with author, Feb. 3, 1990; Charlie Monroe, *The Songs You Have Requested* (self-published, ca. 1939), 15. **"True Life Blues"**: Douglas B. Green, liner notes for *Bill Monroe and His Blue Grass Boys: The Classic Bluegrass Recordings, Vol. 1*, County Records, CCS-104.

56. **Quote**: D. Green, *The Classic Recordings* (CCS-104). **"Kentucky Waltz"**: Ibid.; Rosenberg, *BAH*, 62. The original "Come Back to Me in My Dreams" wasn't released by Columbia until 1980 (CCS-105).

57. Ewing, "Howard Watts," 47; Howard Watts Jr. and Jarrett Watts (Howard Watts's sons), interview, Apr. 13, 2001, and Jarrett Watts, email, May 21, 2001.

58. **Lester Flatt**: "Lester Flatt: His Boyhood and Early Career" (part 2), *TBS*, Mar. 1972, 4. **Andy Boyett**: Lisa Williams, "Lost to the Airwaves: The Most Intriguing Country Acts Seldom Heard," *JCM* 22, no. 1 (2001): 21–22; Morton with Wolfe, *DeFord Bailey*, 36; Walter V. Saunders, "Notes and Queries," *BU*, Sept. 2002, 26–27. **Jim Shumate**: Wayne Erbsen, "Jim Shumate—Bluegrass Fiddler Supreme," *BU*, Apr. 1979, 14–15.

59. **Bill the farmer**: Hurst, "Mellowing Father," 3-S; Author unknown, *Purina's Grand Ole Opry and Checkerboard Fun-Fest Souvenir Album* (Nashville: Early 1945), unnumbered pages 7–8; Hand-drawn map of property, dated Mar. 1943, collection of Jim Mills, 2011. **Tent show season**: Hatch, sheet 44.

60. **Roosevelt**: Kennedy, *Freedom from Fear*, 808. **Opry**: Tom Ewing, "Thirty Years Ago This Month," *BU*, Nov. 1998, 9. **Germany**: C. Daniel et al., *20th Century*, 592.

61. **Watts and others**: Ewing, "Howard Watts," 47. **Wise**: Lance LeRoy, "Chubby Wise: 'Master of Bluegrass Fiddle Soul,'" *BU*, Mar. 1996, 13; Chubby Wise, from *Bill Monroe: Father of Bluegrass Music*. **Williams**: Wayne W. Daniel, "Curley Williams: Country Fiddler, Western Swing Band Leader, Composer of Pop Music Hit," *The Devil's Box*, Spring 1999, 8. **Bradshaw**: "American Folk Tunes," *Billboard*, Dec. 7, 1946, 104; Kingsbury et al., *TE* (98), 519. Bradshaw can be heard playing harmonica on "Lost John" and "Alabama Blues" on *Going to Little Creek* by Uncle Henry's Original Kentucky Mountaineers, a British Archive of Country Music CD, D-020.

62. **Birth of Howard Watts Jr.**: Ewing, "Howard Watts," 47. **Birch on bass**: *Grinder's Switch Gazette*, Aug. 1945, 8. **End of World War II**: C. Daniel et al., *20th Century*, 597–98.

63. **"Lost John" Miller**: *Grinder's Switch Gazette*, Nov., 1945, 6. **Scruggs**: Rosenberg, *Stars*, 258; Rosenberg, *BAH*, 70; Earl Scruggs, interviewed by Douglas B. Green, June 21, 1974: FLA-CMHOF&M, tape OH168-LC, c. 2; Scruggs, *Earl Scruggs and Banjo*, 151.

64. Smith, *Can't You Hear?*, 79–80, 99; Simpson Co., Ky., Archives, Marriage Bond 528.

65. **"Blue Moon"**: Robert Gottlieb and Robert Kimball, *Reading Lyrics* (New York: Pantheon, 2000), 198, 647. **"When My Blue Moon Turns to Gold Again"**: McCloud et al., *DC*, 869. **Quotes**: Dorothy Horstman, *Sing Your Heart Out, Country Boy* (Nashville: Country Music Foundation Press, 1986), 151. **Full moon**: "Keith's Moon Page," http://home.hiwaay.net/~krcool/Astro/moon/fullmoon.htm#00. **March 1945**: Hatch, 43. **First performance**: Dick Hill, "The *Grand Ole Opry*, 1944–45: A Radio Log," *JCM* 5, no. 3 (Fall 1974): 116.

66. **Shumate and quote**: Jim Shumate, interview, Sept. 3, 2005. **Akeman to army**: Edlund, "Monroe—The Master Speaks," 6; Wolfe, "Bluegrass Touches," 11; Kennedy, *Freedom from Fear*, 710. **Andrews**: Rosenberg, *BAH*, 71; Wolfe, *Good-Natured Riot*, 243–44.

67. George D. Hay, *A Story of the Grand Ole Opry* (Nashville: self-published, 1945), 51–52; Ewing, ed., *Bill Monroe Reader*, 12.

68. **Season's end**: Hatch, 48. **Akeman and Childre**: Wolfe, "Bluegrass Touches," 11; McCloud et al., *DC*, 155. **Lew Childre guesting**: Hatch, 46. **Akeman leaving, first quote, and finding Scruggs**: Erbsen, "Jim Shumate," 20. **Second quote**: Roger Siminoff, "Earl Scruggs," *Frets*, July 1981, 25.

69. **Scruggs's audition**: Erbsen, "Jim Shumate," 20; Rosenberg, *BAH*, 70; Siminoff, "Earl Scruggs," 26. **First quote**: E. Scruggs, FLA-CMHOF&M, OH168-LC, c. 2. **Second quote**: Jim Shumate, conversation, May 22, 2001. **Third quote**: Jim Shumate, conversation, July 9, 2001. **Pay**: Henry, "Come Prepared," 74.

70. **First quote**: Don Rhodes, "Lester Flatt: Talking with a Bluegrass Giant," *Pickin'*, Feb. 1979, 26. **Second quote**: Lambert (with Sechler), *Lester Flatt*, 114. **Third quote**: Siminoff, "Earl Scruggs," 26. **Shumate departs**: J. Shumate, interview, 2005. **Fourth quote**: Erbsen, "Jim Shumate," 20.

71. **Joe Forrester**: Murphy Henry, "Joe Forrester: Forgotten Blue Grass Boy," *BU*, Aug. 2002, 46. **Birch**: *Grinder's Switch Gazette*, Jan. and Feb., 1946, 8; ad in *Coalfield Progress*, Norton, Va., June 20, 1946. **Jim Andrews**: Siminoff, "Earl Scruggs," 26; Tony Trischka (with Béla Fleck), "The Earl Scruggs Interview" (part 1), *Banjo Newsletter*, Oct. 2006, 11. **Schedule**: Hatch, 49.

72. **Release date**: Rosenberg and Wolfe, *TMBM*, 297. **Last release**: Ibid., 314. **The record business**: Rosenberg, *BAH*, 61. **Billboard listing**: Joel Whitburn, ed., *Joel Whitburn's Top Country Singles, 1944–1993* (Menomonee, Wisc.: Record Research, 1994), 245; author's survey, *Billboard*, 1944–45. Of the chart's five entries when "Kentucky Waltz" peaked, there were five songs tied at number 4 (*Billboard*, May 4, 1946, 29).

73. **Itinerary**: Hatch, 49–51. **Quote**: Henry, "Joe Forrester," 47–48.

74. **Departure of Forresters**: Henry, "Sally Ann Forrester," 58; Henry, "Come Prepared," 86–87. **Return of Watts**: Ewing, "Howard Watts," 47; Bill Monroe and the Blue Grass Boys, "Little Maggie," *Bluegrass Classics: Radio Shows, 1946–1948*, BGC 80.

75. **Hay intro**: Bill Monroe and the Blue Grass Boys, *Bluegrass Classics* (BGC 80), introduction for "Careless Love." **RB-11**: Kevin Kerfoot, "At Home with Earl Scruggs," *Bluegrass Music Profiles*, Sept./Oct. 2006, 11; *Gibson Instruments Catalog W*, 1935 edition, 42. Based on old photos in author's collection, Dave Akeman also played an RB-11 early in his career.

76. **Wise**: Ewing, "Howard Watts," 47. **Rehearsals**: Rooney, *Bossmen*, 43.

77. **"How Will I Explain?"**: D. Green, *Classic Recordings* (CCS-104); Lucky Saylor (former member of Smith's band), interview, May 22, 2008. **"Blue Yodel No. 4"**: Author's survey of Jimmie Rodgers's "Blue Yodels." **Composer credits**: Lambert (with Sechler), *Lester Flatt*, 113. **Advance royalties**: D. Green, *Classic Recordings* (CCS-104).

78. **First quote**: Rinzler, notes for *Off the Record, Volume 1*, 22. **Second quote**: Siminoff, "Earl Scruggs," 29–30. **Third quote**: Kerfoot, "At Home with Scruggs," 12.

79. **"Heavy Traffic Ahead"**: Rosenberg and Wolfe, *TMBM*, 58; Kerfoot, "At Home with Scruggs," 15; Earl Scruggs, interviewed by Eddie Stubbs, Mar. 14, 2004, Video Oral History Collection, International Bluegrass Music Museum (IBMM), Owensboro, Ky. **"Toy Heart"**: Walter V. Saunders (quoting Pete Kuykendall), "Notes and Queries," *BU*, Feb. 2008, 19. **Baseball suspended**: Trischka (with Fleck), "Scruggs Interview," 20.

80. Merlene Austin (widow of Scottie Monroe) and Francis Harvey (friend of the family), conversations, Mar. 15, 2009.

81. **Series of one-nighters**: Hatch, 53–55. **Scruggs's banjos**: Kerfoot, "At Home with Scruggs," 11; Reno, *Musical History*, 6. **Sunset Park**: Lawrence A. Waltman, *Sunset Park 50th Anniversary Album, 1940–1990* (self-published, 1991), 5.

82. **Tent show**: Hatch, 55–56. **Sessions**: Rosenberg and Wolfe, *TMBM*, 67–69. **Quote**: Tom Ewing, "Fifty Years Ago This Month: Recording the New Bluegrass," *BU*, Sept. 1996, 27. **"Why Did You Wander?"**: Rosenberg and Wolfe, *TMBM*, 67–68.

83. **Quote**: Ewing, "Fifty Years Ago," 27. **First takes**: Rosenberg and Wolfe, *TMBM*, 67–69, 297–98.

84. **"Blue Yodel No. 3"**: Porterfield, *Jimmie Rodgers*, 394. **"Mother's Only Sleeping"**: Rosenberg, *BAH*, 74; Bob Carlin, "Mother Songs Are Not Dead: The Story of the Spencer Brothers," *BU*, Aug. 1996, 35.

85. Bill Myrick, interview, Aug. 13, 2004; Schlappi, *Roy Acuff*, 51–54; McCloud et al., *DC*, 291.

86. B. Myrick, interview, 2004.

87. **Release**: Rosenberg and Wolfe, *TMBM*, 297. **Stanleys**: Jack Tottle, "The Stanley Brothers: For Most of Their Brilliant First Decade, Bristol Was Home," *BU*, Oct. 1987, 27; Gary Reid, email, Mar. 29, 2009; Jeff Miller, email, Apr. 1, 2009. **"Pee Wee" Lambert**: Frank Godbey, "Pee Wee Lambert," *BU*, Jan. 1979, 12–14.

88. **Itinerary**: Hatch, 56. **"Shenandoah Waltz"**: Carpenter and Kissil, "Chubby Wise," 17; LeRoy, "Chubby Wise," 14; McCloud et al., *DC*, 559. It was probably the 1940 Bluebird recording of "Sidewalk Waltz" by Jimmie Revard and his Oklahoma Playboys that Wise heard. Choates's version wasn't recorded and released until 1949 (Andrew Brown, booklet for *Harry Choates: Devil in the Bayou*, Bear Family, BCD 16355 BH, 107; Tim Knight, email, Jan. 28, 2013). **"The Old Cross Road"**: D. Green, *Classic Recordings* (CCS-104). **Watts**: Ewing, "Howard Watts," 48.

89. **"Footprints in the Snow"**: Whitburn, *Top Country Singles*, 245; "Most-Played Juke Box Folk Records," *Billboard*, Dec. 7, 1946, through Jan. 4, 1947. **"Tennessee Waltz"**: Walt Trott, "Redd Stewart Mined Gold with the 'Tennessee Waltz,'" *Nashville Musician*, Jan.–Mar. 1998, 25; Walt Trott, "'Waltz' Writer Succumbs," *NM*, Oct.–Dec. 2003, 24.

90. **Itinerary**: Hatch, 57–59. **First quote**: Ewing, "Fifty Years Ago," 26.

91. **Osbornes**: Rosenberg, *BAH*, 76–77; Neil V. Rosenberg, "Osborne Brothers" (part 1), *BU*, Sept. 1971, 5; Trischka and Wernick, *Masters of Banjo*, 112.

92. **Itinerary**: Hatch, 59–60. **Release**: Rosenberg and Wolfe, *TMBM*, 297.

93. **Songbook**: (Bill Monroe), *Bill Monroe's WSM Grand Ole Opry Song Folio No. 1* (New York: Peer International, 1947). **King Wilkie**: James Monroe, conversation, Apr. 2, 2009.

94. **Stripling**: Wayne W. Daniel, "Chick Stripling: Dancer, Comedian, and Old-Time Fiddler," *BU*, Nov. 1993, 37–38. **Bill's guitar**: Earl Scruggs, interview, July 9, 1996. **Martin herringbones**: Martin Guitar Company, *The Martin Story* (booklet), 1997, 11. **Replacement**: Doug Hutchens, "Rudy Lyle: Classic Bluegrass Banjo Man," *BU*, Apr. 1985, 44.

95. **Castle Recording Studio**: Kingsbury et al., *TE* (98), 88; John W. Rumble, "The Emergence of Nashville as a Recording Center: Logbooks from the Castle Studio, 1952–1953," *JCM*, Dec. 1978, 24. **Hank Williams**: Colin Escott with George Merritt and William MacEwen, *Hank Williams: The Biography* (Boston: Little, Brown, 1995), 68, 272. **Ernest Tubb**: Pugh, *Ernest Tubb*, 375. **Ernest Tubb Record Shop**: *Inside WSM* 7 (3rd Q 1997), 8; Pugh, *Ernest Tubb*, 146–49. **Hay and Denny**: Kingsbury et al., *TE* (98), 142, 233; John Rumble, conversation, Sept. 10, 2009.

96. Hatch, 60–63.

97. Ivan M. Tribe, "The Kentucky Twins," *BU*, June 1986, 54–55.

98. (Bill Monroe), *Bill Monroe's WSM Grand Ole Opry Song Folio No. 1* (New York: Peer International, 1947). *Song Folio No. 1* was reprinted by Peer-Southern in October 1973.

99. Rosenberg and Wolfe, *TMBM*, 297.

100. **Rumored strike**: Rosenberg and Wolfe, *TMBM*, 60–61. **"Blue Grass Breakdown"**: Trischka (with Fleck), "Scruggs Interview," 14.

101. **Itinerary**: Hatch, 64. **Quote**: Mac Martin, letter, Sept. 12, 2007. **Release**: Rosenberg and Wolfe, *TMBM*, 297.

102. H. Watts Jr. and J. Watts, interview, 2001; Jarrett Watts, email, May 13, 2001.

103. Hatch, 65; Danny Jones, interview, Feb. 23, 2012.

104. **Sessions**: Rosenberg and Wolfe, *TMBM*, 71–74; Colin Escott, *The Grand Ole Opry: The Making of an American Icon* (New York: Center Street, 2006), 68. Pictured in the latter is an *Opry* program of Dec. 18, 1943, listing "Bill and Clyde" singing "I'm Going Back to Old Kentucky." **Birch**: M. Leach, interview, 2006; Birch Monroe, souvenir folder of Tallahassee, Fla., postmarked Jan. 30, 1946, sent to Maude and Bertha Monroe, East Chicago, Ind., author's collection; John M. Johnson, letter to Birch Monroe, Tulane Hotel, Nashville, Tenn., dated Dec. 13, 1949, author's collection.

105. **"Tim Brook"**: Russell, *CMR*, 196. **The Carver Boys**: Wolfe, *Kentucky Country*, 41–42.

106. Rosenberg and Wolfe, *TMBM*, 61–62.

107. **Itinerary**: Hatch, 66. **Benny Martin**: Lambert (with Sechler), *Lester Flatt*, 131. **Wise with Williams**: Escott with Merritt and MacEwen, *Hank Williams*, 68, 273.

108. **Itinerary**: Hatch, 66. **Joel Price**: Rosenberg and Wolfe, *TMBM*, 81; Hatch, 66, 68.

109. Rosenberg and Wolfe, *TMBM*, 297.

110. **Get-together**: Lambert (with Sechler), *Lester Flatt*, 7. **First quote**: Rhodes, "Lester Flatt," 27. **Second quote**: Trischka (with Fleck), "Scruggs Interview," 19. **Third quote**: Kerfoot, "At Home with Scruggs," 15.

111. Joe Carlton, "What Goes for 1948?," *Billboard*, Jan. 3, 1948, 17; Neil F. Harrison, "For the Record—Mr. Petrillo," *Billboard*, Jan. 17, 1948, 25.

112. Rosenberg and Wolfe, *TMBM*, 297.

113. **Itinerary**: Hatch, 67. **Wise's departure**: Rosenberg, *BAH*, 78. **Martin and Flatt**: Walt Trott, "Record Reviews," *NM*, Oct.–Dec. 1999, 33.

114. **Mauldin and Gann**: Simpson Co., Ky., Archives, Marriage Bond 446. **Scruggs and Flatt**: Rhodes, "Lester Flatt," 27. **Goad**: Thomas A. Adler, *Bean Blossom: The Brown County Jamboree and Bill Monroe's Bluegrass Festivals* (Urbana: University of Illinois Press, 2011), 61; Hatch, 68. **McCraw**: Bruce Nemerov, "Hubert Davis: Down Home Banjo Picker," *BU*, Jan. 1977, 20.

115. **Reno**: Rooney, *Bossmen*, 51; Reno, *Musical History*, 6. **Size of house**: Bill Vernon, "The Don Reno Story, Part 2: Bill Monroe and Beyond," *MN*, Aug. 1973, 8.

116. **Reno and capo**: Trischka and Wernick, *Masters of Banjo*, 90–91. **Quote**: Hub Nitchie, "BNL Visits with Don Reno," *Banjo Newsletter*, Nov., 1976, 6.

117. **Band lineup**: Reno, *Musical History*, 6. **Price**: Rosenberg and Wolfe, *TMBM*, 81; Eddie Stubbs, Joel Price obituary, *BU*, July 1999, 13; Hatch, 68. **Phelps**: Jackie Phelps,

interviewed by Douglas B. Green, Dec. 19, 1975: FLA-CMHOF&M, OH139; Hatch, 69. **Reno and pay**: Rooney, *Bossmen*, 51.

118. Rhodes, "Lester Flatt," 27.

119. Rooney, *Bossmen*, 51; Kim Swindell Wood, "Gladys Flatt, Wife of Bluegrass Legend Lester Flatt, Has Passed Away," http://myspartanews.com/articles/2014/04/01/news/doc533ab6ede3d80313007650.prt.

120. **Phelps**: J. Phelps, FLA-CMHOF&M, OH139. **Release**: Rosenberg and Wolfe, *TMBM*, 297. **Eanes**: Russell, *CMR*, 391; Pete Kuykendall, "Smilin' Jim Eanes," *BU*, Feb. 1973, 8–9.

121. **Eanes**: Gary B. Reid, "Jim Eanes," *BU*, May 1987, 23. **Wright**: Walt Saunders, "Notes and Queries," *BU*, July 1995, 10. **Reno**: Kuykendall, "Don Reno" (part 2), 14.

122. **Itinerary**: Hatch, 72. **Quote**: Rooney, *Bossmen*, 59. **"Sweetheart" in chart**: "Most-Played Juke Box Folk Records," *Billboard*, June 15, 1948, 43. **July release**: Rosenberg and Wolfe, *TMBM*, 297. **Live recording**: Rosenberg and Wolfe, *TMBM*, 75, 306.

123. **Flatt and Scruggs in Bristol**: Rosenberg, *BAH*, 80. **Wiseman**: Jack Tottle, "Mac Wiseman: The Bristol Years," *BU*, Oct. 1987, 26. **First quote**: Earl Scruggs, "Remembering Don Reno: Banjo's Eclectic Innovator," including "Earl Scruggs Remembers," *Frets*, Apr. 1985, 23. **Second quote**: Nitchie, "BNL Visits with Reno," 5. **Time of trade**: Jim Rollins, email, Oct. 27, 2013; Ralph Stanley via James Alan Shelton, email, Oct. 28, 2013. Stanley was present at the trade prior to the Stanley Brothers leaving WCYB in July 1948.

124. **Itinerary**: Hatch, 73–74. **Quote**: B. Monroe, Rinzler Archives, RINZ-RR-0002. A song that Reno recalled co-writing with Bill on Sept. 15, 1948, "I'm Afraid My Darling's Gone," was recorded by Reno and Harrell in 1972 and released on *Reno-Smiley-Harrell, 1963–1972 Complete King-Starday Recordings, Vol. 3* (Gusto, GT7-2176-2).

125. Nitchie, "BNL Visits with Reno," 7.

126. **Itinerary**: Hatch, 73–75. **Baseball revived and Shenandoah Valley Trio**: Johnnie Sippel, "Folk Talent and Tunes," *Billboard*, Nov. 6, 1948, 33; Vernon, "Don Reno Story, Part 2," 9. **Carger**: Mack Carger, interview, May 5, 2009.

127. **Ball game in Rosine**: F. Harvey, interview, 2006; James Paul Burden, interview, June 8, 2009; Darrel Dukes, interview, June 9, 2009; Bud Raley and Joe Wright, interviewed by Campbell Mercer, June 19 and Aug. 31, 2002; *OCN*, July 9, 1948, 7.

128. **Rich-R'-Tone recordings and Bill's response**: Rosenberg, *BAH*, 80–84; Rosenberg and Wolfe, *TMBM*, 297. **Quote**: R. Stanley, interviewed by M. Seeger, 1966. **Stanley Brothers' recordings**: Gary B. Reid, *Stanley Brothers: A Preliminary Discography* (Roanoke, Va.: Copper Creek, 1984), unnumbered pp. 4–5.

129. **Itinerary**: Hatch, 74–75. **"Wicked Path of Sin"**: "Best-Selling Retail Folk Records," *Billboard*, Nov. 6, 1948, 32. **Election**: C. Daniel et al., *20th Century*, 653. **"Little Community Church"**: "Best-Selling Retail Folk Records," *Billboard*, Nov. 27, 1948, 35 (debut); Dec. 11, 1948, 31 (peak); Jan. 22, 1949, 41 (last appearance).

130. **End of ban**: Kingsbury et al., *TE* (98), 6; "Post-Ban Time, It Says Here," *Billboard*, Dec. 18, 1948, 3, 19; Joe Csida, "Billboard Backstage," *Billboard*, Dec. 25, 1948, 3, 21. **Reissues**: Rosenberg and Wolfe, *TMBM*, 315.

131. **Debut**: Johnnie Sippel, "Folk Talent and Tunes," *Billboard*, Jan. 8, 1949, 26. **Release**: Rosenberg and Wolfe, *TMBM*, 297.

132. **First record**: Neil V. Rosenberg, "The Flatt and Scruggs Discography: The Mercury Sessions, 1948–50," *JCM* 12, no. 3 (June 1989): 47–48. **Wiseman's departure**: Tottle, "Mac Wiseman," 26.

133. Steven D. Price, *Old as the Hills: The Story of Bluegrass Music* (New York: Viking, 1975), 37.

134. **Satherley**: Mac Wiseman, first interview, May 6, 1997. **Songs**: Reid, *Stanley Brothers Discography*, 4.

135. **Release**: Rosenberg and Wolfe, *TMBM*, 298. **Phelps**: J. Phelps, FLA-CMHOF&M, OH139. **Itinerary**: Hatch, 79. **Wiseman**: Doug Green, "Mac Wiseman: Remembering," *MN*, July 1972, 4.

136. Rosenberg, "Flatt and Scruggs Discography: Mercury Sessions," 47–48; Columbia Records session ledger (Stanley Brothers).

137. **Myrick and Carger**: Bill Myrick, interviews, Aug. 13 and Sept. 13, 2004. **Price**: Rosenberg and Wolfe, *TMBM*, 82. **Morgan**: Johnnie Sippel, "Folk Talent and Tunes," *Billboard*, Apr. 30, 1949, 36. **Billboard**: Ibid. **Release**: Rosenberg and Wolfe, *TMBM*, 298. **Itinerary, Lonzo and Oscar, and Stringbean**: Hatch, 80–85. **First drive-in**: Hatch, 81. **Stringbean coaching**: (Bill Monroe), *Bill Monroe's Blue Grass Country Songs* (New York: Bill Monroe Music, 1950), inside front cover. **Quote**: B. Myrick, interviews, 2004.

138. Mac Wiseman, second interview, July 30, 2002; B. Myrick, interviews, 2004.

139. **Bill's absences**: M. Wiseman, second interview, 2002. **B. Martin**: Lambert (with Sechler), *Lester Flatt*, 131. **Ethridge**: Reno, *Musical History*, 6.

140. **Williams on Opry**: Kingsbury and Axlerod, *Country*, 350–51; Escott with Merritt and MacEwen, *Hank Williams*, 104–6. **Number one on both charts**: "Most-Played Juke Box Folk Records," *Billboard*, June 4, 1949, 32, and "Best-Selling Retail Folk Records," same issue, 33.

141. **Stanley release**: Columbia Records session ledger (Stanley Brothers). **Decca**: Kingsbury et al., *TE* (98), 140.

142. **Schedule**: Hatch, 83. **Christian**: Gene Christian, interview, Aug. 1, 2002. **Bess**: Kingsbury et al., *TE* (98), 541.

143. **Itinerary**: Hatch, 83–84. **Bessie went along**: Mac Martin, conversation, Apr. 22, 2009. **Trio went on**: Rooney, *Bossmen*, 58. **Quote**: G. Christian, interview, 2002.

144. Vernon, "Don Reno Story, Part 2," 10; Walt Trott, "Don Reno and Red Smiley: 'Don't Let Your Sweet Love Die,'" *NM*, Jan.–Mar. 1998, 24.

145. Hutchens, "Rudy Lyle," 44.

146. "Most-Played Juke Box Folk Records," *Billboard*, Aug. 6, 1949, 30; Whitburn, *Top Country Singles*, 245.

147. **Lyle and replacements**: Hutchens, "Rudy Lyle," 44–45. **Wise**: Tribe, "Chubby Wise," 11. **Thompson**: Ad, *Pikeville (Ky.) Daily News*, July 23, 1949; Hutchens, "Rudy Lyle," 45.

148. **Itinerary**: Hatch, 86. **Shenandoah Valley Trio and Melissa Monroe**: B. Myrick, interviews, 2004. **Release**: Rosenberg and Wolfe, *TMBM*, 298. **Session owed**: M. Wiseman, first interview, 1997; Rumble, notes for *TMBM (36 to 94)*, 42.

149. Escott with Merritt and MacEwen, *Hank Williams*, 128; Ralph Rinzler, liner notes for *The High, Lonesome Sound of Bill Monroe and His Blue Grass Boys*, Decca Records, DL4780.

150. Peter V. Kuykendall, "Jimmy Martin, Super King of Bluegrass: Bluegrass Music Is His Life," *BU*, Sept. 1979, 11; Brett F. Devan, "The High Lonesome Sound of Jimmy Martin, the King of Bluegrass: A Rare Interview," *BU*, Dec. 1995, 17.

151. B. Myrick, interviews, 2004; Doug Green, "'As My Granddaddy Always Used to Say': An Interview with Jimmy Martin," *BU*, Sept. 1972, 7.

152. **Itinerary**: Hatch, 88. **Shows in Arkansas**: Devan, "Jimmy Martin," 18.

153. **Session**: Rosenberg and Wolfe, *TMBM*, 75–76. **"Can't You Hear Me Callin'?"**: M. Wiseman, first interview, 1997. **"Travelin' Down This Lonesome Road"**: D. Green, *The Classic Recordings* (CCS-104). **"The Girl in the Blue Velvet Band"**: W. W. Bryan, Burnet, Texas (copy of poem); Dave Fredrickson via Sandy Rothman, email, Oct. 24, 2005.

154. M. Wiseman, first interview, 1997.

155. **Itinerary**: Hatch, 89. **1940s at homeplace**: M. Leach, interview, 2006; Merlene Austin, conversation, Mar. 15, 2010. **Quote**: Bill Monroe, from *The Mandolin of Bill Monroe* (instructional video), Smithsonian/Folkways Recordings and Homespun Video (VD-MON-MN01). **"I'm On My Way Back"**: M. Wiseman, first interview, 1997.

156. **Show in Montgomery**: George Merritt (attendee), conversation, May 7, 2009; *Montgomery (Ala.) Advertiser*, Nov. 9, 1949, 2-A. **Dickens**: Paul Kingsbury, Michael McCall, and John W. Rumble, eds., *The Encyclopedia of Country Music*, 2nd ed. (New York: Oxford University Press, 2012), 137. **Still-new**: Escott with Merritt and MacEwen, *Hank Williams*, 286.

157. **Announcement**: Johnnie Sippel, "Folk Tunes and Talent," *Billboard*, Nov. 12, 1949, 35. **Agreement**: Rosenberg, *BAH*, 88; Rumble, *TMBM (36 to 94)*, 54. **Men's room**: Rich Kienzle, "Owen Bradley," *Journal of the American Academy for the Preservation of Old-Time Country Music*, Dec. 1994, 13.

158. **Itinerary**: Hatch, 89–90. **Terhune's films**: "Max Terhune (1891–1973)," http://us.imdb.com/name/nm0855579; "The Three Mesquiteers," http://www.b-westerns.com/trio3m.htm. The films included "Range Justice" and "West of El Dorado" with Johnny Mack Brown and "Law of the West" with Bob Steele.

159. **Releases**: Rosenberg and Wolfe, *TMBM*, 298. **Wait**: Rumble, *TMBM (36 to 94)*, 42.

160. B. Monroe, Rinzler Archives, RINZ-RR-0005; D. Green, "Mac Wiseman," 4; Don Rhodes, "Mac Wiseman," *BU*, July 1975, 18.

CHAPTER FIVE. 1950–1959

1. **Wise and Clements**: Carpenter and Kissil, "Chubby Wise," 12. **Price and Thompson**: Rosenberg and Wolfe, *TMBM*, 81–82.

2. **Itinerary**: Hatch, 90–91. **Bill's revision**: Bill Monroe and Blue Grass Boys, live recording, early 1946, author's collection. **"New Mule Skinner Blues"**: Dorothy Horstman, "Writer Vaughn Horton Is 'Born to Win,'" *Music City News*, Dec. 1976, 8.

3. **Session**: Rosenberg and Wolfe, *TMBM*, 83, 101. **"Blue Grass Ramble" tuning**: Grisman, "Monroe Interview," 7. **"My Little Georgia Rose"**: Jimmy Martin, interviewed by Lance LeRoy, Dec. 20, 2004, Video Oral History Collection, IBMM. **"Memories of You" tuning**: Butch Waller (mandolinist), e-mail, May 14, 2009.

4. **Session**: Rosenberg and Wolfe, *TMBM*, 101–2. **"Alabama Waltz"**: B. Monroe, Rinzler Archives, RINZ-RR-0005. **"I'm On My Way to the Old Home" and "The Old Home"**: Reid, *Stanley Brothers Discography*, 5; Columbia Records session ledger (Stanley Bros.); Rosenberg and Wolfe, *TMBM*, 301.

5. **Itinerary**: Hatch, 92–93. **Myrick's departure**: B. Myrick, interviews, 2004. **Martin**: Jimmy Martin, interviewed 2004, Video Oral History Collection, IBMM.

6. **Releases by Bill and by Flatt and Scruggs**: Rosenberg and Wolfe, *TMBM*, 298, 300; Rosenberg, "Flatt and Scruggs Discography: Mercury Sessions," 48.

7. Ewing, "Howard Watts," 49; Kuykendall, "Jimmy Martin," 12.

8. Rosenberg and Wolfe, *TMBM*, 84–85, 102, 300. Until the forth and final take of "Boat of Love," the lyrics of the third line of its third verse were: "Leave your sins behind. Quit your hesitatin'" (disc 1, cuts 37–40 of *Bill Monroe and the Bluegrass Boys, Castle Studio, 1950–1951, Complete Sessions* [RWA, ACD 12522]).

9. **Itinerary**: Hatch, 94–96. **June 25**: C. Daniel et al., *20th Century*, 680.

10. Dick Bowden, "Russell Petty: One of the Blue Grass 'Boys of Summer' or 'The Crowds Wouldn't Have Come If They Didn't Like the Music,'" *BU*, Mar. 1995, 31–33.

11. Don Cunningham, "Hearing Red: Merle Taylor's Bed-Rock Bluegrass Fiddling," *BU*, Aug. 1982, 29–30.

12. **Itinerary**: Hatch, 98. **Quote**: Cunningham, "Hearing Red," 30.

13. **Melissa**: Columbia Records session ledger (Melissa Monroe). **Molly Bee**: McCloud et al., *DC*, 58. **Brenda Lee**: Kingsbury, McCall, and Rumble, *TE*, 276. **Trio**: Ivan Tribe, booklet for *New Sounds Ramblin' from Coast to Coast: The Early Days of Bluegrass, Vol. 3*, Rounder Records, 1015, 5; Shenandoah Valley Trio's recording of "Cabin of Love," Columbia Records, 20794. Melissa's recordings, released in 1950: "Guilty Tears" / "Oh, How I Miss You" (20752), and in 1951: "You Rule My Heart" / "Stop, Look and Listen" (20783).

14. **Itinerary**: Hatch, 99. **Lyle's recollection**: Hutchens, "Rudy Lyle," 45. **Rainbow Park**: Johnny Sippel, "Folk Talent and Tunes," *Billboard*, May 27, 1950, 40; Rhonda Strickland, "Ola Belle Reed: Preserving Traditional Music without Killing It," *BU*, June 1983, 43; Ralph Reed Jr. (son of Bud and Ola Belle Reed), conversation, May 21, 2009.

15. "Best-Selling Pop Singles," "Most-Played Juke Box Records," "Most-Played Juke Box (Country and Western) Records," and "Best-Selling Retail Folk (Country and Western) Records," *Billboard*, Aug. 26, 1950, 28, 29, 32; "Goodnight, Irene" / "Tzena, Tzena, Tzena" by Gordon Jenkins and his Orchestra and the Weavers (Decca, 27077).

16. Neil V. Rosenberg, "Thirty Years Ago This Month," *BU*, Aug. 1980, 6; Kevin Kerfoot, "Bob Osborne Interview," *Bluegrass Music Profiles*, July–Aug. 2004, 12; Bill Emerson (interviewer), "The Osborne Brothers: Getting Started," *MN*, July–Aug. 1971, 6.

17. **Itinerary**: Hatch, 99. **Quote**: Doug Hutchens, compiler, *Howdy, Folks, Howdy (Volume 1)* (Spencer, Va.: self-published, 2003), 4.

18. **Bill's guitar**: Jimmy Martin, remarks recorded at the Bean Blossom Bluegrass Festival, Sept., 2003, video collection of John Arms, 2011; Larry Wallace (banjo player with Jimmy Martin, 1991–2000), conversation, June 1, 2011. **Recordings and releases**: Rosenberg and Wolfe, *TMBM*, 102–3, 300; Gary B. Reid, booklet for *Reno and Smiley,*

Early Years: 1951–1959, Gusto, GT7-0959-2. **Wiseman with Bill**: Rinzler, liner notes for *The High, Lonesome Sound*.

19. *Bill Monroe's Blue Grass Country Songs* (New York: Bill Monroe Music, 1950).

20. Ibid., 1.

21. B. Myrick, interviews, 2004; Hatch, 101; Doug Hutchens, "Edd Mayfield: The Mystery Man," *BU*, Aug. 1983, 26–27; Joe Carr and Alan Munde, booklet notes for *The Mayfield Brothers: Vintage Recordings, 1948–1956*, Patuxent Music, CD 136, rel. 2006.

22. **Itinerary**: Hatch, 101–2. **"Uncle Pen" release**: Rosenberg and Wolfe, *TMBM*, 300. **Terry**: Hutchens, *Howdy, Folks, Howdy*, 4–5.

23. **Itinerary**: Hatch, 102–4. **Sheet music**: Based on information provided by the anonymous seller of the sheet music, auctioned on eBay, Nov. 10, 2002.

24. **"Letter from My Darling"**: Rinzler, liner notes for *The High, Lonesome Sound*; Frank Wakefield, comment to author, Oct. 20, 2010. **"On the Old Kentucky Shore"**: B. Monroe, Rinzler Archives, RINZ-RR-0002; Leora Baize, Commonwealth of Kentucky Certificate of Death, Vol. 28, file 13710; Editor unknown, *357 Songs We Love to Sing* (Paul A. Schmitt Music / Belwin-Mills, 1938), 88. **"Raw Hide"**: Rosenberg and Wolfe, *TMBM*, 87; *Rawhide*, 20th Century Fox Corp., directed by Henry Hathaway, released 1951; ad (for movie's premiere at local theatre), *Corbin [Ky.] Daily Tribune*, Sept. 4, 1951, 3. **"Poison Love"**: "Advance Folk (Country and Western) Record Releases," *Billboard*, Sept. 9, 1950, 44; "Best Selling Retail Folk (Country and Western) Records," *Billboard*, Mar. 3, 1951, 27.

25. **Itinerary**: Hatch, 102–3. **Weather**: Leon Alligood, "Nashville's Worst Blizzard Crippled City 50 Years Ago," *Tennessean*, Jan. 28, 2001, 1B. **Young**: Gary Nichols and Opal Sims, "Vern Young," *BU*, Nov. 1991, 38; Vern Young, conversation, July 2, 2009.

26. **Arnold's release**: "Advance Folk (Country and Western) Record Releases," *Billboard*, Apr. 7, 1951, 58. **Session**: Rosenberg and Wolfe, *TMBM*, 87–88, 103–4. **From Florida**: Hatch, 104. **Martin on fiddle**: Neil V. Rosenberg, email, June 9, 2009.

27. **Hal Smith**: Pugh, *Ernest Tubb*, 90, 121, 159; Kingsbury et al., *TE* (98), 492; Walt Trott, "Hal Smith, Fiddler and Pioneer Publisher, Dead at 84," *NM*, Oct.–Dec. 2008, 11. **Session**: Rosenberg and Wolfe, *TMBM*, 104.

28. Penny Parsons, email, May 14, 2009; Carl Fleischhauer, "The Public Named Bluegrass Music: An Interview with Everett Lilly," *Old Time Music* 21 (Summer 1976): 5.

29. Hatch, 105–6; Rooney, *Bossmen*, 56–58.

30. **Thompson**: "Singer Asks Share in 'Kentucky Waltz,'" *Tennessean*, Apr. 15, 1951, 6; "Monroe Says He Paid for 'Kentucky Waltz,'" *Tennessean*, May 5, 1951, 3. **Number 1**: "Best-Selling Retail Folk (Country and Western) Records" and "Most-Played Juke Box Folk (Country and Western) Records," *Billboard*, June 2, 1951, 26.

31. **Sessions**: Rosenberg and Wolfe, *TMBM*, 104–5. **Releases**: Ibid., 300–301. **Bill's dissatisfaction**: Rosenberg, *BAH*, 100.

32. **Mauldin**: B. Mauldin, interviewed by R. Rinzler, ca. 1978. **Martin quote**: Jimmy Martin, interviewed by Pete Kuykendall, Jan. 1995. **Martin**: Kuykendall, "Jimmy Martin," 12; Rosenberg, "The Osborne Brothers" (part 1), 7; Rhonda Strickland, "Jimmy Martin: 'King of Bluegrass' Tells It Like It Is," *BU*, July 1986, 17. **Martin and Osborne**: Gary Reid, booklet notes for *The Best of King and Starday Bluegrass*, King, KG-0952-4-2 (rel. 2004), 6; Bobby Osborne, conversation, Jan, 20, 2011.

33. **Pete Pyle**: Pete Pyle, interviewed by Ralph Rinzler, ca. 1978, collection of Dwanna Pyle, Nashville, Tenn., 2012; Green, "Pete Pyle," 25. **Vic Daniels**: Pete Kuykendall, photo of Daniels, *BU*, Jan. 1999, 10. **Carter's call**: Ralph Stanley, conversation, June 6, 2009; James Alan Shelton, email, June 15, 2009. **Stanley Brothers**: Rosenberg, *BAH*, 100; Dave Samuelson, "The Stanley Brothers," *Journal of the American Academy for the Preservation of Old-Time Country Music*, Apr. 1994, 15; Gary Reid, email, Jan. 28, 2016.

34. Gordon Terry, conversation, 2002.

35. **Show**: Johnnie Sippel, "Folk Tunes and Talent," *Billboard*, June 23, 1951, 32; N. V. Rosenberg, "Thirty Years Ago," *BU*, June 1981, 8. **"Sugar-Coated Love"**: George B. Mc-Ceney, "Don't Let Your Deal Go Down: The Bluegrass Career of Ray Davis," *BU*, June 1975, 29. It appears that Tex Williams's release (Capitol 1540) preceded one by Red Kirk (Mercury 6332) ("Advance Folk [Country and Western] Record Releases," *Billboard*, May 19, 1951, 89; ad [for Mercury Records], *Billboard*, June 9, 1951, 15).

36. **Session and release**: Rosenberg and Wolfe, *TMBM*, 89, 105, 300. **Newton**: Kingsbury et al., *TE* (98), 380.

37. **Itinerary**: Hatch, 106. **Session**: Rosenberg and Wolfe, *TMBM*, 105–6. **"Sugar Coated Love"**: Composer: Audrey Butler; publisher: Babb Music. **"You're Drifting Away"**: Bill Monroe and the Blue Grass Boys, live recording, 1946–47, author's collection. **"Get Down on Your Knees and Pray"**: Disc 5, cuts 17–23 of *Bill Monroe and the Bluegrass Boys, Castle Studio, 1950–1951, Complete Sessions* (RWA, ACD 12522).

38. **Lyle**: Hutchens, "Rudy Lyle," 47. **Clark**: Wayne W. Daniel, "Good Old Songs, Good Old Jokes, Good Old Boys: Old Joe Clark and Terry," *BU*, Apr. 1989, 35. **"Touch of the banjo"**: Wolfe, "Bluegrass Touches," 11. **Quote**: David Gates, "Annals of Bluegrass: Constant Sorrow—The Long Road of Ralph Stanley" in *The Bluegrass Reader*, Thomas Goldsmith, ed. (University of Illinois Press, 2004), 333. **Ralph Stanley with Bill**: Samuelson, "The Stanley Brothers," 15; Jack Tottle, "Ralph Stanley: The Stanley Sound," *BU*, May 1981, 17; Walter Saunders, email, Jan. 28, 2016. **Carter's laryngitis**: Ralph Stanley, Lincoln Memorial University (Harrogate, Tenn.), 1976, via Gary Reid, email, Aug. 6, 2009.

39. **Session**: Columbia Records session ledger (Melissa Monroe). **Wise**: Rosenberg, booklet for *Flatt and Scruggs: 1948–1959*, unnumbered page 3. Melissa's recordings released in 1951: "Peppermint Sticks and Lemon Drops" / "Oceans of Tears" (20856) and "I'm Waiting Just For You" / "There's No Room in My Heart (for the Blues)" (20868).

40. **Snow's accident**: Hank Snow with Jack Ownbey and Bob Burris, *The Hank Snow Story* (Urbana: University of Illinois Press, 1994), 334–36. **Bill stood in**: *Halifax [Co., Va.] Gazette*, Aug. 30, 1951, 1.

41. **Drumright**: Joe Drumright, Hutchens's Questionnaire, Mar. 1979. **Tipton**: Barbara L. Green, "The Carl Tipton Family," *BU*, May 1977, 46–47. **Itinerary**: Hatch, 106–7. **Events of that week**: Johnny Vipperman, interview, Sept. 5, 2005. **Salyer**: South Salyer, Hutchens's Questionnaire, Feb. 1979. **Shehan**: Ibid.; Jim Sizemore, "Early Country Music and Bluegrass in East Tennessee: Part II," *Pickin'*, Apr. 1974, 16–17. Carter Stanley and Bill wrote several songs together during the time he was in the band. One, "Say, Won't You Be Mine?," was recorded later by the Stanley Brothers, its melody similar to Carter Stanley's "Let Me Be Your Friend," derived from Bill's "It's Mighty Dark to Travel" (Carter Stanley, interviewed by Mike Seeger, Mar. 1966; Reid, *Stanley Brothers Discography*, 6).

42. **Bill and Charlie reunion**: Ad, *Corbin [Ky.] Daily Tribune*, Sept. 14, 1951, 8. **Series of shows**: N. V. Rosenberg, "Thirty Years Ago," *BU*, Sept. 1981, 8. **"Together again"**: "Musical Monroes: Charlie and Bill Monroe," *Country Song Roundup*, Feb. 1952, 15.

43. **Mayfield**: Hutchens, "Edd Mayfield," 27. **Drumright**: Kathy Kaplan, liner notes for *Backwoods Bluegrass* by Connie and Babe, Rounder Records, 0043, rel. 1975. **Bowers**: J. Vipperman, interview, 2005.

44. **Itinerary**: Hatch, 108. **Show, Logan, and song**: Benjamin "Tex" Logan (as told to John Holder), "Christmas Time's A-Comin'," *BU*, Dec. 1982, 80.

45. **Itinerary**: Hatch, 108. **Brown County Jamboree**: Adler, *Bean Blossom*, 22–23, 35, 37. **"Spurts" Ragsdale**: Ibid., 14, 50.

46. **Telegram**: Bill Monroe, telegram to Tex Logan, Oct. 25, 1951, collection of the IBMM, Owensboro, Ky. **Quotes and original tuning**: Logan (Holder), "Christmas Time's A-Comin'," 80; Tex Logan, conversation, June 18, 2009. **Shorty's help**: Neil V. Rosenberg, email, June 19, 2009. **Terry's tuning**: Glen Duncan, email, June 16, 2009. **Session**: Rosenberg and Wolfe, *TMBM*, 106. Contrary to this source (p. 90), the tuning is not "the same tuning as in 'Black Mountain Rag.'" That tuning is (low to high) A/E/A/C# (Glen Duncan, email, June 16, 2009).

47. **TV**: David Halberstam, *The Fifties* (New York: Villard, 1993), 180–97. **Lucille Ball**: C. Daniel et al., *20th Century*, 153.

48. **Itinerary**: Hatch, 110–11. **Second divorce**: Circuit Court of Davidson Co., Tenn., *Gann v. Gann*, final decree 21303.

49. **Bill's purchase of Brown County Jamboree**: Adler, *Bean Blossom*, 48–52; Rosenberg, "Front Porch Visit," 62. **Sale finalized**: Raymond Huffmaster, email, Feb. 16, 2004. **Dunbar Cave**: Schlappi, *Roy Acuff*, 165–67.

50. **Richardson**: Russ Cheatham, "Charlie and Lee Cline and the Lonesome Pine Fiddlers," *BU*, Feb. 1980, 20. **Terry**: Kingsbury et al., *TE* (98), 534. **Itinerary**: Hatch, 112. **Cline**: Charlie Cline, interview, May 15, 2001.

51. Jack Hurst, "Mellowing Father of Bluegrass," *Nashville Tennessean*, June 25, 1972, 3-S; "James Monroe: From the First to the Second Generation of Monroes," *TBS*, Sept. 1972, 4.

52. Rosenberg and Wolfe, *TMBM*, 301.

53. Rosenberg, "Front Porch Visit," 63; Adler, *Bean Blossom*, 54, 55; P. Pyle, interviewed by R. Rinzler, ca. 1978.

54. **Wakefield**: Dennis Satterlee, *Teardrops in My Eyes: The Music of Harley "Red" Allen* (Kensington, Md.: Plucked String Foundation, 2007), 17; Tom Teepen, "Allen Grass: A Family Affair," *MN*, Feb. 1973, 5; Frank Wakefield, conversation, Mar. 24, 2010; ad, *Dayton (Ohio) Daily News*, Apr. 13, 1952, 15 (2nd sec.). **Jim and Jesse**: McCloud et al., *DC*, 422. **Bill's advice**: Dix Bruce, "Frank Wakefield," *BU*, July 1983, 16; Joseph L. Scott, liner notes for *Frank Wakefield: A Tribute to Bill Monroe*, Patuxent Music, PXCD-227.

55. **Release**: Rosenberg, "Flatt and Scruggs Discography: Mercury Sessions," 48. **Quote**: Earl Scruggs, "Scruggs Style Banjo," *Frets*, Feb. 1983, 50.

56. Hatch, 114.

57. **First quote**: B. Monroe, Rinzler Archives, FP-1993-CT-0262. **Second quote**: Doug Benson, "Bill Monroe: King of Blue Grass Music" (program 1, part 2), *BU*, Dec. 1967, 3. **Bill's mandolin**: Tom Isenhour, email, July 2, 2009.

58. **Itinerary**: Hatch, 115. **Sundays**: C. Cline, interview, 2001. **Price**: Bill Vernon, "Bill Price," *BU*, Mar. 1985, 56. **Baseball season**: Hatch, 115–20. **Martin**: Kuykendall, "Jimmy Martin," 13.

59. Rosenberg, "Osborne Brothers" (part 1), 8.

60. Sonny Osborne, from *Bill Monroe: Father of Bluegrass Music*.

61. **Osborne seeing Bill again**: Sonny Osborne, Hutchens's Questionnaire, Dec., 1978. **Session**: Rosenberg and Wolfe, *TMBM*, 92, 106–7. Cline provided the sound of the "cold wind" (Sonny Osborne via Eddie Stubbs, comment made during a WSM radio tribute to Bill, Sept. 9, 1996). **Newton**: Rosenberg and Wolfe, *TMBM*, 106–11.

62. **Quote**: Martin, interviewed by Kuykendall, 1995. **Location of coffee shop**: Jim Smoak, email, July 27, 2009.

63. **Session**: Rosenberg and Wolfe, *TMBM*, 107. **"Memories of Mother and Dad"**: David Johnston, conversation, Mar. 3, 2007; Glen Duncan, emails, Sept. 27 and 28, 2009. **"Little Girl and Dreadful Snake"**: Jill Raley via Merlene Austin, conversation, July 2009. **"My Dying Bed"**: Rosenberg and Wolfe, *TMBM*, 305. **"Don't Put Off 'til Tomorrow"**: Ibid., 305; P. Pyle, interviewed by R. Rinzler, ca. 1978. **"Country Waltz"**: Rosenberg and Wolfe, *TMBM*, 305.

64. **Session**: Rosenberg and Wolfe, *TMBM*, 108. **"Mighty Pretty Waltz"**: Ad (for Decca Records), *Billboard*, June 7, 1952, 19; Sandy Rothman, email, May 29, 2011; Glen Duncan, email, June 3, 2011. **"Pike County Breakdown"**: S. Osborne, from *Bill Monroe: Father of Bluegrass Music*; S. Osborne, Hutchens's Questionnaire; Sonny Osborne, email, Oct. 10, 2000.

65. Escott with Merritt and MacEwen, *Hank Williams*, 202–8.

66. **First quote**: Benson, "King of Blue Grass" (program 1, part 2), 3. **Second quote**: Laura Eipper, "Bill Monroe's Mandolin Gets an Apologetic Facelift," *BU*, Nov. 1980, 29. **Gibson's repair work**: Tom Isenhour, email, July 2, 2009. **Third quote**: S. Osborne, from *Bill Monroe: Father of Bluegrass Music*.

67. **Itinerary**: Hatch, 119. **Smoak**: Jim Smoak, Hutchens's Questionnaire, 1979; Jim Smoak, interview, July 7, 2009. **Car**: S. Osborne, Hutchens's Questionnaire, 1978; Doug Hutchens, "The Bill Monroe Museum and Bluegrass Hall of Fame: The Dream Comes True," *BU*, Oct. 1984, 33.

68. J. Smoak, interview, 2009; C. Cline, interview, 2001.

69. **Itinerary and Brown County Jamboree**: Hatch, 119–22. **Eisenhower**: C. Daniel et al., *20th Century*, 726. **DJ Convention**: Paul Kingsbury, *The Grand Ole Opry History of Country Music* (New York: Villard, 1995), 98; Kingsbury et al., *TE* (98), 149. **Package show**: N. V. Rosenberg, "Thirty Years Ago," *BU*, Dec. 1982, 6.

70. **Williams's death**: Escott with Merritt and MacEwen, *Hank Williams*, 238–46. **Canton show**: Colin Escott and Kira Florita, *Hank Williams: Snapshots from the Lost Highway* (Cambridge, Mass.: Da Capo, 2001), 156. **Taylor**: N. V. Rosenberg, "Thirty Years Ago," *BU*, June 1983, 7.

71. **Funeral**: Escott with Merritt and MacEwen, *Hank Williams*, 246–48; Roger M. Williams, "Hank Williams" in *Stars of Country Music: Uncle Dave Macon to Johnny Rodriguez*, eds. Bill Malone and Judith McCulloh (Urbana: University of Illinois Press, 1975), 252; George Merritt (based on a recording of the service), conversation, July 19, 2009. **Rosa Parks**: Halberstam, *Fifties*, 539–42.

72. **Itinerary**: Hatch, 123. **Cline**: C. Cline, interview, 2001. **The band in town**: Jim Smoak, email, July 16, 2009.

73. **Collision**: B. Mauldin, interviewed by R. Rinzler, ca. 1978; Neil V. Rosenberg and Charles Wolfe, booklet for *Bill Monroe—Bluegrass: 1950–1958*, Bear Family, BCD 15423, 28. **Quotes**: Nash, *Behind*, 353; Sonny Osborne, from BGRASS-L, Sept. 14, 2000; B. Mauldin, interviewed by R. Rinzler, ca. 1978. **Injuries**: Nash, *Behind*, 353; S. Osborne, from BGRASS-L, 2000. **Bill's eye and his sisters**: James Monroe, conversation, July 23, 2009. **Hospital location**: *Nashville City Directory* (1953). **Leg fractures**: Daniel C. Scullin Jr., MD, conversation, July 23, 2009. **Maude**: Maude Monroe, Practical Nursing certificate, Hume-Fogg Technical and Vocational School, Jan. 6, 1949. **Bertha and Bernard**: "Obituaries: Bernard C. Kurth," http://news.heralddispatch.com/obituaries/index.php?id=42438.

74. **Re: radio show and hospital**: J. Smoak, interview, 2009; Jim Smoak, emails, July 22 and 27, 2009. **Martin**: Martin, interviewed by Kuykendall, 1995. **Cas Walker**: Walt Saunders, Cas Walker obituary, *BU*, Nov. 1998, 28.

75. **Exercise Balls**: B. Mauldin, interviewed by R. Rinzler, ca. 1978. **Benefit**: Pugh, *Ernest Tubb*, 180; N. V. Rosenberg, "Thirty Years Ago," *BU*, Mar. 1983, 11. **Cadillac limo**: S. Osborne, Hutchens's Questionnaire, 1978.

76. *Bill Monroe's WSM Grand Ole Opry Song Folio No. 2* (New York: Peer International, 1953).

77. Carr and Munde, booklet for *The Mayfield Brothers*, 7–8; Hutchens, "Edd Mayfield," 28; *Brown County (Ind.) Democrat*, Apr. 30, 1953, 7, and July 9, 1953, 7.

78. **Back brace**: B. Monroe, Rinzler Archives, RINZ-RR-0005; Nash, *Behind*, 354. **Release**: Neil V. Rosenberg, "The Flatt and Scruggs Discography: Releases, 1949–69," *JCM* 14, no. 1 (Aug. 1991), 40.

79. **Swarthmore festival**: "Swarthmore College," http://en.wikipedia.org/wiki/Swarthmore_College; Alisa Giardinelli (Swarthmore Communications Office), email, Aug. 7, 2009. **Pete Seeger**: Axlerod and Oster with Rawls, *Penguin Dictionary*, 434. **Ralph Rinzler**: Kate Rinzler, *A Source of Wonder* (unfinished biography of Ralph Rinzler); Ralph Rinzler, interviewed by Neil V. Rosenberg, Oct. 18, 1980; Szwed, *Alan Lomax*, 214.

80. **Bill**: Bud Ballad, "Lowdown . . . on the Hoedown," *Pickin' and Singin' News*, May 23, 1953, 2; B. Mauldin, interviewed by R. Rinzler, ca. 1978. **Martin**: Martin, interviewed by Kuykendall, 1995. **White**: L. E. White, Hutchens's Questionnaire, Mar. 1979. **Cline**: Reinhard Pietsch, "Lonesome Pine Fiddlers Discography," *BU*, Nov. 1968, 4. **Sandy**: Tom Ewing, "Leslie Sandy: The Lost Are Found," *BU*, Jan. 2004, 53.

81. **May 24**: Hatch, 123. **Rodgers Celebration**: Pugh, *Ernest Tubb*, 185–91; "Jimmie Rodgers: Hillbilly World to Honor His Memory," *Billboard*, May 16, 1953, 1, 16; Spottswood, booklet for *C. Monroe: I'm Old Kentucky Bound*, 31.

82. **Osborne**: Sonny Osborne, from BGRASS-L, 2000; S. Osborne, Hutchens's Questionnaire, 1978. **Back supports**: Michelle Putnam, conversation, Sept. 13, 2013.

83. **Flatt & Scruggs**: Rosenberg, *Stars*, 265; Scruggs, *Earl Scruggs and Banjo*, 153. **Presley**: McCloud et al., *DC*, 643; Halberstam, *Fifties*, 457–58.

84. Ewing, "Leslie Sandy," 53–54.

85. **Haney**: Gary B. Reid, Carlton Haney obituary, *BU*, May 2011, 17; Kingsbury et al., *TE* (98), 227; Fred Bartenstein, email, Sept. 6, 2009; Barry R. Willis, *America's Music: Bluegrass* (Franktown, Colo.: Pine Valley Music, 1997), 565.

86. **Korean War**: C. Daniel et al., *20th Century*, 727, 738. **Itinerary**: Hatch, 124. **First quote**: Sonny Osborne, from BGRASS-L, Aug. 29, 2000. **Second quote**: Rosenberg, "Osborne Brothers" (part 1), 9.

87. Grisman, "Monroe Interview," 6.

88. Hutchens, "Rudy Lyle," 47.

89. Hatch, 125; Reid, *Stanley Brothers Discography*, 7.

90. **Schedule**: Hatch, 123–27. **Jordanaires**: McCloud et al., *DC*, 430. **Reunion**: Adler, *Bean Blossom*, 56–57. **Quote**: Rosenberg, "Front Porch Visit," 58, 62.

91. **White**: Rosenberg, "Osborne Brothers" (part 1), 9. **Session and tuning**: Rosenberg and Wolfe, *TMBM*, 93, 108.

92. **Itinerary**: Hatch, 126–27. **Sandy**: Ewing, "Leslie Sandy," 54.

93. Rosenberg and Wolfe, *TMBM*, 108–10, 300–302.

94. **Session**: Rosenberg and Wolfe, *TMBM*, 108–9. **Bradley Studio**: Rosenberg and Wolfe, *TMBM*, 82; McCloud et al., *DC*, 94. **"John Henry"**: Rosenberg and Wolfe, *TMBM*, 43; Norm Cohen, *Long Steel Rail: The Railroad in American Folksong* (Urbana: University of Illinois Press, 1981), 66; Neil V. Rosenberg, "Bill Monroe's 'John Henry, The Steel Driving Man': A Study in Textual Variation," American Folklore Society paper, Oct. 1983, 4; Russell, *CMR*, 175, 459, 581, 827–28, 873, 887, 888; author's recollection and/or personal journal.

95. **Session**: Rosenberg and Wolfe, *TMBM*, 109, 302. **"Sitting Alone"**: Bill Monroe, personal communication with author, 1989; John Arms, email, Apr. 26, 2014. **"Plant Some Flowers"**: C. Cline, interview, 2001; "Jimmie Davis," http://en.wikipedia.org/wiki/Jimmie_Davis. **"Changing Partners"**: "Honor Roll of Hits," *Billboard*, Dec. 26, 1953, 24. **"Y'All Come"**: Rosenberg and Wolfe, *TMBM*, 94.

96. **Session**: Rosenberg and Wolfe, *TMBM*, 109–10. **"Happy on My Way"**: Green, "Pete Pyle," 25; P. Pyle, interviewed by R. Rinzler, ca. 1978. **"I'm Working on a Building"**: Ralph Rinzler, liner notes for *A Voice from On High*, DL7-5135; Live recording, ca. 1947, author's collection. **Stanley Brothers recording**: Reid, *Stanley Brothers Discography*, 7. **"He Will Set Your Fields on Fire"**: Rinzler, "The Daddy," 7. **Estes**: Ken Beck, "Ask Showcase," *Tennessean (Showcase)*, Apr. 9, 2000, 4.

97. **Bill's intent**: Rhodes, "Monroe, the Father," 16. **Land purchase**: State of Tennessee, Sumner County Deed Book 156, p. 35; Tennessee Title Co., contract of sale, dated June 11, 1954, collection of Jim Mills, 2011. **Help from Bessie**: Bill Monroe via Julia LaBella, conversation, Aug. 4, 2009. **Log cabin**: Jan Otteson, "Bluegrass 'Father,' Monroe, Is at Home on the Farm," *Music City News*, Sept., 1977, 13. **Dairy barn**: Ronni Lundy, "Bill Monroe," *Louisville Times (Scene)*, Sept. 10, 1983, 23.

98. **Lyle**: Hutchens, "Rudy Lyle," 48. **Smoak**: J. Smoak, interview, 2009. **"Little Robert"**: Reid, booklet notes for *The Best of King and Starday Bluegrass*, 6; Kuykendall, "Jimmy Martin," 12; Tom Morgan, "Enos Johnson: Part of an East Tennessee Tradition," *BU*, Nov. 1991, 58. **Cline's departure**: Pietsch, "Lonesome Pine Fiddlers Discography," 4; Jim Smoak, email, Aug. 18, 2009.

99. J. Smoak, interview, 2009; Martin, interviewed by Kuykendall, 1995; Devan, "Jimmy Martin," 18; Edward L. Stubbs and Richard Weize, booklet discography for *Jimmy Martin and the Sunny Mountain Boys*, Bear Family, BCD-15705 (rel. 1994), 38.

100. **Itinerary**: Hatch, 127–29. **Youngblood**: J. Smoak, interview, 2009; Jerry Prescott, "Jack Youngblood: Mississippi Fiddler," *BU*, Aug. 1995, 51; Kingsbury et al., *TE* (98), 185.

"**Lazy Jim**" **Day**: Simon, *Cowboy Copas*, 206, 211; Damian Morgan, "60 Years on the Roam Brought Youngblood Home," *Advertiser News* (Hattiesburg, Miss.), July 2, 1997, B-1.

101. **Swarthmore Folk Festivals**: Fred Stollnitz (Swarthmore, class of 1959), email, Oct. 12, 2009. **Mike Seeger and Flatt and Scruggs**: Mark Greenberg, "Mike Seeger," in *Artists of American Folk Music*, edited by Phil Hood (New York: GPI, 1986), 105. **Seegers and Rinzler**: Peggy Seeger, *Smithsonian Folklife Festival 2000* guidebook (Washington, D.C.: Smithsonian Institution, 2000), 91; R. Rinzler, interviewed by N. V. Rosenberg, 1980.

102. **Writing "Cheyenne"**: J. Smoak, Hutchens's Questionnaire, 1979; J. Smoak, interview, 2009; Prescott, "Jack Youngblood," 51. **Cheyenne**: Kelsie B. Harder, ed., *Illustrated Dictionary of Place Names: United States and Canada* (New York: Facts On File, 1985), 99. **Youngblood**: Jim Smoak, email, Aug. 21, 2009; Columbia Records session ledger (Jack Youngblood).

103. **Three fiddles**: Cunningham, "Hearing Red," 31. **Session**: Rosenberg and Wolfe, *TMBM*, 110; J. Smoak, interview, 2009. **Castle Studio-Tulane Hotel**: Zepp, "Tulane Hotel," 6B; Havighurst, *Air Castle*, 191–92.

104. **Session details**: J. Smoak, interview, 2009. **Fiddle harmony parts**: Glen Duncan, email, Aug. 26, 2009.

105. Rosenberg and Wolfe, *TMBM*, 96, 110, 305; Wolfe, *G-NR*, 171–72.

106. **Quote**: Walt Trott, "Rock Hall of Fame Claims Sideman Scotty Moore," *NM*, Jan.–Mar. 2000, 12. **Moore and Black**: Ibid.; "Bill Black," http://en.wikipedia.org/wiki/Bill_Black. **Perkins**: Carl Perkins and David McGee, *Go, Cat, Go: The Life and Times of Carl Perkins* (New York: Hyperion, 1996), 11–12, 38, 79. **Release**: Ibid., 78. **Moore's words**: Trott, "Scotty Moore," 12.

107. **Itinerary**: Hatch, 131–32. **Death date**: Harry C. Monroe, tombstone, Rosine Cemetery, Rosine, Ky. **Divorce**: Ohio County, Ky., Circuit Court, decree 7233. **Hotel**: Jenny Serna and David Mahan (grandson) via Merlene Austin, conversations, Nov. 1, 2012; David Mahan, email, Jan. 3, 2013. **Rosine Methodist Church**: Boyce Taylor, "Rosine," *OCN*, Oct. 2, 1953, 6. **Funeral**: "Harry C. Monroe Dies in Indiana," *OCM*, Aug. 27, 1954, 1; David Mahan, conversation, Nov. 19, 2011. The new Methodist church in Rosine was completed in October 1953.

108. **Smoak**: J. Smoak, interview, 2009. **Quote**: C. Stanley, interviewed by M. Seeger, 1966. **Session**: Reid, *Stanley Brothers Discography*, 7.

109. **Stanleys**: C. Stanley, interviewed by M. Seeger, 1966. **Session**: Rosenberg and Wolfe, *TMBM*, 110.

110. **Itinerary**: Hatch, 132. **Quotes**: Bill Monroe and Leslie Sandy ("Uncle Puny"), Marvin Hedrick (recordist), Brown County Jamboree, Sept. 19, 1954. **Memphis listings**: "Country and Western Territorial Best Sellers," *Billboard*, Sept. 25, 1954, 57.

111. **Sandy**: Ewing, "Leslie Sandy," 54–55. **Haney and Hicks**: Ed Davis, "Bobby Hicks: A Living Legend Returns," *MN*, June 1975, 6. **Hicks**: Reid, "Jim Eanes," 27; Traci Todd, "A Conversation with Bobby Hicks," *BU*, Mar. 1998, 38; Bobby Hicks, interview, May 17, 2004.

112. **Presley on Opry**: Bobbie Ann Mason, *Elvis Presley* (New York: Viking Penguin, 2003), 33, 37; Buddy Killen with Tom Carter, *By the Seat of My Pants: My Life in Country*

Music (New York: Simon and Shuster, 1993), 109. **First quote**: Bruce, "An Interview with Bill Monroe," 20; Jason DeParle, "Bill Monroe Still Has Lots to Sing but Little to Say," *New York Times*, June 9, 1994, B3. **Second quote**: Red O'Donnell, "Nashville Report," *Record World*, July 14, 1973, 44.

113. **Hay ownership**: *Pickin' and Singin' News*, Oct. 15, 1954, 1. **Bill's feature article (with ad)**: George D. Hay, "Bill Monroe Celebrates 15 Years with *Opry*," *Pickin' and Singin' News*, Nov. 15, 1954, 3, 22. **Quote**: Green, "Charlie Monroe Story" (part 2), 11. **Bessie at Andrew Jackson**: Andrew Jackson Hotel, bill for Bessie Mauldin's 1955 phone calls and cover letter to her, 1956: collection of Michael Dunn, 2009.

114. **Mayfield**: Hutchens, "Edd Mayfield," 29. **Itinerary**: Hatch, 133–35. **Hicks and Davis**: Nemerov, "Hubert Davis," 20.

115. **Session**: Rosenberg and Wolfe, *TMBM*, 111. **"Roanoke"**: Rooney, *Bossmen*, 68. **Itinerary**: Hatch, 131, 133. **Bill's idea**: Bobby Hicks, interviewed by John Rumble, Mar. 25, 1994: Frist Library and Archive, Country Music Hall of Fame and Museum (hereafter, FLA-CMHOF&M), OHC357-LC. **"You'll Find Her Name Written There"**: Ken Griffis, "The Harold Hensley Story," *John Edwards Memorial Foundation Quarterly* 20 (Winter 1971): 149; A. W. Hauslohner, "The Harold Hensley Story," *The Devil's Box*, Spring 1997, 34–35; John Rumble, email, Apr. 17, 2013; "Tennessee Ernie Ford," http://www.ernieford.com; Weize with Sax and Spottswood, "C. Monroe: The Discography," *C. Monroe: I'm Old Kentucky Bound*, 52.

116. N. V. Rosenberg, "Thirty Years Ago," *BU*, Jan. 1985, 5. A recording of Bill and the band on this show performing "Blue Moon of Kentucky" is included in *The Music of Bill Monroe from 1936 to 1994*, MCA, MCAD4-11048. Bill is heard singing, "*I said* blue moon of Kentucky . . . ," just like Presley. The banjo player ("unidentified") sounds like Rudy Lyle.

117. **Session**: Rosenberg and Wolfe, *TMBM*, 113. **Quote**: Bruce, "Interview with Bill Monroe," 21. **Smith and Houser**: "Chester R. Smith Succumbs at 78," Bob Pinheiro, http://www.modestoradiomuseum.org/chester%20smith.html; Walter V. Saunders, "Notes and Queries," *BU*, Dec. 2014, 17–18.

118. Rosenberg, *BAH*, 106–7.

119. **Davy Crockett**: C. Daniel et al., *20th Century*, 760. **Release date**: Rosenberg and Wolfe, *TMBM*, 301. **Quote**: Rooney, *Bossmen*, 68.

120. N. V. Rosenberg, "Thirty Years Ago," *BU*, Nov. 1984, 5; "Opry Stars Sign Television Deal for 35 Pictures," *Pickin' and Singin' News*, Jan. 31, 1955, 1; Pugh, *Ernest Tubb*, 198–99; Rosenberg and Wolfe, *TMBM*, 111–12. In 1955, Bill and the band filmed five of their six appearances on the show (episodes 17, 21, 22, 23, and 37).

121. Hatch, 138.

122. **Brock and Crase**: Fred Bartenstein, "Noah Crase: 'It's Not Easy Done'" (part 2), *BU*, July 1985, 23; Noah Crase, interview, Sept. 24, 2009; Robert Leach, "Carlos Brock," *BU*, Apr. 2000, 73. **Phelps**: Carlos Brock, interview, Nov. 11, 2009.

123. Bartenstein, "Noah Crase," 24–25.

124. **Brock and guitar**: Leach, "Carlos Brock," 74. **Second herringbone**: Hutchens, "Rudy Lyle," 45.

125. Reid, *Stanley Brothers Discography*, 8; C. Stanley, interview by M. Seeger, 1966.

126. R. Rinzler, interviewed by N. V. Rosenberg, 1980; ads, *Cecil (Md.) Democrat*, Apr. 21 and May 5, 1955, via G. Reid, email, 2009; Rinzler, *Stars*, 204.

127. **Tent show**: N. V. Rosenberg, "Thirty Years Ago," *BU*, June 1985, 9. **Itinerary**: Hatch, 139–40; C. Brock, interview, 2009. **Haney**: Fred Bartenstein, "The Carlton Haney Story," *MN*, Sept., 1971, 8. **Smith**: Roger Smith, interview, Mar. 23, 2009; Marvin Hedrick, interviewed by Neil V. Rosenberg, Aug. 1972.

128. **Tent show**: Bill Sachs, "Folk Talent and Tunes," *Billboard*, July 2, 1955, 24. **Brattleboro**: C. Cline, interview, 2001; B. Hicks, interview, 2004. **Collar bone**: Daniel C. Scullin Jr., MD, email, Sept. 21, 2009. **New River Ranch**: Ad, *Cecil (Md.) Democrat*, July 28, 1955, via G. Reid, email, 2009. **Brock**: C. Brock, interview, 2009. **Canada**: N. V. Rosenberg, "Thirty Years Ago," *BU*, Aug. 1985, 10.

129. "Joe Stuart," *TBS*, Feb. 1972, 8–9; Judy Paris, "Joe Stuart on . . . ," *Pickin'*, Feb. 1977, 30.

130. "Carlton Haney," Fred Bartenstein, http://www.bluegrassmuseum.org; Fred Bartenstein, emails, Sept. 6 and 23, 2009; Adler, *Bean Blossom*, 63.

131. *Swarthmore College Student Directory, 1955–56*, Ralph Rinzler Folklife Archives and Collections, Smithsonian Institution; Judy and David Werman (sister and brother-in-law), conversation, Sept. 26, 2009.

132. **Session**: Rosenberg and Wolfe, *TMBM*, 113. **Location**: Kienzle, "Owen Bradley," 14. **"Tall Timber"**: Rinzler, liner notes, *Bluegrass Instrumentals*. **"Brown County Breakdown"**: Rosenberg and Wolfe, *TMBM*, 98. **Crase comment**: Bartenstein, "Noah Crase" (part 2), 24. **Release dates, Bill and Reno and Smiley**: Rosenberg and Wolfe, *TMBM*, 98, 305.

133. **Itinerary**: Hatch, 140–41. *Sunset Valley Barn Dance*: Kingsbury et al., *TE* (98), 510. **Carson**: Howard Pine, "Pine Country Echoes," *Countryside* (formerly *Upper Midwestern Country and Western News Scene*), July 1974, 27. **Bill and Bessie**: B. Hicks, interview, 2004. **"Big Mon"**: Rinzler, liner notes, *Bluegrass Instrumentals*; Rosenberg and Wolfe, *TMBM*, 135.

134. Dick Vallenga with Mick Farren, *Elvis and the Colonel* (New York: Delacourte, 1988), 87–88.

135. C. Cline, interview, 2001; N. V. Rosenberg, "Thirty Years Ago," *BU*, Dec. 1985, 6; Arnold Terry, interview, Oct. 21, 2008, and conversation, Oct. 16, 2009.

136. **Itinerary**: A. Terry, interview, 2008. **Newman**: McCloud et al., *DC*, 586–87. **Shenandoah Valley Trio**: Bill Monroe and his Blue Grass Boys, live recording, Brown County Jamboree, Sept. 19, 1954, author's collection. **Town Hall Party**: Ibid., 814–15. **Clements**: Arnold Terry, interviewed by Tom Adler, Nov. 26, 2002.

137. **Itinerary**: Rosenberg, "Thirty Years Ago," *BU*, Dec. 1985, 6; A. Terry, interview, 2008; N. V. Rosenberg, "Thirty Years Ago," *BU*, Jan. 1986, 6; Bill Monroe's 1956 datebook, collection of Jim Mills, 2011. **Bill and Bessie**: A. Terry, interview, 2008.

138. A. Terry, interview, 2008; Hatch, 142; Kingsbury et al., *TE* (98), 35; B. Monroe's 1956 datebook, collection of J. Mills, 2011.

139. **Time off**: A. Terry, interview, 2008; B. Monroe's 1956 datebook, collection of J. Mills, 2011. **"Mid-Day Merry-Go-Round"**: Kingsbury, McCall, and Rumble, *TE*, 328. **Baker**: Alice Foster, "Kenny Baker," *BU*, Dec., 1968, 10; Brett F. Devan, "Kenny Baker:

One of the Masters," *BU*, Feb. 1991, 21; Kenny Baker, from *Bill Monroe: Father of Bluegrass Music*.

140. **Presley**: Mason, *Elvis Presley*, 47–70. **Itinerary**: Hatch, 142–47; B. Monroe's 1956 datebook, collection of J. Mills, 2011. **Decca**: Author's survey of *Billboard*, Jan.–Dec. 1956. **Martin**: Stubbs and Weize, booklet discography for *Jimmy Martin*, 38. **Holly**: Carr and Munde, booklet for *The Mayfield Brothers*, 4–5; John Goldrosen and John Beecher, *Remembering Buddy: The Definitive Biography of Buddy Holly* (London, England: Omnibus, 1996), 15–16, 35, 179–80.

141. **Itinerary**: B. Monroe's 1956 datebook, collection of J. Mills, 2011. **Saylor**: Ira Gitlin, "Lucky Saylor: A Forgotten Blue Grass Boy," *BU*, May 1993, 40–41; Lucky Saylor, interview, May 22, 2008. **Cadillac**: "Super-Depreciated Cadillac Brings Suit," *Tennessean*, Sept. 27, 1958, 6.

142. **Single release**: Rosenberg and Wolfe, *TMBM*, 302. **EPs**: Rosenberg and Wolfe, *TMBM*, 304.

143. **Terry/Green**: A. Terry, interview with author, 2008; Yates Green, interview, May 25, 2005. **Itinerary**: Hatch, 144–45; B. Monroe's 1956 datebook, collection of J. Mills, 2011. **Lyle**: Hutchens, "Rudy Lyle," 48. **Foster and Gerrard**: Bill C. Malone, *Music from the True Vine: Mike Seeger's Life and Musical Journey* (Chapel Hill, N.C.: University of North Carolina Press, 2011), 40; Alice Gerrard, emails, Oct. 28, 2009, and May 20, 2010. Several recordings from May 13, 1956, are included on *Bill Monroe and the Bluegrass Boys, Live Recordings 1956–1969 Off the Record, Volume 1*, Smithsonian-Folkways, SF CD 40063.

144. **Texas and California**: N. V. Rosenberg, "Thirty Years Ago," *BU*, May 1986, 6; B. Monroe's 1956 datebook, collection of J. Mills, 2011. **Stripling**: Y. Green, interview, 2005.

145. **Bessie**: Y. Green, interview, 2005. **James**: "James Monroe," 4.

146. **Green**: Y. Green, interview, 2005. **ABC-TV show**: N. V. Rosenberg, "Thirty Years Ago," *BU*, June 1986, 6; Walt Saunders, "Notes and Queries," *BU*, Aug. 2010, 16; Havighurst, *Air Castle*, 192. **Crase**: Bartenstein, "Noah Crase," 25. **"Uncle Pen"**: "Most Played by Jockeys" chart, *Billboard*, June 9, 1956, 43, and June 16, 1956, 41. A kinescope of this performance is included in the documentary *Bill Monroe: Father of Bluegrass Music*, Original Cinema, OC-1001. *Great Falls [Mont.] Tribune*, Oct. 29, 1955, 2.

147. Rosenberg, "Thirty Years Ago," June 1986, 6; R. Smith, interview, 2009; Harley Bray, interview, Feb. 18, 2009.

148. **Itinerary**: Rosenberg, "Thirty Years Ago," June 1986, 6; N. V. Rosenberg, "Thirty Years Ago," *BU*, July 1986, 6. **Retirement**: Bobby Atkins, interview, May 27, 2010; Gentry, *A History and Encyclopedia*, 275.

149. **Release**: N. V. Rosenberg, "Thirty Years Ago," *BU*, Dec. 1986, 14. **Lonnie Donegan**: Peter D. Goldsmith, *Making People's Music: Moe Asch and Folkways Records* (Washington, D.C.: Smithsonian Institution Press, 1998), 259–60; "Best-Selling Pop Records in Britain," *Billboard*, Jan. 28, 1956, 22, and "Honor Roll of Hits," *Billboard*, Apr. 14, 1956, 42; Tony Russell, email, Nov. 1, 2009. **Claim**: Rosenberg, *BAH*, 119.

150. Reid, *Stanley Brothers Discography*, 9; Ralph Stanley via James Alan Shelton, email, Nov. 10, 2009; Gary Reid, email, Nov. 3, 2009.

151. **Hicks**: B. Hicks, interview, 2004. **C. Smith**: Charlie Smith, emails, Feb. 7, 2010. **Williams**: Tommy Williams, interview, Jan. 5, 2012. **Tate**: Ivan Tribe, "Clarence 'Tater'

Tate: A Quarter Century of Bluegrass Fiddling," *BU*, Nov. 1973, 7–8; Ray Thigpen, "Clarence 'Tater' Tate: A Fiddler Who's Paid His Dues," *BU*, Dec. 1986, 38; B. Monroe's 1956 datebook, collection of J. Mills, 2011.

152. **Sept. 23 at Ranch**: Rinzler, notes for *Off the Record, Volume 1*, 9–11; Mike Seeger, insert notes for *American Banjo: Three-Finger and Scruggs Style*, Smithsonian/Folkways, CD SF 40037, released 1990, unnumbered page 3. **"LP"**: Oliver Read and Walter L. Welch, *From Tin Foil to Stereo: Evolution of the Phonograph* (Indianapolis: Sams, 1976), 319–20. Three selections from Sept. 23, 1956, are included on *Bill Monroe and the Bluegrass Boys, Live Recordings 1956–1969, Off the Record, Volume 1*, Smithsonian Folkways, SF CD 40063.

153. Rosenberg, *BAH*, 107, 135; Walt Trott, "Carl Smith Welcomed a Whole New Way of Life," *NM*, Oct.–Nov. 2002, 19; Havighurst, *Air Castle*, 190–94; John Rumble, conversation, Sept. 10, 2009.

154. Perkins and McGee, *Go, Cat, Go*, 177–91, 215–16, 219–20.

155. **Johnson**: Morgan, "Enos Johnson," 56–58; Neil V. Rosenberg with Edward L. Stubbs, booklet notes for *The Osborne Brothers: 1956–1968*, Bear Family, BCD 15598 (rel. 1995), 4. **Meadows**: B. Monroe's 1956 datebook, collection of J. Mills, 2011; Ivan Tribe, "Joe Meadows: Mountain State Fiddler," *BU*, Oct. 1978, 32; Joe Meadows, Hutchens's Questionnaire, 1979; Reid, *Stanley Brothers Discography*, 8.

156. **Sun session**: Perkins and McGee, *Go, Cat, Go*, 220–30; Colin Escott and Martin Hawkins, *Sun Records: The Discography* (West Germany: Bear Family Records, 1987), 96, 128, 225; Colin Escott, email, Feb. 26, 2017. **Monroe releases**: Rosenberg and Wolfe, *TMBM*, 297. Recordings from this jam session weren't released until the 1980s. There is considerable uncertainty concerning when Cash left ("Million Dollar Quartet," https:// en.wikipedia.org/wiki/Million_Dollar_Quartet).

157. **Vanover**: Carl Vanover, interview, Dec. 16, 2009.

158. Rosenberg and Wolfe, *TMBM*, 302.

159. **Release**: N. V. Rosenberg, "Thirty Years Ago," *BU*, Jan. 1987, 6. **Quote**: Ralph Rinzler, booklet notes for *American Banjo: Tunes and Songs in Scruggs Style*, Folkways Records, FA 2314. **Rinzler**: R. Rinzler, interviewed by N. V. Rosenberg, 1980; Axlerod and Oster with Rawls, *Penguin Dictionary*, 407. **Rinzler in Europe**: Richard Gagné, "Ralph Rinzler: Professional Biography," *Folklore Forum* 27, no. 1 (1996): 21, 23, 25.

160. **Metzel**: Bill Sachs, "Folk Talent and Tunes," *Billboard*, Aug. 13, 1955, 53; Bob Metzel, Hutchens's Questionnaire, date unknown; Rita M. Hough, "Bobby's a Busy Guy," *Country and Western Jamboree (Yearbook, 1959)*, 97–98. Metzel and his band, the Blue Valley Ramblers, played in Knoxville in the early 1950s. He moved to California in 1961 and died there in 1991 (Gary Reid, email, Dec. 28, 2014). **Meadows**: Tribe, "Joe Meadows," 32; J. Meadows, Hutchens's Questionnaire, 1979. **Letter**: Bessie Mauldin, letter to Edd Mayfield, Feb. 1, 1957, courtesy of Fred Mayfield (son).

161. **Stover**: N. V. Rosenberg, "Thirty Years Ago," *BU*, Mar. 1987, 15; Hank Edenborn, compiler, *Don Stover: A Discography* (Finleyville, Pa.: White Oak, 1996), 5; Hank Edenborn, email, Nov. 19, 2009. **Terry**: Kingsbury et al., *TE* (98), 534–35.

162. **Birch**: Rosenberg, "Front Porch Visit," 63; Kyle and Cordie Wells, interviewed by Tom Adler, Nov. 3, 2002; Tom Adler, emails, Mar. 19, 2004, and July 15, 2010. **Twigg**

Industries: "Our Town: Martinsville," http://www.indiana.edu/~radiotv/wtiu/ourtown/martinsville.html.

163. **Opry tent show**: N. V. Rosenberg, "Thirty Years Ago," *BU*, Apr. 1987, 9; Donald Teplyske, emails, Jan. 5, 2011; Roger White, *Walk Right Back: The Story of the Everly Brothers* (London: Plexus, 1998), 34–35. **Everly Brothers**: McCloud et al., *DC*, 273; Nash, *Behind*, 349. **Release and country charts**: Ads (for Cadence), *Billboard*, Apr. 6, 1957, 42, 57; "Most Played C&W by Jockeys," *Billboard*, May 13, 1957, 73. **Everlys' Opry membership**: "Country Artist of the Week: Don Everly," *Cash Box*, June 5, 1976, 35. Cadence recordings by Gordon Terry ("Johnson's Old Gray Mule" / "Service with a Smile" and "Black Mountain Rag" / "Orange Blossom Special"), released at the same time, went nowhere (author's survey, *Billboard*, May–June, 1957).

164. Donald Teplyske, "Jack Paget," *That High Lonesome Sound* (published by the Waskasoo Bluegrass Music Society, Edmonton, Alberta, Canada), Jan., 2002, 6; Jack Paget, interview, Dec. 12, 2009.

165. **Recent releases**: ad (for Jim Reeves), *Billboard*, Apr. 13, 1957, 72; ad (for Jimmy Newman), *Billboard*, Apr. 27, 1957, 58. **Session**: Rosenberg and Wolfe, *TMBM*, 131. **Terry solo**: Glen Duncan, email, Nov. 26, 2009.

166. **Albums**: McCloud et al., *DC*, 3, 485, 637, 748, 821, 855, 890. **Session**: Rosenberg and Wolfe, *TMBM*, 131.

167. **Sandy**: Ewing, "Les Sandy," 55. **Showdates**: Hatch, 148.

168. **Session**: Rosenberg and Wolfe, *TMBM*, 131; Ewing, "Les Sandy," 55; Glen Duncan, email, Dec. 3, 2009. **"A Good Woman's Love"**: Michael Streissguth, "Cy Coben: With a Pen in His Hand and a Song in His Heart," *JCM* 21, No. 3, 24–29; McCloud et al., *DC*, 477. **"Cry, Cry Darlin'"**: A. Terry, interview, 2008; McCloud et al., *DC*, 587. **"I'm Sittin' on Top of the World"**: Gottlieb and Kimball, *Reading Lyrics*, 41–45; Russell, *CMR*, 504.

169. Rosenberg and Wolfe, *TMBM*, 131–32; Ewing, "Les Sandy," 55. In the latter, I incorrectly stated that Les Sandy played on the May 14 session.

170. **Session**: Rosenberg and Wolfe, *TMBM*, 131–32, 145 (notes 1 and 2). **Stover quote**: Edenborn, *Don Stover: A Discography*, 30. **"Out in the Cold World"**: Russell, *CMR*, 548; Reid, *Stanley Brothers Discography*, 5. **"Roane County Prison"**: Wolfe, "Fiddler in Shadows," 52. **"In Despair"**: Bill Monroe, personal communication with author; Rosenberg and Wolfe, *TMBM*, 118. **Itinerary**: Hatch, 148.

171. **Sandy**: Ewing, "Les Sandy," 55. **Stover**: Jack Tottle, "Big Banjo from Boston: The Don Stover Story," *BU*, Mar. 1973, 8; Bill Monroe's 1957 Federal Income Tax forms, collection of Michael Dunn, 2009. **Graves**: Ernie Graves, interview, Jan. 6, 2010. **Duncan**: Bill Duncan, interview, Feb. 3, 2008.

172. Foster, "Kenny Baker," 10; Rooney, *Bossmen*, 94.

173. **Barn**: James Monroe, conversation, Jan. 7, 2010. **Living on farm**: B. Duncan, interview, 2008. **Cadillac/Buick**: "Super-Depreciated Cadillac," 6; R. Smith, interview, 2009.

174. **"Sputnik"**: C. Daniel et al., *20th Century*, 806; Halberstam, *Fifties*, 624–25. **First Bluegrass Album**: Rosenberg, "The Flatt and Scruggs Discography: The Columbia Recordings, 1950–59," *JCM* 13, no. 1 (Dec., 1989): 42–44; Rosenberg, "Flatt and Scruggs Discography: Releases, 1949–69," 40–41, 43.

175. Kingsbury et al., *TE* (98), 227, 393–94, 438; N. V. Rosenberg, "Thirty Years Ago," *BU*, Oct. 1987, 13.

176. **Haney**: Bartenstein, "Carlton Haney Story," 9. **"Live and Let Live"**: Ad, *Country Music Reporter*, Oct. 6, 1956, 7.

177. **Wiseman release**: Gary Reid, email, Jan. 11, 2010. **Single release**: Rosenberg and Wolfe, *TMBM*, 302. **"Sally-Jo"**: Doug Kershaw, email to Richard Thompson, July 23, 2006. The single mentioned here appears to have been the last of Bill's Decca recordings released in both 45 rpm and 78 rpm formats.

178. **Session**: Rosenberg and Wolfe, *TMBM*, 132. **Duncan**: B. Duncan, interview, 2008. **Tuning**: Doug Kershaw, email, Jan. 31, 2010. **Elrod**: Rosenberg, "Thirty Years Ago," Oct. 1987, 13; McCloud et al., *DC*, 186. **"Brand New Shoes"**: Dave Payne Sr., "Duncan was a member of Bill Monroe's Bluegrass Boys in 1957 and 1960," *Parkersburg News and Sentinel*, Jan. 20, 2008, 1D. **Album release**: Rosenberg and Wolfe, *TMBM*, 305.

179. Alana White, "Earl Snead," *BU*, May 1991, 62. Earl T. Snead Sr. was born in Danville, Va., on Oct. 29, 1939. He died on Sept. 9, 2002.

180. **Bradley**: Rosenberg and Wolfe, *TMBM*, 118; Liz Ferrell, "Owen Bradley: A WSM Pioneer and So Much More," *Inside WSM* 10 (2nd Q 1998): 2. **Cohen**: Kingsbury et al., *TE* (98), 102–3. **Mayfield**: Carl Mayfield (son), conversation, Aug. 3, 2013. **Quote**: B. Monroe, Rinzler Archives, RINZ-RR-0005. **Smith**: Charlie Smith, email, Feb. 5, 2010.

181. **Sessions**: Rosenberg and Wolfe, *TMBM*, 105–6, 133–34. **Holt**: Walt Trott, "The Jordanaires," *NM*, Oct.–Dec. 2001, 25. **Quote**: Kenny Baker, conversation, Jan. 15, 2010. **Ford's album**: Kingsbury et al., *TE* (98), 177; ad (for *Hymns*), *Billboard*, Dec. 29, 1956, 23.

182. **Songs previously recorded**: Russell, *CMR*, 211, 740–41, 728, 815, 849, 916, 953; McCloud et al., *DC*, 106; Cohen, *Long Steel Rail*, 615. **"Wayfaring Stranger"**: B. Monroe, onstage interview, 1963; Tennessee Ernie Ford, *Spirituals*, Capitol T818.

183. N. V. Rosenberg, "Thirty Years Ago," *BU*, Feb. 1988, 10.

184. Art Edelstein, "John Herald," in *Artists of American Folk Music*, 97; Mark Greenberg, "Bob Yellin," in *Artists of American Folk Music*, 101; Eric Weissberg, email, Jan. 30, 2003.

185. **Session**: Rosenberg and Wolfe, *TMBM*, 134. **Snead**: White, "Earl Snead," 62. **Hicks**: B. Hicks, interview, 2004.

186. **Itinerary**: Hatch, 152–53. **Fire in the Barn**: Tom Adler, email, Sept. 3, 2002.

187. **Adcock**: Don Rhodes, "Eddie and Martha Adcock: Finding Their Place in Blue-grass Music," *BU*, Apr. 1982, 36; Penny Parsons, "The Eddie Adcock Story: Exploring New(Grass) Horizons," *BU*, Mar. 1994, 17; Martha Adcock, email, Feb. 7, 2003; Eddie Adcock, conversation, Feb. 10, 2010. **Country Gentlemen**: Rosenberg, *BAH*, 138–39.

188. **Release**: Rosenberg and Wolfe, *TMBM*, 305; McCloud et al., *DC*, 684. **Liner notes**: Charles Lamb, liner notes for *Knee Deep in Blue Grass* by Bill Monroe and his Blue Grass Boys, Decca Records, DL 8731.

189. **Mayfield**: Hutchens, "Edd Mayfield," 30; B. Monroe, Rinzler Archives, RINZ-RR-0005; Mrs. Jo (Mayfield) Butler, conversation, Jan. 25, 2010; Fred Mayfield, conversation, Feb. 4, 2010; Doug Hutchens, email, Feb. 3, 2010 (including excerpts from his interview with Bill in fall 1982). Butch Robins has written, "At the old Pulaski Hospital on Randolph Avenue, Edd was refused admittance because he was a musician (in those days,

traveling entertainers didn't have the best reputations for paying bills)" (Butch Robins, *What I Know 'bout What I Know* [self-published, 2003], 14). **The Goins Brothers**: Marty Godbey, "The Goins Brothers," *BU*, Aug. 1983, 16–20; Melvin Goins, conversation, Feb. 8, 2010. Fred and Carl Mayfield's sister, LaDonna Mayfield, was born shortly after her father's death (Mrs. Jo Butler and Fred Mayfield, as above).

190. Rosenberg and Wolfe, *TMBM*, 305; liner notes for *I Saw the Light* by Bill Monroe, DL 8769.

191. Robert "Red" Cravens, interview, Feb. 25, 2009.

192. **Itinerary**: Hatch, 153–54. **C. Smith on Opry**: Charlie Smith, email, Feb. 2, 2010. **Bill back on road**: R. Smith, interview, 2009; N. V. Rosenberg, "Thirty Years Ago," *BU*, Aug. 1988, 11. **Emerson with Gents**: Robert Kyle, "History of the Country Gentlemen" in *The Country Gentlemen 25th Anniversary* (Kinston, N.C.: LeeWay, 1982), 11.

193. Kaplan, liner notes for *Connie and Babe: Backwoods Bluegrass*, 1975; Connie Gately, interview, Feb. 3, 2010; Connie Gately, email, Feb. 5, 2010.

194. B. Hicks, interview, 2004; "The Billboard Hot 100 Chart," *Billboard*, Sept. 29, 1958, 43; C. Gately, interview, 2010.

195. **Mandolins**: Charlie Smith, email, Feb. 11, 2010; N. V. Rosenberg, "Thirty Years Ago," *BU*, Nov. 1988, 18; Connie Gately, emails, Feb. 14, 2010. **"Scotland"**: "Hot C&W Sides" chart, *Billboard*, Nov. 3, 1958, 48.

196. Glenn Roberts, "Jack Cooke: A Bluegrass Music Pioneer . . . Well, Almost," *BU*, Sept. 2005, 37–38.

197. **At Opry**: C. Gately, interview, 2010; Connie Gately, email, Feb. 5, 2010. **Pennington**: Keith Pennington (son), email, Mar. 18, 2010.

198. **Session**: Rosenberg and Wolfe, *TMBM*, 135. **Smith**: Charlie Smith, email, Feb. 11, 2010. **"Gotta Travel On"**: C. Gately, interview, 2010; Kingsbury et al., *TE* (98), 207. **"No One But My Darlin'"**: Walt Saunders, "Notes and Queries," *BU*, Nov. 2011, 16. **"Big Mon"**: Rinzler, liner notes, *Bluegrass Instrumentals*. **"Monroe's Hornpipe"**: Charlie Smith, email, Feb. 17, 2010.

199. **Release**: Rosenberg and Wolfe, *TMBM*, 302. **Rinzler**: K. Rinzler, *A Source of Wonder*.

200. Charlie Smith, interview, Feb. 22, 2010.

201. Charlie Smith, email, Feb. 14, 2010; C. Smith, interview, 2010.

202. **Running Over**: Rosenberg and Wolfe, *TMBM*, 136; C. Smith, interview, 2010. **Hudgins**: Jim Glaser, email, Mar. 5, 2010; Earl White, email, Mar. 6, 2010; Cowboy Joe Babcock, email, Mar. 7, 2010. **Cooper**: C. Smith, interview, 2010. **"Stoney Lonesome"**: Ibid.; "Stony [sic] Lonesome, Indiana," http://en.wikipedia.org/wiki/Stony_Lonesome,_Indiana.

203. **"Folksong '59"**: Rosenberg, *BAH*, 150–51. **Lomax**: Robert Cantwell, *When We Were Good: The Folk Revival* (Cambridge, Mass.: Harvard University Press, 1996), 164–66; Szwed, *Alan Lomax*, 235–37. **Quote**: R. Rinzler, interviewed by N. V. Rosenberg, 1980. **Earl Taylor and the Stoney Mountain Boys**: Recordings, Earl Taylor and the Stoney Mountain Boys, produced by Alan Lomax for United Artists, *Folk Songs from the Bluegrass* (UAL 3049) and *Folk Song Festival at Carnegie Hall* (UAL 3050).

204. **"Gotta Travel On"**: "Hot C&W Sides," *Billboard*, Mar. 2, 1959, 43; Whitburn, *Top Country Singles*, 245. **March and April**: Charlie Smith, email, Feb. 19, 2010. **The Country Boys**: Roland White, first interview, June 30, 2011.

205. **Release**: N. V. Rosenberg, "Thirty Years Ago," *BU*, May 1989, 9. **Booklet**: Mike Seeger, booklet for *Mountain Music Bluegrass Style*, Folkways Records, 1, 3.

206. **Hicks**: Rosenberg, "Thirty Years Ago," May 1989, 9; McCloud et al., *DC*, 835; B. Hicks, interview, 2004. **Smith**: Charlie Smith, email, Mar. 1, 2010.

207. Rosenberg, *BAH*, 152–53; "Newport Folk Festival Discography," Stefan Wirz, http://www.wirz.de/music/newport.htm; Jim Smoak, email, Mar. 3, 2010. Three instrumentals from this appearance were included in vol. 3 of *Folk Festival at Newport* (Vanguard, VSD-2055).

208. **Smith**: Charlie Smith, email, Mar. 1, 2010. **Fiddlers**: Roberts, "Jack Cooke," 38. **Pennington**: Keith Pennington (son), conversation, Mar. 2, 2010; Ken Dick (WHIS-TV), email, Mar. 3, 2010.

209. Warranty Deed 1129, recorded in Brown Co., Ind., property records, Aug. 21, 1959; Adler, *Bean Blossom*, 52.

210. Alan Lomax, "Bluegrass Background: Folk Music with Overdrive," *Esquire*, Oct. 1959, 108.

211. Liner notes for *New Folks*, Vanguard Records, VRS-9096, rel. 1961.

212. **Maynard**: N. V. Rosenberg, "Thirty Years Ago," *BU*, Dec. 1989, 6; Charlie Smith, email, Mar. 3, 2010; Jimmy Maynard, interview, Mar. 18, 2010. **McPeake**: Joe Ross, "An Interview with Curtis McPeake," *BU*, July 1992, 43; Curtis McPeake, interview, Mar. 11, 2010. **Scruggs**: N. V. Rosenberg, "Thirty Years Ago," *BU*, Oct. 1985, 8; Rosenberg, *BAH*, 166.

213. **Release**: Rosenberg and Wolfe, *TMBM*, 392. **Opry twentieth anniversary**: Kingsbury et al., *TE* (98), 144.

214. Bill Workman, "Tony Ellis," *BU*, Nov. 1986, 50; Tony Ellis, first interview, Feb. 25, 2010.

215. **Session**: Rosenberg and Wolfe, *TMBM*, 136. **Drumright**: J. Maynard, 2010. **B. Martin**: Rosenberg and Wolfe, *TMBM*, 319. **"Lonesome Wind Blues"**: McCloud et al., *DC*, 656; Ivan Tribe, email, Mar. 8, 2010. **"Thinking About You"**: McCloud et al., *DC*, 427. **"Come Go with Me"**: Diane Diekman (Robbins biographer), email, Mar. 7, 2010. **Cooke**: T. Ellis, first interview, 2010.

216. T. Ellis, first interview, 2010.

CHAPTER SIX. 1960–1969

1. Kingsbury et al., *TE* (98), 371–72; Havighurst, *Air Castle*, 201–4.

2. **Cash**: Kingsbury et al., *TE* (98), 86. **Cash tour**: T. Ellis, first interview, 2010. **Bessie's car**: Del McCoury, conversation, Nov. 11, 2010. **Itinerary**: Tony Ellis, email, Mar. 15, 2010; N. V. Rosenberg, "Thirty Years Ago," *BU*, Jan. 1990, 9.

3. T. Ellis, first interview, 2010.

4. Lomax, "Bluegrass Background," 108; Rosenberg, *BAH*, 154–158; Rosenberg, *BAH*, 158.

5. **Fendermen and pop chart**: "The *Billboard* Top 100," May 23, 1960, 34, July 11, 1960, 44, and Sept. 5, 1960, 30; "Jim Sundquist and His Fendermen," http://fendermen.com. **"Hot C&W Sides"**: Whitburn, *Top Country Singles*, 118; "Hot C&W Sides," *Billboard*, July 11, 1960, 48.

6. T. Ellis, first interview, Feb. 2010; B. Green, "Carl Tipton Family," 46–47; Bill Monroe and his Blue Grass Boys, live recording, Brunswick, Md., Aug. 9, 1960, author's collection.

7. H. Bray, interview, 2009; R. Cravens, interview.

8. **"Blue Grass Day"**: H. Conway Gandy, "Don Owens: The Washington, D.C., Connection," *BU*, Nov. 1987, 68–72; Eddie Stubbs, "Don Owens: A Pioneering Figure in Bluegrass and Country Music," *BU*, June 1998, 26–34; Willis, *America's Music*, 473–74; Gary Reid, email, Jan. 14, 2011; Fred Bartenstein, email, Jan. 15, 2011. **Bill's band and quote**: Bill Monroe and his Blue Grass Boys, live recording, Watermelon Park, Aug. 14, 1960, from the collection of Bill Keith.

9. **Divorce**: *Carolyn Monroe v. William S. Monroe*, Circuit Court, Davidson Co., Tenn., Decree No. 34918. **Relative values**: "Seven Ways to Compute," http://www.measuringworth.com/uscompare. **Telephone**: Hurst, "Mellowing Father," 3-S; Julia LaBella, conversation, Sept. 19, 2013. **Lucy and Desi**: C. Daniel, *20th Century*, 845.

10. **Rinzler**: R. Rinzler, interviewed by N. V. Rosenberg, 1980; Goldsmith, *Making People's Music*, 263–64. An album of Rinzler's field recordings, *Old Time Music at Clarence Ashley's* (Folkways, FA 2355), recorded at Ashley's daughter's house, was released in 1961.

11. **Buchanan**: Frank Buchanan, interview, May 24, 2005; Tony Ellis, email, Apr. 13, 2010. **Smith**: Bobby Smith, Hutchens's Questionnaire, 1979; "Bobby Smith," *BS*, Dec., 1972, 4–5; Tony Ellis, email, Mar. 24, 2010. **Ellis**: Tony Ellis, second interview, Mar. 22, 2010.

12. **Ellis**: T. Ellis, second interview, 2010. **Butler**: Jim Maynard via Charlie Smith, email, Mar. 13, 2010; McCloud et al., *DC*, 118–19.

13. **"Sold Down the River"**: Kingsbury et al., *TE* (98), 248; Rosenberg, "Flatt and Scruggs Discography: Mercury Sessions," 47. **"Linda Lou"**: N. V. Rosenberg, "Thirty Years Ago," *BU*, July 1991, 6; Wayne W. Daniel, "Emory and Linda Lou Martin: Sweethearts of Renfro Valley," *Old Time Country*, Fall 1992, 10–11. **"You Live in a World All Your Own"**: Michel Ruppli, compiler, *The King Labels: A Discography, Vol. 1* (Westport, Conn.: Greenwood, 1985), 3. **"Little Joe"**: Rosenberg and Wolfe, *TMBM*, 22.

14. **"Seven Year Blues"**: MCA Records, Inc., *Historical Catalogue, Vol. IV*, (Universal City, Calif.: MCA Records-International, 1980), 1715. **"Time Changes Everything"**: Russell, *CMR*, 964. **"Lonesome Road Blues" and afterward**: C. McPeake, interview, 2010.

15. T. Ellis, second interview, 2010.

16. **"Big River"**: Rosenberg and Wolfe, *TMBM*, 138; Escott and Hawkins, *Sun Discography*, 40; Johnny Cash, "The Best of the Johnny Cash TV Show: 1969–71," Disc 2, Columbia Legacy 88697-040269, released 2007. **"Flowers of Love"**: Rosenberg and Wolfe, *TMBM*, 138; Tony Ellis, email, Mar. 2, 2016. **"It's Mighty Dark to Travel"**: Rosenberg and Wolfe, *TMBM*, 110, 132. **"Blue Grass Part 1"**: Ibid., 123. **"The Sound"**: Evan Reilly, email, Apr. 7, 2010.

17. Hatch, 162–66.

18. **Itinerary**: Hatch, 162. *The Great Bill Monroe*: Rosenberg and Wolfe, *TMBM*, 299.

19. **Photo**: N. V. Rosenberg, "Thirty Years Ago," *BU*, May 1990, 10. **Itinerary**: Hatch, 163–65. **Skaggs**: McCloud et al., *DC*, 735; Larry Nager, booklet notes for *Bill Monroe and the Blue Grass Boys: Live - Volume One*, Copper Creek, RHY-1015, 14–15; Best of the Flatt and Scruggs *TV Show, Vol. 3*, Shanachie DVD: SH 613, released 2007.

20. N. V. Rosenberg, "Thirty Years Ago," *BU*, June 1991, 6; Neil V. Rosenberg, compiler, *Bill Monroe and His Blue Grass Boys: An Illustrated Discography* (Nashville: Country Music Foundation Press, 1974), 4; Neil V. Rosenberg, "Picking Myself Apart," *Journal of American Folklore* 108 (1995): 279.

21. **"All Blue Grass Show"**: Rosenberg, *BAH*, 177–81; N. V. Rosenberg, "Thirty Years Ago," *BU*, July 1991, 6; Margaret Worrell, "Letters," *BU*, May 1976, 6; Live recording in author's collection, Oak Leaf Park, Luray, Va., July 4, 1961. **Second "Blue Grass Day"**: Fred Bartenstein, email, Jan. 26, 2011.

22. B. Atkins, interview, 2010.

23. Rosenberg, *BAH*, 181; N. V. Rosenberg, "Thirty Years Ago," *BU*, Sept. 1991, 6; Uncredited, liner notes for *New Folks*, Vanguard Records, VRS-9096.

24. **Release**: N. V. Rosenberg, "Thirty Years Ago," *BU*, Oct. 1991, 6. **Starday**: Kingsbury et al., *TE* (98), 504. **Lonesome Pine Fiddlers**: Bill Monroe, liner notes for *The Lonesome Pine Fiddlers*, Starday Records, SLP 155; M. Godbey, "Goins Brothers," 20–21.

25. **Sessions**: B. Atkins, interview, 2010; Rosenberg and Wolfe, *TMBM*, 138–39. **Spicher**: Buddy Spicher, interview, May 12, 2014. **Williams**: Tom Morgan, "Benny Williams: Super Sideman from the Sticks," *BU*, May 1982, 68.

26. **"Little Maggie"**: Reid, *Stanley Brothers Discography*, 16. **"Shady Grove"**: "Discography of Blue Grass Recordings," Charley Pennell (compiler), www.ibiblio.org/hillwilliam/chuckhome.html. **"Nine Pound Hammer"**: Merle Travis, *Folk Songs of the Hills*, Capitol Records, AD50, rel. 1947; M. Seeger, booklet notes for *Mountain Music Bluegrass Style*. **"I'm Going Back to Old Kentucky"**: Rosenberg and Wolfe, *TMBM*, 71, 138, 220, 255. **"Toy Heart"**: Ibid., 68, 138. **"Live and Let Live"**: Russell, *CMR*, 936; D. Green, "Pete Pyle," 22. **All songs**: J. Maynard, interview, 2010.

27. **Carnegie Hall show**: Hurst, *Nashville's Opry*, 296–97. **Flying the troupe**: C. McPeake, interview, 2010.

28. **Ellis and Lester**: T. Ellis, second interview, 2010; Tony Ellis, email, Apr. 21, 2010. **McPeake and Maynard**: C. McPeake, interview, 2010.

29. C. McPeake, interview, 2010.

30. **Session and songs**: Rosenberg and Wolfe, *TMBM*, 124, 139. **Bluegrass recordings**: "Discography" website, Pennell (compiler). The photo of Bill and Benny Williams on the dust jacket cover of Rosenberg and Wolfe's *The Music of Bill Monroe* was taken at this session by an unknown photographer.

31. **Session**: Rosenberg and Wolfe, *TMBM*, 139–40. **Ellis quote**: Tony Ellis, email, Apr. 8, 2010. **Recorded previously**: Neil V. Rosenberg, email, Mar. 24, 2010. **"John Hardy"**: Workman, "Tony Ellis," 49. **"Bugle Call Rag"**: Tony Ellis, email, Apr. 8, 2010.

32. T. Ellis, second interview, 2010.

33. Smith, *Can't You Hear*, 297 (note 98); Tony Ellis, email, June 2, 2010. The State of Tennessee provides death records to relatives only.

34. **Ellis**: T. Ellis, first and second interviews, 2010; Workman, "Tony Ellis," 50. **Frolics**: Kingsbury et al., *TE*, 195. **Mom Upchurch's**: Walt Trott, "'Mom' Upchurch Opened Her Home to Young Pickers," *NM*, Jan.–Mar. 2002, 36–37. **Bertha**: Tom Adler, email, Mar. 19, 2004.

35. **Releases**: Rosenberg and Wolfe, *TMBM*, 302, 304. **The Twist and "Peppermint Twist—Part 1"**: Bronson, *Number One Hits*, 101–4.

36. **John at homeplace**: Merlene Austin, conversation, Apr. 21, 2010. **Itinerary**: Hatch, 167. **John's death**: Commonwealth of Kentucky, Certificate of Death, file 116-62-4025.

37. **Session and album release**: Rosenberg and Wolfe, *TMBM*, 140–41, 296. **The album**: Dave Samuelson, "Classic Album," *Journal of the American Academy for the Preservation of Old-Time Country Music*, Apr., 1996, 27. **Itinerary**: Hatch, 168.

38. **Buchanan**: F. Buchanan, interview, 2005. **"Red" Stanley**: Walt Saunders, "Notes and Queries," *BU*, Oct. 2002, 22; Godbey, *Crowe on the Banjo*, 28. **Tour with Wiseman**: Workman, "Tony Ellis," 50. **Quote**: Kevin Kerfoot, "Frank Buchanan, Bluegrass Boy #37," *Bluegrass Music Profiles*, July/Aug., 2007, 20.

39. **Cover story**: Pete Welding, "Earl Scruggs—and the Sound of Bluegrass," *SO*, Apr.–May 1962, 4–7. **Rinzler**: Peter K. Siegel, booklet notes for *Friends of Old Time Music: The Folk Arrival, 1961–1965*, Smithsonian/Folkways, SFW CD 40160 (rel. 2006), 13. **Greenbriar Boys**: Ad, *SO*, Apr.–May 1962, 50; Rosenberg, *BAH*, 181–82; R. Rinzler, interviewed by N. V. Rosenberg, 1980; Ralph Rinzler, liner notes for *The Greenbriar Boys*, Vanguard, VRS-9104.

40. **Sessions**: Rosenberg and Wolfe, *TMBM*, 141–43. **Buchanan**: F. Buchanan, interview, 2005. **Bradley studio**: McCloud et al., *DC*, 94.

41. **Carson**: Pine, "Pine Country Echoes," 26. **Songs**: Rosenberg and Wolfe, *TMBM*, 141. **First quote**: B. Monroe, Rinzler Archives, RINZ-RR-0005. **Second quote**: F. Buchanan, interview, 2005.

42. **Session**: Rosenberg and Wolfe, *TMBM*, 141. **"When the Bees Are in the Hive"**: Original sheet music, published by F. A. Mills, New York, 1904; Russell, *CMR*, 236. **"Big Ball in Brooklyn"**: F. Buchanan, interview, 2005; Rosenberg and Wolfe, *TMBM*, 127. **"Columbus Stockade Blues"**: F. Buchanan, interview, 2005; T. Ellis, first interview, 2010.

43. **Session/Silverstein**: Rosenberg and Wolfe, *TMBM*, 142, 161; Stubbs and Weize, booklet discography for *Jimmy Martin*, 42. **"Blue Ridge Mountain Blues"**: F. Buchanan, interview, 2005; Russell, *CMR*, 716. **"How Will I Explain about You?"**: Rosenberg and Wolfe, *TMBM*, 69. **"Foggy River"**: Frank Buchanan, conversation, Dec. 23, 2005; *MCA Records, Inc., Historical Catalogue, Vol. IV*, 880.

44. **Session/personnel**: Rosenberg and Wolfe, *TMBM*, 142. **"The Old Country Baptizing"**: Jim Shumate, conversation, July 9, 2001; "Discography" website, Pennell (compiler). **"I Found the Way" and "This World Is Not My Home"**: Rosenberg and Wolfe, *TMBM*, 18, 20.

45. **Session**: Rosenberg and Wolfe, *TMBM*, 142–43. **"Way Down in My Soul"**: N. V. Rosenberg, "Thirty Years Ago," *BU*, Apr. 1983, 6. **"Drifting Too Far"**: Rosenberg and Wolfe, *TMBM*, 18. **"Going Home"**: "Discography" website, Pennell (compiler); Tom Mindte, email of July 19, 2016.

46. **Session**: Rosenberg and Wolfe, *TMBM*, 143. **"On the Jericho Road"**: "Discography" website, Pennell (compiler); Russell, *CMR*, 211, 714; Ruppli, *King Labels*, 10. **"We'll**

Understand It Better": "Discography" website, Pennell (compiler); Russell, *CMR*, 643. **"Somebody Touched Me"**: Booklet notes for *The Early Days of Bluegrass, Volume 1*, Rounder Records 1013, 6; Rosenberg and Wolfe, *TMBM*, 127. "The Old Country Baptizing" and "Somebody Touched Me" would not be released until 1973, probably due to recent recordings by others. (Rosenberg and Wolfe, *TMBM*, 305–6.)

47. F. Buchanan, interview, 2005.

48. **First quote**: Rooney, *Bossmen*, 79. **Second quote**: Rinzler, *Stars*, 204. **Third quote**: Rooney, *Bossmen*, 79.

49. Rosenberg, *BAH*, 180; Malone, *True Vine*, 59.

50. **Appearance**: Ad, *Delaware Co. (Pa.) Daily Times*, 18. **Release**: Rosenberg and Wolfe, *TMBM*, 305. **First quote**: Rinzler, *Stars*, 204. **Second quote**: Rooney, *Bossmen*, 79.

51. **Events of June 24**: Alice Gerrard, email, May 19, 2010. **Foster and Stanleys**: Rosenberg, "Thirty Years Ago," May 1990, 10. **Rinzler and Stanleys**: Siegel, booklet notes for *Friends of Old Time Music*, 13.

52. **Further events of June 24**: Joan Shagan (one of the friends), interview, May 19, 2010; Hazel Dickens, interview, May 19, 2010; Mike Seeger, interviewed by Gary Reid, ca. November 2007; Rooney, *Bossmen*, 79. **Negotiations**: Rinzler, *Off the Record, Volume 1*, 5.

53. **Ellis**: Workman, "Tony Ellis," 50. **Deese**: Pat J. Ahrens, "David Deese: From Blue Grass Boy to Briarhopper," *BU*, Dec., 2007, 45–46; David Deese, interview, May 25, 2010. **Smith and Williams**: Charlie Smith, email, Mar. 5, 2010; D. Deese, interview, 2010.

54. **Reference book**: Gentry, *A History and Encyclopedia*, 1, 273. **Release**: Rosenberg and Wolfe, *TMBM*, 315. **Liner notes**: Frank Sheffield, liner notes for *The Father of Blue Grass Music*, RCA Camden Records, CAL-719.

55. **Itinerary**: Hatch, 170. **Food on the road**: Ahrens, "David Deese," 46–47; D. Deese, interview, 2010. **Interstate system**: Tom Lewis, *Divided Highways* (New York: Viking, 1997), 168.

56. **The fair**: Ralph Rinzler, "Bill Monroe: A Man and His Music," *Pickin'*, Dec., 1976, 7; David Deese, interview, 2010; "Fair Will Get Underway Tonight in Felts Park for Remainder of Week," *Galax Gazette*, Aug. 20, 1962, A1. **Richard Rinzler**: Siegel, booklet for *Friends of Old Time Music*, 13. **First quote**: Rinzler, *Off the Record, Volume 1*, 5. **Second quote**: Richard Rinzler, email, July 22, 2010.

57. **Location**: Ad, *Galax Gazette*, Aug. 27, 1962, B4. **First quote**: Richard Rinzler, email, July 22, 2010. **Second quote**: Rinzler, *Stars*, 204. **The notes**: B. Monroe, from interview notes, Rinzler Archives: RR343, Box 9. **Third quote**: Rooney, *Bossmen*, 79. **The article**: R. Rinzler, interviewed by N. V. Rosenberg, 1980.

58. **Deese**: D. Deese, interview, 2010. **Fill-ins**: Lonnie Hoppers, Hutchens's Questionnaire, date unknown. **Labor Day weekend**: Hatch, 170. **Ray and Melvin Goins**: M. Godbey, "Goins Brothers," 20. **Cohen**: Siegel, booklet for *Friends of Old Time Music*, 10. **Film, title, and first documentary**: Rosenberg, *BAH*, 173–74. **Audio**: John Cohen, *That High Lonesome Sound*, Shanachie VHS 1404; Rosenberg and Wolfe, *TMBM*, 145, note 14.

59. **Keith**: Tony Trischka, "Bill Keith," *BU*, Dec. 1975, 12; Trischka and Wernick, *Masters of Banjo*, 176–77; N. V. Rosenberg, "Thirty Years Ago," *BU*, Mar. 1992, 6. **"Beverly**

Hillbillies": N. V. Rosenberg, "Thirty Years Ago," *BU*, Sept. 1992, 6; Rosenberg, *BAH*, 259–63. **Number One**: "Hot Country Singles," *Billboard*, Jan. 19, 1963, 14.

60. **Itinerary**: Rosenberg, "Thirty Years Ago," Sept. 1992, 6; N. V. Rosenberg, "Thirty Years Ago," *BU*, Oct. 1992, 6. **Hoppers**: Don Ginnings, "Lonnie Hoppers," *BU*, Mar. 1983; Lonnie Hoppers, interview, June 13, 2010.

61. L. Hoppers, interview, 2010; F. Buchanan, conversation, June 17, 2010; Kerfoot, "Frank Buchanan," 21.

62. Rosenberg, "Thirty Years Ago," Oct. 1992, 6; L. Hoppers, interview, 2010; Lonnie Hoppers, email, June 17, 2010.

63. **Crisis**: Terry H. Anderson, *The Sixties* (New York: Pearson Longman, 2004), 34–35; C. Daniel et al., *20th Century*, 889. **Appearance**: Rosenberg, "Thirty Years Ago," *BU*, Oct. 1992, 6. **Weger**: N. V. Rosenberg, "Thirty Years Ago," *BU*, July 1992, 6; Rosenberg, *Monroe Discography*, 22; "Obituaries: Harry Weger," http://tribstar.com/obituaries/x1155686402/ HarryWeger. **Quote**: Rosenberg, *Monroe Discography*, 22. **Release**: Rosenberg and Wolfe, *TMBM*, 305.

64. **Sessions**: Rosenberg and Wolfe, *TMBM*, 143–44. **Off crutches**: Lonnie Hoppers, conversation, June 20, 2010. **"Careless Love"**: Alice Foster, "Kenny Baker," *BU*, Dec. 1968, 9; "St. Louis Blues (1958)," http://www.blackclassicmovies.com/Movie_Database/films/ st_louis_blues.html; "Discography" website, Pennell (compiler). **"I'm So Lonesome"**: Mac Wiseman, conversation, June 10, 2009. **"Jimmy Brown the Newsboy"**: Rosenberg and Wolfe, *TMBM*, 129. **"Pass Me Not"**: Hutchens, *Howdy, Folks, Howdy*, 8; Reid, *Stanley Brothers Discography*, 14; Rosenberg and Wolfe, *TMBM*, 306. **"The Glory Land Way"**: Rosenberg and Wolfe, *TMBM*, 129. **"Farther Along"**: Weize with Sax and Spottswood, "C. Monroe: The Discography," *C. Monroe: I'm Old Kentucky Bound*, 48.

65. **Session**: Rosenberg and Wolfe, *TMBM*, 144. **"Big Sandy River" and "Baker's Breakdown"**: Lonnie Hoppers, email, June 23, 2010. **"Darling Corey"**: Spottswood, "Alan Lomax," 21. **First to record it**: "Discography" website, Pennell (compiler); Neil V. Rosenberg, booklet for *Flatt and Scruggs—1959-1963*, Bear Family, BCD 15559 (rel. 1992), 17; Rosenberg, "Flatt and Scruggs Discography: Releases, 1949–69," 44; Rosenberg and Wolfe, *TMBM*, 303.

66. **Flatt and Scruggs at Johns Hopkins**: Scruggs, *Earl Scruggs and Banjo*, 3; Penny Parsons (from the late Paul Warren's datebook), email, July 8, 2010; Bill Keith, email, June 9, 2011. **Keith meeting Scruggs**: Rosenberg, *BAH*, 183; Bill Keith, email, July 1, 2010.

67. **"Cindy"**: Neil V. Rosenberg, email, June 26, 2010. **"Master Builder" and "Let Me Rest"**: Rosenberg and Wolfe, *TMBM*, 130.

68. Ginnings, "Lonnie Hoppers," 34–35; Ad, *Roanoke Times*, Dec. 25, 1962, 26.

69. **Hoppers**: L. Hoppers, interview, 2010. **Yarbrough and Landers**: Rual Yarbrough, interview, Mar. 12, 2007; Patricia Glenn, "The Master Sergeant of Music—Jake Landers," *BU*, June 1982, 42–43.

70. **First portrait**: Rinzler, "The Daddy," 5–8. **Circulation**: Mark D. Moss (*Sing Out!* editor), email, July 6, 2010. **Rinzler quote**: Gagné, "Ralph Rinzler," 27.

71. **First folk festival**: N. V. Rosenberg, "Thirty Years Ago," *BU*, Feb. 1993, 6. **Also appearing**: Joe Hickerson, email, Aug. 20, 2010. **First quote**: R. Rinzler, interviewed

by N. V. Rosenberg, 1980. **The trip there**: Jake Landers, interview, July 5, 2010. **Second and third quotes**: Rinzler, *Stars*, 204–5; Rinzler, notes for *Off the Record, Volume 1*, 6. **Rinzler, bass**: Mike Hall, "Campus Report: The University of Chicago Folklore Society," *Hootenanny*, Dec., 1964, 33.

72. B. Monroe, onstage interview, 1963; R. Rinzler, interviewed by N. Rosenberg, 1980.

73. **Second show**: Rosenberg, "Thirty Years Ago," Feb. 1993. **Landers and Yarbrough**: J. Landers, interview, 2010. **Cooke and McCoury**: D. McCoury, interview, 2007.

74. **Crowd and show**: Recording of show in author's collection. **Founder**: Siegel, booklet notes for *Friends of Old Time Music*, 13. **Bill's offer**: D. McCoury, interview, 2007; Gwen Taylor, "Del McCoury," *BU*, June 1973, 18.

75. **Keith in Nashville and at Opry**: Bill Keith, first interview, Sept. 5, 2010; Bill Keith's diary, entries of Feb. 9–18, 1963. **Flatt and Scruggs itinerary**: Penny Parsons, email, Sept. 15, 2010. **First quote**: C. Gately, interview, 2010. **Second quote**: R. Yarbrough, interview, 2007. **Third quote**: K. Baker, from *Bill Monroe: Father of Bluegrass Music*. **Fourth quote**: Bill Keith, from *Bill Monroe: Father of Bluegrass Music*.

76. **Keith's call**: B. Keith, first interview, 2010. **Amherst and Reserve**: R.J. Kelly, "Bill Keith: 'Sharing a Banjo Tightrope,'" *BU*, Jan. 1985, 14. **Yarbrough and Landers**: R. Yarbrough, interview, 2007; J. Landers, interview, 2010.

77. **Uncertainty**: Bill Keith, second interview, Sept. 6, 2010; Bill Keith, conversation, Oct. 7, 2010. **First quote**: Bill Keith, email, July 11, 2010. **Second quote**: R. Rinzler, interviewed by N. V. Rosenberg, 1980. **Third quote**: Bill Keith, email, July 12, 2010.

78. Bill Keith, email, July 14, 2010.

79. **The audition**: Brett F. Devan, "The Del McCoury Band: State-of-the-Art Bluegrass Purists," *BU*, Aug. 1990, 20–21; D. McCoury, interview, 2007; Bill Keith, email, July 14, 2010. **Keith quote**: Bill Keith, emails, July 12 and 27, 2010. **McCoury quote**: Jay Orr and Michael Gray, "The Father of Bluegrass," *Nashville Banner*, Sept. 10, 1996, A2. **Opry debut**: Bill Keith, diary entry, Mar. 16, 1963; Ronnie McCoury (son), email, July 19, 2014; Bill Monroe and Blue Grass Boys, live recordings, collections of N. V. Rosenberg and the author. **Learning songs**: McCoury, interview, 2007. Jake Landers, email, July 25, 2014.

80. Rinzler, notes for *Off the Record, Volume 1*, 6.

81. **Keith**: Eric von Schmidt and Jim Rooney, *Baby, Let Me Follow You Down: The Illustrated Story of the Cambridge Folk Years* (Garden City, N.Y.: Anchor, 1979), 158; B. Keith, first interview, 2010. **Session**: Rosenberg and Wolfe, *TMBM*, 168–69. **"Sailor's Hornpipe"**: Bill Keith, interviewed by Nick Barr, Nov. 19, 2007, Video Oral History Collection, IBMM. **Earlier recordings**: Russell, *CMR*, 91, 205, 292–93, 480. **Change**: Decca "Record Personnel" Sheet, Mar. 20, 1963. **"Were You There?"**: Rosenberg and Wolfe, *TMBM*, 35, 305.

82. **Session**: Rosenberg and Wolfe, *TMBM*, 169. **Phelps**: Rosenberg and Wolfe, *TMBM*, 113. **Keith**: B. Keith, first interview, 2010. **"Pike County Breakdown"**: Neil V. Rosenberg, email, Dec. 8, 2012. **"Shenandoah Breakdown"**: Joe Drumright, Hutchens's Questionnaire, 1979. **"Santa Claus"**: Rinzler, liner notes, *Bluegrass Instrumentals*.

83. N. V. Rosenberg, "Thirty Years Ago," *BU*, Apr. 1993, 6; Rosenberg and Wolfe, *TMBM*, 147.

84. **May 3–5**: Rosenberg and Wolfe, *TMBM*, 150; N. V. Rosenberg, "Thirty Years Ago This Month," *BU*, May 1993, 6. **May 10–11**: Rosenberg and Wolfe, *TMBM*, 150; Sandy Roth-

man, email, May 20, 2010. **Quote**: Bill Monroe, remarks recorded by Roosevelt Watson, May 11, 1963, Berkeley, Cal., author's collection. Bill had previously visited California in 1955, 1956, and 1959.

85. Sandy Rothman, email, July 31, 2010.

86. Ralph Rinzler, booklet notes for *Bill Monroe and Doc Watson: Live Duet Recordings, 1963–1980, Off the Record, Volume 2*, Smithsonian Folkways, SF CD 40064, 5; Ralph Rinzler, "Doc Watson: Folksinging Is a Way of Life," *SO*, Feb.–Mar. 1964, 11; Doc Watson, comment made during a WSM radio tribute to Bill, Sept. 9, 1996; Uncredited, insert notes for *Bill and Doc Sing Country Songs*, FBN-210.

87. **Rinzler**: Charles Wolfe and Neil V. Rosenberg, booklet notes for *Bill Monroe—Bluegrass: 1959–1969*, Bear Family, BCD 15529, 2; B. Keith, second interview, 2010. **Baker**: Foster, "Kenny Baker," 10. **Other fiddlers**: N. V. Rosenberg, "Thirty Years Ago," *BU*, June 1993, 6; Buddy Pendleton, conversation, Aug. 3, 2010.

88. Rosenberg, "Thirty Years Ago," *BU*, June 1993, 6; Bill Monroe, remarks recorded June 2, 1963, Brown County Jamboree, author's collection.

89. K. Rinzler, *A Source of Wonder*; R. Rinzler, interviewed by N. V. Rosenberg, 1980; Bartenstein, "Carlton Haney Story," 10.

90. **Releases**: Rosenberg and Wolfe, *TMBM*, 305; Rosenberg, "Thirty Years Ago," *BU*, June 1993, 6. **Bluegrass Special**: Liner notes for *Bluegrass Special*, Bill Monroe and his Blue Grass Boys, Decca Records, DL 4382. **Early Blue Grass Music**: Roy Horton, liner notes for *Early Blue Grass Music by the Monroe Brothers*, RCA Camden, CAL-774.

91. Schmidt and Rooney, *Baby, Let Me Follow*, 156, 157; Sandy Rothman, email, Jan. 24, 2004.

92. Neil V. Rosenberg, email, July 15, 2010; Schmidt and Rooney, *Baby Let Me Follow*, 159, 162.

93. Neil V. Rosenberg, letter to Ralph Rinzler, June 8, 1963; Neil V. Rosenberg, emails, July 15 and 22, 2010.

94. Rooney, *Bossmen*, 80–81; Rinzler, notes for *Off the Record, Volume 1*, 20–21.

95. **Newport**: Rinzler, *Stars*, 217; Cantwell, *When We Were Good*, 298. **Lineup, July 26**: "About Phil Ochs," http://phil-ochs.blogspot.com.

96. Bill Sachs, "Country Music Corner," *Billboard*, Aug. 3, 1963, 14.

97. Author's recollection and/or personal journal.

98. Marriage Record 4538, Overton Co., Tenn.; James Monroe, conversation, Oct. 7, 2010.

99. McCloud et al., *DC*, 604; Rosenberg with Stubbs, booklet notes for *The Osborne Brothers, 1956–68*, 23.

100. **Rinzler's return to NYC**: Rosenberg, *BAH*, 186, R. Rinzler, interviewed by N. V. Rosenberg, 1980. **Marvin**: Rosenberg and Wolfe, *TMBM*, 147. **Release**: Rosenberg and Wolfe, *TMBM*, 147, 302.

101. "Folk Festival at Newport Revived," *SO*, Apr.–May 1963, 76; Siegel, booklet notes for *Friends of Old Time Music*, 15; Rosenberg and Wolfe, *TMBM*, 147; Szwed, *Alan Lomax*, 349; Gagné, "Ralph Rinzler," 28.

102. N. V. Rosenberg, "Thirty Years Ago," *BU*, Oct. 1993, 6; Neil V. Rosenberg, email, Aug. 28, 2010; Bill Monroe, remarks recorded Oct. 11, 1963, Brown County Jamboree, author's collection.

103. **Haerle**: Bill Keith, conversation, Oct. 7, 2010; "CMH Records," en.wikipedia.org/wiki/CMH_Records. **Rosenberg and Bill**: Neil V. Rosenberg, emails, Apr. 24, 1999, and Aug. 29, 2010.

104. N. V. Rosenberg, "Thirty Years Ago," *BU*, Nov. 1993, 6; Neil V. Rosenberg, booklet notes for *Bill Monroe and the Blue Grass Boys: Live at Mechanics Hall*, Acoustic Disc, ACD-59, unnumbered page 9.

105. **Kennedy assassination**: David Farber and Beth Bailey with contributors, *The Columbia Guide to America in the 1960s* (New York: Columbia University Press, 2001), 19; Gene Brown, ed., *The Kennedys: A New York Times Profile* (New York: Arno, 1980), 120–22. **Bus**: Bill Keith, Hutchens's Questionnaire, 1979; Edward L. Stubbs et al., booklet notes for *Johnnie and Jack and the Tennessee Mountain Boys*, Bear Family, BCD 15553, 32. **Itinerary**: Rosenberg, "Thirty Years Ago," Nov. 1993, 6.

106. **Itinerary**: Rosenberg, "Thirty Years Ago," Nov. 1993, 6. **Events at WWVA**: B. Keith, second interview, 2010.

107. B. Keith, second interview, 2010; "When the Bus Broke Down: Playing with Bill Monroe," Al Ross, http://power-pickers.com/playing-with-bill-monroe.

108. Robert "Tut" Taylor, conversations, Jan. 5, 2008, and Sept. 5, 2010; Tom Isenhour, emails, Sept. 9 and 21, 2010. Bill used the case for the next twenty years. It can be seen on the covers of the *Road of Life* and *The Weary Traveler* LPs.

109. Ibid.; Neil V. Rosenberg, "Bill Keith Discography, Part I," *Banjo Newsletter*, June 1975, 7. Six tunes featuring Keith's picking were released on *12-String Dobro!: Tut Taylor and the Folkswingers with 12-String Guitar* (ST-1816).

110. Rooney, *Bossmen*, 82–83.

111. **Cooder**: Mayne Smith, email, Sept. 15, 2010; Bill Keith, email, Sept. 16, 2010. **Diamond**: Bobby Diamond, conversation, Oct. 2, 2010; D. McCoury, interview, 2007. Diamond's real name was Robert F. Rook Jr. (Bobby Diamond obituary, *BU*, Dec. 2011, 7.) **Held over**: Ed Pearl, letter to Ralph Rinzler, Rinzler Archives, RR343, box 9.

112. Bronson, *Number One Hits*, 143; Uncredited, "Hot 100," *Billboard*, Feb. 2, 1964, 20; Betsy Towner, "Live!: TV Moments That Forever Changed Us," *AARP Bulletin*, Oct., 2010, 43.

113. **"Hootenanny"**: Jim Clark, letter to Ralph Rinzler, Rinzler Archives, RR343, box 9; recording of show, courtesy of Tom Isenhour. **McCoury**: Devan, "Del McCoury Band," 21.

114. Rosenberg and Wolfe, *TMBM*, 174; Don O'Neil, "Ken Clark," *BU*, Apr. 1971, 12.

115. D. McCoury, interview, 2007; Rosenberg and Wolfe, *TMBM*, 174–75, 193 (note 5); Audrey Lambert, email, Oct. 6, 2010; "Play Boys," Charles Denning, http://www.ajlambert.com/history/hst_pb.pdf.

116. **McCoury**: Devan, "Del McCoury Band," 21. **Session**: Rosenberg and Wolfe, *TMBM*, 175, 306. **"Last Old Dollar"**: Ken Marvin, from a tape of a show in Mar. 1964, author's collection.

117. Bill Sachs, "Country Music Corner," *Billboard*, Feb. 15, 1964, 20.

118. Bessie Mauldin, letter to Ralph Rinzler, Rinzler Archives, RR343, box 9.

119. **Release**: Rosenberg and Wolfe, *TMBM*, 305. **Songs**: Rosenberg and Wolfe, *TMBM*, 105, 113, 136. **Jim and Jesse**: Scott Hambly, liner notes for *The Jim and Jesse Story*, CMH

Records, CMH-9022, rel. 1980; Jesse McReynolds, conversation, Jan. 18, 2011. **Devine**: Kingsbury et al., *TE* (98), 209.

120. Ralph Rinzler, "The Nashville Scene: The Roots of Bluegrass," *Hootenanny*, Mar. 1964, 54–55.

121. **Session**: Rosenberg and Wolfe, *TMBM*, 152, 175. **Bessie and Baker**: Rosenberg and Wolfe, *TMBM*, 317, 319. **"Louisville"**: Bill Monroe, personal communication with author. **"Over in the Gloryland"**: Russell, *CMR*, 582, 926; McCloud et al., *DC*, 106. **Bessie**: Marks, "Common-Law Wife," 25.

122. Blair Jackson, *Garcia: An American Life* (New York: Viking Penguin, 1999), 51–63; Sandy Rothman, emails, Sept. 14, 2001, and Nov. 3, 2010.

123. George Jones with Tom Carter, *I Lived to Tell It All* (New York: Villard Books / Random House, 1996), 97–101; Bill Sachs, "Country Music Corner," *Billboard*, June 6, 1964, 33; Fred Bartenstein, email, Sept. 4, 2011.

124. **Band on May 24**: N. V. Rosenberg, "Thirty Years Ago," *BU*, May 1994, 6; Walt Saunders, "Notes and Queries," *BU*, Sept. 2000, 19–21. **Garcia and Rothman**: Jackson, *Garcia*, 63–64; Sandy Rothman, email, Sept. 14, 2001.

125. Rosenberg and Wolfe, *TMBM*, 299, 305.

126. Sandy Rothman, emails, Nov. 5–8, 2010.

127. Paul, "James Monroe," 4; Sandy Rothman, email, Nov. 11, 2010.

128. **Rothman on banjo**: Sandy Rothman, email, Jan. 8, 2011. **Bill's singles**: Rosenberg and Wolfe, *TMBM*, 303. **Arkin**: Steve Arkin, first interview, Jan. 6, 2011.

129. S. Arkin, first interview, 2011; Steve Arkin, Hutchens's Questionnaire, July 1979; Robins, *What I Know*, 39.

130. Sandy Rothman, email, Nov. 8, 2010.

131. Rosenberg, *BAH*, 204; R. Rinzler, interviewed by N. V. Rosenberg, 1980; Cantwell, *When We Were Good*, 302–3; Bartenstein, "Carlton Haney," IBMM website; T. Ewing, "Thirty Years Ago," *BU*, Dec. 1994, 6.

132. **Vietnam**: Farber and Bailey, *America in the 1960s*, 36–38; C. Daniel et al., *20th Century*, 919. **Osbornes on Opry**: Rosenberg with Stubbs, booklet notes for *The Osborne Brothers: 1956–1968*, 2; Bobby Osborne, conversation with author, Jan. 20, 2011.

133. Steve Arkin, second interview, Jan. 11, 2011; S. Arkin, first interview, 2011, Sandy Rothman, email, Nov. 26, 2002.

134. Walt Saunders, "Notes and Queries," *BU*, Nov. 1999, 15; Doug Hutchens, email, Oct. 30, 2011.

135. Richard Brown, interview, July 2, 2014; "Bill Monroe for Breakfast: Day 2, Part 1," http://wwwyoutube.com/watch?v=nLjLcytlSxo; "etree.org Community Bittorrent Tracker," http://bt.etree.org/details.php?id+503167; Richard Brown, email, July 20, 2014.

136. Sandy Rothman, emails, Nov. 8, 2010, Jan. 2, 2011, Jan. 12, 2011, and Jan. 15, 2011; "Me and My Old Banjo," Julian Winston, http://julianwinston.com/music/me_and_my_old_banjo.php; Rosenberg and Wolfe, *TMBM*, 153.

137. **Concerts in North**: Ralph Rinzler, letter to Bill Monroe, Oct. 2, 1964, Rinzler Archives, RR343, box 9; T. Ewing, "Thirty Years Ago," *BU*, Oct. 1994, 6. **Lowinger**: Gene Lowinger, *I Hear a Voice Calling: A Bluegrass Memoir* (Urbana: University of Illinois Press, 2009), 20. **Bush**: Roger Bush, conversation, Mar. 9, 2011.

138. **Rowan**: Schmidt and Rooney, *Baby, Let Me Follow*, 64, 209, 213. **Early anniversary**: "Blue Grass Music Now Making Hit," *Nashville Banner*, Nov. 5, 1964, 36.

139. Don Lineberger, letter, Oct. 25, 2002; Rosenberg and Wolfe, *TMBM*, 155–56, 177, 311. "Second Fiddle to a Steel Guitar," originally released in 1965, was rereleased in 1991 by Vic Lewis Video (VLV 008-96820).

140. **Orchestra Hall**: Don Lineberger, letter, Aug. 20, 2002. **Advertisement**: Ad, *Chicago Tribune*, Oct. 25, 1964.

141. Rinzler, letter to B. Monroe, Oct., 2, 1964; Lowinger, *I Hear a Voice*, 20; Schmidt and Rooney, *Baby, Let Me Follow*, 213. Four selections from this show were included on *Bill Monroe and the Bluegrass Boys: Live Recordings 1956–69, Off the Record, Volume 1*, SFCD 40063.

142. Rosenberg and Wolfe, *TMBM*, 153; Neil V. Rosenberg, email, Jan. 17, 2011.

143. Jeff Harrison, "Pete Rowan: Master of Many Styles," *Pickin'*, July 1979, 24; "He Saw the Light," David Hill, http://www.westword.com/2001-12-06/music/he-saw-the-light; Bill Monroe, remarks recorded Nov. 8, 1964, Brown County Jamboree, author's collection.

144. **Charlie and Betty Monroe**: Green, "Charlie Monroe" (part 3), 14–15; Several knowledgeable sources in Ohio County, Ky., who prefer to be anonymous. **Mortgages**: Ohio County, Ky., Mortgages, books 62, 241; 65, 16; 66, 42; 67, 160. **Land Sale**: Ohio County, Ky., Deed Book 164, 75–78.

145. Saunders, "Notes and Queries," Nov. 1999, 15–16.

146. **Session**: Rosenberg and Wolfe, *TMBM*, 147, 178. **"I Live in the Past"**: Virginia Mae Stauffer obituary, *Sturgis (Mich.) Journal*, Nov. 22, 2011, A2. Stauffer was born in St. Joseph Co., Mich., on Sept. 29, 1940; she died on Nov. 12, 2011. **"Old, Old House"**: T. Ewing, "Thirty Years Ago," *BU*, Apr. 1995, 6; Rosenberg and Wolfe, *TMBM*, 303.

147. **April 2**: Bill Monroe and Doc Watson, recorded at Swarthmore College, Apr. 2, 1965: Rinzler Archives, FP-RINZ-7RR-0151. **Dartmouth**: Lowinger, *I Hear a Voice*, 20–21; Gene Lowinger, email, Feb. 12, 2011.

148. **Deployment and protest**: Farber and Bailey, *America in the 1960s*, 40; C. Daniel, *20th Century*, 931–33. **Brown County Music Corp.**: Jim Peva, letter to author, Oct. 25, 1994. **Bill and band**: Neil V. Rosenberg, "Bluegrass at Bean Blossom: Chronological List" (of tapes, 1964–69), his collection.

149. Lowinger, *I Hear a Voice*, 22–25, 83; Gene Lowinger, emails, Feb. 14 and 18, 2011.

150. *Bluegrass Instrumentals*: Rosenberg and Wolfe, *TMBM*, 305; Rosenberg, *BAH*, 208; Neil V. Rosenberg, email, Feb. 19, 2011. **Price tag**: Bill Keith, email, Mar. 1, 2011.

151. *The Original Blue Grass Sound*: Rosenberg and Wolfe, *TMBM*, 299. **Eight unreleased**: Ibid., 68, 69, 73, 74.

152. T. Ewing, "Thirty Years Ago," *BU*, June 1995, 10; Nancy Talbott, "Tex Logan: Fiddler in Two Worlds," *MN*, Dec. 1974, 10; Bob Black, conversation, Feb. 20, 2011. "Cotton-Eyed Joe," recorded at the first party on June 17, 1965, was released on *Bill Monroe and the Bluegrass Boys: Live Recordings 1956–69, Off the Record, Volume 1*, SFCD 40063.

153. Charles Wolfe, *In Close Harmony: The Story of the Louvin Brothers* (Jackson, Miss.: University Press of Mississippi, 1996), 118–20.

154. Schmidt and Rooney, *Baby, Let Me Follow*, 214; Peter Rowan, interview, Apr. 1, 2011; Lowinger, *I Hear a Voice*, 34, 36; Rosenberg and Wolfe, *TMBM*, 179–80.

155. Peva, letter, 1994; Jim Peva, letter to Bill Monroe, June 16, 1965.

156. Rosenberg, *BAH*, 243–44; Schmidt and Rooney, *Baby, Let Me Follow*, 259; Byron Berline, Hutchens's Questionnaire, July 1979.

157. Lowinger, *I Hear a Voice*, 35–36; Gene Lowinger, emails, Feb. 21 and 24, 2011.

158. **Grier**: Lamar Grier, email, Oct. 9, 2009; Hub Nitchie, "Interview: Lamar Grier," *Banjo Newsletter*, July 1978, 8; Lamar Grier, "My Life and Times as a Blue Grass Boy with Bill Monroe," unpublished memoir, unnumbered pages 3–4. **Lineberger**: Saunders, "Notes and Queries," *BU*, Nov. 1999, 17; Bill Monroe's 1965 account notebook, collection of Danny Clark, Owensboro, Ky., Oct. 6, 2011.

159. Ad (for Ray Charles LP), *Billboard*, Aug. 21, 1965, 31; "Ray Charles," Marilyn Williams, http://www.encyclopedia.com/topic/Ray_Charles.aspx; "Top LPs" chart, *Billboard*, Sept. 11, 1965, 62, through Oct. 16, 1965, 48.

160. Rosenberg, *BAH*, 206–7; Carlton Haney Promotions, flier for the "Roanoke Blue Grass Music Festival," 1965; Bartenstein, "Carlton Haney Story," 10, 18. Butch Robins has noted that Haney had produced country music shows at Cantrell's Horse Farm on Sundays prior to the first festival. (Robins, *What I Know*, 38.)

161. Rosenberg, *BAH*, 209; L. Mayne Smith, "An Introduction to Bluegrass," *Journal of American Folklore*, July–Sept., 1965, 245; L. Mayne Smith, "Additions and Corrections," *BU*, Jan. 1967, 5; Mayne Smith, "First Bluegrass Festival Honors Bill Monroe," *SO*, Jan. 1966, 65; Mayne Smith, emails, Dec. 7, 1998, and Jan. 23, 1999.

162. Ahrens, "David Deese," 47; Lamar Grier, email, Oct. 9, 2009.

163. Bill Monroe, remarks recorded Sept. 5, 1965, Roanoke Blue Grass Festival, Fincastle, Va., author's collection.

164. **Fill-ins**: Bill Monroe's 1965 account notebook; Godbey, *Crowe on the Banjo*, 79; T. Ewing, "Thirty Years Ago," *BU*, Sept. 1995, 6. **Grier**: Lamar Grier, emails, Oct. 9, 2009, and Mar. 13, 2011; Grier, "My Life and Times," unnumbered page 5. **The bus**: Tim Dillman and Wayne Lewis, conversations, Apr. 21, 2011; Allen Mills, email, Apr. 24, 2011.

165. Grier, "My Life and Times," unnumbered p. 6; Rosenberg, "Chronological List" (1964–69); Bill Monroe and his Blue Grass Boys, live recording, Brown County Jamboree, Nov. 7, 1965, author's collection; Lowinger, *I Hear a Voice*, 36.

166. Lowinger, *I Hear a Voice*, 30–31; Gene Lowinger, email, Feb. 24, 2011; Kingsbury et al., *TE*, 195.

167. Lowinger, *I Hear a Voice*, 38–39; Lamar Grier, email, Oct. 9, 2009.

168. T. Ewing, "Thirty Years Ago," *BU*, Jan. 1996, 6. An album by Jones and Montgomery, titled *Blue Moon of Kentucky*, was released in January 1966 (United Artists, T-90832). (Ad for Jones-Montgomery LP, *Billboard*, Feb. 5, 1966, 33.)

169. Grier, "My Life and Times," unnumbered p. 5; Lamar Grier, emails, Oct. 9, 2009, and Apr. 20, 2011.

170. **Trip to Montreal**: Grier, "My Life and Times," unnumbered p. 13. **Greene**: Joe Ross, "From Bluegrass to Classical and Back Again: Fiddler Richard Greene Comes Full Circle," *BU*, July 1994, 52; Richard Greene, interview, Mar. 27, 2011; Satterlee, *Harley "Red"*

Allen, 82–83; Doug Benson, "Bill Monroe: King of Blue Grass Music" (program 2, part 1), *BU*, Feb. 1968, 11–12. **January 27**: Richard Miller, email, Mar. 27, 2011.

171. Richard J. Brooks, "An Interview with Richard S. Greene, Virtuoso Violinist," *BU*, Nov. 1984, 19; Bill Monroe and his Blue Grass Boys, live *Opry* recordings, 1966, author's collection.

172. Grier, "My Life and Times," unnumbered p. 19.

173. Ross, "Fiddler Richard Greene," 52; R. Greene, interview with author, 2011; Nitchie, "Interview with Grier," 8.

174. T. Ewing, "Thirty Years Ago," *BU*, May 1996, 6, and June 1996, 6; Grier, "My Life and Times," unnumbered pp. 7, 17; Richard Thompson (and Ken Harris), email, Apr. 13, 2011; Bill Clifton, email, May 27, 2011.

175. "He Saw the Light," David Hill, http://www.westword.com/2001-12-06/music/he-saw-the-light; Ralph Rinzler, letter to Bill Monroe, May 31, 1966, Rinzler Archives, RR343, box 9.

176. Rosenberg and Wolfe, *TMBM*, 107, 110, 181, 305. Bill and the band were welcomed back to the States with a party at Tex Logan's on June 20, and three performances from that night were included on *Bill Monroe and the Bluegrass Boys: Live Recordings 1956–69, Off the Record, Volume 1*, SFCD 40063.

177. **Booking**: Rinzler, letter to B. Monroe, May 1966, Rinzler Archives. **The Black Poodle**: "Printer's Alley," http://en.wikipedia.org/wiki/Printer%27s_Alley. **The Theft**: James Monroe, conversation, May 5, 2011. **Rowan and Bill**: Peter Rowan, email, May 20, 2011.

178. T. Ewing, "Thirty Years Ago," *BU*, July 1996, 13; Fred Geiger, "One Way of Looking at the First International Bluegrass Festival in Warrenton, Virginia," *BU*, Aug. 1966, 1; Grier, "My Life and Times," unnumbered p. 19.

179. **Bill, playing and farming**: Richard Greene, email, Apr. 13, 2011; Benson, "King of Blue Grass," program 2, part 1), 12. **Cattle**: David Davis (cattleman), conversation, Aug. 9, 2011.

180. **Itinerary**: Lamar Grier, "Partial Bill Monroe Itinerary with Lamar Grier," July 1995; "Personal Appearances," *BU*, Aug. 1966, 8. **Bill and Doc**: Rosenberg and Wolfe, *TMBM*, 150, 181; Rosenberg, "Flatt and Scruggs Discography, Columbia Recordings, 1965–69," 34. Two tunes recorded at the party were released on *Bill Monroe and Doc Watson, Live Duet Recordings, 1963–1980, Off the Record, Volume 2*, SF CD 40064.

181. **Festival**: T. Ewing, "Thirty Years Ago," *BU*, Sept. 1996, 6; Rosenberg, *BAH*, 278; Neil V. Rosenberg, "Reflections on Roanoke," *BU*, Jan. 1967, 3. **Hall of Fame**: Kingsbury et al., *TE* (98), 113, 617. **Fan club**: Marvine Johnson, *Bill Monroe Fan Club Newsletter*, undated (late 1966), 3; *Bill Monroe Fan Club Journal* 1, p. 1; Marvine (Johnson) Loving, conversation, July 2, 2013.

182. **Sparkman**: "John Sparkman," http://en.wikipedia.org/wiki/John_Jackson_Sparkman. **Bill and the band**: Grier, "My Life and Times," unnumbered pp. 15, 17. Senator Sparkman was reelected in November 1966.

183. **Session**: Rosenberg and Wolfe, *TMBM*, 178, 182. **"When My Blue Moon Turns to Gold Again"**: Russell, *CMR*, 936; E. Scruggs, interview, 1996. **"I Wonder Where You Are Tonight"**: Bill Monroe, remarks recorded 1966, Roanoke Bluegrass Festival, author's

collection; Russell, *CMR*, 391. **"Turkey in the Straw"**: Grier, "My Life and Times," un-numbered p. 15.

184. T. Ewing, "Thirty Years Ago," *BU*, Oct. 1996, 6; Gary Reid, emails, Aug. 21, 2009, and Apr. 26, 2011.

185. **Session**: Rosenberg and Wolfe, *TMBM*, 182. **Spicher**: Brooks, "An Interview with Richard S. Greene," 19–20. **"Pretty Fair Maiden"**: Rosenberg and Wolfe, *TMBM*, 157; Sandy Rothman, email, Feb. 25, 2013; Richard Greene, email, Feb. 25, 2013. **"Log Cabin in the Lane"**: Reid, "Jim Eanes," 28. **"Paddy"**: Bill Monroe, recorded at the 1965 Roanoke Bluegrass Festival, author's collection; Lamar Grier, email, Apr. 28, 2011; Rosenberg and Wolfe, *TM*, 309. "Paddy on the Turnpike" was not released on LP until 1985, and then only by Rebel-MCA in Canada on *Classic Bluegrass Instrumentals* (REB-850).

186. **Itinerary**: T. Ewing, "Thirty Years Ago," *BU*, Nov. 1996, 6. **Montreal**: Doug Benson, emails, Apr. 25, 2011, and Jan. 11, 2012. **Radio shows**: Doug Benson, email, July 27, 2011. **Quote**: Benson, "King of Blue Grass" (program 1, part 2), 7.

187. **Funeral of Carter Stanley**: Stanley, *Man of Constant Sorrow*, 57–58, 151, 246–47; Gary Reid, emails, May 9 and 10, 2011.

188. **Session**: Rosenberg and Wolfe, *TMBM*, 182–83. **"That's All Right"**: "Blue Grass Music Now Making Hit," 36. **"It Makes No Difference Now"**: Ronnie Pugh and Paul Kingsbury, "Songs They Gave Away," *JCM* 13, no. 1 (1989): 10; "Ray Charles," Marilyn Williams, http://www.encyclopedia.com/topic/Ray_Charles.aspx. **"Dusty Miller"**: Richard Greene, email, Apr. 28, 2011; Wolfe, *Devil's Box*, 138–39; Glen Duncan, email, May 28, 2011.

189. **Session**: Rosenberg and Wolfe, *TMBM*, 183. **"Midnight on Stormy Deep"**: Russell, *CMR*, 542. **"All the Good Times"**: Russell, *CMR*, 633. **"Soldier's Joy"**: R. Greene, interview, 2011; Rinzler, *Stars*, 206–7; Grisman, "Monroe Interview," 5.

190. Morgan Co. (Ind.) Health Dept., Certificate of Death, book 28, p. 29; T. Ewing, "Thirty Years Ago," *BU*, Jan. 1997, 7; Grier, "My Life and Times," unnumbered p. 7.

191. **Session**: Rosenberg and Wolfe, *TMBM*, 183. **"Blue Night"**: Alan Steiner, "Peter Rowan: Wandering Boy Returns to His Roots," *BU*, Feb. 1979, 12–13; Kirk McGee, *Mister Kirk: 54 Years of Country Pickin'*, MBA Records, NR11331. **"Grey Eagle"**: Paul F. Wells, "'Bluegrass Was Really My Center': An Interview with Richard Greene," *Pickin'*, Nov. 1975, 15. **Releases**: Neil V. Rosenberg, email, Dec. 6, 2012; Rosenberg and Wolfe, *TMBM*, 306.

192. **Berline**: Byron Berline, interview, May 29, 2011. **Grier**: Grier, "My Life and Times," unnumbered p. 16. **Song**: Neil V. Rosenberg, booklet notes for *Won't You Come and Sing For Me?*, Folkways, FT-31034, 3.

193. **Rowan's departure date**: Nitchie, "Interview: Lamar Grier," 8; Uncredited, "Personal Appearance Calendar," *BU*, Mar. 1967, 16. **Quote**: P. Rowan, interview, 2011.

194. **Greene's departure date**: T. Ewing, "Thirty Years Ago," *BU*, Mar. 1997, 8. **Quote**: Brooks, "An Interview with Richard S. Greene," 20–21.

195. George Gruhn and Jim Hatlo, "Bill Monroe: 'Bluegrass Is a Pure Music,'" *Frets*, Sept., 1986, 38.

196. B. Berline, interview, 2011.

197. **Blackwell**: Al Osteen, "Curtis Blackwell and the Dixie Bluegrass Boys," *BU*, Nov. 1968, 15. **Land**: Arlie Metheny, "Mitchell Land and His Stone Mountain Bluegrass

Company," *BU*, Mar. 1989, 59. **Sonka**: Mylos "Myles" Sonka, conversation, June 8, 2011. **Williams**: B. Berline, interview with author, 2011.

198. K. Rinzler, *A Source of Wonder*; Ralph Rinzler, letter of Nov. 11, 1966, Rinzler Archives, RR343, box 9; Mitch Greenhill (son), conversation, June 10, 2011.

199. Wayne Whitt, "1,000 Dignitaries Join Tribute to Evans Family," *Nashville Tennessean*, Apr. 7, 1967, 1, 3; B. Berline, interview, 2011; B. Berline, Hutchens's Questionnaire, July 1979; Grier, "My Life and Times," unnumbered p. 9.

200. **Itinerary**: "Personal Appearances," *BU*, Apr. 1967, 18. **Gene Martin**: Schlappi, *Roy Acuff*, 99. **Repair**: B. Berline, interview, 2011; "The Grammer Guitar: History," http://www.grammerguitar.com/-history.html.

201. Satterlee, *Harley "Red" Allen*, 95–96; Grier, "My Life and Times," unnumbered p. 20.

202. Doug Green, first interview, June 14, 2011; Bill Monroe and his Blue Grass Boys, live recording, Brown County Jamboree, Apr. 30, 1967, author's collection.

203. T. Ewing, "Thirty Years Ago," *BU*, May 1997, 8; D. Green, first interview, 2011; Doug Green, "The Thrill of a Lifetime," *Bill Monroe Fan Club Newsletter No. 3*, ca. Sept. 1967, 4.

204. Ewing, "Thirty Years Ago," May 1997, 8; Grier, "Partial Bill Monroe Itinerary," 1995; Grier, "My Life and Times," unnumbered p. 7; Bill Monroe, remarks recorded May 14, 1967, Ash Grove, author's collection; R. White, first interview, 2011. Bill also offered the guitar job to Roland White's brother Clarence White and to Bill Lowe, a talented Kentuckian then living in Los Angeles. Both declined the offer. (David Dickey, conversation, Mar. 1997, and Bill Lowe, email, June 11, 2001.)

205. Grier, "Partial Bill Monroe Itinerary," 1995; D. Green, first interview, 2011.

206. Rosenberg and Wolfe, *TMBM*, 174, 305.

207. T. Ewing, "Thirty Years Ago," *BU*, June 1997, 9; Adler, *Bean Blossom*, 92, 97; Neil V. Rosenberg, email, July 11, 2011.

208. Adler, *Bean Blossom*, 92; Greg Moore, email, July 21, 2011; Neil V. Rosenberg, email, July 6, 2011.

209. Grier, "Partial Bill Monroe Itinerary," 1995; Doug Benson, emails, May 18 and 28, 2011; Robins, *What I Know*, 49; Butch Robins, email, May 8, 2004.

210. Grier, "Partial Bill Monroe Itinerary," 1995; Grier, "My Life and Times," unnumbered p. 9; David Robinson, "Vic Jordan," *Pickin'*, Aug. 1974, 6; Vic Jordan, interview, July 14, 2011.

211. T. Ewing, "Thirty Years Ago," *BU*, Aug. 1997; Rosenberg, "Flatt and Scruggs Discography: Mercury Sessions," 47.

212. **Session**: Rosenberg and Wolfe, *TMBM*, 184; Decca "Record Personnel" Sheet, Aug. 23, 1967. **Stauffer**: V. Stauffer obituary, *Sturgis Journal*, 2011; V. Jordan, interview, 2011.

213. **"Roanoke festival"**: Ad (festival schedule), *BU*, Aug. 1967, unnumbered page between pages 9 and 10. **Grant**: Arlie Metheny, "Bill and Juarez Grant's Salt Creek Park, 19-Going-On-20," *BU*, Sept. 1988, 21–22; Bill Grant, conversation, July 23, 2011.

214. **Berline**: B. Berline, Hutchens's Questionnaire, July 1979; John Delgatto, "The Country Gazette," *BU*, Nov. 1972, 6. **Uncle Pen's tunes**: B. Monroe, Rinzler Archives, RINZ-RR-0005.

215. **Deejay Convention**: T. Ewing, "Thirty Years Ago," *BU*, Oct. 1997, 6; Randy Wood, interview, Mar. 11, 2012. **Inductees**: Kingsbury et al., *TE* (98), 181–82, 483, 617; McCloud et al., *DC*, 304.

216. Benson, "King of Blue Grass" (program #1, part 1), 6; Benson, "King of Blue Grass" (program #1, part 2), 3. Three more installments, mainly featuring Greene and Rowan, appeared in the February, May, and June 1968 issues.

217. **Williams**: B. Berline, Hutchens's Questionnaire, July 1979. **Session**: Rosenberg and Wolfe, *TMBM*, 184. **Clements**: Benjamin "Tex" Logan, "Vassar Clements: A Musician's Musician," *MN*, May 1973, 12; Doug Tuchman, "Vassar Clements," *Pickin'*, Jan. 1975, 4. **"Train 45"**: Neil V. Rosenberg, "Osborne Brothers Discography," *BU*, June 1967, 3; Reid, *Stanley Brothers Discography*, 12; Stubbs and Weize, booklet discography for *Jimmy Martin*, 39; Russell, *CMR*, 380, 583. **"Kentucky Mandolin"**: Rosenberg and Wolfe, *TMBM*, 159, 175.

218. V. Jordan, interview, 2011; Roland White, second interview, Aug. 4, 2011; T. Ewing, "Thirty Years Ago," *BU*, Mar. 1998, 8, and Apr. 1998, 8.

219. **King**: Farber and Bailey, *America in the 1960s*, 45; Anderson, *Sixties*, 109. **Opry and Wendell**: Havighurst, *Air Castle*, 226.

220. Ewing, "Thirty Years Ago," *BU*, Apr., 1998, 8; T. Ewing, "Thirty Years Ago," *BU*, May 1998, 10; V. Jordan, interview, 2011; R. White, second interview, 2011.

221. V. Jordan, interview, 2011; Roland White, interview with Tom Adler, Oct. 21, 1999.

222. Adler, *Bean Blossom*, 102; R. White, second interview, 2011.

223. *Brenda Harris Monroe v. James William Monroe*, Petition for Absolute Divorce, Fourth Circuit Court of Davidson County, Tennessee, no. 53319, filed May 29, 1968; James Monroe, conversation, Aug. 17, 2011.

224. Rosenberg and Wolfe, *TMBM*, 305; Ralph Rinzler, letter to Harry Silverstein, Feb. 23, 1968, Rinzler Archives, RR343, box 9.

225. Ad (for festival), *BU*, May 1968, 25; Adler, *Bean Blossom*, 102, 104; Neil V. Rosenberg, email, Aug. 20, 2011; Mitchell Land, "Impressions of the Bean Blossom Festival," *Bill Monroe Fan Club Newsletter*, No. 6, July 1968, unnumbered p. 12; R. White, second interview, 2011.

226. Norman Carlson, "Bill Monroe's Bluegrass Festival," *BU*, Aug. 1968, 5; Metheny, "Bill and Juarez Grant's Salt Creek Park," 22; Marvine (Johnson) Loving, conversation, July 2, 2013.

227. **Gospel in Barn**: Carlson, "Bill Monroe's Blue Grass Festival," unnumbered p. 19. **Sullivan Family**: Enoch and Margie Sullivan with Robert Gentry, *The Sullivan Family: Fifty Years in Bluegrass Gospel Music* (Many, La.: Sweet Dreams, 1999), 90–93. **Preacher**: Bettie Leonard, "A Week-End [sic] I'll Never Forget," *International Bill Monroe Fan Club Newsletter* 7 (Oct. 1968): 5.

228. Ewing, "Thirty Years Ago," *BU*, Mar. 1998, 8; Neil V. Rosenberg, email, Aug. 21, 2011.

229. Ad (for festival), *BU*, Mar. 1968, 19; ad (for festival), *BU*, June 1968, 25; ad (for festival), *BU*, Aug. 1968, 23.

230. **Camp**: Ad (for festival), *BU*, June 1968, 21. **Gorman**: Suzanne Sullivan, "Skip Gorman: From Jimmie Rodgers to Monroe to Old Wyoming," *BU*, July 1999, 61; Skip

Gorman, email, Aug. 28, 2011. **Rooney**: Barbara Thomas, *International Bill Monroe Fan Club Newsletter* 7 (Oct. 1968): 6; Kingsbury et al., *TE* (98), 458; Jim Rooney, interview, Dec. 5, 2011.

231. V. Jordan, interview, 2011; R. White, second interview, 2011; Charles Faurot, emails, July 18 and 19, 2011; Doug Green, email, Aug. 28, 2011; Fred Bartenstein, email, Aug. 29, 2011; Kurt Mosser, "Fred Bartenstein: The Right Place at the Right Time," *BU*, May 1999, 26–28; T. Ewing, "Thirty Years Ago," *BU*, July 1999, 6; Rosenberg, *BAH*, 307; David Freeman, email, Sept. 3, 2011.

232. Carl Goldstein, "Berryville Bluegrass Festival," *BU*, Oct. 1968, 5; Charlie Smith, email, Sept. 3, 2011; Rosenberg and Wolfe, *TMBM*, 110.

233. Boyce Taylor, "Rosine News," *OCM*, Oct. 5, 1968, 5; James Hines, conversation, July 18, 2011.

234. Lawrence Waltman (owner of Sunset Park), conversation with author, July 30, 2011; D. Green, first interview, 2011; Divorce Decree, Probate Court of Davidson Co., Tenn., case 53319, Oct. 3, 1968; Agreed Order, case no. 53319, Sept. 30, 1980.

235. Farber and Bailey, *America in the 1960s*, 47; Rosenberg and Wolfe, *TMBM*, 169, 184.

236. Rosenberg and Wolfe, *TMBM*, 135, 306; Wolfe and Rosenberg, booklet notes for *Bill Monroe—Bluegrass: 1959–1969*, 23; Neil Rosenberg, email, Dec. 6, 2012. This recording of "Walls of Time" would not be released in the States until 1991.

237. Rosenberg, *BAH*, 311–14; "Sonny Tells It Like It Is," *BU*, June 1969, 7–15; ad (for festival), *BU*, May 1976, 36; Rosenberg, *Monroe Discography*, 88; Bruce, "An Interview with Bill Monroe," 23; Roland White, email, Oct. 10, 2011.

238. **Itinerary**: V. Jordan, interview, 2011. **Break-up**: T. Ewing, "Thirty Years Ago," *BU*, Feb. 1999, 6; Rhodes, "Lester Flatt," 29. **White**: R. White, second interview, 2011.

239. Rosenberg and Wolfe, *TMBM*, 305; Ralph Rinzler, liner notes for *Bill Monroe and Charlie Monroe*, DL 7-5006; T. Ewing, "Thirty Years Ago," *BU*, Mar. 1999, 6; Weize with Sax and Spottswood, "C. Monroe: The Discography," *C. Monroe: I'm Old Kentucky Bound*, 53.

240. V. Jordan, interview, 2011; R. White, second interview, 2011; Barry Brower, "Remembering the Kentucky Colonels: The Bluegrass Life of Roland White," *BU*, Feb. 1987, 29; Vic Jordan and Roland White, conversations, Sept. 21, 2011; Michelle Putnam, "Vic Jordan: Still Pickin' Away," *BU*, Dec. 1991, 28.

241. Pete Kuykendall, "James Monroe," *BU*, July 1973, 10; James Monroe, conversation, Sept. 22, 2011.

242. Doug Green, second interview, Sept. 28, 2011; Bill Monroe and his Blue Grass Boys, recorded at the Astro Inn, Columbus, Ohio, Mar. 21, 1969, author's collection; Brian Aldridge (Howard's son), email, Sept. 28, 2011.

243. Patricia Glenn, "Rual Yarbrough," *BU*, Oct. 1978, 11; R. Yarbrough, interview, 2007; Rosenberg and Wolfe, *TMBM*, 185.

244. **Session**: Rosenberg and Wolfe, *TMBM*, 185. **"I Haven't Seen Mary in Years"**: J. W. Layden, "Damon Black," *BU*, July 1988, 44–45; James Monroe, conversation, Sept. 23, 2011; "Mel Tillis," http://www.lpdiscography. com/?page=main#?page=discography&interpret=355; RCA Victor recording sessions on microfilm, Country Music Hall of Fame

Library, Nashville, Tenn.; "Porter Wagoner Albums," http://www.sing365.com/music/lyrics.nsf/Porter-albums. **"Fireball Mail"**: Schlappi, *Roy Acuff*, 153; Rosenberg, "Flatt and Scruggs Discography: Releases, 1949–69," 43. **"The Dead March"**: Rosenberg and Wolfe, *TMBM*, 160. **Sidemen**: Ibid., 160; Walt Trott, "Bass Fiddler Dies," *NM*, Apr.–June 2003, 26.

245. James R. Morris, email, Oct. 7, 2011.

246. **Session**: Rosenberg and Wolfe, *TMBM*, 185–86. **Williams**: T. Williams, interview, 2012. **"Cripple Creek"**: Rosenberg, "Flatt and Scruggs Discography: Releases, 1949–69," 43; R. Yarbrough, interview, 2007. **"What about You?"**: Rosenberg and Wolfe, *TMBM*, 160, 296; Neil V. Rosenberg, email, Dec. 6, 2012. **"With Body and Soul"**: D. Green, second interview, 2011; Rosenberg and Wolfe, *TMBM*, 160, 303. **"Methodist Preacher"**: Rosenberg and Wolfe, *TMBM*, 186.

247. R. Yarbrough, interview, 2007.

248. Rosenberg and Wolfe, *TMBM*, 303, 306; T. Ewing, "Thirty Years Ago," *BU*, May 1999, 6.

249. Davis, taped replies, tape 1.

250. Ads (for festival), *BU*, Apr. 1969, 10, and May 1969, 19–20; Rosenberg, *BAH*, 282; Adler, *Bean Blossom*, 110; Kingsbury et al., *TE* (98), 323.

251. Robins, *What I Know*, 56–60; Uncredited, "Show Dates for Bill Monroe and the Bluegrass Boys," *Bill Monroe Fan Club Newsletter* 8 (Apr. 1969): 7; Calvin Robins, "Notes and Bits," *Bill Monroe Fan Club Newsletter* 9 (July 1969): 13.

252. J. Landers, interview, 2010.

253. Rosenberg and Wolfe, *TMBM*, 300–301, 305; Rinzler, liner notes for *A Voice from On High*, DL7-5135.

254. Alice Foster, "Festival of American Folklife," *BU*, June 1969, 21–22; Monroe Brothers et al., recorded at the Festival of American Folklife, July 3, 1969, author's collection; Doug Green, second interview, 2011; James R. Morris, email, Oct. 7, 2011.

255. **Marriage of Charlie and Martha**: *Ohio County, Kentucky, Marriage License and Bonds (1966–1969)* 73:452; "Charlie Monroe Weds," *OCT-N*, July 21, 1969, 2A; ad (for Charlie), *MN*, Jan.–Feb. 1975, 16; Wendell Allen, "Deaths," *OCT-N*, July 27, 1989, 2A; Green, "Charlie Monroe" (part 3), 15. **Martha and Bill**: Smith, *Can't You Hear*, 214–15; Jimmy Martin via Gloria Belle Flickinger, conversation, June 13, 2012.

256. Doug Green, emails, June 17 and Oct. 3, 2011; Eugenia Snyder, "Bill Yates: A Master of Support," *BU*, Sept. 1983, 52.

257. Ewing, "Thirty Years Ago," *BU*, July 1999, 6; Bill Monroe (from interviews with Alice Foster), "My Life in Blue Grass," Newport Folk Festival program booklet, 1969.

258. Farber and Bailey, *America in the 1960s*, 49–51, 246, 306.

259. **"Bluest Man in Town"**: Dick Staber, conversations, May 5, 2004, and Feb. 6, 2012; Dennis Satterlee, "Dick Staber," *BU*, May 2004, 77. McCoury was the first to record "Bluest Man in Town" in 1971 (Grassound 102), and he would record it with Bill in 1985. **Manson and Woodstock**: Farber and Bailey, *America in the 1960s*, 226, 257.

260. **Salt Creek Festival**: Ad (for festival), *BU*, Aug. 1969, 23. **The bus**: R. Wood, interview, 2012; Bill Yates, interview, Oct. 31, 2011; Robins, *What I Know*, 60; Gene Lowinger, email, Nov. 2, 2011. **Rattlesnake rattle**: Doug Hutchens, email, Mar. 8, 2012; Black, *Come*

Hither, 109; "Rattlesnake Rattles," http://stoneplus.cst.cmich.edu/zoogems/rattles.html. **Leonard**: Judy Paris, "So You Want to Be President," *Pickin'*, Sept. 1975, 17.

261. R. Wood, interview, 2012; George Gruhn, conversation, Mar. 22, 2012; ad (for GTR), *BU*, June 1970, 22.

262. Richard K. Spottswood, "There Was Bluegrass at Camp Springs," *BU*, Oct. 1969, 7; T. Ewing, "Thirty Years Ago," *BU*, Aug. 1999, 6; Cover photo, *MN*, Aug. 26, 1969.

263. **"To Tell the Truth"**: Bill Monroe, letter to the Bill Monroe International Fan Club's *Bluegrass Special*, Journal no. 3 (Nov. 1969), 1; Marshall Akers ("To Tell the Truth" webmaster), conversation, Nov. 9, 2011. After the show aired, *MN* reported that "2 out of the 4 panelists guessed (Bill)." (*MN*, Feb., 1970, 7.) **"Bill Monroe Day"**: "'Bill Monroe Day' Is Set In Kentucky by Governor," *Messenger* (Madisonville, Ky.), Sept. 20, 1969; Ann Brown, "Police-Firemen Show Saturday Night 'Best,'" *Messenger* (Madisonville, Ky.), Oct. 20, 1969, 1; Neil V. Rosenberg, email, Jan. 7, 2012. Bill's performance of "Body and Soul" appeared in Rachel Liebling's *High Lonesome*, released in 1991. "The Nashville Sound," SMMVD28419, was rereleased in 2005 by S'More Entertainment.

264. Boyce Taylor, "Rosine Personals," *OCT*, Oct. 2, 1969, 10; "Charlie Monroe Making Come-Back in Music Field," *OCT*, Oct. 2, 1969, 13.

265. Rosenberg and Wolfe, *TMBM*, 177, 187, 191; Vic Gabany, email, Jan. 7, 2012.

266. **Session**: Rosenberg and Wolfe, *TMBM*, 187. **"Land of Lincoln"**: David Freeman, liner notes for Kenny Baker, *Dry and Dusty*, County Records, 744; Rosenberg and Wolfe, *TMBM*, 161, 191. **"Going Up Caney"**: *Kentucky Atlas and Gazetteer* (Yarmouth, Me.: DeLorme, 1997), 46; B. Yates, interview, 2011; David Mahan (Harry Monroe's grandson), conversation, Nov. 19, 2011. **"The Lee Weddin Tune"**: *HH*, Nov. 5, 1919, 5, and Apr. 21, 1920, 1.

267. B. Yates, interview, 2011; Glen Mowrey, *Bluegrass Special*, Journal no. 3 (November 1969), 3; "Skip" Payne, interview, Nov. 22, 2011; R.C. Harris, email, November 23, 2011.

268. J. Rooney, interview, 2011.

269. Rosenberg and Wolfe, *TMBM*, 161, 187.

270. Rosenberg and Wolfe, *TMBM*, 131–32, 305.

CHAPTER SEVEN. 1970–1979

1. T. Ewing, "Thirty Years Ago," *BU*, Jan. 2000, 6; Rosenberg and Wolfe, *TMBM*, 188; Sandy Rothman, email, Mar. 26, 2012; "Grave Search Results," https://www.findagrave.com. Harry Silverstein was born on Sept. 6, 1930.

2. Rosenberg and Wolfe, *TMBM*, 189; Kristen M. O'Hare (curatorial assistant, *Grand Ole Opry* Museum), survey of *Opry* souvenir programs, 1970–72.

3. Rosenberg and Wolfe, *TMBM*, 188; S. Payne, interview, 2011.

4. Jim Rooney, email, June 17, 2004; Jim Rooney, conversation, Aug. 31, 2011; J. Rooney, interview, 2011.

5. **Kent State**: C. Daniel et al., *20th Century*, 1019–20. **Parton**: RCA Victor recording sessions on microfilm, Country Music Hall of Fame Library, Nashville, Tenn.; McCloud et al., *DC*, 621; Tom Roland, *The Billboard Book of Number One Country Hits* (New York: Billboard Books, 1991), 49; T. Ewing, "Thirty Years Ago," *BU*, June 2000, 10, and Sept. 2000, 6.

6. Ad (for festivals), *BU*, May 1970, 12; Author's survey, all issues of *BU*, 1970–79.

7. Adler, *Bean Blossom*, 114–16; "Early Festivals," Doug Hutchens, http://doughutchens.blogspot.com.

8. *Newsweek* staff, "Pickin' and Singin'," *Newsweek*, June 29, 1970, 85.

9. **Decca**: Rosenberg and Wolfe, *TMBM*, 306; Ralph Rinzler, correspondence with various Decca executives, May–July, 1970, Rinzler Archives, RR343, Box 9. **Columbia**: Rosenberg and Wolfe, *TMBM*, 51–52, 68–76, 299.

10. Carlton Haney, "Blue Grass Music—It's Time to Organize," *MN*, Feb. 1970, inside front cover; Fred Bartenstein, "Notes on the North Carolina Blue Grass Music Festival and Festivals in General," *MN*, Sept.–Oct. 1970, 10–11; Willis, *America's Music*, 566; ad (for festival), *MN*, July–Aug. 1970, 21; Carlton Haney, remarks recorded at the Camp Springs Bluegrass Festival, Sept. 6, 1970.

11. Fred Bartenstein, interview, Nov. 30, 2011; Carlton Haney, remarks recorded at the Camp Springs Bluegrass Festival, Sept. 6, 1970; Fred Bartenstein, email, Dec. 2, 2011; Ronnie Reno, email, Dec. 5, 2011.

12. Marks, "Common-Law Wife," 25; Sandy Rothman, email, Nov. 28, 2011.

13. **Festival**: Ewing, "Thirty Years Ago," *BU*, Sept. 2000, 7; Jack Hicks, interview, Feb. 19, 2012. **Band**: Walt Saunders, "Notes and Queries," *BU*, Nov. 2011, 19.

14. Marty Stuart, comment made during a WSM radio tribute to Bill, Sept. 10, 1996; Marty Stuart, "Memories of Bill Monroe," *Southern Living*, Sept., 1999, 110; E. and M. Sullivan with Gentry, *Sullivan Family*, photo section page 14, 170.

15. T. Ewing, "Thirty Years Ago," *BU*, Oct. 2000, 6; Bill Monroe, letter dated Dec. 22, 1970, *Bill Monroe Fan Club Newsletter*, 1; Neil V. Rosenberg, email, Jan. 18, 2011. Johnny Cash celebrated Bill's induction on his primetime ABC-TV show of November 11, 1970, introducing him as "the creator of the purest form of country music." Bill sang "Blue Moon of Kentucky," later included on Disc 2 of *The Best of the Johnny Cash TV Show: 1969–71*, Columbia-Legacy, 88697-040269.

16. Ad (for festival), *BU*, Nov. 1970, 12–13; Doug Hutchens, emails, Jan. 18 and 23, 2012.

17. Glenn, "Rual Yarbrough," 11–12; R. Yarbrough, interview, 2007; Glen Mowrey, *Bill Monroe Fan Club Newsletter*, Dec. 1970, 14.

18. Rosenberg and Wolfe, *TMBM*, 189; Vic Gabany, email, Jan. 27, 2012; Doug Hutchens, conversation, Jan. 28, 2012; Neil V. Rosenberg, email, Jan. 29, 2012; Kingsbury et al., *TE* (98), 235.

19. Rosenberg and Wolfe, *TMBM*, 189–90; Ewing, "Thirty Years Ago," Oct. 2001, 6. "Lonesome Moonlight Waltz" was recorded by the California bluegrass band High Country and released in October 1971 on their *Dreams* album (Raccoon, BS-2608), seven months before Bill's Decca release of May 1972.

20. R. C. Harris, interview, Jan. 26, 2012.

21. Rosenberg and Wolfe, *TMBM*, 190.

22. Ibid., 190–91; **"Poor White Folks"**: Bill Monroe, Rinzler Archives, FP-1993-CT-0262; **"Kiss Me Waltz"**: Russell, *CMR*, 389, 699, 902; **"Jenny Lynn"**: Harrison and Klotter, *NH*, 161; **"Heel and Toe Polka"**: Rinzler Archives, FP-1993-CT-0262; **"Milenburg Joy"**: Cantwell, *Breakdown*, 47.

23. **Presley**: Ernest Jorgensen, *Elvis Presley: A Life in Music—The Complete Recording Sessions* (New York: St. Martin's, 1998), 297, 420. **Harris**: R. C. Harris, interview, 2012; R. C. Harris, email, Feb. 1, 2012.

24. Marion Kuykendall, "Notes and Queries," *BU*, Feb. 1971, 20.

25. **Bossmen**: T. Ewing, "Thirty Years Ago," *BU*, Apr. 2001, 6. **Band**: R. C. Harris, email, Feb. 1, 2012; Glen Mowrey, "Featured Bluegrass Boy Jack Hicks," *Bill Monroe Fan Club Journal* 5 (Oct. 22, 1971). **Release**: Rosenberg and Wolfe, *TMBM*, 306.

26. T. Ewing, "Thirty Years Ago," Apr. 2001, 6; Hurst, *Nashville's Opry*, 335; Kingsbury et al., *TE* (98), 464; T. Ewing, "Thirty Years Ago," *BU*, Aug. 2001, 6; Escott, *Grand Ole Opry*, 163, 199–201.

27. **James**: Kuykendall, "James Monroe," 12. **Stewart**: Walt Saunders, "Notes and Queries," *BU*, Nov. 2011, 19; Fred Robbins, email, Feb. 12, 2012; Travis Stewart, interview, Feb. 12, 2012.

28. Doug Hutchens, interview, Jan. 18, 2012; Doug Hutchens, email, Feb. 6, 2012; Doug Hutchens, conversation, Feb. 9, 2012; ad (for festival), *BU*, May 1971, 7.

29. Ad (for festival), *BU*, May 1971, 3; Robert Cantwell, "Believing in Bluegrass," *Atlantic Monthly*, Mar. 1972, 54, 58; Doug Hutchens's blog, "Bill Monroe and the Blue Grass Boys, Summer 1971," dated Mar. 25, 2011.

30. Festival program (Bean Blossom), *BU*, June 1971, 4; Lambert (with Sechler), *Lester Flatt*, 64; Rhodes, "Lester Flatt," 29; Hutchens's Blog, "Lester Flatt," dated May 12, 2011; "Bill Monroe's Bean Blossom—June 1971" (audio recordings), Ken Landreth, http://frobbi.org/landrethcollection.html.

31. Danny Jones, interview, Feb. 23, 2012; George B. McCeney, "Record Reviews," *BU*, June 1970, 25–26.

32. Hutchens's blog, "Bill Monroe," Mar. 25, 2011.

33. Rosenberg and Wolfe, *TMBM*, 303; Hutchens's blog, "Bill Monroe," Mar. 25, 2011.

34. Hutchens's blog, "Frontier Ranch, June 27th, 1971," dated Feb. 14, 2012.

35. Hutchens, *Howdy, Folks Howdy*, 12–13; Doug Hutchens, email, Feb. 6, 2012; Dave Samuelson, email, Mar. 18, 2012.

36. B. Monroe, Rinzler Archives, RINZ-RR-0005; Russell, *CMR*, 88; Hutchens's Blog, "Cosby, Tennessee, July 2nd, 3rd, and 4th," dated Feb. 16, 2012.

37. Ad (for festival), *BU*, Mar. 1971, 7; Hutchens, *Howdy, Folks, Howdy*, 13.

38. D. Jones, interview, 2012; Doug Hutchens, emails, Jan. 18 and Feb. 6, 2012.

39. Ad (for festival), *BU*, Aug. 1971, inside back cover; Doug Hutchens, email , Feb. 15, 2001.

40. McCloud et al., *DC*, 708–9; "Discography" website, Pennell (compiler); Neil V. Rosenberg, "The Flatt and Scruggs Discography: The Columbia Recordings, 1960–64," *JCM* 13, no. 2 (Aug. 1990): 3.

41. *TBS*, Oct. 1971, 4–6, 7, 8; Kingsbury, McCall, and Rumble, *TE*, 356, 604.

42. Ad (for show), *Brown County Democrat*, Nov. 4, 1971; Glen Duncan, emails, Aug. 6 and Dec. 15, 2011.

43. T. Ewing, "Thirty Years Ago," *BU*, Jan. 2002, 6.

44. Sandy Rothman, email, Mar. 18, 2012; Author's recollection and/or personal journal; Sandy Rothman, email from John Arms, Dec. 5, 2015.

45. **Sessions**: Rosenberg and Wolfe, *TMBM*, 191–92. **Overdub vs. "live"**: Sandy Rothman, email, Mar. 26, 2012; Vic Gabany, email, Mar. 26, 2012. **Hicks's picking**: J. Hicks, interview, 2012. **Jewel Breeding**: Carl Fleischhauer and Neil V. Rosenberg, *Bluegrass*

Odyssey: A Documentary in Pictures and Words, 1966–86 (Urbana: University of Illinois Press, 2001), 156–57; Trischka and Wernick, *Masters of Banjo*, 13; J. Hicks, interview, 2012.

46. **Wood**: Janice Brown McDonald, "Randy Wood: Woodworking Wizard," *BU*, May 1989, 36; R. Wood, interview, 2012. **White and Down Home Folks**: Kingsbury, McCall, and Rumble, *TE*, 558. "Indian Blood" was included in the first album by *Buck White and the Down Home Folks*, County 735, released in Aug. 1972 (T. Ewing, "Thirty Years Ago," *BU*, Aug. 2002, 6).

47. Fleischhauer and Rosenberg, *Bluegrass Odyssey*, 3, 4, 191; Rooney, *Bossmen*, 62–63, 72, 74, 78, 87, 95, 100; S. Rothman, emails, Mar. 30 and Apr. 1, 2012; Carl Fleischhauer, emails, Apr. 1 and 2, 2012; Neil V. Rosenberg, emails, Apr. 2, 2012, and Dec. 6, 2016; Merlene Austin, conversation, Apr. 5, 2012; Carl Fleischhauer, report on visit to Rosine, Kentucky, Apr. 1972, Rinzler Archives, RR343, box 9; Carl Fleischhauer, nine proofsheets of exposures made in or near Rosine, Kentucky, Apr. 1972, author's collection.

48. Rosenberg and Wolfe, *TMBM*, 303; T. Ewing, "Thirty Years Ago," *BU*, May 2002, 6.

49. **Bill Monroe's Uncle Pen**: Rosenberg and Wolfe, *TMBM*, 166, 306; Hurst, "Mellowing Father," 3-S. **Festivals**: Author's survey, all issues of *BU*, 1972; Jack Hurst, "Bill Monroe's Bean Blossom Top Festival," *Tennessean*, June 19, 1972, 6; Adler, *Bean Blossom*, 125. **Mandolin**: Jim Rooney, "Sketches of Bill Monroe," *Country Music*, Oct., 1972, 47; Jim Rooney, email, Apr. 15, 2012; Darryl Wolfe, unpublished list: "Gibson F5 Lloyd Loar Mandolins," dated May 28, 1986; Adler, *Bean Blossom*, 126. Adler offers an alternate version of this event, of "a widow whose husband had requested that, after his death, her first offering of his prize Lloyd Loar Gibson mandolin for sale would be to Monroe. She brought the instrument to the festival; Monroe bought it" (Adler, *Bean Blossom*, 126).

50. T. Ewing, "Thirty Years Ago," *BU*, Aug. 2002, 6; *Lester Flatt and the Nashville Grass, 1976* (souvenir booklet).

51. T. Ewing, "Thirty Years Ago," *BU*, Aug. 2002, 6; Rosenberg, *BAH*, 317–18; Jack Hurst, "Bill Monroe: From Refined Oil to Slick Music," *Chicago Tribune*, Oct. 12, 1977; T. Ewing, "Thirty Years Ago," *BU*, Nov. 2002, 6. The Nitty Gritty Dirt Band's three-record *Will the Circle Be Unbroken* album (United Artists, UAS-9801) was released in late 1972.

52. Adler, *Bean Blossom*, 128; Tom Adler, email, Apr. 19, 2012.

53. C. Daniel, *20th Century*, 1049, 1057.

54. Uncredited (Marion Kuykendall), "General Store," *BU*, Dec. 1972, 6; Green, "Charlie Monroe" (part 3), 15.

55. **Bluegrass Express**: Ad (for shows), *BU*, Jan. 1973, 21; James Monroe, conversation, May 25, 2012. **Johnson**: C. Daniel et al., *20th Century*, 1060–61.

56. T. Ewing, "Thirty Years Ago," *BU*, Feb. 2003, 6; William Henry Koon, liner notes for *Muleskinner-Live: The Video*, Sierra Home Video, SHV 1001; John Delgatto, email, Dec. 5, 2002; T. Ewing, "Thirty Years Ago," *BU*, May 2004, 6; John Delgatto, email, May 10, 2012. Calling themselves "Muleskinner," Greene et al. recorded an album for Warner Brothers, *Muleskinner: A Potpourri of Bluegrass Jam* (BS 2787), released in May 1974.

57. Kingsbury, McCall, and Rumble, eds., *TE*, 132; Rosenberg and Wolfe, *TMBM*, 306; Pugh, *Ernest Tubb*, 406, 412.

58. **Stuart**: Maria Gajda, "Muleskinner Newsletter," *MN*, June 1973, 5. **Fowler**: Bob Fowler, interview, Mar. 16, 2007.

59. Guy Stevenson, interview, May 14, 2012.

60. **Bean Blossom**: Ad (for festival), *BU*, May 1973, 30. **Albums**: T. Ewing, "Thirty Years Ago," *BU*, Jan.–Mar. 2003. **Bill's suggestion**: Rosenberg and Wolfe, *TMBM*, 195. **Recording**: B. Fowler, interview, 2007; G. Stevenson, interview, 2012.

61. Rosenberg and Wolfe, *TMBM*, 206; Kingsbury, McCall, and Rumble, eds., *TE*, 242.

62. Rosenberg and Wolfe, *TMBM*, 207, 303. Bill's first "official" MCA single, released in March 1974, combined "Swing Low, Sweet Chariot" with "Down Yonder" (40220).

63. B. Fowler, interview, 2007; Bill Box, interview, June 2, 2012.

64. G. Stevenson, interview, 2007; Gregg Kennedy, Hutchens's Questionnaire, date unknown.

65. B. Box, interview, 2012.

66. Gregg Kennedy, email, Apr. 21, 2005; Jack Hicks, email, June 10, 2012; J. Hicks, interview, 2012; Ben Pedigo, interview, June 28, 2012; Author's survey, all issues of *BU*, 1970–79.

67. Ad (for festival), *BU*, Aug. 1973, 34; Carl Fleischhauer, report on trip to Louisville-Rosine, Ky., Sept. 14–16, 1973, Rinzler Archives, RR343, box 9; Boyce Taylor, "Rosine Society News," *OCT*, Aug. 16, 1973, sec. 1, 6; Boyce Taylor, "Rosine Society News," *OCT*, Sept. 13, 1973, 1.

68. Richard Hefner, interview, June 10, 2012; Hazel Smith, "Monroe Homecoming," *BU*, Nov. 1973, 19.

69. **Property**: Ohio Co., Ky., Deeds, book 304, p. 547. **Rafferty**: Merlene Austin (great-niece), conversations, June 2012. **Ceremony**: R. Hefner, interview, 2012; C. Fleischhauer, report on trip, Rinzler Archives, RR343, box 9; Doug McHattie, recordings of Uncle Pen monument dedication ceremony, Sept. 16, 1973, collection of Carl Fleischhauer, Port Republic, Md.

70. B. Pedigo, interview, 2012; Jim Moratto, email, Apr. 16, 2016; ads (for festivals), *BU*, Sept. 1973, 3, 4.

71. **LP release**: Rosenberg and Wolfe, *TMBM*, 306. **Single release**: T. Ewing, "Thirty Years Ago," *BU*, Nov. 2003, 6. **Single in charts**: T. Ewing, "Thirty Years Ago," *BU*, Jan. 2004, 6. **LP in charts**: Joel Whitburn, ed., *Joel Whitburn's Top Country Albums, 1964–1997* (Memomonee Falls, Wisc.: Record Research, 1997), 110; T. Ewing, "Thirty Years Ago," *BU*, Mar. 2004, 6, and Apr. 2004, 6.

72. Kingsbury, McCall, and Rumble, eds., *TE*, 489–90; Gregg Kennedy, "Comments on the Bill Monroe Schedule/Diary" (memoir), unnumbered p. 10.

73. **Banjo players**: Kennedy, "Comments," 8, 9, 12. **Moratto**: Ibid., 13; Jim Moratto, email, Apr. 16, 2016. **Interview**: Steve Rathe, "Bill Monroe," *Pickin'*, Feb. 1974, 4, 8. **Rumors**: Bill Williams, "Nashville Scene," *Billboard*, July 7, 1973, 34.

74. **Festivals**: Author's survey, all issues of *BU*, 1970–79. **Agency**: Ad (for Monroe agency), *BU*, Feb. 1974, 21; Hazel Smith, "Chuck Campbell," *Bill Monroe Fan Club Newsletter* 18 (Apr. 14, 1974), 3; ad (for Monroe agency), *MN*, Apr. 1974, 47.

75. Author's recollection and/or personal journal; Hurst, *Nashville's Opry*, 328.

76. Kennedy, "Comments," 19; Thomas Goldsmith, booklet for *Flatt on Victor Plus More*, Bear Family, BCD 15975FI, released in 1999, 27; Gregg Kennedy, conversation, June 12, 2012. All of the concert's recordings, including three by Bill and the Blue Grass Boys, were released in 2000 in a Bear Family boxed set, *Flatt on Victor Plus More*, BCD 15975FI.

77. Tribe, "Charlie Monroe," 19; Cecil Hall, interview, July 14, 2012; Ed Davis, "Best Friends Are Tarheels," *MN*, Apr. 1975, 12.

78. "The International Festivals of Country Music at Wembley," http://www.stanlaundon.com/wembley.html; B. Box, interview, 2012.

79. Bob Fowler, conversation, Aug. 29, 2012; Charmaine Lanham, email, Sept. 10, 2012; J. T. Gray, email, Sept. 10, 2012; Bill Michaels, "Bluegrass Camelot Survives! Celebrating Thirty-One Years of Magic at the Station Inn," *BU*, July 2005, 41.

80. **James's first**: T. Ewing, "Thirty Years Ago," *BU*, May 2004, 6. **Album releases**: Author's survey, "Thirty Years Ago This Month," *BU*, 1972–74. **MCA performers**: Stubbs and Weize, booklet discography for *Jimmy Martin*, 42; Bobby Osborne and Neil Rosenberg, Sonny Osborne, Edward L. Stubbs, and Richard Weize, booklet discography for *Osborne Brothers, 1968–74*, BCD 15748-DI, released 1995, 23. **Quote**: Bill Monroe, liner notes for *Something New! Something Different! Something Good!*, Atteiram Records, API-L-1507. This recording, retitled *James Monroe: His First Solo Album*, was reissued on CD in 2011 (Gusto, GT7-2249-2).

81. Uncredited, "Bill Monroe's Blue Grass Fest," *Cash Box*, Aug. 3, 1974, 32; Author's recollection and/or personal journal.

82. T. Ewing, "Thirty Years Ago," *BU*, June 2004, 6; Freeman, liner notes for *Charlie Monroe on the Noonday Jamboree*; David Freeman, email, July 20, 2012. In July 1974, County released an album of selected performances from the other discs, *The Songs of Charlie Monroe and the Kentucky Pardners*, with notes by Bill Vernon, who'd encouraged Charlie to take his recordings to County.

83. T. Ewing, "Thirty Years Ago," *BU*, July 2004, 6; Franklin D. "Bud" Brewster, interview, July 9, 2012.

84. Jim Moratto, email, Apr. 16, 2016; Ralph Lewis, interview, July 26, 2012; Marc Pruett, email, Aug. 4, 2010; Stephanie P. Ledgin, "Spotlight on Randy Davis," *Pickin'*, Nov. 1976, 10.

85. Dwight Dillman, interview, Aug. 2, 2012; Dwight Dillman, email, Aug. 16, 2012.

86. Author's recollection and/or personal journal.

87. C. Daniel et al., *20th Century*, 1069, 1076, 1082.

88. C. Hall, interview, 2012; Tribe, "Charlie Monroe," 19; Davis, "Best Friends," 12.

89. Neil V. Rosenberg, "Sound Intelligence: Discography as Ethnography," unpublished lecture, Music, Media, and Culture series, Memorial University, St. John's, Newfoundland, Mar. 19, 2003; Neil V. Rosenberg, email, Nov. 24, 2003; Uncredited (Marion Kuykendall), "General Store," *BU*, Oct. 1974, 5.

90. Ohio Co., Ky., Deeds, book 209, 173–76; Uncredited, "Bluegrass Musicland Park Schedules May 9 Opening," *Amusement Business*, Apr. 5, 1975.

91. D. Dillman, interview, 2012.

92. Black, *Come Hither*, 25–28, 32, 92; R. Lewis, interview, 2012.

93. Black, *Come Hither*, 34; Charles K. Wolfe, *The Grand Ole Opry: The Early Years, 1925–35* (London, England: Old Time Music, 1975), 6; Wolfe, *G-NR*, iv; Wolfe, "Bluegrass Touches," 7.

94. Ed Davis, "Best Friends," 12; "Muleskinner Newsletter," *MN*, Dec. 1974, 4; North Carolina Department of Human Resources, Division of Health Services, Vital Records Branch, Certificate of Death 33545; Daniel C. Scullin, Jr., MD, emails, Sept. 24–30, 2012.

95. Rosenberg and Wolfe, *TMBM*, 131, 142, 143, 144, 169, 175, 188, 306.

96. James Monroe, conversation, May 25, 2012.

97. **First Japan tour**: Black, *Come Hither*, 47–52, 162. **Previous tours**: Rosenberg, *BAH*, 310, 328; Marion Kuykendall, "News and Notes from the Bluegrass World," *BU*, Apr. 1971, 25; Walt Saunders, Everett Lilly obituary, *BU*, July 2012, 10. **Set of LPs**: "Discography" website, Pennell (compiler); Toru Mitsui, email, Dec. 9, 2012. Before Bill's visit to Japan, in October 1973, a four-LP boxed set, *Bill Monroe and His Blue Grass Boys (1950–60)*, was released by Japanese Victor, under contract with MCA. Many of its fifty-six recordings had been released in the United States only on singles. None of the fifty-six were from 1960. Five live instrumental performances recorded at Osaka on December 13, 1974, were released in 2005 on Bob Black's *Ladies on the Steamboat* CD (Green Valley).

98. Black, *Come Hither*, 44; "Ash Grove Music Foundation," http://www. ashgrovemusic. com.

99. Rosenberg and Wolfe, *TMBM*, 192, 206–8, 209–20. James would also record and release his second album for Atteiram, *Midnight Blues*, in 1975. (Walter V. Saunders, "Record Reviews," *BU*, Feb. 1976, 23.)

100. Rosenberg and Wolfe, *TMBM*, 154, 208–9; R. Lewis, interview, 2012; Bob Black, email, Sept. 23, 2012; Jack Hicks, email, Sept. 24, 2012.

101. Rosenberg and Wolfe, *TMBM*, 154, 209; Winsett, ed., *Best of All*, 63; author's recollection and/or personal journal; B. Monroe, Rinzler Archives, RINZ-RR-0004.

102. Black, *Come Hither*, 106; R. Lewis, interview, 2012; Bill Monroe, personal communication with author, Feb. 3, 1990.

103. Price, *Old as the Hills*, 31, 35; Bob Artis, *Bluegrass* (New York: Hawthorn, 1975), 20–21, 21.

104. Lawayne Satterfield, "Monroe Talks," *Music City News*, May 1975, 12–13; Roland, *Number One Country Hits*, 57–58, 72–73, 87–88, 108, 136.

105. Black, *Come Hither*, 63–64; ad (for festival), *BU*, Apr. 1975, 5; Reinhard Pietsch, booklet notes for *Far across the Blue Water: Bill Monroe in Germany (1975 and 1989)*, Bear Family Records, BCD 16624 EK, 7.

106. Black, *Come Hither*, 58–59; R. Lewis, interview, 2012.

107. Black, *Come Hither*, 61–63, 163; Rolf Sieker, "On Tour with Bill Monroe in Germany 1975," booklet for *Far across the Blue Water*, BCD 16624 EK, 29–30. Bear Family Records released *Far Across The Blue Water: Bill Monroe in Germany (1975 and 1989)* in 2004, a collection of live recordings that includes Bill's shows of May 17, 1975.

108. Bill Clifton et al., *European Tour '75 Souvenir Program*, reproduced in the booklet for *Far across the Blue Water*, BCD 16624 EK, 10–13; Rosenberg and Wolfe, *TMBM*, 306.

109. Rosenberg and Wolfe, *TMBM*, 213–14; Carl Queen, conversation, Mar. 6, 1999; T. Ewing, "Thirty Years Ago," *BU*, Dec. 2005, 6; ad (for festival), *BU*, June 1975, 35; "Personal Appearance Calendar," *BU*, June 1975, 39.

110. Ad (for Black Diamond Strings), *BU*, May 1974, 28; ad (for Black Diamond Strings), *BU*, July 1975, 22; Black, *Come Hither*, 71–73.

111. T. Ewing, "Thirty Years Ago," *BU*, July 2005, 6; Rinzler, *Stars*, 205, 219; Marks, "Common-Law Wife," 25; Murphy Hicks Henry, "Bessie Lee Mauldin," *BU*, Aug. 2013, 37.

112. **Release**: Ewing, "Thirty Years Ago," *BU*, July 2005, 6. **Charlie in Rosine**: Jan Stone (columnist), "Those Were the Days," *OCT-N*, July 8, 2010, 3B; Uncredited, "Monroe Returns For Performance," *OCT*, July 31, 1975, 15.

113. Black, *Come Hither*, 79; ad (for festival), *BU*, Aug. 1976, 9; ad (for festival), *BU*, Aug. 1977, 28; ad (for festival), *BU*, Aug. 1978, 29.

114. C. Hall, interview, 2012.

115. Frank W. Martin, "The Hills—and Everywhere Else—Are Alive with the Sound of Bill Monroe's Unique Bluegrass," *People Weekly*, Sept. 1, 1975, 46–48; Black, *Come Hither*, 163.

116. **Sept. 19–21, 1975**: Uncredited (Marion Kuykendall), "General Store," *BU*, Sept. 1975, 9; "Charlie Monroe, Carl Story to Appear at Rosine, Windy Hollow This Weekend," *OCT*, Sept. 18, 1975, 9. **Windy Hollow Park**: Byron Oost, conversation, Oct. 11, 2012; Floyd Stewart, interview, Oct. 20, 2012. **Charlie in hospital**: Daniel C. Scullin Jr., MD, emails, Oct. 18 and 21, 2012.

117. "Charlie Monore [sic] Performs at Rosine, Windy Hollow," *OCT*, Sept. 25, 1975, 16; Danny Jones, conversation, Nov. 1, 2012; F. Stewart, interview, 2012.

118. Bill Vernon, "Last Respects to the Giant, Charlie Monroe," *Pickin'*, Jan. 1976, 17; Wendell Allen, "Charlie Monroe Remembered by Bluegrass Music Fans," *OCT*, Oct. 2, 1975, section 1, 7.

119. Black, *Come Hither*, 86; R. Lewis, interview, 2012; Vernon, "Last Respects," 14; Ralph Lewis (via son Marty Lewis), email, Nov. 3, 2012.

120. Merlene Austin, conversations, Oct. 24 and 25, 2012; Black, *Come Hither*, 87; C. Hall, interview, 2012. In 1976, Pine Mountain Records released a two-record set, *Memories of Charlie Monroe* (PMR 246–247). Live recordings of Charlie on one record came from shows with the Dominion Bluegrass Boys and Slim and Wilma Martin in 1974. On the other were studio recordings by Wendell Allen and the gospel-singing Phipps Family, owners of the Pine Mountain label, singing songs they sang at Charlie's funeral.

121. Black, *Come Hither*, 164; Author's recollection and/or personal journal.

122. Black, *Come Hither*, 99–105, 164–65; Neil V. Rosenberg, emails, Dec. 6, 2012; "Discography" website, Pennell (compiler); Toru Mitsui, email, Dec. 11, 2012.

123. Rosenberg and Wolfe, *TMBM*, 208–9, 306; Owen Bradley, liner notes for *The Weary Traveler* (MCA 2173).

124. **Tour**: Black, *Come Hither*, 165. **Session**: Rosenberg and Wolfe, *TMBM*, 214–15; James Monroe, conversation, Nov. 7, 2012. **Release**: T. Ewing, "Thirty Years Ago," *BU*, Dec. 2006, 6.

125. R. Lewis, interview, 2012; Author's recollection and/or personal journal; Bob Jones, email, Nov. 1, 2012; Bob Jones, Hutchens's Questionnaire, Jan. 8, 1979.

126. Black, *Come Hither*, 80; Bob Jones, email, Nov. 1, 2012.

127. **Session**: Rosenberg and Wolfe, *TMBM*, 215–16; Bob Black, email, Nov. 9, 2012. **Three of twelve**: Douglas B. Green, liner notes for *Kenny Baker Plays Bill Monroe*, County 761; author's recollection and/or personal journal. **Release**: T. Ewing, "Thirty Years Ago," *BU*, Nov. 2006, 6. According to Glen Duncan, Bill credited Buddy Spicher with developing the second part of "Road to Columbus." (Glen Duncan, email, Jan. 12, 2015.)

128. Kelly Delaney, "The Father of Bluegrass Is at Home on the Farm," *Music City News*, May 1976, 5; Wesley Decker (cattleman), conversation, Nov. 23, 2012.

129. Hume, "Daddy Bluegrass," 22–27.

130. **Recording**: Rosenberg and Wolfe, *TMBM*, 216–17. **Singing flat**: Daniel C. Scullin Jr., MD, email, Nov. 11, 2012. This radio show recording, just over twenty-five minutes in length, was released as an album, *Bill Monroe: Live Radio*, on Country Road (CR-02) in 1982 and reissued as a CD (CR-02-CD) in 2000.

131. Bob Jones, emails, Nov. 14 and Dec. 3, 2012; Paul Morris, "Wayne Lewis," *BU*, Sept. 1981, 42–43; Ron Eldridge, conversation with WSM deejay Hairl Hensley, broadcast of Sept. 9, 1996; Kenny Baker, conversation, 2010; Black, *Come Hither*, 165.

132. Adler, *Bean Blossom*, 52–53; Brown County, Indiana, Warranty Deed 8993, pp. 131–33, May 28, 1976; ad (for festival), *BU*, May 1976, 36.

133. Kingsbury, McCall, and Rumble, eds., *TE*, 209, 602; Roland, *Number One Country Hits*, 84, 117, 151, 198, 239; Rosenberg and Wolfe, *TMBM*, 217; Tom T. Hall, email, Nov. 29, 2012; T. Ewing, "Thirty Years Ago," *BU*, Sept. 2006, 6. Tom T. Hall's *The Magnificent Music Machine* (Mercury, SRM-1-1111) was released in September 1976.

134. Julia LaBella, first interview, Nov. 28, 2012; Ad (for festival), *BU*, June 1976, 41; Peter Wernick, *Bluegrass Songbook* (New York: Oak, 1976), 19.

135. Black, *Come Hither*, 166; J. LaBella, first interview, 2012; Julia LaBella, second interview, Mar. 27, 2013.

136. David Freeman, *County Sales Newsletter*, Sept.–Oct. 1976, 7; Eberhard Finke, email, Oct. 18, 2012; Rienk Janssen, email, Oct. 18, 2012; T. Ewing, "Thirty Years Ago," *BU*, Mar. 1977, 6; Neil V. Rosenberg, email, Feb. 5, 2016.

137. Black, *Come Hither*, 118–19; Bob Black, interview, Aug. 19, 2012; Bill Holden, interview, Feb. 16, 2013; Bill Holden, Hutchens's Questionnaire, 1986; liner notes for *Frost on the Pumpkin*, County 770, rel. 1977.

138. **Session**: Rosenberg and Wolfe, *TMBM*, 217. **"Cabin in Caroline"**: Rosenberg, "Flatt and Scruggs Discography: Mercury Sessions," 47. **"No Place to Pillow My Head"**: T. Ewing, "Thirty Years Ago," *BU*, Mar. 2003, 6. **"My Sweet Blue-Eyed Darling"**: J. LaBella, second interview, 2013; Donald Stauffer (brother), conversation, Jan. 10, 2013. Flatt's recording of "No Place to Pillow My Head" was released in 1973 on his *Country Boy* LP (RCA Victor, APL1-0131).

139. **Session**: Rosenberg and Wolfe, *TMBM*, 217–18. **"Monroe's Blue's"**: Black, *Come Hither*, 97–98, B. Black, interview, 2012. **"The First Whippoorwill"**: Rosenberg and Wolfe, *TMBM*, 106. **"Lucky Lady"**: Bill Monroe, liner notes for *Bill Monroe Sings Bluegrass, Body and Soul*, MCA-2251; Harless "Tootie" Williams, conversation, Apr. 3, 2013.

140. C. Daniel et al., *20th Century*, 1117.

141. J. LaBella, first interview, 2012; Julia LaBella, email, Jan. 24, 2013.

142. Julia LaBella, email, May 17, 2012; J. LaBella, first interview, 2012; J. LaBella, second interview, 2013; author's recollection and/or personal journal.

143. Nash, *Behind*, 338. The tune would later be titled "My Last Days on Earth."

144. Masuo Sasabe, email to Sandy Rothman, forwarded to author by permission, Nov. 6, 2012; Rosenberg and Wolfe, *TMBM*, 304, 306; ad (for show), *San Francisco Chronicle*, Jan. 16, 1977; Butch Waller, emails, Jan. 13 and 21, 2013; J. LaBella, second interview, 2013.

145. B. Holden, Hutchens's Questionnaire, 1986; B. Holden, interview, 2013.

146. Larry Beasley, interview, Jan. 31, 2013.

147. **Rinzler and Cantwell**: Robert Cantwell, interview, Jan. 29, 2013; Judith McCulloh, email, Feb. 9, 2013. **Observation**: Cantwell, *Breakdown*, 9–10. ***Coal Miner's Daughter***: Kingsbury, McCall, and Rumble, eds., *TE*, 294.

148. Ad (for festival), *BU*, May 1977, 30; L. Beasley, interview, 2013; Rhodes, "Monroe, the Father," 12–13.

149. "Personal Appearance Calendar," *BU*, June 1977, 50; Jim Peva, "Thirty Years of Bean Blossom Recollections," *BU*, Jan. 1998, 38.

150. L. Beasley, interview, 2013; B. Holden, interview, 2013.

151. Bobby Osborne, email, Feb. 15, 2013; Robins, *What I Know*, 125. John Oxford of Oklahoma, who made knives for Bill and Baker, said the blades were "sharp enough to cut the South Wind." (John R. Oxford, letter, *Bill Monroe International Fan Club Newsletter* 1 (Sept. 1984): 11–12.)

152. **Sessions**: Rosenberg and Wolfe, *TMBM*, 218. **Stauffer and LaBella**: J. LaBella, first interview, 2012. **"My Favorite Memory"**: Osborne Brothers Discography, Bobby Osborne and Neil Rosenberg, with additions by Sonny Osborne, Edward L. Stubbs, and Richard Weize, booklet for *The Osborne Brothers, 1956–1968*.

153. **Session**: Rosenberg and Wolfe, *TMBM*, 219. **"Pinewood Valley"**: B. Holden, interview, 2013; Barbara L. Green, "'We're Not Getting Rich, but We're Having Lots of Fun': Buddy Spicher and the Pinewood Valley Ranch," *BU*, Sept. 1978, 22–24. **"Wabash Cannon Ball"**: Ad (for Acuff-Rose agency), *Billboard*, Aug. 20, 1977, AR-20.

154. B. Holden, interview, 2013; J. Bryan, interview, 2013; Alanna Nash, "Sam Bush, New Grass Revival, and Leon Russell," *BU*, Oct. 1973, 22; Uncredited, "Personal Appearance Calendar," *BU*, Oct. 1974, 29–30; T. Ewing, "Thirty Years Ago," *BU*, May 2007, 6.

155. James Bryan, interview, Feb. 22, 2013; Al and Aleta Murphy, email to author, Feb. 5, 2013; Glen Duncan, email, Mar. 15, 2013. Bryan later recorded three of Bill's tunes ("Nanook of the North," "Monroe's Farewell to Long Hollow," and "Reelfoot Reel") on his first album, *Lookout Blues* (Rounder 0175), released in 1983. Bryan said Bill pronounced "Nanook" as "Ney-nook" and told him it was written "about a beautiful lady."

156. Otteson, "Bluegrass 'Father' Monroe," 13.

157. C. Daniel et al., *20th Century*, 1128.

158. "Donald Evans killed Thursday in car-truck accident," *OCN*, Sept. 8, 1977, 1; Rev. Mike Taylor, conversation, Mar. 6, 2013.

159. **"For Country People"**: Rooney, *Bossmen*, 34; *Newsweek* staff, "Pickin' and Singin'," 85. **Rift in the Genre**: Becky Homan, "Can Bluegrass Survive?" *Louisville Times* (*Scene* magazine), Oct. 15, 1977, 3–4.

160. Ralph Rinzler, Rinzler Archives, letter to Bill Monroe, Sept. 13, 1977; Robert Cantwell, email, Mar. 23, 2013; "Personal Appearance Calendar," *BU*, Sept. 1977, 30.

161. J. LaBella, second interview, 2013.

162. J. Bryan, interview, 2013; Rosenberg and Wolfe, *TMBM*, 306; Grisman, "Monroe Interview," 7. The tune would later be titled "My Last Days on Earth."

163. T. Ewing, "Thirty Years Ago," *BU*, Mar. 1999, 6; T. Ewing, "Thirty Years Ago," *BU*, Nov. 2007, 6; Tom Gray, emails, Mar. 19 and 20, 2013; Pete Kuykendall, email, Mar. 19, 2013; Winnie Willard, photo in "General Store," *BU*, Jan. 1978, 8; Winnie Willard-Richardson, email, Mar. 31, 2013.

164. Ad (for Monroe agency), *BU*, Dec. 1977, 5; author's recollection and/or personal journal.

165. Rosenberg and Wolfe, *TMBM*, 203, 219; Cantwell, *Bluegrass Breakdown*, 223–24; Robert Cantwell, email, Apr. 5, 2013; Julia LaBella, conversation, Apr. 6, 2013; Butch Robins, conversation, Apr. 6, 2013; Vic Gabany (*Opry* engineer), conversation, Apr. 9, 2013.

166. **Session**: Rosenberg and Wolfe, *TMBM*, 219–20. **"Six Feet Under"**: F. Brewster, interview, 2012.

167. **Session**: Rosenberg and Wolfe, *TMBM*, 220. **Act 3**: T. Ewing, "Thirty Years Ago," *BU*, Dec. 2003, 6. **Rosenthal**: Kenneth Best, "Phil Rosenthal," *BU*, Sept. 2002, 56. **"Corrina, Corrina"**: Russell, *CMR*, 236.

168. **Session/Release**: Rosenberg and Wolfe, *TMBM*, 220, 306. **Bradley's Barn**: Kingsbury, McCall, and Rumble, *TE*, 47. **"Golden River"**: Russell, *CMR*, 392. **"Those Memories"**: Kingsbury, McCall, and Rumble, *TE*, 391.

169. Joe Edwards, "The 'Father of Bluegrass' Just Can't Give It Up," *Miami Herald*, Mar. 5, 1978, 8L.

170. Rosenberg and Wolfe, *TMBM*, 221, 309; J. Bryan, interview, 2013; Uncredited (Marion Kuykendall), "General Store," *BU*, Apr. 1978, 14; Ad (for Monroe Recording Co.), *BU*, May 1978, 14; James Monroe, conversation, Apr. 12, 2013; Ad (for County Sales), *BU*, Sept. 1984, 37. Five selections from *Satisfied Mind* were included on *James and Bill Monroe: Bluegrass Special Memories*, Raintree, RR-599D, a CD released in 1999.

171. Julia LaBella, email, Apr. 1, 2013.

172. Ad (for festival), *BU*, June 1978, 27; McCloud et al., *DC*, 671; Don Wayne Reno, "In Memoriam," *Banjo Newsletter*, Dec. 1996, 5; Mike Drudge, "The Reno Brothers: Continuing a Musical Legacy," *BU*, Dec. 1990, 29.

173. "The F-5L Mandolin—A Turning Point in the History of Gibson's Acoustic String Instruments," Roger Siminoff, http://www.mandolincafe.com; Roger Siminoff, conversation, June 8, 2013; Dan Del Fiorentino, email, June 10, 2013.

174. Rosenberg and Wolfe, *TMBM*, 309; ad (for County Sales), *BU*, Aug. 1978, 31. That summer, leadership of the Bill Monroe Fan Club passed to Lynda Bowman, then of Meadows of Dan, Va. Unfortunately, Ms. Bowman could not be located. (Uncredited [Marion Kuykendall], "General Store," *BU*, July 1978, 8.)

175. Doug Hutchens, conversation, Apr. 23, 2013; Uncredited (Marion Kuykendall), "General Store," *BU*, Oct. 1978, 9; Uncredited (Marion Kuykendall), "General Store," *BU*, Dec. 1978, 8.

176. Lambert (with Sechler), *Lester Flatt*, 70, 72, 77; Uncredited (Marion Kuykendall), "General Store," *BU*, Mar. 1979, 11–12; Don Rhodes, "Carrying On without Lester," *BU*, Nov. 1979, 34.

177. Bill Monroe, remarks recorded June 16, 1979, during recording of *Bill Monroe: Bean Blossom '79*, MCA 3209; Rosenberg and Wolfe, *TMBM*, 221–22; James Bryan, Hutchens's Questionnaire, Apr. 1979.

178. Ad (for festival), *BU*, June 1979, 75; Robins, *What I Know*, 137; Adler, *Bean Blossom*, 138; Raymond Huffmaster, email, Apr. 17, 2002.

179. "Personal Appearance Calendar," *BU*, June 1979, 47; Mark Hembree, interview, May 8, 2013; Mark Hembree, email, May 12, 2013.

180. **Renovation of cabin and "the little house"**: Julia LaBella, third interview, July 15, 2013. **Improvements**: Carlos Brock, conversation, Aug. 5, 2013. **James's house**: James Monroe, conversation, Aug. 7, 2013.

181. Ad (for festival), *BU*, Aug. 1979, 52; Doug Hutchens, conversation, May 16, 2013; Marty Godbey, "Blue Grass Boy Turns Detective," *BU*, July 1979, 46.

182. Ad (for festival), *BU*, Sept. 1979, 38; author's recollection and/or personal journal.

183. Mary Starkey, first interview, May 26, 2013. A photograph of Starkey with Bill, taken at Frontier Ranch in 1972, is included in Fleischhauer and Rosenberg's *Bluegrass Odyssey* (p. 156).

184. "Personal Appearance Calendar," *BU*, Sept. 1979, 41; "About Ford's, 1978–1987," http://www.fordstheatre.org; Robins, *What I Know*, 140; *Time*, Oct. 15, 1979.

185. McCloud et al., *DC*, 736–37; Ivan Tribe, email, May 29, 2013; James William Skinner (son), email, June 2, 2013; Jimmie Skinner, "He Knew," liner notes for Bill Monroe, *Bluegrass Memories*, MCA 2315. On the back cover of *Bluegrass Memories*, the last word in the poem's third line ("sing") is corrected here.

186. "Personal Appearance Calendar," *BU*, Dec. 1979, 39–40; Eipper, "Bill Monroe's Mandolin," 29; Rendal Wall, email, June 22, 2013.

CHAPTER EIGHT. 1980–1989

1. Author's survey, "Personal Appearance Calendar," *BU*, Jan.–Apr. 1980.

2. Larry Sledge, conversation, Aug. 2, 2013; Norman Blake, conversation, July 31, 2013. The unnamed tune mentioned here would later be titled "My Last Days on Earth." Bill donated the mandolin under the bed, a 1964 Gibson F-5 (serial number 181350) and a hat given to him by Lester Flatt, to the Country Music Hall of Fame in the summer of 1981 (Uncredited [Marion Kuykendall], "General Store," *BU*, Sept. 1981, 10; John Rumble, email, Aug. 8, 2013).

3. Lee Rector, "Monroe's Mandolin Is Also Legendary," *Music City News*, Apr. 1980, 17.

4. C. Daniel et al., *20th Century*, 1171, 1174; Simon Winchester, email, June 21, 2013.

5. Ad (for festival), *BU*, May 1980, 9; Calvin Robins obituary, *BU*, July 1980, 11; Robins, *What I Know*, 19, 152–54.

6. Ads (for shows), *OCT*, June 26, 1980, 14; July 17, 1980, 3; Oct. 16, 1980, 2; Dawn Jones, "Letters" ("Bean Blossom—People Helping People"), *BU*, Sept. 1980, 6.

7. "Bluegrass Museum Proposed," *OCT*, July 17, 1980, 1; Belinda Mason, "Monroe Unhappy with Ohio County," *OCT-N*, Aug. 4, 1983, 1A.

8. Uncredited (Marion Kuykendall), "General Store," *BU*, Sept. 1980, 10; "Monroe Opens Bluegrass Club," *Tennessean (Showcase)*, July 27, 1980, 33; James Monroe, conversation, July 5, 2013.

9. Uncredited (Marion Kuykendall), "General Store," *BU*, Sept. 1980, 11; Rendal Wall, email, June 22, 2013. Bill can be seen playing the F5-L on August 7, 1980, when he and the band and Doc Watson played for President and Mrs. Carter on the South Lawn of the White House, on the final segment of *The Mandolin of Bill Monroe* instructional video (VD-MON-MN01).

10. Ad (for festival), *OCT*, Aug. 21, 1980, 15A.

11. Jim Hatlo, "Monroe's Mandolin" in *The Big Book of Bluegrass: The Artists, The History, The Music*, edited by Marilyn Kochman (New York: GPI, 1984), 21; Rendal Wall, email, June 22, 2013; Hatlo, "Bill Monroe's Mandolin," 37; Eipper, "Bill Monroe's Mandolin," 29.

12. "Personal Appearance Calendar," *BU*, Nov. 1980, 46–47; "Monroe's Bluegrass Remains a Cut Above," *San Jose (Calif.) Mercury*, Nov. 18, 1980, 1E–2E.

13. C. Daniel et al., *20th Century*, 1182.

14. Richard Thompson, email, July 17, 2013; Michael Toland (manager, National Productions, KLRU-TV, Austin, Texas), email, July 17, 2013; "Austin City Limits," http://en.wikipedia.org/wiki/Austin_City_Limits.

15. Ad (for festival), *BU*, Nov. 1980, 41; C. Daniel et al., *20th Century*, 1183.

16. Uncredited (Marion Kuykendall), "General Store," *BU*, Feb. 1981, 9; Kingsbury, McCall, and Rumble, *TE*, 277.

17. Robins, *What I Know*, 157.

18. **Sessions**: Rosenberg and Wolfe, *TMBM*, 246–47. **"Old Ebenezer Scrooge"**: Julia LaBella, conversation, Aug. 8, 2013; Leonard Maltin, ed., *Leonard Maltin's 2012 Movie Guide* (New York: Penguin, 2011), 246. **"Come Hither to Go Yonder"**: Julia LaBella, conversation, Aug. 8, 2013. **"Right, Right On"**: Bill Monroe and the Blue Grass Boys, live recording, Feb. 1979, http://www.youtube.com. **"Lochwood"**: Ad (for festival), *BU*, Sept. 1972, 18. **"Old Dangerfield"**: Julia LaBella, conversation, Aug. 8, 2013. **"Fair Play"**: Ibid. **"Melissa's Waltz for JB" and "Lady of the Blue Ridge"**: Larry Sledge, conversation, Aug. 2, 2013. LaBella said that while on the road with Bill, she saw a Catholic church named Our Lady of the Blue Ridge and suggested it to him as a possible title for a tune he had written. **Untitled tune**: Larry Sledge, conversation, Aug. 2, 2013; Norman Blake, conversation, July 31, 2013; Mark Hembree, interviewed by Joseph Gray, Mar. 27, 2011, Video Oral History Collection, IBMM; Sandy Rothman, emails, Aug. 15 and 16, 2013. This untitled tune was later titled "My Last Days on Earth." **"Evening Prayer Blues"**: Morton with Wolfe, *DeFord Bailey*, 67.

19. J. LaBella, third interview, 2013.

20. **Bill and LaBella**: J. LaBella, third interview, 2013. **Cancer diagnosis**: Daniel C. Scullin Jr., MD, emails, Aug. 8 and 10, 2013. **Quote from Bill**: Nash, *Behind Closed Doors*, 339. **Releases**: David Freeman, *County Sales Newsletter* 111 (March 1981): 4, and 112 (May–June 1981): 3.

21. **Recuperation**: J. LaBella, third interview, 2013; author's recollection and/or personal journal. **Opry**: Wendell Allen, "Rosine Society News," *OCT-N*, Apr. 2, 1981, 9A.

22. Uncredited (Marion Kuykendall), "General Store," *BU*, Apr. 1981, 9; James Monroe, conversation, Mar. 3, 2014; Terry Heaton (newsman who filmed at the site), email, Mar. 8, 2014.

23. **Showdates**: "Personal Appearance Calendar," *BU*, Apr. 1981, 84–86. **Mixing session**: Rosenberg and Wolfe, *TMBM*, 247. **Bill's approval**: J. LaBella, third interview, 2013. **McElhiney**: Walt Trott, "Trumpet Player's Final bow," *NM*, Apr.–June 2002, 18. **Quote**: Ray Edlund, "A Talk with the Master—Bill Monroe," *Bluegrass Breakdown*, May/June 1982, 14. **String players**: Rosenberg and Wolfe, *TMBM*, 247; "Conni Ellisor," http://ellisormusic. com. According to Rosenberg and Wolfe, Bill's "My Last Days" was "used in a popular movie, *All the Pretty Horses*" (released in 2000). However, it is not Bill's recording in the film's soundtrack but rather similar-sounding mandolin playing by Marty Stuart. (Rosenberg and Wolfe, *TMBM*, 225; Maltin, ed., *Movie Guide*, 27–28.)

24. **Bean Blossom**: Adler, *Bean Blossom*, 142; Glen Duncan, emails, Aug. 21, 2013. On June 12, 1981, MCA released Bill's last 45 rpm single, "My Last Days on Earth" / "Come Hither to Go Yonder" (51129), the latter's title corrected before the release of *Master of Bluegrass* (Rosenberg and Wolfe, *TMBM*, 304).

25. Robins, *What I Know*, 159–63, 183–84; Uncredited, "Personal Appearance Calendar," *BU*, June 1981, 72, and July 1981, 48; Rosenberg and Wolfe, *TMBM*, 307; Paul Kovac, emails, Apr. 7, 2014.

26. R. C. Harris, interview, 2012; Michelle Putnam, "Blake Williams: The Sparta Flash," *BU*, Jan. 1990, 54–55; Blake Williams, emails, Aug. 27, 2013.

27. David Freeman, *County Sales Newsletter* 114, Sept.–Oct. 1981, 3; Rosenberg and Wolfe, *TMBM*, 56, 296.

28. **Appearance**: Uncredited (Marion Kuykendall), "General Store," *BU*, Nov. 1981, 8; "Personal Appearance Calendar," *BU*, Sept. 1981, 50–51; Kimberly Williams, email, Sept. 2, 2013. **Sanders**: "Col. Harland Sanders," http://en.wikipedia.org/wiki.Colonel_Sanders; Nash, *Behind*, 341.

29. **Musicland festivals**: "Bluegrass Festival Planned," *OCT-N*, May 26, 1981, 10-B; ad (for festival), *OCT-N*, July 23, 1981, 13A; "Monroes to Speak at Local Museum," *OCT-N*, Sept. 3, 1981, 4B. **Brown Co. Jamboree**: Tom Adler, email, Mar. 20, 2013; Uncredited (Marion Kuykendall), "General Store," *BU*, Jan. 1982, 5. **Moving to farm**: J. LaBella, third interview, 2013.

30. Kingsbury, McCall, and Rumble, *TE*, 218–19; Blake Williams, email, Sept. 11, 2013; author's recollection and/or personal journal.

31. James Monroe, conversation, Sept. 13, 2013; Wendell Allen, "Rosine Personals," *OCT-N*, Feb. 18, 1982, 7A; Damon Black, letter to Ralph Rinzler, Feb. 20, 1982, RR343, box 9.

32. Wendell Allen, "Rosine Society News," *OCT-N*, Mar. 11, 1982, 6A; Merlene Austin, conversation, Mar. 29, 2013.

33. Darrel Dukes, conversation, Sept. 18, 2013; Wendell Allen, "Rosine Society News," *OCT-N*, May 6, 1982, 12B; "Monroe Stricken," *OCT-N*, May 6, 1982, 13B; Blake Williams, email, Dec. 5, 2014; Commonwealth of Kentucky Certificate of Death, 116-82-10187; John D. Miller (festival attendee), conversation, June 21, 2014; Uncredited, "Farewell to Music Legend," *OCT-N*, May 20, 1982, 1A.

34. Birch Monroe obituary, *BU*, June 1982, 4; Adler, *Bean Blossom*, 144.

35. Doug Fulmer, "Ronnie and Rob McCoury: Sons of Tradition," *BU*, Feb. 1994, 63; Ronnie McCoury, email, July 20, 2010.

36. "National Heritage Fellowship Award," http://en.wikipedia.org/wiki/National_Heritage_Award; Rosenberg and Wolfe, *TMBM*, 225–27. Ten of the recordings discussed here were released twenty-four years later in a Bear Family boxed set, *Bill Monroe: Bluegrass 1981–1994, My Last Days on Earth*, BCD 16673.

37. Julia LaBella, fourth interview, Sept. 25, 2013; Daniel C. Scullin Jr., MD, emails, Sept. 27 and 28, 2013; Mark Hembree, email, Sept. 27, 2013; Blake Williams, email, Sept. 30, 2013.

38. J. LaBella, fourth interview, 2013.

39. Godbey, "Happy Birthday, Bill Monroe," 14–16; Doug Hutchens, emails, Oct. 3, 2013. Bill would use this mandolin case throughout the rest of his career.

40. Toru Mitsui, email, Sept. 1, 2013; John Rumble, email, Sept. 3, 2013. The remaining unreleased Decca recording, 1962's "Big Ball in Brooklyn," was finally released in 1991 in the Bear Family boxed set *Bill Monroe: Bluegrass, 1959–1969* (BCD-15529).

41. James Monroe, conversation, Sept. 13, 2013; Ralph Rinzler, letter (to himself), dated Oct. 4, 1982, Rinzler Archives, RR343, box 9.

42. Dan Mazer, "Kathy Chiavola," *BU*, July 1993, 55–56; Kathy Chiavola, first interview, Apr. 23, 2015.

43. Jack Hurst, "Mandolin Music Mellows Burns-Monroe 'Feud,'" *Chicago Tribune*, Nov. 26, 1982; Kenneth "Jethro" Burns, "'Cept Old Bill," Athens Music, recorded July 18, 1983, and released on *Jethro Burns and Red Rector: Old Friends*, Rebel Records (REB-1626).

44. Rosenberg and Wolfe, *TMBM*, 227–28, 249–51; Vic Gabany, emails, Oct. 13 and 14, 2013; Kingsbury, McCall, and Rumble, *TE*, 602. Overdubbed harmony vocals on "Old Riverman" were sung by Randy Thompson and Kathy Chiavola. Chiavola had recorded many "demo" sessions at Walter Haynes's studio (K. Chiavola, interview, Apr. 23, 2015).

45. Uncredited (Marion Kuykendall), "General Store," *BU*, Mar. 1983, 10–11.

46. Henry, "Bessie Lee Mauldin," 37.

47. Havighurst, *Air Castle*, 237, 240; Kingsbury, McCall, and Rumble, *TE*, 575–56; Escott, *Grand Ole Opry*, 214; Blake Williams, second interview, Jan. 9, 2014.

48. **Tour itinerary**: Uncredited, "Personal Appearance Calendar," *BU*, Apr. 1983, 60–61. **Recording**: Rosenberg and Wolfe, *TMBM*, 251. **Grand Marshall**: Uncredited (Marion Kuykendall), "General Store," *BU*, July 1983, 10; "Pegasus Parade," http://en.wikipedia.org/wiki/Pegasus_Parade.

49. Rosenberg and Wolfe, *TMBM*, 227, 251, 306; Uncredited (Marion Kuykendall), "General Store," *BU*, March 1983, 10. *Bill Monroe and Friends* was in *Billboard*'s "Top Country LPs" chart for six weeks, peaking in March 1983 at an extremely modest number 61 (of 75). It was Bill's last appearance in the music business magazine's charts (Whitburn, *Top Country Albums*, 110).

50. Morton with Wolfe, *DeFord Bailey*, 1–11; David C. Morton, conversation, Oct. 21, 2013.

51. Beth Tweedell, "The Telluride Bluegrass and Country Music Festival," *BU*, June 1984, 70; Edlund, "Monroe—The Master Speaks," 8.

52. Ad (for tour), *BU*, Apr. 1983, 58; "Grand Ole Gospel Time," http://www.jimmys-now.com/grand.html; Blake Williams, first interview, Oct. 17, 2013; Melinda Williams, "Bill Monroe in Israel," *BU*, Nov. 1983, 46. In the latter, banjoist Wendy Holcombe and saxophonist Donnie "Sax" Sanders were mentioned as opening acts at the concerts.

53. Dee Dee Prestige (Diana Christian), first and second interviews, Oct. 24 and 25, 2013; "Dee Dee Prestige," http://flutterbear.org/contact-Us.html.

54. B. Williams, first interview, 2013; M. Williams, "Bill Monroe in Israel," 46; Mark Hembree, email, Aug. 5, 2013.

55. Ad (for festival), *BU*, Mar. 1983, 94; Mason, "Monroe Unhappy," 20A; Belinda Mason, "Festival a Success . . . Almost," *OCT-N*, Aug. 4, 1983, 1A; Wendell Allen, "Rosine Society News," *OCT-N*, Aug. 4, 1983, 4A.

56. "Personal Appearance Calendar," *BU*, Sept. 1983, 55; B. Williams, first interview, 2013. According to James Monroe, the Musicland Park property was sold, a few lots at a time, by 1997. (James Monroe, conversation, Oct. 28, 2013.)

57. Sandy Rothman, "Bill Monroe's Birthday Party," *BU*, Dec. 1983, 32–33. Doug Hutchens continued to organize birthday salutes to Bill through 1989, when his teaching duties forced him to stop. Celebrations were held at different locations with a variety of gifts, but always including a new Randy Priest felt hat and a specially decorated card of well-wishes (Doug Hutchens, email, Apr. 14, 2014).

58. **Session**: David Davis, conversation, Oct. 16, 2013; Robert Montgomery, email, Mar. 10, 2014; Uncredited (Fred Geiger), "General Store," *BU*, Dec. 1983, 8–9. The recordings discussed here were not released until 1993, on a cassette titled *The Early Days of Bluegrass: A Tribute to the Father of Bluegrass*. It was privately issued by Thurmond several years after he asked Davis to take over leadership of the Warrior River Boys.

59. Arthur Menius, "A Bluegrass Hall of Fame," *BU*, Feb. 1984, 10; Register of Deeds, Davidson Co., Tenn., Deed Book 6169, p. 673. Donations were solicited for a "Walkway of Stars" and a statue, but not enough money was raised to pay for the latter.

60. Rosenberg and Wolfe, *TMBM*, 251; "The Bottom Line," http://www.bottomline cabaret.com. The set would be released in 1999 on a CD titled *Lookin' Back* (Silver Eagle, SEA-CD-70007).

61. **January 1984**: "Personal Appearance Calendar," *BU*, Jan. 1984; author's recollection and/or personal journal. **SPBGMA**: "SPBGMA," www.spbgma.com/about/index.html; Nancy Cardwell, "SPBGMA: Indoor Event Pioneers," *BU*, Jan. 1993, 78.

62. Rosenberg and Wolfe, *TMBM*, 228, 253, 287n30.

63. Ad (for museum), *BU*, Apr. 1984, 67; Hutchens, "The Bill Monroe Museum," 10–11, 31–34; Ewing, ed., *Bill Monroe Reader*, 168–69; Glen Duncan, email, Nov. 4, 2013; Diana Christian, conversation, Nov. 6, 2013; "Monroe Vows Caution after Incidents," *Nashville Banner*, Dec. 18, 1985, A15.

64. Mark Hembree, email, Nov. 4, 2013; Kingsbury, McCall, and Rumble, *TE*, 355–56; Thigpen, "Clarence 'Tater' Tate," 39; Blake Williams, conversation, Mar. 3, 2014. Williams took over Hembree's duties selling Bill Monroe merchandise at "the record table" at this point (Blake Williams, email, Dec. 15, 2014).

65. Ad (for County Sales), *BU*, Sept. 1984, 37; Diana Christian, conversation, Nov. 6, 2013; Carolyn Monroe, Tennessee Dept. of Health and Environment, Certificate of Death, file 84-021461.

66. **Festival**: "Personal Appearance Calendar," *BU*, Aug. 1984, 50; "Rains Hurt Attendance at Bluegrass Festival," *OCT-N*, Aug. 9, 1984, 1A, 16A. **LP**: Ad (for County Sales), *BU*, Oct. 1984, 51.

67. Pugh, *Ernest Tubb*, 84–85, 311–13.

68. *Bill Monroe International Fan Club Newsletter* 1 (Sept. 1984): 2–5, 18–19.

69. "Personal Appearance Calendar," *BU*, Oct. 1984, 53; Kenny Baker, interviewed by Randall Franks for "Southern Style" (a syndicated newspaper column), Feb. 22, 2006; Blake Williams, email, Nov. 10, 2013; Blake Williams, conversation, Mar. 3, 2014.

70. Roland, *Number One Country Hits*, 469, 511, 557, 590.

71. **Hawaii**: Uncredited (Fred Geiger), "General Store," *BU*, Jan. 1985, 10. **Bluegrass 45**: "Bluegrass 45," *bluegrass45.com*. **In Japan**: Kohei Yoshida (photographer), *Bill Monroe* (souvenir photo book) (Hyogo, Japan: BOM, 1985); Tatsuya Imai, email, Oct. 1 and 2, 2006.

72. **Franks**: Randall Franks, interview, Nov. 19, 2013. **McInturff**: Lundy, "Bill Monroe," 20. Randy Franks, email, Mar. 3, 2014.

73. C. Daniel et al., *20th Century*, 1238, 1249.

74. Dale Morris, interview, Nov. 12, 2013.

75. **LP and single**: Rosenberg and Wolfe, *TMBM*, 299; Roland, *Number One Country Hits*, 421–22. **Filming**: Nash, *Behind*, 341; Ricky Skaggs with Eddie Dean, *Kentucky Traveler: My Life in Music* (New York: HarperCollins, 2013), 249.

76. Skaggs with Dean, *Kentucky Traveler*, 248.

77. D. Morris, interview, 2013.

78. **Duncan**: Walt Trott, "Hoosier Glen Duncan, a Man of Varied Music Skills," *NM*, July–Sept. 2006, 19–20; Glen Duncan, first interview, Dec. 16, 2013; Kathy Chiavola, second interview, May 20, 2015.

79. G. Duncan, first interview, 2013; Wolmuth, "Bio," 54; "Evangel Temple," http://jimmysnow.com/evangel.html; "Bill Monroe Weds In Quiet Ceremony," *Tennessean*, 1D; Glen Duncan, email, May 1, 2016.

80. **Recordings**: Rosenberg and Wolfe, *TMBM*, 229–30, 253–55; G. Duncan, first interview, 2013; Black, *Come Hither*, 41–42; Charlie Sizemore, email of Jan. 12, 2014. **Hall of Famers**: Hutchens, "Bill Monroe Museum," 31–32. **Digital Technology**: Emory Gordy Jr., conversation, Dec. 23, 2013; Emory Gordy Jr., emails, Dec. 28, 2013–Jan. 1, 2014.

81. "Personal Appearance Calendar," *BU*, July 1985, 63–67; Lawrence Waltman, photo (courtesy of), *BU*, Oct. 1985, 59.

82. "Bluegrass Fest Aug. 9–11," *OCT-N*, Aug. 1, 1985, 1A; ad (for festival), *OCT-N*, July 24, 1986, 4A.

83. G. Duncan, first interview, 2013; B. Williams, second interview, 2014; Robert Sherborne, "Bill Monroe Believes He May Be in Danger," *Tennessean*, Dec. 18, 1985, 1A and 14A; author's recollection and/or personal journal.

84. Sherborne, "Bill Monroe Believes," 14A.

85. **Vandalism**: Thomas Goldsmith and Donna Dearmore, "Bill Monroe's trademark mandolin vandalized," *Tennessean*, Nov. 15, 1985, 2E; "Bill Monroe Break-In," *BU*, Dec. 1985, 8; Hazel Smith, "People" ("It's a Crying Shame"), *Country Music*, Mar./Apr. 1986,

19. **Aftermath**: Bill Monroe, remarks recorded Nov. 15, 1985, Nightstage nightclub, Cambridge, Mass., author's collection; Roger Siminoff, "Bill Monroe's F-5: Worst-Case Repair," *Frets*, Feb. 1986, 40; B. Williams, second interview, 2014; Glen Duncan, second interview, Jan. 6, 2014; Susan Derrington (wife), conversations, Feb. 17 and 20, 2014; B. Hawkins, interview, 2003; Evan Reilly, email, Jan. 23, 2014. **Christmas**: Uncredited (Fred Geiger), "General Store," *BU*, Jan. 1986, 12. The fireplace poker was part of a set given to Bill for his birthday that year by the Blue Grass Boys (Hutchens, email, Apr. 14, 2014).

86. Sherborne, "Bill Monroe Believes," 1A and 14A; G. Duncan, first interview, 2013.

87. B. Williams, second interview, 2014; author's recollection and/or personal journal.

88. G. Duncan second interview, 2014; B. Williams, second interview, 2014.

89. Trott, "Hoosier Glen Duncan," 20; G. Duncan, second interview, 2014; Marty Godbey, "The Lost Fiddler: Art Stamper," *BU*, Nov. 1982, 24–25.

90. Charmaine Lanham, "Bill Monroe's Mandolin Is Restored," *BU*, Apr., 1986, 40–41; Hatlo, "Bill Monroe's Mandolin," 37; David Harvey, conversation, Jan. 29, 2014; author's recollection and/or personal journal. Bill never recorded "The Lloyd Loar," but it was recorded by Skip Gorman on *The Old Style Mandolin, Vol. 2: Monroesque* (Old West 002), released in 2003 (Skip Gorman, email, Feb. 4, 2014). Derrington and crew would take their time on Bill's other Loar (72214), returning it to him in May 1986 without fanfare (author's recollection and/or personal journal).

91. B. Williams, second interview, 2014; Paul Brown, "An Interview with Art Stamper," *Old-Time Herald*, Winter 2000/2001, 24.

92. Author's recollection and/or personal journal; Rosenberg and Wolfe, *TMBM*, 231, 256; G. Duncan, first interview, 2013; "Personal Appearance Calendar," *BU*, Dec. 1983, 55.

93. Rosenberg and Wolfe, *TMBM*, 256; Chris Hirsch, email, Jan. 11, 2014; Stewart Evans, emails, Feb. 12, 2004, and Jan. 26, 2014.

94. **Session**: Rosenberg and Wolfe, *TMBM*, 104, 257; G. Duncan, second interview, 2014. **CDs**: Uncredited (Fred Geiger), "General Store," *BU*, May 1986, 17; "Compact Disc," http://en.wikipedia.org/wiki/Compact_Disc.

95. **Montgomery**: Author's recollection and/or personal journal; Johnny Montgomery, interview, July 23, 2013.

96. Michelle Putnam, "Wayne Lewis: Portrait of a Blue Grass Boy—Then and Now," *BU*, Feb. 1988, 18; author's recollection and/or personal journal.

97. Cleo Davis obituary, *BU*, Sept. 1986, 20; Uncredited (Al Steiner), "General Store," *BU*, Dec. 1986, 13; author's recollection and/or personal journal.

98. **Session**: Rosenberg and Wolfe, *TMBM*, 257; Emory Gordy Jr., emails, Feb. 7, 2014. **"God Holds the Future"**: Russell, *CMR*, 632, 749. **"Farther On"**: Ibid., 194. **"The Old Crossroad/Crossroads"**: Rosenberg and Wolfe, *TMBM*, 72. When Bill and the band taped the Nashville Network's "New Country" on November 11, 1986, they performed "God Holds the Future" and "Farther On," then still possible inclusions for Bill's "new album" (*Bluegrass '87*). "God Holds the Future in His Hands" was later included in the Bear Family boxed set *My Last Days on Earth* (author's recollection and/or personal journal; ad [for County Sales], *BU*, Aug. 1987, 54).

99. Ad (for festival), *OCT-N*, Aug. 21, 1986, 13-B; ad (for festival), *BU*, Aug. 1986, 43.

100. Promotional flier, 1986 Camp Springs, N.C., festival (courtesy Mark Squires); Mike Wilson, email, Feb. 19, 2014; ads (for festivals), *BU*, Aug. 1981, 23; Aug. 1982, 73; Aug. 1983, 30; Aug. 1984, 3; Aug. 1985, 3; Mark Squires, interview, Feb. 10, 2014.

101. Wolmuth, "Bio," 48–50, 53–54; David Grisman, George Gruhn, Jim Hatlo, and John McGann, "Bill Monroe at 75," *Frets*, Sept. 1986, 30–32, 37–44, 53.

102. **Cake**: Uncredited (Al Steiner), "General Store," *BU*, Nov. 1986, 12. **Montgomery and Tate**: author's recollection and/or personal journal. **Squires**: M. Squires, interview, 2014; Mark Squires, emails, Feb. 11, 2014; author's recollection and/or personal journal.

103. Ad (for festival), *BU*, Sept. 1986, 2; Wayne Lewis, conversation, Feb. 24, 2014; author's recollection and/or personal journal; President Ronald Reagan, letter to Bill Monroe, Sept. 10, 1986, "General Store," *BU*, Nov. 1986, 12; Jack Leiderman, conversation, Feb, 23, 2014.

104. Billy Joe Foster, interviewed by Alan Munde, Dec. 8, 2009 (part 1), Video Oral History Collection, IBMM; author's recollection and/or personal journal.

105. Adler, *Bean Blossom*, 167–68; Frank Overstreet, "Ashes of Bean Blossom," *BU*, Apr. 1987, 47.

106. Author's recollection and/or personal journal; Billy Joe Foster, 2009 interview (part 2), V.O.H.C., IBMM.

107. Author's recollection and/or personal journal.

108. Author's recollection and/or personal journal; Wolmuth, "Bio," 54.

109. Rachel Liebling, booklet notes for *High Lonesome: The Story of Bluegrass Music* (soundtrack CD), CMH, CD-8007; Rosenberg and Wolfe, *TMBM*, 238; Rachel Liebling, emails, Mar. 11 and July 7, 2014.

110. Author's recollection and/or personal journal; James Monroe, ed., *Bill Monroe: 50 Years of Music*, self-published, Nashville, Tenn., 1986. The booklet's cover art was drawn by commercial artist Hsieh Ke-Yi, known as "Jim" Hsieh (1944–2008), a native of China who lived and worked in the Nashville area (see "Jim Hsieh: drawing.painting.music," http://jh44.wordpress.com/about).

111. Author's recollection and/or personal journal; "Hemphill Brothers Coach Company," http://en.wikipedia.org/wiki/Hemphill_Brothers_Coach_Company.

112. Author's recollection and/or personal journal; Dixie Hall, compiler and editor, *The Animaland Cookbook, Vol. II: Pet Project of the Stars* (Nashville, Tenn.: Animaland, 1993), 99. (Bill's recipe was reprinted in *The Bluegrass Music Cookbook*, compiled by Penny Parsons, Ken Beck, and Jim Clark and published in Winston-Salem, N.C., by John F. Blair in 1997.)

113. "Divorces Filed," *News-Examiner* (Gallatin, Tenn.), 10A; Circuit Court of Sumner Co., Tenn., Divorce Decrees, 168: 379.

114. Billy Joe Foster, 2009 interview (part 2), V.O.H.C., IBMM.; Daniel C. Scullin Jr., MD, email, June 5, 2014; Author's recollection and/or personal journal.

115. Author's recollection and/or personal journal.

116. Willard C. "Woody" Allen, conversation, March 25, 2014.

117. Author's recollection and/or personal journal; Roland White, conversation, March 27, 2014.

118. Author's recollection and/or personal journal; Adler, *Bean Blossom*, 168–71.

119. Blake Williams, email, March 27, 2014; Billy Joe Foster, 2009 interview (part 2), V.O.H.C., IBMM; author's recollection and/or personal journal.

120. Author's recollection and/or personal journal; Daniel C. Scullin Jr., MD, email, Apr. 2, 2104.

121. Billy Joe Foster, 2009 interview (part 2), V.O.H.C., IBMM; Mike Feagan, interview, Apr. 16, 2014.

122. Author's recollection and/or personal journal; *Bill Monroe Fan Club Newsletter* 8 (May 1987): 22.

123. Author's recollection and/or personal journal.

124. Doug Hutchens, emails, Feb. 1, 2013, Apr. 11, 2014, and Apr. 2, 2015. Designed by West Virginia artist Fred Huffman, the belt buckles were fabricated by Award Design Medals of Noble, Oklahoma, near Oklahoma City.

125. Joe Stuart obituary, *BU*, Oct. 1987, 13.

126. Author's recollection and/or personal journal; M. Feagan, interview, 2014.

127. Author's recollection and/or personal journal.

128. "Grammy Lifetime Achievement Award," http://en.wikipedia.org/wiki/Grammy_Lifetime_Achievement_Award; Rosenberg and Wolfe, *TMBM*, 258; McCloud et al., *DC*, 837. On an unknown date in 1987, Bill recorded two instrumental tunes, via overdubbing, for an album by guitarist Glenda Faye Kniphfer, a member of the Right Combination, the all-girl band of session producer Porter Wagoner. "Down Yonder" and "Ozark Rag," the latter one of Bill's original compositions for guitar, were released in late 1987 on *Glenda Faye: Flatpickin' Favorites*, Flying Fish, FF 432.

129. Author's recollection and/or personal journal.

130. Rosenberg and Wolfe, *TMBM*, 258, 305–6; author's recollection and/or personal journal.

131. Rosenberg and Wolfe, *TMBM*, 233, 258–59; author's recollection and/or personal journal.

132. Rosenberg and Wolfe, *TMBM*, 259; author's recollection and/or personal journal; Blake Williams, email, Apr. 4, 2014.

133. Rosenberg and Wolfe, *TMBM*, 259; Roberta Cude, "Wayne Jerrolds: Tennessee Fiddler," *BU*, Sept. 1982, 26–28; Wayne Jerrolds, interview, May 10, 2014; author's recollection and/or personal journal. Jerrolds has since retitled his song "Blue Tennessee Waltz."

134. Rosenberg and Wolfe, *TMBM*, 234, 259–60; Brett F. Devan, "Bobby Smith and the Boys from Shiloh: Pioneer Second Generation Artist," *BU*, Nov. 1984, 14; Putnam, "Blake Williams," 54; author's recollection and/or personal journal.

135. Rosenberg and Wolfe, *TMBM*, 260; author's recollection and/or personal journal; Emory Gordy Jr., emails, Feb. 17, 2004, and Apr. 29, 2014. Producer Gordy, hoping to set the record straight about the albums, wrote to the author and emphasized the techniques that were *not* used to record them: "Bill did no overdubbing, did not use headphones on anything, and did not sing additional vocal takes on open tracks of the master tape."

136. Author's recollection and/or personal journal; James Monroe, conversation, Apr. 30, 2014.

137. Author's recollection and/or personal journal.

138. Author's recollection and/or personal journal; *Acts of the General Assembly of the Commonwealth of Kentucky*, 1988, 346.

139. Ad (for sale of park), *BU*, Apr. 1988, 86; author's recollection and/or personal journal.

140. Author's recollection and/or personal journal; Billy Joe Foster, 2009 interview (part 2), V.O.H.C., IBMM; M. Feagan, interview, 2014.

141. Author's recollection and/or personal journal; Michelle Putnam, "Bill Monroe: A Tradition Ends, A New Venture Begins," *BU*, Aug. 1988, 55.

142. Dee Dee Prestige (Diana Christian), second interview, 2013; author's recollection and/or personal journal.

143. Author's recollection and/or personal journal; Billy Joe Foster, conversation, Oct. 11, 2004.

144. Ad (for festival), *BU*, June 1988, 66; Putnam, "Bill Monroe," 54.

145. Author's recollection and/or personal journal.

146. Author's recollection and/or personal journal; Charlie Appleton, "'Womanizing' Led to Monroe Tussle, Ex-Girlfriend Says," *Nashville Banner*, May 3, 1989, A1.

147. Author's recollection and/or personal journal.

148. Author's recollection and/or personal journal; Billy Joe Foster, 2009 interview (part 3), V.O.H.C., IBMM.

149. Ad (for festival), *BU*, Sept. 1988, 27; Author's recollection and/or personal journal; MaryE Yeomans, email, Mar. 18, 2017; B. Spicher, interview, 2014.

150. Author's recollection and/or personal journal; C. Daniel et al., *20th Century*, 1322; Circuit Court of Sumner Co., Tenn., Divorce Decrees 68:383.

151. Author's recollection and/or personal journal; W. Jerrolds, interview, 2014.

152. Author's recollection and/or personal journal; Roberta Roberts Cude, "The Boone Creek Bluegrass Band," *BU*, Sept. 1987, 31–34; Scottie Baugus, interview, May 14, 2014.

153. **The Ploy**: Jack Hurst, "He's Just Plain Bill," *Chicago Tribune*, Sept. 16, 1988, 1B; ad (for festival), *BU*, Jan. 1989, 20, and February 1989, 31. **Grammy**: Wendell Allen, "Rosine Happenings," *OCT-N*, Jan. 19, 1989, 5A.

154. "Grammy Award," http://en.wikipedia.org/wiki/Grammy.com; Rosenberg and Wolfe, *TMBM*, 234; author's recollection and/or personal journal.

155. S. Baugus, interview, 2014; Scottie Baugus, email, May 21, 2014.

156. Billy Rose, first interview, May 21, 2014; author's recollection and/or personal journal.

157. Thomas Goldsmith and John Watson, "Woman Says *Opry*'s Monroe Kicked Her, Hit Her with Bible," *Tennessean*, May 3, 1989, 1A; Appleton, "Womanizing," A1, A8; *San Francisco Chronicle*, May 4, 1989.

158. "Steve Buchanan: Protector of All Things *Opry*" by Cindy Watts, http://blogs.tennessean.com/tunein/2014/02/02; author's recollection and/or personal journal.

159. Catherine Thompson, "Charges against Monroe Dropped," *Tennessean*, May 11, 1989, 4A; Donna Davis, "Monroe glad assault charge behind Him," *Nashville Banner*, May 11, 1989, B1.

160. Author's recollection and/or personal journal; James Monroe, conversation, May 20, 2014; McCloud et al., *DC*, 300–301; ad (for James Monroe), *BU*, Sept. 1994, 85.

161. Author's recollection and/or personal journal; Rosenberg and Wolfe, *TMBM*, 296. The recording the band made that day was released ten years later on *Bill Monroe: Live from Mountain Stage* (Blue Plate Music, BPM-400).

162. **Bean Blossom**: Black, *Come Hither*, 140; Rosenberg and Wolfe, *TMBM*, 262–63. **Rosine**: B. Rose, first interview, 2014; Rachel Liebling, email, May 25, 2014; Steve Geary (son), conversation, May 28, 2014; Rosenberg and Wolfe, *TMBM*, 263.

163. Author's recollection and/or personal journal; Black, *Come Hither*, 143; Sandra Wohlers (Bear Family), email, May 30, 2014; Ellie Pesavento (agent), GroundSpeed tour schedule, July 29–31, 1989; Liz Meyer, booklet notes for *Far across the Blue Water: Bill Monroe in Germany (1975 and 1989)*, BCD 16624 EK, 46; Rosenberg and Wolfe, *TMBM*, 263–65. *Far across the Blue Water*, released in 2004, includes an audio recording of the Streekermoor show on two CDs, a DVD with an amateur video of the show, and an interview with Bill on July 31, 1989.

164. Ad (for County Sales), *BU*, Oct. 1989, 58; Dick Spottswood, "Bear Family: Doing It Right," *BU*, Mar. 1994, 42.

165. Author's recollection and/or personal journal. Liebling's documentary film, *High Lonesome: The Story of Bluegrass Music*, premiered two years later, in 1991. It was released on videotape in 1994 and on DVD in 1997.

166. Larry Smith, "Country Gold Hits Japan," *Performance*, Oct. 27, 1989; Billy Rose, conversation, June 2, 2014; Blake Williams, email, June 3, 2014; Toru Mitsui, email, June 7, 2014; author's recollection and/or personal journal.

167. Rosenberg and Wolfe, *TMBM*, 278, 306, 310; author's recollection and/or personal journal; author's collection, "Bill Monroe's 50th Anniversary," Nashville Network production, Oct. 28, 1989; Daniel C. Scullin Jr., MD, email, Dec. 15, 2014. "Kentucky King," co-written by Larry Cordle and Jim Rushing, was recorded by Cordle, Glen Duncan, and Lonesome Standard Time in March 1992 for their *Lonesome Standard Time* CD (Sugar Hill, SH-CD-3802). Bill played mandolin on a "Watermelon Hangin' on the Vine" tagged ending for it.

168. Don Rhodes, "Bill Monroe: Still a Star, Still a Good Guy," *Augusta (Ga.) Chronicle*, Nov. 19, 1989, 8D; Joe Edwards, "Bluegrass Veteran Monroe Still Celebrates Milestones," *Columbus (Ohio) Dispatch*, Dec. 17, 1989, 3G; author's recollection and/or personal journal.

169. Author's recollection and/or personal journal; Blake and Kimberly Williams, emails, June 9 and 10, 2014; Daniel C. Scullin Jr., MD, email, Dec. 15, 2014.

CHAPTER NINE. 1990–1996

1. Author's recollection and/or personal journal; "Bruce Hornsby," http://en.wikipedia.org/wiki/Bruce_Hornsby; Uncredited (Murphy Henry), "General Store," *BU*, Mar. 1990, 19.

2. "Farm Aid," http://en.wikipedia.org/wiki/Farm_Aid; author's recollection and/or personal journal; Escott, *Grand Ole Opry*, 205.

3. Author's recollection and/or personal journal; Diana Christian, conversation, June 17, 2014; Javonda Charlene Smith, first interview, Oct. 21, 2014; Javonda Charlene Smith, third interview, Nov. 11, 2014.

4. Rosenberg and Wolfe, *TMBM*, 236–37, 266–67, 276.

5. "Briefly," *OCT-N*, May 31, 1990, 1A; Steve Geary (son), conversation, June 20, 2014; Uncredited (possibly Wendell Allen), "Rosine Happenings," *OCT-N*, June 7, 1990, 4B.

6. Steve Gebhardt, interview, June 20, 2014.

7. Rosenberg and Wolfe, *TMBM*, 271–76, 308; S. Gebhardt, interview, 2014; Ad (for festival), *BU*, May 1990, 67; Steve Gebhardt, emails, June 27, 29, and 30, 2014; Jacky Christian, conversation, July 7, 2014. Gebhardt's *Bill Monroe, Father of Bluegrass Music* was released on videotape in 1993 and on DVD in 1999.

8. Billy Rose, second interview, Sept. 11, 2014; Uncredited (Murphy Henry), "General Store," *BU*, Nov. 1987, 13; Rosenberg and Wolfe, *TMBM*, 266–67; Johnny Campbell (brother), email, Sept. 12, 2014.

9. Author's recollection and/or personal journal; McCloud, *DC*, 437–38, 1018; John Rumble, email, Sept. 19, 2014.

10. Diana Christian, conversation, Oct. 4, 2014.

11. J. C. Smith, first interview, 2014; Melissa Monroe obituary, *BU*, Jan. 1991, 14; Daniel C. Scullin Jr., MD, emails, Oct. 26 and 28, 2014; Julia LaBella, fifth interview, Nov. 17, 2014; Denise (Painter) Easter, interview, Oct. 14, 2014.

12. Peter V. Kuykendall, "Editorial," *BU*, July 1991, 26; "Death Notices," *Tennessean*, Dec. 4, 1990, 5B; author's recollection and/or personal journal.

13. Stanley, *Man of Constant Sorrow*, 419; Javonda Charlene Smith, second interview, Oct. 28, 2014.

14. Author's recollection and/or personal journal.

15. Bill Monroe, personal communication with author; LaBella, fifth interview, 2014.

16. **Millard:** North Carolina Death Index, 1931–1994 (accessed from http://www. myheritage.com); Wayne Erbsen, "Tommy Millard," 25. **Bill:** J. C. Smith, second interview, 2014; Daniel C. Scullin Jr., MD, email, Nov. 8, 2014. The Bear Family's second boxed set of Bill's Decca recordings, *Bill Monroe: Bluegrass 1959–1969*, BCD 15529, was released in the spring of 1991 (ad [for County Sales], *BU*, June 1991, 68).

17. Adler, *Bean Blossom*, 175; Murphy Henry, "General Store," *BU*, Aug. 1991, 17; Author's recollection and/or personal journal.

18. Lowinger, *I Hear a Voice*, 57–58.

19. J. C. Smith, second interview, 2014.

20. D. (Painter) Easter, interview, 2014; author's recollection and/or personal journal; Robins, *What I Know*, 186; J. C. Smith, second interview, 2014. Without Bill, between August 9 and September 1, 1991, the Blue Grass Boys played an *Opry* matinee and the Opryland Bluegrass Festival with Terry Eldredge (then with the Osborne Brothers) singing tenor and chopping mandolin, and three shows in Ohio, Virginia, and Maryland with Ricky Skaggs substituting for Bill.

21. Author's recollection and/or personal journal; Blake Williams, emails, March 3, Nov. 18, and Dec. 15, 2014; Adler, *Bean Blossom*, 164, 173.

22. Author's recollection and/or personal journal; Daniel C. Scullin Jr., MD, email, Nov. 24, 2014; Eleanor Reid, letter to *Bill Monroe Fan Club Journal*, Dec. 1991, 14; Peva, *Bean Blossom: Its People and Its Music*, 73; Murphy Henry, "General Store," *BU*, July 1991, 12.

23. **Changes:** James Monroe, conversations, Dec. 2 and 4, 2014; author's recollection and/or personal journal; Adler, *Bean Blossom*, 176; Peva, *Bean Blossom: Its People and Its Music*, 39. **Cabin:** "The Cabin's Gone," *OCT-N*, Oct. 31, 1991, 1A, 4A; Merlene Austin, conversation, Dec. 17, 2014.

24. Author's recollection and/or personal journal; "Bypass Surgery and Memory," http://www.health.harvard.edu./fhg/updates/update0206c.shtml; Peva, *Bean Blossom*, 75.

25. Author's recollection and/or personal journal; Rosenberg and Wolfe, *TMBM*, 279, 307; ad (for Homespun Video), *BU*, Jan. 1993, 57; Susan Robinson (Homespun), email, Jan. 2, 2015. *The Mandolin of Bill Monroe, Video One* (VD-MON-MN01) was released in late 1992 with a companion *Video Two* (VD-MON-MN02), an analysis by former newgrass nemesis Sam Bush.

26. Mike Kelley, liner notes for *Ralph Stanley: Saturday Night and Sunday Morning*, Charles R. Freeland, CD-9001; Rosenberg and Wolfe, *TMBM*, 278, 288, note 71; "Charles R. Freeland (1938–2014)," http://www.legacy.com/obituaries/washingtonpost/obituary.aspz?pid=172138142. The two songs were released together in 1992 on the two-CD set *Ralph Stanley: Saturday Night and Sunday Morning*, CD-900127, and separately on cassettes: *Saturday Night*, CT-640, and *Sunday Morning*, CT-643.

27. LaBella, fifth interview, 2014.

28. Ad (for festival), *BU*, June 1992, 87; Author's recollection and/or personal journal. The Hall of Fame and Museum at Bean Blossom finally opened on September 4, 1992, during an under-advertised and poorly attended country music "Legends" weekend.

29. Lowinger, *I Hear a Voice*, 58–59, 60.

30. Author's recollection and/or personal journal; Neil V. Rosenberg, email, Jan. 12, 2015.

31. Kingsbury, McCall, and Rumble, *TE*, 63; Ronnie Pugh, booklet notes for *Carl Butler: A Blue Million Tears*, Bear Family, BCD 16118 AH, 13.

32. Author's recollection and/or personal journal.

33. C. Daniel et al., *20th Century*, 1388; "William Howard Taft," http://en.wikipedia.org/William_Howard_Taft; "Bill Clinton," http://en.wikipedia.org/Bill_Clinton.

34. Schlappi, *Roy Acuff*, 56–57.

35. Author's recollection and/or personal journal.

36. Author's recollection and/or personal journal.

37. Author's recollection and/or personal journal; Robert Bowlin, interview, Feb. 2, 2015.

38. Author's recollection and/or personal journal; R. Bowlin, interview, 2015.

39. "Lifetime Achievement Award," http://www.grammy.org/recording-academy/awards/lifetime-awards.

40. Ad (for festivals), *Bill Monroe Fan Club* (newsletter), Mar. 1993, unnumbered p. 5; ad (for festivals), *BU*, Apr. 1993, 95; author's recollection and/or personal journal.

41. Stanley, *Man of Constant Sorrow*, 418.

42. Author's recollection and/or personal journal; Ernie Sykes, interview, Feb. 13, 2015; Lowinger, *I Hear a Voice*, photo 34, 66; Gene Lowinger, email, Feb. 13, 2015. In his memoir, Lowinger included a photo of Sykes warming up with the band before the Huntington

show. Sykes guested on a couple of tunes, singing and playing bass while Tate twinned with Bowlin.

43. Lowinger, *I Hear a Voice*, 69–70; E. Sykes, interview, 2015; Gene Lowinger, email, Feb. 14, 2015; author's recollection and/or personal journal.

44. Author's recollection and/or personal journal; "Nashville Now," http://en.wikipedia. org/wiki/Nashville_Now; Havighurst, *Air Castle*, 245.

45. **True Believer:** Vic Gabany, emails, Jan. 27, 2012, and Feb. 22, 2015; author's recollection and/or personal journal. **CDs:** ad (for County Sales), *BU*, Nov. 1993, 46.

46. Author's recollection and/or personal journal; Rosenberg and Wolfe, *TMBM*, 261, 268.

47. Rosenberg and Wolfe, *TMBM*, 281–82; Vic Gabany, email, Feb. 25, 2015; Robert Bowlin, email, Mar. 7, 2015; author's recollection and/or personal journal; Bill Monroe, personal communication with author; "Discography" website, Pennell (compiler).

48. Ad (for tour), *BU*, Jan. 1994, 12; James Monroe, conversation, Mar. 2, 2015; Jimmy Zmudka (booking agent), conversation, Mar. 1, 2015.

49. J. C. Smith, third interview, 2014.

50. Author's recollection and/or personal journal; Daniel C. Scullin Jr., MD, email, Mar. 3, 2015.

51. Daniel C. Scullin Jr., MD, email, Apr. 1, 2015; Claire Levine, "The Northwest's Rainy Season and How Bluegrass Fans Survive: Wintergrass," *BU*, Jan. 1995, 28.

52. B. Hawkins, interview, 2003; Julia LaBella, conversation, Mar. 2, 2015; author's recollection and/or personal journal.

53. Mary Starkey, second interview, Mar. 4, 2015; Daniel C. Scullin Jr., MD, email, Mar. 5, 2015.

54. Author's recollection and/or personal journal; Ad (Feller Brown: for Bill's farm), *Tennessean*, Apr. 10, 1994; M. Starkey, second interview, 2015; ad ("May the Circle Be Unbroken: The Truth about Bill and James Monroe"), *BU*, Sept. 1994, 85.

55. **Auction:** Glen Duncan, third interview, Mar. 15, 2015. **Bidding:** James Monroe, conversation, Mar. 18, 2015. **Price:** Mary Starkey, conversation, Mar. 16, 2015. In April 1994, Bear Family released the third boxed set of Bill's Decca-MCA recordings, *Bill Monroe: Bluegrass 1970–1979*, BCD 15606 DI (ad [County Sales], *BU*, June 1994, 44).

56. Rosenberg and Wolfe, *TMBM*, 187, 282–83; author's recollection and/or personal journal; ad (for MCA recording), *BU*, Aug. 1994, 29. Only one tune from the Gabany sessions, "Boston Boy," was released by MCA in July 1994 on a Country Music Foundation–produced four-CD set, *The Music of Bill Monroe from 1936 to 1994*, MCAD4-11048.

57. Christine Kreyling, "Hallowed Hall: Saving the Ryman, We Saved Our Own Soul," *Nashville Scene*, Sept. 8, 1994, 7–9; Havighurst, *Air Castle*, 243; ad (for Ryman shows), *BU*, May 1994, 45; Kingsbury, McCall, and Rumble, *TE*, 602; Jay Orr, "Monroe, Krauss Ring in Summer Bluegrass Concert Series," *Banner*, June 15, 1994, C1; Tom Roland, "Two Blades of Bluegrass Grow at Ryman Auditorium," *Tennessean*, June 15, 1994, 4D.

58. Author's recollection and/or personal journal.

59. Richard Kurin, "'So Long, It's Been Good to Know You: A Remembrance of Festival Director Ralph Rinzler," 1995 Festival of American Folklife program booklet, 12; Smithsonian Institution for Folklife Programs and Cultural Studies, *Ralph Rinzler: A*

Celebration of Life, video of 1994 memorial service, Washington, D.C., released 1995; Julia LaBella, conversation, March 11, 2015.

60. Tommy Goldsmith, "Bill Monroe and Earl Scruggs: Together Again," *BU*, Sept. 1994, 9; author's recollection and/or personal journal.

61. Rosenberg and Wolfe, *TMBM*, 284; K. Chiavola, first interview, 2015. "Stay Away from Me" was released in 1996 on *The Harvest* by Kathy Chiavola, Demon Records, FIENDCD 779.

62. Javonda Charlene Smith, *Bill Monroe and Friends: Inside the Life of Bill Monroe* (West Conshohocken, Pa.: Infinity, 2008), 75–91; Charlene Smith, email, Mar. 27, 2015; Julia LaBella, Bill Monroe's 1994 birthday party invitation, author's collection; Sandy Rothman, email, Mar. 13, 2015.

63. Rosenberg and Wolfe, *TMBM*, 284–85; Butch Robins, email, Mar. 28, 2015; Mike Compton, emails, Apr. 26, May 27, and May 28, 2015.

64. Author's recollection and/or personal journal; James W. Monroe II, interview, June 10, 2015; James W. Monroe II, email, June 12, 2015.

65. Rosenberg and Wolfe, *TMBM*, 285; Byron Berline, email, May 28, 2015; Daniel C. Scullin Jr., MD, email, June 3, 2015; author's recollection and/or personal journal. Byron Berline's *Fiddle and A Song* (Sugar Hill, SH-CD-3838) was released in 1995.

66. Rosenberg and Wolfe, *TMBM*, 258, 285; Walt Saunders, "Notes and Queries," *BU*, Mar. 2011, 14; Gary Brewer, conversation, June 5, 2015. Gary Brewer's *Guitar* (Copper Creek, CCCD-0137) was released in 1995.

67. Author's recollection and/or personal journal; Levine, "Wintergrass," *BU*, Jan. 1995, 28–29; Daniel Gore, "With Body and Soul: Notes from Wintergrass '95," *BU*, Feb. 1996, 50–51.

68. Author's recollection and/or personal journal; Lonnie Jones, interview, July 2, 2015.

69. Rosenberg and Wolfe, *TMBM*, 244, 285–86; Mike Compton, emails, June 30 and July 14, 2015. Jimmy Campbell's *Pieces of Time* (Red Clay Records, RC-CD-113) was released in 1996.

70. Vic Gabany, email, Dec. 16, 2015.

71. Declaration by the House of Representatives of the Commonwealth of Kentucky, dated Apr. 30, 1995; proclamation by Brereton C. Jones, governor of the Commonwealth of Kentucky, Apr. 28, 1995.

72. Author's recollection and/or personal journal.

73. "Big Plans for Old Barn," *OCT-N*, Apr. 9, 1992, 1A, 16A; Mason, "Monroe Unhappy," 20A; Hoyt and Eleanor Bratcher, interview, July 22, 2015.

74. "Personal Appearance Calendar," *BU*, June 1995, 82; Vic Gabany, email, Dec. 16, 2015; Vic Gabany (recordist), live recording, "Bill Monroe/Kenny Baker Reunion, Bean Blossom, 1995."

75. Author's recollection and/or personal journal; Daniel C. Scullin Jr., MD, email, Mar. 30, 2015.

76. Mary Starkey, third interview, Aug. 13, 2015; Julia LaBella, conversation, Aug. 18, 2015.

77. David Blackburn, "Bill Monroe's Biggest Booster Shares His Passion for Rosine," *Owensboro (Ky.) Messenger-Inquirer*, July 16, 2001, 1C, 3C; Brad Allen, ed., *Blue Moon*

News, Mar. 1996 (vol. 6), 1–2; Aaron Hutchings, interview, Aug. 20, 2015; Frances Harvey, conversation, Aug. 21, 2015.

78. Steve Vied, "Monroe Plays, Sings, Even Dances as Plaque Honoring Him Is Unveiled," *Owensboro Messenger-Inquirer*, Sept. 22, 1995, 1A, 2A; Julia LaBella, conversation, Aug. 18, 2015; Dudley Cooper (then Ohio County judge-executive), conversation, Aug. 25, 2015; Eleanor Bratcher, conversation, Aug. 26, 2015; Jim Peva, conversation, Aug. 30, 2015; Bill Wallace, conversation, Aug. 31, 2015.

79. Becky Johnson, email, Aug. 21, 2015; Richard Thompson, email, Aug. 28, 2015. Becky Johnson's photograph of Bill lifting the award to Heaven appeared in the November 1995 issue of *BU* on page 9.

80. Videotape of Bill Monroe at the Ole Barn, Rosine, Ky., Sept. 22, 1995; Vied, "Monroe Plays," 2A; Julia LaBella, conversation, Aug. 18, 2015; Text of National Medal of Arts certificate; "National Medal of Arts," https://en.wikipedia.org/wiki/National_Medal_of_Arts. The presentation ceremony is available online at: http://www.c-span.org/video/?67492–1/national-arts-humanities-awards.

81. Julia LaBella, conversation, Jan. 3, 2016.

82. Author's recollection and/or personal journal. Bill played his last show on the road at the Shaumburg, Ill., Center for the Arts on Nov. 10, 1995, with Mike Bub filling in on bass for Tate.

83. Kathy Seibel, first interview, Jan. 7, 2016.

84. Author's recollection and/or personal journal; Daniel C. Scullin Jr., MD, email, Oct. 27, 2015.

85. Gore, "With Body," 50–51; author's recollection and/or personal journal.

86. Pete Kuykendall, conversation, Jan. 23, 1996; "Letters," *BU*, Mar. 1996, 9; Jack Flippen, "Nobody Does It Like Bill," *BU*, Apr. 1996, 38–43. In the summer of 1996, former Blue Grass Boy Sandy Rothman self-published the first edition of *True Life News*, a newsletter that included several letters not published by *Bluegrass Unlimited*.

87. LaBella, fifth interview, 2014.

88. Author's recollection and/or personal journal; Billy Smith, conversation, Nov. 19, 2015; Rosenberg and Wolfe, *TMBM*, 286–87, 325.

89. Author's recollection and/or personal journal; Kingsbury, McCall, and Rumble, eds., *TE*, 394.

90. *Friday Night Opry*, audio recording of eight o'clock show, Mar. 15, 1996, Vic Gabany, recordist.

91. James Monroe, conversation, Dec. 19, 2015; author's recollection and/or personal journal.

92. Author's recollection and/or personal journal.

93. **Location:** "Bill Monroe Moves to Another Hospital," *Tennessean*, Apr. 13, 1996. **Pacemaker:** Daniel C. Scullin Jr., MD, email, Nov. 22, 2015. **Visit:** Author's recollection and/or personal journal; Ernie Sykes, conversation, Dec. 18, 2015.

94. Peva, *Bean Blossom*, 75; D. (Painter) Easter, interview, 2014; Julia LaBella, email to Sandy Rothman, Mar. 8, 2002.

95. **Beverly:** Author's recollection and/or personal journal; Seibel, first interview, 2016. **Northcrest:** James Monroe, conversation, Jan. 10, 2016. The Beverly Healthcare and Rehabilitation Center is now the "Golden Living Center."

96. Kathy Seibel, second interview, Jan. 12, 2016; Seibel, first interview, 2016.

97. Kathy Seibel, letter to Sandy Rothman, postmarked Sept. 27, 1996; Seibel, second interview, 2016.

98. Kathy Seibel, third interview, Jan. 14, 2016; Wilma Millsaps, conversation, Jan. 22, 2016.

99. Kathy Seibel, second and third interviews, 2016.

100. Kathy Seibel, second and third interviews, 2016; Seibel, letter, Sept. 27, 1996.

101. John Keith, "The Last Time I Saw Mr. Monroe," The Bluegrass Blog (website), Nov. 29, 2010; John Keith, conversation, Jan. 24, 2016; Melvin Goins, conversation, Jan. 24, 2016.

102. Kathy Seibel, second interview, 2016; Seibel, letter, Sept. 27, 1996; Kathy Seibel, third interview, 2016.

103. Kathy Seibel, letter to Sandy Rothman, postmarked Dec. 30, 1996.

104. State of Tennessee, Office of Vital Records, death certificate of William Smith Monroe; Kathy Seibel, third interview, 2016. The quotation from the Bible first appears in Psalms 98:4.

SELECTED BIBLIOGRAPHY

Adler, Thomas A. *Bean Blossom: The Brown County Jamboree and Bill Monroe's Bluegrass Festivals*. Urbana: University of Illinois Press, 2011.

Black, Bob. *Come Hither to Go Yonder: Playing Bluegrass with Bill Monroe*. Urbana: University of Illinois Press, 2005.

Daniel, Clifton, and John W. Kirshon, eds. *20th Century Day by Day: The Ultimate Record of Our Times*. London: Dorling Kindersley, 2000.

Havighurst, Craig. *Air Castle of the South: WSM and the Making of Music City*. Urbana: University of Illinois Press, 2007.

Kingsbury, Paul, ed., with the assistance of Laura Garrard, Daniel Cooper, and John Rumble. *The Encyclopedia of Country Music: The Ultimate Guide to the Music*. Compiled by the staff of the Country Music Hall of Fame and Museum. New York: Oxford University Press, 1998.

Kingsbury, Paul, Michael McCall, and John W. Rumble, eds. *The Encyclopedia of Country Music*, 2nd ed. Compiled by the staff of the Country Music Hall of Fame and Museum. New York: Oxford University Press, 2012.

McCloud, Barry, et al. *Definitive Country: The Ultimate Encyclopedia of Country Music and Its Performers*. New York: Berkley Publishing Group, 1995.

Nash, Alanna. *Behind Closed Doors*. New York: Knopf, 1988.

Rinzler, Ralph. "Bill Monroe." In *Stars of Country Music: Uncle Dave Macon to Johnny Rodriquez*, edited by Bill Malone and Judith McCulloh. Urbana: University of Illinois Press, 1975.

Rooney, James. *Bossmen: Bill Monroe and Muddy Waters*. New York: Dial, 1971.

Rosenberg, Neil V. *Bluegrass: A History*. Urbana: University of Illinois Press, 1985.

Rosenberg, Neil V., and Charles K. Wolfe. *The Music of Bill Monroe*. Urbana: University of Illinois Press, 2007.

Russell, Tony. *Country Music Records: A Discography, 1921–1942.* New York: Oxford University Press, 2004.

Wolfe, Charles K. *A Good-Natured Riot: The Birth of the Grand Ole Opry.* Nashville: Country Music Foundation Press, 1999.

INDEX

Acuff, Roy, 72, 75; "Great Speckled Bird," 77, 136; on *Opry*, 87; recorded "Mule Skinner Blues," 110; first *Opry* tent show, 113; demanded higher pay, 136–37; and Keith's banjo picking, 252; Lifetime Achievement Award, 421; death, 444

Adcock, Eddie, 218

Akeman, Dave ("Stringbean"), 117–18; banjo playing style, 120; as baseball player, 123; in army, 129; teamed with Childre, 129; featured with Bill, 148; coached ball team, 151; murder of, 340

"Alabama Waltz" (song), 159

albums, 113–14; of Rodgers songs, 167, 169; with Martin, 177, 179; "LP," 208. *See also specific album titles*

Aldrin, Edwin ("Buzz"), Jr., 309

Allen, Harley ("Red"), 176, 252; audition, 293

Allen, Wendell (Rosine historian), 50; Fleishhauer and Rothman visit, 333; Charlie Monroe Day, 353; Charlie Monroe Festival, 354; Rosine Band, 354; comment, 435

Allen, Willard C. ("Woody," state representative), 417

"All the Good Times Are Past and Gone" (song), 72, 290

"Along About Daybreak" (song), 143, 153; LP release, 400

American Banjo Tunes and Songs in Scruggs Style (Folkways album), 209–10, 249

Andrew Jackson Hotel, 165, 181

Andrews, Jim, 129, 131

"Angels, Rock Me to Sleep" (song), 167, 410

Antioch College (Yellow Springs, Ohio), first bluegrass concert, 228

Arkansas Democrat (newspaper), 76, 77, 78

Arkie, Arkansas Woodchopper (Luther Ossenbrink), 48, 54, 57

Arkin, Steve, 269, 270

Armstrong, Neil, 309

Ash Grove (folk music club), 256, 281; bands filled in at, 293; Fowler as bartender at, 336; burned down, 348

"Ashland Breakdown" (tune), 349

Ashley, Clarence ("Tom"), 228

Atchison, Shelby ("Tex"), 54, 354–55

Atkins, Bobby, 234, 235

Atkins, John, liner notes, 351–52

Atlanta, Ga., 67, 78, 111, 114

Atlanta Journal (newspaper), 78

Atteiram Records, 342–43

Austin City Limits (TV show), 382, 408

"Back Up and Push" (tune), 131, 149

Bailey, DeFord, 110, 116, 395

Baize, Cleve, 16

Baize, Leora, 35, 61

Baker, Billy, 229, 234, 260

Baker, Johnnie, 399

Baker, Kenny, 197; in and out of band, 213, 218, 247, 252, 257, 297, 369, 400–401; mention of Uncle Pen's tunes, 213–14; living in little house, 214; sang baritone, 216; played shows with Bill, 239; first original tunes recorded, 249; first solo album, 301; finding replacements, 344; and Tom Ewing, 358–59; cut hand, 365; reunited with Bill, 457

"Baker's Breakdown" (tune), 249

Ball, Lucille, 174

"Banks of the Ohio" (song), 331

barrel house (Sinclair Oil Refinery), 47

Bartenstein, Fred, 301, 318, 359

baseball: William Monroe as shortstop, 4; Bill first played, 23–24; Charlie and, 31, 47; Bill's tent show, 123; game in Rosine, 148; Bill's plans for 1949, 151; Russell Petty, 160–61; in songbook, 165; 1951 season, 167

Baugus, Scottie, 427, 428

Bean Blossom (album, MCA), 340

Bean Blossom bluegrass festivals. See Monroe's Bean Blossom bluegrass festivals

Beasley, Larry, 363, 364

Beatles, 264–65

"A Beautiful Life" (song), 73

Beaver Dam, Ky., 2

Bell Cove (nightclub): Bill sitting in, 421; filming High Lonesome, 431; birthday parties, 452

"Ben Dewberry's Final Run" (song), 169; released in Japan, 356

Benson, Doug: arranged appearances, 282, 288–89; interviews, 288–89; Bluegrass Unlimited installments, 296–97

Berline, Byron, 277–78; told Bill about draft, 291; on album cover, 294; session, 295; left band, 296; Bill recorded with, 453

Berryman, Winifred (great-great-grandmother), xvi

Bessire, Jim: as house band bassist, 233; as helper, 275; as road manager for James,
399; as manager of Bill Monroe Museum, 399; as road manager for Bill, 440; and Bowlin, 444; and Starkey, 449; visited Bill at Medical Center, 464

The Best of Bill Monroe (album, MCA), 352

Best of Bill Monroe and His Blue Grass Boys (album, MCA, released in Europe only), 351–52

Beverly Healthcare and Rehabilitation Center (Springfield, Tenn.): Bill taken to, 465; Millsapses visited, 465; Goins band played, 466; Bill and Seibel, 465, 466, 467

Beverly Hillbillies (TV show), theme song, 247

"Beyond the Gate" (song), 315

"Big Ball in Brooklyn" (song), 240

"Big Mon" (tune), written and forgotten, 202; resurrected, 222

Big Plans: first, Monroe Bluegrass Musicland Park, 346; second, Monroe Manor, 351, 380, 385; third, Bill Monroe Museum and Bluegrass Hall of Fame, 398, 399; fourth, Bill Monroe's Bluegrass Country, 415, 424; fifth, Uncle Pen's cabin reconstruction and new stage, 441; sixth, monthly festivals at Bean Blossom, 445

"Big River" (song), 231

"Big Sandy River" (tune), 249, 255

"Bile Them Cabbage Down" (song), Opry audition, 85

Bill and James Monroe's Festival Park and Campground, 443. See also Brown County Jamboree Park

Billboard charts: "Most Played Juke Box Folk Records," 131, 153; "Best Selling Retail Folk Records," 149; "Best-Selling Retail," 150; "Hot C & W Sides," 221, 223; country singles, 247; announcement, 260–61

Bill Monroe: Bean Blossom '79 (album, MCA), 374–75

Bill Monroe: Columbia Historic Edition (album, Columbia), 400

Bill Monroe: 50 Years of Music (commemorative booklet), 415

Bill Monroe: The Classic Recordings, Vols. 1 & 2 (albums, County/CBS Records), 385

Bill Monroe and Charlie Monroe (album, Decca), 303

Bill Monroe and Friends (album, MCA), 394

Bill Monroe & James Monroe: Father & Son (album, MCA), 330–31, 336

Bill Monroe and Kentuckians (newspaper listing), 77, 78

Bill Monroe and Stars of the Bluegrass Hall of Fame (album, MCA), 405

Bill Monroe and the Bluegrass Boys: Live at the Opry (CD and cassette, MCA), 429, 432; Grammy nomination, 434

Bill Monroe and the Boys, 454

"Bill Monroe Appreciation Day," 455

Bill Monroe Associates (Rinzler's agency), 257, 258

Bill Monroe Bluegrass Festival (Ohio County, Ky.): preliminary proclamation, 394; first, 397; second, 400; third as Bill's last, 405–6

Bill Monroe Bluegrass Hall of Fame and Museum, 399; construction began, 441. *See also* Bill Monroe Museum and Bluegrass Hall of Fame

Bill Monroe—Bluegrass 1950–1958 (boxed set, Bear Family), 431

Bill Monroe Bluegrass Special (bootleg albums, BS1 and BS3), released, 360

Bill Monroe Fan Club: Johnson as founder, 286; Mowery as president, 299; Leonard as president, 309; Ramsey as president and Stamey as vice president, 400; *Newsletter* ad, 445

Bill Monroe Museum and Bluegrass Hall of Fame, 398–99, 415. *See also* Bill Monroe Bluegrass Hall of Fame and Museum

Bill Monroe's Best (album, Harmony-Columbia), 268

Bill Monroe's Bluegrass Country ("the Club"), 415, 424, 426, 429

Bill Monroe's Blue Grass Country Songs (songbook), 164–65

Bill Monroe's Country Music Hall of Fame (album, Decca), 322

Bill Monroe's Greatest Hits (album, Decca), 299

Bill Monroe Singles Collection (album, Japanese Victor), 392

Bill Monroe Sings Country Songs (album, Vocalion-Decca), 266

Bill Monroe's Uncle Pen (album, Decca), 333

Bill Monroe's WSM Grand Ole Opry Song Folio No. 1 (songbook), 140

Bill Monroe's WSM Grand Ole Opry Song Folio No. 2 (songbook), 182–83

Bill Monroe with Lester Flatt and Earl Scruggs: "The Original Bluegrass Band" (album, Rounder), 373–74

"Bill's Dream" (tune), 266

Birmingham, Ala., 78

Black, Bob: hired, 346–47; early morning calls, 350; nickname, 357; let go, 360–61; touring with Bill, 430–31

Black, Damon: pitched song to James, 304; "Tall Pines," 311; asked to write Bill's biography, 388; James dissatisfied, 392

Black Poodle (nightclub), 284, 285, 288

Blackwell, Curtis, 291

Blake, Norman and Nancy: picking sessions with Bill, 379–80; Norman recording with Bill, 383

Bluebird (RCA Victor record label), 54; and Jimmie Rodgers, 55; new recordings, 55; sessions without Monroe Brothers, 73–74; first session with Bill and Blue Grass Boys, 111–12; first Bill Monroe release, 112

"Blue Goose" (tune), 365

Bluegrass (book, Artis), 349–50

Bluegrass: A History (book, Rosenberg), 332, 333

The Blue Grass All-Stars (road baseball team), 168

The Blue Grass Ballclub (Nashville baseball team), 168

Blue Grass Boys: demands of road, 109; backed Smith, 110; baseball, 123; Flatt, Scruggs, and Wise, 138; after Bill's wreck, 182; Bill's favorite "game," 205; dogs ate better than, 206; worked on Bill's farm, 213; Rinzler's advice, 264–65; recruited son James, 269; auditioning, 271; played without Bill, 273; Bill's outlook on, 291; matching outfits, 297; built the stage, 298; birthday salutes, 391, 397–98; played without pay, 396–97; dedicated Birch's tombstone, 397; and wives at wedding, 404; boycotted benefits, 456; played *Opry* without Bill, 463; visited Bill at Medical Center, 464. *See also* fill-ins

Bluegrass Breakdown (book, Cantwell), 5, 324–25, 370

"Bluegrass Breakdown" (bus nickname), 277, 280, 282, 293

"Blue Grass Breakdown" (tune), 141, 142, 150

Bluegrass Classics Radio Shows 1946–48 (bootleg album, BGC 80), 387

Bluegrass Country (TV show), 335

Bluegrass '87 (album, MCA), 411, 416

Bluegrass Express tours, 330, 335

Bluegrass Fan Fest (IBMA), 426. *See also* Bluegrass with Class

Bluegrass Festival of the United States, birthday salute at, 387. *See also* Kentucky Fried Chicken Festival

Bluegrass Instrumentals (album, Decca), 275

Bluegrass Memories (album, MCA), 365

bluegrass music, xv, 35; and Bill's guitar playing, 111; growing popularity of, 116; Wise and, 119; naming of, 167; Rinzler on, 210; Seeger on, 224; Lomax on, 225; Bill's "My Life in," 308; growing mainstream acceptance, 310; Bill's *Newsweek* comment about, 317; Bill's observation about friends, 371; Bill on different playing styles, 395–96

Bluegrass Musicland Park. *See* Monroe's Bluegrass Musicland Park

"The Bluegrass (Music) Story" (at Haney's festivals), 279, 280, 287, 301; sixth and last, 318

"Blue Grass Part 1" (tune), 232; retitled, 237

Blue Grass Quartet, 84, 87–88, 151, 164, 251

Bluegrass Ramble (album, Decca), 247

"Blue Grass Ramble" (tune), 159

Bluegrass Special (album, Decca), 257

"Blue Grass Special" (tune), 126

Blue Grass Special (vehicle): Chevrolet, 124, 126; GMC, 262; breakdown, 341; broken into, 407; last, 416

The Bluegrass Star (magazine), 329

"Blue Grass Stomp" (tune), 155, 157

Blue Grass Style (album, Vocalion-Decca), 313

Bluegrass Talent Agency. *See* Monroe's Bluegrass Talent Agency

Blue Grass Time (album, Decca), 294

Bluegrass Unlimited (magazine), 285; "Bill Monroe: King of Blue Grass Music," 296–97; size, 320; on Bill's breakfast, 322; on former Blue Grass Boys, 374; obituary for Birch, 389; cosponsored belt buckles, 419–20; ad for festivals, 445; "Wintergrass '95" article, 461

Bluegrass with Class (Owensboro, Ky.), 411. *See also* Bluegrass Fan Fest

Blue Moon Boys, 192, 194

"Blue Moon of Kentucky" (song), xx; writing of, 128–29; release, 141; recorded by Elvis, 192; recorded by Bill without banjo, 193; Rose Maddox recording, 238; and Ray Charles, 278; and George Jones and Melba Montgomery, 281–82; and the moon landing, 309; named "state bluegrass song," 424; Bill sang at farm auction, 450; Bill sang at National Medal of Arts dinner, 459; Bill recorded with Billy and Terry Smith, 462

"Blue Night" (song), 290

"Blue Ridge Mountain Blues" (song), 240–41

"Blue Savannah Waltz" (song), 422

Blue Sky Boys, 67; at WGST, 80

"Bluest Man in Town" (song), 309

"Blue Yodel No. 4" (song), 133, 140

"Blue Yodel No. 7" (song), 115, 149

"Boat of Love" (song), 160

Bonnie and Clyde (movie), 295

"Bonny" (song): James Monroe recording, 313; vocal rerecorded, 314; released on album, 330; rerecorded for *Satisfied Mind* album, 371

Bossmen: Bill Monroe and Muddy Waters (book, Rooney), 312–13, 315, 322. *See also* Rooney, Jim

"Boston Boy" (tune), 447

Bowers, James ("Gar"), 172, 174

Bowlin, Robert, 444

Boyett, Andy, 127

Box, Bill, 337, 342, 344

Bradley, Owen: as Cohen's assistant, 167, 174; as instrumentalist, 167, 174, 216; studio, 187; as producer, 216; assistant Silverstein succeeds, 240; assistant Haynes succeeds, 320; liner notes for *Weary Traveler* album, 356

Bradley Film and Recording Studio, 201; sold to Columbia, 239

Bradley's Barn, 272, 330; Bill's last session at, 371

"Bradley Studio," 187

Bradshaw, Elliott ("Curley"), 120, 127–28

"Brakeman's Blues" (song), 167

"Brand New Shoes" (song), 215

Bratcher, Hoyt and Eleanor, 456

Bray, Harley, 207

Breeding, Jewell, as subject of "My Old Kentucky and You," 330

Brewer, Gary, 448, 454

Brewster, Franklin D. ("Bud"), 343–44

Briggs Manufacturing Company (Detroit, Mich.), 31, 34

Brock, Carlos, 198; and Bill's guitar, 199; left band, 200; and houses, 376

Brother Birch Plays Old Time Fiddle Favorites (album, Atteiram), 352

Brown, Carolyn, 60; and move to South Carolina, 61; pregnancy and common-law marriage, 66; photo, 93. See also Monroe, Carolyn

Brown, Richard ("Richie"), 271

"Brown County Breakdown" (tune), 202, 275

Brown County Fox Hunters (band), 176, 183

Brown County Jamboree (Bean Blossom, Ind.), 173; Mayfield and Richardson, 183; live recording, 193–94; Bill visiting on Sundays, 229; Cravens and Brays, 229; Monroe Family Day, 262; end of "predictable seasons," 389

Brown County Jamboree Barn, 173; fire, 218; improvements, 274; demolished, 414

Brown County Jamboree Park (aka Monroe's Festival Park and Campground): purchased, 174; property paid off, 224; minifestival at, 329; ownership transferred to Bill, 359; advertised as for sale, 424. See also Bill and James Monroe's Festival Park and Campground

Brown County Music Corporation, 274, 277

Bryan, James: hired to replace Baker, 366; Baker returned, 369; picking sessions with Bill, 379–80

Bryant, Boudleaux and Felice: Boudleaux recorded with Bill, 178; Osborne Brothers and "Rocky Top," 300; "Daddy Bluegrass," 340

Bub, Mike, 457

Buchanan, Frank, 230, 238, 247

Buchanan, Steve, 429

Buck White and the Down Home Folks, 332. See also White, Buck

Buddy Lee Attractions, 382, 384

"Bugle Call Rag" (tune), 236

Burns, Kenneth ("Jethro"), 393–94

Burns Station Sound Studio, "Bill Monroe and Friends" sessions, 394

Bush, George H. W., 426–27; invited Bill to White House, 432

Bush, Roger, 271

Bush, Sam, on Bill, 368

"The Butcher Boy" (song), 9–10; and footstones, 40

Butler, Carl (and Pearl): Smoak on banjo with, 180; Carl recorded with Bill, 231; Carl's death, 443

Butler County, Ky., xxv; 6

Byrd, Jimmy, 227

"Cabin in Caroline" (song), 361

"Cabin of Love" (song), 162, 170

"Cacklin' Hen" (tune), 16

Calhoun, Bill, 75

Calumet (region), 36

Campbell, Jimmy, 436–37, 444, 447; asked Bill to record, 455

Canada: Bill's first visit, 201; with Cash, 227; at McGill University, 282; and interviews with Benson, 288–89; Country Music Hall, 295

"Candy Gal" (tune), 311

Cantwell, Robert, 9, 363

"Can't You Hear Me Callin'?" (song), 155, 157, 160; Joe Stuart on, 408; attempt to record with Stanley, 442

Capitol Records: and Rose Maddox, 238; and Beatles, 264; "Daddy Bluegrass," 340

"Careless Love" (song), 248

Carl Story and Rambling Mountaineers, 354–55, 363

Carlton Haney's Labor Day bluegrass festivals: first, Roanoke, 278–80; second, Roanoke, 286–87; third, Berryville, 296; fourth, Berryville, with music camp, 300–301; fifth, Camp Springs, 310; twenty-second, and Squires, 412

Carnegie Hall: "Folksong '59," 223; Opry package show, 235; New York Folk Festival, 276; with Boys of the Lough, 423

Carpenter, Boyd (aka "Hillbilly Kid"), 70, 71

Carson, Chuck, 202, 239

Carter, Jimmy, 361; Bill played for, 377

Carter Family, 38; and *Smokey Mountain Ballads*, 114

Cash, Johnny, 209, 227, 340

Castle Recording Studio, 139, 150; Bill's first session, 155; 1950 session, 158, 164, 167, 168, 187; Bill's last session, 191

C. E. Crowder's Store (Horton, Ky.), 36, 37

Cedarwood Publishing Co., 274

C. F. Martin and Co., Bill's guitar sent to factory, 164

"Changing Partners" (song), 188

"Chappie" (Bessie Mauldin's dog), 180, 198, 206

Charles, Ray, 278, 289

Charlie Monroe Blue Grass Festival, 354

Charlotte, N.C., 62–63, 64; Oberstein hears Monroe Brothers, 66

"Cheap Love Affair" (song), 239

"Cheyenne" (tune), 190–91, 196, 197

Chiavola, Kathy, 393, 403–4, 452

Chicago World's Fair (1933 and 1934), 56, 59

Christian, Diana (stage name for Dee Dee Prestige), 425, 434, 437. *See also* Prestige, Dee Dee

Christian, Gene, 153

"Christmas Time's A-Comin'" (song), 173–74, 175, 365

Church, Porter, 229

"Cindy" (song), 249

Civil War, xvii–xviii

Clark, Manuel ("Old Joe"), 171, 172, 174

Clarkston Hotel (Nashville, Tenn.), 199, 253

"classic bluegrass band," 193; first release of recordings on LP, 232; later releases, 268, 276; reissues of previous reissues, 317; "Why Did You Wander," 360; entire album, 373–74; final releases, 385, 400

Clements, Vassar, 158; left band, 161; trip to West Coast, 203; rejoined band, 234; session with Bill, 297

Clifton, Bill, 233, 283

Cline, Charlie, 169, 174; on fiddle and banjo, 177; Bill angry with, 178; left band, 181; returned to Nashville, 183; returned to Lonesome Pine Fiddlers, 184; on fiddle,

187; rejoined Fiddlers, 189; "three-fiddle thing," 191; showed Bill's guitar to Brock, 199; on mandolin, 201; return from navy, 221

Cline, Danny, 229

"Clinging to a Saving Hand" (song), 348

Clinton, Bill, 444; Bill played for, 445; awards National Medal of Arts to Bill, 459

"Close By" (song), 189, 191, 301

coal, in Kentucky, xxiii

Cohen, John, 246, 250

Cohen, Paul (Decca producer), 156–57; "New Mule Skinner Blues," 158; assistant of, 167; moved to Coral, 216

Columbia, S.C., 61, 62

Columbia Records: Acuff recording, 110; Bill signed with, 116; Bill's 1945 session, 126; Bill's 1946 sessions, 135–36; requests more, 140–41; Bill's 1947 sessions, 142–43; Stanley Brothers, 150, 152–53; Bill's 1949 session, 155; Bill's departure from, 156–57; Melissa records for, 162, 171; Shenandoah Valley Trio records, 162; Youngblood's recordings, 190, 191; first bluegrass album, 214. *See also names of specific songs, tunes, and albums*

"Columbus Stockade Blues" (song), 240

"Come Back to Me in My Dreams" (song), 126, 213

"Come Go with Me" (song), 226

"Come Hither to Go Yonder" (tune), 383

compact disc (CD), first bluegrass on, 410

Compton, Mike, 453, 455, 456

Conway, Tony, 421, 461

Cooder, Ryland ("Ry"), 264

Cooke, Jack, 221, 251–52, 271

co-op songwriting process, 133

Copas, Lloyd ("Cowboy"), 190

"Corinna, Corinna" (song), 370

"Cotton Fields" (song), 236

"Country Boy" (music video), 403

Country Boys, 223. *See also* Kentucky Colonels (formerly the Country Boys)

Country Current (U.S. Navy Band), 458–89

Country Gentlemen, 274, 294, 309

Country Music (magazine), feature article on Bill, 358

Country Music Association (CMA), 227

Country Music Hall of Fame, 286, 296

Country Road (radio show), 358

The Country Show: With Stars of the Grand Ole Opry (TV show), 197–98

"Country Waltz" (song), 179

County Records, 301, 343

"The Coupon Song" (song), 115

Cox, James M. (presidential candidate), 24

Crase, Noah, 198, 199, 206

Cravens, Robert ("Red"), 220

Crazy Barn Dance (WBT), 63

Crazy Water Crystals, 62–63, 64, 67, 68; sponsorship dropped, 69; sponsorship regained, 69; sponsorship ended, 71, 73

"Cripple Creek" (tune), 236, 305

Cripple Creek Boys, 230, 234, 236

Cross, Hugh, 50

"Crossing the Cumberlands" (tune), 283, 302

Cross Roads Follies (radio show), 79–80

Crowe, J. D., 280

"Cry, Cry Darlin'" (song), 212

Cupp, Dana, 440, 444

"Dancin' in Branson" (tune), 409

Dandurand, Tommy, 29; and band, 254

Daniels, Vic, 169

"Danny Boy" (song), 236

Darby, Tom, 37–38

Darby and Tarlton (duet), 37–38

"Dark as the Night, Blue as the Day" (song), 222, 225

"Darling Corey" (song), 114, 249

Davis, Cleo, 78; and ad for guitar picker, 96; let go, 111; had no capo, 117; possible original band recording, 306; death, 411

Davis, David, 398

Davis, Hubert, 195–96

Davis, Karl, 53

Davis, Randy, 344, 375

Davis, Ray, 170

Day, James Alvie ("Lazy Jim"), 190

"The Days Gone By" (song), 416, 422

"The Dead March" (tune), 304

Decca Records, 88, 153; signing sealed with handshake, 157; first sessions, 158–59; simultaneous releases, 159; session, 160; Weavers record, 163; sessions, 164, 166–67, 168–69, 170, 173–74; release, 175; sessions, 178–79; everything released, 187; sessions, 187–89, 191, 193, 196, 197, 201–2; offer for Elvis, 202; Jimmy Martin release, 204; single release and first EPs, 205; release, 209; twenty-fifth session, 211–12; single release promoting album, 215; instrumental session, 217; *I Saw the Light*, 219–20; single release, 222; session, 222–23; single release, 225; sessions, 236; single release, 237; sessions, 239–42; sessions with Keith, 254–55; single release, 255; as label of Bill, Martin, and Osbornes, 261; single release, 261; sessions, 265, 265–66, 274, 287, 289, 290, 290, 295, 297, 302, 304, 305; single release, 305–6; James Monroe session, 313; sessions, 314, 315, 320–21, 322; single release, 326; sessions, 330–31, 331; single release, 333; name change, 336; lost Charlie's discs, 343. *See also names of specific songs, tunes, and albums*

Deese, David, 244, 245, 246, 279–80

Deliverance (movie, Warner Brothers), soundtrack, 336

Delmore Brothers, 50; debut on *Opry*, 55; recording in Chicago, 56; and Monroe Brothers' first session, 66; songs of, 73; last song on *Opry*, 80; consulted with Bill, 80; left Greenville, 82

Denny, Jim, 140, 208, 274

Derrington, Charlie (Gibson luthier), 407, 408

Detroit, Mich., 31, 34, 45, 46

"Devil's Dream" (tune), 35, 254–55; releases, 261, 351

Devine, Ottis ("Ott"), 225

Diamond, Bobby, 264

Dillman, Dwight, 344, 346

Disc Jockey Convention ("Deejay Convention"), 181, 288, 296

"Dog House Blues" (song), 111

Dollar Crystal Company, 58, 60

Don Reno and Bill Harrell and Tennessee Cutups, 308, 318

Don Reno and Red Smiley and Tennessee Cutups: managed by Haney, 201; recorded, 202; *Old Dominion Barn Dance*, 214; brought to *Opry*, 214; breakup, 270

"Don't Forget Me" (song), 71

"Don't Put Off 'til Tomorrow" (song), recorded, 178–79; released, 307

"Down Yonder" (song and tune): as fiddlers' "roll call," 337; on Bill's last show, 463

"Drifting Too Far from the Shore" (song), 67, 68, 241

Drumright, Joe, 171, 220, 228

duets, 37

Duffey, John, 294, 369–70

Duncan, Bill ("Chum"), 213–14, 215

Duncan, Glen: heard Baker fiddle, 329–30; hired, 403–4; on *Austin City Limits*, 408; left band, 408; gave tape to Gordy, 409

Durham, Hal (*Opry* manager), 443

"Dusty Miller" (tune), 289

Dylan, Bob, 348

Eanes, Jim, 113, 146

Earl Scruggs: His Family and Friends (documentary), 315

Earl Scruggs Revue, 314–15, 316

Earl Taylor and Stoney Mountain Boys, 223

Early Bird Bluegrass Show, 329

Early Blue Grass Music by the Monroe Brothers (album, Camden-RCA Victor), 257

East Chicago, Ind., 36, 49

Eisenhower, Dwight, 180

Eldredge, Terry, 441, 464

Elizabethtown and Paducah Railroad (E&P), xxiii

Ellis, Tony, 226, 229–32, 234–37; credited Lyle for break, 240; banjo on gospel songs, 241; left band for good, 244

Elrod, Jimmy, 215, 271

Emerson, Bill, 220

Esquire (magazine), 224–25, 228

Estes, Milton, 189

Ethridge, Floyd, 118, 119, 152

"Evening Prayer Blues" (tune), 328, 384

Everly Brothers, 211

Ewing, Tom, 261; sat in with Bill and band, 330; auditions, 344–45, 410; drove Bill to Bean Blossom, 410–11; lesson in showmanship, 418; quit and rejoined twice, 424, 427, 428; escorted Bill, 452; visited Bill at Medical Center, 464

"Fair Play" (tune), 383

"A Fallen Star" (song), 211–12

Fan Fair, 399, 424

"Farther Along" (song), 87, 249

"Farther On" (song), 349, 411

The Father of Blue Grass Music (album, RCA Victor), 244–45

Favorite Hymns and Mountain Songs (songbook), 68

Feagan, Mike, 419–21, 424

Feast Here Tonight (album, RCA Victor), 353

Fendermen (duo), 228

Festival of American Folklife (Smithsonian Institution), 307

"Fiddlers Blues" (tune), 455

"Fiddler's Pastime" (tune), 357

Field, Henry, 59–60

Fields, Monroe, 329, 336

fill-ins (in order of appearance): McGarr, 118; Ethridge, 118, 119, 152; Goad, 145; McGraw, 145; Hankinson, Stan, 150; Young, 166; Stanley, 171; Vipperman, 172; Gunther ("Little Robert Van Winkle"), 189; Hubert Davis, 195–96; Tommy Williams, 208, 305; Metzel, 210; Elrod, 215; Cravens, 220; Emerson, 220; Byrd, 227; Church, 229; Danny Cline, 229; Carl Butler, 231; Rosenberg, 233; Lester, 235–36; Ray Goins, 246; Landers, 250, 251; Pendleton, 257; Sage, 257; Ross, 263; Cooder, 264; Diamond, 264; Roberts, 269; McCormick, 271; Marvin, 271; Thurmond, 271; Roger Bush, 271; Lilly, 272; Logan, 272; Winston, 274; Crowe, 280; Blackwell, 291; Land, 292; Sonka, 292; Mowery, 329; Buck White, 336; Hefner, 339; Lee, 341; Brewster, 343; O'Bryant, 363; Huffmaster, 375; Kovac, 386; R. C. Harris, 386; Johnnie Baker, 399; Sato, 402; Imai, 402; Saburo Watanabe, 402; Franks, 402; Kenny Jones, 412; Huskey, 412; Forrest Rose, 412; Billy Rose, 423, 426; Sprouse, 426; Sykes, 446, 457; Bub, 457

Fincher, James Wesley ("J. W."), 62–63

"Fireball Mail" (song), 304

"Fire on the Mountain" (tune), 86, 267, 317

"The First Whippoorwill" (song), 174, 175; attempted as trio, 361

Flatt, Lester, 109; joined Happy-Go-Lucky Boys, 113; played with Charlie, 122; filled in, then hired, 127; skeptical about

Scruggs, 130; get-together at trailer, 144; gave notice and left band, 144, 145; reunited with Bill, 325; visited Bill's bus, 326–27; recorded song Bill wrote, 334; death, 374. *See also* Flatt and Scruggs

Flatt and Scruggs: first release, 149; second release, 150–51; release of "Foggy Mountain Breakdown," 160; "bluegrass" as substitute, 167; Martin and, 169; release of "Pike County Breakdown," 176; *Martha White Biscuit Time*, 184; Martha White Mills TV show, 197; on *Opry*, 197; rehearsing in *Opry* hallway, 220–21; "Ballad of Jed Clampett," 247; *Bonnie and Clyde*, 295; end of partnership, 302–3

Fleischhauer, Carl, 332–33

"Flowers of Love" (song), 232, 237

Foggy Mountain Jamboree (album, Columbia), 214

"Foggy Mountain Top" (song), 36, 331

"Foggy River" (song), 241

Foley, Red, 53, 57, 72; replacing Acuff, 137; Country Music Hall of Fame, 296

Folkways Records, 208, 209, 224

"Footprints in the Snow" (song): and Hugh Cross, 50; in the grease house, 82; Bill's recording, 126; release, 137; rerecorded, 178; Rose Maddox recording, 238

Ford, Ernie ("Tennessee Ernie"), 180, 196

Ford, Gerald, 345

Forget Me Not (book, McHenry), xxv, 13

Forrester, Howard ("Howdy"), 116–19; returned, 131; gave notice, 132; as agent, 366

Forrester, Joe, 131–32

Forrester, Wilene ("Sally Ann"), 116, 120, 132

Foster, Alice (née Gerrard), 206; at Sunset Park, 243, 291, 292; and "My Life in Blue Grass," 308

Foster, Billy Joe: hired, 413–14; at father's home, 418; leaves of absence, 419, 426

Foster, Jeremy, 205–6, 208, 228

"Four Walls" (song), 211–12

Fowler, Bob, 336, 337, 342

foxhounds (J. B.'s), 12, 33

fox hunting, 14, 33, 181, 189; with Hicks, 207

Frank, Joe, 54, 72, 296

Franks, Randy, 402

Freeman, David, 343

Frets (magazine), 412

Friday Night Frolics (radio show), 237, 253, 269, 281

"Friday Night at the Opry" (tune), 447

Friday Night Opry (radio show), 281, 287

Friends of Old Time Music, 243, 251–52

"Frog on the Lilypad" (tune), 442, 447

Frontier Ranch (music park), 326–27, 377, 436

Gabany, Vic (independent producer), 446–47, 451–52, 456–57

Gabany studio sessions, 447, 450–51

"Galley Nipper" (tune), 442

Gannaway, Albert (producer, *The Country Show*), 197–98

Garcia, Jerry, 267, 268

Garren, Walter ("Amos"), 84, 110

Gary, Ind., 36

Gately, Connie, 220, 221, 252

Gaylord Entertainment Company, 395, 450

Geary, Stoy, 430, 435

Gebhardt, Steve (filmmaker), 436

General Hospital (Nashville, Tenn.), 182

Gentry, Linnell, 244

Gerrard, Alice. *See* Foster, Alice (née Gerrard)

"Get Down on Your Knees and Pray" (song), 170

"Get Up John" (tune), 187; tuning used in "In Despair," 213; album release, 275; rerecorded, 321

Gibson Musical Instruments: catalog, 72; Bill and band toured, 140; Martin using guitar from, 164; F-5 sent to factory and returned, 176–77, 179–80, 185–86; executives came to *Opry*, 186; F-5 sent to factory and returned, 221, 223; Siminoff and, 373; Wall at *Opry*, 378; agreement announced, 380; Bill playing F-5L, 381; F-5 restored and returned, 381; team pieced mandolin together, 407

Gillespie Service Station (Greenville, S.C., sponsor), 68

Gillespie Tire Company (sponsor), 80, 82, 83

"The Girl in the Blue Velvet Band" (song), 155, 157, 321

Girls of the Golden West (duo), 55, 72

"Give Me Wings" (song), 423

"The Glory Land Way" (song), 249

Glosson, Lonnie, 53; on KARK, 76

Goad, Dorothy and Mildred. *See* Girls of the Golden West

Goad, Tommy, 145

Godbey, Marty, *Bluegrass Unlimited* article, 376

"God Holds the Future in His Hands" (song), 68, 411

Goff, Caroline, 6, 7, 13

Goff, Nola ("Nolie"), 13

Goff, Robert, 6, 13

"Going Across the Sea" (tune and song), 35, 430

"Going Home" (song), 241

"Going Up Caney" (tune and song), 311–12, 326

Goins, Ray, 246

Goins Brothers: shows with Bill and Mayfield, 218–19; Lonesome Pine Fiddlers, 235; at *The High Lonesome Sound* filming, 246; on Bill's bus, 309

"Golden River" (song), 371

"The Golden West" (tune), 405, 453

Golden West Cowboys (band), 86, 87

"The Gold Rush" (tune), 295

Good, Dolly and Millie. *See* Girls of the Golden West

"Goodbye Old Pal" (song), 126, 141, 213

"A Good Woman's Love" (song), 212

Gordy, Emory, Jr. (MCA producer): suggested album with Hall of Famers, 404; *Planes, Trains, and Automobiles* session, 419; called for banjo tune, 422; last production, 423

Gorman, Charles ("Skip"), 300–301

"Gotta Travel On" (song), 222; on *Billboard* chart, 223

Grammy Awards: Skaggs gave award to Bill, 403; Acuff and Williams lifetime achievement awards, 421; *Southern Flavor* nominated and awarded, 427; *Live at the Opry* nominated, 434

Grand Ole Opry (radio show), 37, 55, 72; Crazy as first sponsor, 73, 75, 77; and War Memorial, 84, 120; moved to Ryman, 121; cancelled (1945), 127; cancelled (1968), 297; cosponsored belt buckle, 419–20

Grand Ole Opry tent shows, 113, 116, 117; Bill's, 120; Tent Show No. 1 (revival), 200; at county fairs, 211

Grant, Bill, 296, 299, 309

Graves, Burkett ("Uncle Josh," "Buck"), 173, 327–28, 454

Graves, Ernie, 213

The Great Bill Monroe (album, Harmony-Columbia), 232

Greenbrair Boys, 217; trip to Union Grove, 228; recorded, 234; touring with Baez, 234; album, 239; *Opry* appearance, 239; last album with Rinzler, 261; and Greene, 282

Green, Clarence and Armolee, 362; refuge for LaBella, 384; sang at Bill's church, 421

Green, Doug: filled in as lead singer, 293; bass on Baker's first solo album, 301; filled in for James on bass, 302; joined band, 304; left band, 308

Green, Yates, 205, 206

Greene, Richard, 282, 288–89, 291

Greenhill, Manuel ("Manny," talent agent), 249

Green Spot Orangeade (sponsor), 84, 85

Greenville, S.C., 63–64

"Grey Eagle" (tune), 290; as fiddlers' "roll call," 337; released in Japan, 356

Grier, Lamar, 278, 280; on "Turkey in the Straw," 287–88; recorded with Hazel and Alice, 291; urged White to join band, 293; left band, 295

Grisman, David, 262, 369

Gunther, Ralph ("Little Robert Van Winkle"), 189

Haerle, Martin, 262

Haire, Charles ("Chuck"), 76, 77

Hall, Cecil (leader of Dominion Bluegrass Boys): Charlie Monroe paired with, 342; Charlie's breakup with, 345; renewed friendship, 353–54; pallbearer at Charlie's funeral, 355

Hall, Roy, 112, 113

Hall, Tom T., 359

Hammond, Ind., 36; Monroes find work in, 49; WWAE radio, 49

Haney, Lawrence Carlton ("Carlton"), 185; Bill called to book bass player, 194; came to Nashville to manage Bill, 198; assigned to help Birch, 200; threatened with axe, 201; organized *New Dominion Barn Dance*, 214; first "Blue Grass Day," 229; Maddox album,

238; first "Blue Grass Festival," 250; met Rinzler, 257; visited Newport, 270; multi-day festivals, 278–80, 286–87, 296, 300–301, 318; promotional ideas for bluegrass, 317–18; Bill severed ties with, 318

Hankinson, Mel and Stan ("Kentucky Twins"), 140; Stan as fill-in, 150

"Happy on My Way" (song), 176, 188

Harding, Warren, 24

"Hard Times Have Been Here" (song), 370

Harris, Ailsey Q. (great-grandmother), xvi–xvii

Harris, "R. C.," 321, 322, 386

Hartford Herald (newspaper), xviii, xxvii, 1; and logging, 2–3; and Jennie McHenry's funeral, 13; and World War, 17; and arrest of Shultz, 26–27; and Old Fiddlers Contest, 35

Hartford, Ky. (Ohio County seat), xvii; Rosine established in, xxv

Harvey, Frances, 6, 7

Harvey, Mae (Goff), 6, 7

Hastings, Lincoln: as farmhand and Bill's driver, 460; as Bill's caregiver, 462, 463, 465

Hatch Show Print Company (for show posters), 88

"Have a Feast Here Tonight" (song), 371

Hawkins, Bill ("Hawk"), 114; took damaged mandolins to bank, 407

Hay, George D.: at WLS, 29; hired by WSM, 34; auditioned Bill and band, 85, 87; published *Opry* book, 129; wrote feature article about Bill, 194–95

Hayes, Joseph ("Red"), 304, 311

Haynes, Walter (MCA producer), 320; and *Friends* album, 394–95

"Heavy Traffic Ahead" (song), 133, 153

Hedrick, Marvin, 193, 259, 274

Hee Haw (TV show), 228; Thompson's picking on theme, 321; Bill's appearance, 387–88

"Heel and Toe Polka" (tune): Malissa Monroe played, 9; Forrester played, 120; Bill recorded, 322

Hefner, Richard, 339

Hembree, Mark, 375, 399

Hemphill Brothers Coach Company, 416

Hendley, Fisher, 63

Hermitage Hotel, 180

"He Will Set Your Fields on Fire" (song), 72, 188–89

Hicks, Bobby, 194, 195–96; fox hunting with Bill, 207; drafted, 207–8; returned, 221; and "Dark as the Night," 222; left band, 224; fiddled with Spicher, 409–10

Hicks, Jack, 319; joined band, 322; left, 338; Bill chided, 340–41

High Lonesome (documentary), 430–31

The High Lonesome Sound (documentary), 246

The High, Lonesome Sound of Bill Monroe and his Blue Grass Boys (album, Decca), 284

"Highway of Sorrow" (song), 169, 265

Hills & Home (album), release of "Why Did You Wander," 360

A History and Encyclopedia of Country, Western, and Gospel Music (book, Gentry), on Bill as "Father of Blue Grass Music," 244

Holcomb, Roscoe, 246

Holden, Bill, 360–61, 363, 364, 366

Holly, Charles ("Buddy"), 205

Holt, Culley, 216, 240

"Home Again" (poem), xxiv

Homecoming Bluegrass Festival. *See* Monroe Homecoming Bluegrass Festival

"Honky Tonk Swing" (tune), 115, 131

Hoosier Hotshots, 57

Hootenanny (TV show), 255, 265

Hoppers, Lonnie, 247, 250

Horse Branch, Ky., 24, 26, 28

Horton, George Vaughn, 158, 231

Horton, Ky., xvii

Horton School, 8, 19; and Bill, 41; photo, 89

Hotel Charlotte (Charlotte, N.C.), 70, 71, 73

"House of Gold" (song), 217

Howdy Judge (book, Hay), 86

"How Old Are You?" (song), 9

"How Will I Explain About You?" (song), 132, 141, 241, 385

Huff, Wanda, 425–26, 428–29

Huffmaster, Raymond, 375

Hurt, Charles ("Chick"), 54

Huskey, Roy, Jr., 412

Hutchens, Doug, 316, 320, 323, 326, 328; documenting former Blue Grass Boys, 374; organized birthday salutes, 391, 397; arranged for belt buckle, 419–20

Hymns (album, Capitol), 216

"I Am Ready to Go" (song), 71
"I Believed in You, Darling" (song), 187, 205
"I'd Like to Be Over Yonder" (tune), 453
"I (Have) Found the Way" (song), 241
"I Haven't Seen Mary in Years" (song), 304, 330, 371
"I Hear a Sweet Voice Calling" (song), 142, 147; with Osbornes, 287, 404
"I Hear My Savior Calling" (song), 199
"I Hope You Have Learned" (song), 187
"I Live in the Past" (song), 274, 317
Illinois Central Railroad, 2
"I Love the State of Virginia" (song), 410
I'll Meet You in Church Sunday Morning (album, Decca), 268
"I'll Meet You in Church Sunday Morning" (song), 160, 265, 442
Imai, Tatsuya, 402
"I'm Blue, I'm Lonesome" (song), 154
"I'm Going Back to Old Kentucky" (song): included in songbook, 140; recorded, 142; released, 154; rerecorded by Bill, 235; rerecorded by Bill and James, 371
"I'm On My Way [Back] to the Old Home" (song), 156, 159, 175
"I'm So Lonesome I Could Cry" (song), 248–49
"I'm Thinking Tonight of My Blue Eyes" (song), 83
"I'm Travelin' On and On" (song), 142, 143, 144; LP release, 385
"I'm Working on a Building" (song), 188
"In Despair" (song), 213
instruments. *See* Monroe, William Smith ("Bill")—instruments
International Bluegrass Music Association (IBMA), 411, 426; Hall of Honor, 441
International Festival of Country Music ("Wembley"), 342, 379, 395
"In the Pines" (song), 178
I Saw the Light (album, Decca), 216–17, 218, 219–20
I Saw the Light (posthumous Hank Williams album, MGM), 217
"I Saw the Light" (song), 156; at funeral, 181
Israel, Tour to, 396–97

"Is the Blue Moon Still Shining?" (song), 297
"It Makes No Difference Now" (song), 289
"It's Me Again, Lord" (song), 315
"It's Mighty Dark to Travel" (song), 143, 149, 232
"It's Sad to Be Alone" (song), 334
"I Want to Go with You" (song), 302
"I Was Left on the Street" (song), 239
"I Will Sing for the Glory of God" (song), 315
"I Wonder Where You Are Tonight" (song), 113, 287

"Jack Across the Way" (tune), 447
Jackson, Carl, 337
Jackson, Tommy, 166, 212
"Jake Satterfield" (song), 370
James Monroe and Midnight Ramblers: first show, 323; Franks died in crash, 364
James Monroe's Bluegrass Club, 381
James Monroe's bluegrass festival (Cosby, Tenn.), 327–28
James Monroe Sings Songs of "Memory Lane" of His Uncle Charlie Monroe (album, Atteiram), 356
Jamieson, Bob ("Handy"), 75, 76, 77, 78; photo, 95
Jam-Up and Honey (Tom Woods and Lee Davis Wilds), 113
J. B. & A. S. Monroe General Store, xx–xxi
"Jekyll Island" (tune), 409
J. E. Mainer's Mountaineers, 61–62, 63, 73
Jenkins, DeWitt ("Snuffy"), 63, 71, 117
"Jenny Lynn" (tune), 35, 322
Jerrolds, Wayne, 427, 428
Jerusalem Ridge (near Rosine, Ky.), 5, 14, 16
"Jerusalem Ridge" (tune): as possibly inspired by "Indian Blood," 332; at *Opry* with Collins, 337–38; original recording, 349; Baker's recording, 357; and Baker quitting, 400–401
Jim and Jesse ("Jesse and James," Jim and Jesse and Virginia Boys): picking style, 176; joined *Opry*, 266; Jesse recording with Bill, 383
"Jimmy Brown the Newsboy" (song), 249
"John Hardy" (tune), 236
"John Henry" (song), 85
Johnson, Enos, 208–9

Johnson, Lyndon, 270

Johnson, Marvine, organized fan club, 286

Jones, Bob, 356–57, 358

Jones, Danny, 325–28; at the Charlie Monroe festival, 354–55

Jones, George: "Brand New Shoes" (song), 215; Madison Square Garden, 268; "Blue Moon of Kentucky" with Montgomery, 281–82

Jones, Kenny, 412

Jordan, Vic, 295, 301, 303

"Journey's End" (song), 236

"Just a Song of Old Kentucky" (song), 68

"Just Over in the Gloryland" (song), 435

KARK (Little Rock, Ark.), 75, 77

Karl and Harty, 50, 53

"Katy Hill" (tune), 86, 149; rerecording rejected, 321

Kay, Lambdin, 80

Keith, Bill ("Brad"): won banjo contest, 246–47; and Scruggs, 249; audition and *Opry* debut, 252–54; called "Brad," 254; sessions with Bill, 254–55; Bill's praise, 255; recorded with Taylor without Bill's permission, 263–64; accused by Melissa, 264; left band, 264; jam session at Rinzler's, 271; filled in, 271, 272; brought Rowan to Nashville, 273; visited Bill on tour in France, 443

Kennedy, Gregg, 337, 344

Kennedy, John: and Cuban missile crisis, 248; assassination, 262

Kenny Baker Plays Bill Monroe (album, County), 357

Kentucky: bluegrass festivals in (*see* Monroe's Kentucky bluegrass festivals); state bluegrass song, 424; "Bill Monroe Appreciation Day," 455

Kentucky Blue Grass (album, Decca), 317

Kentucky Blue Grass Boys, 75–78

"Kentucky Colonels" (nickname of Monroe Brothers and Byron Parker), 64, 65

Kentucky Colonels (formerly the Country Boys), 271, 293. *See also* Country Boys

Kentucky Fried Chicken Festival, 391, 412. *See also* Bluegrass Festival of the United States

Kentucky Headhunters: "Walk Softly on My Heart" (song), 437; at Bean Blossom festival (with Bill sitting in), 441

"Kentucky Jewel" (tune), 331

"Kentucky Mandolin" (tune), 297

Kentucky Pardners (Charlie Monroe's Kentucky Pardners), 84, 85, 87; with Akeman, 118; with Flatt and brother Birch, 122; "Mother's Only Sleeping," 136; at Brown County Jamboree, 207; Monroe Family Tribute, 307; County label album, 343; and Cecil Hall, 345; in Rosine, 354; Charlie Monroe festival, 354–55

"Kentucky Songbirds" (nickname of Monroe Brothers), 51, 65, 69

"Kentucky Waltz" (song), 116, 126, 131; on *Billboard* chart, 131; inspiring "Tennessee Waltz," 138; rerecorded, 166–67, 321

Kershaw, Doug, and "Sally Jo" (song), 215

"Kewpie" (Bessie Mauldin's dog), 198, 206

KFNF (Shenandoah, Ia.), 59–60

Killen, Buddy, 206

Kilpatrick, Walter David ("D."), 208

King Records: Martin and Osborne, 169; Reno and Smiley, 202, 217

"Kiss Me Waltz" (tune), 322

Knee Deep in Bluegrass (album, Decca), 218

Korean War, 160

Kovac, Paul, 386

Kurth, Bernard Charles and Bertha, 77; divorce, 182. *See also* Monroe, Bertha Lee

Kuykendall, Pete, 285; filled in for Bill, 441; offered qualified apology, 461

LaBella, Julia Anne: met Bill, 359–60; invited to Nashville, 360; "Beautiful Julia LaBella" (song), 362; tour of farm, 362; Bill's proposal, 368; followed Bill to Stauffer's, 368–69; married Williams, 384; divorced Williams and reunited with Bill, 384, 385; married Phelps, 391; reappeared with guitar, 437; found Bill with visitor, 438; job with WSM, 443; filled in for Starkey, 449; took Bill to Rinzler service, 452; hosted birthday party, 452–53; took over housekeeping and driving, 458–59; quit as caregiver, 462

"Lady of the Blue Ridge" (tune), 383

Lair, John, 48, 72

Land, Mitchell: as fill-in, 292; repaired bus, 293; with Stone Mountain Boys, 294; band contest winners, 299

Landers, Jacob ("Jake"): as fill-in, 250, 251; verses for "Walk Softly," 253, 306

"Land of Lincoln" (tune), 311, 451

"Last Old Dollar" (song), 265–66, 317

Lee, Travis, 341

"The Lee Weddin Tune" (tune), 311–12

"Legend of the Blue Ridge Mountains" (song), 265

Leiderman, Jack, 413

Lennon, John, 382

Leonard, Bettie (fan club president), 309

Lester, Bobby Joe, 235–36

Lester Flatt and the Nashville Grass, 303, 325, 327–28

Lester Flatt Live! Bluegrass Festival with Guest Bill Monroe (album, RCA Victor), 341–42

"Let Me Rest at the End of My Journey" (song), 162, 249–50

"Let the Gates Swing Wide" (song), 405

"Let the Light Shine Down on Me" (song), 197

"Letter from My Darling" (song), 166, 442

Lewis, Ralph, 344, 356

Lewis, Wayne, 358–59, 410; took Bill to hospital, 462

Liebling, Rachel, and *High Lonesome* (documentary), 415, 430, 431

"Life's Highway" (song), 423

"Life's Railway to Heaven" (song), 217

Light Crust Doughboys, 76

Lilly, Everett, 167

"Linda Lou" (song), 231

Lineberger, Don, 270, 273–74, 278

"Little Cabin Home on the Hill" (song), 140, 147, 276; recorded by Elvis Presley, 322; rerecorded in memory of Flatt, 374

"Little Community Church" (song), 142, 143; release and *Billboard* chart, 149

"The Little Girl and the Dreadful Snake" (song), 178

"Little Joe" (song), 231

"Little Maggie" (song), 235

"Little Red Shoes" (song). See "Who's Gonna Shoe Your Pretty Little Feet?"

Little Rock, Ark., 75, 76

Live at McClure (album, Rebel), 352

"The Lloyd Loar" (tune), 409

Loar, Lloyd (acoustical engineer): and A-4, 53; and F-5, 125

"Lochwood" (tune), 383

Logan, Benjamin Franklin ("Tex"), 173, 276

"Log Cabin in the Lane" (song), 288

logging, 2–3

Lomax, Alan, 113–14; and Ralph Rinzler, 210; and "Folksong '59," 223; *Esquire* article, 224–25

Lomax, John, 113–14

"Lonesome Moonlight Waltz" (tune), 321, 333

Lonesome Pine Fiddlers, 163, 169, 235

"A Lonesome Road" (song), 215

"Lonesome Truck Driver's Blues" (song), 170

"Lonesome Road Blues" (song), 231

"Lonesome Valley" (song). See "You've Got to Walk that Lonesome Valley"

"Lonesome Wind Blues" (song), 226

Lone Star Bluegrass Festival, 328–29

"Long Black Veil" (song), 274, 317

Long Hollow Jamboree, 454, 460

"The Long Bow" (tune), 410

Lonzo and Oscar, 151. *See also* Ken Marvin

"Lord, Protect My Soul" (song), 164

"Louisville Breakdown" (tune), 267, 303

Louisville Courier Journal (newspaper), xviii, xxiii

Louisville Times (newspaper), quotes Bill on "newgrass," 367

Louvin, Ira (of the Louvin Brothers), death and funeral, 276–77

"Love, Please Come Home" (song), 331, 414

Loving, Marvine, organized fan club, 286

Lowinger, Gene: filling in, 271, 272, 274; hired, 275; introduced as "Jewish boy," 275, 278, 281; and synagogue, 281; left band, 281; photographed Bill, 439, 446

Lyle, Rudy: filled in, 153; drafted, 171; returned to claim job, 186; left band, 189

"Lucky Lady" (tune), 361

Mac and Bob (McFarland and Gardner), 37, 49–50

Macon, Dave ("Uncle Dave"), 86, 87; on quartet, 88; first *Opry* tent show, 113; *Smoky Mountain Ballads*, 114; tent shows with Bill, 116, 120

Mac Wiseman and the Country Boys, 218

Maddox, Rose, 223, 238

Magness, Tommy, 110, 112, 113, 118

"Malissa's Waltz for J.B." (tune), 383

mandolin, Malissa's choice as instrument for Bill, 21, 22–23. *See also* Monroe, William Smith ("Bill")—instruments

Mandolin World News (magazine), 369

Manny Greenhill's Folklore Productions, 292

"Mansions for Me" (song), 134, 135, 139

Manson, Charles, 309

Martin, Benny, 143, 144, 152; recorded with Bill, 226

Martin, Gene, repaired Bill's mandolin, 292

Martin, Jimmy, 154–55, 163–64; left band, 169; recorded for King, 169; working with Sonny Osborne, 177, 178; returned to Knoxville, 182; gave notice, 189–90; first Decca single, 204; Haynes and, 320; coaxed Charlie out of retirement, 335; dropped by MCA, 343; refused to shake Bill's hand, 454

Martin, William ("Mac"), 141

Marvin, Ken: as Rinzler's representative, 261, 265–66; as fill-in, 271. *See also* Lonzo and Oscar

"Mary at the Homeplace" (song), 265

"Mary Jane, Won't You Be Mine?" (song), 349

Mason's Restaurant (Goodlettsville), 360; as site of second birthday salute, 397–98

"Master Builder" (song), 249

Master of Bluegrass (album, MCA), 382, 383–84, 385–86

Mauldin, Bessie Lee, 65; with Bill in Charlotte, 75; 1963 photograph with band, 103; brought to Nashville, 114; and Nelson Gann, 128, 137, 144, 151, 174; extremely jealous, 152; on Jimmy Martin, 169; Bill bought bass for, 169; singing with band, 180; dogs, 180, 198; injured in car wreck, 181–82; played bass, 187, 198; and "Cheyenne," 190; first session, 201; and Green, 206; and Mayfield, 210; moved into cabin, 214; and Ellis, 226; Bill enjoined from marrying, 230, 234; bathing on the road, 244; complaint letter to Rinzler, 266; last session, 267; common-law claim, 353; death, 394

Mayfield, Carl and Fred (Edd Mayfield's sons), 183

Mayfield, Edd, 165; audition, 172; and "The First Whippoorwill," 174; left band, 177; Brown County Jamboree house band, 183; rejoined and left again, 190, 195; called for gospel album, 216; death, 218–19

Mayfield, Jody (Edd Mayfield's wife), 183

Maynard, Jimmy, 225, 235, 236, 271

MCA Records: Decca name change, 336; at Bean Blossom, 336; sessions, 348–49; and other labels, 352; single release, 386; Cathedral Caverns session, 389; *Friends* album sessions, 394, 395; *Hall of Fame* sessions, 404–5; *Bluegrass '87* sessions, 409–10; *Live at the Opry* sessions, 429; *Cryin' Holy* sessions, 435; affiliation with Bill ended, 442

McCormick, Kelly, 271

McCoury, Del: FOTM concert, 251–52; audition, 253–54; hired to play guitar, 254; Rosine visit, 259–60; Baker's first solo album, 301; at Bean Blossom festival with son Ronnie, 389

McCoury, Ronnie, 389, 459

McCulloh, Judith, 363

McDaniel, Emmett ("Lefty"), 75

McGarr, Clarence ("Mac"), 118

McGee, Sam and Kirk, 87, 120

McGraw, Lloyd, 145

McHenry, Henry D., xxiii–xxv, xxvii

McHenry, Ky., xxv

McHenry, Martha Jane ("Jennie," "Rosine"), xxiii–xxv, xxvii, 5, 13

McInturff, Betty (Monroe Talent secretary), 402, 415

"McKinley's March" (tune), 314, 351

McPeake, Curtis, 225; used instead of Ellis, 230; at Carnegie Hall, 236; banjo on "Blue Moon of Kentucky," 282

Meadows, Joe, 209, 210

"Memories of Mother and Dad" (song), 25, 178

"Memories of You" (song), 159

Memphis, Tenn., 75

Mercury Records, 149, 150; simultaneous releases, 160; three albums at once, 217

"Methodist Preacher" (tune), 305

Metzel, Bob, 210

Mid-Day Merry-Go-Round (WNOX), 75, 204

"Midnight on the Stormy Deep" (song), 290

Midnite Jamboree (radio show), 140, 276

"A Mighty Pretty Waltz" (song), 179

"Milenburg Joy" (tune): as "Milenburg Joys," 58; recorded, 322

Millard, Tommy ("Snowball"), 82, 83, 84, 439

Miller, Betty, 67–68. *See also* Betty Monroe

Miller, "Lost John," 128, 130

Millsaps, Bill and Wilma (and Snowbird Mountain Boys), 465

"Mississippi Waltz" (tune), 357

Mollie McCarthy and Ten Broeck (race horses), xviii–xix

"Molly and Tenbrooks" (song), xix; listed as "Ten-Brooks and Molly," 140; recorded previously, 142; Stanley Brothers recorded, 148–49; Bill's original release, 184; rerecorded, 213; second version, 215; Rose Maddox recording, 238; album release, 276; Tom T. Hall recorded, 359

Monroe, Andrew (great-grandfather), xvi–xvii

Monroe, Andrew Smith (J. B.'s brother), xvii, xviii, xx–xxi, 2–3, 8; Bill worked for, 42; death, 50

Monroe, Arabella (J. B.'s sister), xvii

Monroe, Bertha Lee (Bill's sister), 6; and guitar, 17; cooking chores, 26; and J. B.'s estate, 40; moved, 40, 48; job at Queen Anne Candy, 49; photo, 89; rooming house with Ellis, 227–28; death of Maude, 237; lived with Birch, 237, 308; lived with Charlie, 301–2; helped at Jamboree, 323; at Bill's farm, 387; moved back to Rosine, 388; lived with Dukeses, 389; visits to Long Hollow Jamboree, 456; death, 470. *See also* Kurth, Bertha

Monroe, Betty (Charlie's first wife), 67–68; death, 290. *See also* Miller, Betty

Monroe, Birch (Bill's brother), 4, 8; fiddling, 11, 17; and pneumonia, 18; and fiddle, 21; and Bill, 22–23; birthday, 26; left home, 31, 36; and Leora Baize, 35; first radio show, 36; home in 1927, 39; and joyride, 41–42; in Detroit, 45; in Calumet, 46; and WWAE, 49, 50, 51; recruited to dance, 52–53; played for churches, 55; on WJKS, 55–56;

at World's Fair, 56, 59; played at Maguon Ave., 57; on the road for WLS, 57; dropped out to support sisters, 59; visited Rosine, 58; photos, 89, 91; played with Charlie, 122; worked for Bill, 124; played bass, 128; sang bass and played fiddle, 131; as fill-in on bass, 137; left band to marry, 142; lived at Monroe homeplace, 156; agreed to manage Jamboree, 174–75; clashed with Haney, 201; moved to Martinsville, 210–11; owner of Jamboree property, 224; Monroe Family Day, 262; loaned James records, 356; transferred Jamboree property to Bill, 359; and Bertha at Bill's farm, 387; moved back to Rosine, 388; death, 388–89

Monroe, Burch (J. B.'s brother), xvii, 4; in string band, 16; and Birch, 17; house burning, 24; and J. B.'s estate, 40; death, 160

Monroe, Carolyn (Bill's first wife), 70, 74; and Cleo Davis, 79; handled bookings, 81; pregnancy, 84, 88; divorce, 230; served as personal secretary, 230, 268; helped with Bluegrass Express tour, 335; death, 400. *See also* Carolyn Brown

Monroe, Charles Pendleton (Bill's brother), 4, 8, 12–13; and guitar, 13, 17, 21; and Bill, 22–23; and horse, 30; and baseball, 31; left home, 31, 36; buying records, 31–32; learned first song, 32; first radio show, 36; home in 1927, 39; and stack of hay, 40; and joyride, 41–42; and knife injury, 42; in Detroit, 42, 45; in Calumet, 46; helped Bill find work, 47; fired at Sinclair, 48; job at Standard Oil, 49; and WWAE, 49, 50, 51; danced for WLS, 52–53; auditioned for Frank, 54–55; played for churches, 55; on WJKS, 55–56; at World's Fair, 56, 59; played at Maguon Ave., 57: on the road for WLS, 57; and Texas Crystals, 58, 62; visited Rosine, 58; at KFNF, 59–60; moved to Omaha, 60; teamed with Parker, 61; moved to South Carolina, 61, 62; new guitar, 61; visited Rosine, 61; auditioned for WBT, 63; moved to Charlotte, 63; and WFBC program, 63; played kerosene circuit, 64; end of Crazy sponsorship on WBT, 64; and Eli Oberstein, first recording session, 66; trip to Atlanta, 67; marriage, 67; new sponsor,

68; first record release, 68; second session, 68–69; sponsorship dropped by Crazy, 69; third session, 69–70; moved to Raleigh, 70; fourth session, 70; played banjo, 71; fifth session, 71–72; singing "White House Blues," 73; sixth session, 73; and breakup, 74–75; first recordings on his own, 77, 79; formed Kentucky Pardners, 84; and WSM audition, 84, 117; photos, 91, 94, 97; bought land and built house near Horton, 117, 122; songwriting, 122; recorded for RCA Victor, 136; Jimmie Rodgers Tribute, 183–84; "You'll Find Her Name Written There," 196; joint appearance with Bill, 200; trip to West Coast, 203–4; retired, 207; refused to sing at 1962 Rosine show, 242; visited by Bill, Rinzler, and McCoury, 259–60; refused to play at Monroe Family Day, 262; sold Monroe land, moved to Indiana, 273; death of wife, Betty, 290; moved back to Kentucky, 301–2; release of *Who's Calling You Sweetheart*, 303; at Festival of American Folklife, 307; remarried, 307; failed Decca record deal, 311, 314; with Dominion Bluegrass Boys, 342, first County album, 343; re-formed Kentucky Pardners, 345; diagnosed with cancer, 347; "Charlie Monroe Day," 353; renewed friendship with Hall, 353–54; Charlie Monroe Bluegrass Festival, 354–55; death, 355

Monroe, Charlotte (Harry and Nolie's daughter), 16

"Monroe City Breakdown" (tune), 417

Monroe, Della (Bill's second wife): marriage, 404; in *People* magazine article, 412; left home, 414; nightclub investment concern, 415; divorce filing, 416–17; removed furniture and burned wedding photo, 418. *See also* Streeter, Della

Monroe, Geanie (Whitehead) (wife of Bill's brother Speed), 46, 50–51; death, 388

Monroe, George (former slave), xvii

Monroe, Harry Carlisle (Bill's brother), 2, 8, 11; married Nolie, 15; and World War, 17; purchased inventory of J. B.'s estate, 40; death, 192

Monroe, Ida Anne (J. B.'s sister), xvii

Monroe, James (president), xvi, xvii, xviii

Monroe, James Buchanan ("Buck," "J. B."; Bill's father), xvii; education, xvii–xviii; nicknamed "Buck," xviii; farmer, xix; and general store, xx–xxi; and Malissa Vandiver, xxvi–xxvii; wedding, 1–2; logging, 2–3, 4; bought land, 4–5, 8; worked land, 12; and Bill, 13–14; and death of Malissa, 25; and Bill's appendicitis, 28; reining in Bill, 33; health decline and death, 36–37, 39–40; Bill's son James named for, 113

Monroe, James William (Bill's son): birth, 113; visited tent show, 124; recalled "the bus," 124–25; farm work, 175; disassembled barn, 214; married, 261; joined band, 269; first session, 274; sang lead, 287; divorce, 299, 302; on taking guitar spot, 303–4; 1969 session, 313; formed band, 323; first solo album, 342–43; guitar on Bill's sessions, 348; tribute album for Charlie, 356; last session with Bill for MCA, 371; house built, 376; "James Monroe's Bluegrass Club," 381; and Bill's biography, 388, 392; and Birch's tombstone, 397; fourth solo album, 399; assumed Bill's business affairs, 415; visited Bill at nursing home, 466

Monroe, James William, II ("Jimbo"; Bill's grandson): birth, 266; custody, 302; and Birch's tombstone, 397; with Bill on trip to Japan, 431–32; sang on *Opry*, 453

Monroe, John (Bill's great-great-grandfather), xv–xvii, 8

Monroe, John Henry ("Jack"; J. B.'s brother), xvii; as "J. H.," xx, xxi; logging, xxvii, 2–3, 4, 5; fiddling, 11; Monroe brothers at house of, 35; and J. B.'s estate, 40; invited Bill to stay, 41; Bill worked for, 43; death, 65

Monroe, John Jesse (Bill's grandfather), xvii, xxvii

Monroe, John Justine (and wife Clara, Bill's brother), 2, 8; fiddling, 11; and World War, 19; birthday, 26; bass singer, 30; purchased inventory from J. B.'s estate, 40; moved to cabin, 40; and the Calumet, 41, 46; home again, 45; return to Detroit, 45; married Clara Wilson, 50; visited Mammoth Cave, 61; meeting with Bill, 75; death, 237–38; "Someday they'll come and look at this house," 238

Monroe, Lydia Charlotte (Stevens) (Bill's grandmother), xvii, xx, 21

Monroe, Malissa (Bill's mother): and music, 3–4, 5; fiddled for dance, 6–7, 7, 8; as musical influence, 9–10; as disciplinarian, 14; and Bill, 14, 20–21, 22–23; and Speed, 20; illness and death, 24–25. *See also* Vandiver, Malissa Anne

Monroe, "Martha" (Myrtha Draper, Charlie's second wife), 307–8

Monroe, Maude Bell (Bill's sister), 2, 8; and music, 17; and tuberculosis, 21; cooking chores, 26; moved in with uncles, 40; moved to Whiting, 48; job at Queen Anne Candy, 49; photo, 89; moved to Nashville, 182; rooming house with Ellis, 227–28; death, 237

Monroe, Melissa Kathleen (Bill's daughter): birth, 69; stayed with John and Clara, 113; sang on *Opry*, 149; rode with ball club, 161; first session, 162; second session, 171; Monroe Family Day, 262; emotional problems, 263; traveled with band, 270, 421; helped Bill move, 385; at assisted living facility, 419; and Diana Christian, 434–35; moved in with Bill, 435; illness and death, 437–38

Monroe, Rosetta (Speed Monroe's daughter), 20, 58, 456

Monroe, Scottie (Speed's son), 58

Monroe, Speed Vorhees (Bill's brother), 2, 8; and World War, 17, 19, 20, 26; moved to cabin, 40; married Geanie Whitehead, 46; put Bill on train, 47; and health of Uncle Pen, 51; lived at homeplace, 58; photo, 89; moved to Cleveland, 113; moved to Nashville, took charge of Bill's farm, 134; returned to Rosine, 192; death, 290

Monroe, Susan Mary (J. B.'s sister), xvii, 4; visit to Rosine, 24, 65

Monroe, William (J. B.'s brother), xvii, 4, 8; death, 118

Monroe, William Smith ("Bill"): ancestors, xv–xvii, xxi–xxv; birth, 7–8; vision problems, 8–9; and school, 18, 19, 43; and insults, 19; and singing, 23; and baseball, 23–24; shyness, 25; farm duties, 25–27; appendicitis, 28; and Shultz, 29–30, 32–33, 38; at Crowder's store, 37; playmates, 38; left homeplace, 41; farming, 41–42; left Uncle Pen's home, 47; job at Sinclair barrel house, 47–48; as sole breadwinner, 48; on WWAE, 49, 50–52; played for square dances, 52; danced for WLS, 52–53; audition for Frank, 54–55; played for churches, 55; on WJKS, 55–56; at World's Fair, 56, 59; eye operation, 56–57; at Maguon Ave., 57; and Texas Crystals, 58, 62; visited Rosine, 58, 61; on KFNF, 59–60; moved to Omaha, 60; teamed with Parker, 61; moved to South Carolina, 61, 62; auditioned for WBT, 63; moved to Charlotte, 63; on WFBC, 63, 82; accident, 64; and Crazy sponsorship on WBT, 64; moved to Greenville, 65; and Eli Oberstein, 66; first Bluebird recording session, 66; mandolin playing as remarkable, 67; Gillespie Service Station as sponsor, 68; first release, 68; and Crazy sponsorship, 68–69; Bluebird recording sessions, 68–70, 71–72, 73; moved to Raleigh, 70; breakup with Charlie, 74–75; first band, 75–76, 78; on KARK, 76–77; in Birmingham, 78; Atlanta and Cleo Davis, 78–80; on WWNC, 80–82; band name, 81; grease house as rehearsal space, 82; and singing, 82–83; as teacher, 83; on bluegrass, 83; left WFBC, 85; photos, 89, 91, 94, 96–97, 101–8; first sessions with Blue Grass Boys, 111–12, 114–15; first house in Nashville, 115; and recording bans, 116–17, 144; Columbia Records, 116–17; offered Jenkins job, 117; carrying Blue Grass Boys, 118; met Reno, 121; baseball, 123, 134; Columbia sessions, 126, 135–36, 142–43; first farm, 127; and end of World War II, 128; first biographical writing about, 129; auditioned Scruggs, 130; hired Forrester, 131; first Columbia release as first hit, 131; Forrester quit, 132; Watts and Wise returned, 132; refining musical interplay, 132; second hit, 138; first songbook, 139; and Hankinson Twins, 140; Wise and Scruggs quit, 144; Flatt and Watts quit, 145; sent for Eanes, 146; played on Flatt and Scruggs's radio show, 147; Shenandoah Valley Trio, 148; Bill's songs by others, 148–49; more baseball, 148, 151, 165, 167–68;

recording ban ended, 149; RCA recordings rereleased, 149; Columbia signed Stanleys, 150; bands imitating style, 150–51; first drive-in appearance, 151; left Columbia, 154; at fair with Williams, 154; visit to Monroe homeplace, 155; let Wiseman go, 157; first Decca session, 158–59; heard Mayfield, 165; recorded with Taylor, 166; filled in for Snow, 171; reunion shows with Charlie, 172; Brown County Jamboree, 174, 176; fox hunting, 181; car wreck and recovery, 181–84; Jimmie Rodgers Tribute, 183–84; gave Stanleys a song, 186; second farm, 189; feature article, 194–95; on *The Country Show*, 198; broke collarbone, 200; met Carson, 202; bought new Cadillac, 205; signed with Denny Artist Bureau, 208; first album, 212–13; Cadillac repossessed, 214; first gospel album, 216–17; at *New Dominion Barn Dance*, 220; in *Esquire* magazine, 224; first "Blue Grass Day," 229–30; changed outlook on music, 229–30; remarks at "All Blue Grass Show," 233–34; at Carnegie Hall (1961), 235–36; uncredited appearance on Rose Maddox album, 238; recorded older songs, 240; stopped singing, 241; played in Rosine, 242; tape of "All Blue Grass Day" remarks, 241–42; Rinzler interview, 243, 245; first show advertised as "Blue Grass Festival," 250; *Sing Out!* article, 250–51; first folk revival audience, 251; with two banjo pickers, 253–54; sessions with Keith, 254–55; promoting banjo album, 256; visit to Keith and friends, 258; replaced Birch as Jamboree manager, 258–59; visited Rosine, 259–60; Monroe Family Day, 262; Rinzler's advice, 264–65; George Jones at Madison Square Garden, 268; jam session at Rinzler's, 271; *Second Fiddle to a Steel Guitar*, 272; consulting on recordings, 274; meeting Byron Berline and father, 277–78; first multiday festival, 278–80; making amends at synagogue, 281; trips to Montreal, 282, 288–89; mentoring young bandsmen, 283; working on farm, 285–86; and fan club, 286; announced session, 287; Carter Stanley's funeral, 289; black-tie dinner, 292; Bill's first festival, 294–95; and Stauffer, 295; and Uncle Pen's tunes, 296; building a stage at Bean Blossom, 298; at "Summer Music Camp," 300–301; with six fiddles, 301; James and guitar spot, 303; "lost" session, 305; proposed original band recording, 306; Festival of American Folklife, 307; disunion of Charlie and Bill, 307–8; at Newport Folk Festival, 308; "My Life in Bluegrass," 308; rattlesnake rattle, 309; playing with Baker, 310; on *To Tell the Truth*, 310; "Bill Monroe Day," 310–11; helping Scruggs Revue, 314–15; Scruggs documentary, 315; second Kentucky festival, 316; ended relationship with Haney, 318; and Country Music Hall of Fame, 319; on Ryman board of advisors, 322–23; reunited with Flatt, 325; invitation to Hutchens, 326; Flatt visit, 326–27; playing with Josh Graves, 327–28; Nashville Songwriter's Hall of Fame, 329; the Dirt Band, 334–35; Hall of Fame show, 335; multiple fiddles at Bean Blossom, 337; first Monroe Homecoming festival, 338; monument and tombstone in Rosine Cemetery, 339; rumors of retirement, 341; rumored firing of band, 344; interviewed by Wolfe, 347; cutting back on Monroe festivals, 347–48; recorded with Stanley and Birch, 352; endorsements, 352; and band at Charlie's funeral, 355; recorded James's tribute to Uncle Charlie, 356; recorded with Baker, 357; singing flat, 358; recorded with Tom T. Hall, 359; Jamboree ownership, 359; preferred an autobiography, 363–64; funeral of Donald Evans, 367; asked again about retirement, 371; gardened, 371–72; a song for Flatt, 374; renovated cabin, 375–76; nullified Blue Grass Boys project, 376; played for President Carter, 377; picking sessions at farm, 379–80; asked again about retirement, 382; "drowning out" banjo break, 383; colon cancer, 384; first festival observation of birthday, 387; invited Birch and Bertha to stay at farm, 387; National Heritage Fellowship Award, 389; health problems, 389–90; Hutchens's first birthday salute, 391; TNN debut broadcast, 395; Pegasus Parade, 395; Israel tour and baptism, 396–97;

Monroe, William Smith ("Bill") (*continued*):
second birthday salute, 397–98; as first
inductee in SPBGMA Hall of Greats, 399;
Cadillac vandalized, 406; wore bulletproof vest, 407, 418, 426; letter from
President Reagan, 413; wrote new tunes
at every show, 417; heard shots fired, 418;
dehydration, 419; recording with Candy,
419; retirement announced (the "ploy"),
420–21; "drug reaction," 423; Carnegie
Hall, 423; "disturbance" at the farm, 428–
29; case dismissed, 429; filming at Monroe
homeplace, 430; invited to White House
by President Bush, 432; Grammy Awards
and Farm Aid IV, 434; filming for another
documentary, 436; health problems, 439,
440, 442; sat in with Kentucky Headhunters, 441; mandolin instruction video, 442;
MCA dropped, 442; recorded with Stanley
again, 442; number of bookings declined,
444; inaugural festival for President Clinton, 445; recommended Stanley for *Opry*,
445–46; falls and fractures, 448, 449; farm
for sale, 449–50; at Rinzler memorial
service, 452; reunion performance with
Scruggs, 452; recorded with Chiavola, 452;
recorded with Robins, 453; recorded with
Berline and Scruggs, 453–54; recorded
with Campbell, 455; and Martin, 455;
asked for memorial plaque in Rosine, 456;
pneumonia, 457; at unveiling of plaque,
459; National Medal of Arts, 459–60; more
health problems, 460; recorded with the
Smith brothers, 462; last show, on *Friday
Night Opry*, 462–63; final health problems
and death, 463–67. *See also* Big Plans
—family relationships: mother's musical
influence, 9–11; father, 13–14, 33, 36–37;
niece born at house, 16; Uncle Pen, 11–12,
19, 33, 41, 43–45; playing with Charlie
and Birch, 22–23, 35, 45; death of mother,
24–25; father's death and estate, 40; birth
of Melissa, 69; breakup with Charlie,
74–75; reunion shows with Charlie, 172;
birth of grandson, 266; disunion of Charlie and Bill, 307–8; birthday present from
James, 339; Charlie's funeral, 355; recorded
James's tribute to Uncle Charlie, 356; death
of Melissa, 438. *See also names of family
members*
—instruments: first mandolin, 20–21, 22;
new mandolin, 53–54, 61; played fiddle on
shows, 71; found F-5, 125–26; guitar stolen,
139; sent F-5 to Gibson, 176–77, 179–80,
185–86, 221; playing F-4, 221–22; price tag
on mandolin, 275–76; misplaced mandolin, 287; F-5 repair, 292; another F-5, 334;
promoted Ibanez mandolins, 356; main
mandolin restored, 380, 381; F-5s damaged, 406–7; main mandolin returned,
408–9
—and *Opry*: audition and debut, 85–87; tour,
138; tenth anniversary, 155; Presley apologized at, 194; live ABC-TV show, 206;
using musicians paid by, 220; twentieth
anniversary, 225; last from Ryman, 341; fiftieth anniversary on, 432; unsteady on feet
at, 433; recommended Stanley for, 445–46;
fifty-fifth anniversary, 453
—romantic partners: brief romance, 46;
met Carolyn Brown, 60; met Bessie
Lee Mauldin, 65; married Carolyn, 70;
Mauldin and "Blue Moon of Kentucky,"
128–29; Mauldin returns, 137, 151–52, 159,
180, 194–95, 202, 214; divorce from Carolyn, 230; Mauldin's last road trip, 266;
Virginia Stauffer as love interest, 274;
Mauldin lawsuit, 353; met Julia LaBella,
360, 362; at Stauffer's, 362–63; proposed to
LaBella, 368; married Della Streeter, 404;
separation and divorce from Streeter, 414,
416–17. *See also* Brown, Carolyn; LaBella,
Julia; Mauldin, Bessie Lee; Monroe, Carolyn; Monroe, Della; Stauffer, Virginia;
Streeter, Della
—specific songs, tunes, and albums: "Kentucky Waltz," 116, 131; "Blue Moon of Kentucky," 128–29; "Footprints in the Snow,"
138; "Let Me Be Your Friend," 152; wrote
"Uncle Pen," 161–62; rerecorded "Kentucky
Waltz," 166–67; "Kentucky Waltz" lawsuit,
168; "Christmas Time's A-Comin'," 173;
release of *The Great Bill Monroe* and *Mr.
Blue Grass*, 232; *Bluegrass Special* released,
257; "Wayfaring Stranger" for Speed, 290;
"Evening Prayer Blues," 328; release of *Bill*

Monroe's Uncle Pen, 333; "Six Feet Under," 343–44; "My Last Days on Earth," 362–63; singing "Mule Skinner Blues" with Parton, 370; played tape of "My Last Days," 386; forgot lyrics of "Blue Moon," 438; played guitar while singing "Mule Skinner Blues," 444. *See also names of specific songs, tunes, and albums*

—tours and trips: on the road for WLS, 52–53, 55, 56–57; "kerosene circuit," 64–65; trip to Atlanta, 67; demands of the road, 110; and rushed recording session, 114–15; Jam-Up and Honey tent show, 116; first own tent show, 120–21; purchased tent and airport limo, 123–24; Northeast, 134–35; *Opry* tour, 138; abbreviated tent show, 138–39; Michigan and West Virginia, 140; last tent-show season, 146–48; purchased first bus, 149–50; playing at movie theaters, 157; long series, 192; *Opry* tent show, 200; West Coast, 202–4, 206; with Reno and Smiley, 207; California, 223; Johnny Cash's, 227; in station wagon, 234; with Ray Price and Pee Wee King, 247; California, 255–56; purchased used bus, 262; Canada and Michigan, 266; bus brake problems, 282; Canada, 282; England, 283–84; West Coast, 293–94; Canada for *Country Music Hall* taping, 295; second overseas trip, 302; separate compartment on bus, 309; Bluegrass Express, 335; California, 335–36; with Lester Flatt, 341–42; England, 342; Japan, 348; Europe, 351; band vacation in Hawaii, 356; with James's band, 356, 363, 379; West Coast, 381–82; Israel, 396–97; lost items, 414; "farewell" (as part of "ploy"), 421; Switzerland, 426; bus breakdown, 426; Northeast, 426; Europe, 430–31; Japan, 431–32; with James, 448; Florida "vacation," 462

Monroe Brothers: Charlie and Birch, 36; trio, 45, 49, 50, 51, 55, 56, 57; Charlie and Bill, 54, 58–74; remembered by Lester Flatt, 110; *Smoky Mountain Ballads*, 114; Scruggs and, 130; reunion shows, 172; reunion of trio, 186

The Monroe Brothers: Their Life, Their Songs (songbook), 73

"Monroe Family Tribute" at Smithsonian, 307

Monroe festivals, 334, 336; Bill and Flatt's, 335; unsuccessful weekend, 338; Corona, Ca., 339, 341; season of thirteen evaluated, 347

Monroe Homecoming Bluegrass Festival: first (1973), 338–39, 360; others, 367, 381; last (1983), 397

Monroe house (at homeplace), 17–18; Fleischhauer and Rothman's visit, 332–33; possible move to Musicland Park, 346; possible move to Ohio County Park, 380

Monroe Manor, 385

Monroe Recording Company, 371

Monroe's Bean Blossom bluegrass festivals: "Celebration," 294–95; with Sunset Jam Session, 299–300; visited by *Opry* manager Wendell, 306; with huge crowd and Scruggs Revue, 316–17; covered by *Newsweek*, 316–17; Cantwell's impressions for *Atlantic Monthly*, 324–25; reunion with Flatt, 325; crowd estimates, 334, 343; "Autumn" festival, 368, 406, 440–41; tornado-like weather, 380; twenty-first, 418; uncertain future, 424, 425, 430; death of two couples, 438; recorded sets, 451, 456–57

Monroe's Bluegrass Musicland Park, 346, 351, 380

Monroe's Bluegrass Talent Agency, 341, 370

"Monroe's Blues" (tune), 361

"Monroe's Hornpipe" (tune), 222

Monroe's Kentucky bluegrass festivals: Ashland, 319; Jackson, 334–35, 353; other locations, 353

Monroe's Lone Star Bluegrass Festival, 328–29

Montgomery, Johnny, 410, 412

Montgomery Ward (record label), 54

Moody, Clyde, 73; in and out of band, 111, 113, 115, 125; baseball talent, 123; Haney and, 185; Melissa Monroe and, 185

Moore, Larry (and wife), 52

Moratto, Jim, 340, 344

Morris, Dale, 402–3

Morris, James R. (Smithsonian Institute), 304–5

"Mother's Not Dead, She's Only Sleeping"
(song), Charlie's version, 136
"Mother's Only Sleeping" (song), Bill's ver-
sion, 135, 139, 331
Mountain Music Time (radio show), 81
Mountain Stage (radio show), 430
Mount St. Helens (volcano), 380
Mowery, Glen, 299, 309, 329
Mr. Blue Grass (album, Decca), 232
"Muddy Waters" (song), 370
Muhlenberg County, Ky., xxii, xxiii, xxv
"Mule Skinner Blues" (song, "Blue Yodel No.
8"), 47, 82; audition for *Opry*, 85, 86, 87;
Acuff recorded, 110; recorded by Bill, 111;
releases, 112, 149; rerecorded, 321; at *Opry*
anniversary, 453; recorded with Smith
brothers, 462
Muleskinner News (magazine), 310
Music City News (periodical): Bill's inter-
views, 350, 357; feature story, 366; on man-
dolin restoration by Gibson, 380
"Music Valley Waltz" (song), 409
My All-Time Country Favorites (album,
Decca), 248
"My Carolina Sunshine Girl" (song), 168;
Japan release, 356
"My Dying Bed" (song), 178, 284
"My Father's Footsteps" (tune), 453
"My Florida Sunshine" (song), 366
"My Last Days on Earth" (tune): writing of,
362–63; mentioned in Grisman interview,
369; recorded, 383; title, 384; additions
(and Bill's comments), 385–86
"My Little Georgia Rose" (song), 152, 159;
Bill's second recording, 191; release, 284;
rerecorded but rejected, 321
"My Long Journey Home" (song), 66–68
"My Louisiana Love" (song), 361
"My Old Kentucky and You" (song), sung to
Jewell Breeding, 330; recorded, 331; single
release, 333
Myrick, Bill, 136–37; rejoined organization,
151; left, 159; and Mayfield Brothers, 165
"My Rose of Old Kentucky" (song), 142, 146;
Maddox recording, 238
"My Sweet Blue-Eyed Darling" (song), 361
"My Sweet Memory" (song), 365

Nashville Now (TV show), 420, 446

Nashville Songwriters Association, Hall of
Fame, 329
The Nashville Sound (documentary), 311
National Academy of Recording Arts and
Sciences, Lifetime Achievement Awards,
421, 445. *See also* Grammy Awards
National Barn Dance (radio show), 56, 72
National Life and Accident Insurance
Company, 85; plan to tear down Ryman,
322–23; sold WSM-TV, 394; sold *Opry* and
Opryland USA, 394; and Nashville Net-
work, 394–95
"Never Again" (song), 267, 317
"Never Leave the A String" (tune), 442
New Country (TV show), 414
New Dominion Barn Dance (radio show),
214, 270
"New John Henry Blues" (song), 187–88;
U.K. release, 207; U.S. release, 261
Newman, Jimmy C., 211, 212
"New Mule Skinner Blues" (song), 159
Newport Folk Festival: and Scruggs, 224; Bill
at 1963 festival, 260; Bill at 1965 festival,
277–78
New River Ranch (country music park, Ris-
ing Sun, Md.): Seeger took Rinzler to, 200;
Lyle with Bill, 205; Mayfield with Bill, 208
News and Observer (newspaper, Raleigh,
N.C.), 70
Newsweek (magazine), on Bill as "father of
bluegrass," 316–17
Newton, Ernie, 166; new technique, 170;
recorded with Bill, 178; played on plat-
form, 191
New York Ramblers, 271, 274
"Nine Pound Hammer" (song), 68, 235
Nixon, Richard, 302, 335; at Opry House, 341;
resigned, 345
"No Place to Pillow My Head" (song), 361
"Northern White Clouds" (tune), 425, 447
nostalgia, as growing national trend, 29

Oak Leaf Park (country music park, Luray,
Va.) "All Blue Grass Show," 233
Oberstein, Eli (RCA Victor producer), 66
O'Bryant, Alan, 363
Ohio County, Ky., xvi, xvii; and railroad,
xxiii, xxv; and Joseph Vandiver, xxvii; and
forest, 3; life in, 5–6; and Arnold Shultz,

15; and singing conventions, 15; 1921, 24; and Old Fiddlers Contest, 35; flooding and measles outbreak, 41; first Homecoming festival, 338; Chamber of Commerce and bluegrass museum, 380; "Bluegrass Music Capitol of the World," 394; Bill's unhappiness with, 397

Ohio County Messenger (newspaper), 58, 61, 65

Ohio County News (newspaper), 36, 45

Ohio County Times (newspaper), 311

Old as the Hills: The Story of Bluegrass (book, Price), 349–50

"The Old Brown County Barn" (tune), 405

"The Old Country Baptizing" (song), 241, 347

"The Old Crossroad" (song, "There's Just One Way to the Pearly Gates"), 69–70

"The Old Cross Road" (song), 137, 151; as only song Martin knew, 155; rerecorded, 411

"Old Dangerfield" (tune), 383

Old Dominion Barn Dance (radio show), 214, 218

"Old Ebenezer Scrooge" (tune), 383

"Old Farm Blues" (tune), 451

"The Old Fiddler" (song), 160

Old Fiddlers Contest (Ohio County, Ky.), 35

"The Old Gray Mare Came Tearing Out of the Wilderness" (tune), 322

"Old Joe Clark" (tune and song), 9, 23; on *Mountain Music Bluegrass Style* (Seeger and Yellin, 1959), 236; recorded by Bill, 236

"The Old Kentucky Blues" (tune), 454

"Old Lonesome Waltz" (tune), 453

"Old, Old House." *See* "There's an Old, Old House"

Old Time Picking Parlor, 331, 332

Ole Barn Jamboree (Rosine, Ky.), 456, 458–59

Omaha, Neb.: Texas Crystals, 58; WAAW, 60–61

"On and On" (song), 187, 205

"The One I Love Is Gone" (song), 291

"One of God's Sheep" (song), 265

"On My Way Back Home" (song), 73

"On the Old Kentucky Shore" (song), 166

Opryland USA, 323, 333; Opry House at, 341; mentioned in endorsement, 352; sold, 394–95; hotel at, 404

"Orange Blossom Special" (tune and song), 110

The Original Blue Grass Sound (album, Harmony-Columbia), 276

Osborne, Bobby, 163, 169

Osborne, Sonny: worked with Jimmy Martin, 177; played "Raw Hide" on *Opry*, 177; recorded with Bill, 178; returned to school, 179; rejoined band and left again, 184, 185

Osborne Brothers (Bobby and Sonny): first college concert, 228; recorded for Decca, 261; joined *Opry*, 270; and "Mule Skinner Blues," 270; at Brown County Jamboree, 277; sang "I Hear a Sweet Voice Calling" with Bill, 287; at Bean Blossom festival, 300; went all-electric, 302; dropped by MCA, 343; toured with Bill, 430–31

"Out in the Cold World" (song), 213; reissued on gospel album, 347

Overseas trips: England, 283–84; Italy and Germany, 302; England, 342; Japan, 348; Europe, 351; Japan, 355–56; Japan, 363; England, 379; Britain and Europe, 395; Japan, 401–02; Switzerland, 426; Switzerland and Germany, 430–31; Japan, 431–32; France, 443

Owens, Don ("Blue Grass Day" producer), 229

Owens, Tom (WLS square dance producer), 29, 52

"Ozark Rag" (tune), 454

"Paddy on the Turnpike" (tune), 288

Painter, Fred and Denise, 438, 464–65

"Panhandle Country" (tune), 217

Parker, Byron ("The Old Hired Hand") and Deanne, 61, 62, 64, 68, 69, 70; quit Monroe Brothers, 71; Bill tried to sing like, 72, 78

Parker, Colonel Tom, as Presley's new manager, 202

Parker, Linda (of WLS), 53; started at WWAE, 56

Park Place Retirement Center, Melissa as resident at, 419, 421

Parton, Dolly, recorded "Mule Skinner Blues," 315

"Pass Me Not" (song), 249, 347

Pat (gray mare), 40; Bill riding to school, 41

Payne, William ("Skip"), 312, 315, 319

Peach, Willis (Rosine barber), 42

"Peach Picking Time in Georgia" (song), 169, 266

Pearl, Ed (Ash Grove owner), 263

Pedigo, Ben, 338, 339

Pendleton, Buddy, 257

Pennington, "Buddy," 221, 224

People (Weekly) (magazine), Bill featured in, 354, 412

Perkins, Carl: up-tempo "Blue Moon," 192; guest on *Opry*, 208; "Million Dollar Quartet," 209

Petty, Russell, 160–61

Peva, Jim: Brown County Music Corporation, 275; given lifetime pass to Bean Blossom, 364; on Bill's ability to "pull himself together," 442; visited Bill at Medical Center with wife Ailene, 464

Phelps, Alan (Dobro player and bus driver), 390; married LaBella, 391

Phelps, Jackie, 145; replaced Mayfield, 195; played guitar break, 196; left to work with Hawkins, 198; worked with Bill, 207; recorded with Keith, 255

Phillips, Sam (Sun Records producer), 184; arranged *Opry* appearance for Presley, 194

Pickin' (magazine), interview with Bill in, 340–41

Pierce, Ray (driver to WJKS), 56

Pigeon Ridge (hill in Kentucky), xvii, 2, 4, 5

Pigeon Roost, Ky. *See* Rosine, Ky.

"Pike County Breakdown" (tune), 176, 179, 255

"Pinewood Valley" (tune), 365–66

Pinnacle Boys, 343–44

Planes, Trains, and Automobiles (movie), "Blue Moon of Kentucky" in, 419

"Plant Some Flowers by My Grave" (song), 188, 248

the "ploy" (attempt to increase Bill's price), 421–22, 424, 425, 427

"Pocahontas" (tune), 450–51

"Poison Love" (song), 166

Poole, James Clay ("Charlie Poole Jr."), 72–73

"Poor White Folks" (tune), 322

Potter, Dale, 189; took charge of fiddlers, 212; joined band, 224; stroke, 227; recorded with Bill, 231

Prairie Ramblers, 54; recording in Chicago, 56

presidents: Monroe, xvi, xvii, xviii; Taft, 8; Harding, 24; Franklin Roosevelt, 55, 112, 125, 127; Eisenhower, 180; Kennedy, 248, 262; Lyndon Johnson, 270; Nixon, 302, 335, 341, 345; Ford, 345; Carter, 361, 377; Reagan, 382, 388, 402, 413; George H. W. Bush, 426–27, 432; Clinton, 444, 445, 459

Presley, Elvis, 184; first Sun session, 192; and "Blue Moon of Kentucky," 194; increasing success of, 204; and "Million Dollar Quartet," 209; recorded "Little Cabin Home on the Hill," 322; death, 366

Prestige, Dee Dee, 396, 399–400. *See also* Christian, Diana (stage name for Dee Dee Prestige)

"Pretty Fair Maiden in the Garden" (song), 288

Price, Bill ("Billy"), 177

Price, Joel, 143, 145; and Bromo, 149; in and out of band, 150, 158, 169

Prince Albert Smoking Tobacco Show (portion of *Opry*), 88

"The Prisoner's Song" (song), 167

Pure Food and Drug Administration, 73

"Put My Little Shoes Away" (song), 34, 191; released in Great Britain, 207

"Put My Rubber Doll Away" (song), 231

Pyle, Pete, 112; joined band, 113; second session, 114; drafted, 115–16; rejoined band, 169; and Brown County Fox Hunters, 176

radio: first commercial station, 24; and nostalgia trend, 29

Ragsdale, Denzel ("Spurts," "Silver Spur"), 173, 203, 206

Rains, Dr. Newton J., 24; and Bill's appendicitis, 28

Raleigh, N.C., 70, 72

Ralph Stanley's bluegrass festival (McClure, Va.), first, 324

Ramsey, Hazel ("Libby"), as fan club president, 400

Rawhide (movie), 166

"Raw Hide" (tune), 166; album release, 275

RCA Victor: and Jimmie Rodgers, 47, 53; Bluebird label, 54; and Mainer's Mountaineers, 61–62; Monroe Brothers sign with, 66; Monroe Brothers six sessions:

66–67, 68–69, 69–70, 70–71, 71–72, 73; Monroe Brothers releases, 68, 71; Charlie's sessions, 77, 79; contacting Bill, 111; Bill's first session, 111–12; *Smoky Mountain Ballads*, 113–14; Bill's second session, 114–15; Bill ended association with, 116–17; Eddy Arnold's "Kentucky Waltz," 166; winning bid for Elvis Presley, 202; released *The Father of Blue Grass* album, 244–45; Porter Wagoner's "Uncle Pen," 206; Bill a guest on *Lester Flatt Live!*, 341–42

Reagan, Ronald, 382; Bill played for, 388; re-elected, 402; congratulatory letter to Bill, 413

"Reasons Why" (song), recorded, 349

the record business: beginnings, 24; and companies, 29 (*see also names of specific companies*)

Red Cravens and the Bray Brothers, 206, 229

Red Smiley and the Bluegrass Cut-Ups, 317; and death of Red Smiley, 331

"Remember the Cross" (song by Howard and Alice Watts), 141–42, 151; album release, 385; Bill recorded with Seldom Scene, 404

Renfro Valley Barn Dance (radio show), 72

Reno, Don, 68; meeting Bill, 121; finding Bill after World War II service, 145; on using a capo, 145; trading banjos with Scruggs, 147; left band, 153; guest with Bill in Virginia, 220; first "Blue Grass Day," 229; cutting Danny Jones's hair, 328; at Bean Blossom, 372

Reno, Don Wayne (Don's son), met Bill, 372

Richardson, Larry, 169, 174, 177

Rich-R'-Tone, 148

"Right, Right On" (tune), 383

Rinzler, Ralph, 183, 190; went with Seeger to see Stanleys and Bill, 200; changed middle name, 201; liner notes, 209–10; studied in France, 210; returned to U.S., 222; joined Greenbriar Boys, 225; met Ashley, 228; returned to South, met Watson, 230; reaction to *Sing Out!*, 242; asked Bill for interview, 242; asked Stanleys for help, 242; offered to open doors, 243; interview with Bill, 245–46; *Sing Out!* article, 250–51; sang bass, 251; and Bill Keith, 253; teamed Bill with Watson, 256; moved to

Nashville, 257; met Haney, 257; confronted Bill about Birch, 258; asked Rosenberg to replace Birch, 259; visited Rosine with Bill, 259–60; moved base to New York, played with Greenbriar Boys, 261; joined board of directors, 261; investigated Bill's unreleased recordings, 262; "The Roots of Bluegrass," 267; recruited Arkin, 269; invited Haney to Newport, 270; first use of "high lonesome sound" for Bill's music, 272; consulted on recordings, 274; liner notes, *Bluegrass Instrumentals*, 275; first multiday festival, 278–80; liner notes, *The High, Lonesome Sound*, 284; the Smithsonian's Folklife Festival, 292; liner notes, *Bill Monroe and Charlie Monroe*, 303; injured in accident, 304; *Stars of Country Music* monograph, 352–53; met potential collaborator Cantwell, 363; offer of help with autobiography rejected, 368; traveled with Bill, end of autobiography effort, 392; executive producer of instructional video, 442; death, 451–52

Rinzler, Richard, 245–46

"River of Death" (song), 164

Rivers, Jerry, 401–2

Road of Life (album, MCA), 347

"Road of Life" (song), 315, 347

"Road to Columbus" (tune), 357; Starkey believed written for her, 377

"Roane County Prison" (song), 213

"Roanoke" (tune), 196, 197

Roberts, Gene, 269

Robins, "Butch": brief stint with band, 295; won Bean Blossom banjo contest, 306; filled in and traveled with band, 306; helped build Bill's compartment, 309; rejoined band, 366; taping tunes, 382; left band, 386; visited Bill at farm, 440; recorded with Bill, 453; invited to play at Ole Barn Jamboree, 456

Robins, Calvin, 295; followed band to Ohio, 306; recruited Hutchens to help, 316; Bill at funeral of, 380

rock and roll: early, 111; "revolution," 187

"Rocky Road Blues" (song), 126, 131, 321

Rodgers, Jimmie, 38; and "Mule Skinner Blues," 47, 96; death, 55

"Roll in My Sweet Baby's Arms" (song), 70, 86; sung by Bill, Flatt, and Martin, 335

"Roll On, Buddy, Roll On" (song), 265

Rooney, Jim, 249; visit from Bill and Mauldin, 258; at "Summer Music Camp," 301; *Bossmen: Bill Monroe and Muddy Waters*, 312–13, 315, 322

Roosevelt, Franklin, 55, 112; helped end recording ban, 125; death, 127

Roscoe Holcomb: The High Lonesome Sound (album, Folkways), 246

Rose, Artie, 271

Rose, Billy: filled in, 423, 426; hired, 428; trip to Rosine, 430; let go, 436–37

Rose, Forrest, 412

Rosenberg, Neil: as fill-in, 233; asked Bill to autograph album, 248; management of Jamboree, 249, 262, 268; heard band without Bill, 273; first *Bluegrass Unlimited* article, 286–87; bluegrass book, 332–33; Bill Monroe discography, 345–46; liner notes for first classic band album, 373–74

"Rosine" (tune), 435

Rosine, Ky., xxi; as Pigeon Roost, xxv; 5; life in, 6; and Dr. Schanzenbacher, 8; singing convention, 15; and Dr. Rains, 24; and Bill driving, 27; and Bill's appendicitis, 28; and Arnold Shultz, 29; and choir, 30; and tie yard, 32; Bill's first visit home, 58; mention in songbook, 68; Bill's visit with John Monroe, 75; train depot, 90; baseball game, 148; show in ballpark, 242; Bill, Rinzler, and McCoury visited, 260; Bill's visit with Charlie, 301–2; Fleischhauer and Rothman visited, 332–33; first Monroe Homecoming festival, 338–39; film crew visited, 430; 1990 show in, 435; Bill at Ole Barn Jamboree, 456, 458–59

Rosine Cemetery: Joseph Vandiver grave, 5; Malissa Monroe buried in, 25; Cecil Vandiver buried in, 33; J. B. Monroe buried in, 39; Pen Vandiver buried in, 51; Bill and Martin visited, 178; Bill, Rinzler, and McCoury visited, 260; Bill and Rose visited, 430

Ross, Al, 263

"Rotation Blues" (song), 170

Rothman, Sandy, 255–56; and Garcia head east, 267; petrified at Jamboree, 268; Bill's invitation, 269–69; asked to play shows, 269; left band, 271; sang "There's an Old, Old House," 274; convinced Bill to let Ewing sit in, 330; asked by Fleischhauer to visit Rosine, 332; attended birthday party, 453

Rowan, Peter: filling in, 271–72, 273; hired, 274; and "Walls of Time," 277; bus accident, 282; and "The Last Thing on My Mind," 284; and theft of Bill's guitar, 284; baritone part in trios, 287; interviewed by Benson, 288–89; "Midnight on the Stormy Deep," 290; left band, 291

"Roxanna Waltz" (tune), 366, 447

Ryman Auditorium (originally Union Gospel Tabernacle), 2; plan to tear down, 322–23; Bill's last *Opry* show at, 341; depicted on buckle, 420; renovation, 451

Sage, Bill, 257

"Sailor's Hornpipe" (tune), 255, 275

"Sailor's Plea" (song), 168, 169

"Sally Goodin" (tune), 35; Scruggs audition, 130; recorded with Berline, 295; with six fiddles, 301; rerecorded with Berline and Scruggs, 453

"Sally Jo" (song), 215

"Salt Creek" (tune), 254

Salt Creek Bluegrass Festival (Hugo, Okla.), 309

Salyer, South, 172

Sandy, Les ("Uncle Puny"), in and out of band, 183, 184–85, 187, 193, 194, 212, 213

"Santa Claus" (tune), 255, 275

Satherley, Art (Columbia producer), 126, 135, 142

Satisfied Mind (album, Atteiram), Bill's uncredited participation in, 371

Sato, Paul, 402

Saylor, Lucky, 205

"Scotland" (tune), 217; on *Billboard* chart, 221

Scott, Gladys and Rusty (comedy team), 73, 75

Scruggs, Earl, 121; joined Lost John band, 128; auditioned and hired by Bill, 130–31;

"fancy" banjo, 132; replaced banjo, 134; grievances, 144; left band, 144; traded banjos with Reno, 147; at Newport Folk Festival, 224; *Sing Out!* article, 239; took Keith to *Opry*, 252; reunited with Bill at Skaggs's "Bluegrass Night," 452; recorded with Bill and Berline, 453–54; with wife Louise at Melissa's visitation, 458

Seckler, Curly, 87

Second Fiddle to a Steel Guitar (movie), 272

Seeger, Mike, 190; took Rinzler to see Stanleys and Bill, 200; produced banjo album, 208; producer, *Mountain Music Bluegrass Style*, 224; called Bill "the father of bluegrass," 224; at Rinzler memorial service, 452

Seeger, Pete, 183

Seibel, Kathy (recreation director, Beverly Healthcare and Rehabilitation Center), 460, 465, 467

Seldom Scene (band), 369, 370, 404

"Seven Year Blues" (song), 231

"Shady Grove" (song), 235

"Shake My Mother's Hand for Me" (song), 115

Shehan, "Shorty," 172, 174, 233

Shenandoah, Ia., 58, 59, 60

"Shenandoah Breakdown" (tune), 255

Shenandoah Valley Trio: and baseball shows, 148; after baseball season, 154; recorded for Columbia, 162, 168

Sherrill, Homer ("Pappy"), 63; about kerosene circuit, 64; with Blue Ridge Hillbillies, 67; Byron Parker band, 71

"She's Young (and I'm Growing Old)" (song), 305

"Shine, Hallelujah, Shine" (song), 142, 143, 144; LP release, 385; rerecorded, 435

"Shining Path" (song), 134, 135; LP release, 400

"Show Me the Way" (song), 348–49

Shultz, Arnold, xxv, 15, 20; played in band, 26; arrested, 26–27; Bill heard, 29–30; played a dance with Bill, 32–33; and Old Fiddlers Contest, 35; played with Wilson et al., 35; death, 38; taught Atchison, 54

Shumate, Jim, 127, 129; recommended Scruggs, 129–30; last night with band, 131; with Flatt and Scruggs, 147

Sieker, Rolf (driver in Europe), 351

Silver Eagle Cross Country Music Show (radio show), 399

Silverstein, Harry (Decca producer), 240, 274, 314

Siminoff, Roger (luthier), 373

singing conventions, 15

singing school, 15

Sing Out! (magazine), 239, 250–51

Sings Bluegrass, Body and Soul (album, MCA), 363

"Sinner, You Better Get Ready" (song), 71

"Sitting Alone in the Moonlight" (song), 188, 209

"Sittin' on Top of the World" (song), 212, 215, 323

"Six Feet Under (the Ground)" (song), 343–44, 370

Sixteen All-Time Greatest Hits (album, Columbia), 317

"Six White Horses" (song), 111, 112

Skaggs, Ricky, 232–33; Bill overdubbed break on "Wheel Hoss," 399; "Uncle Pen," 401; "Country Boy" video, 403; awarded Grammy for "Wheel Hoss," 403

Skinner, Jimmie, 377–78

slaves, Monroe family's, xvii

Sledge, Larry, 379–80, 383

"Slow and Easy Blues" (tune), 447

Smith, Arthur ("Fiddlin' Arthur"), 66; session with Blue Grass Boys, 112; *Smoky Mountain Ballads*, 114; and "Dusty Miller," 289

Smith, Billy and Terry (sons of Hazel Smith), 462

Smith, Bobby, 230, 235

Smith, Charlie: audition, 207–8; a "regular" at *Opry*, 220; composed tune for Bill, 222; played on the road, 224; navy cruise, 224; introduced Bill to Maynard, 225; left band, 244

Smith, Hal, 167, 169

Smith, Javonda Charlene ("Charlene"): as caregiver for Melissa, 435, 437; and Bill's health, 439, 440; ended relationship, 448; hosted Bill's birthday party, 452

Smith, Mayne, and origin of bluegrass, 279

Smith, Roger, 200; called to play in St. Louis, 206; at New Dominion Barn Dance, 220; Brown County Music Corporation, 274–75

Smith, Sue, 438

Smoak, Jim: hired, 180; left band, 182; rejoined band, 189, 190–91; quit band, 192

Smoky Mountain Ballads (RCA Victor album), 113–14

"Smoky Mountain Schottische" (tune), 442, 447

Snead, Earl, 216; banjo on *Bill Monroe's Country Music Hall of Fame* album, 321; let go, 322

Snow, Rev. Jimmie: arranged Tour to Israel, 396; baptized Bill in River of Jordan, 397; married Bill and Della Streeter, 404

"Sold Down the River" (song), 231

"Soldier's Joy" (tune): Bill first heard, 16; recorded, 290; as fiddlers' "roll call," 337; released in Japan, 356

"Somebody Touched Me" (song), 242, 347

Sonka, Mylos ("Miles"), 292

Southern Flavor (album, MCA), 421, 424

"Southern Flavor" (tune), 421–22

Southern Radio Corporation (Charlotte, N.C.), 66

Spanish-American War, 3

Spicher, "Buddy," 235; on *Second Fiddle to a Steel Guitar* soundtrack, 272; substituted for Baker in studio, 365; in studio, 409–10; fiddled with Hicks, 409–10; on the road, 426

splicing (tape): "Get Down on Your Knees," 170; "A Mighty Pretty Waltz," 179; "Going Home," 241; "On the Jericho Road," 242; "Soldier's Joy," 290

Spottswood, Richard, 285

Sprouse, Blaine, 361, 426

Squires, Mark, 412, 414

Staber, Dick, writing "Bluest Man in Town," 309

Stamey, Mary Ruth (fan club vice president), 400

Stamper, Art, 408, 409

Stanley, Carter: offered to be lead singer for Bill, 169; last show with Bill, 172; and "Blue Moon of Kentucky," 192–93; at "All Blue Grass Show," 233–34; vouched for Seeger

and Rinzler, 243; at Black Poodle, 288; death, 289

Stanley, Ralph: as fill-in, 171; Bill recorded with, 352, 442; Bill's recommendation for *Opry* membership, 445

Stanley, "Red," 238–39, 241, 244

Stanley Brothers (and Clinch Mountain Boys): first saw Bill, 111; Lambert's influence, 137; Bill's displeasure with, 148–49; Carter writing songs, 150; Ralph's second thoughts, 169; Ralph picked banjo with Bill, 171; Ralph in car wreck, 171; signed with Mercury Records, 186; suggested by Seeger to Rinzler, 190; Bill and Cline at session, 193; Carter endorsed Seeger and Rinzler, 243

Starday Records, 235

Starkey, Mary, 376–77; asked to be caregiver for Bill, 449; and Big Plan debts, 450; quit "hanging out," 457

Stars of Country Music (book, ed. Malone and McCulloh), 352–53

Stauffer, Virginia, 102; "I Live in the Past," 274; traveled with band, 293, 295; drove Green home, 294; and Bill, 295; at Bean Blossom, 298; "With Body and Soul," 305; "Road of Life," 315, 347; and Bill, 318; at Bean Blossom, 323; "Show Me the Way," 348–49; Bill lived with, 362, 365, 368; Christmas song, 365; Bill moved out, 385

"Stay Away from Me" (song), 409; recorded with Chiavola, 452; Bill sang on last show, 463

Stevenson, Guy, 336, 337

Stewart, Arthur T. ("T," Noble's father), 39

Stewart, Floyd, 355

Stewart, Noble, 35, 38–39

Stewart, Travis, 323, 325

Stone, David (WSM announcer), 85, 202

Stone, Harry (WSM station manager), 85

"Stone Coal" (tune), 422

Stoneman, Donna, 238

"Stoney Lonesome" (tune), 222–23

"Stormy" (one of Bill's dogs), with Bill on cover of *Bluegrass '87*, 416

Story, Carl, 118, 119

A Story of the Grand Ole Opry (book, Hay), 129

Stover, Don, 210, 213

"Strawberry Point" (tune), 417

Streeter, Della: at Old Time Pickin' Parlor, 332; father of, 404; married Bill, 404. *See also* Monroe, Della

Stringfield, Hubert, 21

Stripling, "Chick," 139, 206

Stuart, Joe, 201; taped picking banjo by Seeger, 208; guitar on "Four Walls," 212; fiddled on Bill's first album, 212–13; returned to banjo, 213; left band, 216; returned and left again twice, 224, 225, 247, 250; last session on banjo, 267; helped build bunk beds on bus, 309; switched to bass, 319; replaced Jones on guitar, 328; left band to work with Sullivan Family, 336; filled in for Lewis, 407–8; and Bean Blossom festival, 418; illness and death, 418, 420

Stuart, Marty, 319

"Sugar Coated Love" (song), 169–70

"Sugar Loaf Mountain" (tune), 422

Sullivan Family: unadvertised appearance, 299–300; Bill's festival in partnership with, 316; Stuart worked with, 336; gospel shows with Bill, 356; 1994 Winter Tour, 448

"Summertime Is Past and Gone" (song), 149, 321

Sunset Park (country music park), band's five-day stand at, 134–35; poster from, 405

Sunset Valley Barn Dance (Minneapolis–St. Paul, Minn.), 202

"Sweetheart, You Done Me Wrong" (song): in Bill's first songbook, 140; recorded, 142; released, 146; on the charts, 147; rerecorded, 331

"Sweet Mary and the Miles in Between" (song), 313, 314

Swing Billies, 72–73; "White House Blues," 188

"Swing Low, Sweet Chariot" (song), 167; as fiddlers' "roll call," 337

Sykes, Ernie, 446, 457

Taft, William, 8

"Take Courage Un' Tomorrow" (song), 423

"Tallahassee" (tune), 321, 326

"Tall Pines" (song), recorded but shelved, 311; new vocal dubbed, 331

"Tall Timber" (tune), 202, 275

Tarlton, Jimmie, 37–38

Tate, Clarence ("Tater," and wife Lois): hired, 208; left band, 209; Bill's recuperation at Tate home, 385; hired as bass player, 399; fiddled on trip to Japan, 401; showed Franks how to play bass, 402; on fiddle and bass, 409, 412; and bus breakdown, 418; vocals, 423; arranged for fill-ins, 423, 457; and plan to rehire Ewing, 428; on fiftieth *Opry* anniversary, 437; Lois injured in car wreck, 441; fiddled with Bill Monroe and the Boys, 454; boycotted benefits, 456

Taylor, "Red": hired, 161; helped write "Uncle Pen," 161–62; left band, 165; recorded with Bill, 166; played on road, 189; on fiddling trio, 191; returned to band and left again, 218, 220

Taylor, Rev. Mike, and funeral of Donald Evans, 367

Taylor, Robert ("Tut"), 263, 296

Telluride Bluegrass Festival, 395–96

"Tennessee Blues" (tune), 111, 126

Tennessee Christian Medical Center (Madison): Bill transferred to, 463–64; Bill's visitors at, 464–65

Terhune, Max, 50; and movie *Rawhide*, 166

Terry, Arnold, 203–4

Terry, Gordon, 163–64; came to Nashville, 165; returned, 169; simplified tuning for "Christmas Time's," 173; left band, 174; played on road, 189; and fiddling trio, 191; returned to band, 210; sang bass on gospel album, 216; filled in during Cash tour, 227

"Texas Blue Bonnet" (tune), 365

Texas Crystals (sponsored Monroe Brothers), 58–62

"Texas Gallop" (tune), 314

"Texas Lone Star" (tune), 409–10, 422

"Thank God for Kentucky" (song), 349

"That Home Above" (song), 142, 143, 385

"That's All Right" (song), 289

"That's Christmas Time to Me" (song), 365

"There's an Old, Old House" (song), 274, 349; with Chiavola, 452

"There Was Nothing We Could Do" (song), 25, 239, 255

"Thinking About You" (song), 226

"This World Is Not My Home" (song), 68, 241, 347, 430

Thompson, Bobby: and Lineberger, 270; banjo on *Bill Monroe's Country Music Hall of Fame* album, 321; and *Bill Monroe's Uncle Pen* album, 322

Thompson, Jack, 153–54, 158

Thompson, James S. (Texas Crystals president), 58, 59, 61

Thompson, Tommy ("the Singing Range Rider"): lyrics for "Kentucky Waltz," 116; tent show appearances, 136; "Kentucky Waltz" lawsuit, 168

"Those Gambler's Blues" (song), 169; released in Japan, 356

"Those Memories of You" (song), 371

Three Tobacco Tags, 63, 70

Thurmond, Garry, 271, 398

"Time Changes Everything" (song), 231

Together Again (album, MCA), 370–71

"Tombstone Junction" (tune), 442, 447

"Tomorrow I'll Be Gone" (song), 223, 225

Tour to Israel, 396–97

"Two Finger Waltz" (tune), 451

"Toy Heart" (song), 134, 135, 150, 235

"Train 45 (Heading South)" (song), 297

"Travelin' Blues" (song), 167

"Travelin' this Lonesome Road" (song), 155, 157, 160, 276

Tronson, Rube, and Texas Cowboys, 53, 57, 54; with Tommy Dandurand band, 254

"True Life Blues" (song), 126, 137; as last song of Bill's last show, 463

Tubb, Ernest, Record Shop, 139–40; death and funeral, 400

Tulane Hotel: Mauldin at, 114; Shumate and Scruggs met at, 130; Scruggs auditioned at, 130; Castle Recording Studio at, 139; torn down, 191

"Turkey in the Straw" (tune), 16, 35, 288

Turner, Jesse Granderson ("Grant"), 125, 182

"Uncle Pen" (song), 161–66; Porter Wagoner recorded, 206; Rose Maddox recorded, 238; sung at monument dedication, 339; Ricky Skaggs recorded, 401

Uncle Pen's cabin: Bill moved in, 41; Pen fiddled on back porch, 43–44; remembered, 333; possible relocations, 346, 380; reconstruction of, 441

"Used To Be" (song), 201, 266

Vandiver, Anna Belle (Johnson, Pen's wife), 4; separation, 5; divorce, 26

Vandiver, Cecil (Pen's son), 4, 26; tombstone, 339

Vandiver, Elizabeth (Miller, Bill's great-grandmother), xxii

Vandiver, George (Bill's great-great-grandfather), xxii

Vandiver, George H. (Bill's great-grandfather), xxii

Vandiver, James Pendleton ("Uncle Pen"), xxiii, xxvi; and Ohio County, xxvii; 1, 4; separation, 5; musical influence, 11–12, 19; helping Charlie, 13; family visits, 14; and musical, 16; and teaching Bill, 22; and death of Malissa, 25; divorce, 26; played with Monroe brothers, 27–28; and trading, 26; played with Bill, 33, 44; and death of Cecil, 33–34; lived with Wilsons, 34; and a loan for Birch, 35; deaths of ex-wife and daughter, 36; accident, 37; pneumonia, 39; cared for family, 40; left Monroe house, 40; and cabin, 40; cooking, 42; said goodbye to Bill, 47; death, 50–51; photo, 92; monument, 339

Vandiver, Joseph M. (Bill's grandfather), xxii–xxiii; and separation, xxvii; death, 5

Vandiver, Lena B. (Pen's daughter), 5, 26

Vandiver, Mahala ("Aunt Halley," Malissa's sister), xxiii, 14

Vandiver, Malissa Ann, xxiii, xxvi; met J. B. Monroe, xxvi; courtship, xxvi–xxvii; marriage, 1. *See* Malissa Monroe

Vandiver, Martha (Beales, Joseph M.'s first wife), xxii

Vandiver, Martha Jane (Malissa's sister), xxii, 5

Vandiver, Munerba Jane (Pharris, Bill's grandmother), xxii–xxiii, xxvii

Vandiver, Nancy (Bill's great-great-grandmother), xxii

Vandiver, William J. (Joseph M.'s son), xxii, xxvii, 5, 8

Vanguard Records: recorded Scruggs, 224; recorded Greenbriar Boys and Baez, 234; recorded Bill, 260

Vanover, Carl, 209, 210

Vietnam War, 270, 273; first protest, 274; Kent State, 315; ended, 335

Vipperman, Johnny, 172

"Virginia Darlin'" (tune), 295

A Voice from On High (album, Decca), 306–7

"A Voice from On High" (song), 186, 188

WAAW (Omaha, Neb.), 60

"Wabash Cannonball" (song), 366

Wade Mainer and Sons of the Mountaineers, 115

Wade Mainer and Zeke Morris ("Singing Rangers"), 66; and "What Would You Give," 67; no borrowing, 71; Mainer at Bean Blossom festival, 306

Wagoner, Porter: and "Uncle Pen," 206; recorded "I Haven't Seen Mary in Years," 304; and Dolly Parton, 315

"Wait a Little Longer, Please Jesus" (song), 197

Wakefield, Frank, 176, 252

Walker, Caswell ("Cas"), 182, 265

"Walk Softly on My Heart" (song): verses by Landers, 253, 306; Bill recorded, 311; Christian sang on *Friday Night Opry*, 434; and Kentucky Headhunters, 437; Bill recorded with the Smith brothers, 462

"Walking in Jerusalem" (song), 178

Wall, Rendal ("Ren"), and mandolin repair, 378

Wallace, Bill (and son Bill Jr.), and Bill's Rosine plaque, 458

"Walls of Time" (song), 277, 293, 302, 331; released in Japan, 356

Waltman, Lawrence (owner of Sunset Park), 405

Watanabe, Saburo, 402

"Watermelon Hanging on the Vine" (song and tune, aka "Watermelon on the Vine"), 34, 69, 451

Watermelon Park (Berryville, Va.), "Blue Grass Day," 229–30

Watson, Arthel ("Doc"), 230, 256; shared week with Bill at Ash Grove, 263; jam session at Rinzler's, 271; at Logan's party, 286; recording with Flatt and Scruggs, 286

Watson, "Tex," 200; drove bus, 263

"Watson Blues" (tune), 349

Watts, Howard ("Cedric Rainwater"), 122–23; in and out of band, 126–27, 128, 137, 141, 145; with Flatt and Scruggs, 147; asked Bill for job back, 160; joined Drifting Cowboys, 160; recorded with Bill again, 170; death, 314

"Way Down in My Soul" (song), 241

"Wayfaring Stranger" (song), 217, 290, 452

WBT (Charlotte, N.C.), 62–63

Weary Traveler (album, MCA), 356

"Weary Traveler" (song), 349, 355

Weger, Harry (managed Brown County Jamboree, 1962), 248

Wehle, Billy, 120, 200

"We'll Understand It Better" (song), 242

Wendell, E. W. ("Bud"), 297, 306

"We Read of a Place That's Called Heaven" (song), 69

"(We're Going) Just Over in the Glory Land" (song), 267, 347

"Were You There?" (song), 115, 255, 347

Wesbrooks, Willie ("Bill," "Cousin Wilbur"), 76, 77, 110; humorous bass playing, 115; left band, 122

WFBC (Greenville, S.C.), 63, 64, 65, 80; return to, 82, 83–84

WGST (Atlanta, Ga.), 67, 80

WHAS (Louisville, Ky.), 87

"What About You?" (song), 305; released in Japan, 356

"What a Wonderful Life" (song), 422, 423

"What Is Home Without Love?" (song), 68

"What Would the Profit Be?" (song), 71

"What Would You Give in Exchange?" (song), 66–67, 68; sequels, 71–72; with Davis, 79; as Delmore Brothers' last song on *Opry*, 80; rerecorded, 331

wheelers (wheel cattle, wheel horses), 3

"Wheel Hoss" (tune, "Wheel Horse"), 3; Bill recorded, 196; Bill overdubbed break on Skaggs's recording, 399; Skaggs gave Grammy for song to Bill, 403

"When My Blue Moon Turns to Gold Again" (song), 287

"When the Bees Are in the Hive" (song), 55, 240

"When the Cactus Is in Bloom" (song), 167

"When the Golden Leaves Begin to Fall" (song), 164, 331

"When the Phone Rang" (song), 222–23, 266

"When You Are Lonely" (song), 142; Reno making up verses, 147; released, 149; on the *Billboard* chart, 153

"Where Is My Sailor Boy?" (song), 71

White, Buck, 336

White, L. E., 183, 187

White, Roland, 293, 294; square dancing, 299; Baker's first solo album, 301; on Flatt and Scruggs, 303; and new bus, 303; left band, 303; drove bus, 417–18

Whitehead, Ruth (Speed Monroe's stepdaughter), 51, 58

"White House Blues" (song, "From Buffalo to Washington"), 73, 187

"White Horse Breakdown" (tune), 366

"White Rose" (song), 422, 443

Whiting, Ind., 36

"Who's Gonna Shoe Your Pretty Little Feet?" (song), 370. *See also* "Little Red Shoes"

"Who Will Call You Sweetheart" (song), 207

"Why Did You Wander?" (song), 133, 141, 360

"Wicked Path of Sin" (song), 134, 148; on *Billboard* chart, 149

Williams, Benny: recorded, 235; played guitar on sessions, 236; rejoined, 244; left band, 247; and *Second Fiddle to a Steel Guitar*, 272; replaced Berline, 297; injured and left band, 297; married LaBella, 384

Williams, Blake: joined band, 386–87; advised Bill to collect pieces, 406–7; left band, 440

Williams, Cohen (Martha White owner), 197

Williams, Hank, 139; as guest on *Opry*, 152; at state fair with Bill, 154; singing "I Saw the Light" with Bill, 156; fired by *Opry*, 179; death and funeral, 181; Lifetime Achievement Award, 421

Williams, Tommy, 208, 305

Willis, Dr. Pal T.: and Uncle Pen's injury, 37; and J. B. Monroe, 39; and Uncle Pen's illness, 51

Willis, "Tex," 125, 126–27

"Will You Be Loving Another Man?" (song): Flatt's solo with Charlie, 122; composer credit includes Bill, 133; released, 140; royalties split, 144; album release, 276

Wilma Lee and Stoney Cooper (and Clinch Mountain Clan), 148

Wilson, Clarence: and banjo at musical, 16; and Pen Vandiver, 34; and Arnold Shultz, 35; as banker for Uncle Pen, 35; appraiser, 40

Wilson, Flossie, photo, 92

Winston, Julian ("Winnie"), 274

Wintergrass Bluegrass Festival (Tacoma, Wash.), 448, 454

WIS (Columbia, S.C.), 62

Wise, "Chubby," 119; leave of absence, 126–27, 132; recorded with Williams, 143; in and out of band, 144, 153, 158; with Flatt and Scruggs, 167; reunion with Bill, Keith, and McCoury, 436

Wiseman, Mac: with Flatt and Scruggs, 147; Bill offered job, 150; and Mauldin, 152; let go, 157; at first "Blue Grass Day," 229; at "All Blue Grass Show," 233; tour with Blue Grass Boys, 239; and "I'm So Lonesome I Could Cry," 248–49; at Haney's first festival, 280; at Newport Folk Festival, 308; and Tour to Israel, 396

"Wishing Waltz" (song), 187

"With Body and Soul" (song), 305, 311

WJKS/WIND (Gary, Ind.), 55–56

WLS (Chicago, Ill.), 29; *Barn Dance* stars, 48–50; *Barn Dance* moved, 50. *See also* *National Barn Dance*

WMC (Memphis, Tenn.), 75

WNOX (Knoxville, Tenn.), 75

women's suffrage (1920), 24

Wood, Randy, 296; helped build bunk beds on bus, 309; traveled with band, 310; Bill asked him to sleep with mandolin, 331–32

Woodstock Music and Art Fair, 309

Wooten, Art, 31, 83; left band, 110; rejoined band, 113; joined navy, 117; death, 411

World's Fair. *See* Chicago World's Fair

World War I, 17, 20

World War II, 84; Pearl Harbor, 115

WPTF (Raleigh, N.C.), 70, 71, 72, 73–74

Wright, Doyle, 146

Wright brothers, 4

WSB (Atlanta, Ga.), 79; Wiseman featured, 149

WSM (Nashville, Tenn.), 34, 84, 88; benefit for Bill, 182

WSM Artist Service Bureau, 109; Bill unwilling to pay percentage, 229

WSM Barn Dance (radio show), 34. See *Grand Ole Opry*

WWAE (Hammond, Ind.), and Bill's radio debut, 49; increased number of country music shows, 50; Monroe Brothers first radio show, 51

WWNC (Asheville, N.C.), 80

WWVA (Wheeling, W.Va.), 84

"Y'All Come" (song), 188

Yarbrough, Rual: filling in, 250; University of Chicago Folk Festival, 251; joined band, 304; helped build bunk beds for bus, 309; left band, 320

yarding timber, 32

Yates, Bill, 308; built compartment on bus for Bill, 309; sang lead on "Going Up Caney," 312; left band, 312

"You'd Better Get Right" (song), 199

"You Live in a World All Your Own" (song), 231

"You'll Find Her Name Written There" (song), 196, 209

Young, Vern, 166

Youngblood, Jack, 190

"You're Drifting Away" (song), 170, 435

"You've Got to Walk That Lonesome Valley" (song), 68, 69

Zinkan, Joe, 304

Zmudka, Jimmy (Buddy Lee agent), 448

TOM EWING was guitarist/lead singer of Bill Monroe and his Blue Grass Boys for ten years. He is the editor of *The Bill Monroe Reader* and writes the "Thirty Years Ago This Month" column for *Bluegrass Unlimited.*

MUSIC IN AMERICAN LIFE

Only a Miner: Studies in Recorded Coal-Mining Songs   *Archie Green*

Great Day Coming: Folk Music and the American Left   *R. Serge Denisoff*

John Philip Sousa: A Descriptive Catalog of His Works   *Paul E. Bierley*

The Hell-Bound Train: A Cowboy Songbook   *Glenn Ohrlin*

Oh, Didn't He Ramble: The Life Story of Lee Collins, as Told to Mary Collins
    Edited by Frank J. Gillis and John W. Miner

American Labor Songs of the Nineteenth Century   *Philip S. Foner*

Stars of Country Music: Uncle Dave Macon to Johnny Rodriguez
    Edited by Bill C. Malone and Judith McCulloh

Git Along, Little Dogies: Songs and Songmakers of the American West   *John I. White*

A Texas-Mexican *Cancionero*: Folksongs of the Lower Border   *Américo Paredes*

San Antonio Rose: The Life and Music of Bob Wills   *Charles R. Townsend*

Early Downhome Blues: A Musical and Cultural Analysis   *Jeff Todd Titon*

An Ives Celebration: Papers and Panels of the Charles Ives Centennial Festival-
    Conference   *Edited by H. Wiley Hitchcock and Vivian Perlis*

Sinful Tunes and Spirituals: Black Folk Music to the Civil War   *Dena J. Epstein*

Joe Scott, the Woodsman-Songmaker   *Edward D. Ives*

Jimmie Rodgers: The Life and Times of America's Blue Yodeler   *Nolan Porterfield*

Early American Music Engraving and Printing: A History of Music Publishing
    in America from 1787 to 1825, with Commentary on Earlier and Later Practices
    Richard J. Wolfe

Sing a Sad Song: The Life of Hank Williams   *Roger M. Williams*

Long Steel Rail: The Railroad in American Folksong   *Norm Cohen*

Resources of American Music History: A Directory of Source Materials from Colonial
    Times to World War II   *D. W. Krummel, Jean Geil, Doris J. Dyen, and Deane L. Root*

Tenement Songs: The Popular Music of the Jewish Immigrants   *Mark Slobin*

Ozark Folksongs   *Vance Randolph; edited and abridged by Norm Cohen*

Oscar Sonneck and American Music   *Edited by William Lichtenwanger*

Bluegrass Breakdown: The Making of the Old Southern Sound   *Robert Cantwell*

Bluegrass: A History   *Neil V. Rosenberg*

Music at the White House: A History of the American Spirit   *Elise K. Kirk*

Red River Blues: The Blues Tradition in the Southeast   *Bruce Bastin*

Good Friends and Bad Enemies: Robert Winslow Gordon and the Study of
    American Folksong   *Debora Kodish*

Fiddlin' Georgia Crazy: Fiddlin' John Carson, His Real World, and the World of
    His Songs   *Gene Wiggins*

America's Music: From the Pilgrims to the Present (rev. 3d ed.)   *Gilbert Chase*

Secular Music in Colonial Annapolis: The Tuesday Club, 1745–56   *John Barry Talley*

Bibliographical Handbook of American Music   *D. W. Krummel*

Goin' to Kansas City   *Nathan W. Pearson Jr.*

"Susanna," "Jeanie," and "The Old Folks at Home": The Songs of Stephen C. Foster
    from His Time to Ours (2d ed.)   *William W. Austin*

Songprints: The Musical Experience of Five Shoshone Women   *Judith Vander*

"Happy in the Service of the Lord": Afro-American Gospel Quartets in Memphis
  Kip Lornell
Paul Hindemith in the United States   *Luther Noss*
"My Song Is My Weapon": People's Songs, American Communism, and the Politics
  of Culture, 1930–50   *Robbie Lieberman*
Chosen Voices: The Story of the American Cantorate   *Mark Slobin*
Theodore Thomas: America's Conductor and Builder of Orchestras, 1835–1905
  Ezra Schabas
"The Whorehouse Bells Were Ringing" and Other Songs Cowboys Sing
  Collected and Edited by Guy Logsdon
Crazeology: The Autobiography of a Chicago Jazzman   *Bud Freeman,*
  as Told to Robert Wolf
Discoursing Sweet Music: Brass Bands and Community Life
  in Turn-of-the-Century Pennsylvania   *Kenneth Kreitner*
Mormonism and Music: A History   *Michael Hicks*
Voices of the Jazz Age: Profiles of Eight Vintage Jazzmen   *Chip Deffaa*
Pickin' on Peachtree: A History of Country Music in Atlanta, Georgia
  Wayne W. Daniel
Bitter Music: Collected Journals, Essays, Introductions, and Librettos   *Harry Partch;*
  edited by Thomas McGeary
Ethnic Music on Records: A Discography of Ethnic Recordings Produced in the United
  States, 1893 to 1942   *Richard K. Spottswood*
Downhome Blues Lyrics: An Anthology from the Post–World War II Era
  Jeff Todd Titon
Ellington: The Early Years   *Mark Tucker*
Chicago Soul   *Robert Pruter*
That Half-Barbaric Twang: The Banjo in American Popular Culture   *Karen Linn*
Hot Man: The Life of Art Hodes   *Art Hodes and Chadwick Hansen*
The Erotic Muse: American Bawdy Songs (2d ed.)   *Ed Cray*
Barrio Rhythm: Mexican American Music in Los Angeles   *Steven Loza*
The Creation of Jazz: Music, Race, and Culture in Urban America   *Burton W. Peretti*
Charles Martin Loeffler: A Life Apart in Music   *Ellen Knight*
Club Date Musicians: Playing the New York Party Circuit   *Bruce A. MacLeod*
Opera on the Road: Traveling Opera Troupes in the United States, 1825–60
  Katherine K. Preston
The Stonemans: An Appalachian Family and the Music That Shaped Their Lives
  Ivan M. Tribe
Transforming Tradition: Folk Music Revivals Examined   *Edited by Neil V. Rosenberg*
The Crooked Stovepipe: Athapaskan Fiddle Music and Square Dancing
  in Northeast Alaska and Northwest Canada   *Craig Mishler*
Traveling the High Way Home: Ralph Stanley and the World of Traditional
  Bluegrass Music   *John Wright*
Carl Ruggles: Composer, Painter, and Storyteller   *Marilyn Ziffrin*
Never without a Song: The Years and Songs of Jennie Devlin, 1865–1952
  Katharine D. Newman

The Hank Snow Story   *Hank Snow, with Jack Ownbey and Bob Burris*

Milton Brown and the Founding of Western Swing   *Cary Ginell,*
  with special assistance from Roy Lee Brown

Santiago de Murcia's "Códice Saldívar No. 4": A Treasury of Secular Guitar Music
  from Baroque Mexico   *Craig H. Russell*

The Sound of the Dove: Singing in Appalachian Primitive Baptist Churches
  Beverly Bush Patterson

Heartland Excursions: Ethnomusicological Reflections on Schools of Music
  Bruno Nettl

Doowop: The Chicago Scene   *Robert Pruter*

Blue Rhythms: Six Lives in Rhythm and Blues   *Chip Deffaa*

Shoshone Ghost Dance Religion: Poetry Songs and Great Basin Context   *Judith Vander*

Go Cat Go! Rockabilly Music and Its Makers   *Craig Morrison*

'Twas Only an Irishman's Dream: The Image of Ireland and the Irish in American
  Popular Song Lyrics, 1800–1920   *William H. A. Williams*

Democracy at the Opera: Music, Theater, and Culture in New York City, 1815–60
  Karen Ahlquist

Fred Waring and the Pennsylvanians   *Virginia Waring*

Woody, Cisco, and Me: Seamen Three in the Merchant Marine   *Jim Longhi*

Behind the Burnt Cork Mask: Early Blackface Minstrelsy and Antebellum American
  Popular Culture   *William J. Mahar*

Going to Cincinnati: A History of the Blues in the Queen City   *Steven C. Tracy*

Pistol Packin' Mama: Aunt Molly Jackson and the Politics of Folksong   *Shelly Romalis*

Sixties Rock: Garage, Psychedelic, and Other Satisfactions   *Michael Hicks*

The Late Great Johnny Ace and the Transition from R&B to Rock 'n' Roll
  James M. Salem

Tito Puente and the Making of Latin Music   *Steven Loza*

Juilliard: A History   *Andrea Olmstead*

Understanding Charles Seeger, Pioneer in American Musicology   *Edited by Bell Yung*
  and Helen Rees

Mountains of Music: West Virginia Traditional Music from *Goldenseal*
  Edited by John Lilly

Alice Tully: An Intimate Portrait   *Albert Fuller*

A Blues Life   *Henry Townsend, as told to Bill Greensmith*

Long Steel Rail: The Railroad in American Folksong (2d ed.)   *Norm Cohen*

The Golden Age of Gospel   *Text by Horace Clarence Boyer;*
  photography by Lloyd Yearwood

Aaron Copland: The Life and Work of an Uncommon Man   *Howard Pollack*

Louis Moreau Gottschalk   *S. Frederick Starr*

Race, Rock, and Elvis   *Michael T. Bertrand*

Theremin: Ether Music and Espionage   *Albert Glinsky*

Poetry and Violence: The Ballad Tradition of Mexico's Costa Chica   *John H. McDowell*

The Bill Monroe Reader   *Edited by Tom Ewing*

Music in Lubavitcher Life   *Ellen Koskoff*

Zarzuela: Spanish Operetta, American Stage   *Janet L. Sturman*

Bluegrass Odyssey: A Documentary in Pictures and Words, 1966–86   *Carl Fleischhauer*
  and Neil V. Rosenberg

That Old-Time Rock & Roll: A Chronicle of an Era, 1954–63   *Richard Aquila*
Labor's Troubadour   *Joe Glazer*
American Opera   *Elise K. Kirk*
Don't Get above Your Raisin': Country Music and the Southern Working Class
   Bill C. Malone
John Alden Carpenter: A Chicago Composer   *Howard Pollack*
Heartbeat of the People: Music and Dance of the Northern Pow-wow   *Tara Browner*
My Lord, What a Morning: An Autobiography   *Marian Anderson*
Marian Anderson: A Singer's Journey   *Allan Keiler*
Charles Ives Remembered: An Oral History   *Vivian Perlis*
Henry Cowell, Bohemian   *Michael Hicks*
Rap Music and Street Consciousness   *Cheryl L. Keyes*
Louis Prima   *Garry Boulard*
Marian McPartland's Jazz World: All in Good Time   *Marian McPartland*
Robert Johnson: Lost and Found   *Barry Lee Pearson and Bill McCulloch*
Bound for America: Three British Composers   *Nicholas Temperley*
Lost Sounds: Blacks and the Birth of the Recording Industry, 1890–1919   *Tim Brooks*
Burn, Baby! BURN! The Autobiography of Magnificent Montague
   Magnificent Montague with Bob Baker
Way Up North in Dixie: A Black Family's Claim to the Confederate Anthem
   Howard L. Sacks and Judith Rose Sacks
The Bluegrass Reader   *Edited by Thomas Goldsmith*
Colin McPhee: Composer in Two Worlds   *Carol J. Oja*
Robert Johnson, Mythmaking, and Contemporary American Culture
   Patricia R. Schroeder
Composing a World: Lou Harrison, Musical Wayfarer   *Leta E. Miller*
   and Fredric Lieberman
Fritz Reiner, Maestro and Martinet   *Kenneth Morgan*
That Toddlin' Town: Chicago's White Dance Bands and Orchestras, 1900–1950
   Charles A. Sengstock Jr.
Dewey and Elvis: The Life and Times of a Rock 'n' Roll Deejay   *Louis Cantor*
Come Hither to Go Yonder: Playing Bluegrass with Bill Monroe   *Bob Black*
Chicago Blues: Portraits and Stories   *David Whiteis*
The Incredible Band of John Philip Sousa   *Paul E. Bierley*
"Maximum Clarity" and Other Writings on Music   *Ben Johnston, edited by Bob Gilmore*
Staging Tradition: John Lair and Sarah Gertrude Knott   *Michael Ann Williams*
Homegrown Music: Discovering Bluegrass   *Stephanie P. Ledgin*
Tales of a Theatrical Guru   *Danny Newman*
The Music of Bill Monroe   *Neil V. Rosenberg and Charles K. Wolfe*
Pressing On: The Roni Stoneman Story   *Roni Stoneman, as told to Ellen Wright*
Together Let Us Sweetly Live   *Jonathan C. David, with photographs by Richard Holloway*
Live Fast, Love Hard: The Faron Young Story   *Diane Diekman*
Air Castle of the South: WSM Radio and the Making of Music City   *Craig P. Havighurst*
Traveling Home: Sacred Harp Singing and American Pluralism   *Kiri Miller*
Where Did Our Love Go? The Rise and Fall of the Motown Sound   *Nelson George*
Lonesome Cowgirls and Honky-Tonk Angels: The Women of Barn Dance Radio
   Kristine M. McCusker

California Polyphony: Ethnic Voices, Musical Crossroads *Mina Yang*

The Never-Ending Revival: Rounder Records and the Folk Alliance *Michael F. Scully*

Sing It Pretty: A Memoir *Bess Lomax Hawes*

Working Girl Blues: The Life and Music of Hazel Dickens *Hazel Dickens and Bill C. Malone*

Charles Ives Reconsidered *Gayle Sherwood Magee*

The Hayloft Gang: The Story of the National Barn Dance *Edited by Chad Berry*

Country Music Humorists and Comedians *Loyal Jones*

Record Makers and Breakers: Voices of the Independent Rock 'n' Roll Pioneers *John Broven*

Music of the First Nations: Tradition and Innovation in Native North America *Edited by Tara Browner*

Cafe Society: The Wrong Place for the Right People *Barney Josephson, with Terry Trilling-Josephson*

George Gershwin: An Intimate Portrait *Walter Rimler*

Life Flows On in Endless Song: Folk Songs and American History *Robert V. Wells*

I Feel a Song Coming On: The Life of Jimmy McHugh *Alyn Shipton*

King of the Queen City: The Story of King Records *Jon Hartley Fox*

Long Lost Blues: Popular Blues in America, 1850–1920 *Peter C. Muir*

Hard Luck Blues: Roots Music Photographs from the Great Depression *Rich Remsberg*

Restless Giant: The Life and Times of Jean Aberbach and Hill and Range Songs *Bar Biszick-Lockwood*

Champagne Charlie and Pretty Jemima: Variety Theater in the Nineteenth Century *Gillian M. Rodger*

Sacred Steel: Inside an African American Steel Guitar Tradition *Robert L. Stone*

Gone to the Country: The New Lost City Ramblers and the Folk Music Revival *Ray Allen*

The Makers of the Sacred Harp *David Warren Steel with Richard H. Hulan*

Woody Guthrie, American Radical *Will Kaufman*

George Szell: A Life of Music *Michael Charry*

Bean Blossom: The Brown County Jamboree and Bill Monroe's Bluegrass Festivals *Thomas A. Adler*

Crowe on the Banjo: The Music Life of J. D. Crowe *Marty Godbey*

Twentieth Century Drifter: The Life of Marty Robbins *Diane Diekman*

Henry Mancini: Reinventing Film Music *John Caps*

The Beautiful Music All Around Us: Field Recordings and the American Experience *Stephen Wade*

Then Sings My Soul: The Culture of Southern Gospel Music *Douglas Harrison*

The Accordion in the Americas: Klezmer, Polka, Tango, Zydeco, and More! *Edited by Helena Simonett*

Bluegrass Bluesman: A Memoir *Josh Graves, edited by Fred Bartenstein*

One Woman in a Hundred: Edna Phillips and the Philadelphia Orchestra *Mary Sue Welsh*

The Great Orchestrator: Arthur Judson and American Arts Management *James M. Doering*

Charles Ives in the Mirror: American Histories of an Iconic Composer *David C. Paul*

Southern Soul-Blues   *David Whiteis*

Sweet Air: Modernism, Regionalism, and American Popular Song
 Edward P. Comentale

Pretty Good for a Girl: Women in Bluegrass   *Murphy Hicks Henry*

Sweet Dreams: The World of Patsy Cline   *Warren R. Hofstra*

William Sidney Mount and the Creolization of American Culture   *Christopher J. Smith*

Bird: The Life and Music of Charlie Parker   *Chuck Haddix*

Making the March King: John Philip Sousa's Washington Years, 1854–1893
 Patrick Warfield

In It for the Long Run   *Jim Rooney*

Pioneers of the Blues Revival   *Steve Cushing*

Roots of the Revival: American and British Folk Music in the 1950s   *Ronald D. Cohen
 and Rachel Clare Donaldson*

Blues All Day Long: The Jimmy Rogers Story   *Wayne Everett Goins*

Yankee Twang: Country and Western Music in New England   *Clifford R. Murphy*

The Music of the Stanley Brothers   *Gary B. Reid*

Hawaiian Music in Motion: Mariners, Missionaries, and Minstrels   *James Revell Carr*

Sounds of the New Deal: The Federal Music Project in the West   *Peter Gough*

The Mormon Tabernacle Choir: A Biography   *Michael Hicks*

The Man That Got Away: The Life and Songs of Harold Arlen   *Walter Rimler*

A City Called Heaven: Chicago and the Birth of Gospel Music   *Robert M. Marovich*

Blues Unlimited: Essential Interviews from the Original Blues Magazine
 Edited by Bill Greensmith, Mike Rowe, and Mark Camarigg

Hoedowns, Reels, and Frolics: Roots and Branches of Southern
 Appalachian Dance   *Phil Jamison*

Fannie Bloomfield-Zeisler: The Life and Times of a Piano Virtuoso
 Beth Abelson Macleod

Cybersonic Arts: Adventures in American New Music   *Gordon Mumma,
 edited with commentary by Michelle Fillion*

The Magic of Beverly Sills   *Nancy Guy*

Waiting for Buddy Guy   *Alan Harper*

Harry T. Burleigh: From the Spiritual to the Harlem Renaissance   *Jean E. Snyder*

Music in the Age of Anxiety: American Music in the Fifties   *James Wierzbicki*

Jazzing: New York City's Unseen Scene   *Thomas H. Greenland*

A Cole Porter Companion   *Edited by Don M. Randel, Matthew Shaftel,
 and Susan Forscher Weiss*

Foggy Mountain Troubadour: The Life and Music of Curly Seckler   *Penny Parsons*

Blue Rhythm Fantasy: Big Band Jazz Arranging in the Swing Era   *John Wriggle*

Bill Clifton: America's Bluegrass Ambassador to the World   *Bill C. Malone*

Chinatown Opera Theater in North America   *Nancy Yunhwa Rao*

The Elocutionists: Women, Music, and the Spoken Word   *Marian Wilson Kimber*

May Irwin: Singing, Shouting, and the Shadow of Minstrelsy   *Sharon Ammen*

Peggy Seeger: A Life of Music, Love, and Politics   *Jean R. Freedman*

Charles Ives's *Concord*: Essays after a Sonata   *Kyle Gann*

Don't Give Your Heart to a Rambler: My Life with Jimmy Martin, the King of Bluegrass
 Barbara Martin Stephens

Libby Larsen: Composing an American Life   *Denise Von Glahn*
George Szell's Reign: Behind the Scenes with the Cleveland Orchestra
  Marcia Hansen Kraus
Just One of the Boys: Female-to-Male Cross-Dressing on the American Variety Stage
  Gillian M. Rodger
Spirituals and the Birth of a Black Entertainment Industry   *Sandra Jean Graham*
Right to the Juke Joint: A Personal History of American Music   *Patrick B. Mullen*
Bluegrass Generation: A Memoir   *Neil V. Rosenberg*
Pioneers of the Blues Revival, Expanded Second Edition   *Steve Cushing*
Banjo Roots and Branches   *Edited by Robert Winans*
Bill Monroe: The Life and Music of the Blue Grass Man   *Tom Ewing*

The University of Illinois Press
is a founding member of the
Association of American University Presses.

Text designed by Lisa Connery
Composed in 10.75/14 Minion Pro
with Alternate Gothic No 1 D and Trend Rh Sans display
at the University of Illinois Press
Cover designed by Dustin J. Hubbart
The cover photo appeared on the back cover of *Bill Monroe's
Blue Grass Country Songs* (Bill Monroe Music, 1950)
Manufactured by Sheridan Books, Inc.

University of Illinois Press
1325 South Oak Street
Champaign, IL 61820-6903
www.press.uillinois.edu